The Ecology of WHALES and DOLPHINS

The Ecology of WHALES and DOLPHINS

D. E. Gaskin

Department of Zoology,
University of Guelph, Ontario, Canada

HEINEMANN
LONDON AND EXETER, NEW HAMPSHIRE

Heinemann Educational Books Ltd
22 Bedford Square, London WC1B 3HH

LONDON EDINBURGH MELBOURNE AUCKLAND
HONG KONG SINGAPORE KUALA LUMPUR NEW DELHI
IBADAN NAIROBI JOHANNESBURG
EXETER (NH) KINGSTON PORT OF SPAIN

First published 1982

British Library Cataloguing in Publication Data

Gaskin, D. E.
    The Ecology of Whales and Dolphins
    1. Cetacea – Behaviour
    2. Mammals – Behaviour
    I. Title
    599.5'0451   QL737.C4

    ISBN 0-435-62286-2

Library of Congress C.I.P. Data

Gaskin, D. E. (David Edward), 1939–
    The Ecology of Whales and Dolphins.
    Includes bibliographies and indexes.
    1. Cetacea – Ecology.   I. Title.
    QL737.C4G24 1982   599.5'045   82-11703

    ISBN 0-435-62286-2

Filmset in Monophoto Plantin and
printed in Great Britain by
BAS Printers Limited,
Over Wallop, Hampshire

For the late Harold Barnes,

formerly of the Dunstaffnage Marine
Research Station, Oban, Scotland

ACKNOWLEDGEMENTS

I would like to thank David M. Lavigne and Gary J. D. Smith of my department, two anonymous senior academic readers in the United Kingdom, and two in the United States, who provided valuable criticisms of many sections of this book. The late Dr Harold Barnes of the Dunstaffnage Marine Laboratory in Scotland gave detailed criticism of earlier drafts of several sections which helped to shape their final form. A number of present and former graduate students, particularly D. B. Yurick, W. Y. Yasui, A. P. Watson and B. M. Braune, assisted with challenging discussions on several of the controversial topics covered in this volume. I also want to record my warm thanks to all my associates and colleagues who so willingly provided photographs for this volume; they are numerous, and acknowledgement is given in the appropriate captions. My wife, Maureen, gave much assistance with the preparation of the figures, and Mrs Irene Teeter of the Department of Zoology, University of Guelph, provided sterling assistance by typing the major drafts of the text, despite the considerable demands upon her time made by the task.

CONTENTS

INTRODUCTION

This book grew from a review paper written for *Oceanography and Marine Biology* in 1976 with much steady prodding by the editor, the late Harold S. Barnes of the Dunstaffnage Marine Biological Station at Oban, Scotland. Several of my colleagues, and finally Hamish MacGibbon of Heinemann Educational Books in London, encouraged me to expand and update the text of the original paper, and to add new chapters on energetics, social structure, population studies, management and contaminants; the present volume is the result.

The number of scientific articles published about cetaceans in each five-year period since 1950 has risen almost exponentially, concurrent with a great increase in the number of scientists and publishing amateur naturalists (some of the latter having a high level of competence indeed) who have become interested in these animals. Even the task of updating the sections included in the original review just to take into account new work published during the last four years proved to be a formidable undertaking. Those familiar with the earlier work will note that I have not hesitated to modify or discard statements when these no longer appear consistent with recent findings, or when revised conclusions seem necessary. The approximate cut-off date of literature citations is January 1980.

This book covers some difficult, and often controversial topics; many of my ideas can and should be criticized. We know so little about these animals that many of my conclusions simply have to be wrong. If this book successfully maps some areas of ignorance and stimulates even a few to undertake more research and re-examine present assumptions, then as a contribution it will have served a useful function.

I think the introduction to my 1976 paper is still valid, and explains to some extent the reasons why 'Saving the Whale' has become such an emotionally charged issue:

In recent years some of the attributes of Cetacea have attracted much attention. This interest in their physiology and behaviour, the controversy about the level and nature of delphinid intelligence, and their growing use as live exhibits in Marineland displays, has not only acutely increased general awareness about cetaceans, but also focussed attention on these animals in a rather special way.

Partly as a result of this awareness, the nineteen seventies may be remembered as the decade in which cetaceans became political animals. 'The Whale' has become in truth a semi-mythological beast, an embodiment of composite attributes not vested in any single species, threatened both by man the hunting primitive and man the technological polluter, and therefore in this age of mass-media generated *causes célèbres*, uniquely suited to adorn lapel buttons and bumper stickers. In North America the poor animal has become thoroughly integrated into the 'counter-culture' of the university campuses and the discothèques. At a more sophisticated level naturalists and biologists with little or no personal experience of Cetacea have become embroiled in the emotionally charged issue of drastic depletion of populations of the large commercially valuable species, blue, fin, sei, humpback, minke, and sperm whales by the major whaling nations. Their concern has spread into the much broader issue of control of resources which are truly international, and may be said to belong to no single nation.

I have deliberately avoided intensive, illustrated reviews of physiological and functional anatomical adaptations. Rather than focusing on an individual whale as a vehicle for interesting phenomena (echolocation, for example) and examining the mechanisms in great detail, I have attempted to restrict such functional discussion to a minimum and concentrate instead on considering cetaceans primarily at the population level, in relation to their environment in time and space.

A few words about the structure of the book may be useful. Some reviewers are critical of texts with the chapters referenced separately, preferring the literature in a single block at the end. I chose to follow the former system, at the risk of the repetition of a certain number of major works for two reasons. First, although the relative handful of specialist readers may use bibliographies principally to search for contributions by *author*, fifteen years of university teaching experience have taught me that senior undergraduates, graduate students and well-informed lay readers are far more interested in searching the literature by *topic*. Not only do these people form the great majority of the readers of a volume like this, they also need more assistance than the specialists in undertaking such searches. To compensate for this approach to some degree, I have added an author index to the scientific name and general subject indices. This will also assist in the identification of multiple-author papers when the reader cannot remember the name of the senior author. Second, I felt that a numerical style of referencing interfered far less with the flow of the text than the more conventional method of having citations of author and date in parentheses. If all the references were concentrated at the end of the book, their numbers are such that the text would have many four-figure citations, greatly detracting from the advantages of this type of layout.

CHAPTER 1

Distributional ecology of Cetacea

Seasonal migrations

The annual migrations of Cetacea appear to represent an evolved compromise between differing requirements for breeding and maximum feeding potential (108). As a consequence, the study of the distributional ecology of these animals becomes largely a study of the distributional ecology of their prey species, and an analysis of the factors which may limit the ability of cetaceans to reproduce or rear calves to maturity. The latter conditions will invariably lie well within maximum tolerance levels for the simple maintenance of the adult animal. Relatively more is known of the migrations of the large Cetacea, simply because their commercial importance has focused most attention (and research funds) upon them. But although distributional data are scanty for many species of small or intermediate size, we can say that those cetaceans which occur in temperate zones or high latitudes at some time of year usually have some kind of generalized (or very specific) pole-ward movement in spring and a reverse movement in autumn in the respective hemispheres. Those restricted to tropical waters often exhibit major onshore–offshore movements.

Long-term studies on two species of *Stenella* in the eastern tropical Pacific reveal several levels of movements (92). Recaptures of marked animals by tuna purse-seining boats indicate maximum daily travel of up to 89 nautical miles/day; the average is significantly less, about 30 miles/day. Over longer periods, of months or as much as a year, animals were recorded moving from 500 to 600 nautical miles. The research workers carrying out the study were cautious in interpreting the results since they suspected that a periodic component was present, based on use of a large home-range zone perhaps 200–300 miles in diameter. Nevertheless, the study of mark recoveries on a seasonal basis suggested quite strongly that there was an inshore (that is, easterly, towards the tropical Americas) movement in autumn and winter, and an offshore movement during the spring and summer.

In another recent paper N. Miyazaki and his co-workers studied the migrations of *Stenella coeruleoalba* and *S. attenuata* in waters of the North Pacific adjacent to the Japanese mainland (71). They concluded that both species inhabited a region influenced by the warm Kuro Shio Current, but that although *S. coeruleoalba* tended to be distributed further north than *S. attenuata*, both species concentrated in an area where the relatively warm water intruded into colder water near the coast. These species are only rarely taken much north of latitude 33°N in winter, but frequently reach latitude 46°N in summer months. *S. attenuata* appears to be restricted to slightly warmer waters than *S. coeruleoalba*. Radiotelemetric tracking of common dolphins off the west coast of the United States (31) shows that large concentrations of *Delphinus* may move more than 100 kilometres in 24 hours, and over longer periods forage several hundred kilometres before returning along a roughly similar track. Close relationships were noted between herd movements and prominent features of bottom topography, although the latter were probably influencing oceanographic conditions to some extent.

T. Kasuya (51) has recently summarized data on the distribution of Dall's porpoise *Phocoenoides dalli* (and cf. *truei*) in the waters of the western North Pacific. He recognized three populations (see also Chapter 7), two largely of the *dalli* type in the Sea of Okhotsk and the more northern waters of the Pacific proper respectively, and one of colour form *truei* off the east coasts of Honshu and Hokkaido. The problem of whether these represent species (1, 83), subspecies (51) or polyphasic morphs (47) remains undecided, except some significant genetic isolation is indicated. Specimens taken in the eastern North Pacific appear, almost invariably, to be *P. truei* (51).

All three groups show a movement which appears to be north-easterly in the spring and summer months, and south-westerly in the autumn and winter months. To a large extent these animals are moving within the influence of the cool Oya Shio waters moving down from the Bering Sea. The Kurile chain appears to form some kind of natural topographic boundary, but the reason why is not understood. *Phocoenoides* is essentially a cool-water porpoise, and is rare off Japan in water regimes with a surface temperature greater than 17°C. Movements off California are not fully understood (73), but appear to have an onshore–offshore component. Dall's porpoises can be found in Californian waters in some numbers in any month of the year and range to about latitude 30°N; they are commonest in the winter months (55, 56, 73).

The northern right whale dolphin *Lissodelphis borealis* population is distributed in temperate waters between 30°–50°N. While the movements of this species are still rather poorly known, a recent summary (57) suggests that at least part of the population moves south and inshore during the spring, then north and offshore at the onset of autumn. In the shelf waters of southern California, where the annual temperature range is from about 7.5° to 19°C, numbers begin to increase in the autumn, peak in mid-winter and decline again in spring and early summer when they presumably move north again. It is not known if the species ranges right across the Pacific, or if it is confined to the cooler marginal waters. The pelagic squid *Loligo opalescens* seems to be an important food item in the diet of the right whale dolphin, and the peak occurrence of both species in Californian waters coincides closely. Right whale dolphins are frequently seen in the vicinity of the offshore Californian banks, such as the Cortes Bank and the San Juan Seamount. In the latter area I saw (winter 1971–2) a small school of right whale dolphins apparently foraging in the top metre or so, in close company with *Grampus griseus*.

Migrations of some Indo-Pacific core-type species are known, but data are limited. If seasonal movements take place in the northern Indian Ocean they might correlate with wet and dry seasons and the onset of monsoon winds, or similar phenomena.

The finless porpoise is a characteristic species of the eastern Indo-Pacific core region, but the only major study on this animal has been made in a peripheral part of its range, the Inland Sea of Japan (52). Extending from about 33°–35°N, this area has high water temperatures in summer (up to 28°C), but by March they can be as low as 6°C. The wide range can to some extent be attributed to the shallow depth of the Inland Sea. *Neophocoena* is a common species in the region, with a decidedly inshore distribution pattern. More than 80 per cent of the individuals sighted during the study in question were found within one mile of shore, and less than 1 per cent were more than three miles out. A strong preference for rocky promontories and passages with fairly strong currents was noted. The Japanese researchers noted some changes in density with the seasons; the highest density was reported in April, and numbers were lowest in early winter. Decline in density during the summer months was attributed to females with calves leaving the Inland Sea. Migration routes and changes of density within the Inland Sea were also studied; it appeared that the migration was from west to east for part of the year, and then from east to west. Almost all animals seemed to leave via the eastern passages of the Kii Channel near Osaka Bay. During the return movement, densities increased first in the eastern part of the Inland Sea, and then spread westwards. The rather drastic changes in surface temperature during the year were regarded as having little obvious effect on these animals, which is surprising considering their small size. Nor did migration to follow stocks of the principal food species, *Ammodytes personatus*, seem to account for the types of movement noted. The researchers suggested that the Inland Sea provided a suitable area for parturition and mating during the early part of the spring–summer period when temperatures were increasing steadily. After the critical period for the newborn calves had passed, the females then moved offshore, leaving the non-breeding animals to exploit the summer fish shoals.

Another characteristic Indo-Pacific core cetacean group is the humpbacked dolphins of the genus *Sousa*. Detailed studies of the South African species (probably *S. lentigenosa* Owen) have been made in recent years, especially of the population present in Plettenberg Bay on the southern coast (102, 103). This is another species which is consistently found very close to shore, working backwards and forwards along stretches of sandy shore with reef outcrops. Individuals were observed to ignore mullet schools, even though they will eat this species in captivity, and instead to concentrate on taking reef organisms. Some fluctuations in sea surface temperature occur in Plettenberg Bay during the course of the year, but this did not appear to exercise any significant effect on the humpbacked dolphins' movements. In fact, although a good deal of local movement was noted – and this species, in contrast to *Tursiops aduncus* which was also present, tended to be concentrated at the western–north-western side of the bay – long-term movement could not be detected. The population appeared to be non-migratory, and to be present all the year round.

The work of the author and his associates on the distribution and movements of *Phocoena phocoena* in eastern Canadian waters is still incomplete (39), but data justify belief in the general kind of seasonal oscillation indicated by D. J. Neave and B. S. Wright (76) for the population in the Bay of Fundy approaches. Our observations show that a few harbour porpoises, however, do remain in coastal waters of southern New Brunswick and Nova Scotia throughout the winter months, in waters which may become as cold as 1.5°C (42). Similar seasonal movements have been reported for European populations of the species; for example, there is cumulative evidence to suggest a southward movement during winter in the North Sea and a penetration of the eastern Baltic Sea by the species only in summer (45, 72, 99, 111, 121). There is a recognizable seasonal migration in through the Danish Straits in spring, and out again in late autumn or early winter. A possible influx of harbour porpoises into the eastern end of the English Channel in or by June is suggested from data given by F. C. Fraser (34). A. G. Tomilin summarized data on the distribution of the species in Russian waters (107). It certainly penetrates as far as the Kara Sea in summer, but is not common there. It is seasonally abundant in the White Sea and other northern waters to the west of the Kara Sea. In the Black Sea region it is most abundant in the southern part of the Sea of Azov, in Kerch Strait and the adjacent portions of the Black Sea. Though relatively rare to the east of this region, it is well known on the coasts of Romania, Bulgaria and European Turkey.

There is evidence of distinct migrations of killer whales *Orcinus orca* in the northern North Atlantic and the Norwegian Sea (50). Killer whales appear to follow the winter herring schools into coastal areas and remain in rather specific localities until May. Peaks recorded off northern Scotland and Iceland are between July and September, and coincide with important herring movements in those waters.

Studies on the Atlantic bottlenosed whale *Hyperoodon ampullatus* suggest that these animals move almost entirely over truly pelagic waters, avoiding even the continental shelf in their search for concentrations of the squid *Gonatius fabricii* (7, 8, 21). The species seems to make a summer and early autumn feeding migration into the Norwegian Sea, concentrating at different times off northern Iceland, then again off Spitsbergen, before moving southward again. The population may winter in relatively southern waters between Iceland and Norway, or even around the British Isles and other west European shores. Specimens have been recorded in the Baltic in the months between August and November, and around Britain most commonly in September–October (8).

Three studies on the migratory movements of narwhal *Monodon monoceros* in the Canadian Arctic have been published in recent years (27, 43, 63). Not unexpectedly, the direction, nature and timing of the migrations of this species are largely dictated by the presence or absence of heavy ice cover. Presumably as a result of retaining the maximum level of reproductive flexibility in such an unstable and unpredictable environment, it has a very poorly defined annual cycle, although most calving, and much of its intensive feeding, is believed to be concentrated in the summer months. The greater part of the population in the Canadian Arctic concentrates in summer in the Lancaster Sound region, between Devon, Baffin and Bylot Islands. It is presumed to winter in open water offshore in the wide expanse of Baffin Bay. Narwhal around Thule in north-west Greenland may represent a separate population or be part of the same stock. The Lancaster Sound animals begin to move westward past Bylot and Devon Islands in the latter part of May, and the migration stream increases in numbers as the summer progresses. The number of animals in Lancaster Sound appears to reach a maximum in July–August, decreasing rather rapidly thereafter. In earlier years some pods penetrated as far west as the Gulf of Boothia, and perhaps Prince of Wales Island. This movement may no longer occur.

The reproductive cycle of the sperm whale *Physeter catodon*, with its long gestation period, does not at first sight appear to fit an annual periodicity of movement, but in reality the phases are seasonally synchronized, and at least part of the global population performs poleward movements in spring and early summer (11, 23, 82, 85, 87). Some males may remain in relatively high or intermediate latitudes (37), but others certainly return, as evidenced by a Russian whale mark fired into a sperm at latitude 62°S which was recovered off Durban at 30°S (11). The same author drew attention to other marks fired into whales at 6°S and 20°–22°S recovered off Saldanha Bay at 33°S. High-latitude schools of sperm whales are composed almost entirely of males. The pole-ward movements of females accompanied by calves is much more restricted, perhaps by the minimum-temperature tolerance of the latter, which might be about 14°C (37).

S. Ohsumi and his colleagues (87, 89) carried out a detailed global study based on density patterns in sperm whale sighting and catch records between 1965 and 1974. They concluded that general distributions in the North Pacific and the Southern Ocean differed somewhat in character. In the North Pacific there was a rather even distribution of density in all latitudes surveyed (40°–60°N), whereas in the southern hemisphere there was relatively high density between 40°–45°S, low density from 45°–60°S (except in the anomalous New Zealand sector, see also my own analysis (37)) and quite high density again above 60°S. Sperm whales appeared to be more abundant in the Indian and Pacific Ocean sectors than in the Atlantic sector of the Southern Ocean, but the authors made no mention of possible factors which might cause this. Previous extensive overexploitation by European whaling vessels is one obvious possibility to be considered; sperm whale stocks take a long time to recover from heavy exploitation, since their reproductive rate is one of the lowest known for any marine mammal (12).

Good summaries of the complex migration patterns of sperm whales have been provided by P. B. Best (9–12) and R. Gambell (35). These migrations contain some unique features which, at first sight, are rather bewildering. There is marked sexual segregation among the adults (see Chapter 4 for further discussion of the social structure), with many of the males forming 'bachelor' schools of varying sizes. Although male schools are the only ones to penetrate high latitudes, as mentioned above, they are by no means confined to those latitudes. In my own work around New Zealand I had no records of 'bachelor' herds north of 35°S in the data available, but I stand corrected by Best, who has determined that they can occur well into tropical latitudes.

One of the most puzzling features of sperm whale movements is that at the height of the mating season in the southern hemisphere (spring and early summer, though it is protracted in many areas), the majority of the bachelor schools appear to be distributed allopatrically to the mixed-sex schools containing the fertilizable females. Although this can be explained in terms of the rather unique social structure of the sperm whale, it appears to lead to a lack of ready replacements if 'school-masters' are killed during tropical or subtropical whaling, with a singularly detrimental effect on the reproductive and replenishment rates of this polygynous animal. E. Mitchell and V. M. Kozicki have suggested that areas within all oceans be delimited to give realistic protection to sperm whales during mating and calving periods (70).

Despite their segregation, bachelor schools and mixed-sex schools appear to have generally similar distribution patterns and migratory movements, both carrying out the seasonal swing towards and away from the poles mentioned earlier. There is a general overlapping of ranges in low latitudes in mid-winter, when some reassortment may take place. S. Ohsumi calculated that only 10–20 per cent of all sexually mature males become school-masters in any given year. Sexual selection appears to take place during the spring. Once this process is completed the surplus males leave and make their way to higher latitudes. A sequence of migratory events has been detected; schools of medium-sized bachelor males depart for higher latitudes earlier and return to low latitudes later than mixed-sex schools, and the largest animals leave earlier still and return last of all. This has probably evolved under the dictate of energetic requirements.

The degree of average movement during a period is poorly known. M. V. Ivashin (48) recorded a male which moved a total of 7400 km before recovery, and a sperm whale marked in Canadian waters was taken seven years later by Spanish whalers (70), confirming that males may and can move from one subregional population to another, but probably at a slow rate. Best (11) calculated from mark returns that the average annual movement was of the order of about 850 nautical miles (about 1410 km) for males, and about 372 (620 km) for females, strongly suggesting that the 'home range' or foraging region of bachelor schools was considerably larger than that of mixed-sex schools.

The annual migrations of baleen whales from low latitudes in winter to high latitudes in summer are more sharply defined than those of the larger odontocetes, and in evolutionary ecological terms represent the sum of responses to various Pleistocene and post-Pleistocene conditions. Such migratory patterns enable these filter-feeding species to exploit the intense seasonal productivity of certain waters in high latitudes, yet still mate and calve in relatively warm waters with rather low (but constant) productivity, which may serve to minimize some of the potential problems of reproduction and neonate survival (but see p. 108). Baleen whale reproductive cycles are relatively well known and since this has much bearing on the annual migratory cycle, the basic data are summarized in Table 1.1. Quite probably the exploitation of these prey concentrations in high latitudes by blue, fin and sei has permitted the establishment of higher population levels than in the case of species such as Bryde's whale, *Balaenoptera edeni*, which dwell in areas of generally lower productivity.

We must remember, however, that even in the tropics, areas of intensive production may occur where upwellings bring nutrients into the epipelagic layer. Such upwelling may occur around oceanic islands and along continental slopes, and so it is no accident that such waters may contain and support quite large populations of Bryde's whales, for example, in the vicinity of the Bonin chain, further out into the subtropical North Pacific (13, 86, 96), and off the coast of Cape Province. Bryde's whale is generally distributed in waters of 20–30°C, although some individuals occur in temperatures down to 15°C.

Table 1.1   Reproductive data for commercially exploited large whale species, pertaining to migratory cycles

Species	Gestation period (months)	Lactation period (months)	Peak of pairing	Calving	References and comments
Balaena mysticetus	(9–10)	(12)	N: Feb.–Mar.	?	Slijper, 1962; all data approximate
Eschrichtius gibbosus	13	7	N: Nov.–Jan.	Dec.–Feb.	Rice and Wolman (98)
Balaenoptera musculus	11+	7	S: Apr.–June	Mar.–June	Harrison, 1969, p. 260
Balaenoptera physalus	11.25	7	N: Nov.–Mar. S: Apr.–July		Harrison, 1969; Mackintosh (61)
Balaenoptera borealis	12	6	N: Nov.–Feb. S: Apr.–Aug.	S: Apr.–Aug.	Harrison, 1969; Gambell, 1968
Balaenoptera acutorostrata	10–11	4–5	N: Jan.–May S: Aug.–Nov.	N: Nov.–Mar. S: June–Aug.	Harrison, 1969
Megaptera novaeangliae	12	10.5	S: Aug.–Sept.	S: July–Aug.	Harrison, 1969, after Dawbin and Chittleborough, various dates
Physeter catodon	16.4	24–25	N: Apr. S: Oct.	N: June–Oct. S: Dec.–Apr.	Ohsumi, 1965
	14.6	24–25	S: Nov.–Dec.	S: Feb.–Mar.	Best, 1968

Notes

Best, P. B. 1968. 'The sperm whale (*Physeter catodon*) off the west coast of South Africa. 2. Reproduction in the female', *Investl. Rep. Div. Sea Fish. S. Afr.* vol. 66, pp. 1–32.

Gambell, R. 1968. 'Seasonal cycles and reproduction in sei whales of the southern hemisphere', *Discovery Rep.* vol. 35, pp. 31–134.

Harrison, R. J. 1969. 'Reproduction and reproductive organs' in H. T. Andersen (ed.) *The Biology of Marine Mammals*, New York, Academic Press, pp. 253–348.

Ohsumi, S. 1965. 'Reproduction of the sperm whale in the northwest Pacific', *Sci. Rep. Whales Res. Inst.* vol. 19, pp. 1–35.

Slijper, E. J. 1962. Chapter 4, ref. 96.

I will have cause to discuss the migratory patterns of the large baleen whales in different contexts in Chapters 6 and 7, and I do not wish to reiterate the general descriptions here. The movements of blue, fin and sei are rather diffuse, and sometimes take place well away from coastal regions. Right, humpback and gray whales, on the other hand, migrate through coastal waters for much of the way, or carry out almost the whole of their migration along a continental coastline. It is important to realize that not all members of a population necessarily take part in these migrations. In the case of the North Atlantic right whale, for example, though records for the Gulf of Maine northwards are almost invariably from the months of summer and early autumn (97), and records from Florida from the depth of winter (Jan.–March), between these extremes right whales might be seen off the long intermediate stretch of the eastern seaboard of the United States in virtually any month of the year. It is only *in average terms* that one can describe the seasonal north–south swing of the population. Not all gray whales move right up into the Bering Sea during the summer months; immature animals, or adults which are otherwise not breeding in a given season, may be seen off the coast from Oregon up to northern British Columbia during the summer months, especially off the coast of Vancouver Island, where they seem to feed for several months (26) (see Chapter 2). Similarly, although perhaps 85 per cent (95, 120) to 90 per cent (2) of the western North Atlantic humpback whale population is concentrated in winter over the line of banks that stretch in an arc from Grand Turk (especially the Silver, Mouchoir and Navidad Banks) down to the Lesser Antilles, some remain around Bermuda in the summer and may in fact go no further north, and others, though admittedly not in large numbers, can be seen off the Massachusetts coast even in winter (115). Whether or not a large baleen whale follows the 'typical' migratory pattern or not can depend on a number of factors; its previous reproductive history, its nutritional state, its state of health, its age and social status, and the ocean environmental conditions extant in the season in question.

Possible factors initiating migration

Although much information has been accumulated over the years on distributions, changes in distributions, and migrations, very little has been discovered about the factors which might initiate migration in Cetacea, or the ways in which they may orientate or navigate, particularly when out of sight of land.

W. H. Dawbin (28, 29) discussed possible factors which might stimulate humpback whales, *Megaptera novaeangliae*, to leave the Antarctic feeding grounds and begin to migrate northwards, and also those which might determine the routes taken by the animals. The southern humpback apparently only requires coastal conditions while in the tropics for breeding. Favourable water temperatures in the western South Pacific are in the 25°C range, a value in good agreement with that given by T. Nemoto (78) for the breeding of North Pacific humpback whales around the Ryukyu Islands. In the southern hemisphere, females with newborn calves are the last to arrive on the Antarctic feeding grounds and the first to leave for the breeding grounds again at the end of the season. On the other hand, pregnant females are the first to arrive and the last to leave, thereby storing up the maximum possible food reserves prior to parturition and lactation. Dawbin plotted sea surface-temperature changes during the Antarctic feeding season and decided that the rate of change was much too small to be likely to initiate the type of differential migrations among females described above. The temperature range encountered is considerably less than that experienced by the animals on any phase of the migrations.

He concluded that change in day length was a much more likely factor to initiate migration. Lactating females leave the Antarctic and begin to move northwards when the mean day length at latitude 60°S drops to about 8.5 hours; pregnant females do not leave until it decreases to about 6.5 hours. The migration rate is relatively slow; humpbacks move through about 15° of latitude per month, with no apparent differences in the rate of movement between males and females, or females in various stages of the reproductive cycle.

During their northward or southward migrations humpbacks were deflected by coastlines running at angles across their north–south route (such as the east and west coasts of New Zealand). On a very local scale they have been observed to alter course to avoid turbid outwash from estuaries, but on the grand scale the migration routes could not be correlated with water mass, current movements or bottom topography. For example, on the northward migration off the east coast of New Zealand the humpbacks move with a north-flowing cold current for the first part of the passage past the archipelago, and into a south-flowing warm current for the second part, crossing both subsurface rises and canyons roughly at right angles to their passage.

Cetacean orientation and navigation

Our knowledge of the orientation and navigation of gray whales in the eastern North Pacific has been discussed by G. C. Pike (94) and K. S. Norris (84). Both concluded that the animals probably utilized all manner of sensory data available to them in order to fix position relative to the coast and to ascertain their direction of travel. Norris thought that gray whales generally appeared to follow bottom topography parallel to the coast during migration, but when they arrived at an anomalous region, such as subsurface canyon, the well-known 'spy-hopping' behaviour occurred. The whale carrying out this kind of behaviour rises vertically from the surface until the whole head is clear, and sustains the posture for some seconds, sometimes turning on its axis. It appears that the animal is looking for the coastline or other features such as islands, although how well mysticetes can see out of water is a matter of some dispute. In general they seem to merely be satisfied to keep the coastline either to the right or left of themselves, depending on the migration phase and thus the direction in which they are travelling. On the last stretch of the southward migration to the breeding lagoons the animals tend to move through quite shallow water close to shore, and it has been suggested that olfaction might play a part in detecting the semi-enclosed fresh or brackish water fed areas for which they are searching, although it is debatable whether or not whales possess an olfactory sense in the way that we understand it. There is no firm evidence that gray whales cease migration movements after dark (98).

Abundant underwater sounds, produced by fish, invertebrates, wave action against the shore and so on may be used by cetaceans to fix their position at least with respect to depth of water beneath them (84). The strange low-frequency pulses emitted by fin whales (and probably other rorquals) might function as a rather crude depth-sounding mechanism even though not of a frequency suitable for use in echolocation. Others, for example R. Payne (91), have suggested that these signals may be used in long-distance communication, but at such low frequencies they are almost universally directional. They also appear to contain little possible information content.

We really have no idea how truly pelagic species such as blue, sei, sperm and bottlenosed whales are able to orientate themselves and navigate across thousands of miles of open ocean. There are some data to suggest that sperm and bottlenosed whales may be influenced by the seasonal movements of water currents, but the migratory rorquals tend to cross latitudinal water masses more or less at right angles, as is apparent in the case of Southern Ocean humpbacks (29). Orientation with respect to the average position of the sun and moon may be involved in the movements of these animals; stellar navigation might be a possibility, since recent studies indicate good visual acuity in some cetaceans, both above and below water (46, 119). Nevertheless, these mammals do navigate and we may be fairly certain that a very high degree of learned behaviour is involved; the young whales almost certainly learn the route by accompanying experienced adults. Some authorities are worried that depletion of gene pool may lead to extinction in those cetacean populations reduced to a very small size by hunting, but depletion of the information pool is almost certainly as acute a problem in such cases, and just as important for their survival.

Cetacean breeding grounds

With the passage of time, whale populations have discovered and exploited major global sources of prey species concentrations in upwelling areas and along ocean fronts. Relatively little feeding by rorquals takes place during the low-latitude phases of their migrations (61, 62). Adult gray whales do not appear to feed on either their northward or southward migration although immature animals, which often do not make a complete migration (see pp. 61–2), may feed (26, 118). Humpbacks rarely feed when moving pole-ward; M. Nishiwaki showed that virtually no feeding occurred on the Ryukyu breeding grounds in the North Pacific (81), and there is also a very low level of feeding by rorquals off South Africa (4); winter distribution of fin whales did not correlate with distribution of euphausiid concentrations. By implication, this is probably also true for other rorqual species except *Balaenoptera edeni*. Such evidence as we have suggests that the breeding grounds of rorquals are determined by relatively simple parameters of which sea temperature is probably the most important. Coastal localities with shallow water are important for humpbacks (for example, the margins of the Koro Sea, Fiji (29), waters close to Maui, Hawaii, and the shallow platform reef banks of the Antilles) (2, 95, 120) (Figure 1.1); gray whales (the shallow bays of the eastern coast of Baja, California); and right whales (the coastal coves from South Carolina to Florida (97), bays of Campbell Island (36), the coast of Tristan da Cunha and the Golfo San Matias, Argentina). Little is known of the breeding grounds of blue and fin; they do not seem to require shallow water for successful calving. Their calving areas are probably offshore in most oceans, and perhaps more dispersed than those of the coastal breeding species, although localized winter concentrations of blue whales have been noted in the tropical Pacific off Central America (113, 114). Sei whales penetrate subtropical waters during winter months, where they collect their 'white scars' which are believed to be caused by bites by the small warm-water shark *Issistius brasiliensis* (49, 104, 105). Warm water appears essential for sperm whale breeding, but no one has been able to identify any other specific requirement. In any case, the distinction between breeding and feeding areas is vague in this species, particularly in the case of the females. Very little work has been carried out on breeding requirements of small odontocetes, although it is worth pointing out that different observers (36, 116, 117) have recorded very large seasonal concentrations of dolphins gathering in New Zealand waters, particularly

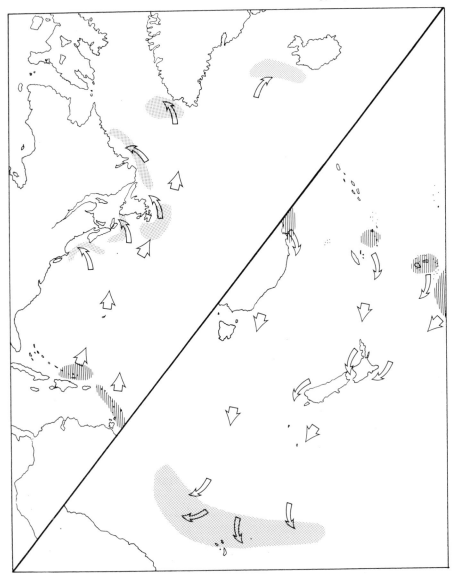

Figure 1.1 Migratory routes of the humpback whale, *Megaptera novaeangliae*, compared: western North Atlantic and western South Pacific. In the former region (upper left), the humpback whales breed in restricted areas of the Antilles (vertical striping), with up to 85 per cent of the animals on a very few offshore banks to the south-east of the Bahamas, and disperse to feed in coastal and offshore bank regions from Massachusetts to Greenland and Iceland during the summer months. In the western South Pacific (lower right) the breeding grounds are more dispersed, but the feeding grounds are generally well offshore, though many humpbacks have traditionally been taken around the Balleny Islands (stippled area). In both regions the populations follow the same general pattern, feeding during the summer months, then migrating into low latitudes for a relatively short period of calving and mating followed by a leisurely return migration.

Lagenorhynchus obscurus, with probable mating activity. I also reported a similar large concentration of right whale dolphins off the east coast of the South Island on one occasion. In other regions, up to one thousand northern right whale dolphins have occasionally been seen at one time (36). The specific oceanographic conditions present at the time of these unusual (800–5000+) concentrations of animals in restricted areas were not known.

Oceanographic structure of feeding grounds

Factors determining feeding areas are much more complex and most baleen whaling is carried out in both hemispheres over the major feeding grounds. Investigation of the oceanographic conditions which favour concentrations of prey species will thus perhaps enable us to unravel, in a large part at least, the reasons for the great short-term variations observed in whale distributions, and also analyse any long-term changes which may occur in these distributions. This very variation, and its influence on the relative movements of whales into and from the whaling grounds and on catch per unit effort, is one of the factors which most often frustrates accurate determination of population sizes and recruitment rates. Detailed season-by-season monitoring of feeding ground conditions is an essential part of global whale research.

Baleen whale feeding grounds in high latitudes have been classified into three major kinds, with subcategories (Figure 1.2) (74, 75). The first and structurally the simplest are those which occur on ocean fronts between major water masses. The second kind are oceanic eddy grounds; these may be of two types, either dynamic (that is, tongues or salients formed on ocean fronts) or topographic (that is, back eddies brought about as a result of water mass deflection by islands, capes, promontories or other surface features). The third kind are those grounds in areas of upwelling: these may also be divided into dynamic (brought about by ocean gyre movement or induced by cyclones or anticyclones) (5, 6, 100), and topographical (induced by sea mounts, subsurface ridges or edges of continental shelves). In all cases the most favourable whaling grounds are associated either with seasonal vertical stability of the water column, which facilitates the build up of phytoplankton and zooplankton, or with shear zones adjacent to upwellings where a high level of nutrients not only fosters high productivity of these organisms, but also favours their retention and accumulation in relatively local areas. Other zones may be just as productive, but the plankton is dispersed to other areas by water movements as rapidly as it is produced, with the formation of no local concentrations.

Upwelling and shear regions generate high productivity over quite wide

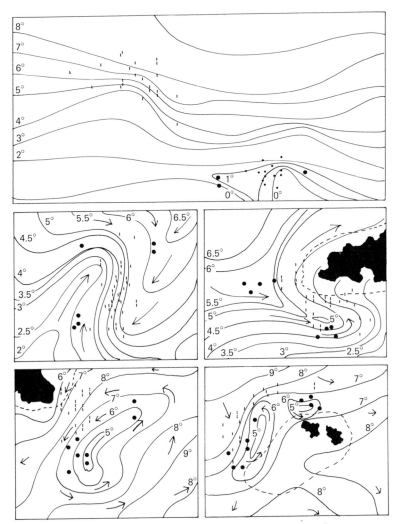

Figure 1.2 Classification of whaling ground types: top – ocean front type; centre – eddy type (left: dynamic, right: topographic); bottom – upwelling type (left: dynamic, right: topographic) (classification after Nasu) (75). Surface temperatures in degrees centigrade; solid lines represent isotherms; broken lines represent coastal shelf; typical species distributions are included; vertical bars represent fin whales; small closed circles (top figure only) represent minke whales; large closed circles represent sperm whales. After Gaskin (38).

areas, but only in recent years have they really begun to receive the attention that they deserve and there has been a tendency to talk of 'upwelling ecosystems' as a hierarchical structure distinct from the surrounding region. The problem of definition of such systems has been discussed in principle and detail by several authors in a recent symposium volume (16). Some workers confessed themselves unable to arrive at a hard-and-fast conclusion as to whether an upwelling constituted an independent marine ecosystem or not. On the basis of the description of 'ecosystem' by F. E. Smith (106) as 'a functional unit with recognisable boundaries and an internal homogeneity', upwelling areas fall short in several respects. They may be seasonal in strength or occurrence, especially if arising through divergence influenced by a wind field rather than just a coast line. Consequently 'internal homogeneity' may be difficult to demonstrate. Further problems are introduced when one attempts to define the 'boundary' of an upwelling. Studies of vertical transport and velocities are abundant in the literature; the nature and magnitude of horizontal transfer has been less studied. Classical analysis assumes constant mixing coefficients; field studies show that upwellings are often differentiated, with a frontal zone being present at the offshore edge of many upwellings where a sharp change in water characteristics occurs. In these areas, the system seems to be strongly governed by diffusion processes and advection (3, 44). There are other instances where such a frontal zone does not exist at all.

R. Margalef (64) argued that an upwelling could not be regarded as simply 'inflow (with nutrients) coming from depth', since analysis indicated that upwellings consisted of a number of active circulation cells. In some parts of an upwelling *depletion* of oxygen and some elements and compounds could be demonstrated.

Margalef concluded that we should consider the largest model possible – that of the 'world ocean'. Upwellings could be considered as 'points of stress' in the system or 'local deformations of the ecological field'; in functional terms they were points where *supplementary energy* was being applied to the ecosystem as a whole, in a way that was analogous to the application of fertilizers (or mechanization, irrigation, etc.) in agriculture. Upwellings are less mature subsystems than the areas around them, and vertical movement within the subsystem prevents any organizational sophistication. There is much variability, therefore, and the food-chains as a consequence tend to be short. It is suggested that in such systems opportunistic feeders would hold a strategic and tactical advantage. Shortened food-chains favour high fish production (101), as is observed in the case of the Peruvian anchoveta *Engraulis ringens*. Furthermore, small clupeoid fishes in upwelling areas tend to be largely phytophagous (that is, feeding on phytoplankton) (59). The *duration* of production in such regions may be far more important than the intensity (24, 25). Long duration of production would certainly favour the types of feeding strategies used by baleen whales and probably those of odontocete whales too. Whales can certainly be classified as opportunistic feeders. The potent combination of high local productivity of considerable duration, with

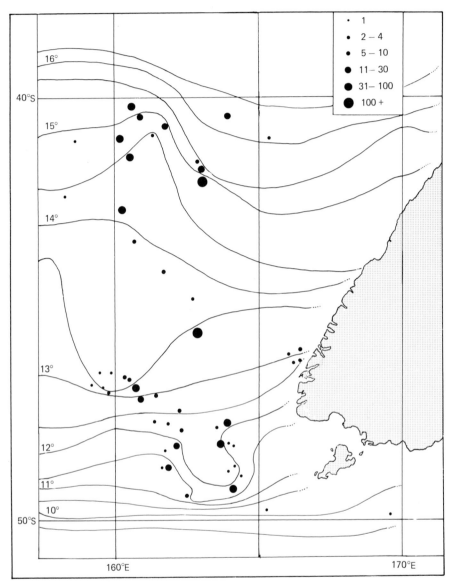

Figure 1.3   Distribution of sei whales sighted from *Chiyoda Maru No. 5* in summer of 1966/7 off south-western New Zealand, in relation to isotherm salients (data from reports by K. Nasu and D. E. Gaskin, cruise biologists). After Gaskin (38).

a shortened food-chain greatly favours the establishment of significant baleen whale populations (18, 19, 33, 38).

The relationships which may be observed between baleen and sperm whale distributions and the various types of oceanographic structures of

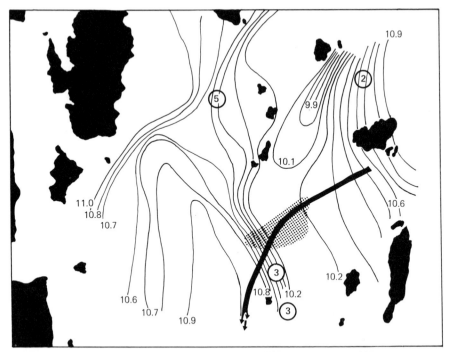

Figure 1.4   Distribution of Cetacea in the Head Harbour region of New Brunswick, Canada, during a day in August 1978, with respect to surface isotherm salients and location of concentration of food species. Temperatures in degrees centigrade. Numbers represent the size of tight schools of *P. phocoena*, broad track with arrows the movements of three fin whales during a twenty-minute period. Stippled area is a large subsurface school of fish, probably Atlantic herring, detected by sonar. All animals moving inshore or down passage (towards bottom of page, more or less south), with incoming tide. From data collected by author, G. J. D. Smith and D. B. Yurick.

the whaling grounds, are better illustrated rather than described (Figures 1.2–1.4). Within a given area baleen whales often noticeably concentrate on isotherm 'tongues' or salients where relatively warm water penetrates into a cold water mass or vice versa (38, 53, 90). Sperm whales may concentrate on the edges of cyclonic zones of upwelling and in regions where steep horizontal and vertical gradients coincide, particularly where the vertical gradient is of the order of 5°C/surface 100 m (37). In certain areas favourable intermediate water feeding conditions may exist even though surface conditions appear unfavourable (113). Because of the inclination of isopyknic surfaces, convergence zones may curve away from the surface position of the convergence with increasing depth. In other areas they are sometimes further displaced by divergence zones.

Variations in the positions of whaling grounds may be studied by comparative calculations to locate the mathematical centre of the topological zone comprising the whaling ground in successive years, following the formulae devised and used by M. Uda (109, 110) and K. Nasu (74, 75). Competition between species may occur; T. Nemoto (78) observed that other rorquals seemed to leave when sei whales arrived on the grounds, but was unable to determine whether this was a primary effect or the result of a change in distribution of food species. Similar successions have been observed off South Africa (4).

The influence of oceanographic conditions on the distribution of baleen whales and sperm whales in the eastern part of the tropical Pacific was discussed by A. F. Volkov and I. F. Moroz (113). Studies during 1975 revealed alternating sequences of high and low abundance of baleen whales between 14°N and 10°S in the surveyed region between longitudes 80°W and 110°W.

Low abundance between 10°N and 14°N was related to the presence in these latitudes of 'quasistationary' (that is, stable in geographic location) 'stale' tropic water moving in with the anticyclonic drift circulation. Biomass at all trophic levels is characteristically low in this region. Between 7°N and 10°N a zone of high abundance was encountered; biomass productivity at all trophic levels was at least twice that found in the northern zone. This productivity was correlated with presence of upwelling along the northern tropical divergence. Baleen whales were to be found associated with the northern and southern boundaries of this zone. The importance of zooplankton concentrations within Langmuir convergences in such areas with respect to baleen whale feeding has been discussed in a recent paper by P. F. Brodie and his co-workers (19).

South of the north tropical convergence a zone of downwelling was recorded, with low productivity and biomass, and correspondingly small numbers of baleen whales. Further south still, in the vicinity of the equatorial divergence, productivity and baleen whale abundance were once more relatively high, although Volkov and Moroz drew attention to the distribution of the whales again being associated with the periphery of the divergence.

These authors reported that they were less able to relate the distribution of sperm whales in the region to oceanographic phenomena immediately discernible in surface waters. They pointed out that the feeding behaviour of sperm whales is largely tied to prey, especially cephalopods, distributed in intermediate and deep waters. Although the majority of marine mammals exploit food species occurring in the upper 50–100 metres of the ocean, some small pelagic odontocetes such as *Stenella* sp. regularly forage down to 250 metres in the 'acoustical scattering layer' on or below the thermocline in tropical waters (31, 93). The sperm whale has become adapted to a trophic habitat involving even deeper regions of the ocean, and is one of the few marine mammals (except perhaps for some ziphiids, such as *Hyperoodon*) which can readily exploit the cephalopod populations of the lower regions of the continental slope (22, 58).

A series of seasonal changes of whaling-ground location in the Southern Ocean was studied by T. Nemoto (79) with particular respect to the distribution of the fin whales in Antarctic areas III–IV between 1958 and 1961. The abundance of fin whales in the pack-ice waters of these areas in 1958–9 was correlated with an abundance of immature *Euphausia superba*; however, in 1959–60 the number of *E. superba* in the same region was very low, and correspondingly low density of fin whales was recorded. The whales tended to remain well north of the pack and may have been taking other prey species such as *E. vallentini*. During 1960–1 a westward shift of the main concentration of fin whales appeared to be associated with encroachment of cold water from the east wind drift over the Kerguelen-Gaussberg Ridge. The resulting conditions produced mixing, boundary eddies, and consequent good feeding conditions for the whales. Still further west these conditions did not occur, and the density of fin whales was far lower. Deflection of the east wind drift in that region is apparently a fairly common phenomenon, resulting in dispersal of *E. superba* further northwards in this region than elsewhere (66, 78).

Influence of zooplankton distributions and behaviour on feeding of baleen whales

Further consideration of conditions governing zooplankton distributions is relevant here. Analysis of variation in dispersal of key zooplankton species, such as calanoid copepods and euphausiids, yields data basic to a study of the movements and dispersal patterns of animals higher in the trophic web. Though fish and squid form the greatest fraction of odontocete diet and are important components in the food of some baleen whales, they too are ultimately dependent upon zooplankton. For example, a study of herring movements may ultimately become largely a study of changes in copepod distributions. Changes in the distributions of phytoplankton and zooplankton species generally result from alterations in the relative positions of water masses and currents. These can usually be detected in a practical way by significant changes in surface temperatures, vertical profiles, and current strengths and directions. On an oceanic scale, distributions of copepods and euphausiid species are, however, relatively constant except for rather regular seasonal changes. Even major alterations in oceanographic conditions generally cause changes of abundance only in the peripheral zones of a species' normal range. Such variations have been observed in euphausiid distributions (17), fluctuations were correlated with irregular changes in the boundaries of the

California Current, Kuro Shio Current, North Pacific Drift and similar water masses.

The ultimate form of localized euphausiid concentration is the 'surface swarm' or 'surface raft', when individuals are so densely packed together that they form reddish patches visible for some distance. The reasons for formation of such swarms, even whether they be the results of active or passive processes, are little known (69). Y. Komaki (54) suggested that mixing of cold offshore water with warm coastal waters produced conditions under which the euphausiids swarmed. The euphausiids almost always concentrated at the very edge of the cold water; however, this merely indicates rather precisely the conditions under which such swarming occurs, and is in agreement with the author's own observations on swarming of *Meganyctiphanes norvegica* off the coast of Brier Island, south-western Nova Scotia, and in Head Harbour Passage, southern New Brunswick, and leaves us little wiser as to the reason for the swarming. In the two Canadian localities the surface rafts are almost invariably formed in conjunction with less obvious but very abundant concentrations of calanoid copepods. In the Brier Island region they appear to be actively feeding (20). Other studies on *M. norvegica* have shown that the swarmers might be aggregating in the pre-breeding periods (15). In Head Harbour Passage and adjacent areas, where swarms are consistently present in summer during most seasons (41), we have observed some mating behaviour. Such irregular swarming, however, differs in several ways from real pre-spawning aggregation (69). Swarms of *Euphausia superba* may first form during the larval stages and become semi-permanent aggregations (66). Although, J. Mauchline (68) has suggested that photophores might play some role in deep water or at night, the mechanisms of swarm maintenance are really unknown. P. F. Brodie and his colleagues (19) have pointed out that swarming in post-breeding euphausiids in the last year of their life is rather inexplicable; since the animals are past breeding, it can have no selective value, and it is hard to see how it could have evolved. This supports the hypothesis of some kind of traumatic or purely physical concentrating action beyond the control of individual euphausiids.

The feeding behaviour and diving capabilities of baleen whales dictate that in practice we are largely interested in what is happening in the upper 100 metres of the whaling grounds. Vertical migrations of zooplankton have been the subject of much intensive research, and the reader is referred to monographs by J. W. S. Marr (66) (on *E. superba*), J. Mauchline and L. R. Fisher (69), and M. E. Vinogradov (112) for detailed treatment.

Vinogradov suggested that there is little real ecological distinction between such zooplankton species as *Calanus finmarchicus* which lay eggs in the surface layers, and those such as *C. cristatus* which deposit their eggs in relatively deep water but have larvae which rise quite early in development to complete their metamorphosis in surface layers. In both cases the greatest effect of feeding by these groups is in the surface layers. Studies of northern hemisphere zooplankton, important in the diet of some whale species (or the fish upon which they feed), show that in the winter months they concentrate in areas where relatively warm intermediate water occurs below the lower limit of the influence of winter convection. If the intermediate water layer is very cold (for example, as in parts of the Sea of Okhotsk), then zooplankton are generally scarce. Species with this kind of winter distribution include *C. cristatus* and *C. plumchrus*; in one area of the North Pacific and Bering Sea region right whales and relatively young fin whales feed on the former, and in another area right and sei whales feed upon the same species (88). A few species of zooplankton such as *Parathemisto* sp. and *Metridia* sp. may sometimes appear in surface waters even during winter, but only locally (112).

In the normal course of events the calanoids will begin to migrate upwards into surface layers for feeding and reproduction during the spring. This movement is generally completed by the end of May and is correlated with the arrival of the first baleen whales in the high-latitude feeding grounds of the North Atlantic and North Pacific. By the end of June a typical summer distribution pattern has appeared, with the bulk of the zooplankton biomass between about 10 and 50 metres below the surface. As summer comes to an end the calanoids again begin to descend, *Calanus cristatus* first and *C. plumchrus* a little later. *Eucalanus* spp. may remain in the surface layers until quite late in the season, providing local feeding for rather small numbers of whales. But by the end of October the vertical distribution pattern is approaching that of the typical winter situation. Secondary diurnal migrations have been recognized in all cases studied, but these are generally of rather small amplitude and intensity except in the case of *Calanus finmarchicus* (112). The latter species appears to fill the same niche in the North Atlantic that *C. cristatus* and *C. plumchrus* occupy in the North Pacific.

Similar vertical migrations have been recorded in the Southern Ocean. During the southern winter (June–September) the zooplankton most important in the diet of baleen whales, such as *Euphausia superba*, *E. vallentini*, *Calanus acutus*, *C. propinquus* and the hyperiid amphipod *Parathemisto gaudichaudi*, concentrate between 200 and 250 metres below the surface. By the end of October they have moved up to the 100 metre zone, and during summer into the 0–50 metre zone, often with the formation of surface swarms in suitable areas. Species such as *Euphausia superba* carry out diurnal migrations of some significance during the summer months. At the same time the main semi-circumpolar currents carry the zooplankton away from the Antarctic continent and concentrate them in the vicinity of the Antarctic convergence or divergence. The possible influence of southern cyclones in inducing upwelling in these regions, with resulting effects on plankton and whale concentrations, should not be overlooked (5, 6). At the end of April the zooplankton of the Southern Ocean begin to descend once more to about 200 metres. The sinking mechanism appears to involve uptake of water into the tissues after winter moult, with a consequent slight but significant change in specific gravity (14). Return of the zooplankton towards the Antarctic continent is effected by their encountering currents in the intermediate water with a marked southward component (60). The pattern resembles that found in the northern hemisphere, and also correlates closely with major baleen whale distributions both in time and space. In all cases the baleen whales appear to be able to exploit these prey populations with complete success only when the bulk of the biomass is in the upper 100 metres (53).

Diurnal feeding patterns in Cetacea

The diurnal migrations of euphausiids such as *E. superba* have considerable influence on feeding times of fish and whales and, in turn, an important bearing on problems of daily food intake discussed elsewhere (pp. 83–7). Feeding patterns have been analysed in the case of several species of baleen whale (77–9, 80) and most particularly for the sei whale by A. Kawamura (53). As might be expected, feeding patterns are rather variable and depend on local conditions. But twice-daily feeding is quite common in fin and sei, with different species being taken at different times. For example, *Calanus simillimus* is taken in the evening, and *C. tonsus* generally during daylight hours, although the quantities of the latter were often well below half the stomach capacity.

In the case of odontocete Cetacea, rather less data are available. Sperm whales may feed most efficiently at night (67). Since squid rise into surface layers after dark (110), feeding under such conditions would require less energy to be exerted by the whales. Sperm whales making feeding dives in daylight hours may be an indication of indifferent feeding conditions (40). The presence of lantern fish (*Myctophus* spp.) in sperm whale stomachs does not necessarily indicate deep feeding, since these species may rise to the surface at night (30). Nevertheless, studies on the diet and feeding habits of delphinids in the eastern Pacific strongly indicate that these small odontocetes regularly forage down to depths between 120 and 250 metres to feed upon mesopelagic species such as *Myctophus* spp. (32, 93). More recently W. E. Evans, by monitoring dolphins bearing radiotelemetric packages (31, 65), has shown conclusively that dive depths are closely correlated both by day and night with the depth of the deep scattering layer (acoustical scattering layer), the zone within which *Myctophus* and similar genera are most abundant.

References

1   Andrews, R. C. 1911. 'A new porpoise from Japan', *Am. Mus. Nat. Hist.*, vol. 3, pp. 31–52.

2   Balcomb, K. C. and Nichols, G. 1978. 'Western North Atlantic humpback whales', *Rep. Int. Whal. Commn*, vol. 28, pp. 159–64.

3   Bang, N. D. 1973. 'Characteristics of an intense ocean frontal system in the upwell regime west of Cape Town', *Tellus*, vol. 25, pp. 256–65.

4   Bannister, J. L. and Baker, A. de C. 1967. 'Observations on food and feeding of baleen whales at Durban', *Norsk Hvalfangsttid.*, vol. 56, pp. 78–82.

5   Beklemishev, C. W. 1960. 'Southern atmospheric cyclones and the whale feeding grounds of the Antarctic', *Nature*, vol. 187, pp. 530–1.

6   Beklemishev, C. W. 1961. '(Influence of atmospheric cyclones on the distribution of feeding whales in the Antarctic)', *Trudy Inta okeanol. A.N. SSSR*, vol. 51, pp. 122–41.

7   Benjaminsen, T. 1972. 'On the biology of the bottlenose whale, *Hyperoodon ampullatus* (Forster)', *Norw. J. Zool.*, vol. 20, pp. 233–41.

8   Benjaminsen, T. and Christensen, I. 1979. 'The natural history of the bottlenose whale, *Hyperoodon ampullatus* (Forster)' in H. E. Winn and B. L. Olla (eds.), *Behavior of Marine Animals: Current Perspectives in Research Vol. 3: Cetaceans*, New York and London, Plenum Press, pp. 143–64.

9   Best, P. B. 1967. 'The sperm whale (*Physeter catodon*) off the west coast of South Africa 1. Ovarian changes and their significance', *Investl. Rep. Div. Sea Fish. S. Afr.*, vol. 61, pp. 1–27.

10 Best, P. B. 1969. 'The sperm whale (*Physeter catodon*) off the west coast of South Africa 3. Reproduction in the male', *Investl. Rep. Div. Sea Fish. S. Afr.*, vol. 72, pp. 1–20.

11 Best, P. B. 1974. 'The biology of the sperm whale as it relates to stock management' in W. E. Schevill (ed.), *The Whale Problem: A Status Report*, Cambridge, Mass., Harvard University Press, pp. 257–93.

12 Best, P. B. 1979. 'Social organization in sperm whales, *Physeter macrocephalus*' in H. E. Winn and B. L. Olla (eds.), *Behaviour in Marine Animals: Current Perspectives in Research Vol. 3: Cetaceans*, New York and London, Plenum Press, pp. 227–89.

13 Berzin, A. A. 1978. 'Whale distribution in tropical eastern Pacific waters', *Rep. Int. Whal. Commn.*, vol. 28, pp. 173–7.

14 Beyer, F. 1962. 'Absorption of water in crustaceans and the standing stock of zooplankton', *Rapp. P.-v. Reun. Cons. perm. int. Explor. Mer.*, vol. 153, pp. 79–85.

15 Bigelow, H. B. and Sears, M. 1939. 'Studies of the waters of the continental shelf, Cape Cod to Chesapeake Bay. III. A volumetric study of the zooplankton', *Mem. Mus. comp. Zool. Harvard*, vol. 54, pp. 179–378.

16 Boje, R. and Tomczack, M. 1978. *Upwelling Ecosystems*, Berlin, Heidelberg and New York, Springer-Verlag.

17 Brinton, E. 1962. 'The distribution of Pacific euphausiids', *Bull. Scripps Instn. Oceanogr.*, vol. 8, pp. 51–270.

18 Brodie, P. F. 1977. 'Form, function and energetics of Cetacea: a discussion' in R. J. Harrison (ed.), *Functional Anatomy of Marine Mammals*, vol. 3, London, Academic Press, pp. 45–56.

19 Brodie, P. F., Sameoto, D. D. and Sheldon, R. W. 1978. 'Population densities of euphausiids off Nova Scotia as indicated by net samples, whale stomach contents, and sonar', *Limnol. Oceanogr.* vol. 23, pp. 1264–7.

20 Brown, R. G. B., Barker, S. P. and Gaskin, D. E. 1979. 'Daytime surface swarming by *Meganyctiphanes norvegica* (M. Sars) (Crustacea, Euphausiacea) off Brier

Island, Bay of Fundy', *Can. J. Zool.*, vol. 57, pp. 2285–91.

21 Christensen, I. 1973. 'Age determination, age distribution and growth of bottlenose whales, *Hyperoodon ampullatus* (Forster), in the Labrador Sea', *Norw. J. Zool.*, vol. 21, pp. 331–40.

22 Clarke, M. R. 1979. 'The head of the sperm whale', *Scientific American*, vol. 240, pp. 128–41.

23 Clarke, R. 1956. 'Sperm whales of the Azores', *Discovery*, Rep. 28, pp. 237–98.

24 Cushing, D. H. 1971. 'Upwelling and the production of fish', *Adv. Mar. Biol.*, vol. 9, pp. 255–334.

25 Cushing, D. H. 1978. 'Upper trophic levels in upwelling areas' in R. Boje and M. Tomczack (eds.), Upwelling Ecosystems, Berlin, Heidelberg and New York, Springer-Verlag, pp. 101–10.

26 Darling, J. 1977. 'Population biology and behaviour of the grey whale (*Eschrichtius robustus*) in Pacific rim National Park', M.Sc. thesis, University of Victoria, British Columbia.

27 Davis, A., Richardson, W. J., Johnson, S. R. and Renaud, W. F. 1978. 'Status of the Lancaster Sound narwhal population in 1976', *Rep. Int. Whal. Commn*, vol. 28, pp. 209–16.

28 Dawbin, W. H. 1956. 'The migrations of humpback whales which pass the New Zealand coast', *Trans. R. Soc. N.Z.*, vol. 84, pp. 147–96.

29 Dawbin, W. H. 1966. 'The seasonal migratory cycle of humpback whales' in K. S. Norris (ed.), *Whales, Dolphins, and Porpoises*, Berkeley and Los Angeles, University of California Press, pp. 145–70.

30 Doogue, R. B. and Moreland, J. M. 1964. *New Zealand Sea Angler's Guide*, Wellington, Reed, 3rd edn.

31 Evans, W. E. 1974. 'Radiotelemetric studies of two species of small odontocete cetaceans' in W. E. Schevill (ed.), *The Whale Problem: A Status Report*, Cambridge, Mass., Harvard University Press, pp. 385–94.

32 Fitch, J. E. and Brownell, R. L. Jr. 1968. 'Fish otoliths in cetaceans stomachs and their importance in interpreting feeding habits', *J. Fish. Res. Bd. Canada*, vol. 25, pp. 2561–74.

33 Fordyce, R. E. 1977. 'The development of the circum-Antarctic current and the evolution of the Mysticeti (Mammalia: Cetacea)', *Palaeogeography, Palaeoclimatology, Paleoecology*, vol. 21, pp. 265–71.

34 Fraser, F. C. 1953. 'Reports on Cetacea stranded on the British coasts from 1938 to 1947', *Bull. Brit. Mus. (Nat. Hist.)*, vol. 13, pp. 1–48.

35 Gambell, R. 1972. 'Sperm whales off Durban', *Discovery*, Rep. 35, pp. 199–358.

36 Gaskin, D. E. 1968. 'The New Zealand Cetacea', *Fish. Res. Bd. N.Z. Mar. Dept.* (new series), vol. 1, pp. 1–92.

37 Gaskin, D. E. 1971. 'Distribution and movements of sperm whales *Physeter catodon* L. in the Cook Strait region of New Zealand', *Norw. J. Zool.*, vol. 19, pp. 241–59.

38 Gaskin, D. E. 1976. 'The evolution, zoogeography and ecology of Cetacea', *Oceanogr. Mar. Biol. Ann. Rev.*, vol. 14, pp. 247–346.

39 Gaskin, D. E. 1977. 'Harbour porpoise *Phocoena phocoena* (L.) in the western approaches to the Bay of Fundy 1969–75', *Rep. Int. Whal. Commn.*, vol. 27, pp. 487–92.

40 Gaskin, D. E. and Cawthorn, M. W. 1967. 'Diet and feeding habits of the sperm whale (*Physeter catodon* L.) in the Cook Strait region of New Zealand', *N.Z.J. mar. Freshwat. Res.*, vol. 1, pp. 156–79.

41 Gaskin, D. E. and Smith, G. J. D. 1979. 'Observations on marine mammals, birds, and environmental conditions in the Head Harbour region of the Bay of Fundy' in D. J. Scarratt (ed.), *Evaluation of recent data relative to potential oil spills in the Passamaquoddy area, Fisheries & Marine Service, Canada, Technical Report*, no. 901, pp. 69–86.

42   Gaskin, D. E., Smith, G. J. D. and Watson, A. P. 1975. 'Preliminary study of movements of harbor porpoises (*Phocoena phocoena*) in the Bay of Fundy using radiotelemetry', *Can. J. Zool.*, vol. 53, pp. 1466–71.

43   Greendale, R. G. and Brousseau-Greendale, C. 1976. 'Observations of marine mammals at Cape Hay, Bylot Island during the summer of 1976', *Fisheries & Marine Service Canada, Technical Report*, no. 680, pp. 1–25.

44   Hagen, E. 1974. 'Ein einfaches Schema der Entwicklung von Kaltwasserrauftriebszellen vor der nordwestafrikanischen Kuste', *Beitr. Meeresk.*, vol. 33, pp. 115–25.

45   Harmer, S. F. 1927. 'Report on Cetacea stranded on the British coasts from 1913 to 1926', *Brit. Mus. Nat. Hist.*, vol. 10, pp. 1–91.

46   Herman, L., Peacock, M. F., Yunker, M. P. and Madsen, C. J. 1975. 'Bottlenosed dolphin double-slit pupil yields equivalent aerial and underwater diurnal acuity', *Science*, vol. 189, pp. 650–652.

47   Houck, W. J. 1976. 'The taxonomic status of the species of the genus *Phocoenoides*', FAO of the UN, Scientific Consultation on Marine Mammals, Bergen, Norway, 31 August–7 September, 1976, document ACMRR/MM/SC/114.

48   Ivashin, M. V. 1967. '(Whale globe-trotter)', *Priroda*, Moscow, pp. 105–7.

49   Jones, E. 1971. '*Isistius brasiliensis*, a squaloid shark, the probable cause of crater wounds on fishes and small cetaceans', *Fish. Bull.*, vol. 69, pp. 791–8.

50   Jonsgård, Å. and Lyshoel, P. B. 1970. 'A contribution to the knowledge of the biology of the killer whale', *Norw. J. Zool.*, vol. 18, pp. 41–8.

51   Kasuya, T. 1976. 'Preliminary report of the biology, catch and populations of *Phocoenoides* in the western North Pacific', FAO of the UN, Scientific Consultation on Marine Mammals, Bergen, Norway, 31 August–7 September 1976, document ACMRR/MM/SC/21, pp. 1–20.

52   Kasuya, T. and Kureha, K. 1979. 'The population of finless porpoise in the Inland Sea of Japan', *Sci. Rep. Whales Res. Inst.*, vol. 31, pp. 1–44.

53   Kawamura, A. 1974. 'Food and feeding ecology in the southern sei whale', *Sci. Rep. Whales Res. Inst.*, vol. 26, pp. 25–144.

54   Komaki, Y. 1967. 'On the surface swarming of euphausiid crustaceans', *Pacific Sci.*, vol. 21, pp. 433–48.

55   Leatherwood, J. S. 1974. 'A note on gray whale behavioral interactions with other marine mammals', *Mar. Fish. Rev.*, vol. 36, pp. 45–50.

56   Leatherwood, J. S. and Fielding, M. R. 1974. 'A summary of distribution and movements of Dall porpoises *Phocoenoides dalli* off southern California and Baja California', FAO of the UN, ACMRR meeting at La Jolla, 16–19 December 1974, working paper, no. 42.

57   Leatherwood, J. S. and Walker, W. A. 1979. 'The northern right whale dolphin *Lissodelphis borealis* Peale in the eastern North Pacific' in H. E. Winn and B. L. Olla (eds.), *Behavior of Marine Animals; Current Perspectives in Research Vol. 3: Cetaceans*, New York and London, Plenum Press, pp. 85–141.

58   Lockyer, C. 1977. 'Observations on diving behaviour of the sperm whale' in M. Angel (ed.), *A Voyage of Discovery*, Oxford and New York, Pergamon Press, pp. 591–609.

59   Longhurst, A. R. 1971. 'The clupeoid resources of tropical seas', *Oceanogr. Mar. Biol. Ann. Rev.*, vol. 9, pp. 349–85.

60   Mackintosh, N. A. 1937. 'The seasonal circulation of the Antarctic macroplankton', *Discovery*, Rep. 16, pp. 367–412.

61   Mackintosh, N. A. 1965. *The Stocks of Whales*, London, Fishing News Books.

62   Mackintosh, N. A. 1966. 'The distribution of southern blue and fin whales' in K. S. Norris (ed.), *Whales, Dolphins, and Porpoises*, Berkeley and Los Angeles, University of California Press, pp. 125–44.

63   Mansfield, A. W., Smith, T. G. and Beck, B. 1975. 'The narwhal *Monodon*

monoceros, in eastern Canadian waters', *J. Fish. Res. Bd. Canada*, vol. 32, pp. 1041–6.

64 Margalef, R. 1978. 'What is an upwelling ecosystem?' in R. Boje and M. Tomczak (eds.), *Upwelling Ecosystems*, Berlin, Heidelberg and New York, Springer-Verlag, pp. 11–12.

65 Martin, H., Evans, W. E. and Bowers, C. A. 1971. 'Methods for radio tracking marine mammals in the open sea', *Trans. IEEE Conference on Engineering in the Ocean Environment, September 1971*, San Diego, California, pp. 44–9.

66 Marr, J. W. S. 1962. 'The natural history and geography of the Antarctic krill (*Euphausia superba* Dana)', *Discovery*, Rep. 32, pp. 33–464.

67 Matsushita, T. 1955. '(Daily rhythmic activity of the sperm whales in the Antarctic Ocean)', *Bull. Jap. Soc. scient. Fish.*, vol. 20, pp. 770–3.

68 Mauchline, J. 1960. 'The biology of the euphausiid crustacean, *Meganyctiphanes norvegica* (M. Sars)', *Proc. R. Soc. Edinb.*, B (Biol.), vol. 67, pp. 141–70.

69 Mauchline, J. and Fisher, L. R. 1969. 'The biology of euphausiids', *Adv. mar. Biol.*, vol. 7, pp. 1–454.

70 Mitchell, E. and Kozicki, V. M. 1978. 'Sperm whale regional closed seasons: proposed protection during mating and calving', *Rep. Int. Whal. Commn*, vol. 28, pp. 195–8.

71 Miyazaki, N., Kasuya, T., Nishiwaki, M. and Dawbin, W. H. 1974. 'Distribution and migration of two species of *Stenella* in the Pacific coast of Japan', *Sci. Rep. Whales Res. Inst.*, vol. 26, pp. 227–43.

72 Møhl-Hansen, U. 1954. 'Investigations of reproduction and growth of the porpoise (*Phocoena phocoena* (L.)) from the Baltic', *Vidensk Medd. Dan. Naturhist. Foren. Khobenhaven*, vol. 116, pp. 369–96.

73 Morejohn, G. V. 1979. 'The natural history of Dall's porpoise in the North Pacific Ocean' in H. E. Winn and B. L. Olla (eds.), *Behavior of Marine Animals; Current Perspectives in Research Vol. 3 : Cetaceans*, New York and London, Plenum Press, pp. 45–83.

74 Nasu, K. 1963. 'Oceanography and whaling ground in the subarctic region of the Pacific Ocean', *Sci. Rep. Whales Res. Inst.*, vol. 17, pp. 105–55.

75 Nasu, K. 1966. 'Fishery oceanography study on the baleen whaling grounds', *Sci. Rep. Whales Res. Inst.*, vol. 20, pp. 157–210.

76 Neave, D. J. and Wright, B. S. 1968. 'Seasonal migrations of the harbor porpoise (*Phocoena phocoena*) and other Cetacea in the Bay of Fundy', *J. Mammal.*, vol. 49, pp. 259–64.

77 Nemoto, T. 1957. 'Foods of baleen whales in the northern Pacific', *Sci. Rep. Whales Res. Inst.*, vol. 12, pp. 33–89.

78 Nemoto, T. 1959. 'Food of baleen whales with reference to whale movements', *Sci. Rep. Whales Res. Inst.*, vol. 14, pp. 149–290.

79 Nemoto, T. 1962. 'Food of baleen whales collected in recent Japanese Antarctic whaling expeditions', *Sci. Rep. Whales Res. Inst.*, vol. 16, pp. 89–103.

80 Nemoto, T. and Kawamura, A. 1977. 'Characteristics of food habits and distribution of baleen whales with special reference to the abundance of North Pacific sei whale', *Rep. Int. Whal. Commn* (special issue 1), pp. 80–7.

81 Nishiwaki, M. 1959. 'Humpback whales in Ryukyuan waters', *Sci. Rep. Whales Res. Inst.*, vol. 14, pp. 49–87.

82 Nishiwaki, M. 1966. 'Distribution and migration of the larger cetaceans in the North Pacific as shown by Japanese whaling results' in K. S. Norris (ed.), *Whales, Dolphins, and Porpoises*, Berkeley and Los Angeles, University of California Press, pp. 171–91.

83 Nishiwaki, M. 1967. 'Distribution and migration of marine mammals in the North Pacific area', *Bull. Ocean Res. Univ. Tokyo*, vol. 1, pp. 1–64.

84 Norris, K. S. 1966. 'Some observations on the migration and orientation of marine

mammals', *Proc. 27th Ann. Biol. Colloq., Corvallis*, pp. 101–25.

85 Ohsumi, S. 1966. 'Sexual segregation of the sperm whale', *Sci. Rep. Whales Res. Inst.*, vol. 20, pp. 1–16.

86 Ohsumi, S. 1979. 'Bryde's whale in the North Pacific in 1977', *Rep. Int. Whal. Commn*, vol. 29, pp. 265–6.

87 Ohsumi, S., Masaki, Y. and Wada, S. 1977. 'Seasonal distribution of sperm whales sighted by scouting boats in the North Pacific and southern hemisphere', *Rep. Int. Whal. Commn*, vol. 27, pp. 308–23.

88 Omura, H. 1958. 'North Pacific right whale', *Sci. Rep. Whales Res. Inst.*, vol. 13, pp. 1–52.

89 Omura, H. 1973. 'A review of pelagic whaling operations in the Antarctic based on the effort and catch data in 10° squares of latitude and longitude', *Sci. Rep. Whales Res. Inst.*, vol. 25, pp. 105–203.

90 Omura, H. and Nemoto, T. 1955. 'Sei whales in the adjacent waters of Japan, III Relation between movement and water temperature of the sea', *Sci. Rep. Whales Res. Inst*, vol. 10, pp. 79–87.

91 Payne, R. and Webb, D. 1971. 'Orientation by means of long range acoustic signaling in baleen whales', *Ann. NY Acad. Sci.*, vol. 188, pp. 110–42.

92 Perrin, W. F. 1975. 'Distribution and differentiation of populations of dolphins of the genus *Stenella* in the eastern tropical Pacific', *J. Fish. Res. Bd. Canada*, vol. 32, pp. 1059–67.

93 Perrin, W. F., Warner, R. R., Fiscus, C. H. and Holts, D. B. 1973. 'Stomach contents of porpoise, *Stenella* sp., and yellowfin tuna, *Thunnus albacares*, in mixed species aggregations', *Fishery Bull. Fish. Wildl. Serv. US*, vol. 70, pp. 1077–92.

94 Pike, G. C. 1962. 'Migration and feeding of the gray whale (*Eschrichtius gibbosus*)', *J. Fish. Res. Bd. Canada*, vol. 19, pp. 815–38.

95 Price, W. S. 1979. 'Western Atlantic humpback whale – *Megaptera novaeangliae*', *A report prepared for the People's Trust for Endangered Species*, London, England, mimeo.

96 Privalikhin, V. I. and Berzin, A. A. 1978. 'Abundance and distribution of Bryde's whale (*Balaenoptera edeni*) in the Pacific Ocean', *Rep. Int. Whal. Commn*, vol. 28, pp. 301–2.

97 Reeves, R. R., Mead, J. G. and Katona, S. 1978. 'The right whale, *Eubalaena glacialis*, in the western North Atlantic', *Rep. Int. Whal. Commn*, vol. 28, pp. 303–12.

98 Rice, D. W. and Wolman, A. A., 1971. 'The life history and ecology of the gray whale (*Eschrichtius robustus*)', *Am. Soc. Mammalogists, Special Publ.*, no. 3.

99 Ropelewski, A. 1957. 'Morswin (*Phocoena phocoena* L.) jako przyłow w polskim rybołowstwie bałtyckim', *Prace MIR w Gdyni*, vol. 9, pp. 427–37.

100 Ruud, J. T. 1932. 'On the biology of southern Euphausiidae', *Hvalråd Skr.*, vol. 2, pp. 1–105.

101 Ryther, J. H. 1969. 'Photosynthesis and fish production in the sea', *Science*, vol. 166, pp. 72–6.

102 Saayman, G. S. and Tayler, C. K. 1973. 'Social organisation of inshore dolphins (*Tursiops aduncus* and *Sousa*) in the Indian Ocean', *J. Mammal.*, vol. 54, pp. 993–6.

103 Saayman, G. S. and Tayler, C. K. 1979. 'The socioecology of humpback dolphins (*Sousa* sp.)' in H. E. Winn and B. L. Olla (eds.), *Behavior of Marine Animals; Current Perspectives in Research Vol. 3: Cetaceans*, New York and London, Plenum Press, pp. 165–226.

104 Shevchenko, V. I. 1970. '(Puzzling white scars on whale body)', *Priroda, Moscow*, no. 6, pp. 72–3.

105 Shevchenko, V. I. 1977. 'Application of white scars to the study of the location and migrations of sei whale populations in Area III of the Antarctic', *Rep. Int. Whal. Commn* (Special Issue 1), pp. 130–4.

106 Smith, F. E. 1970. 'Analysis of ecosystems' in D. E. Reichle (ed.) *Analysis of Temperate Forest Ecosystems. Ecological Studies I*, Berlin, Heidelberg and New York, Springer-Verlag, pp. 7–18.

107 Tomilin, A. G. 1967. *Cetacea. vol. 9, Mammals of the USSR and Adjacent Countries*, translation by Israel Program for Scientific Translation, Jerusalem, and edited by V. G. Heptner.

108 Townsend, C. H. 1935. 'The distribution of certain whales as shown by logbook records of American whaleships', *Zoologica*, vol. 19, pp. 1–50.

109 Uda, M. 1954. 'Studies of the relation between the whaling grounds and the hydrographic conditions (I)', *Sci. Rep. Whales Res. Inst.*, vol. 9, pp. 179–87.

110 Uda, M. 1959. *The Fisheries of Japan*, Nanaimo Biological Station, Fisheries Research Board of Canada.

111 Van Utrecht, W. L. 1959. 'Wounds and scars in the skin of the common porpoise, *Phocoena phocoena* (L.)', *Mammalia*, vol. 23, pp. 100–22.

112 Vinogradov, M. E. 1970. *Vertical Distribution of the Oceanic Zooplankton*, translated by Israel Program for Scientific Translation, Jerusalem.

113 Volkov, A. F. and Moroz, I. F. 1977. 'Oceanological conditions of the distribution of Cetacea in the eastern tropical part of the Pacific Ocean', *Rep. Int. Whal. Commn*, vol. 27, pp. 186–8.

114 Wade, L. S. and Friedrichsen, G. L. 1979. 'Recent sightings of the blue whale, *Balaenoptera musculus*, in the northeastern tropical Pacific', *Fishery Bull.*, vol. 76, pp. 915–19.

115 Watkins, W. A. 1979. Personal communication, September 1979.

116 Webb, B. F. 1973. 'Cetaceans sighted off the west coast of the South Island, New Zealand, summer 1970 (note)', *N.Z.J. mar. Freshwat. Res.*, vol. 7, pp. 179–82.

117 Webb, B. F. 1973. 'Dolphin sightings, Tasman Bay to Cook Strait, New Zealand, September 1968–June 1969', *N.Z.J. mar. Freshwat. Res.*, vol. 7, pp. 399–405.

118 Wellington, G. M. and Anderson, S. 1978. 'Surface feeding by a juvenile gray whale *Eschrichtius robustus*', *Fishery Bull.*, vol. 76, pp. 290–3.

119 White, D., Cameron, N., Spong, P. and Bradford, J. 1971. 'Visual acuity of the killer whale (*Orcinus orca*)', *Exp. Neurol.*, vol. 32, pp. 230–6.

120 Winn, H. E., Edel, R. K. and Taruski, A. G. 1975. 'Population estimate of the humpback whale (*Megaptera novaeangliae*) in the West Indies by visual and acoustic techniques', *J. Fish. Res. Bd. Canada*, vol. 32, pp. 499–506.

121 Wołk, K. 1969. '(Migratory character of the Baltic population of the porpoise, *Phocoena phocoena* (L.))', *Przeglad Zoologiczny*, vol. 13, pp. 349–51.

CHAPTER 2

Diet and feeding behaviour of Cetacea

The recognized taxonomic division of Cetacea into Mysticeti and Odontoceti reflects their different feeding methods. The baleen whales are 'strainers' (Filtrales) and the toothed whales 'graspers' (Raptoriales). Several authors have provided ecological classifications based on diet and feeding methods (34, 35, 42, 68, 92, 149). Toothed whales can be divided into three groups: the fish-eaters (ichthyophagi), squid-eaters (teuthophagi), and flesh-eaters (sarcophagi). The food of baleen whales consists largely of planktonic or micronektonic crustaceans and/or relatively small pelagic fish, so these species are often grouped into a fourth ecological class, the planktonophagi (see Figures 2.1 and 2.2).

All toothed whales are monophydont, and the permanent teeth remain largely undeveloped. As we have seen earlier, the trend away from normal mammalian dentition began in the archaeocetes, and this has culminated in the homodont dentition of the odontocetes. Some further trends of either tooth loss or secondary specialization or both, have occurred in the Ziphiidae (especially in the genus *Mesoplodon*), in *Phocoenoides*, in *Physeter* and in *Globicephala*.

Odontocete dietary patterns

The only true member of the sarcophagi is the killer whale *Orcinus orca*. Systematic accounts of the diet of killer whales are rather rare, although there are some useful data scattered in several papers from different parts of the world (21, 54, 101, 130, 165). These authors point out that fish and squid make up the largest fraction of the diet. It has been suggested that there may be quite heavy predation during the salmon run in the Puget Sound region, but factual evidence was lacking. Off the coast of Japan, cod were the most abundant fish species recorded in stomachs of killers, supplemented by flat fish such as halibut. Castello found the remains of eagle sting ray *Myliobatis* in the stomach of a killer whale examined on the coast of southern Brazil (21); broken stings were found embedded in the jaw and snout. Killer whales in Antarctic waters are reputed to take penguins at sea, and in northern waters marine mammals form a smaller,

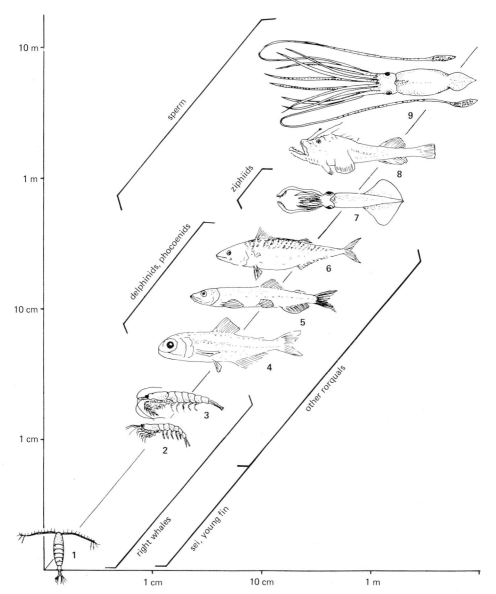

Figure 2.1 Size ranges of preferred food items of cetacean groups on a logarithmic scale: 1. calanoid copepods; 2. *Thysanoessa*; 3. *Euphausia* and *Meganyctiphanes*; 4. myctophid lantern fish; 5. capelin; 6. mackerel; 7. onychoteuthid squid; 8. bathypelagic angler fish; 9. architeuthid squid, sporadically eaten by sperm whales. Redrawn from Gaskin (42).

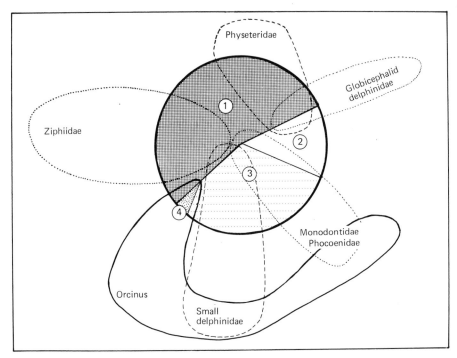

Figure 2.2   Schematic diagram of the feeding patterns of odontocete Cetacea: 1. squid; 2. demersal fish; 3. pelagic fish; 4. birds and seals. Lines attempt to delineate roughly proportional preferences, for example, the Ziphiidae are obligate teuthophagi, sperm whales take some fish in coastal and seamount areas but are generally squid-feeders (facultative teuthophagi), small delphinids subsist largely on small pelagic fish, but take some squid, and killer whales take some squid, birds, seals, pelagic fish, and also some small cetaceans. Redrawn after Gaskin (42).

but still very significant, fraction of the diet, after fish. In the North Pacific, Dall's porpoise (*Phocoenoides dalli*), is probably taken more often than any other, but harbour porpoise (*Phocoena phocoena*), Steller sea-lions (*Eumetopias jubatus*), elephant seals (*Mirounga angustirostris*) and Californian sea-lions (*Zalophus californianus*) are other well-known items of diet. Nishiwaki and Handa (101) also recorded the blue–white dolphin (*Stenella coeruleoalba*) as being eaten on a number of occasions, and there are several cases on record of larger whales, specifically minke, sei and blue, being attacked (44, 130, 147). These larger whales may be literally torn to pieces during attacks by packs of killer whales, but not all tissues are necessarily eaten. Handcock (44) reported that killers attacking a single minke whale ate only the blubber, dorsal fin and tongue. There is at least one confirmed record of an attack on a right whale off the coast of British Columbia; I have observed killer whales harassing a female sei whale with a calf in Antarctic waters, and recently a series of photographs were published of an attack by killer whales on a small adult blue whale in the eastern North Pacific (147).

The truly ichthyophagous cetaceans are typified by the pelagic dolphins of the genera *Stenella* and *Delphinus*, but even these may eat significant numbers of suitable-sized squid when the opportunity arises. All such cetaceans are obviously opportunistic feeders and, as a result, studies in different geographical areas under different conditions can yield very divergent conclusions. For example, on the basis of otolith identifications and counts, lantern fish (Myctophidae) accounted for nearly 90 per cent of the total contents in stomachs of five species of Delphinidae from four genera from the North Pacific (37). Stomachs of *Stenella coeruleoalba* taken off the coast of Japan likewise contained large quantities of myctophids (90), but these were supplemented by considerable numbers of the semi-pelagic shrimp *Bentheogennema borealis*. A study of the diet of spotted dolphin (*Stenella attenuata*) and spinner dolphin (*S. longirostris*) taken in association with yellowfin tuna (*Thunnus albacares*) in the tropical eastern Pacific, revealed the major component by volume and numbers to be the well-known ommastrephid squid, *Dosidicus gigas* (115). Onychoteuthid and enoploteuthid squid were also recorded. Among fish remains, those of various myctophids were abundant, but other families, especially exocoetids, were also important. Quite significant differences have been noted between the dietary components of the two common species of *Stenella* in the tropical Pacific, and workers have concluded that while the spotted dolphin feeds largely on epipelagic species, the spinner dolphin feeds at deeper levels, and at different times of day to its spotted relative.

As a general rule all these pelagic forms have a slender rostrum with many teeth, and these are sharply pointed and adapted to grasping relatively small fish. A short beak with fewer teeth is found in neritic species such as the beluga (*Delphinapterus leucas*), harbour porpoise (*Phocoena phocoena*) and other phocoenids. *P. phocoena* takes both nekto-pelagic species, such as herring (*Clupea harengus*) and mackerel (*Scomber scombrus*), and bentho-pelagic fish, such as cod (*Gadus morhua*) and redfish (*Sebastes marinus*) (125, 140, 143). The teeth of phocoenids tend to be apically spatulate and chisel-shaped, and are set each at an acute angle to the line of the jaw, providing an efficient shearing mechanism. When available, squid such as *Illex* and *Loligo* are also readily eaten (140). In the diet of beluga or white whale in the St Lawrence region dominant items are capelin (*Mallotus villosus*) and sand launce (*Ammodytes americanus*), together with remains of unidentified squid, probably *Illex*, and various nereids, crustaceans and gastropod molluscs (154). Very different results have been published by Russian workers. The diet in the White Sea has

Figure 2.3   The small mouth and anterio-ventrally flattened snout of the pygmy
sperm whale suggests that it may feed near or on the bottom of the sea.
Although squid are a relatively common item of diet, fish and even crabs have
been recovered from stomachs of captured or stranded specimens. Photograph
courtesy of Seaworld, Orlando, Florida, USA (Dr E. Asper).

been reported as changing as the season progresses; with flatfishes and
Cyclopterus sp. (lumpfish) being eaten in the early summer, cod and
shrimps in mid-summer, and herring and flatfish in the late summer (65,
153). At most times the diet was supplemented by white fish such as
haddock (*Melanogrammus aeglefinus*). In a later study in the same area
haddock were found to be the major item of diet from June to July (64).
Differences were noted between the diet in 1955 and that in 1956,
reflecting the availability of various species. Flatfish were a more
significant fraction in 1955 than in the next season. Unexpected items such
as remains of gastropods, amphipods and nereids had probably been
liberated from fish stomachs, and not eaten directly by the belugas. In the
Barents and Kara Seas, food items consisted of smelt (*Osmerus mordax*),
Arctic cod (*Boreogadus saida*), Atlantic salmon (*Salmo salar*), Arctic char
(*Salveninus alpinus*), and whitefishes (*Coregonus* spp.). In the waters
around far eastern Russia major food items included keta salmon
(*Oncorhynchus keta*) and saffron cod (*Eleginus navaga*) (6). So the beluga is
seen to have a broad dietary range, although almost all the fish eaten are of
medium or small size, and are taken from relatively shallow waters. The
catholic tastes of this species have been attributed in part to the fact that it

not only has a very wide geographical range, but has also penetrated rivers of the temperate and boreal north not accessible to other odontocete cetaceans (64). It takes both benthic and pelagic fish, and exploits all the available abundant food fish resources of the neritic zone to its advantage.

The teuthophagous cetaceans generally have a characteristic reduction of maxillary teeth (as in the sperm whales) (Figure 2.3), or an anterior emphasis in the distribution of teeth in both jaws (as in the pilot whale), or partial or complete loss of all functional teeth (as in many Ziphiidae). In *Phocoenoides dalli* the teeth are present but small, and almost buried by dermal papillary tissue. To compensate for loss or reduction of dentition, the palate of teuthophagous cetaceans may be rugose or ribbed, providing a surface suited to holding slippery-bodied cephalopods. In some species there has been selection in favour of increased diving capacity to facilitate protracted feeding around the thermocline, or on the bottom. Both the sperm whale (*Physeter catodon*) and the Atlantic bottlenosed whale (*Hyperoodon ampullatus*) have dive times which may attain or exceed one hour's duration.

All the Ziphiidae appear to be teuthophagous, although relatively little is known of detailed feeding habits. *Gonatius fabricii*, *Sepia* and *Loligo* are major dietary items of the Atlantic bottlenosed whale (34, 68), although in certain seasons and areas herring and cod are taken in significant quantities (45, 133). In the North Pacific the ziphiid species *Berardius bairdii* also eats *Gonatius fabricii*, as well as saffron cod (149). Both of the best known globicephalids, the pilot whale (*Globicephala melaena*) and the false killer whale (*Pseudorca crassidens*) prey on squid, supplemented by fish (39, 138, 151). There appears to be a close relationship between the distribution of the pilot whale population off the east coast of Newfoundland and the mesopelagic short-finned *Illex illecebrosus*. After several successive years during which squid were plentiful in inshore areas an abrupt disappearance was observed in late August 1957, and the following year was also one in which squid were scarce in coastal regions. Few pilot whales were seen, and of those taken, the majority had been feeding on Atlantic cod. The main pilot whale population seemed to have followed the squid, clearly indicating that these were preferred to fish.

Because of its great commercial importance the sperm whale has been more thoroughly studied than any other odontocete, and proportionally more is known of its diet. A number of detailed regional studies have been published (1, 15, 23, 40, 43, 82, 96, 108, 118, 128, 129, 132). Pelagic populations of the species are markedly teuthophagic. Inshore populations, on the other hand, take proportionally more fish (43, 132). Sperm whales taken near Iceland fed predominantly on *Cyclopterus lumpus*, *Sebastes* sp. and *Lophius piscatorius* rather than cephalopods. Most of the fish taken are considered to be benthic or bentho-pelagic species, and from

Table 2.1   Basic summary of diets of some odontocete Cetacea

Species	Region	Items of diet	References
Sperm whale	North Atlantic	Fish: including *Cyclopterus, Sebastes, Lophius*, etc. Squid: Ommastrephidae, Onychoteuthidae	23, 132
	South Atlantic	Squid, some sharks and teleost fishes	40
	Southern Ocean	Squid: Ommastrephidae, Onychoteuthidae, etc.	82
	North Pacific	Squid: Gonatidae, Cranchiidae, Octopodoteuthidae, Histioteuthidae, Onychoteuthidae, Ommastrephidae	15, 108, 118, 129
	Western South Pacific	Fish: including *Genypterus, Hoplostethus, Polyprion, Jordanidia* Squid: Architeuthidae, Histioteuthidae, Ommastrephidae, Onychoteuthidae	43
North Atlantic bottlenosed whale	North Atlantic	Squid: Gonatidae, Myopsidae, Oegopsidae Fish: *Clupea, Gadus* locally	34, 45, 68, 133
Baird's beaked whale	North Pacific	Fish: *Eleginus* Squid: Gonatidae	149
Pilot whale	North Atlantic	Fish: *Gadus* Squid: Ommastrephidae	39, 138
False killer whale	North Atlantic	Squid and fish	38, 151
Killer whale	South Atlantic North Pacific	Fish: *Myliobatis* Fish: *Oncorhynchus?* Mammals: *Phocoenoides, Stenella, Phoca*, etc.	21 54, 101, 130, 165
White whale	East Canada	Fish: *Mallotus, Ammodytes* Squid: *Illex*	154
	North-west USSR	Fish: *Cyclopterus, Clupea, Melanogramma, Osmerus, Salmo, Salveninus, Coregonus*	65, 153
	North-east USSR	*Oncorhynchus, Eleginus*	6

Species	Region	Items of diet	References
Harbour porpoise	North Atlantic	Fish: *Scomber, Sebastes, Clupea, Aphya* Squid: *Illex, Loligo*	125, 140, 143
Common dolphin	Tropical east Pacific	Fish: Myctophidae	37
Blue–white dolphin	Tropical east Pacific	Fish: Myctophidae Squid: Ommastrephidae Crustacea: Bentheogennema	37, 90
Spotted, striped or spinner dolphins	Tropical east Pacific	Fish: Myctophidae, Exocoetidae Squid: Ommastrephidae, Enoploteuthidae, Onychoteuthidae	37, 115

his data H. S. J. Roe (132) concluded that sperm whales off Iceland feed on the bottom in depths of at least 500 metres. Although medium-sized onychoteuthid and ommastrephid squid probably make up the majority of the food of sperm whales in most parts of the world, the stomachs may be found to contain all kinds of squid, from the huge architeuthids – although these are less commonly eaten than some popular accounts would have one believe – to relatively small histioteuthids with mantle lengths of only a few centimetres. Speculation on feeding mechanisms, and daytime versus night-time feeding have been discussed elsewhere (24, 41, 80). When all the information is considered the sperm whale emerges as a facultative teuthophage with the ability to take squid and fish by active hunting or perhaps also by some kind of passive stratagem involving luring food species, from surface waters, mid-water regions near or below the thermocline, or from the ocean floor. There is some indication that groups of sperm whales fan out at different depths to increase effectiveness of foraging, and communicate while doing so (155).

From all the foregoing examples discussed it should be obvious that Eschricht's ecological classification of odontocetes by diet pattern is quite useful in a general way, but that rigid categorizations are impractical. Most odontocetes are opportunistic feeders, and preferences are often dictated by circumstances. Some species, for example the two North Atlantic species of *Lagenorhynchus*, *L. albirostris* (white-beaked dolphin) and *L. acutus* (white-sided dolphin), may be said to overlap the two major categories almost completely. They appear to take fish species generally, but will feed on squid whenever the opportunity presents itself (45). *L. acutus* could be defined as nektonoichthyophagous, preferring salmonids, mackerel and herring, and *L. albirostris* as benthoichthyophagous, preferring cod, whiting and capelin (63).

Use of echolocation in odontocete feeding

Odontocetes may hunt by sight in clear water, or by detecting noises made by their prey, or by active echolocation. I have observed harbour porpoises picking mackerel from the edge of an almost stationary school; these animals were almost certainly hunting by sight alone. In the summer of 1981 a school of white-sided dolphins cruised into Lord's Cove, Deer Island, N.B., and swam right up to the salmon-rearing pens of Marine Research Associates Ltd. These animals had presumably been outside the island chain when they detected noise made by the crowded fish, since we have no record of that species entering that particular cove in more than a decade. In the Lagoa dos Patos in southern Brazil the waters are so turbid with brown sediment that underwater visibility is only a few centimetres. Bottlenosed dolphins feeding on mullet in this body of water are presumed to hunt by echolocation, perhaps after initially hearing sounds made by their prey.

No aspect of odontocete feeding has stimulated as much discussion in the last two decades as their production of high-frequency echolocatory sounds. Odontocetes are capable of emitting a wide range of sounds, some audible to the human ear, some not. They may be roughly divided into two categories, click sequences, or pure tone or modulated whistles. The clicks are the sounds most directly related to echolocation.

Species such as the bottlenosed dolphins *Tursiops truncatus* and *T. gilli* have been shown experimentally to carry out complicated behaviour in total darkness, in conjunction with the emission of intense trains of broadband clicks which are undoubtedly being used by the animals to scan their environment acoustically. The bottlenosed dolphin appears to be able to control the frequency of its click-trains to some extent; the high-frequency sounds (2.0–220 kHz) have been called 'discrimination clicks', and the low-frequency (0.25–1.0 kHz) 'orientation clicks', since theory indicates that information gathered in this way will be less precise and give a more generalized profile of the features of the environment than the high-frequency sounds. A recent article by Altes attempts to provide comprehensive mathematical models for echolocation theory (3).

The origin of these sounds is still a matter of much controversy. One school of thought has vigorously maintained that all sounds associated with echolocation arise in the nasal diverticula surrounding the blowhole (MacKay (75) recently outlined evidence for involvement of the spermaceti organ in sound production), and a hypothesis has been formulated for the sounds being produced by recycling of air through the system (102–5). The air stream is presumed to pass over the nasal plugs, and vibrations within asymmetrical features in these result in click-trains being produced by the right plug and the whistles by the left plug. In a recent paper P. E. Purves and G. Pilleri (124) have enumerated objections to these ideas, based on their own anatomical investigations of the structures involved. They pointed out that all odontocetes appear to produce clicks, but that only some of the advanced genera possessed all the specialized features discussed by Norris and his co-workers. They and others (69, 123) have postulated the major involvement of the larynx in at least some sound production, situated as it is in the very specialized nasopharyngeal region. Many data are in direct conflict, and the matter is very far from resolution.

Dolphins have been observed to make echolocatory sounds without correlative expiration so, regardless of the mechanisms, some degree of air recycling must be involved to produce movement within either the nasal sacs or over the larynx. The latter lacks developed vocal cords, but has complex folds and musculature. Some workers have maintained that the larynx is set too deeply within the head to be involved in echolocation, but Purves and Pilleri (124) asserted that if the sounds were produced by the epiglottic 'spout' of the larynx, the vibrations could be transmitted to the bones of the rostrum by the palatopharyngeal muscles, and that in addition the glottis is acoustically partially isolated from the ears by the peribullar air spaces and is, therefore, on two counts, very favourably placed to be a sound emitter in these animals. A recent study by MacKay and Liaw using ultrasonic techniques of investigation appears, however, to have thrown further doubt on the idea of significant laryngeal involvement in the production of these sounds (76).

There is no doubt that the sense of hearing is very acute in Odontoceti, and that these animals are capable of detecting and analysing 'minute quanta of sound energy' (84, 85). The site of hearing in cetaceans, whose external ear opening is, however, reduced to a pinhole-like aperture, is as much in dispute as the mechanism of sound production. Because of this reduction of the external ear structure Reysenbach de Haan (127) and Dudok van Heel (32) assumed that most sound was received via bone and soft tissue conduction, and Purves (122) summarized evidence to indicate that the reduced meatic region was probably still the major site of sound reception. Norris and his co-workers, on the other hand (102–5), proposed that most sound returned via the intramandibular fat body, the posterior portion of the mandible being very thin and directly adjacent to the wall of the tympanic bulla. In the face of the proliferation of contradictory theories, attempts have been made to obtain incontrovertible data by the implantation of electrodes against the cochlea itself, to measure potential changes that would directly reflect the performance of the ear under experimental conditions (84). Utilizing methods of surgical operation McCormick and his co-workers managed to implant the electrodes and study cochlear potentials in the bottlenosed dolphin and the white-sided dolphin, *Lagenorhynchus obliquidens*, despite severe complications introduced by the thick hypodermal blubber layer and the anastomosing retial vessels in the region of the ear which bled profusely and were difficult to ligature completely (84).

The results indicated that hearing was most effective in the immediate vicinity of the ear itself, as predicted by Reysenbaach de Haan and Purves; no differences in cochlear potentials were, however, noted even when an experimental vibrator was applied as near as 4 centimetres from the aperture of the meatus. Furthermore, the examination of a number of preserved heads showed that the meatus was almost certainly non-functional, since in some individuals it was occluded with mucus, and in others absent below the hypodermis. Dampening of sound transmission was found to occur when the innermost part of the ossicular chain was tampered with, but when the malleus was actually removed the potentials were only reduced by 4 dB. Changing the tension of the tympanum had a result of somewhat greater magnitude, bringing about an 18 dB change in the cochlear potentials. But they also reported that sound was received via the sides of the head, and the lower jaw below the gape, thereby supporting the possibility of Norris and his co-workers being correct in most aspects of their hypothesis. Further studies by McCormick's group (85), complementing the earlier studies of Bullock and others (19), provide even stronger evidence that the lateral section of the mandible, together with the ipsilateral melon, are most sensitive to sound within the general head region of dolphins. Several recent biochemical and biophysical studies have indicated that unusual triglycerides and wax esters in the melon and jaw fat of odontocetes may play a significant role in sound propagation (72, 73).

Of more general interest and application, and perhaps less specifically contentious, are the ideas outlined by K. S. Norris (103) concerning the possible ways in which the echolocatory mechanisms first came to be used by odontocetes. The ancestors of whales presumably possessed normal acute hearing for airborne sounds. In water the terrestrial ear is hardly any more efficient than adjacent areas of the head; not only does sound travel several times faster than in air, but objects struck by sound waves under water may resonate and become secondary sound sources which can convey information to an animal possessing a system for evaluating such information. Norris assumed that these animals first fortuitously used airborne sounds while in the water and largely submerged, but nevertheless emitted a component which could be picked up by totally submerged individuals. Once this kind of signalling was established and of advantage to facilitate the animals' feeding and reproductive behaviour, selection pressures through the Eocene and Oligocene favoured adaptations in structures of the cranial region serving to refine and improve sound production and reception in a completely aquatic environment. Modifications were presumed to have occurred by the time modern odontocete families were established, that is, by the Lower Miocene at the latest. Indeed, Norris suggested that the success of these odontocetes in competition with archaeocetes may have resulted from their possession of a relatively sophisticated echolocatory food-finding system.

More recently, G. Fleischer (38) made a detailed comparative study of the structure of the cochlea in a series of cetacean skulls representing both living and extinct forms. His findings confirmed the above view that the adaptation of the odontocete cochlea for echolocation occurred during the Oligocene. The Squalodontidae were in possession of structures suited to reception of high-frequency signals, and the development of acoustical shielding in the dorso-anterior region of the head is strongly indicative of their ability to produce such sounds as well. By the Miocene, Fleischer concluded that all odontocetes studied were adapted to the use of high-frequency sounds. This was not the case for *Zyghorhiza*, nor apparently for any Archaeoceti. The Mysticeti were also found to have a specialized cochlea, but one developed for perception of low-frequency sounds, indirectly making it appear doubtful that high-frequency echolocation plays any role in the food-finding behaviour of these animals.

Mysticete feeding and dietary patterns

In the baleen whales the whole anterior end of the animal has become modified (cf. pp. 185–6). The head is very large in proportion to the rest of the body, accommodating the greatly enlarged buccal cavity. The straining apparatus varies in detail from family to family, but essentially consists of a double series of elongate, subtriangular horny plates, 130–480 in number, set in the roof of the mouth. The plates are set more or less at right angles to the longitudinal axis of the mouth. The inner edge of each plate is 'fringed' or 'frayed'. The baleen fringes of one plate overlap those of the next, forming a fibrous 'mat' in the roof of the mouth. After the whale has taken a mouthful of food, pressure of the tongue against this 'mat' drives the water out through the spaces between the plates. The tongue movement is also directed posteriorly with the result that the mass of food is carried towards the rear of the buccal cavity and comes to lie adjacent to the entrance to the throat and oesophagus. The fusion of the mandibular rami in baleen whales differs from that found in the toothed whales; in the former articulation is by fibrous ligaments rather than a bony symphysis. This facilitates the extraordinary gape observed in these animals, and also provides a cushioning system against the stress of sudden entry of large volumes of water when the mouth is opened. In the right and gray whales the left and right rows of plates do not meet in the anterior midline. Even in the rorquals the baleen is greatly modified at the tip of the snout, appearing more like very stiff bristles than plates. The survival of vibrissae at the anterior extremities of the jaws in baleen whales is probably associated with tactile contact with food organisms.

Methods for straining small food organisms from the environment have arisen independently at all levels of the marine food web. The whale shark, for example, feeds by a mechanism analogous to that of the baleen whales. Nevertheless, the straining system of the baleen whale is one of the most bizarre adaptations found in the order Mammalia. It is interesting to speculate about those selection pressures which led to the suppression of normal dentition and directed development of the baleen plate system. The gray and pygmy right whales are probably the most primitive surviving baleen whale species, but even in these we see a straining system which is the result of a long evolutionary process, and is primitive only by comparison with other modern species. Most authors have avoided discussion of the evolution of baleen, and concentrated instead on the evolution of the mysticete and odontocete skulls (62). A. B. Howell (49) considered the problem in comparison with the condition found in *Phocoenoides*, where the teeth are small and virtually non-functional. Here the margins of the jaws have dermal ridges of hard tissue on each side of the tooth rows, often masking the latter completely. In the teuthophagous beaked whales and the sperm whale the palate has similarly become equipped with rugose or ribbed or ridged papillae suited to grasping the slippery bodies of squid. Embryological study of the origin of baleen in the foetus reveals that the plates arise from dermal papillae on the regular palate (152). The diet of the early mysticete forms is conjectural, however, and we still have little idea how the metamorphosis from short papillae to functional plates was achieved.

There are two basic methods of feeding in baleen whales – 'skimming', most often seen in right whales (but often in sei whales also) and 'gulping', typified by finbacks and other rorquals. The morphology of the buccal cavity differs considerably between right whales and rorquals, being significantly arched and closed in at the sides in the former. During their feeding runs, the jaws seem to be held open at about 10–15°; much less than the gape observed in fin whales. The morphology of the buccal cavity of rorquals, especially the functional aspects of baleen and the movements of the lower jaw, have been discussed by several authors (70, 120, 158). A. Pivorunas (120) has emphasized the outward curve of the tips of the baleen plate rows in adult rorquals, which forces the whale to rotate the lower jaw first one way, then the other, as it closes its mouth. D. G. Lillie (70) noted that the arrangement of the adductor muscles facilitated such a movement.

Pivorunas also examined the functional aspects of baleen fringe size and structure in relation to diet. The nature of the fringe differs from species to species, and can be related to the size of food item (92). Pivorunas determined that two types of fringe, fine and coarse, co-existed in the fin whale, the former dominating in the medial position on each plate (the fringing was possibly denser in this location too). The easy collapse of this area into a fine 'mat' provided a reasonably efficient temporary sealed surface during the actual feeding process. The fringes close to the apex of each plate are stiff, coarse and dense. This portion of the baleen appears to be trapped against the inner surface of the lower jaw and the tongue during feeding, forming a posterio-lateral seal. Pivorunas noted that 'only a semi-ovoid area in the central and rearward portion' of the baleen of a rorqual actually took part in the filtration of water from the gulped food mass. He cautioned those who would make comparative estimates of feeding capacity based upon the total exposed area of baleen in these whales, since it was not known if the truly functional feeding surface was comparable in all balaenopterid species.

There are practical limitations to the density of fringes which can be developed to real effect; after a certain density of fibres is reached, any increase, though perhaps serving to further improve the retention of small food organisms, so inhibits the rate of extrusion of water that no net increase in efficiency of the mechanism is obtained. Pivorunas agreed with earlier comments by T. Nemoto that fringe *density per se* was not primarily correlated with the size and type of food taken. The fineness of fringes seemed to be more important, and this was in turn a function of the angle formed between the inner (functional) margin of the plate and the longitudinal axes of the baleen tubules from which the fibres arise. Pivorunas also developed a mathematical formula which attempted to relate and describe fringe characteristics and baleen plate characteristics.

The divergent feeding habits of mysticetes, and their exploitation of different ecological niches in what at first sight seems to be a rather homogenous environment, is a very interesting study. The minke whale (Figure 2.4) demonstrates the most marked ichthyophagy in the genus *Balaenoptera*, at least in the northern hemisphere, where most studies of its diet have been made (53, 134, 139, 144, 150). Only in high northern latitudes do pelagic crustaceans such as *Meganyctiphanes norvegica* make up the major part of the diet (107). In boreal and temperate regions the species is a predator of gadoids, clupeoids and scombroids, especially in coastal waters. The southern form of the minke generally exploits *Euphausia superba* populations (106, 107). S. Ohsumi (106) has recently reported on the diet of a series of minke whales taken in the Antarctic in the 1971–2 season by a Japanese fleet. All the stomachs contained *Euphausia superba*, with no other species present, and contents ranged in wet weight from 50.4 kg to 136.4 kg, much more than was recorded by earlier

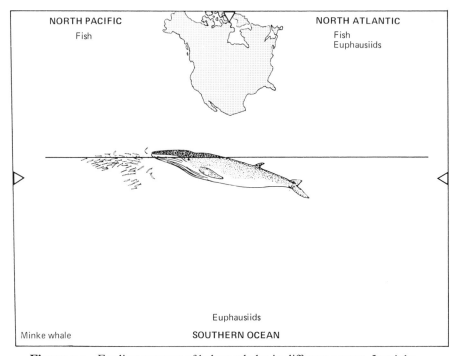

NORTH PACIFIC
Fish

NORTH ATLANTIC
Fish
Euphausiids

Euphausiids

Minke whale   SOUTHERN OCEAN

Figure 2.4   Feeding patterns of baleen whales in different oceans, I: minke whale.

workers. Minke had fresh stomach contents during the middle of the afternoon, indicating that daytime feeding had been taking place. Limited data suggested that these minke were not selecting for particular size classes of euphausiid.

In the western North Pacific the minke exploits coastal stocks of saffron cod (*Eleginus navaga glacialis*) and this appears to be the main food species in eastern Russian waters, at least in spring and summer (150); however, in the Bering Sea pelagic pteropods and Arctic cod are also eaten in some quantity (142). In eastern Canadian waters the minke is a relatively common animal, but generally occurs as scattered solitary individuals (1–2 km apart) dispersed to feed from tidal current slicks, often very close to shore. These animals are usually in search of herring or capelin. In the Antarctic, schools of 5–10 are not uncommon in certain areas (personal observations) and on occasions much larger schools are encountered (150). The species penetrates far into leads in coastal and offshore pack-ice in the summer months.

Careful observations have shown that minke, probably the same individuals, regularly return year after year to the same locations in coastal waters, sometimes alone, sometimes in the company of larger rorquals. During the summer of 1974 a single minke was observed by the author

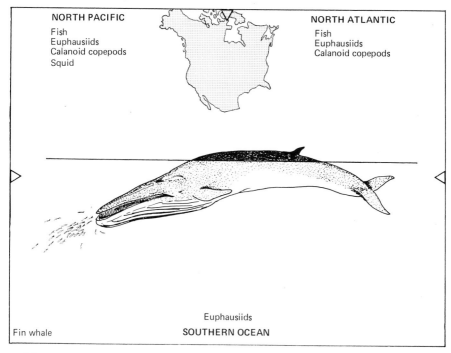

Figure 2.5 Feeding patterns of baleen whales in different oceans, II: fin whale.

over a period of nearly three weeks, working a single tidal streak off the south-western shore of Nova Scotia, and feeding among fin whales. Its behaviour was relatively unobtrusive; the animal was sometimes visible from the boat, sliding among schools of herring perhaps 1–5 metres below the surface. At intervals of three to five minutes it would rise to breathe, rarely more than one or two breaths being taken in any single sequence. The 'blow' was visible only when the animal was outlined against the shore. In July 1974 a minke remained in the channel between White and Nubble Islands, off the Charlotte County coast of southern New Brunswick, for several successive days, working from one side of the passage to the other for the duration of the flood tide. This animal also appeared to be feeding on herring, surfacing in the fashion described above. Minke observed over successive seasons in the mouth of the Saguenay River, a major tributary of the St Lawrence, often behave in more flamboyant fashion. These animals were pursuing large schools of capelin (the presence of which was determined by experimental trawling following reception of strong sonar reflections). At intervals these whales would break through the surface with the whole head and much of the thoracic region exposed for an instant. At least one identified individual was present in several successive seasons (L. Pippard, personal communication).

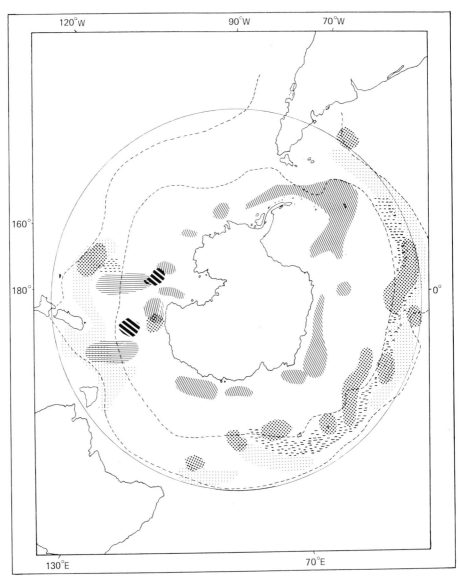

Figure 2.6 Distribution of major baleen whale food species in the Southern Ocean: broken lines indicate Antarctic and Subtropical Convergences: stipple, *Calanus tonsus*; horizontal lines, *C. simillimus*; heavy diagonal shading, *C. propinquus*; short bars, *Euphausia vallentini*; oblique lines, *Euphausia superba*; heavy stipple, *Parethemisto gaudichaudii*. Largely adapted from Marr, (66, Chapter 1) and Kawamura (59); redrawn from Gaskin (42).

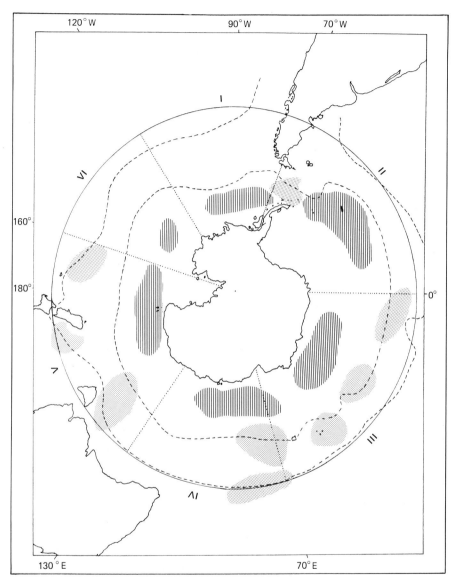

Figure 2.7 Major whaling areas of the Southern Ocean: stipple indicates sei whales; vertical striping, blue and fin whales. Largely adopted from Mackintosh (78) and Kawamura (59); redrawn from Gaskin (42).

The diet of the fin whale is well known (Figure 2.5), since large commercial catches have been extensively sampled by biologists in the higher latitudes of the major oceans of the world. The staple item of diet in many areas of the Southern Ocean is *Euphausia superba* (78); this species is taken in particularly large quantities in the pack-ice waters of Antarctic areas III and IV (see Figures 2.6 and 2.7) (93). Even so, stomachs of fin whales taken in subantarctic latitudes frequently contain large quantities of *Thysanoessa macrura* and *Euphausia vallentini* (95). The latter species is largely distributed between the subtropical and Antarctic convergences to about 54°S in summer (Figure 5.8). It is especially abundant where subsurface ridges occur, for example the Kerguelen-Gaussberg ridge (south-east from Kerguelen through Heard Island), the Atlantic–Antarctic Ridge, the Falkland Shelf and the Auckland Island Shelf (92). The rarer *Euphausia crystallorophias* Holt and Tattersall has also been recorded from fin whale stomachs in intermediate latitudes (92). In southern subtropical latitudes fin appear, however, to feed infrequently (7, 77).

The diet of fin whales in the northern hemisphere is more diverse. Several Russian scientists have given detailed accounts of the diet of fin whales in the Chukchi Sea, Gulf of Anadyr and adjacent bays of Russian far eastern coastal waters (121, 150, 163). Animals taken relatively close to shore had been eating herring, Japanese sardine (*Sardinella melanosticta*) and capelin. Similarly fin in the Aleutian coastal area are reported as feeding largely on capelin and Alaskan pollack (*Theragra chalcogramma*) (92). Away from the coast, however, *Thysanoessa raschii, T. inermis* and *T. longipes* were generally the dominant food items, the last named particularly in the vicinity of the Commander Islands. Off Kamchatka and the northern side of the Aleutians *Calanus cristatus* and *C. plumchrus* are also eaten in large quantities, and *Euphausia pacifica* is taken when present in suitable concentrations (92). The dominance of these two species as crustacean food items in the pelagic Aleutian area was confirmed by T. Nemoto (92). Crustaceans particularly predominate in the diet in the summer months, but as the whales move southwards in the autumn the ommastrephid squid *Ommastrephes* (= *Nototodarus*) *sloani pacificus* is eaten in some quantities around the Kurile Islands (14). Off the coasts of Alaska and British Columbia the major summer prey is *Thysanoessa spinifera* (4, 48).

Seasonal variations in diet have also been recorded in different areas of the North Atlantic. In the summer months fin whales tend to concentrate in areas where herring and mackerel have also gathered to feed on pelagic crustaceans, specifically *Meganyctiphanes norvegica* and *Thysanoessa inermis* (47). Large quantities of fish may be eaten by the whales along with the euphausiids. *Calanus finmarchicus* is often taken by young North

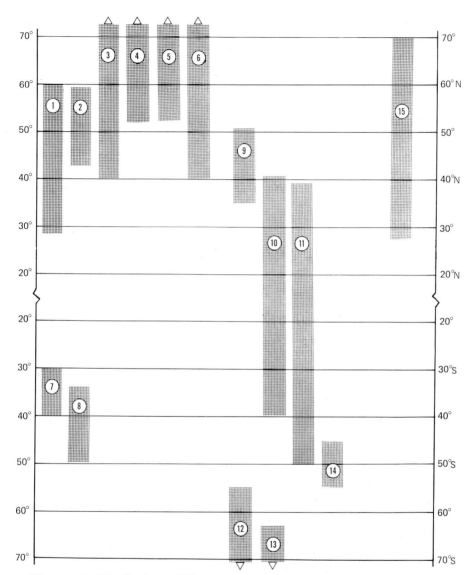

Figure 2.8 Distributions of *Thysanoessa, Euphausia* and *Meganyctiphanes* species by latitude: largely adapted from tabular information provided by Mauchline and Fisher (69, Chapter 1): 1. *T. spinifera*; 2. *T. longipes*; 3. *T. inermis*; 4. *T. macrura*; 5. *T. vincina*; 6. *T. raschii*; 7. *T. capensis*; 8. *T. australis*; 9. *E. pacifica*; 10. *E. recurva*; 11. *E. similis*; 12. *E. superba*; 13. *E. crystallorophias*; 14. *E. vallentini*; 15. *M. norvegica*. After Gaskin (42).

Figure 2.9 Fin whale engaged in leisurely side-feeding off the outer island chain in the Head Harbour region of southern New Brunswick, Canada. Visible is the ventral surface of the right fluke. Scars are most likely the result of contact with the floating debris which is so common in the Bay of Fundy with its large tidal amplitudes. Photograph by G. J. D. Smith.

Atlantic and Barents Sea fin whales, since these animals have a much finer fringe to the baleen than the adults and can successfully exploit the small copepods (150). Fish appear to be eaten more exclusively in the winter months (47, 153). Fin (and sei) whales taken by the whaling station on the Atlantic coast of Nova Scotia had been feeding on euphausiids and copepods, whereas those taken in Newfoundland waters had been eating capelin almost exclusively (89).

The feeding behaviour of fin whales is interesting and rather characteristic. During August 1974 the author was fortunate enough to be able to film this behaviour at close quarters, from a silent boat off the south-western coast of Nova Scotia (42). During summer in this region, which is part of the Bay of Fundy approaches, copepods and euphausiids, preyed on by schools of herring and mackerel, begin to rise into the surface layers over or adjacent to the long series of offshore banks and ledges as the strong Fundy flood tide starts to run. Shortly after the tide turns, the fin whales, which have dispersed both inshore and offshore during the ebb period, begin to gather in the vicinity of the ledges and prey on the euphausiids. The latter become concentrated at or near the surface in a tidal streak some ten miles in length.

The euphausiids, largely *Meganyctiphanes*, were being constantly harassed by large schools of mackerel, and began to form tight masses in the upper one or two metres. The fin whales exploited this situation; five

Figure 2.10   Fin whale engaged in energetic lunging side-feeding among large surface swarms of *Meganyctiphanes norvegica* and schools of Atlantic herring and mackerel off Brier Island, Nova Scotia, August 1974. Photograph by D. E. Gaskin.

large animals began to feed within a restricted area of radius about 0.25 km around the observation boat. Typically a whale would advance on a concentration of euphausiids in a shallow ascent, clearly visible beneath the water; on some occasions shortly before breaking the surface the animal commenced a roll to its side (Figure 2.9), simultaneously opening the mouth. Generally the animals rolled to the right, but not invariably so. With the mouth gaping open at an angle of 30° or more, the whale, with violent fluke beats and lateral extension of the pivotal flipper beneath the surface, turned in a half-circle in barely its own body length, rotating on its axis again as the mouth closed, to bring it back into a dorso-ventral plane at the conclusion of the turn. This manoeuvre appeared to drive euphausiids or fish across the arc of the animal's turning circle, or at least permit the whale to scoop up prey as they attempted to double back past it to escape. Side-swimming facilitates rapid change of direction in the horizontal plane (131). At the peak of the feeding lunge more than half the head and lower jaw and the whole of one flipper were exposed above the surface of the water (Figure 2.10). Feeding in the dorso-ventral plane at the surface was observed on two occasions; the subjective impression of the observers was that this seemed to be a less effective method only infrequently used by the fin whales. On both occasions it seemed that the whales might be feeding specifically on fish rather than euphausiids, but this could not be verified.

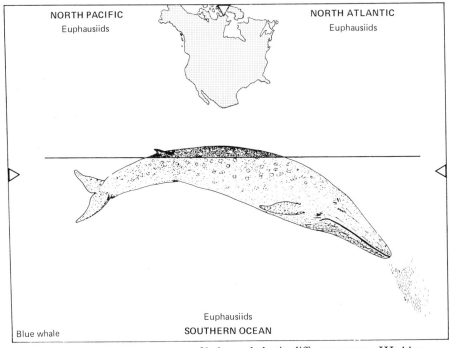

Figure 2.11   Feeding patterns of baleen whales in different oceans, III: blue whale.

About twenty fin whales were observed by W. A. Watkins and W. E. Schevill, feeding on schooling fish 8–10 km north of Race Point, Massachusetts in late April and early May 1975, in company with other species (157). The fin whales approached the fish just below the surface, not opening their mouths until close to the schools. The smaller the fish school being preyed upon, the larger the gape. The throat expansion was considerable, and was greatest immediately after the mouth closed, suggesting a much higher water-to-prey ratio than in some other species, such as the sei whale (see p. 56). In this situation, side-feeding appeared to be the exception rather than the rule. The animals swam into the fish concentrations in normal upright plane, with the dorsal fin or part of the head sometimes breaking the surface, and the body easily visible from the air. Three or more passes at a school were often made in rapid succession.

On another occasion these workers reported fin whales feeding at a greater depth, about 15–20 metres, in clear water over a sandy floor. The fish were concentrated just off the bottom. The whales approached the fish quite slowly, rolling to show the ventral surface as they apparently sprinted briefly to take the moving school. Circling behaviour of surface-feeding fin whales was noted on several occasions both from ships and from the air by Watkins and Schevill, but this did not seem to include any purposeful 'herding' of fish as has been suggested by other workers. Watkins and Schevill drew attention to the very large range of variation in the feeding behaviour of fin whales; the nature and density of the prey species appeared to be important, or the size of the school in the case of small fish; the degree of satiation also seemed to modify behaviour. They noted that whales could be seen swimming rapidly towards feeding concentrations with fin whales already present, from as much as 7–10 km distant, and speculated that calls made during feeding were alerting whales over quite a wide area.

Although the blue whale is another macroplanktonophagous species, in contrast to the fin whale it shows marked stenophagy (Figure 2.11). In the Southern Ocean it feeds almost exclusively on *Euphausia superba*, with other items being taken only by accidental ingestion (79, 117). In the North Pacific the diet is largely composed of *Thysanoessa inermis*, *T. longipes* and *Nematoscelis megalops* (92, 150, 163). In the North Atlantic only *Thysanoessa inermis*, *Temora longicornis* and *Meganyctiphanes norvegica* have been recorded (2, 47, 86).

During feeding the blue whale is generally said to display none of the stylized behaviour exhibited by the fin whale. The blue whale generally appears to be a slower and clumsier species than the fin, although there is no doubt that the animal possesses enormous stamina and endurance (150). It is sometimes difficult to decide whether or not a blue whale is actually feeding, except that it may surface less often than when just travelling, and may blow more frequently when it does surface. This may, however, be only a subjective impression, and there are few data in the literature from extended series of observations. Just recently R. Sears completed a season of observations on blue whales engaged in summer feeding in the vicinity of the Mingan Islands (137), in the northern Gulf of St Lawrence. On numerous occasions he recorded these animals engaging both in side-feeding and lunge-feeding, in a similar fashion to fin whales.

As a consequence of the rapid growth of its commercial importance in the last decade in both the Antarctic and the North Pacific the diet of the sei whale has been the subject of intensive study (Figure 2.12). It is a euryphagous species which generally frequents somewhat warmer waters than the blue, fin and humpback whales, and has a less pronounced migratory pattern. Its diet varies extensively by region and season. In the western South Atlantic, for example, the sei regularly penetrates further south than in other sectors, and in the higher latitudes of the region it may eat *Euphausia superba* almost exclusively (79, 86). Most animals found in the colder waters around South Georgia tend to be large, fully mature individuals, immature ones making up less than 10 per cent of the catch (83). In the vicinity of the Bounty and Antipodes Islands, near the

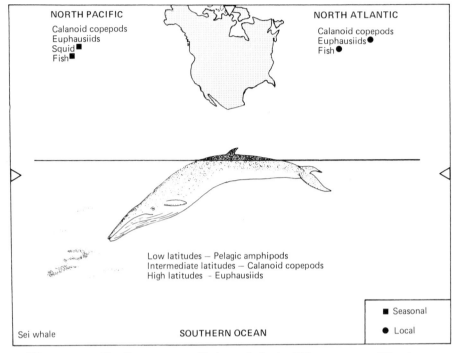

Figure 2.12   Feeding patterns of baleen whales in different oceans, IV: sei whale.

boundary of Antarctic areas V and VI (see Figure 2.7), *E. vallentini* is an important prey species, together with the very locally abundant *Clausocalanus laticeps* which forms dense shoals in suitable areas. In waters directly south of the New Zealand archipelago a massive 'bloom' of *Calanus tonsus* may frequently occur. This species is found in waters of 9.5–12.0°C, and the 'bloom' may be relatively short-lived (18, 36, 52), but is, nevertheless, intensively exploited by sei when available (57, 59).

In the Indian Ocean another endemic subantarctic species of calanoid, *C. simillimus*, is taken in waters of 5–10°C by sei to a northern limit of about 45°S (61). This species is extensively eaten together with *C. tonsus* in the vicinity of the Crozet Islands. Records of *C. propinquus* and *Calanoides acutus* in this area (116) have been dismissed by A. Kawamura as almost certain misidentifications, since these are surface species only in high Antarctic latitudes, and further north occur only in deep water. In the same region *Drepanopus pectinatus* is also eaten, and in lower latitudes, larger quantities of the pelagic amphipod *Parathemisto gaudichaudii* (97). *Drepanopus pectinatus* has also been found in the stomachs of sei captured near Kerguelen, and *Calanus tonsus* and *Clausocalanus arcuicornis* have been recorded as food items in the coastal waters of Cape Province (7, 12).

Sei are reported to prefer copepods to amphipods when the choice was available to them. Sei off the coast of Patagonia appeared to feed upon *Munida gregaria* and its pelagic post-larval stage (*Grimothea* or 'lobster krill') (81).

The general conclusion is that euphausiids are most important in the diet of sei in Antarctic areas IV–VI (Australia–western South Pacific), amphipods in areas III–IV (Indian Ocean), while calanoids are of considerable supplementary importance in areas V and VI (see Figs 2.6, 2.7). In the course of his detailed analysis of sei feeding patterns in Antarctic waters A. Kawamura (57) determined that a latitudinal succession of food species could be recognized, in addition to the regional differences outlined above. With due allowances for these regional (longitudinal zone) differences he found an approximate sequence – from north to south – roughly as follows. In low latitudes, *Calanus tonsus*, a little further south *C. simillimus*, then *Euphausia vallentini*, *Parathemisto gaudichaudii* and in the vicinity of the Antarctic convergence *Euphausia vallentini* again, and finally in the highest latitudes penetrated by sei, *E. superba*. Some variation was noted during the course of any single season, for example, *Calanus tonsus* was most abundant in December, and *C. simillimus* in January and February. It is rather difficult to determine whether the sei moved south because the supply of *C. tonsus* declined, or whether the decline is a reflection of the whales having moved south for some other reason, leaving the zone of maximum abundance of *C. tonsus*. Kawamura also noted that at any given time an individual sei whale was a stenophagous feeder, that is, stomachs containing more than one prey species were found infrequently.

Earlier reports of the diet of sei whales in the North Atlantic were summarized by R. Collett (25) and J. G. Millais (86), and showed that *Calanus finmarchicus*, *Thysanoessa inermis* and smaller quantities of *Temora longicornis* and *Meganyctiphanes norvegica* were eaten. Relatively few sei have been taken in the North Atlantic in recent years and those were mainly from the now-dormant Canadian land stations. E. Mitchell (89) examined the stomach contents of these animals, and reported that while copepods were the main dietary item, euphausiids were sometimes taken almost exclusively. He presented the interesting idea that the timing and location of the migration track of the sei whale population in this region may closely coincide with that of the western North Atlantic right whale, and in competition for patchy, localized concentrations of zooplankton, the right whale might not have been able to rebuild its population from the residue left after the intensive over-exploitation prior to total protection. Such problems are discussed in more detail in Chapter 8; in most cases a hypothesis like Mitchell's cannot be tested given our present limited abilities to study interactions of pelagic populations in the wild.

Until recently sei were the most important baleen whales of the North Pacific catch, and consequently their feeding habits are well known (94). The four calanoid species – *Calanus pacificus, C. plumchrus* (especially the adult female and copepodite V stages) (145, 146), *C. cristatus* and *C. glacialis* – are heavily exploited by sei, supplemented by *Eucalanus elongatus, Metridia ochotensis, M. pacifica, Thysanoessa inermis, T. longipes* and a few other species of lesser importance (67). *T. raschii* were taken on those occasions when concentrations were present (14). Sei eat quantities of fish and squid in the North Pacific when the need arises or the opportunity is presented. The fish most commonly taken include *Sardinops sagax, Engraulis japonica, E. mordax, Mallotus villosus* and *Myctophum aspersum* (67). Sei have also been reported feeding on schools of immature Arctic cod (142). *Ommastrephes sloani pacificus* becomes a locally important food item near the Kurile Islands as the sei begin to move southwards during the autumn months (14). The squid taken are relatively small, with mantle lengths in the 15–20 cm range. Other squid have been recorded as occurring in sei stomachs from time to time in this region, specifically *Loligo opalescens* and *Gonatius fabricii* (67).

In general terms, however, the key to the movements of sei in the North Pacific appears to lie in the distributional ecology of *Calanus pacificus* and related species (58). In recent years Japanese vessels have been permitted to take limited catches of sei whales south of the usual 40°N boundary for factory ship operations, and the prey species have been studied by Kawamura (58). The surveyed area extended from 40°N to 34°N and 165°E to 165°W, but significant concentrations of sei were taken only in the vicinity of the Emperor Seamount chain (34–40°N by 165–180°E). These animals were feeding extensively on the copepodite IV and V stages of *C. pacificus* in waters of about 8–11°C, supplemented by some Pacific saury (*Cololabis saura*), Japanese mackerel (*Scomber japonicus*), Japanese sardine (*Sardinella melanosticta*) and euphausiids. The fish appeared to have concentrated in the region to feed on the copepod swarms. Information is very limited from other North Pacific sectors, but we have the report of L. H. Matthews (81) that off the Pacific coast of Mexico sei appear to compete with blue whales for local concentrations of the anomuran galatheid *Pleuroncodes planipes*. Feeding behaviour in the sei differs according to diet. It has been described as taking small pelagic crustaceans by swimming slowly along just beneath the surface, with a lateral rolling motion which brings first one and then the other side of the jaws up to touch the surface (71), and then rolling right over while closing the mouth. The author observed several sei feeding on one occasion in the Antarctic in what was virtually a latero-ventral position, the animals holding this orientation for a hundred yards or more. G. M. Allen (2) reported that sei chasing fish followed schools just under the surface, but

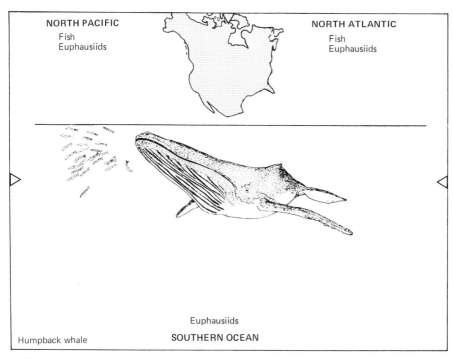

NORTH PACIFIC
Fish
Euphausiids

NORTH ATLANTIC
Fish
Euphausiids

Euphausiids

Humpback whale   SOUTHERN OCEAN

Figure 2.13   Feeding patterns of baleen whales in different oceans, V:
humpback whale.

with the dorsal fin exposed, so that the animal obviously retained an
upright posture (compare with comments on dorsal feeding by fin whales,
pp. 50–2). T. Nemoto and A. Kawamura (94) have classified the sei whale
primarily as a skimming feeder.

Watkins and Schevill of the Woods Hole Marine Laboratory observed a
sei whale feeding with right whales off Race Point, Massachusetts in late
April 1975 (157). This animal ignored schools of fish completely, and like
the right whales, concentrated on patches of plankton. It swam only a
metre or so below the surface, with the dorsal fin frequently trailing along
the interface, opening its mouth at irregular intervals with visible, but not
particularly great distention of the buccal region. It did not seem to follow
the densest ribbons or patches of plankton nearly as consistently as the
right whales.

The diet of humpback whales (Figure 2.13) in the southern hemisphere
has been investigated (31) with special reference to the New Zealand
region, and the vicinity of South Georgia. In high latitudes the prey
species is almost exclusively *Euphausia superba*, probably supplemented
by *E. vallentini* in areas where that species replaces *E. superba*, and some
Thysanoessa macrura. The results of W. H. Dawbin's detailed study of the

Figure 2.14   In the Head Harbour region of southern New Brunswick, Canada, euphausiid shrimp and herring gather in slick areas along current boundaries and eddies. Humpback whales exploit these concentrations. In this case an animal spent some time simply lying among the floating weed. August 1980, photograph courtesy of G. J. D. Smith.

species in New Zealand waters may be summarized as follows. On the northward migration through coastal waters the Antarctic area V humpbacks take little or no food, although on sporadic occasions they were recorded as feeding on very localized concentrations of a species identified as *Nyctiphanes australis*, which occurs in coastal waters of more than 13.5°C and salinities between 34.05 and 34.72 per thousand (8, 16). Humpbacks are supposed to exploit swarms of *Munida gregaria* which occur from Cook Strait southwards in the spring and summer months (October–February). Humpbacks particularly concentrate in the Foveaux Strait region between Stewart Island and the South Island while moving south. Yet Dawbin noted that in this area the main organism which could be obtained from surface tows was *Nyctiphanes australis* and not *Munida gregaria*. Humpbacks feed on *Euphausia spinifera*, *E. hemigibba* (29), *E. recurva*, *E. Lucens*, *Nyctiphanes capensis* off Western Australia and *Thysanoessa gregaria* off South Africa (12). Humpbacks have been protected in the North Atlantic for many years except for a small number taken under special scientific licence from Canadian land stations. As a consequence, there are few recent data on their diet. The most important prey species are said to be *Meganyctiphanes norvegica* and *Thysanoessa inermis* (2). Both herring and capelin are eaten off the coasts of northern Europe; other less important items recorded have been pteropod molluscs and unidentified cephalopods (150), but these are probably taken incidentally.

Russian and Japanese workers have amassed detailed information on the diet and feeding habits of humpbacks in the North Pacific, Bering Sea and Chukchi Sea. In the latter regions the most important single item is *Mysis᾿ oculata* (150), supplemented by herring, capelin and other crustaceans such as *Thysanoessa longipes* and *Pandalus goniurus*. In the vicinity of the Kurile Islands *Euphausia pacifica* is often taken (14); the diet varies greatly with time and locality. For example, humpbacks in the coastal regions of the Chukchi Sea feed on large quantities of saffron cod (navaga) and Arctic cod (164). The latter are also taken in Alaskan waters (4). M. Nishiwaki reported *Euphausia similis* and *Pseudoeuphausia latifrons* from the stomachs of humpbacks taken near the Ryukyan Islands (99, 100).

The dark baleen of humpbacks is relatively coarse and stiff and this correlates well with the absence of small planktonic forms such as *Calanus* spp. in the stomachs and the wide variety of pelagic and benthic fish and crustaceans which have been recorded as being eaten by the species. The feeding behaviour of humpback whales has been observed by the author on a number of occasions, most recently off the western coast of Nova Scotia in August 1974 and off southern New Brunswick in August 1979 and 1980 (Figure 2.14). In general, the feeding of this species resembles that of the fin whale (50, 55, 150) – there is the same lunging, breaching final rush at the school or shoal of prey, often with the same simultaneous roll to one side accompanied by a turn around or across the direction of movement of the prey (Figure 2.15). Despite its clumsy appearance the humpback is an agile species which seems to be able to exploit shoals of benthic or near-benthic organisms as readily as pelagic ones. This may be assumed from the frequent presence of animals such as *Pandalus* sp. in the stomach, and the fact that the migrations of the humpback often take it through very shallow water. The greatly elongate flippers are used to give the animal good hydrodynamic control; the author has seen humpbacks holding vertical positions just beneath the surface for some seconds, with either flukes or snout uppermost, without apparent difficulty.

An extremely interesting method of feeding by humpback whales was recently described and filmed in Glacier Bay, Alaska (33, 55, 111). When these animals encountered swarms of krill on or below the surface one or sometimes two individuals would swim in an upward spiral from below, expelling air in a chain of bubbles from the blowhole (Figure 2.16). The rising bubbles formed a transitory circular 'curtain', coralling the small crustaceans and causing them to mass in the centre of the ring, as far as possible from the confused peripheral water. The whale or whales then rose to feed on the resulting concentration. Although the usual 'curtain' was smaller, one or more humpbacks were sometimes observed to form rings as great as a hundred feet in diameter.

The feeding methods utilized by Alaskan humpback whales vary

Figure 2.15   Humpback whale feeding on its side after a lunge, upper jaws with baleen visible at right: Glacier Bay, Alaska. Photograph courtesy of Dr C. Jurasz, Sea Search Ltd, Auke, Alaska, USA.

Figure 2.16   Humpback whale under the surface of Glacier Bay, Alaska, begins to form a 'bubble curtain' during feeding on swarming pelagic shrimp. Photograph courtesy of Dr C. Jurasz, Sea Search Ltd, Auke, Alaska, USA.

according to the nature of the prey species and the available density. Charles and Virginia Jurasz (55) categorized feeding into 'lunge feeding', 'flick feeding' and the 'bubble-net feeding' method described above. In 'flick' feeding, what appears at first to be a normal dive becomes a forward movement as the tail is suddenly flexed forward, generating a wave which appears to concentrate euphausiids as the whale moves through the wave and takes them. This whole sequence was reported to last about three seconds. Lunge feeding varied considerably, and could be carried out laterally, vertically or with the body virtually upside down. These methods were used when food was concentrated and abundant. Two or more whales were sometimes seen in what was referred to as co-operative lunge feeding. Up to four animals could be involved. The prey was observed to be *Euphausia pacifica*, *Clupea harengus* and *Mallotus villosus*, with walleye pollack seeming to be accidently ingested on occasion while they themselves were feeding on euphausiids.

W. A. Watkins and W. E. Schevill reported the feeding behaviour of a single humpback among a group of several baleen whale species observed together in a large slick area about 8–10 km north of Race Point, Massachusetts, in late April and early May 1975 (156). Lunge feeding seemed to be the only method used by this animal, which was seen to select relatively dense schools of fish on which to feed, and it usually approached the fish from below, at an angle of 20–40°. Its momentum frequently carried it out of the water, so that the lunge terminated in a considerable splash visible for some distance.

The bottom feeding habit is most fully developed in the gray whale. American scientists have concluded that virtually no adults feed during their northward or southward migrations along the coast of Pacific America (131) (although see references 26 and 118 in Chapter 1). Quantities of zoea larvae of the littoral crab *Pachycheles rudis* and the brachyuran *Fabia* sp. have been found, but in only two of 136 stomachs sampled. Although *Pleuroncodes planipes* is often abundant off the coast of Baja California in winter, Californian workers have been unable to verify an earlier suggestion (81) that gray whales might feed on this crustacean; even though gray whales were observed in the vicinity of dense surface swarms, no evident feeding behaviour was seen and the report by J. Cousteau and P. Diole (26) of feeding behaviour in the Gulf of California is, therefore, also suspect. Nevertheless, Mizue (91) has recorded winter–spring feeding of two gray whales in the northern Yellow Sea on the anomuran decapod *Nephrops thomsoni*. J. Darling recently completed a thesis from Victoria University in British Columbia. In this he gave results of several seasons of observations of gray whales which spent the summer off the west coast of Vancouver Island instead of migrating the whole distance to the Bering Sea (30). Many of these animals seemed to be immature, judging by their size. Although stomachs could not be sampled, direct underwater observations of feeding whales, or of the bottom in their vicinity strongly suggested that they were taking significant quantities of sessile polychaetes, tubeworms and *not* amphipods. The great majority of feeding was carried out in kelp bed areas just outside the surf line, in a very few metres of water. In August 1978 I was fortunate enough to watch about half a dozen of these animals for several hours on three different occasions, south of Berkeley Sound, BC. The behaviour certainly appeared consistent with feeding, but it was virtually impossible to confirm this by surface observations. At no time did the animals rear from the water showing muddied snouts, as has been reported by some observers in Alaskan waters.

Several scientists have studied the feeding of gray whales in the Bering Sea, Bering Strait and Chukchi Sea during summer (119, 150, 161, 162, 164). Their data clearly shows that gammaridean amphipods form the major food, especially *Amplisca macrocephala*, except in the coastal region adjacent to Cape Navarin where it is largely replaced by *Atylus carinatus* and near St Lawrence Island where it is supplemented by *Amplisca eschrichti*. In many of the stomachs examined these workers also found lesser quantities of cumaceans, bottom-dwelling mysids, isopods, molluscs, hydroids and polychaetes. The relatively small quantities of the latter abundant benthic organisms are a strong indication that the gray whale is a highly selective bottom-feeder (131). They suggested that it stirs up sediment with the snout and then filters the turbid disturbed water just above the bottom, taking the amphipods which remain swimming, while less motile or less buoyant organisms quickly settle again. Support for this hypothesis comes from observers who have reported seeing feeding gray whales surface in shallow waters with muddied snouts (119). Gray whales from Russian eastern coastal catches have been described as having scarred and abraded snouts and jaws (150). The very stiff, coarse, relatively short baleen plates, with strong inner marginal bristles, are well adapted for bottom scouring or 'ploughing'. Evidence of consistently greater wear on the baleen plates of the right side has been cited as evidence of side-swimming behaviour during feeding along the bottom (56).

A limited number of observations were made on a young gray whale held captive for a time at Sea World, San Diego, in 1971 (126). This animal was trained to take full-grown squid (*Loligo opalescens*) which were dropped (dead) into the tank in batches. This animal took food from the bottom while swimming right over on her side – actually at an angle of about 120° – and seemed to use tongue movements to increase the volume of the mouth so that the lower lip was depressed and food flowed in, almost as a result of a 'suction' mechanism. Sometimes turbid water could be seen squirting from the sides of the animal's mouth. The actual movements of the buccal region appeared to be quite complex and rather variable. The lips could be moved independently on the left and right sides, and the animal was able to curl them away from the baleen. Although most gray whales appear to feed on their right side, this animal was trained to take food on the left side without difficulty. During the period that food was being ingested distention of the gular region was seen, and the gular grooves were significantly expanded.

Bryde's whale is another largely ichthyophagous species with relatively coarse baleen, although its diet is less well known. Significant numbers of this animal are taken in only a few localities, but it does appear to be the only baleen whale which feeds to any degree in relatively warm waters. *Euphausia recurva* has been found in the stomach of a Bryde's whale taken off Durban (7); however, other data showed that this species mainly exploits shoaling fish, especially the 'South African pilchard' *Sardinops ocellata* in the whaling grounds off Saldanha Bay (11, 12).

In a more recent paper P. B. Best (13) showed that the situation was actually quite complex. He carried out a study of 128 Bryde's whales landed at the Donkergat whaling station in South Africa between 1962 and 1965, and concluded that two distinct, allopatric forms occurred in South African waters. This interesting discovery has been considered in detail in Chapter 3, but for the moment I want to draw particular attention to his finding that the inshore form was smaller, had relatively narrow baleen plates (length : breadth quotient 2.22–2.43) and fed on anchovies *Engraulis capensis*, maasbankers *Trachurus trachurus* and pilchards *Sardinops ocellata*. The offshore form was larger, had relatively broad baleen plates (length : breadth quotient 1.83–2.24), and fed on euphausiids (*E. lucens* and *E. recurva*, *Nyctiphanes capensis* (also found in one inshore Bryde's whale) and *Thysanoessa gregaria*). Of lesser importance were instances of mesopelagic fish such as *Lestidium*.

Bryde's whales observed by the author on several occasions in the Hauraki Gulf off the north-eastern coast of the North Island of New Zealand appeared to be feeding (in a fashion similar to that described earlier for the minke whale) on dense shoals of an unidentified fish to which local fishermen applied the vague name of 'mullet'; no specimens were obtained. A. Kawamura (60) reported on the stomach contents of a large sample of Bryde's whales taken in the Coral Sea, South Pacific and Indian Ocean in 1976–7. *Euphausia recurva* and *E. diomedae* were abundant food items in all areas, and *Thysanoessa gregaria* was also common, particularly in the Coral Sea and South Pacific animals. The anchovy *Engraulis australis* is eaten off south Western Australia (22). Other euphausiids have been recorded as being eaten by Bryde's whale off South Africa, including *Nyctiphanes capensis*, *Euphausia lucens* and *Thysanoessa gregaria* (12). 'Sei' whales taken around the Bonin Islands were feeding on *T. gregaria*, *Myctophum aspersum* and a small gonostomid fish *Yarrella* sp. (= *Y. microcephala*, according to Nemoto) (92) and, on one occasion, the small molid, *Ranzania typus* (98). Some, if not all these whales, were probably Bryde's whales. Bryde's whales taken off the Wakayama prefecture of Japan had been eating *Euphausia similis* in early summer, and Japanese anchovy *Engraulis japonica* in late summer. To the south-east of the Japanese archipelago and into the cental subtropical North Pacific, Bryde's whales appear to take largely euphausiids, supplemented by various schooling fish (94).

The right whales are the true microplanktonophagi among whales. The baleen plates are proportionately longer and more slender than those of rorquals, possess far finer fringes on their inner margins and are well adapted to feeding on the smaller size ranges of pelagic shoaling crustaceans.

The usual diet of the Atlantic or Biscayan right whale *Eubalaena glacialis glacialis* consists of *Calanus finmarchicus* (Figure 2.17) (2). When the species winters off the eastern seaboard of the United States, however, the larger *Thysanoessa inermis* is eaten, and there is one record of a right whale taking small pelagic pteropod molluscs (46). A number of right whales (*Eubalaenia glacialis seiboldii*) have been taken in the North Pacific and the Sea of Okhotsk on special scientific licences (66, 109, 110). Important food items recorded were *Calanus plumchrus* and *C. cristatus*, supplemented by some *Metridia* sp. Distributions were not apparently uniform; animals taken south of Kodiak Island in the Gulf of Alaska were eating *Calanus plumchrus*, those caught north of the eastern Aleutians were eating *C. cristatus*, and those from the Sea of Okhotsk a mixture of *C. plumchrus* and *Metridia* sp. Only in the stomachs of two animals shot off the coast of Japan were both *Calanus plumchrus* and *C. cristatus* noted in significant admixture, together with small quantities of another copepod tentatively identified as *C. finmarchicus* (= *C. pacificus* or *C. glacialis*? – see footnote on page 145 of Shih, Figueira and Grainger) (141), and some larval stages of *Euphausia pacifica*.

Both the nominal subspecies of the northern hemisphere feed on small zooplankton (or micronekton) of about 2–7 mm (or up to 16 mm when *Thysanoessa* is included), whereas the southern subspecies *E. g. australis* eats the much larger *E. superba* (55–65 mm). The sparse fossil record of Balaenidae in the southern hemisphere and the general micro-planktonophagous habit of the group have been taken as indications that the right whale was a relatively recent arrival in the Antarctic Ocean which had adapted to one of the major food sources in high latitudes. A baleen whale can more easily switch to feeding on a relatively large food organism than vice versa; whales with coarse-fringed baleen would have

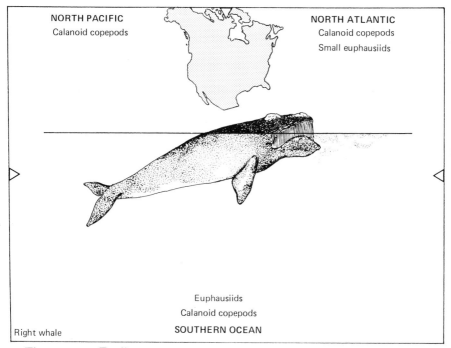

Figure 2.17 Feeding patterns of baleen whales in different oceans, VI: right whale.

the greatest difficulty retaining enough small calanoids to provide a meal.

Little is known of the diet of the endemic southern hemisphere pygmy right whale, other than that stomach contents of animals taken in the South Atlantic contained *Calanus* spp. (51).

The fine-fringed baleen of the Greenland right whale or bowhead suggests that it too is largely a copepod feeder, although there is very little reliable information on species composition. Studies have been made of the figures of probable food species illustrated by W. Scoresby in 1820 (136), and the list includes many such as ctenophores which are really rather unlikely to be more than incidental items (47). The major items of diet were probably *C. finmarchicus* (at least in the Atlantic sector; in the Bering Sea and adjacent regions of the Pacific Arctic the species involved is probably *C. glacialis*), and the pteropod mollusc *Limacina helicina*.

In keeping with the small size of their prey species the right whales have developed a feeding behaviour pattern quite different from that of the rorquals. Atlantic right whales have been studied for a number of years in waters near Cape Cod by scientists from the Woods Hole Marine Laboratory (156), and both surface and subsurface feeding have been observed. In the former the whales would seek out dense surface patches of

Figure 2.18   Right whales have been observed to undertake feeding runs, then
to surface and agitate large volumes of water through their mouths while making
short lunging rushes, apparently cleaning clinging food particles or debris from
the baleen plates. Photography courtesy of Drs M. and B. Würsig, Santa Cruz,
University of California, USA.

zooplankton, specifically *Calanus finmarchicus* and the young stages of
euphausiids (probably *Thysanoessa*), and cruise back and forth through
these concentrations with the mouth open, exposing the baleen plates, and
just the snout projecting from the water (Figure 2.18). When using
hydrophones in the vicinity of whales engaged in this behaviour W. A.
Watkins and W. E. Schevill heard a characteristic rattling sound,
apparently produced by the lapping of water over partially submerged
baleen plates (156). They noticed that water backed up in the mouth so
that the level was significantly higher than that of the surrounding sea;
water could be seen flowing out between the posterior plates. Sometimes
the tongue was visible, possibly being held forward to minimize the flow of
water into the central part of the mouth and maximize flow towards the
fringed surfaces of the baleen plates. Subsurface feeding was seen from
small aircraft; whales were observed swimming with open mouths up to
10 metres below the surface; and it was inferred that deeper feeding might
also occur, since 10 metres was the limit of visibility. Right whales feeding
in this manner remained submerged for periods of four to six minutes.

Table 2.2   Basic summaries of baleen whale diets

Species	Region	Items of diet	References
Bowhead whale	European Arctic	Crustacea: *Calanus*	47
	Beaufort and Chukchi Seas	Crustacea: *Calanus*	
Right whale	North Atlantic	Crustacea: *Calanus, Meganyctiphanes, Thysanoessa*	156
	North Pacific	Crustacea: *Thysanoessa, Calanus*	42
	Southern Ocean	Crustacea: *Calanus, Euphausia*	42
Blue whale	North Atlantic	Crustacea: *Thysanoessa, Temora, Megancytiphanes*	2, 47, 86
	North Pacific	Crustacea: *Thysanoessa, Nematoscelis*	92, 150, 163
	Southern Ocean	Crustacea: *Euphausia*	79, 117
Fin whale	North Atlantic	Crustacea: *Thysanoessa, Meganyctiphanes, Calanus* (by young animals) Fish: *Clupea, Mallotus*	47, 89, 150, 153
	North Pacific, Chukchi Sea	Crustacea: *Calanus, Thysanoessa, Euphausia* Fish: *Sardinella, Theragra* Squid: Ommastrephidae	14, 48, 92, 121, 150, 163
	Southern Ocean	Crustacea: *Euphausia, Thysanoessa*	78, 92, 95
Sei whale	North Atlantic	Crustacea: *Calanus, Temora, Meganyctiphanes*	25, 86, 89
	North Pacific	Crustacea: *Calanus, Eucalanus, Metridia, Thysanoessa* Fish: *Engraulis, Sardinops, Cololabis,* Myctophidae	14, 67, 94, 144, 145
	Southern Ocean	Crustacea: *Calanus, Parathemisto, Clausocalanus*	7, 12, 57, 59, 61, 97
Bryde's whale	North Pacific	Crustacea: *Euphausia, Thysanoessa*	60
	South-east Indian Ocean	Fish: *Engraulis*	22
(inshore form)	South Atlantic	Fish: *Engraulis, Trachurus, Sardinops*	11, 12, 13
(offshore form)		Crustacea: *Euphausia, Nyctiphanes, Thysanoessa*	11, 12, 13
Humpback whale	North Atlantic	Crustacea: *Meganyctiphanes* Fish: *Clupea, Mallotus*	2, 150, 156, and personal observations
	North Pacific and Bering Sea	Crustacea: *Mysis, Pandalus, Pseudoeuphausia, Thysanoessa* Fish: *Clupea, Mallotus, Boreogadus*	14, 99, 100, 150
	Southern Ocean	Crustacea: *Euphausia, Nyctiphanes, Thysanoessa*	12, 29, 31
Gray whale	Eastern North Pacific, Bering Sea, Chukchi Sea	Crustacea: *Pachycheles, Fabia, Pleuroncodes, Nephrops, Atylus, Amplisca,* Polychaeta	30, 81, 91, 119, 131, 150, 161, 162, 164

The present author and his co-workers observed a school of right whales in the Campobello Island region of the western Bay of Fundy for about one week in August 1971 (5). These animals were in close proximity to fin whales feeding on euphausiids, which at least on the ebb tide were shoaling near or at the surface around White Island; calanoid copepods were also abundant. No obvious skimming feeding by the right whales was, however, observed; if they were feeding at all it was below the surface. All individuals were diving for extensive periods; these were not measured exactly because of the near-impossibility of telling one whale from another at any distance. Our subjective impression was that animals were submerging for 5–10 minutes each.

Mysticete sound production

The possible role of acoustics in food location by mysticetes has been a fiercely contended issue. It has been known for a number of years that humpback whales are singularly vocal, and that other rorquals and right whales also produce specific underwater sounds (148) – for example, fin whales produce signals in the 20 Hz range (135); clicks and variable whistles have also been reported (112, 159). Right whale sounds have been categorized as 'belches' (below 500 Hz), 'simple moans' (160 Hz narrow-band), 'complex moans' (about 235 Hz, but wider-band) and distinctive pulses (very short bursts of sound lasting about 0.06 second extending from 30 to 2100 Hz) sometimes associated with miscellaneous phonations below about 1900 Hz (27). Several types of sounds have also been recorded from blue whales (28).

None of the sounds produced could, however, be unequivocally related to echolocation, although this has been tentatively claimed (9, 10). Narrow-band pulses, largely between 21 and 31 kHz, have been recorded in the vicinity of a blue whale which appeared to be feeding (9), and sonic pulses between 4 and 7.5 kHz (click-trains with repetition rate of 6.75 ± 1.02 per second) were taped near a minke whale (10). The observers noted cautiously that, in contrast to observations on delphinid echo-locatory sounds, the quality remained more or less constant despite movements of the minke whale relative to the recording equipment. This *could* represent broadly directional presentation in contrast to the highly directional nature of the delphinid signal pulses (105), but also opens some doubt that these sounds were really being made by the baleen whales. Even assuming that these sounds actually were produced by the whales, it seems likely that the baleen whale would gain less specific data by a relatively unsophisticated method of acoustical scanning of the environment for potential food. Since, however, these species are exploiting schooling prey, rather than chasing food items singly, such a system could be very well adapted to their needs. The frequency differences beween blue (21–31 kHz) and minke (4–7.5 kHz) signals were discussed by P. Beamish and E. Mitchell (9, 10), who suggested that this correlated quite well with the different sizes of the food items (respectively, euphausiids, 2–5 cm, and herring and capelin, *c.* 8–20 cm) preferred by the two species, since 'the acoustic plane wave amplitude reflection from an organism . . . is proportional to the cube of the mean radius of the organism' (10). The blue is stenophagous and planktonophagous, the North Atlantic minke largely ichthyophagous. These authors put forward the hypothesis that selection of small prey might lead to selection for a shift towards higher frequency emissions, and that stenophagy could result in a narrow spectral peak.

More recently Beamish has had the opportunity to blindfold a temporarily captive humpback whale to see if it could run a simple maze of obstacles. The animal failed to do so. While this does not show conclusively that humpback whales cannot echolocate, it certainly puts the concept in grave doubt once again.

Colour patterns – possible roles in predation

The origins of colour patterns in baleen whales have been discussed by E. Mitchell, who attempted to relate them to the evolution of differing dietary regimes in the group (88). He suspected that euryphagy in the fin whale was a relatively recent development, and that the baleen whales as a whole first differentiated as fish feeders in the nekton. He also outlined the need for rorquals to be concealed from their prey. *Balaenoptera physalus* and *B. acutorostrata* are both nektonoeuryphagic; the dark body, pale baleen (asymmetrically coloured in the fin whale), and in the case of the North Atlantic minke the white flipper blaze, could present a simple but effective disruption of the body outline to the prey species. P. F. Brodie has also suggested that sudden presentation of the white blaze, by altering the angle of the flippers, could serve to disrupt and 'herd' schools of fish (17). In the same paper he suggested that the humpback might use the pale pigmentation on its extremely elongate flippers to actively herd fish towards the mouth, relying on the relative inconspicuousness of the head region, which is black dorsally. The humpback also has very dark baleen.

The body is rather evenly dappled in both blue and sei whales and this would serve to blend into the background. Since these tend to be planktonophagous, Mitchell considered that protection from predators was most important in this case but there is little evidence that, other than a possible preference for minke, killer whales would attack any particular large baleen whale species in preference to another.

The significance of the various forms of colour patterns found in small odontocetes has been similarly discussed in two interesting speculative papers by A. V. Yablokov (160) and E. Mitchell (87). Yablokov recognized

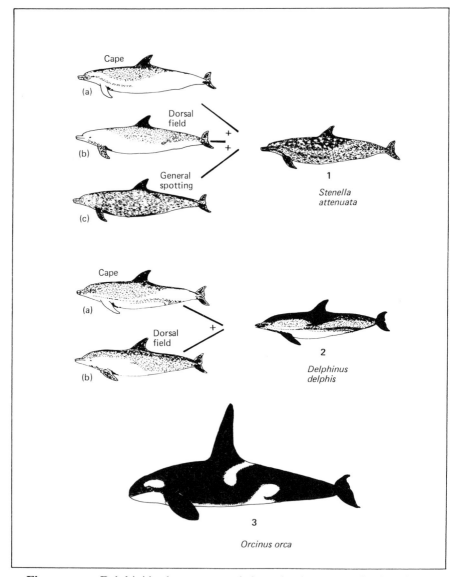

Figure 2.19   Delphinid colour patterns: below, simple counter-shading of the killer whale, also found in Dall's porpoise and *Cephalorhynchus*; above and centre, components which make up total body pigmentation patterns of 1. *Stenella attenuata* (formerly *graffmani*) and 2. *Delphinus delphis*. Originally adapted and modified from drawings and data given by Perrin (113) and Mitchell (87); redrawn from Gaskin (42).

three surface patterns; uniform (plain or evenly marked), counter-shaded, and those with clearly demarcated pigmented areas. Mitchell established a terminology for pattern components in odontocetes; 'saddled' (the most generalized and possibly the most primitive), 'striped', 'spotted', and 'criss-crossed'. The composition of the body patterns in *Stenella* cf. *longirostris* in the central and eastern Pacific have also been presented by W. F. Perrin (113, 114) and analysed into components in a manner similar to that adopted by Mitchell (Figure 2.19).

After a detailed analysis of colour patterns in *Delphinus* and *Stenella*, Mitchell concluded that the saddled pattern afforded protection from being seen by predators or prey through counter-lighting effect, that the spotted pattern blended directly with a background of dappled water, especially with sunlight penetrating it; and that the criss-crossed pattern utilized both counter-shading and outline disruption. In many delphinids the head outline is altered or masked by lip and eye patches or stripes. Yablokov gives data to support the hypothesis that the odontocetes feeding largely below the euphotic zone tend to be uniformly pigmented, and that the counter-shaded forms feed in the upper layers on nektonic food species. His conclusions, and those of Mitchell, are in general agreement with the data on food species composition referred to earlier (37). Some species have rather intermediate feeding patterns but this is only to be expected in such opportunistic feeders as the Delphinidae.

Yablokov discounted the importance of protection from predators in selection for colour patterns; Mitchell seemed less sure that this was entirely true. Certainly the frequency with which *Phocoenoides* and *Stenella coeruleoalba* occur in killer whale stomachs in the North Pacific (101) indicates significant predation. Both Yablokov and Mitchell discussed the probable importance of sharp patterns in facilitation of visual cues during active schooling behaviour of small odontocetes, and the latter author pointed to the laterally placed eyes of these animals.

The value of the spotted body pattern has also been discussed (20, 87). Mitchell concluded that this was predator camouflage (compare with the spotting of a leopard) to facilitate approaching prey, rather than camouflage *from* predators, although a dual purpose might be served.

The whole topic of the evolution of pigmentation patterns in cetaceans and its use in any interpretation of phylogeny as well as ecology and ethology is particularly fascinating, but singularly lacking in direct observational interactive behavioural data. Only the major points can be considered here, and the reader is referred to the previously cited papers by Yablokov and Mitchell for more detailed treatment; the bibliography of Mitchell's paper is particularly useful. For further discussion of the role of tone, pattern and camouflage in aquatic organisms, reference can be made to the volume by Lythgoe entitled *The Ecology of Vision* (74).

References

1 Akimushkin, I. I. 1955. '(Feeding of the cachalot)', *Dokl. Akad. Nauk SSSR*, vol. 101, pp. 1139–40.
2 Allen, G. M. 1916. 'The whalebone whales of New England', *Mem. Soc. nat. Hist. Boston*, vol. 8, pp. 107–322.
3 Altes, R. A. 1980. 'Models for echolocation' R.-G. Busnel and J. F. Fish (eds.), *Animal Sonar Systems*, New York and London, Plenum Press, published in co-operation with NATO Scientific Affairs Division, pp. 625–71.
4 Andrews, R. C. 1909. 'Observations on the habits of the finback and humpback whales of the eastern North Pacific', *Bull. Am. Mus. nat. Hist.*, vol. 26, pp. 213–26.
5 Arnold, P. W. and Gaskin, D. E. 1972. 'Sight records of right whales (*Eubalaena glacialis*) and finback whales (*Balaenoptera physalus*) from the lower Bay of Fundy', *J. Fish. Res. Bd. Canada*, vol. 29, pp. 1477–8.
6 Arseniev, V. A. 1937. '(Some data on the white whale, its migrations and fishery in Sakhalin Island)', *Bull. Pacific Sci. Inst. Fish. Oceangr. Vladivostok*, vol. 10, pp. 19–26.
7 Bannister, J. L. and Baker, A. de C. 1967. 'Observations on food and feeding of baleen whales at Durban', *Norsk Hvalfangsttid.*, vol. 56, pp. 78–82.
8 Bary, B. M. 1956. 'Notes on ecology, systematics, and development of some Mysidacea and Euphausiacea (Crustacea) from New Zealand', *Pacific Sci.*, vol. 10, pp. 431–67.
9 Beamish, P. and Mitchell, E. 1971. 'Ultrasonic sounds recorded in the presence of a blue whale *Balaenoptera musculus*', *Deep-Sea Res.*, vol. 18, pp. 803–9.
10 Beamish, P. and Mitchell, E. 1973. 'Short pulse length audio frequency sounds recorded in the presence of a minke whale (*Balaenoptera acutorostrata*)', *Deep-Sea Res.*, vol. 20, pp. 375–86.
11 Best, P. B. 1960. 'Further information on Bryde's whale (*Balaenoptera edeni* Anderson) from Saldhana Bay, South Africa', *Norsk Hvalfangsttid.*, vol. 49, pp. 201–15.
12 Best, P. B. 1967. 'Distribution and feeding habits of baleen whales off the Cape Province', *Investl Rep. Div. Sea Fish. S. Afr.*, vol. 57, pp. 1–44.
13 Best, P. B. 1974. 'Two allopatric forms of Bryde's whale off South Africa', *Rep. Int. Whal. Commn* (special issue 1), pp. 10–38.
14 Betesheva, E. I. 1954. '(Data on the feeding of baleen whales in the Kurile region)', *Trudy Inst. Okeanol.*, vol. 11, pp. 238–45.
15 Betesheva, E. I. and Akimushkin, I. I. 1955. '(Food of the sperm whale (*P. catodon*) in the Kurile Islands)', *Trudy Inst. Okeanol.*, vol. 18, pp. 86–94.
16 Brinton, E. 1962. 'The distribution of Pacific euphausiids', *Bull. Scripps Instn Oceanogr.*, vol. 8, pp. 51–270.
17 Brodie, P. F. 1977. 'Form, function and energetics of Cetacea: a discussion' in R. J. Harrison (ed.), *Functional Anatomy of Marine Mammals*, vol. 3, London, Academic Press, pp. 45–56.
18 Brodskii, K. A. 1964. 'Distribution and some morphological features of the Antarctic species of *Calanus* (Copepoda)', *Issled. Fauny Morei*, vol. 2, pp. 189–250.
19 Bullock, T. H., Grinell, A. D., Ikezeno, E., Kameda, K., Katsuki, Y., Nomoto, M., Sato, O., Suga, N. and Yanagisawa, K. 1968. 'Electrophysiological studies of central auditory mechanisms in cetaceans', *Z. vergl. Physiol.*, vol. 59, pp. 117–56.
20 Caldwell, D. K. and Caldwell, M. C. 1966. 'Observations on the distribution, coloration, behavior and audible sound production of the spotted dolphin, *Stenella plagiodon* (Cope)', *Los Angeles County Mus. Contrib. Sci.*, vol. 104, pp. 1–28.
21 Castello, H. P. 1977. 'Food of a killer whale: Eagle sting ray, *Myliobatis* found in the stomach of a stranded *Orcinus orca*', *Sci. Rep. Whales Res. Inst.*, vol. 29, pp. 107–11.

22 Chittleborough, R. G. 1959. '*Balaenoptera brydei* Olsen on the west coast of Australia', *Norsk Hvalfangsttid.*, vol. 48, pp. 62–6.

23 Clarke, R. 1956. 'Sperm whales of the Azores', *Discovery*, Rep. 28, pp. 237–98.

24 Clarke, M. R. 1979. 'The head of the sperm whale', *Scientific American*, vol. 240, pp. 128–41.

25 Collett, R. 1886. 'On the external characters of Rudolphi's rorqual (*Balaenoptera borealis*)', *Proc. zool. Soc. London*, vol. 18, pp. 243–65.

26 Cousteau, J.-Y. and Diole, P. 1972. *The Whale: Mighty Monarch of the Sea*, translated by J. F. Bernard, Garden City, NY, Doubleday.

27 Cummings, W. C., Fish, J. F. and Thompson, P. O. 1972. 'Sound production and other behavior of southern right whales, *Eubalaena glacialis*', *San Diego Soc. Nat. Hist. Trans.*, vol. 17, pp. 1–14.

28 Cummings, W. C. and Thompson, P. O. 1971. 'Underwater sounds from the blue whale, *Balaenoptera musculus*', *J. acoust. Soc. Am.*, vol. 50, pp. 1193–8.

29 Dall, W. and Dunstan, D. J. 1957. '*Euphausia superba* Dana from a humpback whale, *Megaptera nodosa* (Bonnaterre) caught off southern Queensland', *Norsk Hvalfangsttid.*, vol. 46, pp. 6–9.

30 Darling, J. 1977. 'Population biology and behaviour of the grey whale (*Eschrichtius robustus*) in Pacific Rim National Park, British Columbia', M.Sc. thesis, University of Victoria, British Columbia.

31 Dawbin, W. H. 1956. 'The migrations of humpback whales which pass the New Zealand coast', *Trans. R. Soc. N.Z.*, vol. 84, pp. 147–96.

32 Dudok van Heel, W. H. 1962. 'Sound and Cetacea', *Netherlands J. Sea Res.*, vol. 1, pp. 407–507.

33 Earle, S. 1979. 'Humpbacks: the gentle whales', *Nat. Geogr. Mag.*, vol. 155, pp. 2–17.

34 Eschricht, D. F. 1845. 'Undersøgelser over Hvaldyrene. Fjerde Afhandling. Om naebhvalen', *K. danske Vidensk. Selsk. naturvid. mat. Afh.*, vol. 11, pp. 321–78.

35 Eschricht, D. F. 1849. *Zoologisch-Anatomische-physiologische Untersuchungen über die nordischen Waltiere*, Leipzig.

36 Farran, G. P. 1929. 'Crustacea, Part X. Copepoda', *Nat. Hist. Rep. Br. Antarct. Terra Nova Exped.*, vol. 8, 203–306.

37 Fitch, J. E. and Brownell, R. L. Jr. 1968. 'Fish otoliths in cetaceans stomachs and their importance in interpreting feeding habits', *J. Fish. Res. Bd. Canada*, vol. 25, pp. 2561–75.

38 Fleischer, G. 1976. 'Hearing in extinct cetaceans as determined by cochlear structure', *J. Palaeontol.*, vol. 50, pp. 133–52.

39 Fraser, F. C. and Norman, J. R. 1937. *Giant Fishes, Whales, and Dolphins*, London, Putnam Press.

40 Gambell, R. 1972. 'Sperm whales off Durban', *Discovery*, Rep. 35, pp. 199–358.

41 Gaskin, D. E. 1972. 'Luminescence in a squid *Moroteuthis* sp. (probably *ingens* Smith), and a possible feeding mechanism in the sperm whale *Physeter catodon* L.', *Tuatara*, vol. 15, pp. 86–8.

42 Gaskin, D. E. 1976. 'The evolution, zoogeography and ecology of Cetacea', *Oceanogr. Mar. Biol. Ann. Rev.*, vol. 14, pp. 247–346.

43 Gaskin, D. E. and Cawthorn, M. W. 1967. 'Diet and feeding habits of the sperm whale (*Physeter catodon* L.) in the Cook Strait region of New Zealand', *N.Z.J. mar. Freshwat. Sci.*, vol. 2, pp. 156–79.

44 Handcock, D. 1965. 'Killer whales kill and eat a minke whale', *J. Mammal.*, vol. 46, pp. 341–2.

45 Harmer, S. F. 1918. 'Report on Cetacea stranded on the British coasts during 1917', *Bull. Brit. Mus. Lond.*, vol. 5, pp. 1–21.

46 Hentschel, E. 1937. 'Naturgeschichte der nord-atlantische Wale und Robben'

in Lübbert u. Ehrenbaum (ed.), *Handbuch Seefischerei NordEuropas*, Stuttgart, Schweizerbart, pp. 1–54.

47 Hjort, J. and Ruud, J. T. 1929. 'Whaling and fishing in the North Atlantic', *Rapp. P.-v. Réun. Cons. perm. int. Explor. Mer.*, vol. 56, pp. 5–123.

48 Hollis, H. 1939. 'Biological report of the United States Bureau of Commercial Fisheries', *Norsk Hvalfangsttid.*, vol. 1, pp. 1–4.

49 Howell, A. B. 1930. *Aquatic Mammals: Their Adaptations to Life in Water*, Springfield, Ill., Charles C. Thomas.

50 Ingebrigtsen, A. 1929. 'Whales caught in the North Atlantic and other seas', *Rapp. P.-v. Réun. Cons. perm. int. Explor. Mer.*, vol. 56, pp. 1–26.

51 Ivashin, M. V., Shevchenko, V. I. and Yukhov, V. L. 1972. '(Pygmy right whale *Caperea marginata* Cetacea)', *Zool. Zhr.*, vol. 51, pp. 1715–23.

52 Jillett, J. B. 1968. '*Calanus tonsus* (Copepoda, Calanoida) in southern New Zealand waters with notes on the male', *Aust. mar. Freshwat. Res.*, vol. 19, pp. 19–30.

53 Jonsgård, Å. 1951. 'Studies on the little piked or minke whale (*Balaenoptera acutorostrata* Lacépède)', *Norsk Hvalfangsttid.*, vol. 40, pp. 209–32.

54 Jonsgård, Å. and Lyshoel, P. B. 1970. 'A contribution to the knowledge of the biology of the killer whale', *Nytt. mag. for Zool.*, vol. 18, pp. 41–8.

55 Jurasz, C. M. and Jurasz, V. P. 1979. 'Feeding modes of the humpback whale, *Megaptera novaeangliae*, in southeast Alaska', *Sci. Reps. Whales Res. Inst.*, vol. 31, pp. 69–83.

56 Kasuya, T. and Rice, D. W. 1970. 'Note on baleen plates and on arrangement of parasitic barnacles of gray whale', *Sci Rep. Whales Res. Inst.*, vol. 22, pp. 39–43.

57 Kawamura, A. 1970. 'Food of sei whale taken by Japanese whaling expeditions in the Antarctic season 1967/68', *Sci. Rep. Whales Res. Inst.*, vol. 22, pp. 127–52.

58 Kawamura, A. 1973. 'Food and feeding of sei whale caught in the waters south of 40°N in the North Pacific', *Sci. Rep. Whales Res. Inst.*, vol. 25, pp. 219–36.

59 Kawamura, A. 1974. 'Food and feeding ecology in the southern sei whale', *Sci. Rep. Whales Res. Inst.*, vol. 26, pp. 25–144.

60 Kawamura, A. and Satake, Y. 1976. 'Preliminary report on the geographical distribution of the Bryde's whale in the North Pacific with special reference to the structure of the filtering apparatus', *Sci. Rep. Whales Res. Inst.*, vol. 28, pp. 1–35.

61 Kawamura, A. and Hoshiai, T. 1969. 'Data on copepods collected in the 7th Japanese Antarctic research expedition 1965–66', *Ant. Rec.*, vol. 36, pp. 69–73.

62 Kellogg, R. 1928. 'The history of whales – their adaptations to life in the water', *Q. Rev. Biol.*, vol. 3, pp. 29–76, 174–208.

63 Kellogg, R. 1940. 'Whales, giants of the sea', *Nat. Geogr. Mag.*, vol. 77, pp. 35–90.

64 Kleinenberg, S. E., Yablokov, A. V., Bel'kovitch, B. M. and Tarasevitch, M. N. 1969. 'Beluga (*Delphinapterus leucas*), investigation of the species', translated by Israel Program for Scientific Translation, Jerusalem.

65 Klumov, S. K. 1939. '(The beluga in the Soviet Union. Resources and Whaling)', *Trudy Inst. VNIRO*, vol. 12, pp. 1–6.

66 Klumov, S. K. 1962. '(Right whale (Japanese) of the Pacific Ocean)', *Trudy Inst. Okeanol.*, vol. 58, pp. 202–97.

67 Klumov, S. K. 1963. '(Feeding and helminth fauna of whalebone whales in the main whaling grounds of the world ocean)', *Trudy Inst. Okeanol.*, vol. 71, pp. 94–194.

68 Kükenthal, W. 1888. 'Bericht über eine Reise in das Eismeer und nach Spitzbergen im jahre 1886', *Geogr. Blätter*, vol. 11, pp. 1–43; *Z. Nat., Jena*, vol. 26, pp. 469–89.

69 Lawrence, B. A. and Schevill, W. E. 1956. 'The functional anatomy of the delphinid nose', *Bull. Mus. Comp. Zool.*, vol. 114, pp. 103–51.

70 Lillie, D. G. 1910. 'Observations on the anatomy and general biology of some members of the larger Cetacea', *Proc. zool. Soc. London* (1910), pp. 769–92.

71 Liouville, J. 1913. *Cetaces de l'Antarctique*, Paris, 2e Expedition antarctique français (1908–1910).

72 Litchfield, C. and Greenberg, A. J. 1974. 'Unusual tri-glycerides and wax esters in the head fats of the Pacific beaked whale *Berardius bairdi*', *J. Am. Oil Chem. Soc.*, vol. 51, p. 515A.

73 Litchfield, C., Karol, R. and Greenberg, A. J. 1974. 'Role of lipids in the acoustical function of the dolphin melon', *J. Am. Oil Chem. Soc.*, vol. 51, p. 516A.

74 Lythgoe, J. N. 1979. *The Ecology of Vision*, Oxford, Clarendon Press.

75 MacKay, R. S. 1980. 'A theory of the spermaceti organ in sperm whale sound production' in R.-G. Busnel and J. F. Fish (eds.), *Animal Sonar Systems*, New York and London, Plenum Press, published in co-operation with NATO Scientific Affairs Division, pp. 937–40.

76 MacKay, R. S. and Liaw, H. M. 1981. 'Dolphin vocalization mechanisms', *Science*, vol. 212, pp. 676–8.

77 Mackintosh, N. A. 1965. *The Stocks of Whales*, London, Fishing News (Books).

78 Mackintosh, N. A. 1966. 'The distribution of southern blue and fin whales' in K. S. Norris (ed.), *Whales, Dolphins, and Porpoises*, Berkeley and Los Angeles, University of California Press, pp. 125–44.

79 Mackintosh, N. A. and Wheeler, J. F. G. 1929. 'Southern blue and fin whales', *Discovery*, Rep. 1, pp. 257–540.

80 Matsushita, T. 1955. '(Daily rhythmic activity of the sperm whales in the Antarctic Ocean)', *Bull. Jap. Soc. scient. Fish.*, vol. 20, pp. 770–3.

81 Matthews, L. H. 1932. 'Lobster-Krill: Anomuran Crustacea that are the food of whales', *Discovery*, Rep. 5, pp. 467–84.

82 Matthews, L. H. 1938. 'The sperm whale, *Physeter catodon*', *Discovery*, Rep. 17, pp. 93–168.

83 Matthews, L. H. 1938. 'The sei whale, *Balaenoptera borealis*', *Discovery*, Rep. 17, pp. 183–290.

84 McCormick, J. G., Wever, E. G., Palin, J. and Ridgway, S. H. 1970. 'Sound conduction in the dolphin ear', *J. acoust. Soc. America*, vol. 48, pp. 1418–28.

85 McCormick, J. G., Wever, E. G., Ridgway, S. H. and Palin, J. 1980. 'Sound reception in the porpoise as it relates to echolocation' in R.-G. Busnel and J. F. Fish (eds.), *Animal Sonar Systems*, New York and London, Plenum Press, published in co-operation with NATO Scientific Affairs Division, pp. 449–67.

86 Millais, J. G. 1906. *The Mammals of Great Britain and Ireland*, London, Longman.

87 Mitchell, E. 1970. 'Pigmentation pattern evolution in delphinid cetaceans: an essay in adaptive coloration', *Can. J. Zool.*, vol. 48, pp. 717–40.

88 Mitchell, E. 1975. 'Whale pigmentation and feeding behavior', *American Zoologist*, vol. 12, pp. 655.

89 Mitchell, E. 1975. 'Trophic relationships and competition for food in Northwest Atlantic whales', *Proc. Can. Soc. Zoologists 1974*, pp. 123–33.

90 Miyazaki, N., Kusaka, T. and Nishiwaki, M. 1973. 'Food of *Stenella caeruleoalba*', *Sci. Rep. Whales Res. Inst.*, vol. 25, pp. 265–75.

91 Mizue, K. 1951. 'Gray whales in the east sea area of Korea', *Sci. Rep. Whales Res. Inst.*, vol. 5, pp. 71–9.

92 Nemoto, T. 1959. 'Food of baleen whales with reference to whale movements', *Sci. Rep. Whales Res. Inst.*, vol. 14, pp. 149–290.

93 Nemoto, T. 1962. 'Food of baleen whales collected in recent Japanese Antarctic whaling expeditions', *Sci. Rep. Whales Res. Inst.*, vol. 16, pp. 89–103.

94 Nemoto, T. and Kawamura, A. 1974. 'Characteristics of food habits and distribution of baleen whales with special reference to the abundance of North Pacific sei and Bryde's whales', *Rep. Int. Whal. Commn* (Special Issue 1), pp. 80–7.

95 Nemoto, T. and Nasu, K. 1958. '*Thysanoessa macrura* as a food of baleen whales in the Antarctic', *Sci. Rep. Whales Res. Inst.*, vol. 13, pp. 193–9.

96   Nemoto, T. and Nasu, K. 1963. 'Stones and other aliens in the stomachs of sperm whales in the Bering Sea', *Sci. Rep. Whales Res. Inst.*, vol. 17, pp. 83–91.

97   Nemoto, T. and Yoo, K. I. 1970. 'An amphipod, *Parathemisto gaudichaudii* as a food of the Antarctic sei whale', *Sci. Rep. Whales Res. Inst.*, vol. 22, pp. 153–8.

98   Nishimoto, S., Tozawa, M. and Kawakami, T. 1952. 'Food of sei whales (*Balaenoptera borealis*) caught in the Bonin Island waters', *Sci. Rep. Whales Res. Inst.*, vol. 7, pp. 79–85.

99   Nishiwaki, M. 1959. 'Humpback whales in Ryukyuan waters', *Sci. Rep. Whales Res. Inst.*, vol. 14, pp. 49–87.

100 Nishiwaki, M. 1960. 'Ryukyuan humpback whaling in 1960', *Sci. Rep. Whales Res. Inst.*, vol. 15, pp. 1–15.

101 Nishiwaki, M. and Handa, C. 1958. 'Killer whales caught in the coastal waters off Japan for the recent 10 years', *Sci. Rep. Whales Res. Inst.*, vol. 13, pp. 85–96.

102 Norris, K. S. 1964. 'Some problems of echolocation in cetaceans' in W. N. Tavolga (ed.) *Marine Bioacoustics*, vol. 1, Oxford, Pergamon Press, pp. 317–36.

103 Norris, K. S. 1968. 'The evolution of acoustic mechanisms in odontocete cetaceans' in E. T. Drake (ed.), *Evolution and Environment*, New Haven and London, Yale University Press, pp. 297–324.

104 Norris, K. S. 1980. 'Peripheral sound processing in odontocetes' in R.-G. Busnel and J. F. Fish (eds.), *Animal Sonar Systems*, New York and London, Plenum Press, published in co-operation with NATO Scientific Affairs Division, pp. 495–509.

105 Norris, K. S. and Evans, W. E. 1967. 'Directionality of echolocation clicks in the rough-tooth porpoise, *Steno bredanensis* (Lesson)' in W. N. Tavolga (ed.), *Marine Bioacoustics*, vol. 2, Oxford, Pergamon Press, pp. 305–16.

106 Ohsumi, S. 1979. 'Feeding habits of the minke whale in the Antarctic', *Rep. Int. Whal. Commn*, vol. 29, pp. 473–6.

107 Ohsumi, S., Masaki, Y. and Kawamura, A. 1970. 'Stock of the Antarctic minke whale', *Sci. Rep. Whales Res. Inst.*, vol. 22, pp. 75–126.

108 Okutani, T. and Nemoto, T. 1964. 'Squids as the food of sperm whales in the Bering Sea and Alaskan Gulf', *Sci. Rep. Whales Res. Inst.*, vol. 18, pp. 111–22.

109 Omura, H. 1958. 'North Pacific right whale', *Sci. Rep. Whales Res. Inst.*, vol. 13, pp. 1–52.

110 Omura, H. and Nemoto, T. 1969. 'Black right whales in the North Pacific', *Sci. Rep. Whales Res. Inst.*, vol. 21, pp. 1–78.

111 Payne, R. 1979. 'Humpbacks: their mysterious songs', *Nat. Geogr. Mag.*, vol. 155, pp. 18–25.

112 Perkins, P. J. 1966. 'Communication sounds of finback whales', *Norsk Hvalfangst-tid.*, vol. 55, pp. 199–200.

113 Perrin, W. F. 1969. 'Color pattern of the eastern spotted porpoise *Stenella graffmani* Lönnberg (Cetacea, Delphinidae)', *Zoologica*, vol. 54, pp. 135–42.

114 Perrin, W. F. 1972. 'Color patterns of spinner porpoises (*Stenella* cf. *S. longirostris*) of the eastern Pacific and Hawaii, with comments on delphinid pigmentation', *Fishery Bull. Fish. Wildl. Serv. US*, vol. 70, pp. 983–1003.

115 Perrin, W. F., Warner, R. R., Fiscus, C. H. and Holts, D. B. 1973. 'Stomach contents of porpoise, *Stenella* sp., and yellowfin tuna, *Thunnus albacares*, in mixed species aggregations', *Fishery Bull. Fish. Wildl. Serv. US*, vol. 70, pp. 1077–92.

116 Pervushin, A. S. 1968. '(Observations of behaviour and feeding of whalebone whales in the area of Crozet Island)', *Okeanol. Akad. Sci. SSSR*, vol. 8, pp. 139–46.

117 Peters, N. 1939. 'Über Grösse, Wachstum, und Altes des Blauwales (*Balaenoptera musculus* L.) und Finnwales (*Balaenoptera physalus* L.)', *Zool. Anz.*, vol. 127, pp. 193–204.

118 Pike, G. C. 1950. 'Stomach contents of whales caught off the coast of British Columbia', *Prog. Rep. Pacif. Cst Stns*, vol. 83, pp. 27–8.

119   Pike, G. C. 1962. 'Migration and feeding of the gray whale (*Eschrichtius gibbosus*)', *J. Fish. Res. Bd. Canada*, vol. 19, pp. 815–38.

120   Pivorunas, A. 1976. 'A mathematical consideration on the function of baleen plates and their fringes', *Sci. Rep. Whales Res. Inst.*, vol. 28, pp. 37–55.

121   Ponomareva, L. A. 1949. '(On the nourishment of the plankton-eating whale in the Bering Sea)', *C.r. Acad. Sci. SSSR*, vol. 68, pp. 401–3.

122   Purves, P. E. 1966. 'Anatomy and physiology of the outer and middle ear in cetaceans' in K. S. Norris (ed.), *Whales, Dolphins, and Porpoises*, Berkeley and Los Angeles, University of California Press, pp. 320–80.

123   Purves, P. E. 1967. 'Anatomical and experimental observations on the cetacean sonar system' in R.-G. Busnel (ed.), *Les Systemes Sonars Animaux, Biologie et Bionique*, Jouy-en-Joas, Laboratoire de physiologie acoustique, Publication INRA-CNRZ, pp. 197–270.

124   Purves, P. E. and Pilleri, G. 1973. 'Observations on the ear, nose, throat and eye of *Platanista indi*' in G. Pilleri (ed.), *Investigations on Cetacea*, vol. V, Berne, Waldau, pp. 13–57.

125   Rae, B. B. 1965. 'The food of the common porpoise', *J. Zool. London*, vol. 146, pp. 114–22.

126   Ray, G. C. and Schevill, W. E. 1974. 'Feeding of a captive gray whale, *Eschrichtius robustus*', *Marine Fish. Rev.*, vol. 36, pp. 31–8.

127   Reysenbach de Haan, F. W. 1957. 'Hearing in whales', *Acta Otolaryngol.*, vol. 134 (Suppl.), pp. 1–114.

128   Rice, D. W. 1963. 'The whale marking cruise of the *Sioux City* off California and Baja California', *Norsk Hvalfangsttid.*, vol. 52, pp. 153–60.

129   Rice, D. W. 1963. 'Progress report on biological studies of larger Cetacea in the waters off California', *Norsk Hvalfangsttid.*, vol. 52, pp. 181–7.

130   Rice, D. W. 1968. 'Stomach contents and feeding behavior of killer whales in the eastern North Pacific', *Norsk Hvalfangsttid.*, vol. 57, pp. 35–8.

131   Rice, D. W. and Wolman, A. A. 1971. 'The life history and ecology of the gray whale (*Eschrichtius robustus*)', *Special Publ. Am. Soc. Mammalogists*, no. 3.

132   Roe, H. S. J. 1969. 'The food and feeding habits of the sperm whales (*Physeter catodon* L.) taken off the west coast of Iceland', *J. Cons. int. Explor. Mer.*, vol. 33, pp. 93–102.

133   Ruud, J. T. 1937. 'Bottlenose', *Norsk Hvalfangsttid.*, vol. 26, pp. 456–8.

134   Scattergood, L. W. 1949. 'Notes on the little piked whale', *The Murrelet*, vol. 30, pp. 3–16.

135   Schevill, W. E. 1964. 'Underwater sounds of cetaceans' in W. N. Tavolga (ed.), *Marine Bio-acoustics*, vol. 1, New York, Pergamon Press, pp. 307–16.

136   Scoresby, W. 1820. *An Account of the Arctic regions, with a History and Description of the Northern Whale Fishery*, Edinburgh, Constable.

137   Sears, R. 1979. 'Observations of cetaceans along the north shore of the Gulf of St Lawrence, August 1979', East Falmouth MA, USA, Mingan Island Cetacean Study, mimeo report.

138   Sergeant, D. E. 1962. 'The biology of the pilot or pot-head whale *Globicephala melaena* (Traill) in Newfoundland waters', *Bull. Fish. Res. Bd. Canada*, vol. 132, pp. 1–84.

139   Sergeant, D. E. 1963. 'Minke whales, *Balaenoptera acutorostrata* Lacépède, of the western North Atlantic', *J. Fish. Res. Bd. Canada*, vol. 20, pp. 1489–504.

140   Sergeant, D. E. and Fisher, H. D. 1957. 'The smaller Cetacea of eastern Canadian waters', *J. Fish. Res. Bd. Canada*, vol. 14, pp. 83–115.

141   Shih, C. T., Figueira, A. J. C. and Grainger, E. H. 1971. 'A synopsis of Canadian marine zooplankton', *Bull. Fish. Res. Bd. Canada*, vol. 176, pp. 1–264.

142   Sleptsov, M. M. 1952. *Kitoobraznye dal'nevostochnykh Morei*, Vladivostok, Izvestiya TINRO.

143 Smith, G. J. D. and Gaskin, D. E. 1974. 'The diet of harbor porpoises (*Phocoena phocoena* (L.)) in coastal waters of eastern Canada, with special reference to the Bay of Fundy', *Can. J. Zool*, vol. 52, pp. 777–82.

144 Stephenson, W. 1951. 'The lesser rorqual in British waters', *Dove Marine Lab. Rep.* (ser. 3), vol. 12, pp. 7–48.

145 Tanaka, O. 1954. 'Notes on *Calanus tonsus* Brady in Japanese waters', *J. Oceanogr. Soc. Jap.*, vol. 10, pp. 126–37.

146 Tanaka, O. 1956. 'Further notes on *Calanus tonsus* Brady in Japanese waters', *J. Oceanogr. Soc. Jap.*, vol. 12, pp. 49–52.

147 Tarpy, C. 1979. 'Killer whale attack!' *Nat. Geogr. Mag.*, vol. 155, pp. 542–5.

148 Thompson, T. J., Winn, H. E. and Perkins, P. J. 1979. 'Mysticete sounds' in H. E. Winn and B. L. Olla (eds.), *Behavior of Marine Animals, Current Perspectives in Research, Vol. 3 : Cetaceans*, New York and London, Plenum Press, pp. 403–31.

149 Tomilin, A. G. 1954. '(Adaptational types among whales [Toward an ecological classification of the Cetacea]), *Zool. Zhr.*, vol. 33, pp. 677–92.

150 Tomilin, A. G. 1967. *Cetacea. Vol. 9, Mammals of the USSR and Adjacent Countries* (V. G. Heptner, ed.), Israel Program for Scientific Translation, Jerusalem.

151 Van Beneden, P. J. 1889. *Histoire Naturelle des Cétacés des Mers d'Europe*, Brussels.

152 Van Utrecht, W. L. 1966. 'On the growth of the baleen plate of the fin whale and the blue whale', *Bijdr. Dierk.*, vol. 35, pp. 1–38.

153 Vinogradov, M. P. 1949. 'Morskie mlekopitayushchie Arktiki', *Trudy Arkticheskoga Instituta Bull*, no. 202.

154 Vladykov, V. D. 1946. *Chasse, biologie et valeur economique du Marsouin Blanc ou Béluga* (Delphinapterus leucas) *du fleuve et du golfe Saint-Laurent*, Québec, Dépt. Pêcheries Prov. de Québec.

155 Watkins, W. A. 1977. 'Acoustic behavior of sperm whales', *Oceanus*, vol. 20, pp. 50–8.

156 Watkins, W. A. and Schevill, W. E. 1976. 'Right whale feeding and baleen rattle', *J. Mammal.*, vol. 57, pp. 58–66.

157 Watkins, W. A. and Schevill, W. E. 1979. 'Aerial observation of feeding behavior in four baleen whales: *Eubalaena glacialis, Balaenoptera borealis, Megaptera novaeangliae*, and *Balaenoptera physalus*', *J. Mammal.*, vol. 60, pp. 155–63.

158 Williamson, G. R. 1973. 'Counting and measuring baleen and ventral grooves of whales', *Sci. Rep. Whales Res. Inst.*, vol. 25, pp. 279–92.

159 Wright, B. S. 1962. 'Notes on North Atlantic whales', *Can.-Fld. Nat.*, vol. 76, pp. 62–5.

160 Yablokov, A. V. 1963. '(Types of colour of the Cetacea)', *Bull. Moscov Soc. Nat. Biol.*, vol. 68, pp. 27–41.

161 Zenkovich, B. A. 1934. '(Research data on Cetacea of far eastern seas (the gray California whale – *Rhachianectes glaucus* Cope))', *Vestnik Akad. Nauk SSSR Dal'nevostochnyi Fil.*, vol. 10, pp. 9–25.

162 Zenkovich, B. A. 1934. '(Some data on whales of the Far East)', *Doklady Akad. Nauk SSSR*, vol. 2, pp. 338–92.

163 Zenkovich, B. A. 1936. '(Migrations of whales)', *Bull. Pacific Sci. Fish. Inst. Ocean. Vlad.*, vol. 10, pp. 3–18.

164 Zenkovich, B. A. 1937. '(The food of far-eastern whales)', *Doklady Akad. Nauk. SSSR*, vol. 16, pp. 231–4.

165 Zenkovich, B. A. 1938. '(On the grampus or killer whale, *Grampus orca* Lin.)', *Priroda*, pp. 109–12.

CHAPTER 3

Metabolic rate and energy budget in Cetaceans

Introduction

The primary factors which would seem to have governed the evolution of the modern Cetacea and, in a more short-term fashion, the development of their movements and migration patterns, are the following.

1   Food sources which may be exploited by Cetacea for net energetic gain are discontinuously distributed in the world ocean: Cetacea must locate these regions, and move when the food sources move.
2   Within these mobile prime areas, the food is frequently available only on a seasonal basis.
3   Even during the periods of seasonal availability, the food is still discontinuously distributed, often with (from the viewpoint of an individual animal) long distances between patches.
4   Presuming that animals can locate and stay with optimal feeding conditions for extended periods, there is a likelihood that these conditions are not optimal for reproductive requirements.
5   Selection will favour those animals which, in making periodic movements, not only find conditions optimal for reproduction, but spend only the time absolutely necessary for essential breeding and nursing activities before returning to high-productivity feeding areas.

The structure and function of the digestive system in Cetacea is consistent with such constraints on the life cycle. Modification of the buccal cavity (according to the nature of the prey) has eliminated the need for mastication in both suborders of Cetacea, an action which might use up valuable seconds of each fleeting period when the whale is in contact with prey. Some of the research on harbour porpoise carried out by my own unit, for example, showed that, on an average daily basis, an individual animal spent about 21 per cent of its time in simple point-to-point locomotion, 3 per cent lying at the surface, but 76 per cent in behaviour interpreted as foraging for food (72). The oesophagus is distensible and able to accommodate a variety of sizes of food items, as is the forestomach, which can function as a crop when food is taken opportunistically.

Digestion appears to be rapid (58) so that the animal is in a maximum state of readiness to take more prey as they are detected. Passage of food and its digestion is aided by the compartmentalization of the stomach region into subunits with cellular division of labour and a great relative increase in surface area. With such a system the cetacean is well adapted to take maximum advantage of food, when encountered (14).

How it deals with the other problems associated with discontinuous food availability depends to a large extent on the capabilities and efficiency of the animal as a whole. There is variation from species to species and group to group and, naturally enough, we find different distributions among cetaceans. As a general rule, the largest species, especially rorquals and right whales, spend at least part of the year in high latitudes, and this stems from the relatively high productivity of these waters and the resulting abundance of food suitable for such cetaceans. Although sperm whales are common in tropical latitudes, even these animals are found to be largely restricted to current boundaries and areas of upwelling where productivity is relatively high.

Nevertheless, since calves have a high surface–volume ratio and thin insulation compared with their parents, it is initially not surprising that the same large rorquals (particularly the humpback) and sperm whales breed in low latitudes. The annual return migrations are, therefore, classically viewed as an evolutionary compromise through which whales are able to exploit both optimal feeding conditions and optimal breeding conditions. The development of the characteristic hypodermal layer of fat blubber is seen as a factor in this evolution, serving as a lipid depot which may be drawn upon in the tropics and subtropics where food is scarce, and as an insulating layer against the cold of high-latitude waters (however, see pp. 107–8).

Concept and value of 'energy budget'

In recent years several workers (7, 32, 41–3) have begun to analyse – from the standpoint of energy inputs and outputs – the large volume of data accrued from scientific studies of large whales of commercial importance. This research comes at an opportune time, since in the last few years we have seen the first serious attempts to study cetaceans in an ecological context, rather than just as commercially exploitable animals.

What, one might ask, is the special significance of a bioenergetic approach to studies of these animals, rather than simply using conventional numerical analysis to examine changes in population size, composition and distribution? The answer, of course, is that ideally one requires both methods, but there are distinct advantages in utilizing the former. The need to understand ecological processes and the dynamics of natural populations becomes more urgent as our use of animal populations becomes more intensive. During recent years there has been reluctant recognition of the limitations inherent in the use of deterministic single-species models to describe population functions. Although such models have had wide acceptance for many years in fisheries and game management, few take any account of the complex relationships which any species has with its environment, and with other living components of an ecosystem. As a result, the limited successes enjoyed by such models in management are hardly surprising, and since the end of the 1960s, the move to systems-analysis approaches has been rapid, assisted by the advent of low-cost high-speed computing.

These analyses focus on the hierarchical structures and interactive aspects of ecosystems, the flow of energy through such systems, the nature and pattern of primary productivity in a given unit, the efficiencies of utilization and transfer of energy from one level to the next, and the relative importance of 'horizontal' links for degradation of usable energy within a trophic level. Rather than just considering numbers, or biomass, such studies can serve to assess the nature and magnitude of the extrinsic and stochastic factors which so strongly influence the structure and relative sizes of populations in the real world. They permit us to quantify and evaluate some of the complexities of community structure, and to begin to perceive the mechanisms governing ecosystem stability. They may aid in the recognition of changes in the relationships of species, and perhaps enable us to detect and forecast the onset of those long-term regular and irregular fluctuations in conditions and population sizes, which so frequently confound predictions based on simple deterministic models. Acquisition of such knowledge cannot help but improve our understanding of the ecology and population dynamics of cetaceans. Furthermore, system management must be improved, for, at least in the foreseeable future, there will be no cessation of the increasing impact of man upon the natural ecosystems of the world, fuelled by the powerful twin driving forces of growing population, and burgeoning consumer demand resulting from increasing expectations in communities which until recently were thankful just to subsist.

The aim of the bioenergetic approach is to prepare a 'balance sheet' to account for the energy inputs and outputs of a series of 'typical' individuals of both sexes at all the critical phases of growth and age, under the major variations of daily and seasonal activity, and physiological stress. When such data are available, they can be combined with information on numbers of whales, their age composition and social structure to calculate the energy budget for the population as a whole, and measure its impact as a trophic unit within the ecosystem. In this way we hope to obtain critical information with respect to the ways in which a population interacts with the other biological components in the system. Those most likely to be affected by changes in the population size, activity and habits of the species in question, of course, are the prey, other species which might be competing for the same prey, and any predators.

At this juncture it might be useful to provide an example of the type of situation in which this kind of information is invaluable. Consider a baleen whale population dependent on a large seasonal krill population in the Southern Ocean. The krill is also eaten by large populations of several species of sea-bird, and at least an equal biomass of groundfish. Decisions are taken to open whaling operations. Will this leave more krill for the other components in this ecosystem? Ecological theory suggests very strongly that it might. What is the normal competitive situation of the whale population with respect to the other organisms – on the assumption that most will be competing for the food supply in the same localized areas of maximum concentration? If, under these circumstances, the biomass and numbers of the other predators increases, can a severely depleted baleen whale population recover or not? What will happen to the ecosystem if we introduce an intensive industrial fishery for the krill? If we out-compete all the major predators of krill in the zones of optimal feeding what will be the result – a drastic reduction in biomass of all these upper trophic level organisms? Or will the ecosystem change its stability pattern by a switch to large numbers of one predator with a great loss of diversity? This is apparently what happened in the Great Plains of North America when the bison replaced a whole cluster of large grazers after the Pleistocene glaciations (possibly as a result of the influence of man's activities according to some authors). I think it is fairly evident that, under the conditions described, we simply could not begin to answer the questions posed above without a thorough knowledge of the energetic inputs and outputs of the various components of the system about to suffer significant interference. This example is a real one, and has close parallels in the controversial man/harp seal/capelin relationship off eastern Canada, the man/pollack/fur seal situation off Alaska, and the man/cod/capelin/humpback whale interaction off Newfoundland (see Chapter 9).

Food content

The entire input of biologically useful energy available to a cetacean throughout its life must naturally come from its food, with the exception, perhaps, of some exceedingly minor contributions such as absorption of some compounds from sea-water by the skin and the involvement of sunlight in the synthesis of vitamin D in the skin. The former possibility has some fairly recent substantiation, the latter is doubted by many cetologists. Vitamin D in these animals is probably obtained only from food organisms.

Quantitative analyses of the calorific value and nutrient composition of food species exploited by whales have dealt almost exclusively with those eaten by the large rorquals, the sperm whale and a few of the small toothed whales. For purposes of simplification most workers have tended to assume a monospecific diet of euphausiids by the large baleen whales, of squid by the sperm whale and of fish by the small odontocetes. Many of the recent data on seal nutrition (15) can, however, also be applied to situations involving cetaceans.

The wet weight of euphausiids includes about 78–80 per cent water (45, 56). The remaining 20–22 per cent constituting the dry weight has been found to have a protein content which can range from 55–88 per cent, lipid from 6–26 per cent, chitin 4 per cent and carbohydrate only 2 per cent (48, 63, 69, 70). The carbohydrate is bound, and probably not available for nutrition. Whole large euphausiids might then be expected to contain about 78–80 per cent water, 1–5 per cent of ash and carbohydrate, 1–4 per cent lipids, and 13–18 per cent protein. Using established conversion values (8), the calorific value of whole euphausiids will be of the order of 1000 kcal/kg. The moisture content of whole squid is somewhat higher, and the levels of protein, lipid and ash correspondingly lower (65). Carbohydrate is negligible. Calorific values for most of the fish eaten by small odontocetes, such as herrings, mackerels, anchovies and smelts (including capelin), fall within the same general range of about 800–1200 kcal/kg. Moisture levels in these range from as low as 62 per cent to as high as 80 per cent, protein from 12–19 per cent and lipids 1–19 per cent, with Atlantic herring *Clupea harengus* having by far the highest percentage of lipids (66). Ash and other residues amount to only 1–4 per cent.

Food intake and feeding rates

Estimates of stomach capacity have been made by a number of authors (6), but the nature of the stomach and the variation which may occur during post-mortem changes in the elastic tissue make such measurements hardly accurate to within 100 per cent. Others have tried a different approach, namely, using some basic morphological and physiological parameters to determine what a given animal should require, and comparing this with observed data on daily feeding rates (7, 32, 41–3).

We have insufficient information to determine whether feeding rates and energy expenditures measured for small odontocetes in oceanaria are representative even for those species, because activity levels may not be comparable with those in the wild state (7). There is evidence that captive odontocetes may overfeed (or be overfed); in particular, captive belugas may become very obese. We do not know if this represents a dietary problem, sheer lack of exercise or a hormonal imbalance, since females are more often affected. Nor do we know if it is really valid to extrapolate to budgets for the large species from data obtained on small species. Because of the sheer size of the larger rorquals, energy budget estimates are likely to contain correspondingly large errors of absolute magnitude. The problem is further complicated by the fact that energy demands in whales naturally vary with species, sex, age, body size at a given age, reproductive state and the thermal regime within which an individual is located at any given time.

Qualitative data on the diets of whale species are plentiful; reliable quantitative data are less easy to come by, and estimates of feeding rates and energy requirements of the large Cetacea are largely theoretical and still quite controversial. Whales may vomit during a chase or when harpooned – this is a particularly well-known phenomenon in the case of sperm whales (11). It has been argued by one Japanese worker (31) that this is not a major source of error, although one of his colleagues (49) earlier presented data to indicate a relationship between chasing time and the quantity of stomach contents in fin and sei, possibly because of food loss from the mouth, but also as a result of increased body temperature during the hunt causing a marginal but significant increase in the rate of digestion or physical breakdown of the food.

Some quantitative estimates of stomach contents are available for most major commercially hunted whale species. Between 100 and 200 kg of euphausiids have been recorded in the stomachs of Bryde's whales taken near the Bonin Islands (50). From Antarctic sei whales up to 600 kg of crustaceans have been estimated to be taken at one time, but this may be near the maximum value. Maxima noted for fin whales have ranged from 425 to 885 kg (30). S. K. Klumov gave a value of 1100 kg for the weight of stomach contents in an Antarctic blue whale (34). Contents of stomachs included all the major crustacean species described in Chapter 2.

Klumov estimated that baleen whales require 'about 30–40 g of food per kg of live weight' in each 24 hour period to sustain themselves. For an 'average-sized' blue whale he calculated that this approximated (assuming twice-daily feeding) to about 2–2.5 tonnes of food every 24 hours. Correspondingly less would be needed by fin and other still smaller rorquals. D. E. Sergeant (62) recalculated possible requirements of rorquals based on available heart–body weight ratios, and his results were in general agreement with those of Klumov. Earlier estimates by Ivashin (26), which suggested that an Antarctic humpback whale required about 4 tonnes of food each day, are probably much too high, but those given by Sergeant and Klumov are also, I think, too high, although not by such a wide margin as those of Ivashin. In view of the numbers of assumptions these authors were forced to make in constructing their dietary energetic models, an error of at least 25 per cent might be very reasonably expected. I think Klumov's error is to place emphasis on maximal stomach contents. My own experience with harpooned whales observed to vomit at or near the surface is that the food loss is either slight – just a dribble of fluid from the mouth with perhaps a few bits and pieces, probably from the oesophagus – or very extensive, but rarely in-between. Which occurs seems to depend on the nature of the wound. Therefore a large volume of fresh food in a stomach is probably representative of a meal. Some recent authors have now published quite extensive series of data on rorqual stomach-content weights (30–2, 49). A. Kawamura is of the opinion that the weight of the average meal is much less than the maximum values recorded in the literature, perhaps only 180–200 kg in the sei and 380–400 kg in the fin whale. Somewhat smaller amounts than for the sei appear to be average for the minke whale. It seems unlikely, considering the long migrations undertaken and the very patchy distributions of the food species present even in relatively productive areas, that rorquals could maintain an average meal weight of anything like the maximum values recorded. Even Klumov admitted that his values were 'optimal' – but how often do such optimal feeding conditions present themselves?

In 1969 D. E. Sergeant made a theoretical study to determine feeding rates in Cetacea of various sizes. He defined feeding rate as the 'daily ration' of V. S. Ivlev (27), expressed as a percentage of body weight. The adult body weights of Cetacea lie in the $10-10^4$ kg range, and Sergeant found an inverse relationship between feeding rate and body weight, both between species and between young and adult specimens of small odontocetes. The young of all the species studied were found to have somewhat elevated underlying metabolic rates, which is to be expected. The feeding rate for all cetaceans fell within the range of 4–13 per cent. Above a body weight of about 6×10^2 kg the feeding rate appeared to become constant within the 4–6 per cent range. The feeding rate for adult rorquals was estimated as about 4 per cent; however, as pointed out above, the extrapolations of theoretical food requirements barely match even the maximal stomach contents recorded in the field. At least one assumption must be out of line with reality. I suggested in 1976 that a feeding rate of about 2.5–3 per cent might be realistic for rorquals. A little later in the same year C. Lockyer published an extensive re-evaluation of growth and energy budgets in the large baleen whales from the southern hemisphere (42), and her conclusions were even more conservative and in line with recorded values for actual intake. She stated (p. 29): 'I conclude that although feeding during the summer months for only a period of 120 days is about 4 per cent of body weight daily, the average throughout the year, allowing for reduced winter feeding at about a tenth of summer amounts (0.4 percent body weight daily) is probably closer to 1.5–2 percent.'

Recently W. Y. Yasui, one of my colleagues at Guelph, completed a preliminary investigation of the energetics of the harbour porpoise, one of the smallest of all cetaceans (74). By plotting Sergeant's data on full logarithmic scale he predicted that a 53 kg harbour porpoise would have a daily feeding rate of about 8.7 per cent. With adjustments for calorific content, this approximated to about 4.6 kg of fish daily. S. Andersen (3) had earlier observed 2.0–5.4 kg of food as being eaten per 24-hour period by this species in captivity, while Dudock Van Heel recorded sexually active specimens consuming food at a still greater rate: 8–10 kg per 24 hours. On the assumption that feeding was reduced during the winter months as the porpoises followed the western North Atlantic herring stocks out of coastal waters and on to the offshore banks, the average annual feeding rate then fell within the general range predicted for an animal of that weight.

Measurements of the weights of daily meals, their contents and gross calorific values give only a first approximation of the food energy which actually becomes available to the animal. The crude calorific values, often determined from the heat of combustion by bomb calorimetric methods, or by using a comparison of the diet composition, and standard values from tables for the equivalent energy liberated by each type of compound, indicate only the potential maximum energy which could be obtained from the meal; in practice this maximum is not realized. Some of the material passes through the digestive tract and out again as faeces; part of this may be in bound form, like the carbohydrate fraction in euphausiids, and not available to the animal because its digestive mechanisms are unable to break that particular chemical bond. Cellulose is such an example; in mammals cellulase enzymes, when present in the digestive system as in ruminants, are produced by symbiotic micro-organisms, not by the mammal itself. Alternatively, a certain amount of digestible material may be 'masked' from digestion during its passage through the alimentary canal. It is necessary, therefore, to consider not just the intake, or 'gross energy' in kcal, but also the amount which is actually digested by the animal (40). It is also unwise to extrapolate a diet for small cetaceans from one or two observations, even if the same prey species is eaten for most of the year. The lipid levels in Atlantic herring, for example, vary each year from a low of as little as 2.5 per cent after the relatively poor winter-feeding conditions, to a high of 15–16 per cent following the peak feeding and depot storage period of late summer and early autumn (66). The percentage of the gross energy intake which may be lost in the ways described above has not been measured with any accuracy in cetaceans; the corresponding value for pinniped species appears to range from a loss of 3 per cent on a pure fish diet to perhaps 9–10 per cent on a mixed diet (40). The digestibility of fish protein is high, because the muscle mass contains a relatively small ratio of tough connective tissue (21).

Subsequent to digestion of the food, some further losses of energy occur from the 'energy assimilated'. Because the endpoints of protein digestion include a number of relatively toxic nitrogenous compounds such as urea, these must be removed in urine. The production of this urine, the cost of carrying out the work needed to maintain the excretion process, together with the loss of gaseous products of digestion such as methane, and the metabolic 'cost' of the digestive process itself, are all further debits to the assimilated energy tally. The last-mentioned occurs because there is an increase in the metabolic rate after ingestion (this has been referred to as the calorigenic effect, heat increments of feeding, or specific dynamic action) (5, 22, 33). Losses through urine production may be about 5 per cent; those through the heat increment, 5–15 per cent. Under some circumstances the 'heat increment' may be useful, rather than being a debit, since it can contribute to maintenance of the deep body-core temperature under hypothermic conditions.

Metabolism and activity

D. M. Lavigne and his co-workers (40) have defined 'net energy' as that amount derived from the daily ration which, after all the marginal assimilation 'costs' indicated above have been paid, is available to the organism for the maintenance of body functions, production of new tissue in growth, and for doing work such as moving the body from place to place in the environment or carrying out more complex activities. It is conventional to consider this net energy as being used for two categories of activity, 'maintenance energy' (for basic metabolic operations, thermo-regulation and general activities) and 'production energy' (that is, those aspects of energetic use related to reproduction and growth).

'Metabolism' is the sum of chemical reactions taking place within an organism, which break down materials to release energy (catabolic reactions) or build up complex molecules or structures and store energy (anabolic reactions). Metabolic rate is very dependent on ambient temperature, inasmuch as this influences the rates of the underlying chemical reactions. The 'warm-blooded' or homoiothermic animals, including the Cetacea, have evolved the ability to divert part of the energy available to them into maintenance of a stable body-core temperature; this has the advantage of controlling the rates of the reactions of body chemistry within a narrow range of variation.

The relationship of metabolic rate and temperature is conventionally expressed as the Q_{10}, that is, the rate of increase for 10°C rise in temperature. Most metabolic rates have a Q_{10} value close to 2; in other words, the rate doubles for each rise of 10°C in ambient temperature.

Metabolic rate in homoiothermic animals is maintained at a stable but relatively high level. The advantage of this is that it frees the organism from the constraints on activity imposed by changes in ambient temperature, maximizes the potential of enzymes to promote high rates of substrate conversion while still keeping them subject to necessary mechanisms of metabolic control (23), and also extends the period of time for which an animal can be maximally active during the inevitable internal build-up of heat (23). The activity of poikilothermic groups such as fish and reptiles, on the other hand, is temperature-dependent to a large extent. Heat for homoiothermic maintenance is commonly liberated from ATP conversion, stimulating more cellular respiration and consequent release of energy as heat. Insulated homoiothermic mammals cope reasonably well with hypothermic environments, but much less well with those which are hyperthermic. Both with respect to heat loss and heat retention, surface–volume ratio is a critical factor. Under normal conditions, metabolic rate is inversely proportional to body size – the larger the animal, the lower the weight-specific metabolic rate.

Where dynamic energetics are concerned, the outputs by Cetacea which have drawn most attention from biologists are the costs of controlling heat loss in a hypothermic environment, locomotory activities and growth.

Estimation of heat loss in Cetacea

The essential problem appearing to face the cetacean then, whether a large or small species, is how to carry out a range of activities (including growth for a significant fraction of its life), while maintaining a muscle core temperature of 36–37°C in an environment which only rarely attains two-thirds of this value, and is frequently barely one-tenth of it. All species are insulated, and the larger species are obviously at a considerable advantage in terms of heat conservation because of their vastly more favourable surface–volume ratio. The topic of thermoregulation creeps into any discussion of energetics in relation to diet, although a discussion of its actual mechanics is beyond the intended scope of this chapter. Four routes for heat loss are immediately evident: through the skin, through respiration and through urine and faeces produced at body temperature. Respiration losses seem to be quite low (about 5 per cent); most heat loss is through the body surface.

The fact that cetaceans have a relatively thick layer of insulation coupled, furthermore, with a heat-exchange system associated with this layer (61), has led to considerable differences of opinion as to how heat loss through the skin should be calculated.

What is the best way to estimate surface area from the point of view of heat loss? P. F. Brodie (7) argued that to include the blubber layer of Cetacea was equivalent to measuring surface area for a rodent and including its winter foodstore! He suggested that total skin surface area was probably not the best criterion to use, and that the true metabolic surface for estimates of heat loss in these animals is not the skin but the surface of the muscle core, since the vascular countercurrent system of the extremities, head and jaw region, and the dermal layer of the whole body, functions in heat exchange rather than heat dissipation. He concluded that a value of 85 per cent of the total epidermal area other than the extremities was a good approximation to the true metabolic surface of a large rorqual. Brodie adopted the formula for a pair of cones with bases apposed, as used by two earlier workers (19, 39). This formula was rejected by Lockyer (42) as giving low values, and she preferred to work with total surface area with slight modifications, as did Yasui (74), studying the harbour porpoise. Brodie concluded that cetacean metabolic rates conformed to a surface rather than volumetric rule, and that use of a volumetric measure, together with a gross overestimate of the body weight of a 55 foot (about 18.2 metres) fin whale, were the reasons which had led J. Kanwisher and G. Sundnes (28, 29) to conclude that the metabolic rate of the large rorquals was probably higher than that of most large terrestrial mammals.

In large rorquals blubber thickness varies with sex, age and size (4). That there are changes in the average thickness during the course of the year in the Antarctic populations has long been known, and several analyses have been published, for example, those on the Australian humpback whales by R. G. Chittleborough (10). Studies by authors on other species have been summarized by C. Lockyer (42). Animals arriving on the Antarctic feeding grounds early in the summer have, on average, a hypodermal layer significantly thinner than that of comparable animals at the end of the season. The implications of this for the variation in oil yield from a given number of whale units according to the timing set for the Antarctic whaling season was not lost on the industry, and detailed studies were made during the early 1950s (4). Consequently, when whales were encountered with thin blubber during the latter part of the feeding season in any area, it was a rather natural assumption to think that such animals had experienced reduced feeding success and were in 'poor condition'. P. F. Brodie (7) re-examined this reasoning, with particular reference to western North Atlantic fin whales. His observations indicated that these animals remained off the coasts of eastern Canada for much of the year, exploiting herring in the autumn and winter, and euphausiids in the spring and summer. Since they were in a region with a relatively reliable, almost year-round food supply, he suggested that the thin blubber layer of these animals reflected not poor feeding success, but precisely the opposite.

With food readily available, there was no need to lay down an extensive fat depot.

Seasonal changes in blubber thickness undoubtedly occur in those populations of rorquals of the southern hemisphere which undertake extensive migrations. Lockyer pointed out that average values from commercial statistics had to be used with care, since inclusion of a significant fraction of pregnant females biased the mean seasonal value upwards. Inclusion of an inordinate number of lactating females with depleted lipid depot, on the other hand, decreased the value of the mean. In his classic paper on blubber structure and function D. A. Parry (53) attempted to use data on seasonal changes in blubber thickness to measure energy consumption. There are, however, serious drawbacks to this approach. First, the lipid content of the hypodermal layer in baleen whales may vary by as much as 50 per cent from one part of the body to another (7, 64). In our own studies on the harbour porpoises of the Bay of Fundy we have found variations of up to 40 per cent in animals of comparable sex, age and body weight, and also variations of a similar magnitude in dolphins of the genus *Stenella* taken in the small whale fishery of St Lucia, West Indies. Secondly, the blubber is by no means the only site of lipid reserve deposition in cetaceans. The liver is important, and so are the rather unusual skeletal bones of these animals which contain significant quantities of oil (7, 42, 64, 68), sometimes as much as 50 per cent of the body total. Because of the influence of these factors, Brodie concluded that variations in blubber thickness are an unreliable parameter on which to base energetic calculations, but estimated that the heat loss for a large rorqual in the subtropics would be barely 50 per cent of that in summer polar waters. Some believe that the large rorquals seem to be over-insulated with respect to tropical and subtropical temperature regimes (28, 29).

Energetic cost of locomotion

Relative to other forms of locomotion swimming is highly economical (60), especially if the body conforms reasonably closely to optimal hydro-dynamic requirements. Nevertheless, locomotion still uses up a very significant fraction of the total energy intake, even in a streamlined marine mammal. It is difficult to estimate this cost directly in terms of actual oxygen consumed, since the problems of taking accurate measurements of oxygen consumption in a moving cetacean are formidable, requiring advanced, light-weight flexible technology. Equipment of this kind has been available theoretically for several years, but most workers have taken the simpler, cheaper route of calculating consumption indirectly, measuring respirations per unit time, tidal volume of air and the amount of oxygen removed from an average intake of breath. These data can then be used in conjunction with the results of (preferably) simultaneous hydrodynamic analysis.

The moving cetacean must overcome the twin forces of inertia and drag during locomotion. Hydrodynamic theory predicts that at high speeds, turbulent flow should occur, even around a streamlined body moving through a liquid medium. In 1936 J. Gray (16) studied the hydrodynamics of dolphins swimming at high speed, and on the basis of what was known then about muscular output in man and other mammals, concluded that dolphins were able to swim several times faster than appeared predictable from the muscular power available. This contradiction became known as 'Gray's paradox'. To account for his observations, Gray concluded that dolphins must possess some mechanism which greatly reduced drag by inducing full laminar flow around the body. Later work has shown that although this is true to some extent, it is not the only explanation of the phenomenon.

By no means all cetaceans possess the build of obvious aquatic sprinters and some, such as the right whales, look cumbersome. The degree to which a body approaches the optimal hydrodynamic shape is measured by the nature of its tapering, called the 'fineness ratio' (9, 47) – basically the relationship between body length and maximum thickness. The position of the latter is also important, and a fineness ratio of about 4.5 is ideal to accommodate the necessary muscle mass and yet permit the maximum degree of streamlining (74). The most streamlined cetaceans, especially the small Delphinidae, closely simulate what is called a 'laminar spindle shape', producing the best hydrodynamic performance (24, 35, 36, 73). To simplify calculations which estimate flow and drag, many workers have assumed that porpoises do indeed conform to this theoretical shape. The porpoise body, however, is not rigidly fusiform but flexes as the animal swims. Furthermore, most workers have minimized the importance of the appendages in contributing to drag; W. Y. Yasui calculated that in the average female adult harbour porpoise the appendages (dorsal fin, flippers and flukes) account for only about 12 per cent of the body surface area, but contribute almost 36 per cent of the total drag (74).

The length of the body, the hydrodynamically 'exposed' surface area, and the viscosity of the medium are significant factors in the calculation of the 'drag coefficient'. For a number of reasons, some indicated above, in practice these calculations are not simple to make with any accuracy on a living animal. Drag, like the power needed to overcome it, is calculated per unit time. There is a functional relationship between the two as would be expected – the greater the drag, the greater the power required to overcome it. The power requirement rises exponentially with increase in swimming speed. Since this relationship exists, if the drag coefficient can be calculated from available data, then the required power can be estimated (on the first-order assumption that the mechanical efficiency is 100 per cent). The calculated theoretical drag multiplied by velocity gives a value in watts. Power needed for locomotion can be expressed in watts, but it can also be expressed as kcal/h or better still, converted to terms of the volume of oxygen used (ml/km per g body weight) so that transport costs can be determined; this is the measure usually employed by those whose subject animals are small enough or amenable to direct estimation of consumption by experimental methods.

Initially the theoretical calculations yield results based on assumptions of muscular homogeneity and 100 per cent mechanical efficiency. Neither of these assumptions is realistic and the estimates require modification. Studies on mammalian locomotory muscle have revealed that the tissue is composed of differing ratios in different species of 'fast twitch' and 'slow twitch' fibres (44), each having a different power output range and response time (73). Ratios also change with age. It is difficult to assess the actual operating efficiency of a muscle mass, but sequential simulations based on assumptions of 100, 75, 50 and 25 per cent mechanical efficiency (in terms of the proportion of swimming metabolism which is actually converted into muscular thrust) can show which gives the best fit with observed performance. Calculations can be further refined by obtaining the output potential of single fibres of each type for a given species, and accurately mapping the relative densities of fibre types in the major muscle masses.

Sometimes the first-order estimates have proved anomalous, especially when matched against the apparent level of assimilated energy from the food intake. For example, after calculating the energy cost for locomotion of southern fin and sei whales on migration in relation to estimates of rate and length of feeding period, A. Kawamura (32) concluded that the accumulated energy reserve seemed barely enough to sustain these animals. If his results were accepted, it would be necessary to assume substantial food intake by large rorquals during the breeding migrations and, as we have seen, the balance of evidence is against significant quantities being consumed in low latitudes. Obviously there is an inconsistency here.

On the basis of anatomical observations, theoretical calculations and experimental work, a number of earlier workers concluded that (a) Gray's paradox had to be explained by skin properties, and (b) that the metabolic rate of cetaceans must be significantly higher than that of terrestrial mammals of corresponding mass. The first conclusion stimulated intensive studies on the dolphin skin, and it was found that enhanced laminar flow does indeed seem to occur. The presence of laminar flow in cetaceans, up to 70 per cent on average in some dolphins (37), gives a much higher efficiency in overcoming water resistance than might otherwise be expected. This laminar flow is believed by most workers to result from the capacity of the skin to form wave or ripple structures at high swimming speeds (1, 2, 55).

Further recent work, however, suggests that it is not necessary to invoke laminar flow alone to explain Gray's paradox. Studies using more refined techniques indicate that the earlier research significantly underestimated the power output of mammalian muscle fibres (73). Re-evaluation of the relationship between calculated drag and the power requirements for harp seals and harbour porpoise indicate that sufficient power *is* generated by the major locomotory muscular masses (40), and that far from being paradoxically high, the net real cost of locomotion in these animals lies close to, or between, that for fish and terrestrial walking or running animals (40, 74). Not only is the available power output now regarded as adequate for sustained swimming, the 'fast twitch' fibres appear to have ample power in reserve for the even more rapid sprints of which most cetacean species are known to be capable.

Metabolic rate

The resting metabolic rate for mammals is predicted from the equation of Kleiber by

$$M = 70W^{0.75}$$

where M is the metabolic rate measured in kcal/day and W is body weight in kilograms.

Apart from Brodie, Lockyer and Yasui, estimates of the metabolic rates of various cetacean species made by earlier workers include A. H. Laurie (39), R. Walmsley (71), P. F. Scholander (61), S. K. Klumov (34), J. Kanwisher and G. Sundnes (28, 29), and D. W. Rice and A. A. Wolman (57). Most, like Lockyer and Yasui, used approximations of total skin surface area to calculate body volume and body weight. Much of the evidence in the earlier literature suggested that the metabolic rate of cetaceans is higher than that of terrestrial mammals of equivalent size (28, 29). The evidence one way or another is still controversial, for seals as well as whales (40, 52), but some recent authors are now leaning to the view that the cetaceans do in fact have metabolic rates quite similar to those of terrestrial mammals. For example, the large relative size of the liver in Cetacea in comparison with that found in the majority of terrestrial mammals, has often been cited as evidence of high metabolic rate. Brodie (7) suggested that a large liver size in the bigger rorquals is not necessarily an indication of high metabolic rate, but instead reflects the importance of the liver in these animals as an organ of lipid storage for periods of fasting during migration, and the great importance of lipid metabolism of these animals. In the limited literature relating to cetacean metabolism there are few data which would conflict with this view. Indeed, much of the evidence cited in support of high metabolic rate in cetaceans is indirect; for example, S. H. Ridgway (58) pointed out that the relatively high proportion of protein in the diet of these animals would probably be an indication of a high rate. Kanwisher and Sundnes recorded high oxygen-consumption rates, but possibly as the result of working with restrained animals.

Metabolic rate can be expressed in terms of oxygen consumption per unit time; we have relatively few data for cetaceans, simply because they are such difficult and expensive experimental animals. Many workers have attempted to use indirect approaches, including the proportional sizes and weights of internal organs, and lung capacity. For most cetacean species we lack extensive reliable data on lung weights and capacities, kidney weights, heart weights and their rates of beating. According to P. F. Scholander (61), the lung capacity in the fin whale would seem to be about 2.5–2.8 per cent, that is somewhat less than in man and the small odontocetes. Tidal exchange and vital capacity of the lungs of cetaceans is efficient, because of the highly elastic nature of the tissues in these animals, but this is more likely to be an adaptation to the diving habit, rather than metabolism *per se*. There is relatively little to indicate that proportional organ weights are very different in large cetaceans from the corresponding values in most terrestrial mammals. Nor do the limited studies of pulse rates suggest a great difference, although most were made under less than ideal circumstances. The proportional size of the heart of the harbour porpoise, one of the smallest of the cold-water cetaceans, is somewhat larger than average (59), but recent work by Yasui (74) casts some doubt on earlier conclusions (28) that the adult animal has a metabolic rate greatly different from a terrestrial mammal of equivalent weight.

Lockyer (42) concluded that the respiratory quotient (RQ) in large rorquals could rise to almost 1.0 after long dives, and probably fall as low as 0.7 during diving, because it seems likely that bradycardia is common to all cetaceans, though only relatively few smaller species have been studied experimentally. The value of 0.82 was thought to be a reasonably representative mean RQ for large rorquals. She also presented several methods for estimating the approximate basal metabolic rate; one of these was to use 10 per cent of the active metabolic rate based on the maximum cruising speed (up to 30 km/h in the large rorquals), and the assumption (after Gray) (16, 17) that about 1.65×10^8 erg/kg of operational musculature is developed at such speeds. Her estimate of basal metabolic rate for a blue whale of 122 tonnes was of the same order of magnitude as that calculated by Laurie (39), namely, $\approx 3.0 \times 10^5$ kcal/day (her value,

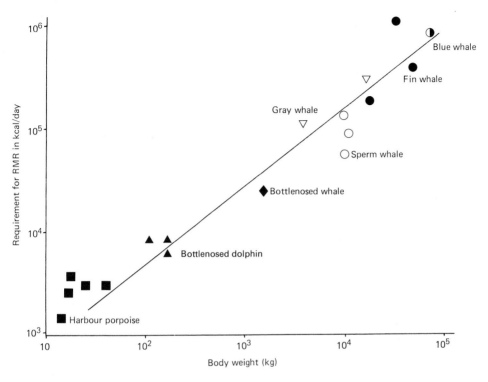

Figure 3.1 Relationship between body weight in kilograms and the kcal per day requirement to maintain resting metabolic rate (RMR) in several species of Cetacea of different sizes. Data drawn from Lockyer (42), and from unpublished data of W. Y. Yasui and D. E. Gaskin for *P. phocoena*.

3.75; his, 2.75). Many assumptions must be made in preparing such estimates, and for a much fuller discussion of the constraints, the reader is referred to Lockyer (1976, pp. 34–44).

Brodie (7) has presented a case for discussing all cetacean metabolic problems in terms of standard metabolism (33) or the synonymous term 'maintenance metabolism' (8), rather than basal metabolism, as is usually employed for man and other terrestrial mammals. The reasoning for this was simple; many cetaceans, especially rorquals, are negatively buoyant, and must continually move in order to plane through the surface to breathe. Resting or basal metabolic rate is, therefore, Brodie considered, a state probably never attained by these animals. The cost to Cetacea of the minimal exertion required to move and breathe is, according to Brodie, quite inseparable from their basal metabolism.

While this viewpoint has general validity, the approach may result in an over-estimate. Watson (72) noted that harbour porpoises spent only some

3 per cent of their observed activity drifting at the surface, but L. Pippard reported to me that she had seen fin whales drifting at the surface at night near Cap Bon Desire in Quebec, blowing at long intervals with only part of the head showing. I have also seen right whales in the Bay of Fundy lying at the surface virtually motionless in calm water for periods of up to 25 minutes.

Although Lockyer came to no specific conclusion, Brodie was not convinced that a critical review of the published data provided any real evidence that the large rorquals had metabolic rates significantly different from those of other mammals, despite statements to the contrary in the literature (see also Figure 3.1).

Energetic cost of growth

Biologists usually assume that most growth energy is channelled into the production of bone, muscle and visceral tissue and regard other uses as negligible in the overall consideration of the budget. This may not be a safe assumption in the case of marine mammals, especially for the post-parturition period; a significant fraction of growth energy may be directed into the addition of body weight in the form of depot fat in the blubber and other organs (40, 74). But in either case, as the animal grows, the proportion of the energy intake required for growth decreases rapidly.

It is not possible to describe the foetal growth rate and post-natal growth rates of cetaceans with a single equation. C. Lockyer found that the expression of foetal growth could be best obtained in the case of blue fin and sperm whales by using

$$W^{1/3} = a(t - t_0)$$

where W is body weight in grams, a a growth velocity constant, t the time in days since conception and t_0 the time in days since conception but before the phase of linear growth.

This may be compared with the situation in pinnipeds, where foetal growth can be described in a variety of species in different families by the expression

$$W = 6 \times 10^{-5}L^{2.74}$$

where W is again the body weight, and L is the body length (but in kg and cm respectively) (40).

The full-term foetus is proportionately large in Cetacea in comparison to most terrestrial mammals, attaining 25 per cent of the body length of the mother in the case of the harbour porpoise (64, 72). One advantage conferred by this may be that the greatest possible surface–volume ratio is attained before the calf is born, a favourable condition in a small cetacean species inhabiting temperate or arctic waters. There is also a need for a mammal born at sea to have a high degree of physical development and precocity in neuromuscular control, if it is to have the maximum chance of immediate post-natal survival.

The energetic cost of pregnancy to a female cetacean does not seem to be very high in the first few months (41, 42), but after the sixth month the cost begins to increase exponentially. For the sperm whale, Lockyer calculated the cost of the first six months as about 6.0×10^4 kcal, but by birth this had risen to a total of 4.58×10^6 kcal. Nevertheless, this seemed to indicate that the pregnant female would only have to increase the intake of food by about 10 per cent during the latter phase of pregnancy, or by an average of only about 5 per cent over the whole period. In terms of total energy, therefore, the loading cost of pregnancy is not really that heavy. Factors in the load are principally the cost of maintaining the pregnant uterus and placenta, and providing the energy for foetal growth and for the necessary increases in the physiological work by the mother's body. Some influences on metabolism are also believed to occur as a result of endocrine changes. Lockyer estimated that the energy of foetal growth in large baleen whales was about 1500 kcal/kg of body weight, amounting to about 0.04×10^8 kcal in blue whales and 0.03×10^8 kcal in fin whales, based on gestation periods of linear growth.

The cost of lactation to the maternal body in cetacean species is significantly higher. Whale and dolphin milk is much richer in fat than that of most terrestrial mammals; in those species examined – blue, fin, sperm and white whale – the fat content ranges from 30–37 per cent, water from 41–54 per cent and solids, largely protein, from 7–22 per cent (18, 38, 51, 54, 67). The calorific content has been calculated, and ranges from about 3700 kcal/kg in the white whale to about 4300 kcal/kg in the large rorquals.

Assimilation efficiencies of cetacean calves appear to be high. Tomilin (67) calculated that a suckling blue whale gains about 81 kg of body weight per day from a daily intake of 90 kg of milk (at a calorific value of about 4140 kcal/kg). The corresponding weight gain in a fin whale suckling was about 53 kg per day, with a similar level of assimilation efficiency. Lockyer (42) calculated assimilation efficiencies for these two species during the suckling stage as about 86 and 93 per cent, respectively.

The measure of 'gross growth efficiency' is estimated from

$$\frac{\text{kcal (net growth)} \times 100}{\text{kcal (food intake)}}$$

In this case 'growth efficiency' is measured in terms of the efficiency of conversion of *calorific* input; a simple comparison of kg of input to kg of body tissue added is misleading because of their very different calorific values. If the measure of the food intake which is actually assimilated is available, the net growth efficiency (again in terms of calories) is calculated from

$$\frac{\text{kcal (net growth)} \times 100}{\text{kcal (assim. intake)}}$$

The calorific value of the growth increment (largely in terms of viscera and muscle) was assumed by Lockyer to be 1500 kcal/kg. The respective values of gross growth efficiency for blue, fin and sperm whales appear to be about 32.6, 26.5 and 14.3 per cent. Net growth efficiencies are naturally higher: 37.8, 28.5 and nearly 21 per cent respectively (41, 42).

Growth rates slow significantly after the first year. Lockyer noted that the calves of large rorquals probably began to feed for themselves at about the seventh month after birth; in the Southern Ocean this would then permit them about four more months of steady feeding. In all years after the first, however, they would have to conform to the summer feeding pattern of adult animals, as they followed the annual migratory cycles. Although assimilation efficiencies in pubertal animals were still about 79–83 per cent, net growth seemed to be reduced at this stage to between 6 and 7 per cent in blue whales and only 5 per cent in fin whales. Assimilation rates in adults remain close to 80 per cent through life, whereas net growth declines to values close to zero.

With relatively few exceptions, the post-natal growth of large cetaceans is adequately described in general terms by the Von Bertalanffy equation

$$L_t = L\infty\,[1 - e^{-k(t-t_0)}]$$

where L_t is body length at any time t, $L\infty$ is the asymptote, $e^{-k(t-t_0)}$ is the exponent, k is the growth coefficient and t_0 is the hypothetical age at which the animal would have had zero body length had it always grown at the rate predicted by this equation (20). In a relatively recent paper, Lockyer (43) concluded that the growth parameter k was sensitive to food availability, after estimating the food requirements for age specific growth in sei whales. She also noted that since the energy cost of lactation was very high, the possibility of there being a two, three or more years reproductive cycle should be considered. W. Y. Yasui (74) found the cost of lactation to be high enough in the harbour porpoise that success might not be assured in all years, and he provided a diagram of alternative reproductive patterns ('strategies' does not seem an appropriate word in such circumstances) which the female might be found to be following under different conditions of energy intake.

At all stages of growth after weaning, the energy budget of the large rorquals of the southern hemisphere requires about a 50 per cent (60–65 per cent in pregnant females) increase in body weight as accumulated fat during the summer feeding period, to permit individuals to survive the winter months (42). The additional depot fat required by pregnant females seems to be obtained by arriving earlier than other animals on the feeding grounds, and leaving later (12, 42). From this we may infer that, on average, feeding success of Antarctic (non-pregnant or male) rorquals is adequate during the usual 120-day period, otherwise we would expect selection for the whole population to remain longer on the feeding grounds than they actually do. The fat store of a young adult blue whale (not pregnant or lactating) was estimated by Lockyer as about 42×10^3 kg, with a calorific content (at 7560 kcal/kg) of 3.17×10^8 kcal per year. Such a budget allows for maintenance, growth in body size, and also a significant contribution to the existing depot fat. It is important to remember that a large fraction of the depot store is 'carried over' from one year to the next, and that the energy budget for a reproducing female only has meaning when estimated over a two-year period to include both gestation and lactation (42). From estimates of the calorific values of food species we may say that this annual intake represents ≈ 578 tonnes of euphausiids, and the mean daily intake some 1.58 tonnes. This would approximate (according to the estimated value for body weight we attach to the concept of 'young adult blue whale') to an average feeding rate of about 3 per cent.

Energy budgets

Construction of an energy budget for a species, by assembling the known data on energy inputs and outputs, provides some degree of feedback during the balancing process (Figure 3.2); to some extent imbalances in the system point out where corrections are needed. If feeding rates have been consistently verified, for example, yet intake does not match apparent requirements, then it is likely that errors of assumption or calculation lie on the right-hand side of the equation. On the other hand, if the requirements can be calculated fairly accurately, but approximate balance is not attained, then the feeding rates and food consumption have probably been underestimated. The assimilation efficiency may be higher than expected, or the cost of locomotion less. The weak points of the budget can be continually re-examined as new data become available, and the overall result tested against what is observed in the wild. The model should, if it is of any use, have some predictive ability.

An energy budget for a large cetacean (sperm whale)

Lockyer provided separate estimates of predicted energy budgets for blue, fin, sei and sperm whales according to sex and maturity stages (41, 42); in young animals a much greater fraction of available energy is channelled into growth than in the mature adult. To illustrate the components of a typical energy budget for a large cetacean, I draw upon her data for the adult sperm whale.

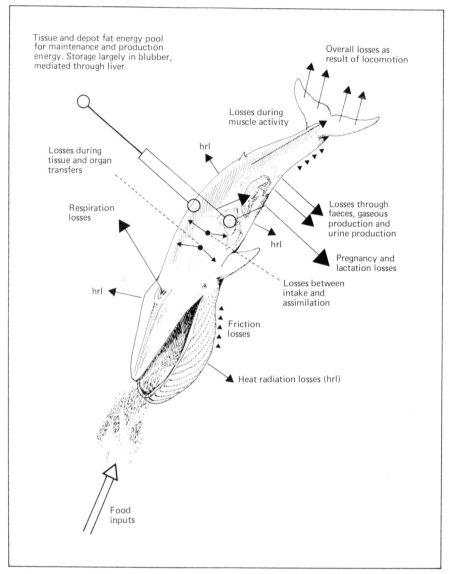

Tissue and depot fat energy pool for maintenance and production energy. Storage largely in blubber, mediated through liver

Overall losses as result of locomotion

Losses during muscle activity

hrl

Losses during tissue and organ transfers

Respiration losses

Losses through faeces, gaseous production and urine production

Pregnancy and lactation losses

hrl

Losses between intake and assimilation

hrl

Friction losses

Heat radiation losses (hrl)

Food inputs

Figure 3.2 Schematic diagram to illustrate the balance of energy inputs, storage and outputs for a cetacean. White arrow indicates the food inputs, which in a baleen whale are usually seasonal. Open circles indicate storage, generally in the form of lipids, in depot fat and the liver. Mobilization of food stores is generally mediated through the liver. Energy losses are indicated by black arrows. There are losses before assimilation of the food, during transfers from organ to organ and tissue to tissue, through heat radiation, respiration, through the faeces and urine; in the adult female, there is a major loss as a result of pregnancy and lactation.

The body weight of *Physeter catodon* at physical maturity may be as much as 50 tonnes in the case of the male, but much less, perhaps 10–12 tonnes, in the case of the female. The stomach capacity of the adult male is as much as 2000 litres. Data collected on whaling ships, together with the estimates of stomach capacity, suggest that food consumption could equal 3 per cent of the body weight per day; perhaps 1500 kg in the male, but only 420 kg in the female.

Lockyer calculated that the annual food intake of the male might be as much as about 550000 kg, compared to slightly more than 150000 kg in the female. The calorific yields of these weights of squid are 43.9×10^7 kcal, and 12.2×10^7 kcal respectively; these represent the total annual energy input. For purposes of calculating the energy outputs, growth in the physically mature male and female can be neglected. The annual increment is negligible, probably much less than 1 per cent. To maintain the theoretical resting metabolic rate the female needs about 1.02×10^5 kcal per day, the male 2.52×10^5 kcal. For active metabolism the equivalent value is 8.2×10^5 kcal and 2.02×10^6 kcal respectively. The yearly total expenditures for maintenance and normal activity amount to 8.97×10^7 kcal in the case of the female, and 31.79×10^7 kcal in the male.

The cost of lactation for the female is high, adding another 2.8×10^7 kcal. Nevertheless, this still appears to leave the female sperm whale with a very slight margin, despite the many assumptions that had to be made in these calculations. Since the margin amounts to less than one day's food intake if converted back into weight of prey, the lactating female must presumably attempt to increase her food intake during this period, or immediately subsequent to it. A comfortable margin may be obtained in reality by spreading the reproductive cycle over a four-year period, as seems to be the case. In the first eight months of gestation the load on the female probably does not exceed her energy reserves. By the end of lactation she may be approaching a 'deficit' situation, and actually starting to draw on other reserves than those in the depot, perhaps with some loss to her own body tissues. This is probably compensated for by the fourth or resting year of the cycle, during which she should be able to make good those losses. Nevertheless, as Lockyer pointed out, if this situation obtains, then it could well explain why sexual segregation has evolved in this species, because the energy demands of adult active males and females are so different.

An energy budget for a small cetacean (harbour porpoise)

At the other end of the scale of size in the Odontoceti, the adult male harbour porpoise may have an average weight of perhaps 53 kg, and the female slightly more, perhaps 54 kg. Unlike the sperm whale, the female is larger and heavier at any given body length, which is just one of the ways in which the harbour porpoise is a rather exceptional odontocete. This size difference may be related to the need for the female to be a little further from the 'ecological knife edge' than the male, when ready to reproduce. While the harbour porpoise is one of the smallest of all cetaceans, and therefore has one of the least favourable surface to volume ratios, it nevertheless penetrates quite cold waters (see p. 228).

The energy budget of this species was first studied by W. Y. Yasui (74), and those preliminary findings have been revised more recently by Yasui and myself. During the development of budget models we took into account what is known about dietary composition, feeding rates, and possible changes in those rates with season and reproductive status. Variation in lipid composition of the prey species at different times of year, and possible differences in prey availability were also considered.

If experimental studies on metabolism, and age determination results from dentinal layering are correct, the balance of present evidence points to this animal having a relatively high metabolic rate (perhaps $2 \times$ BMR) and a relatively short life span (possibly about 13 years). This is coupled with rather late sexual maturation at 3–5 years of age. Yasui and I modelled an energy budget for the species on this basis, using estimates of feeding rates from studies on captive animals, and a conservative assimilation rate of 70 per cent, slightly below the average of the range of values considered by Lavigne and others for the harp seal (40). These data yielded average inputs and surpluses over outputs of 1.6×10^6 kcals and 13 per cent for males, and 1.7×10^6 kcals and 19 per cent for females, respectively. We then modelled a second budget which assumed little more than $1 \times$ BMR (in line with Yasui's original calculations (74)), but used more realistic lipid levels in the major prey species, and daily feeding rates significantly lower than those obtained from captive animals, which some authorities believe to be far too high. We also applied alternative energy budget schemes which took into account possible overall or differential reductions in prey availability. The annual margin of surplus could be shown to be reduced to a very few per cent under such circumstances; depending on the degree of the reduction the value could become negative. In real life this would imply a drain on the standing store of depot fats, or in serious situations, body musculature. The calorific value of the deficit can be converted quite simply to an estimate of the weight loss that would result (8). As might be expected, the lactating female was particularly vulnerable to such reductions of intake, and in some cases we could not see how the animal could wean its calf successfully and still survive, even if we increased the possible efficiency value of assimilation to 80 per cent, which seems very high. If the reproductive load is spread over two or more seasons, with a recovery in energy inputs, the problem is ameliorated.

The harbour porpoise would seem to have rather limited reproductive strategies at its disposal within the constraints of either model if indeed the life span is as short as it appears. In good or excellent feeding conditions sequential years of reproduction are favoured; simultaneous pregnancy and lactation has been recorded in the Bay of Fundy. In poor years a pregnancy may well be missed, with reproduction occurring every second year. Anything less than this would seem to put the species in a difficult situation even for basic survival. The average number of calves per female in its lifetime is unlikely to exceed four, and the average could be as low as between two and three in many cases. Also, extensive migrations would not seem to make any energetic sense for this species. Suggestions that they may regularly cross the North Atlantic are almost certainly out of the question, even if D. B. Yurick had not already shown significant meristic/morphometric differences between the two populations in the western and eastern waters of that ocean (75). Finally, the species must have a relatively restricted adaptive zone, since a distribution in warmer waters would appear more favourable. Although it does occur as far south as West Africa, the major population centres are in cool waters.

Population energetics

Evolutionary considerations

Contemplation of surface–volume ratios of large whales has drawn the attention of many workers studying the International Whaling Statistics to the significant size differences between the blue and fin whales of the northern hemisphere and the Southern Ocean (64). Mayr (46) speculated that these animals obeyed Bergmann's rule, since the temperatures encountered in the Southern Ocean during the summer feeding period were lower than in the North Atlantic.

Recently Brodie (7) has reviewed this problem and others relating to cetacean energetics in some detail (with a useful bibliography), and concluded that Mayr was in error. He assembled evidence to show that the availability of food and feeding patterns in the two hemispheres were significantly different. The Antarctic populations feed for a relatively restricted period (120 days) on dense monospecific swarms of euphausiids or, in the case of the sei whales, on euphausiids, calanoids and amphipods. The populations of the northern hemisphere, on the other hand, feed for a much longer time (often in excess of six months), and usually have a rather diverse diet. North Pacific fin whales, for example, may take calanoids when young, then euphausiids and several schooling fish species in adult life. North Atlantic fin whales take herring, capelin and alewives over an extended period. The exclusion of these northern animals from feeding grounds is, therefore, for a much shorter time than in the case of the southern populations. That large species of southern rorqual fast on the way to the subtropical breeding grounds – or at least take in far too little food for their daily energetic requirements – seems indisputable (42). Brodie (7) concluded that differences in length of feeding period have been a critical factor in selection for optimal body size. In the southern animals, large body size would be favoured, he argues, because it would permit the specific metabolic rate and surface area to be adjusted to allow sufficient storage of lipid reserves and maximal use of these energy stores during the period away from the feeding grounds. In other words, the large body size of the southern blue fin whale is an adaptation to the long period of exclusion from the feeding grounds; a quite different interpretation of the phenomenon to that of Mayr. To justify the former view, it is necessary to consider the value to a large whale, in terms of energetic economics, of remaining in cool feeding grounds when food densities are decreasing. Brodie suggested that from the point of view of energy conservation there might be a threshold at which it would be better to cease feeding and swim (with stored food reserves) into a less thermally demanding water-temperature regime, rather than remain in the feeding grounds under conditions of rapidly diminishing energetic returns. He speculated that since rorquals are negatively buoyant, and must move forward continually in order to be able to breathe, the propulsive energy used in migrating at basal cruising speed might, in fact, be no more than would have been required to remain within a specific area.

Consumption rates of standing crops of prey populations by whale populations

An issue with ominous long-term implications for the future well-being of cetacean populations is the attitude of fisheries management agencies to the purported competition of whales with man and his various high-yield global fisheries industries. Since data are sparse I want only to establish the bare bones of the relationship between whale and prey species biomass.

Although there is a significant squid fishery in several oceans, it totals barely one million tonnes in most years, and there is no real discussion concerning the competition of teuthophagous species such as the sperm whale and the beaked whales with man; this is just simply not an issue at present. Controversies centre around the competition of fish-eating species with man, be they dolphins taking fish off the coasts of Japan, or North Atlantic fin whales and humpback whales taking capelin off the shores of eastern Canada, or the possible impact of a Southern Ocean krill fishery on the recovery of depleted blue, fin and humpback populations. In the St Lawrence river in earlier decades the Quebec Department of Fisheries gave a bounty for white whales, on the premise that they exerted a significant influence on the local catches of schooling fish to the detriment of the income of coastal fishermen.

At the present time we are cautiously starting to explore the possibility that major changes in the balance of the upper trophic levels of the Southern Ocean ecosystem have occurred as a result of the drastic reduction of the size of the population of blue, fin and humpback whales. A major argument revolves around the size of the harvestable 'surplus' of euphausiids which might be available under the different predation levels obtaining if (a) whale populations are permitted to recover, and (b) if they are maintained (or stay) at relatively low levels. There has been much speculation that great increases in numbers of Antarctic pelagic birds and seal populations have occurred as a result of the removal of the large rorqual populations. Frankly, the evidence is tenuous, except in the case of *Arctocephalus gazella*. Since the life cycles of the euphausiid species have evolved through selective forces to maximize or optimalize their survival prospects, it is a moot point what effect the activities of predators have had on these populations. There are a number of theoretical and practical ecological studies which suggest that predation exerts only a marginal effect on populations in comparison to the effects of the availability of food supply and territory suitable for optimal reproduction (13). Was there always a 'surplus' of euphausiids, even when whale populations were at their maximum? Have other predators increased in numbers to take up the 'ecological slack' with the disappearance of the large whales?

Few workers would argue that we are moving into an area of discussion where there are few reliable quantitative values for any aspect of the problem. Our ideas on the 'plateau' populations of the large rorquals of the pre-exploitation period in the Southern Ocean are little more than extrapolated guestimates. Similarly, we have little idea of the overall carrying capacity of the Southern Ocean; published values may be out by as much as an order of magnitude.

It is at this point that we can bring into play the results of some of the studies discussed in the earlier parts of this chapter (Figure 3.3). We have some data on feeding rates in whales and their individual energetic requirements. These can be applied as average values to present stock levels, and then extrapolated back to various proposed hypothetical pre-exploitation levels. Since the whale populations were able to maintain themselves at least for the post-Pleistocene period in these waters, the result has to be at least a first-order approximation to the absolute minimum sustainable yield estimate for the euphausiid populations. Even today, the annual consumption of euphausiids by whales in the Southern Ocean does not appear to be much less than about 40 million tonnes, and in

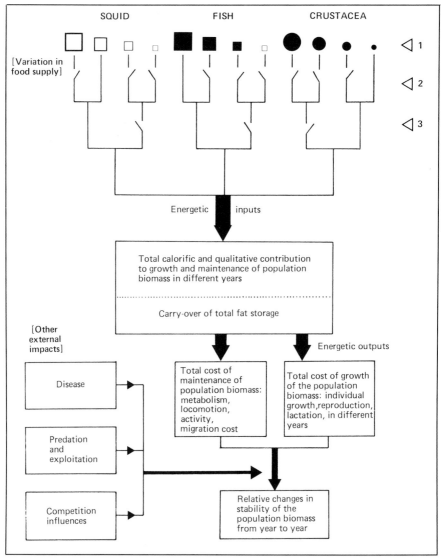

Figure 3.3 Schematic representation of the energetic inputs and outputs for a baleen whale population. The major food sources are considered to be Crustacea, fish or squid. The biomass of any of these groups which is even potentially available to a cetacean population will differ in any given year. This is indicated in line 1 by different sizes of symbols, representing varying *production* of each food species. Whether or not the population of cetaceans can *on average* exploit any of the amounts potentially available to it will depend on its members being in the right place (randomly opening and closing gates of statistical opportunity in line 2), at the right time (randomly opening and closing gates of statistical opportunity in line 3). The total energetic inputs of the population will therefore vary from year to year according to the degree of success with which the population was able to exploit an irregularly available food supply of varying biomass. Further

(continued)

the 1920s could have been as high as 200 million (25). This figure, of course, neglects consumption by Southern Ocean sea-birds, seals and fish. Some data on population levels of birds and fish have been used to suggest that the ratio of 'impact' on the shrimp populations by whales, seals and birds is very roughly of the order 40 :30 :30. It would not seem unreasonable to assume that the annual standing crop of euphausiids in the Southern Ocean is between 600 and 1000 million tonnes. The life-span has been suggested to be as long as four years (26), but studies on *Meganyctiphanes norvegica*, the North Atlantic counterpart to *Euphausia superba*, would point to two or three years being more likely. Under these conditions, the replacement level per annum could be as high as 80 per cent. The sustainable yield from the krill fishery is therefore seen by the industrial fishing nations of the world as being potentially many tens of millions of metric tonnes. If it is pointed out to the reader that the *total* weight yield of global fisheries is 60–70 million tonnes, it is not difficult to see why nations are eyeing this resource so intently. Commercial fishing for krill has already begun, although at the time of writing the yield is only a few tens of thousands of tonnes, and the economics rather marginal, especially with recent increases in fuel costs. I will return later to this complex question of competition between whales and the fishing industries.

Concluding remarks

The approach of critically re-examining every basic assumption about whale populations, especially those which enter into energetic calculations, cannot be too highly encouraged. The question of feeding rates of the larger Cetacea is far from being resolved – can they, for example, tolerate reduced mean feeding success for several successive seasons without incurring an increase in natural mortality? Is distribution of each food species, rather than total biomass, the critical factor governing feeding success each season, as I have implied elsewhere? If this be so, then the rorqual populations of the southern hemisphere may, indeed, be resource limited through the disjunct distribution of food concentrations (with changes in that distribution pattern every season), despite the biomass of food (apparently) being present in excess. As a result, are the natural mortality rates more or less constant for the adults, as has long been assumed in the calculations by the Scientific Committee of the International Whaling Commission? (The data do suggest that they are, although there may be long-term trends.)

---

influences on the stability of the population biomass, particularly in terms of numbers, will be through disease and predation. Competition is likely to augment the pressure of erratic food supply, and will likely operate more to slightly depress biomass potential by weight gain, rather than numbers.

Much of the discussion in this section has been concerned with what happens to rorquals on the feeding grounds. If, on re-calculation, even the smaller cetaceans seem to be adequately insulated to penetrate cold waters, might this also apply to calves of the larger species? Many, myself included, have tended to assume tacitly that the southern rorquals move into subtropical waters to breed because the surface–volume ratio of the small calves is not favourable for prolonged existence in higher latitudes with cooler temperature regimes. Is the answer really so simple? I have begun to doubt that it is. Even this assumption needs to be critically re-examined. We talk of the requirement by these large whales of warm water for breeding, and in the case of the gray and humpback whales, shallow water as well. What exactly are these mysterious breeding requirements? Could conception, rather than calving, be the event which for some reason requires relatively warm water? Since there is a negative temperature gradient through the blubber away from the muscle core, intromission might have to take place deeply in the vagina for optimal movement of spermatozoa. Yet whatever conclusion is reached with respect to the rorquals, we should not forget that the Greenland right whale and the bowhead whale populations carry out their whole life cycle in what are, by the standards for the other baleen whales, very cold waters. This is also true for the narwhal. It is evident that there is not enough information to begin to answer these questions with any degree of confidence. The animals tend to confound our calculations – by present theory the harbour porpoise is inadequately insulated for waters below 5°C, yet they are not infrequently observed where sea temperatures are as low as 1.9°C. Nevertheless, one is still left with a feeling that such species are living on an ecological (that is energetic) knife-edge. If this were really so, then we would need to know it and, preferably, be in a position to quantify the situation. Particularly where coastal regions are concerned, we are already entering a period of extensive habitat modification, and the intensive competition by man for many of the food species of these animals is only one aspect of this process.

References

1 Aleyev, Yu. G. 1965. 'The dolphin body as the aerofoil', *Zool. Zh.*, vol. 44, pp. 626–30.
2 Aleyev, Yu. G. 1970. 'Mobile roughness on the body-surface of nectonic organisms as a means of reducing drag', *Zool. Zh.*, vol. 49, pp. 1173–80.
3 Andersen, S. 1965. 'L'alimentation du marsouin (*Phocoena phocoena* L.) en captivite', *Vie Milieu*, vol. 12, pp. 799–810.
4 Ash, C. E. 1955. 'The fin whales of 1954/5: blubber thickness and factory efficiency', *Norsk Hvalfangsttid*, vol. 44, pp. 550–4.
5 Beamish, F. W. H., Niimi, A. J. and Lett, P. F. 1975. 'Bioenergetics of teleost fishes: environmental influences' in L. Bolis, H. P. Maddrell and K. Schmidt-Nielsen (eds.),

Comparative Physiology – Functional Aspects of Structural Materials, Amsterdam, North-Holland Publishing Co., pp. 187–208.

6   Berzin, A. A. 1972. *The Sperm Whale*, Jerusalem, Israel Program for Scientific Translations.

7   Brodie, P. F. 1975. 'Cetacean energetics, an overview of intraspecific size variation', *Ecology*, vol. 56, pp. 152–61.

8   Brody, S. 1945. *Bioenergetics and growth, with special reference to the efficiency complex in domestic animals*, New York, Hafner Publishing Company.

9   Carmichael, B., Knoll, W., Kramer, M. O. and White, F. 1963. *Project Dolphin*, Report no. 43, Downey, California, North American Aviation, Space and Information Systems Division.

10 Chittleborough, R. G. 1965. 'Dynamics of two populations of the humpback whale, *Megaptera novaeangliae* (Borowski)', *Aust. J. mar. Freshwat. Res.*, vol. 16, pp. 33–128.

11 Clarke, R. 1956. 'Sperm whales of the Azores', *Discovery*, Rep. 28, pp. 237–98.

12 Dawbin, W. H. 1966. 'The seasonal migratory cycle of humpback whales' in K. S. Norris (ed.), *Whales, Dolphins, and Porpoises*, Berkeley and Los Angeles, University of California Press, pp. 145–70.

13 Dempster, J. P. 1975. *Animal Population Ecology*, London, Academic Press.

14 Gaskin, D. E. 1978. 'Form and function in the digestive tract and associated organs in Cetacea, with a consideration of metabolic rates and specific energy budgets', *Oceanogr. Mar. Biol. Ann. Rev.*, vol. 16, pp. 313–45.

15 Geraci, J. R. 1975. 'Pinniped nutrition', *Rapp. P.-v. Réun. Cons. int. Mer.*, vol. 169, pp. 312–23.

16 Gray, J. 1936. 'Studies in animal locomotion. VI. The propulsive powers of the dolphin', *J. Exp. Biol*, vol. 13, pp. 192–9.

17 Gray, J. 1968. *Animal Locomotion*, London, Weidenfield & Nicolson.

18 Gregory, M. E., Kon, S. K., Rowland S. J. and Thompson, S. Y. 1955. 'The composition of the milk of the blue whale', *J. Dairy Res.*, vol. 72, p. 108.

19 Guldberg, G. 1907. 'Ueber das verfahren bei Berechnung des rauminhaltes und gewichtes dder grossen waltiere', *Forh. Vidensk-Selsk. Krist.*, vol. 7, p. 3.

20 Gulland, J. A. (ed.). 1977. *Fish Population Dynamics*, London and New York, John Wiley.

21 Harmoir, G. 1955. 'Fish proteins', *Adv. Protein Chem.*, vol. 10, pp. 227–88.

22 Harris, L. E. 1966. 'Biological energy interrelationships and glossary of energy terms', *National Acad. Sci. Nat. Res. Council Publs.*, vol. 1411, pp. 1–35.

23 Heinrich, B. 1977. 'Why have some animals evolved to regulate a high body temperature', *Amer. Nat.*, vol. 111, pp. 623–40.

24 Hertel, H. 1969. 'Hydrodynamics of swimming and wave riding dolphins' in H. T. Andersen (ed.), *The Biology of Marine Mammals*, New York, Academic Press, pp. 31–63.

25 International Whaling Commission. 1979. 'Report of the special meeting on southern hemisphere minke whales, Seattle, May 1978', *Rep. Int. Whal. Commn.*, vol. 29, App. 3, p. 357.

26 Ivashin, M. V. 1961. '(On the periodicity of feeding of the humpback whale in the southern part of the Atlantic Ocean)', *Byull. mosk. Obshch. Ispyt. Priroda*, vol. 66, pp. 110–15.

27 Ivlev, V. S. 1961. *Experimental ecology of the feeding of fishes*, translated by D. Scott, New Haven, Conn., Yale University Press.

28 Kanwisher, J. and Sundnes, G. 1965. 'Physiology of a small cetacean', *Essays in Marine Physiology* vol. 48, pp. 45–53.

29 Kanwisher, J. and Sundnes, G. 1966. 'Thermal regulation in cetaceans' in K. S. Norris (ed.), *Whales, Dolphins, and Porpoises*, Berkeley and Los Angeles, University of California Press, pp. 398–409.

30 Kawamura, A. 1970. 'Food of sei whale taken by Japanese whaling expeditions in the Antarctic season 1967/68', *Sci. Rep. Whales Res. Inst.*, vol. 22, pp. 127–52.

31 Kawamura, A. 1971. 'Influence of chasing time to stomach contents of baleen and sperm whales', *Sci. Rep. Whales Res. Inst.*, vol. 23, pp. 27–36.

32 Kawamura, A. 1975. 'A consideration of an available source of energy and its cost for locomotion in fin whales with special reference to the seasonal migrations', *Sci. Rep. Whales Res. Inst.*, vol. 27, pp. 61–79.

33 Kleiber, M. 1961. *The Fire of Life, An Introduction to Animal Energetics*, New York, John Wiley.

34 Klumov, S. K. 1963. '(Feeding and helminth fauna of whalebone whales (Mystacoceti) in the main whaling grounds of the world ocean)', *Trudy Inst. Okeanol.*, vol. 71, pp. 94–194.

35 Kramer, M. O. 1960. 'Boundary layer stabilization by distributed damping', *J. Am. Soc. Nav. Eng.*, February 1960, pp. 25–33.

36 Kramer, M. O. 1965. 'Hydrodynamics of the dolphin' in V. T. Chow (ed.), *Advances in Hydroscience*, vol. 2, New York, Academic Press, pp. 111–30.

37 Lang, T. G. 1966. 'Hydrodynamic analysis of cetacean performance' in K. S. Norris (ed.), *Whales, Dolphins, and Porpoises*, Berkeley and Los Angeles, University of California Press, pp. 410–32.

38 Lauer, B. H. and Baker, B. E, 1969. 'Whale milk. I. Fin whale (*Balaenoptera physalus*) and beluga whale (*Delphinapterus leucas*) milk: gross composition and fatty acid constitution', *Can. J. Zool.*, vol. 47, pp. 95–7.

39 Laurie, A. H. 1933. 'Some aspects of respiration in blue and fin whales', *Discovery*, rep. 7, pp. 363–407.

40 Lavigne, D. M., Barchard, W., Innes, S. and Øritsland, N. A. 1976. 'Pinniped bioenergetics'. FAO of the UN, Scientific Consultation on Marine Mammals, Bergen, Norway, 31 August–9 September 1976, document ACMRR/MM/SC/112.

41 Lockyer, C. 1975. 'Estimates of growth and energy budget for the sperm whale, *Physeter catodon*', FAO of the UN, Scientific Consultation on Marine Mammals, Bergen, Norway, 31 August–9 September 1976, document ACMRR/MM/SC/38.

42 Lockyer, C. 1976. 'Growth and energy budgets of large baleen whales from the southern hemisphere', FAO of the UN, Scientific Consultation on Marine Mammals, Bergen, Norway, 31 August–9 September 1976, document ACMRR/MM/SC/41.

43 Lockyer, C. 1978. 'A theoretical approach to the balance between growth and food consumption in fin and sei whales, with special reference to the female reproductive cycle', *Rep. Int. Whal. Comm.*, vol. 28, pp. 243–9.

44 Man'kovskaya, I. N. 1975. '(The content and distribution of myoglobin in muscle tissue of Black Sea dolphins)', *Zh. Evol. Biokhim. Fizicl.*, vol. 11, pp. 221–5.

45 Mauchline, J. and Fisher, L. R. 1969. 'The biology of euphausiids', *Adv. Mar. Biol.* vol. 7, pp 1–454.

46 Mayr, E. 1965. *Animal Species and Evolution*, Cambridge Mass., Belknap Press, Harvard University Press.

47 Mises, R. Von. 1945. *Theory of Flight*, New York, Dover Books.

48 Moiseev, P. A. 1970. 'Some aspects of the commercial use of the krill resources of the Antarctic seas' in M. W. Holdgate (ed.), *Antarctic Ecology*, vol. I, London, Academic Press, pp. 213–16.

49 Nemoto, T. 1957. 'Foods of baleen whales in the Northern Pacific', *Sci. Rep. Whales Res. Inst.*, vol. 12, pp. 33–89.

50 Nishimoto, S., Tozawa, M. and Kawakami, T. 1952. 'Food of sei whales (*Balaenoptera borealis*) caught in the Bonin Island waters', *Sci. Rep. Whales Res. Inst.*, vol. 5, pp. 79–85.

51 Ohta, K., Watarai, T., Oishi, T., Ueshiba, Y., Hirose, S., Yoshizawa, T., Akikusa, Y.,

Sato, M. and Okano, H. 1955. 'Composition of fin whale milk', *Sci. Rep. Whales Res. Inst.*, vol. 10, pp. 151–67.

52 Øritsland, N. A. and Ronald, K. 1975. 'Energetics of the free diving harp seal (*Pagophilus groenlandicus*)', *Rapp. P.-v. Réun. Cons. Int. Explor. Mer.*, vol. 169, pp. 451–4.

53 Parry, D. A. 1949. 'Swimming in whales and a discussion of Gray's Paradox', *J. Exp. Biol.*, vol. 36, pp. 24–34.

54 Pedersen, T. 1952. 'The milk fat of the sperm whale', *Norsk Hvalfangsttid.*, vol. 41, p. 300.

55 Purves, P. E. 1963. 'Locomotion in whales', *Nature*, London, vol. 197, pp. 334–7.

56 Raymont, J. E. G., Srinivagam, R. T. and Raymont, J. K. B. 1971. 'Biochemical studies on marine zooplankton. 8. Further investigations of *Meganyctiphanes norvegica* (M. Sars)', *Deep-Sea Res.*, vol. 18, pp. 1167–78.

57 Rice, D.W. and Wolman, A. A. 1971. 'The life history and ecology of the gray whale (*Eschrichtius robustus*)', *Am. Soc. Mammal. Special Publ.*, vol. 3, pp. 1–142.

58 Ridgway, S. H. 1972. *Mammals of the Sea – Biology and Medicine*, Springfield, Ill., C. C. Thomas.

59 Rowlatt, U. and Gaskin, D. E. 1975. 'Functional anatomy of the heart of the harbor porpoise, *Phocaena phocaena*', *J. Morph.*, vol. 146, pp. 479–94.

60 Schmidt-Nielsen, K. 1972. 'Locomotion: energy cost of swimming, flying and running', *Science*, vol. 177, pp. 222–8.

61 Scholander, P. F. 1940. 'Experimental investigations on the respiratory function in diving mammals and birds', *Hvalråd. Skr.*, vol. 22, pp. 1–131.

62 Sergeant, D. E. 1969. 'Feeding rates of Cetacea', *Fisk. Dir. Skr. Ser. Havunders*, vol. 15, pp. 246–58.

63 Sidhu, G., Montgomery, W., Holloway, G., Johnson, A. and Walker, D. 1970. 'Biochemical composition and nutritive value of krill (*Euphausia superba* Dana)', *J. Sci. Food Agric.*, vol. 21, pp. 293–6.

64 Slijper, E. J. 1962. *Whales*, London, Hutchinson.

65 Spector, W. S. (ed.). 1956. *Handbook of Biological Data*, Philadelphia, W. B. Saunders.

66 Stoddard, J. H. 1968. 'Fat contents of Canadian Atlantic herring', *Fish Res. Bd. Canada Tech.*, Rep. 79, pp. 1–23.

67 Tomilin, A. G. 1946. '(Lactation and nutrition in cetaceans)', *Dokl. Akad. Nauk SSSR*, vol. 52, pp. 277–9.

68 Tomilin, A. G. 1967. *Mammals of the USSR and Adjacent Countries, Vol. 9 Cetacea*, Jerusalem, Israel Program for Scientific Translations.

69 Vinogradova, Z. A. 1960. '(Study of the biochemical composition of Antarctic krill (*Euphausia superba* Dana))', *Dokl. Akad. Nauk. SSSR*, vol. 133, pp. 680–2.

70 Vinogradova, Z. A. 1967. '(The biochemical composition of Antarctic plankton)', (*Biochemistry of Marine Organisms*), Publ. Ukrainian Acad. Sciences, pp. 7–17, Kiev.

71 Walmsley, R. 1938. 'Some observations on the vascular system of a female fetal finback', *Carnegie Inst., Washington Publ. Contrib. Embryol.*, vol. 27, pp. 107–78.

72 Watson, A. P. 1976. 'The diurnal behaviour of the harbour porpoise (*Phocoena phocoena* L.) in the coastal waters of the Bay of Fundy', M.Sc. thesis, University of Guelph, Ontario.

73 Webb, P. W. 1975. 'Hydrodynamics and energetics of fish propulsion', *Fish. Res. Bd. Canada Bull.*, vol. 190, pp. 1–158.

74 Yasui, W. Y. 1980. 'Morphometrics, hydrodynamics and energetics of locomotion for a small cetacean, *Phocoena phocoena* L.', M.Sc. thesis, University of Guelph, Ontario.

75 Yurick, D. B. 1977. 'Populations, subpopulations and zoogeography of the harbour porpoise, *Phocoena phocoena* (L.)', M.Sc. thesis, University of Guelph, Ontario.

CHAPTER 4

Social structure and social behaviour

Introduction

No research on Cetacea has attracted more public attention in recent years than work on their behaviour, communication and intelligence levels (31, 97). Yet surely no aspects are more difficult for the scientist to study effectively. The biologist, educated to respect the 'hard data' of the numbers and weights of population samples or the calculated values from studies of cellular enzymatic reactions and blood chemistry, usually views behavioural work as occupying the 'soft' fringe of biology (meaning that area which abuts on psychology, and is therefore barely respectable).

Essential to the growth of any area of scientific endeavour is the search for ever more reliable measurement of phenomena. Unfortunately, in behavioural studies scientists not only find great difficulty in applying acceptable quantitative measurements to many of their observations, but often cannot even agree on the nature of phenomena being observed. Although it may be true that the totality of behaviour of an organism is the sum of a myriad of neuro-physiological/endocrinological functions, our ability to monitor, let alone analyse, the physiology of behaviour in a complex animal such as a cetacean is hopelessly inadequate. But despite this, we obviously still need some kind of generally acceptable framework within which we can discuss the reactions and behaviour of individuals and groups of organisms.

The two most basic drives that we can recognize in an organism, and which function at the evolutionary level, are those to survive and reproduce – not necessarily in that order at any given moment of the life cycle. Foraging for food and shelter and reproduction requires a certain volume of spatial resources, the absolute amount depending on the characteristics and size of the animal. The organism will therefore attempt to use and occupy those spatial resources essential to its needs at any given time. Reproduction will often not occur successfully if the necessary spatial resource is lacking; under certain circumstances this can lead to sublimated or frustrated pseudo-reproductive behaviour or aggression. Survival until and between reproductions is obviously an essential part of the overall process. That some of the activities of the organism occurring as a result of these essential motivations can be to the detriment of other individuals of the same population is, in the final event, incidental in terms of the operation of natural selection. The single exception is when close kin are involved (112). As we presently understand the mechanics of the evolutionary process, natural selection operates through, and only through, the transmission of the genetic potential of *individuals* in a population. This is an important basic point and I will return to it later, since interpretation of the operation of natural selection is at the root of a basic schism in the modern behavioural literature.

Ideally, starting from consideration of basic drives, we would hope to trace the development of mating systems, territoriality, social structure and social behaviour in our chosen group of study. In practice, of course, this is a rather tall order, requiring much speculation. The framework of such speculation, however, can be derived to some extent from comparisons between species, and dictated by the most parsimonious explanations of observed phenomena. At all stages of the process, *assumptions* of social structure are not to be considered sufficient; such structure must be demonstrated and supported by acceptable evidence (111).

When the lay naturalist sights a school of porpoises, preconceptions derived from popular books, reinforced by subconscious assumptions and prejudices based on general experience within human society, may lead him or her quite naturally to the conclusion that a highly structured community or group is being observed. Intensive and careful study of such a school over an extended period of time by a trained biologist, on the other hand, may result in very different conclusions being drawn. Behaviour, much like beauty, is in the eye of the beholder. I do not want to take up a lot of space discussing general rather than specific cetacean social behaviour, but it is worth stating that many evolutionary biologists find few of the premises of 'group selection' necessary to explain the origin of social behaviour in populations.

Cetaceans, under most circumstances, are schooling species. This is one of the features that attracts our attention. Why do animals form schools anyway? What advantages accrue from such aggregations? Herds and schools appear to form under two conditions; when food sources are concentrated rather than dispersed, and when concealment is more or less non-existent in the environment (107, 111). There is no necessity to ascribe any *function* to such aggregations, the distribution of the prey merely dictates that individuals find advantage in gathering in one place, and if the prey is densely concentrated, the predators will similarly become concentrated in that area. Other authors have cited protection from predation as a probable advantage conferred by membership in a school or herd. In physically diverse habitats animal populations are usually dispersed, and individuals utilize the heterogeneity of the habitat to seek concealment. In open country or in the sea, only camouflage can be used by the individual, and this may become useless the moment the animal moves. The 'predation theory' of schooling postulates that hunting animals tend to attack prey peripheral to a school, or prey moving independently, rather than cohesive groups. The chances of any given individual animal being taken by a predator are therefore statistically far less if it stays deep within a school (12). Obviously this kind of protection can break down when large numbers of predators gather in one place; the very concentration which under low predation density confers advantage to an individual member may facilitate capture under high predation density. When artificial predation by man is introduced, using nets and traps, membership in an aggregation can be disastrous in selective terms. One can simulate a number of levels of predation (discounting the impact of man for the moment) to test the validity of this idea of protection, and it seems to work up to a point. Nevertheless, it can be argued (82) that congregation to exploit a concentrated food source may be the prime operative force, and that any protection so conferred may be an incidental effect. From time to time whole herds or schools can be and are wiped out under natural circumstances – during mass strandings of toothed whale species, for example. This is not necessarily disastrous for the population as a whole; there is no reason at all to require that the feeding–aggregation or protection–aggregation mechanisms be perfect (111). Balanced selection could quite well operate, with competition for a position in the centre of the feeding concentration being countered by the rapid depletion of food under high-density population conditions (111).

It is unlikely that we will be able to devise schemes which explain all the aspects of behaviour that we observe. It is, for example, quite reasonable to anticipate flexible behaviour patterns in marginal or variable environments (107). It is when some authors begin to ascribe *functions* to a herd or school that we reach an area of strong contention among modern behaviourists. If one accepts the idea of group functions, then obviously one can talk about group selection. This is an attractive and seductive idea that has gained wide acceptance, and at first sight some of the examples quoted are quite compelling (119). Nevertheless, some evolutionary biologists and behavioural scientists consider that the basic premises are seriously flawed, make demands beyond the known operations of natural selection, and that the 'case histories' usually cited have alternative, more parsimonious explanations. The student wishing to pursue this topic can do no better, I think, than to read carefully at some stage the sober, lucid book by G. C. Williams on this subject and related areas of evolutionary discussion (111). I will give just one example from his writings of the kind of misinterpretations that are often made, and which at first sight seem to provide convincing explanations of phenomena. Some writers, observing that individual mammals can minimize heat loss by huddling in a herd, have made the totally unnecessary additional assumption that a *function* of the herd, therefore, is to provide warmth. If one accepts this, Williams muses, then one must logically also accept that a *function* of a herd is to facilitate the transmission of infectious diseases! When put in these terms, the danger of ascribing social functions without thinking too deeply about the implications becomes obvious. It is imperative that we examine cetacean behaviour in the strictest possible terms for, if our interpretations are biased by anthropomorphic influences or erroneous assumptions of group functions, these faults will be magnified when we come to consider communication and intelligence levels.

Some comments on the study of behaviour in Cetacea

In this chapter I will certainly not attempt to analyse behaviour of Cetacea in basic physiological terms such as those indicated earlier; their functional neurology is far too poorly known. Because the emphasis throughout this book is at the population level, I want to restrict discussion as much as possible to social structure, social behaviour and the implications of these for behavioural ecology. In keeping with the critical approach outlined above, I intend to start by asking two basic questions:

(1) Is there any real social structure in cetacean populations?
(2) Do cetaceans have highly developed social behaviour?

I am sure that some readers are already appalled that I would doubt either concept. But the fact is that in recent years the authors of one popular book after another have *started* from the basic premise (sometimes explicit, sometimes implied) that the cetaceans represent a high order of social evolution and, by implication, intelligence. Human nature and the press being what they are, some of these accounts have received wide publicity in magazines and newspapers and on television, to the extent that complex dolphin sociology and high cetacean intelligence have joined motherhood and apple pie in the public mythology. The realities of social organization in cetacean populations, I suggest, although interesting, are considerably more mundane than the speculation. Frequently analogies have been drawn in popular literature between dolphins, and chimpanzees and man, with respect to social structure as well as intelligence. In several important ways the major social parallels between many cetacean species and terrestrial mammals lie not with the primates, but with the nomadic plains animals, and the behavioural repertoire and social organization of most species may be less 'advanced' than many people have come to believe, and as much the result of great capacity for mimicry as of creative intelligence.

The behavioural scientist starting a study of a cetacean species faces all the usual difficulties inherent in such research, and more besides. Obviously the simplest approach is to work with captive animals, and here we run into the complex question of just what constitutes valid observation and reliable data. During the 1960s the rapid growth of profit-making seaquaria across North America, then in Europe, Australia and New Zealand, provided opportunities to work with captive dolphins and porpoises (6, 18–24, 27–30, 88, 100), in some cases with small groups the composition of which was stable for several years (27, 100). Conclusions drawn from such work may be misleading. Among the important factors which may seriously distort the behaviour of captive dolphins can be included the size and shape of their pool, and the psychological effects of close confinement which result, even if one uses the largest tank which is economically practical. Small shallow tanks may function as acoustic reverberation chambers, distorting the aural information reaching the dolphin cortex, and close confinement may prevent normal spatial dispersion, leading to abnormal aggression (87), and high death rates from various causes (40). Sensory deprivation may also be an important factor, since most pools are free of growing marine plants, natural substrate, or other marine organisms, for ease of viewing, maintenance of water clarity and hygiene (87). At best, data gathered from studies of captive colonies should be used only when comparison with wild-ranging populations is possible. Most colonies do not represent a natural kinship grouping, because animals are selected for their responsiveness to training, and some individual dolphins are consistently unresponsive and soon discarded (87). During the last few years we have seen the publication of significant studies of wild-ranging cetaceans. For obvious reasons such research is fraught with difficulties, even simply maintaining contact with the study animals can be impossible in marginal weather, and only certain species in accessible areas are amenable to this approach. Nevertheless, such work has yielded very useful insights from which we can start to formulate some tentative generalized conclusions.

Social organization

The cetacean school

Some kind of standardization of terminology is obviously necessary as a prior condition to discussing social organization in these animals. Recently P. B. Best defined types of cetacean associations, with particular reference to sperm whales (10). Because these have general application, I will follow them where possible. The term 'school' is applied only when the behaviour of the animals in the unit provides some evidence for a degree of social cohesion; obviously we are hardly ever going to be in a position to know whether these are kinship groups or not. There is some evidence to indicate that in many cases kinship grouping does not extend much further than mother/calf in these animals (114). 'Aggregation' is a general term employed to describe a number of schools in association, either travelling in the same direction, but with recognizable spacing, or together in the same general area, perhaps feeding and moving in different directions. 'Group' is a vague term used when we are not in a position to apply a more precise term. It may or may not refer to a school.

The ocean-ranging habits of most species of baleen whales make it singularly difficult to learn anything about their school structure, except that females with calves tend to be segregated from other animals on the cool-water feeding grounds. Although as many as ten to twelve fin whales may occasionally be found together, these animals rarely form close-packed schools (2, 69). Both Nemoto and Andrews, studying distribution off Japan and the United States, concluded that fin whales only congregated in large schools on feeding grounds, and that four or five individuals was the normal maximum size for a travelling group. Sei whales are sometimes more gregarious; I have seen six to eight travelling in close formation in the subantarctic Atlantic. We observed a school of fifteen Bryde's whales off the north-west coast of New Zealand on one occasion, although feeding animals of this species seem to break up into singles, twos or threes to pursue fish. Minke whales frequently travel in small schools in the Antarctic, and sometimes these become massed in turn into larger, but somewhat dispersed aggregations. Feeding minke in the coastal waters of the western North Atlantic, on the other hand, are almost invariably seen as singletons.

The school size of right and humpback whales on feeding grounds differs little from that of fin and blue whales. Up to eight right whales were seen in one area off southern New Brunswick in August 1980, but they were too dispersed to be called a school. Two or three animals together is more usual. These two species are virtually the only baleen whales which have been studied extensively on their breeding grounds (26, 75, 113). Here again, groups are rarely much larger than three to five individuals, although a number of such groups of right whales may be ranged a few hundred metres apart along a coastline in suitable areas. Like the rorquals, females with calves often segregate at some distance from other animals. Unless water clarity and other conditions permit divers to enter the water in the immediate proximity of the whales, it is very difficult to determine exactly what behaviour is taking place in these groups. Even when animals are interacting at the surface only a small proportion of the bodies of right and humpback whales can be seen, and it is almost impossible to keep track of specific individuals or even determine the sex of the animals which appear to take different behavioural roles (86).

The school structure of baleen whales, therefore, seems to be somewhat primitive, even with due allowance for the paucity of our knowledge. The only recognizably constant feature is the mother–calf bond. The male parent may or may not stay in the proximity of the female and the offspring, and although there are a number of anecdotal accounts of such a kinship bond, their reliability is suspect. Too often there is a tendency for observers to record what they think they should be seeing.

This relatively simple group organization in baleen whales may at first surprise some readers. Although I am ready to admit that there may well be subtleties in these associations that we do not recognize, it is not necessary to postulate that there *must* be more to the relationships than we seem to see, simply because such simplicity offends a preconceived, opinion that these are highly intelligent animals with complex societal structure. Payne and McVay, for example, suggested that the 'songs' of the humpback whale serve to hold together a loose cluster of individuals during their long migration (76). This would have obvious selective advantages.

I would argue that in fact this small group size and limited infrastructure is highly adaptive to the mode of feeding in baleen whales and the bioenergetic realities which these populations have experienced during their evolution. Individual baleen whales have large absolute body size and require a large volume of food during each day of the feeding season. In the southern hemisphere and many parts of the North Atlantic and North Pacific, we have seen that these animals feed on locally dense shoals of euphausiids or copepods concentrated (on a larger scale) in relatively restricted geographical areas. If the grouping of schools is too tight, they are likely to interfere with one another while feeding, to the detriment of each individual involved. Such behaviour would not confer selective advantage. It does, however, make sense in statistical bioenergetic terms for there to have been selection for individuals to form small, moderately compact groups to exploit locally restricted but highly concentrated patches of shoaling or schooling prey. If these 'sets' of patches are, in turn, distributed over a relatively restricted geographical region, the aggregation of a number of small groups of whales in that area – an aggregation which might be loosely described as a 'large school' – could be an incidental effect, although we certainly cannot rule out the likelihood of acoustic contact over considerable distances.

The only predators which might exert some kind of marginal pressure on the populations of large baleen whales are sharks and killer whales, probably in that order. The large individual body size and rapid swimming speed affords considerable protection against most potential predators, and sharks and killer whales take fish much of the time in any case. Because these predators frequently hunt in packs, no particular protection is afforded by travelling in concentrated schools, especially since the larger the school, the more noise it will make, and killer whales probably hunt at least in part by picking up and homing in on the sounds of potential prey. There would probably be selective advantage for large baleen whales on migration to travel as a dispersed population. In this way, though individuals might fall to hunting packs of killer whales and sharks, the situation in which most members in a medium-sized group might be attacked by a more numerous predator pack is avoided. Packs of sharks have been recorded trailing sperm whale schools in the tropics and subtropics, especially when those schools contain small calves.

We know somewhat more about the school organization of odontocete whales, mainly from mass strandings and from occasional mass captures of whole schools by whalers. The latter information generally results from the drives for pilot whales in places such as Newfoundland and the Faeroe Islands, or for dolphins such as *Stenella* sp. in coastal waters of Japan, but on one or two occasions the International Whaling Commission has issued special scientific kill permits for expeditions to take entire schools of sperm whales.

On the whole, odontocetes are considerably more gregarious than baleen whales, but as might be expected, there are degrees of gregarious-ness, and these can often be related to diet and feeding habits, or simply to habitat. Although we know relatively little about them, the beaked whales are probably the least social of the medium-sizes odontocetes. In southern temperate and subantarctic waters animals of the genus *Mesoplodon*, *Ziphius*, *Tasmacetus*, *Berardius* and *Hyperoodon* are exceedingly difficult to identify at sea, but are usually encountered singly or in groups of two or three (36). *Hyperoodon ampullatus* is most frequently seen in small groups such as those in the northern North Atlantic (8); reports by Nansen (67) that they form much larger schools are partly based on anecdotal information, but it must be remembered that the North Atlantic bottlenosed whale has been extensively hunted over a long period by the Norwegian whalers, and we are observing a much depleted population (60).

Social organization in the sperm whale (Figure 4.1) has been studied more intensively than in any other species, partly because of the commercial importance of this animal, but also because sampling is relatively easy in some industrial whaling circumstances. Dimorphism becomes very marked by late adolescence (although males mature much more slowly than females). The physically mature male may be half as long again as a female of comparable age (10), and weigh about three times as much (57), and the head of the male is proportionately much larger than

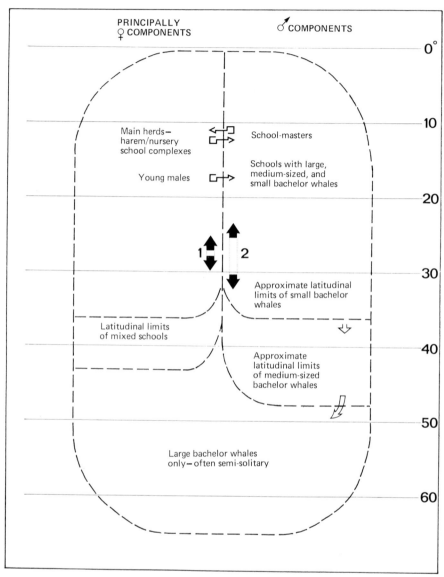

Figure 4.1   Schematic outline of social structure of the sperm whale, redrawn
and modified after Gaskin (34), and incorporating new data from Best (10).
Annual movements of females (1) considerably smaller than those of adult males (2).

that of the female (10). The polygynous habit of the sperm whale has been
commented on by many workers (9, 10, 17, 25, 35, 36, 98); and a significant
degree of sexual segregation has evolved along with the development of
polygyny in this species.

Figure 4.2 Sperm whale school (part only is visible) encountered in the western South Pacific in 1967. A calf is visible with the female on the left. Taken from *Chiyoda Maru No. 5*, photograph by D. E. Gaskin.

The basic social unit is the active breeding school or mixed-sex school (Figure 4.2) (10). Some authors (98, 105) have claimed that several different herds are formed according to the reproductive status of the females, but most evidence suggests that the breeding schools are relatively stable (10, 74); some females may remain together for up to a decade. Even in recent years there has been contention concerning the role of sexually active males in these schools, and argument as to which *are* the sexually active males. Some have suggested that relatively young, small males carry out the main reproductive function in these groups (17). P. B. Best, on the other hand, has recently presented some convincing evidence showing that there is, as believed by the old-time whalers, one large 'school-master', usually of about 15 metres in length (10). The presence of some smaller males within the breeding unit may be incidental. No less than three large males were present in an aggregation observed by the author in the south temperate Pacific Ocean in 1967 (36), but because several discrete, tight subunits could be recognized, it is a moot point whether or not the whole aggregation could safely be referred to as a school, even though the whales were all travelling together. Although when publishing this observation I used the term 'school', I tried to make it obvious that different kinship groups could well have been present in the complex nursery aggregation.

By examining data from a number of sources, Best decided that the number of males of all ages in mixed-sex schools varied considerably, but was usually only about 22 per cent, including young (that is about 78 per cent of the school is female). The female proportion can sometimes be as high as 100 per cent (74). These schools move in relatively tight formations, and the sizes seem to be remarkably constant, about 20–40 individuals (10).

The low production per annum in this species, the slow growth of males to maturity, and the polygynous habit have several interesting effects on the structure of the adult population. The ratio of mature females to males is about 2.6:1 under normal circumstances (10), and the polygynous concentration of the breeding units means that there is probably a ratio of 'inactive' to 'active' bulls of about 4:1. Despite the extended female reproductive cycle, the effective ratio of active females to active males, therefore, is quite high. Several authors have speculated on the effect of the apparent 'surplus' males in the sperm whale population; possibly one of the results could be intensification of competition among males for harem leadership, although other than head-scarring, there is admittedly relatively little direct observational evidence that battles occur for harem control (10).

The balance of evidence assembled by Best (10) points to relatively short annual tenure of the school-masters within the breeding units; mixed-sex schools captured off the coast of South Africa out of the breeding season contained no large mature males. Furthermore, females and large males carry different species of 'whale lice' (*Neocyamus physeteris* and *Cyamus catodontis* respectively), indicating a long history of sexual segregation between the mature fraction of each sex. That a distinct annual cycle of testicular size and activity can be demonstrated in the male sperm whale is totally compatible with Best's findings. Transient presence of breeding males in the family unit has been noted in several species of small odontocete, and can be assumed to confer significant evolutionary advantage to the species in terms of reduced local competition with the growing young for food resources (p. 136). It is not known if male school-masters return to the same group of breeding females each season. If dominance of harems has to be re-established every year the overall tenure could be quite short (in practice reducing the ratio of 'inactive' males given above), and intraspecific competition could be quite fierce among the sexually mature males. Gambell pointed out that sperm whales can detect screw-powered vessels at distances of several miles, so that these may not be good platforms from which to observe normal sperm whale behaviour (32); Best concluded that this might account for the paucity of accounts of fights between male sperm whales during the modern whaling period.

Another possible result of this kind of social structure is the formation of

Figure 4.3   Large solitary male sperm whale sighted off the east coast of the South Island of New Zealand in 1967. Photograph by D. E. Gaskin.

temporary homosexual relationships among males. Although male pairs are frequently observed in some areas, this is really just speculation (35, 36). A more certain result of the polygynous habit is the segregation of the males into 'bachelor' schools. A. A. Berzin (9), C. Lockyer (57) and P. B. Best (10) have also related the sexual segregation to the significantly different food requirements of adult males and females (see Chapter 3, pp. 99–101). Bachelor schools can apparently be found at all latitudes (10), contrary to my own earlier supposition, based on limited data, that they might be primarily a subtropical and temperate-zone phenomenon (35, 36). The smallest males appear to belong to the largest bachelor schools, numbering 10–50 animals. As they start to mature, school size seems to decrease to about 3–15 individuals, and finally the largest males are usually spaced out in loose aggregations, although they may come together in somewhat tighter groups when they travel from one feeding ground to the next (Figure 4.3).

The largest animals in 'harem' units sometimes prove on close inspection to be females (10); in fact Best has suggested that the term 'extended matricentral family' might be applied to the social unit in question (81). Such breeding units, largely distributed in the warmer waters of the world, have, as one might expect, developed migratory movements which are quite unlike those of males which move into high-latitude regions to feed each year.

P. B. Best recently summarized the apparent ontogeny of social organization in the sperm whale, and the changes that must occur in the social and reproductive status of an animal of each sex with age (10). The basic social unit is the mixed school of adult females and their offspring,

Figure 4.4   School of pilot whales *Globicephala melaena* in the Head Harbour Passage region of New Brunswick, Canada, containing animals of all sizes, including calves. Photograph courtesy of G. J. D. Smith, University of Guelph, Ontario.

the male component in these schools being sexually immature. Adult males, fully sexually mature, join these schools only during the breeding season, and even then only 10–25 per cent of all sexually mature males take part in this activity. Segregation of males into bachelor schools presumably begins even before they attain sexual maturity; perhaps some time after weaning. It is not known how soon the full high-latitude–low-latitude annual migratory cycle of males begins; there is some evidence that not all males take part in this, and off New Zealand statistical analyses in fact showed significant differences in direction of movement of bachelor schools, male pairs and solitary sperm whales (35). Although some females also appear to be segregated for a time from the breeding schools, they are presumed to rejoin them before or as they approach puberty. The general social organization of the sperm whale is certainly based on a polygynous mating system, but we lack enough data on behaviour during the mating season and subsequent period of calf-rearing to be quite sure of its exact form (10).

We have limited data on the school composition and size or social structure, of a number of other odontocetes: pilot whale *Globicephala melaena* in the western North Atlantic (Figure 4.4) (93); white whale *Delphinapterus leucas* in the St Lawrence estuary of Canada (Figure 4.5) and the Arctic USSR (48, 70); Harbour porpoise *Phocoena phocoena* in the western North Atlantic (37, 110); Burmeister's porpoise *Phocoena spinipinnis* in the western South Atlantic (118); Dall's porpoise *Phocoenoides dalli* in the eastern and western North Pacific (65); finless

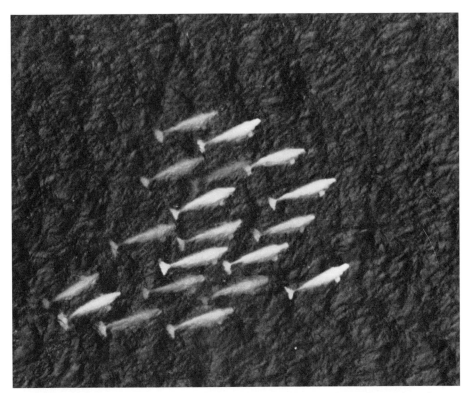

Figure 4.5   A school of nineteen adult white whales in the Saguenay region of the St Lawrence estuary – mostly male animals, which can be recognized by the 'squared' shoulders. Photograph courtesy of Leone Pippard, 1977.

porpoise *Neophocoena phocoenoides* in the western North Pacific (44); northern right whale dolphin *Lissodelphis borealis* in the western North Pacific (52); bottlenosed dolphin *Tursiops truncatus* from south-western Indian Ocean (85, 88); bottlenosed dolphin *Tursiops truncatus* from south-western Indian Ocean (85, 88), western South Atlantic (Figure 4.6) (114, 115) and western North Atlantic (41); dusky dolphin *Lagenorhynchus obscurus* from the western South Atlantic (Figure 4.7) (117); blue–white or striped dolphin *Stenella coeruleoalba* in the eastern North Pacific (61); spinner dolphin *Stenella longirostris* (Figure 4.8) from Hawaii (72); and humpbacked dolphin *Sousa* sp. in the south-western Indian Ocean (Figure 4.9) (87).

There is some evidence pointing to the existence of polygynous mating systems in several of these species, although the apparent continuity of the predominantly female breeding school is not nearly as clearly defined in the literature about these animals as for the sperm whale. School size is very variable; smaller school size seems not so much related to social differentiation or systematic position, as to the habitat occupied by a

Figure 4.6   School of Bottlenosed dolphins *Tursiops truncatus* (or a named form), apparently two females with young, in the Lagoa dos Patos, southern Brazil. Photograph by Hugo P. Castello, supplied by Mrs Maria Cristina Pinedo, of the Universidade do Rio Grande, RS, Brasil.

Figure 4.7   Pair of dusky dolphins *Lagenorhynchus obscurus*, in the Golfo San José, Argentina. Photograph courtesy of Drs M. and B. Würsig, Santa Cruz, University of California, USA.

Figure 4.8   Mobile aggregation of *Stenella* dolphins (probably *longirostris*) off the island of St Lucia, West Indies, in 1972. Photograph courtesy of G. J. D. Smith, University of Guelph, Ontario.

Figure 4.9 Humpbacked dolphin, *Sousa sp.* working close inshore at Umhlanga, RSA. Photograph by Rod Wilson NASMB, courtesy of Dr G. J. B. Ross, of the Port Elizabeth Museum, RSA.

species. The inshore species, such as *Tursiops, Phocoena, Neophocoena* and *Sousa* have schools of quite small average size, although some diurnal and seasonal periodicity has to be taken into account. The pelagic species such as *Stenella coeruleoalba* may have school sizes of up to 500 (61), although these may in practice consist of temporary aggregations of much smaller units. One of the consistently semi-solitary species seems to be *Neophocoena*, where the mother–calf pair was the only social combination that could be recognized by Japanese workers (44). The size of schools in the Inland Sea of Japan rarely exceeded three or four animals.

At the other extreme, the literature on right whale dolphins contains accounts of groups of as many as 2000 animals. It is probably safe to assume that such large numbers represent temporary travelling or feeding aggregations of many small units (52). Seasonal occurrence of very large schools of several species of dolphin off New Zealand have been recorded by the present author (36), including the southern right whale dolphin *Lissodelphis peroni*. Californian workers estimated the arithmetic mean of the school sizes of the North Pacific species sighted by them in recent years as about 42 ± 10 (52). They also recognized three or four basic types of formation among travelling right whale dolphins: a concentrated group; an echelon or line abreast (considered likely to be variants of the same formation); and a spaced set of subgroups. The latter formation was commonly adopted when these animals were travelling in company with other delphinid species. Similar swimming formations have been reported in other pelagic delphinids in various parts of the world (78).

Some further light has been cast on the problem of variation in school size by K. S. Norris and T. Dohl, and B. and M. Würsig, respectively studying the Hawaiian spinner dolphin and dusky dolphin off the coast of Argentina (72, 117). A school of the former species was observed to move slowly around a bay during the morning hours, apparently resting. School size at this time was about 25 individuals, swimming in tight formation, with bodies almost touching. Later in the day they would suddenly become more active, disperse and begin extensive and prolonged diving to forage for prey. At such times several different schools would converge on a single productive area, and the identity of schools would be submerged for a time in the turmoil of a general feeding aggregation. Rather similar changes in diurnal activity were observed in the dusky dolphins. The size of the average non-feeding school in this species was about 6–15 animals, but when anchovy schools were present in surface waters as many as 300 could be counted in a single feeding aggregation.

On a somewhat smaller scale, the diurnal behaviour of harbour porpoises in southern New Brunswick waters also follows this pattern. School size during most of the summer is small, either singles or only 2–3 animals (110); mother, calf and yearling is a frequent unit observed (Figure 4.10). Larger aggregations can occur as temporary phenomena, when animals meet while travelling in the same direction; they may split up after a few minutes or a few hours. Schools of 8–12 are common only in the autumn when they appear to form larger units prior to moving out of coastal waters to wintering grounds on the offshore banks. Under normal circumstances larger aggregations are formed during the summer only when herring schools of significant size enter the island passages; then as many as 30–50 animals may be found engaged in frenzied feeding behaviour within a 1 km² area. Even under these circumstances the aggregations persist only as long as the herring are running close to the surface.

Fluidity of school structure is a feature common to many of these species. Studying *Tursiops* in an Argentine bay (114), Würsig found that while a small 'core' of recognizable individuals remained in the bay for extended periods, others came and went at intervals, so that while the overall number in the study area might not vary that much, there was constant flux in terms of the individuals actually present. He observed some limited stability in subgroups which, on average, had a composition of about 10 per cent calves. Some of the 'core' bottlenosed dolphins would leave for many weeks at a time, returning later. Others were present for extended periods, then were never seen again during the course of the study. These are precisely the kinds of patterns observed by my own team studying recognizable individuals of harbour porpoise off the coast of New Brunswick (110). Würsig noted short-term stability in subgroups of dusky

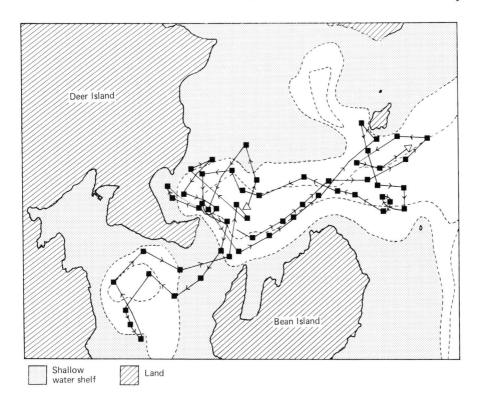

Figure 4.10   Daily pattern of foraging behaviour in Fish Harbour and Lords
Cove, Deer Island, New Brunswick, Canada, of a female harbour porpoise and
calf during two typical days in the summer of 1974. The mother could be
recognized by a characteristic large scar on her back. This pattern, generally
hugging the edges of the basins and shallow trenches, was followed day after day
with relatively minor variation. Squares indicate surfacings with direction of
movement determined. Drawn from unpublished data of A. P. Watson and D. E.
Gaskin, University of Guelph, Ontario.

dolphin in the same region (117) and semi-persistent localized subunits of
humpbacked dolphins were also noted by Saayman and his co-workers on
the coast of South Africa (87).

Although school size has been estimated for most of the species listed
earlier, there is much less information available on school composition.
White whales in the St Lawrence appear to form two basic types of school;
family groups containing females, calves and immatures, and adult groups
(Figure 4.5) (79); the latter having more males than females. The same
kind of school structure may occur in the pilot whale, although segregation
of males does not seem to be as distinct in either of these species as in the
sperm whale (93). Kleinenberg (48) thought that the evidence for a
polygynous mating system in white whales was far from conclusive,

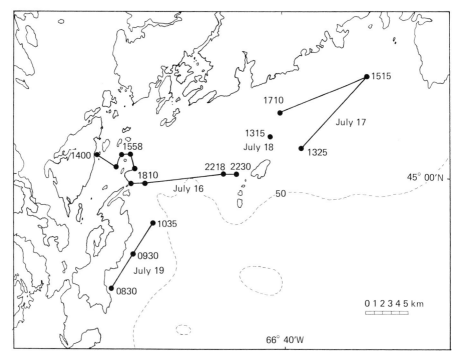

Figure 4.11   Distances traversed by a large male harbour porpoise *Phocoena phocoena* bearing a radio transmitter during a four-day period of July 1974. Animal sometimes moved into areas where a clear signal could not be received. When contacted visually, it appeared to be actively feeding or searching for fish. Redrawn from Gaskin *et al*. (See Chapter 1, reference 42.)

although the persistence of stable groups of females and young, without adult males consistently present, is very like the situation in sperm whale populations. At certain times of year a large proportion of the white whale schools in a given area gather into large aggregations, perhaps for mating, or prior to migration. This phenomenon has been observed in the St Lawrence estuary by L. Pippard and J. Laurin, in the Canadian arctic by D. Sergeant, and in the Chukchi Sea by C. Ray.

My research group has encountered apparent all-male schools of harbour porpoises in the Bay of Fundy (Figure 4.11); all six individuals collected from what appeared to be the same dispersed feeding school of young animals in the Digby Gut, Nova Scotia in 1972 were immature males (37). Irvine and his co-workers found significant segregation by age and sex in western North Atlantic bottlenosed dolphins during extensive tagging and release studies (41). The home range of the group studied was about 85 km², and a polygynous mating system seemed to be operating. Breeding schools contained few adult males or none at all. Subadult males formed bachelor schools, and adult and subadult males rarely mixed.

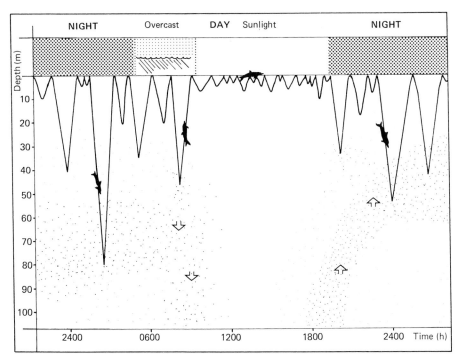

Figure 4.12 Foraging behaviour of the pelagic species *Delphinus delphis* in the subtropical Pacific. Compiled from data and illustrations by Dr W. E. Evans (47, Chapter 7) and other sources. Deep dives are made at night, and under overcast conditions, when potential prey animals of the deep scattering layer rise towards the epipelagic layer. During daytime, only shallow dives are recorded.

These findings parallel those for *Stenella* studied off Japan (61). In the dusky dolphin, on the other hand, Würsig (117) found during tagging studies that the typical non-feeding school contained adults, of both sexes as well as young.

This type of rather casual mixing, with coming and going of subunits, has been related in terrestrial mammals, including ungulates and chimpanzees (83), to patchy and irregular food supply. There are a number of ways, however, in which the social organization of dolphin groups may more closely resemble that of the nomadic plains animals than primates. Dolphins live in a pelagic, three-dimensional environment (Figure 4.12), where concealment is almost impossible beyond the minimal development of disruptive camouflage (59) (see p. 71), and even this is not found in all species. In their use of wide foraging territories and in the way that subunits come together opportunistically into larger feeding aggregations when food is plentiful, whale and dolphin behaviour parallels that of ungulates. Kinship bonds generally appear to be weaker in cetaceans than in primates; there is certainly no evidence of a male–young bond, as can be identified in some higher primates, for example; in most species the mother–calf bond is the only kinship which can be consistently identified. Finally, as parallel or analogous adaptations to enhance neonate survival in two kinds of hostile environment, we find precocious young in both cetaceans and ungulates. The young of primates and canids, on the other hand, require extensive parental care for a variable period after birth, and are incapable of travelling with the adults immediately after parturition. Extended lactation periods are not uncommon. It could be argued that precocious development of the central nervous system in cetaceans, especially of the brain (in addition to the need to have large areas of the cortex involved with the processing of acoustic information) might result in significant restriction of the 'plasticity' of the cerebral cortex during the post-natal period. This might possibly place constraints on the degree of development of certain types of learning or intellectual abilities, depending on the cortical zones most affected. It is becoming more certain that considerable areas of the dolphin cortex are organized in ways quite unlike those of other mammals (see also p. 150) (64).

Table 4.1   Summary of group size and composition (where known) in Cetacea

Species	Range of group sizes	Data on composition	References
Fin whale	1–5	Little known	2, 69
Blue whale	1–5	Little known	69
Sei whale	1–8	Sexually segregated groups known to occur	69, and personal observations Southern Ocean, 1962
Bryde's whale	1–3	Little published information	Personal observations, N. New Zealand 1963, 1964
Minke whale	1–7	Often seen singly on North Atlantic feeding grounds, but in groups sometimes in Antarctic	Personal observations, S. Ocean, 1962, 1967; E. Canada 1969–80.
Right whale	1–5	Females with calves sometimes segregated from others	69, and personal observations, Bay of Fundy, Canada, 1971, 1980
Gray whale	1–3	Tend to be rather solitary on feeding grounds, and in loose dispersed aggregations on migration	69; refs. 30, 130 of Chapter 2
Sperm whale	males 1–50	Immature males and younger non-breeding males form the largest schools	10
	family groups 20–40	Female proportion among the adults in these groups can reach 100 per cent	10
Beaked whales	1–3	Variable, often seen singly	8, 67

Species	Range of group sizes	Data on composition	References
Killer whale	1–15+	Family groups, with or without mature males	ref. 17 of Chapter 8; personal observations off California, New Zealand, and in the Southern Ocean
White whale	3–20+	Family groups with few adult males tend to be segregated from adult groups with a high proportion of males	79
Bottlenosed dolphin	5–10	Family units noted, with few adult males present	44, 88, 114, 116
Dusky dolphin	6–15; up to 300 in feeding aggregations of a temporary nature off Argentina, and some thousands off N.Z.	Usually groups of adults with about 10 per cent proportion of calves	36, 117
Right whale dolphin	42 ± 10, but hundreds or low thousands may travel together	Family groups and mixed groups	52
Humpbacked dolphin	2–5	Small family groups and singles	87, 88
Hawaiian spinner dolphin	c. 25+	Family units, moving in and out of larger more flexible feeding aggregations	72
Blue–white, spinner and spotted dolphins	100–500+	As above	61, and personal observations by author and G. J. D. Smith
Harbour porpoise	2–5, with temporary late summer groups of 20+	Mother–calf pairs and singles are common, also small schools (3–6) of immatures	37, 110
Finless porpoise	1–3	Mother–calf pairs and singles predominate	44

Evolution of polygny in an odontocete (sperm whale)

As we have seen, the polygynous habit may have developed in several, or even many, species of odontocete, but in most cases we lack the data to draw firm conclusions about the selective value of this reproductive mode to these animals. Best has recently discussed the ways in which the polygynous habit may have arisen in the sperm whale, and it is worth briefly summarizing his conclusions (10), which he compared and contrasted with a model devised by G. A. Bartholomew to explain the origins of pinniped polygyny (4).

Development of this mating system must obviously be preceded by gregarious behaviour which spans the breeding season. The main food species are mesopelagic and bathypelagic schooling squid, and there is evidence that sperm whales may undertake a form of co-ordinated hunting (108, 109). W. A. Watkins noted that a school fanned out after diving, yet appeared to continue issuing identifying signals; each animal should therefore know where the others were. Furthermore, these animals often returned to the surface within close distance of each other, despite having dived to depths of several hundred metres (Figure 4.13). The fact that the prey might be termed 'difficult' to hunt would tend to favour selection for a long period of maternal care. The lactation period is indeed very long in this species, up to 22 months (10). The mothers need to dive to depths which could well be beyond the capabilities of young calves, so the evolution of a tight schooling structure permitting the calf to be left among other adults would also be favoured, because this would afford protection against attacks on the calves by sharks. Because these attacks may be quite common in tropical latitudes, sperm whales appear to have developed protective reactions against such predators (17, 71). If positive advantages accrue to individuals from this kind of association, one might expect year-round or long-term stable units to develop. Most dolphins, on the other hand, probably swim too fast or are too agile to fall frequent prey to shark attack.

Unlike pinniped species, sperm whale populations have low annual production rates – Best thought perhaps the lowest of any marine mammal (10). He attributed this to the development of a long lactation period in the species, taking up about 40 per cent of the total length of the female reproductive cycle. The number of females coming into oestrus each season, therefore, is quite low, barely 35 per cent, so that an annual surplus of males is an inevitable by-product of the extended lactation, unless some mechanism arose to change the sex ratio of births. The gregarious nature of the females provides opportunity for a dominant bull to have several sexual encounters without great energetic expenditure, and thus to maximize the chances of passing on his genetic characteristics (10). Because the extended female reproductive cycle inevitably leads to a surplus of sexually active males each year, competition for females is inevitable. The chances of any one male obtaining a whole harem are obviously quite small. Best suggested that there was therefore consider-able selective advantage in the development of delayed sexual maturity in the male of this species, since this might avoid competition reaching counterproductive levels. In the same manner, selection for increase in the length of the gestation period in polygynous or semi-polygynous species

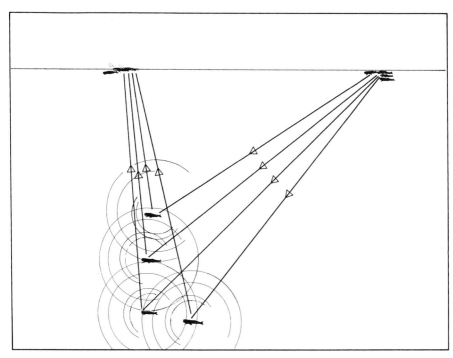

Figure 4.13   Sperm whale communication underwater during foraging.
Compiled from data and illustrations by Dr W. A. Watkins (108) and Watkins and
Schevill (109). The animals disperse after diving and 'signature' frequently while
down, permitting each animal to recognize the identity of all the others and
probably determine their relative positions. School structure often re-forms as
they return to the surface.

would also be favoured, since it would effectively separate the mating
period from the period when the young calves were most dependent on the
mothers (10). There are three species of odontocete for which it is known
for certain that the gestation period exceeds 14 months: the sperm whale
(10), white whale (48), and long-finned pilot whale (93). There are
probably others, particularly among the Ziphiidae.

The origin of sexual dimorphism in the sperm whale is an interesting
problem, and cannot be explained in terms of large body size and
subcutaneous-fat build-up for a period of long territorial defence
postulated by Bartholomew for pinnipeds (4). For one thing, the
dimorphism in the sperm whale includes significant changes in body
proportions as well. The social organization developed among the female–
calf schools would be favoured by exclusion of the males, even the 'school-
masters', once the essential breeding period was over. Differential
migration of males away from the female–young groups is now quite well
documented in polygynous populations of terrestrial mammals, and

would seem to reduce competition for food resources under conditions when the males might profit to the detriment of the recovering females and the growing young (107). It is evident that normal selective processes operating in the competition between males in a polygynous species could favour the development of large body size in that sex, but as Best pointed out, a consequence of this would be a corresponding increase in the nutritional demands of the males relative to females. He believed that any adaptations permitting the male to take food without competition with the females and young would be favoured, and this would include diving to a different depth stratum as well as moving into higher latitudes to feed. There appears to be a correlation between the development of the spermaceti organ and the ability to dive to great depths. As the males start to develop these characteristics before puberty, this reduces the advantage of staying with the female schools and enhances the advantages of joining with other foraging males. Selection would therefore favour the segregation of males from the breeding units at a much earlier age than females (10).

Social behaviour

In this section I want to consider those aspects of behaviour exhibited by cetacean individuals which may affect or influence other animals in their immediate group, or even other groups at some distance. Obviously, this section runs quite naturally into a consideration of communication, and it is difficult, if not impossible, to draw a firm boundary between the two topics. I will try to consistently refer to these aspects as 'social behaviour', and to distinguish them from purely individual facets of behaviour, such as, for example, descriptions of the way in which a lone animal forages for food. I am also specifically excluding from 'social behaviour' the interrelationships between mother and calf, although I have to refer to these from time to time, because it is well established that a basic mother–calf kinship bond exists. For the purposes of this chapter (as stated on p. 115), I will be trying to identify possible behavioural relationships in Cetacea which extend beyond this most basic of mammalian bonds.

Epimeletic or 'care-giving' behaviour

Nurturant behaviour, that is, succour given by the mother to her distressed or injured calf, is well documented (19, 94), and the general evidence for epimeletic behaviour in whales and dolphins was reviewed by M. C. and D. K. Caldwell in a readily available volume some years ago (20). Discussion of this type of epimeletic behaviour is excluded here, for the reasons outlined above.

Accounts of general succorant or 'standing-by' behaviour by whales and porpoises (94) seem, at first sight, rather contradictory. Sometimes whales will remain with an injured animal, on other occasions the injured whale is deserted by its companions. It often does not seem to matter whether the distressed individual is calling or not (19–22), or, when aid is given, whether it is even conscious.

When the observations are reviewed in the literature, it would appear that we can make four generalizations about such behaviour, after discounting some of the anecdotal accounts in which the interpretations seem debatable. First, juveniles do not participate in this kind of activity, unless we include (erroneously in this context, I think), examples of calves standing by an injured or dead mother. Second, the occurrence of succorant behaviour beyond the bounds of mother and calf does not seem to correlate at all with the apparent level of social organization, nor with phylogeny. Scientists studying terrestrial mammal populations have noted, incidentally, that mutual aid and co-operation appears to have developed in those species which have the 'matriarchal' or 'extended matricentral family' type of social structure (11, 81). Third, males will stand by injured females, for example, gray and humpback whales (2, 19), but females only rarely stand by injured males. Fourth, males hardly ever stand by injured males, as far as can be determined. Of course, under many circumstances it is not possible to identify which sex the animals are. In fact when one totals the number of observations of succorant behaviour by each species in the wild, except under whaling conditions, where the presence of screw propeller noise may alter the normal behaviour, they are few in number. One has to be in the right place at the right time to observe it, and that takes a large element of good fortune.

I do not want to repeat here the specific detail already adequately surveyed by the Caldwells, but I would like to review the available information to see what conclusions may be drawn about the origins of this kind of succorant behaviour. In many popular and semi-popular articles it has been cited frequently, and in my opinion without sufficient justification, to illustrate either the high level of social organization in cetacean groups or the high intelligence level of these animals, or both.

Consider the following points. First, the neonate cetacean, like any viviparous mammal, must take its first independent breath a very few minutes after birth or suffer oxygen deprivation which, if it does not cause death, is likely to cause irreparable brain damage. The problem for cetaceans is compounded by the birth taking place in water, an additional difficulty which only Sirenians and the sea otter have overcome among all the other mammalian families. Even the Pinnipedia must move to land or fast ice to give birth. That selection should have occurred for the cetacean mother to support her calf during the first few critical minutes after birth is, therefore, hardly surprising. Secondly, I think it significant that general succorant behaviour does not occur in juveniles. It is manifested, however, by submature females and adult females with or without their own calves. The Caldwells summarized a number of examples of this kind of activity in captive bottlenosed dolphins (19). The behaviour can extend over a period of weeks, and frequently is maintained after death of the distressed or injured animal. There is even a record of an animal which carried a shark on its rostrum for eight days (73).

The last example suggests that the relationship between succorant behaviour and intelligence level is not highly correlated. Furthermore, the concept of a 'helper', is well known to animal behaviourists; it is not a phenomenon confined to the 'higher' mammals, but quite widespread among birds (see review by A. F. Skutch) (95), and may be a regular occurrence in the Californian woodpecker in particular (111), although only a small percentage of breeding pairs will have a helper in any given area. The 'helper', in this case, is viewed as an individual demonstrating some elements of normal parental behaviour, perhaps elicited by specific visual or aural stimuli, but not necessarily at the right time from its own point of view, simply because the control mechanisms of such behaviour are not perfect (111). It would be quite natural, therefore, to expect this kind of behaviour from a pubertal female or from an adult female without a calf at the particular time. The behaviour would have selective advantage to these individuals in the long run, since the time will come when they will have their own young, but the fact that it could, from time to time, be employed to the advantage of an unrelated individual is almost certainly an incidental effect. It is quite wrong, I think, to talk about there being 'group' selection for this kind of behaviour, since it is perfectly explicable in terms of selection advantageous to the individual alone, if we restrict our consideration to the *origin* of this kind of behaviour. That, in the case of an extended matricentral family school (for example, in sperm whales), the existence of this type of response in all the adult females permits calves to be left with other females while the mother dives for food still does not mean that this communal day-care has become a function of the group. There is a cause-and-effect relationship, certainly, but one based on the selective advantage accruing to individuals in such a situation. It is conceptually most important that this is made clear; succorant behaviour is not a *function* of the school.

The other points enumerated earlier can also be considered in evolutionary terms. First, there is no reason why there *should* be any correlation between epimeletic behaviour and phylogeny in Cetacea – unless one accepts 'progress' as a general principle of evolution – rather than a process of independent substitution of one adaptation for another, coupled with diversification and sometimes increase in body size and cellular differentiation (111). Second, there is selective advantage in a male aiding a female which may be carrying his progeny providing that, under normal circumstances, there is a better than even chance that his behaviour will result in the female surviving a period of distress. Obviously this kind of behaviour did not evolve in such a way that it continued to be effective when harpoon-throwing man arrived on the scene, although there are a few accounts of sperm whales apparently trying to sever harpoon lines attached to other animals (17). The possibility that they swam into them accidentally and entangled their jaws cannot be excluded, because there are also accounts of sperm whales swimming steadily on their original course while a companion was harpooned. If males have less than an even chance of aiding females, and their own lives are endangered, selection would favour those that flee and live to impregnate other females. Third, in species in which polygynous mating systems are operating, there is no selective advantage for a male to stand by another injured male, and therefore no reason why this kind of behaviour should develop. Under certain circumstances, however, particularly if no visible or audible threat is apparent, an animal may investigate the stricken individual briefly out of simple (and widespread) mammalian curiosity. Fourth, if the males have completed their role in the season's reproductive process in a polygynously structured population, and there is a surplus of active males, then there is similarly no selective value in females standing by an injured male. A review of the literature suggests that factual support for the idea of females standing by injured males is lacking, and there is some good observational evidence that it does *not* occur in some species – for example, the humpback whale (20). This behaviour usually occurs in those primates such as some tribes of man, in which monogamous life-mating systems have been developed, where the pair-bond frequently appears to override more basic (and evolutionary sensible) instincts.

This may seem a rather cold-blooded evaluation and interpretation of succorant behaviour in Cetacea, probably offending many fondly held conceptions. But the interpretations are based, wherever possible, on what I consider to be the simplest and most economical explanations of what we observe. I am perfectly prepared to believe that social behaviour of a much 'higher' form occurs in these animals. I do not believe, however, that it has yet been demonstrated by experimental or observational results which cannot be interpreted in much simpler terms.

Dominance hierarchies in captive Cetacea

Many aspects of human social behaviour, and our thinking about such concepts in animals, are influenced by the idea of 'leadership'. Almost all human societies defer some level of ultimate decision-making to a 'leader'.

Some animal behaviourists believe that the origin of this social phenomenon can be traced back to what is commonly referred to as the 'peck order' in animal groups – it has been studied experimentally in chickens, and is perfectly familiar to anyone who has worked in a government department.

Some studies indicate that a peck order develops in captive cetacean colonies in a fairly short period of time (6, 100). A 'leader' can usually be identified in these colonies; the relationships among the animals in the group can be determined observationally by examining the distribution of threat gestures (5). Threat gestures that have been identified in delphinids include the 'open mouth display' (one that is common in other mammals as well as dolphins) (107), the 'jaw clap' (62), and direct head presentation in *Phocoena phocoena*. In the latter case an animal half turns its body until the snout is directed at the threatened animal, which then usually turns away (1). Researchers have had some problems distinguishing between 'threat' and 'fear' gestures or reactions in captive delphinids (24, 54). Agonistic behaviour is well marked in bottlenosed dolphins; somehow the idea has spread into much of the popular literature that these animals are completely peaceful – nothing could be further from the truth. Fights both in captivity and the wild can inflict visible and bloody (but probably not dangerous) wounds on both males and females. Many cetaceans, such as Risso's dolphin, the male sperm whales and older bottlenosed dolphins, bear scar patterns made by the raking teeth of their own species (10). The animal at the top of the peck order or 'leader' in a captive dolphin colony need not be a male. If a colony has been dominated by a large adult female, and a new adult male is added, she will frequently attack him savagely. In some cases these fights continue day after day, without any sign of increasing acceptance or social stability; in such circumstances the aquarium has no recourse but to segregate the individuals concerned. One fact of life that has nothing to do with phylogeny or intelligence in mammals is the ability of individuals to develop an almost pathological dislike of other animals in their group or unit.

The fact that we can recognize such hierarchies in captive cetaceans, usually based on body size or personal aggression level, does not mean that we should immediately conclude that this system exists in the same form in the wild. Underwater observations have shown that dolphin schools can have vertical as well as horizontal stratification (30); while swimming underwater *Stenella* schools may have as many as five distinct vertical layers, which re-form again after the animals have surfaced to breathe. However large the tank in which captive colonies are kept, it can provide nothing but travesty of the conditions found in nature (87). In the wild, a small male can keep distance from a bigger male that finds its presence an irritant, and the largely individual nature of delphinid foraging is very different from 'feeding time' in the seaquarium. Generally, to avoid fighting and jostling, the animals must be trained to take their food in strict sequence, unless the institution can afford the luxury of several handlers. It is quite possible that some kind of hierarchical structure, probably matricentral, exists in cetacean schools in the wild, but the fluidity that we observe in wild dolphin groups suggests that there simply may be no stimulus for it to develop, except perhaps for short periods during the peak of the mating season.

Possible co-operative behaviour

Several authors have described dolphins as 'herding' fish (87, 117). There is obvious selective advantage in the evolution of this kind of behaviour, but I would caution the reader against reading too much into use of the word 'herding'. In the human context this generally implies some kind of conscious intent in which we have some foreknowledge of the results of that herding. After watching harbour porpoises feeding for a dozen seasons, I am still not convinced that what occurs should be interpreted as intelligent co-operative behaviour, but rather a convergence in individual porpoise feeding strategies favoured to some extent by the defensive behaviour of the prey. It seems evident that these animals prefer, or need, a certain volume of water in which to manoeuvre successfully, and that they usually pursue a single fish rather than snapping blindly into a school. Furthermore, if they follow the prey rather than coming at it head-on or from the side, it is at a disadvantage in two ways. First, if the prey turns to left or right, or up or down, not only is the distance between prey and predator suddenly reduced, but the prey presents a larger target area for a short but critical period. Second, while being pursued, the prey can see the following predator at best only with its peripheral vision. Under these circumstances it follows (a) that dolphins can gain by following a school of fish rather than rushing into it and dispersing it, and (b) that the need for room to manoeuvre probably dictates that they spread out in a crescent behind a school swimming at the surface. It is not unreasonable for the human observer to conclude that this is co-operative herding, but it may in fact be nothing so sophisticated, merely a number of individuals feeding, with a convergent strategy and a 'nearest-neighbour' distance constraint, resulting in a rather regular formation. This 'herding behaviour' appears to differ little from the herding of herring by feeding silver hake, of mackerel by schools of tuna, and of menhaden by bluefish.

Social behaviour, communication and intelligence

There is a tendency in much of the literature to discuss social behaviour and communication separately, probably because communication within human groups is often related strictly to the passage of information, and is frequently divorced from any other social behaviour (53). Some authors have assumed that this distinction can be made in cetaceans as well, but the validity of this assumption is not well proven, and I am in full agreement with W. E. Evans and J. Bastian, and D. K. and M. C. Caldwell that we probably make a serious mistake, if we attempt to evaluate and interpret cetacean communications out of the immediate social context, or even if we assume *a priori* that 'purpose' is involved in some or any of their communications (30). If one's studies lead to the irrevocable conclusion that purpose is present, well and good, but to *start* by assuming dolphin communication to involve '*exchange* of information between two or more minds' (56) is simply not sound practice. 'Mind' is a word loaded with far too many anthropomorphic connotations to be used lightly when discussing animal behaviour.

There are several good reasons for opposing the use of such anthropomorphisms right from the outset in this kind of analysis. Evans and Bastian made a particularly significant contribution to this discussion, but the subjective approach still seems to dominate the popular literature with respect to drawing parallels between dolphin and man concerning social behaviour and communication. I want to redress the balance to some extent by highlighting what I consider to be some of the important basic differences. First, it is not too difficult to see that *Homo sapiens* has succeeded because he is, like some other 'higher' primates, a generalist, and a gregarious one at that. He runs moderately well, swims moderately well, fights moderately well and can conceal himself moderately well. There are other mammals which can exceed man's capabilities in any one of those categories and a few excel in all, but they are either not as gregarious as man (for example, tiger or large bears), or not as large (for example, weasels). On the other hand, there are a very few species of mammal, such as wolves, which come close to man both in gregariousness and group-fighting ability. The fear which even the name 'wolf' has inspired in temperate-zone communities is in part a measure of the respect with which it was once regarded. Yet the wolf lacked one supreme advantage – an opposable thumb. Physically the wolf-packs might have been the equals or superiors of the man-packs, but not when met by blows from thrown rocks and thrusts from fire-hardened wooden spears.

There are probably very few biologists who would dispute that man's 'progress', (that is, technological specialization) is owed as much to his thumbs and generalized adaptability as to his large and convoluted cortex. The dolphin, on the other hand, is anatomically highly specialized. The price paid for hydrodynamic efficiency is great – loss of lower limbs, confining the order to one type of habitat, streamlining of the body with marked constraints on potential variation in overall shape; loss of a large percentage of the skin receptors; atrophication of the olfactory sense and probably loss of many of the subtleties of the gustatory sense as well; restriction of mobility of the jaws and tongue, loss of differentiation of the teeth along with the adaptation to patchy supply of fast-swimming food species and, perhaps most important of all, loss of separate, flexible digits with the modification of the pectoral extremities into unified paddle-shaped flippers.

The world in which the dolphin lives is such that the value of vision is relatively restricted, and in one species, the blind river dolphin, vision is virtually lost. Before discussing the role of sound in social behaviour, it is worth mentioning that there are other ways in which individual identification and emotional state can be conveyed, and group cohesion facilitated. First, many delphinids are strikingly marked (Figures 4.14 and 4.15). Some of these patterns have been interpreted as disruptive camouflage, but others seem to serve as highly visible identifying markers under water (30, 60). White areas on the ventral and latero-ventral surfaces of the dolphin body reflect light from the surface quite brilliantly under sunlit conditions, and scatter the light at an angle so that the patches are visible for considerable distances in relatively clear water, even when the outline of the animal as a whole may not be (30). The white patches around the mammary/genital region possibly aid the young in finding the nipples in poor visibility (30), or provide a marking position beside which the calf can swim with maximum protection and some assistance from the hydrodynamic flow around the mother (110). It may be significant that these body markings can develop with age (30, 36), suggesting that what may be adaptive in the adult is not necessarily adaptive in the juvenile. This kind of 'flash recognition' system is simple, exists in many groups of animals, and functions well for gregarious species under different conditions. Nevertheless, many coastal marine and fluvial habitats are extremely turbid with consistently limited visibility; consequently the value of visual signalling cues, so important in man, other primates and many groups of terrestrial mammals, is relatively limited.

Study of cetaceans in the wild or in captivity suggests that tactile contact is an important facet of communication among these animals. Much of their behaviour has been assumed by observers to have a strong sexual connotation, because there is much genital/genital, oro-genital, and extremity/genital contact among all ages and both sexes. I think it worthwhile to point out that, in animals with no hindlimbs and unified pectoral extremities in which there is little ability even to rotate the limb, the protrusive penis of the male cetacean may, in fact, have taken over many of the tactile and exploratory roles for which the forelimb is used in other mammals. Some cetacean species appear to have a rather distinct annual sexual cycle, with great changes in the size and activity of the testes

Figure 4.14   School of *Delphinus delphis* riding the bow wave of the *Regina Maris* off the Pacific coast of Baja California, Mexico. Photograph courtesy of Drs M. and B. Würsig, Santa Cruz, California, USA.

in the male. The apparent sexuality of the contacts may be just an assumption of the observer. Nipping with the teeth and butting with the head are also commonly observed during the interplay between individual delphinids. In some species, the penis, as much as the snout, seems to be used by young male dolphins to explore foreign objects encountered. Pushing, butting and flipper contact, including flipper slaps, are also common aspects of right whale behaviour (86).

The development of the acoustic senses in odontocetes, however, has been so great that the biological success of the group seems assured, short of major ocean habitat disruption in the forseeable future. That dolphins and porpoises emit sounds of different kinds has been known for many

Figure 4.15.   School of *Delphinus delphis* riding the bow wave of the *Regina Maris* off the Pacific coast of Baja California, Mexico. Photograph courtesy of Drs M. and B. Würsig, Santa Cruz, California, USA. (The reflection in the water is actually the safety netting slung along the bowsprit of the vessel.)

years (91), but although studies of their echolocating ability have produced much information, major areas of ignorance remain; even the methods by which these sounds are produced and received is still controversial (see Chapter 2, pp. 38–41).

The literature on dolphin echolocation is now substantial; comprehensive reviews and accounts can be found in recent articles by Ayrapet'yants and Konstantinov (3), Bel'kovich and Dubrovskiy (7), Murchison (66) and Natchigall (68). Methodology and procedure is still a major source of difficulty in this type of experimental work (92). Reverberation in the environment can cause serious problems in the interpretation of results, and the acuity of dolphins in detecting experimental objects can depend on the length of training (the animals greatly improve their performance by learning), and sometimes on unconscious or unintentional 'reinforcement' by the experimenter during the procedures.

Busnel and Dziedzic (16) showed that harbour porpoises could detect and avoid metal wires 0.5 mm in diameter, but experienced considerable difficulties with wires of 0.2 mm. Results from studies on the detection thresholds of echolocating dolphins and porpoises still have a number of controversial aspects. They appear capable of discriminating targets at various ranges to about 5′ (minutes of arc) (7). The maximum range at which they can detect objects at the 75 per cent correct-response level seems to depend on the period of training, their familiarity with the experimental environment and the nature of the target. There is no 'single-target dimension', and the size, shape and material composition of the target must be taken into account (68). A number of workers have accepted as an approximate standard the ability to detect a theoretical school of 4000 mackerel or some other fish, of 19 cm individual length, in lateral aspect (7). Murchison (66) calculated an average maximum detection range of about 292 metres by *Tursiops truncatus* for this target; this figure can be compared with estimated values of 100 metres and 350 metres by Russian workers. Bel'kovich and Dubrovskiy (7) also concluded that the maximum range for detection of steel or lead spheres 3 mm in diameter was from 3.0–3.5 metres, and for 12.7 mm spheres, between 7.5 and 9.0 metres.

A number of sounds not associated with 'voice' as such are used by cetaceans for various purposes. Leaping is common among delphinids, and the noise carries a long way under water; this may be one way in which social cohesion may be maintained over moderate distances (116). Leaping or breaching has fascinated observers for many years (96), and there has been much speculation about its 'purpose', but in fact it seems likely that it is just another method of generating a recognizable sound. Tail-slapping is another facet of this kind of behaviour, which can sometimes indicate alarm or distress (20), as can the 'jaw clap', common in bottlenose (20, 21) and white whales (62). Presentation of various body positions is another important way in which those animals can communicate intent or emotional state (30).

Delphinid intracephalic sound generation is a complex problem (see Chapter 2, pp. 38–41). Basically, however, whatever the method of production, it seems reasonable to classify the emissions into only two general categories. First, there are various types of pulsed sounds, which include those referred to by writers as 'yelps' (a male sound associated with sexual arousal), 'squawks, squeaks, yaps and barks'. The latter is a rather high-energy sound which is associated with alarm (24), and travels a long way under water. The controlled rapid-train emissions associated with echolocation also appeared to be produced more or less in the same manner as the others listed above. The second type of emission is a family of pure tone whistles. Because delphinids have been recorded making these simultaneously with the 'click-trains' of echolocation, there is speculation that they are produced at a different site within the head region.

The squawks and similar sounds all seem to convey some information about emotional content (21), and they are often heard being produced when animals in captivity are anticipating food, when juveniles are engaged in play activity, or when one adult interferes with another. The pure tone whistles, on the other hand, are rarely emitted under these circumstances, and some have argued that they constitute language. This is where we enter an area of major controversy, and it is important to bear in mind that most studies have been made on captive, not wild animals. The conclusions of authors who have carried out work in this field fall into three groups; those who believe that there is a dolphin language (for example, J. C. Lilly (56)); those who regard these sounds as quasi-language (for example, R.-G. Busnel (15), and J. J. Dreher (27, 28)); and finally those who regard the case for language at best non-proven, or not supported by experimental evidence at all (for example, D. K. and M. C. Caldwell (21, 22)). It may or may not be significant that one of the most 'phylogenetically primitive' or archaic cetaceans, *Inia geoffrensis*, does not appear to make pure tone whistles (23). However, the fact that *Inia* is a non-social species must also be taken into consideration.

R.-G. Busnel provided an analogy between delphinid whistling and human whistled languages, such as Mazateco and Silbo-Gomero, but obviously doubted that the whistles, even at best, could represent much more than pseudo-language, because of the absence of syntax to convey meaning and sequences of correspondences (15). Even recent reports of apparent use of syntax by chimpanzees and gorillas (80, 89, 90, 103) has been doubted by some workers (102). In a recent article of considerable interest, Epstein and his co-workers (29) suggested that pigeons were capable of communicating information by means of learned symbols, and that one bird appeared to request information of the other in the experiments. Nevertheless, by the authors' own admission, this 'conversational exchange' could also be explained by the prevailing contingencies of reinforcement during the experiment. We must continue to evaluate such work very cautiously indeed. With respect to delphinids, Dreher and Evans (28) were reasonably certain that a whistle with a steadily rising contour was associated with search behaviour, that a rising then falling whistle indicated that an animal was disturbed by something, and that a falling contour indicated acute distress or fright. This does not constitute language, by any means. A. G. Taruski (99) found seven contour categories of whistle in the Atlantic pilot whale; of these, two may have conveyed unidentified information (perhaps of emotional state) but were relatively rare. The other five all appeared to be related to individual signature-type signalling. Taruski also argued that all contours were in fact part of a broad continuum, rather than there being discrete types as suggested by Dreher and Evans.

One author has suggested that the pulsed clicks may function in digital language, and that click-trains might be rather like hieroglyphs (14). Once again, we find the same old assumption that there *must* be a dolphin language. His idea is ingenious; but the stereotypy one finds in sonograms of click-trains hardly supports it, unfortunately. The same author goes on to talk about the psychological pressures that exist to go on regarding the whales as 'lower' animals. I would contend that there also exists, on the other hand, a deep psychological 'need' among segments of our society to 'find' another intelligence (13, 56). The two balance, and one must then insist on the objective approach of mundane scientific method, inadequate and loaded as it is with the inconvenience of that same old 'burden of proof' that it always demands.

That some cetacean sounds, including some of the pure tone whistles, are related to individual signature registration appears almost certain. The Caldwells found that in naive dolphins (22) (those fresh into captivity and not subjected to any training procedures) there was considerable stereotypy of the pure tone whistles produced. Although there were slight changes in frequency, speed of emission, or larger changes in intensity, the essential contour remained easily recognizable in a comparative sonagram, or to the experienced ear, as belonging to a particular animal. Some development of these signatures with age was recognized, just as occurs in the nature and form of the 'sexual yelp' of the male bottlenosed dolphin. There is certainly extra information content both in the signature and the yelp; the emotional state of the animal can be conveyed with the intensity of the whistle, and a female could probably gauge the emotional state and maturity or experience of a male by the type of yelp uttered (80). Shortly after a calf is born the mother bottlenose dolphin whistles constantly, apparently to familiarize and condition the calf to her signature (21).

The Caldwells have rightly stressed the importance of the *context* within which dolphin sounds are emitted. The same sound can have several different meanings depending on circumstances. The way in which it is interpreted will vary according to accompanying body gestures or changes in body position. Although dolphins have lost the ability to convey emotions by facial expressions, other than by open-mouth display, they still have a significant display of 'body language'. The latter is an aspect of human communication which behaviourists have only recently started to take seriously (30), although it seems certain that this type of communication was evolved long before transmission of any verbal messages. Furthermore, in the dolphin's world, as in our own, a sudden silence can convey as much abundant meaning as a change in vocalization. Combinations of body postures and changes in the intensity or frequency of signature could add to the information which could be conveyed. Such 'composite' behaviour is regarded as of overwhelming importance in primates (58). It is quite possible that the pulsed sounds of dolphins also convey significant information through modulation, perhaps giving shades of emotional intensity through variation in emission intensity; this is known to occur in rhesus monkeys (84). Burst pulse emissions may be used to produce signature information in sperm whales (109). Some authors have published data suggesting that 'dialects' can be identified in animals from different regions (62); this is not unexpected. D. Morgan, studying white whale emissions in the wild, found that different types of simple white whale sounds, played back in various sequences, caused different reactions; he suggested that this was evidence for primitive syntax in the signalling of these animals. Obviously there are other possible explanations, and his interpretations were cautious.

First, let us consider the nature of cetacean communication. There is no doubt of the great importance to any animal of obtaining and storing information about its environment. This information can be broadcast by an individual animal if it can signal. The animal may identify itself, or at least its kind and its presence, to attract a mate, or to warn away potential competitors. On the negative side, such calling may attract predators. Can we go further, as Lilly did (54, 55), and propose that the *purpose* for signalling in bottlenosed dolphins is to evoke a response in other individuals? The Caldwells and Evans and Bastian, think not. The value of the calling and the broadcasting of information is that it can provide each individual dolphin with what it needs to know about its environment and the location of its own social group. It is a major conceptual point of departure, even though some readers may not realize it, to advance directly to an assumption that there is a conscious *intent* to convey that knowledge to others, regardless of the fact that the knowledge *may* be conveyed. Evans and Bastian detail some experiments with segregated dolphins, one trained, the other naive, which at first sight appeared to show purposeful transmission of information from one to the other. Yet, after further experimentation involving extensive routines, it became evident that the trained animal, despite what the lay person might have assumed from the initial results, obviously had no grasp of the essential consequences of her actions (30). On the basis of these results one can ask the vital question with respect to succorant behaviour: does the animal aiding a distressed school-mate really *understand* the consequences of helping? There are significant observational data to suggest that succorant behaviour is automatic in female dolphins, an essentially mindless response to certain triggering stimuli, as in the example given earlier of a female bottlenosed dolphin which carried a shark on its melon, taking it to the surface over and over again for days. It is *not* in fact necessary to postulate that the animal has to understand what it does in order for succorant behaviour towards peers to evolve, as long as it confers selective advantage. There are similar records of females taking stillborn calves to the surface over and over again for many hours, and of one doing this with a partly decomposed head (20).

This, I suppose, brings us to the question of cetacean intelligence, which raises immediately the thorny and hoary problem of defining the concept. All animals can be shown to be intelligent to some degree, if one operates on an absolute scale. What we are really asking, of course, is 'Are dolphins as intelligent as man, and if not, how intelligent are they, relative to man, or higher primates?' Some authors insist that the answer to the first question is yes (56); others, myself included, cannot see that the experimental and *objective* behavioural observations support this supposition of high dolphin intelligence; in fact they frequently suggest the opposite. Dolphins can perform quite complex tasks. Bottlenosed dolphins, in particular, are superb mimics, can memorize long routines, and are amenable to training. They are not superb at solving problems, merely quite good by higher vertebrate standards (51) and, as might well be expected, their auditory learning skills are considerable (104). They have been ranked at about the same level as the elephant in test scoring (45). Certainly some dolphin species exhibit individual behaviour of some complexity, and they sometimes spontaneously innovate. But so do many other mammals, a point which tends to be forgotten. I used to have a cat which (despite the 90 per cent sensory cortex in his little brain) learned spontaneously to open doors. Opening doors was an act which now and then brought results in the form of food to which he did not normally have access. But did he have a '*plan*'? He would sometimes open the bedroom door and then stand looking rather bewildered. *Purpose* and *intent* imply some foreknowledge of the specific results of specific actions. The more definitive studies on dolphin behaviour suggest (despite statements to the contrary) that dolphins have not yet been demonstrated to have thought processes of this kind.

Some workers have explored the anatomical route, pointing to the large proportional size of the brain (this is not true for all cetaceans, incidentally), the high degree of convolution of the cerebral cortex and the zonal differentiation (38, 49, 50, 63, 77) as possible evidence of the high intelligence of dolphins, especially since some parallels with primate organization were noted (42, 55). Other recent work, however, also seems to point to significant organizational differences (46, 64). The neurone density in most cetacean brains is not particularly high, and larger brain size does not seem to be correlated with increased neurone density (43, 106). Although the cortex is extensive, it is likely to be taken up with the processing of acoustic information, and there is some reason to believe that these data may be more 'cumbersome' to store and retrieve than visual information. In several respects other than neurone density, the cortex seems to be roughly equivalent in development to that of the elephant (43, 106). The distribution of large pyramidal motor cells resembles that in the ungulates and carnivores. There are other descriptive and interpretive studies which provide evidence that the dolphin brain is essentially different from ours in many significant respects, for example in the thin limbic cortex, weak vertical striation and absence of primate-type granule cells (46).

SUMMARY

Are we, then, in a position to draw some tentative conclusions about cetacean social structure, communication and intelligence? There is a tendency for authors to continue prevaricating, suggesting that more and more information is needed before decisions can be made. I think that certain broad conclusions, however, *can* be drawn at this time.

Statements that assume the existence of a high order of social evolution in the Cetacea are, frankly, not really supported to any extent by the observations of free-ranging populations. The social structure of odontocete populations is often fluid, and in the one species (sperm whale) where some evidence exists for stability of school structure for long periods, we find a polygynous mating system operating, with the males playing virtually no social role, no male-offspring bond, and little evidence of behavioural or social complexity beyond that of an ungulate herd. Mysticete behaviour and social structure is even less complex. It is hard to see how on any criterion they could be ranked much 'higher' than elephants or hippopotami.

Saayman and Tayler (87, 101) studying the movements of humpbacked dolphin groups off the coast of South Africa, have suggested that the fluid nature of the social groupings indicates perhaps, like the society of chimpanzees (39, 70), that the 'unseen' societal bonds are so strong that they can survive long periods of separation. I do not think that the data derived from studies of bottlenosed dolphins by Bernd Würsig necessarily provide support for such a view. The alternative and simpler conclusion, of course, is that the bonds are loose, and animals wander in and out of areas, or depart for good to seek new territories for feeding, because a society does not exist at all in the primate sense. Watson (110) found that harbour porpoises might spend as much as 97 per cent of the daylight hours in apparent foraging behaviour, or simple movement from one feeding area to another. 'Greeting' rituals between groups have been described, but one sees this in dogs too, even in animals that do not know one another. Lowering the head and tail-wagging all serve to minimize potential aggressive behaviour. Gregariousness is strongly adaptive, as indicated earlier, and the evolution of signalling which attracted animals to feeding areas would also be adaptive, but it is not necessary to go on from there to postulate that they are intentionally *calling* one another, even if the same effect is achieved. Such a system can evolve without any intent being present.

With respect to 'communication', we know that cetaceans gather, accumulate and (perhaps unwittingly) broadcast information about their environment. Such evidence as we have suggests that 'intent', as we understand the term, is lacking in this broadcasting. They can signature, both vocally and by body language, and this facilitates social cohesion and recognition of emotional condition. Studies to date of their sound production do not, sadly, even begin to produce evidence of the existence of a 'language' that parallels those of *Homo sapiens*, with their rich variety of syntax.

Finally, where then is the boundary line between the level of intelligence determinable in dolphins on the basis of present information and that of *Homo sapiens*? If I may borrow and embellish a phrase from a paper by the Caldwells, there is abundant evidence that dolphins communicate information about 'what', 'where' and 'who'. There is no substantive evidence that they transmit information about 'when', 'how', or 'why'. So, no matter what some might wish to believe, with respect to Kipling's 'six honest serving men' of learning and intellect (47), the dolphin appears to be three servants short.

References

1 Amundin, B. and Amundin, M. 1971. 'Några etologiska iakttagelser over tumlaren, *Phocoena phocoena* (L.), i fångenskap', *Zool. Revy*, vol. 33, pp. 51–9.

2 Andrews, R. C. 1914. 'Monographs of the Pacific Cetacea. 1. The California gray whale (*Rhachiantectes glaucus* Cope)', *Mem. Am. Mus. Nat. Hist.* (n.s.), vol. 1, pp. 229–87.

3 Ayrapet'yants, E. Sh. and Konstantinov, A. I. 1974. *Echolocation in nature, Nauka,* Leningrad, English translation JPRS 63328.

4 Bartholomew, G. A. 1970. 'A model for the evolution of pinniped polygeny', *Evolution*, vol. 24, pp. 546–59.

5 Bateson, G. 1966. 'Problems in cetacean and other mammalian communication' in K. S. Norris (ed.), *Whales, Dolphins, and Porpoises*, Berkeley and Los Angeles, University of California Press, pp. 569–79.

6 Bateson, G. 1974. 'Observations of a cetacean community' in J. McIntyre (ed.), *Mind in the Waters*, Toronto, McClelland & Stewart, pp. 146–65.

7 Bel'kovitch, B. M. and Dubrovskiy, N. A. 1976. *Sensory bases of cetacean orientation,* Nauka, Leningrad, English translation JPRS L/7157.

8 Benjaminsen, T. and Christensen, I. 1979. 'The natural history of the bottlenose whale, *Hyperoodon ampullatus* Forster' in H. E. Winn and B. L. Olla (eds.), *Behavior of Marine Animals – Current Perspectives in Research. Vol. 3 : Cetaceans,* New York, Plenum Press, pp. 143–64.

9 Berzin, A. A. 1972. *The Sperm Whale*, translated by E. Hoz and Z. Blake, Jerusalem, Israel Program for Scientific Translations.

10 Best, P. B. 1979. 'Social organization in sperm whales, *Physeter macrocephalus*' in H. E. Winn and B. L. Olla (eds.), *Behavior of Marine Animals – Current Perspectives in Research. Vol. 3 : Cetaceans,* New York, Plenum Press, pp. 227–89.

11 Bourlière, F. 1952. 'Classification et caractéristiques des principaux types de groupements sociaux chez les vertébrés sauvages' in *Structure et physiologie des sociétés animales,* Paris, *Colloq, int. Cent. nat. Rech. sci.,* vol. 34, Recherche Scientifique, pp. 71–9.

12 Breder, C. M. 1959. 'Studies on social groupings in fishes', *Bull. Am. Mus. Nat. Hist.,* vol. 117, pp. 395–481.

13 Brenner, M. 1974. 'Say "Rooo-beee!"', in J. McIntyre (ed.), *Mind in the Waters,* Toronto, McClelland & Stewart, pp. 186–90.

14 Bunnell, S. 1974. 'The evolution of cetacean intelligence' in J. McIntyre (ed.), *Mind in the Waters*, Toronto, McClelland & Stewart, pp. 52–66.

15 Busnel, R.-G. 1966. 'Information in the human whistled language and sea mammal whistling' in K. S. Norris (ed.), *Whales, Dolphins, and Porpoises*, Berkeley and Los Angeles, University of California Press, pp. 544–68.

16 Busnel, R.-G. and Dziedzic, A. 1966. 'Acoustic signals of the pilot whale *Globicephala melaena* and of the porpoises *Delphinus delphis* and *Phocaena phocaena*' in K. S. Norris (ed.), *Whales, Dolphins, and Porpoises*, Berkeley and Los Angeles, University of California Press, pp. 607–46.

17 Caldwell, D. K., Caldwell, M. C. and Rice, D. W. 1966. 'Behavior of the sperm whale, *Physeter catodon* L.' in K. S. Norris (ed.), *Whales, Dolphins, and Porpoises*, Berkeley and Los Angeles, University of California Press, pp. 677–717.

18 Caldwell, M. C., Brown, D. H. and Caldwell, D. K. 1963. 'Intergeneric behavior by a captive pilot whale', *Contrib. Sci. Los Angeles County Mus.,* vol. 70, pp. 1–12.

19 Caldwell, M. C. and Caldwell, D. K. 1964. 'Experimental studies on factors involved in care-giving behavior in three species of the cetacean family Delphinidae', *Bull. S. California Acad. Sci.,* vol. 63, pp. 1–20.

20 Caldwell, M. C. and Caldwell, D. K. 1966. 'Epimeletic (care-giving) behaviour in

Cetacea' in K. S. Norris (ed.), *Whales, Dolphins, and Porpoises*, Berkeley and Los Angeles, University of California Press, pp. 755–89.

21   Caldwell, M. C. and Caldwell, D. K. 1967. 'Intraspecific transfer of information via the pulsed sound in captive odontocete cetaceans' in R.-G. Busnel (ed.), *Les Systemes sonars animaux*, Frascati, Sept. 1966, Proc. Symp., pp. 879–936.

22   Caldwell, M. C. and Caldwell, D. K. 1968. 'Vocalization of naive captive dolphins in small groups', *Science*, vol. 159, pp. 1121–3.

23   Caldwell, M. C., Caldwell, D. K. and Evans, W. E. 1966. 'Sounds and behavior of captive Amazon freshwater dolphins, *Inia geoffrensis*', *Contrib. Sci. Los Angeles County Mus.*, vol. 108, pp. 1–24.

24   Caldwell, M. C., Haugen, R. M. and Caldwell, D. K. 1962. 'High-energy sound associated with fright in the dolphin', *Science*, vol. 138, pp. 907–8.

25   Clarke, R. 1956. 'Sperm whales of the Azores', *Discovery*, Rep. 28, pp. 237–98.

26   Dawbin, W. H. 1959. 'New Zealand and South Pacific whale marking and recoveries to the end of 1958', *Norsk Hvalfangsttid.*, vol. 48, pp. 213–38.

27   Dreher, J. J. 1966. 'Cetacean communication: small-group experiment' in K. S. Norris (ed.), *Whales, Dolphins, and Porpoises*, Berkeley and Los Angeles, University of California Press, pp. 503–9.

28   Dreher, J. J. and Evans, W. E. 1964. 'Cetacean communication' in W. N. Tavolga (ed.), *Marine Bioacoustics*, Vol. II, New York, Pergamon Press, pp. 373–93.

29   Epstein, R., Lanza, R. P. and Skinner, B. F. 1980. 'Symbolic communication between two pigeons', *Science*, vol. 207, pp. 543–5.

30   Evans, W. E. and Bastian, J. 1969. 'Marine mammal communication: social and ecological factors' in H. T. Andersen (ed.), *The Biology of Marine Mammals*, New York, Academic Press, pp. 425–75.

31   Fichtelius, K.-E. and Sjölander, S. 1972. *Smarter than Man?*, New York, Ballantine Books.

32   Gambell, R. 1968. 'Aerial observations of sperm whale behaviour based on observations, notes and comments by K. J. Pinkerton', *Norsk Hvalfangsttid.*, vol. 57, pp. 126–38.

33   Gardner, B. T. and Gardner, R. A. 1975. 'Evidence for sentence constituents in the early utterances of child and chimpanzee', *J. Exp. Psychol.: General*, vol. 104, pp. 244–67.

34   Gaskin, D. E. 1971. 'Composition of schools of sperm whales *Physeter catodon* Linn. east of New Zealand' *N.Z.J. mar. Freshwat. Res.*, vol. 4, pp. 456–71.

35   Gaskin, D. E. 1971. 'Distribution and movements of sperm whales (*Physeter catodon* L.) in the Cook Strait region of New Zealand', *Norw. J. Zool.*, vol. 19, pp. 241–59.

36   Gaskin, D. E. 1972. *Whales, Dolphins and Seals – with special reference to the New Zealand Region*, Auckland, Heinemann Educational Books (N.Z.).

37   Gaskin, D. E. and Watson, A. P. Unpublished data.

38   Gihr, M. and Pilleri, G. 1969. 'On the anatomy and biometry of *Stenella styx* Gray and *Delphinus delphis* L. (Cetacea, Delphinidae) of the western Mediterranean' in G. Pilleri (ed.), *Investigations on Cetacea* Vol. I., Berne, Waldau, pp. 15–65.

39   Goodall, J. 1965. 'Chimpanzees of the Gombe Stream Reserve' in I. DeVore (ed.), *Primate Behavior: Field Studies of Monkeys and Apes*, New York, Holt, Rinehart & Winston, pp. 425–73.

40   Hussain, F. 1973. 'Whatever happened to dolphins?', *New Scientist*, vol. 57, pp. 182–4.

41   Irvine, A. B., Scott, M. D., Wells, R. S., Kaufmann, J. H. and Evans, W. E. 1979. *A study of the movements and activities of the Atlantic bottlenose dolphin, Tursiops truncatus, including an evaluation of tagging techniques*, Washington, final report for US Marine Mammal Commission Washington, contracts MM4AC004 and MM5AC0018.

42 Jacobs, M. S. 1974. 'The whale brain: input and behavior' in J. McIntyre (ed.), *Mind in the Waters*, Toronto, McClelland & Stewart, pp. 78–83.

43 Jansen, J. and Jansen, J. K. S. 1969. 'The nervous system of Cetacea' in H. T. Andersen (ed.), *The Biology of Marine Mammals*, New York, Academic Press, pp. 175–252.

44 Kasuya, T. and Kureha, K. 1979. 'The population of finless porpoise in the Inland Sea of Japan', *Sci. Rep. Whales Res. Inst.*, vol. 31, pp. 1–44.

45 Kellogg, W. N. and Rice, C. E. 1966. 'Visual discrimination and problem solving in a bottlenose dolphin' in K. S. Norris (ed.), *Whales, Dolphins, and Porpoises*, Berkeley and Los Angeles, University of California Press, pp. 731–54.

46 Kesarev, U. S. 1969. '(Structural organization of the limbic cortex of the dolphin brain)', *Arkh. Anat. Gistol. Embriol.*, vol. 56, pp. 28–35.

47 Kipling, R. 1910. *Just-so Stories. The Works of Rudyard Kipling*. Vol. XX, New York, Charles Scribner's Sons.

48 Kleinenberg, S. E., Yablokov, A. V., Bel'kovich, B. M. and Tarasevitch, M. N. 1969. *Beluga* (Delphinapterus leucas), *investigation of the species*, Jerusalem, Israel Program for Scientific Translations.

49 Kraus, C. and Pilleri, G. 1969. 'Zur Histologie der Grosshirnrinde von *Balaenoptera borealis* Lesson (Cetacea, Mysticeti)' in G. Pilleri (ed.), *Investigations on Cetacea*, vol. I, Berne, Waldau, pp. 151–70.

50 Kruger, L. 1966. 'Specialized features of the cetacean brain' in K. S. Norris (ed.), *Whales, Dolphins, and Porpoises*, Berkeley and Los Angeles, University of California Press, pp. 232–54.

51 Krushinskii, L. V., Dashevski, B. A., Krushinskaya, N. L. and Dmitreva, I. L. 1972. 'A study on the ability of the dolphin *Tursiops truncatus* (Montagu) to operate with the empirical dimensionality of geometric figures', *Dokl. Akad. Nauk SSSR*, vol. 204, pp. 755–8, translation by Consultants Bureau (Plenum Press, New York).

52 Leatherwood, J. S. and Walker, W. A. 1979. 'The northern right whale dolphin *Lissodelphis borealis* Peale in the eastern North Pacific' in H. E. Winn and B. L. Olla (eds.), *Behaviour of Marine Animals – Current Perspectives in Research. Vol. 3: Cetaceans*, New York, Plenum Press, pp. 85–141.

53 Lenneberg, E. H. 1967. *Biological Foundations of Language*, New York, Wiley.

54 Lilly, J. C. 1962. 'Vocal behavior of the bottlenose dolphin', *Proc. Am. Philos. Soc.*, vol. 160, pp. 520–9.

55 Lilly, J. C. 1963. 'Distress call of the bottlenose dolphin: stimuli and evoked behavioral responses', *Science*, vol. 139, pp. 116–18.

56 Lilly, J. C. 1967. *The Mind of the Dolphin: A Nonhuman Intelligence*, New York, Doubleday.

57 Lockyer, C. 1975. 'Estimates of growth and energy budget for the sperm whale, *Physeter catodon*', FAO of the UN, Scientific Consultation on Marine Mammals, Bergen, Norway, 31 August–9 September 1976, document ACMRR/MM/SC38.

58 Marler, P. 1965. 'Communication in monkeys and apes' in I. DeVore (ed.), *Primate Behavior: Field Studies of Monkeys and Apes*, New York, Holt, Rinehart & Winston, pp. 544–84.

59 Mitchell, E. 1970. 'Pigmentation pattern evolution in delphinid cetaceans: an essay in adaptive coloration', *Can. J. Zool.*, vol. 48, pp. 717–40.

60 Mitchell, E. 1977. 'Evidence that the northern bottlenose whale is depleted', *Rep. Int. Whal. Commn.*, vol. 27, pp. 195–201.

61 Miyazaki, N. and Nishiwaki, M. 1978. 'School structure of the striped dolphin off the Pacific coast of Japan', *Sci. Rep. Whales Res. Inst.*, vol. 30, pp. 65–115.

62 Morgan, D. W. 1979. 'The vocal and behavioral reactions of the beluga, *Delphinapterus leucas*, to playback of its sounds' in H. E. Winn and B. L. Olla (eds.), *Behavior of Marine Animals – Current Perspectives in Research. Vol. 3: Cetaceans*, New York, Plenum Press, pp. 311–43.

63   Morgane, P. J. 1974. 'The whale brain: the anatomical basis of intelligence' in J. McIntyre (ed.), *Mind in the Waters*, Toronto, McClelland & Stewart, pp. 84–93.

64   Morgane, P. J., Jacobs, M. S. and McFarland, W. L. 1980. 'The anatomy of the brain of the bottlenose dolphin (*Tursiops truncatus*). Surface configurations of the telecephalon of the bottlenose dolphin with comparative observations in four other cetacean species', *Brain. Res. Bull.*, vol. 5, Suppl. no. 3.

65   Morejohn, G. V. 1979. 'The natural history of Dall's porpoise in the North Pacific Ocean' in H. E. Winn and B. L. Olla (eds.), *Behavior of Marine Animals – Current Perspectives in Research. Vol. 3 : Cetaceans*, New York, Plenum Press, pp. 45–83.

66   Murchison, A. E. 1980. 'Detection range and range resolution of echolocating bottlenose porpoise (*Tursiops truncatus*)' in R.-G. Busnel and J. F. Fish (eds.), *Animal Sonar Systems*, New York and London, Plenum Press, published in co-operation with NATO Scientific Affairs Division, pp. 43–70.

67   Nansen, F. 1924. *Blant Sel og Bjørn*, Kristiana, J. Dybwads Forlag.

68   Natchigall, P. E. 1980. 'Odontocete echolocation performance on object size, shape and material' in R.-G. Busnel and J. F. Fish (eds.), *Animal Sonar Systems*, New York and London, Plenum Press, published in co-operation with NATO Scientific Affairs Division, pp. 71–95.

69   Nemoto, T. 1964. 'School of baleen whales in the feeding areas', *Sci. Rep. Whales Res. Inst.*, vol. 18, pp. 89–110.

70   Nishida, T. 1968. 'The social group of wild chimpanzees in the Mahali mountains', *Primates*, vol. 9, pp. 167–224.

71   Nishiwaki, M. 1962. 'Aerial photographs show sperm whales' interesting habits', *Norsk Hvalfangsttid.*, vol. 51, pp. 393–8.

72   Norris, K. S. and Dohl, T. P. 1980. 'The behavior of the Hawaiian spinner dolphin, *Stenella longirostris*', *Fishery Bulletin*, vol. 77, pp. 821–49.

73   Norris, K. S. and Prescott, J. H. 1961. 'Observations on Pacific cetaceans of California and Mexican waters', *Univ. Calif. Publ. Zool.*, vol. 63, pp. 291–401.

74   Ohsumi, S. 1971. 'Some investigations on the school structure of sperm whale', *Sci. Rep. Whales Res. Inst.*, vol. 23, pp. 1–25.

75   Payne, R. S. 1972. *Report from Patagonia : the right whales*, New York, Zoological Society.

76   Payne, R. S. and McVay, S. 1971. 'Songs of humpback whales', *Science*, vol. 173, pp. 587–97.

77   Pilleri, G. and Busnel, R.-G. 1968. 'Brain/body weight ratios in Delphinidae', *Acta Anat.*, vol. 73, pp. 92–7.

78   Pilleri, G. and Knuckey, J. 1969. 'The distribution, navigation and orientation by the sun of *Delphinus delphis* L. in the western Mediterranean', *Experimentia*, vol. 24, pp. 394–6.

79   Pippard, L. and Malcolm, H. 1978. *White whales* (Delphinapterus leucas) *observations on their distribution, population and critical habitats in the St Lawrence and Saguenay rivers*, Department of Indian and Northern Affairs and Parks Canada. Project C1632, Contract 76/190.

80   Premack, D. 1971. 'On the assessment of language competence in the chimpanzee' in A. M. Schrier and F. Stollintz (eds.), *Behavior of Non-human Primates*, New York, Academic Press, pp. 185–228.

81   Ralls, K. 1976. 'Mammals in which females are larger than males', *Quart. Rev. Biol.*, vol. 51, pp. 245–76.

82   Rand, A. L. 1954. 'Social feeding behavior of birds', *Fieldiana Zool.*, vol. 36, pp. 1–71.

83   Reynolds, V. and Reynolds, F. 1965. 'Chimpanzees of the Budongo Forest' in I. DeVore (ed.), *Primate Behaviour : Field Studies of Monkeys and Apes*, New York, Holt Rinehart & Winston, pp. 368–424.

84 Rowell, T. W. 1962. 'Agonistic noises in the rhesus monkey (*Macaca mulatta*)', *Symp. Zool. Soc. Lond.*, vol. 8, pp. 91–6.

85 Saayman, G. S., Bower, D. and Tayler, C. K. 1972. 'Observations on inshore and pelagic dolphins on the south-eastern Cape coast of South Africa', *Koedoe*, vol. 15, pp. 1–24.

86 Saayman, G. S. and Tayler, C. K. 1973. 'Some behaviour patterns of the southern right whale *Eubalaena australis*', *Sonder. Z.f. Saugietier. Bd.*, vol. 38, pp. 172–83.

87 Saayman, G. S. and Tayler, C. K. 1979. 'The socioecology of humpback dolphins (*Sousa* sp.)' in H. E. Winn and B. L. Olla (eds.), *Behavior of Marine Animals – Current Perspectives in Research. Vol. 3: Cetaceans*, New York, Plenum Press, pp. 165–226.

88 Saayman, G. S., Tayler, C. K. and Bower, D. 1973. 'Diurnal activity cycles in captive and free-ranging Indian Ocean bottlenose dolphins (*Tursiops aduncus* Ehrenburg)', *Behaviour*, vol. 44, pp. 212–33.

89 Savage-Rumbaugh, E. S., Rumbaugh, D. M. and Boysen, S. 1980. 'Do apes use language?', *Amer. Scientist*, vol. 68, pp. 49–61.

90 Savage-Rumbaugh, E. S. and Rumbaugh, D. M. 1980. 'Reference: the linguistic essential', *Science*, vol. 210, pp. 922–5.

91 Schevill, W. E. and Watkins, W. A. 1962. 'Whale and porpoise voices', *Woods Hole Oceanogr. Inst.*, contr. no. 1320 (*Nat. Hist.*), vol. 9, pp. 11–49.

92 Schusterman, R. J. 1980. 'Behavioral methodology in echolocation by marine mammals' in R.-G. Busnel and J. F. Fish (eds.), *Animal Sonar Systems*, New York and London, Plenum Press, published in co-operation with NATO Scientific Affairs Division, pp. 11–41.

93 Sergeant, D. E. 1962. 'The biology of the pilot or pothead whale *Globicephala melaena* (Traill) in Newfoundland waters', *Bull. Fish. Res. Bd. Canada*, vol. 132, pp. 1–84.

94 Siebenaler, J. B. and Caldwell, D. K. 1956. 'Cooperation among adult dolphins', *J. Mammal.*, vol. 37, pp. 126–8.

95 Skutch, A. F. 1961. 'Helpers among birds', *Condor*, vol. 63, pp. 198–226.

96 Slijper, E. J. 1962. *Whales*, London, Hutchinson.

97 Stenuit, R. 1972. *The Dolphin, Cousin to Man*, New York, Bantam Books.

98 Tarasevitch, M. N. 1967. '(On the structure of cetacean groupings. I. Structure of the groupings of *Physeter catodon* males)', *Zool. Zhur.*, vol. 46, pp. 24–131.

99 Taruski, A. G. 1979. 'The whistle repertoire of the North Atlantic pilot whale (*Globicephala melaena*) and its relationship to behavior and environment' in H. E. Winn and B. L. Olla (eds.), *Behavior of Marine Animals – Current Perspectives in Research. Vol. 3: Cetaceans*, New York, Plenum Press, pp. 345–68.

100 Tavolga, M. C. 1966. 'Behavior of the bottlenose dolphin (*Tursiops truncatus*): social interactions in a captive colony' in K. S. Norris (ed.), *Whales, Dolphins, and Porpoises*, Berkeley and Los Angeles, University of California Press, pp. 718–30.

101 Tayler, C. K. and Saayman, G. S. 1972. 'The social organization and behaviour of dolphins (*Tursiops aduncus*) and baboons (*Papio ursinus*): some comparisons and assessments', *Ann. Cape Prov. Mus. (Nat. Hist)*, vol. 9, pp. 11–49.

102 Terrace, H. S., Petitto, L. A., Sanders, R. J. and Bever, T. G. 1979. 'Can an ape create a sentence?', *Science*, vol. 206, pp. 891–902.

103 Thompson, C. R. and Church, R. M. 1980. 'An explanation of the language of a chimpanzee', *Science*, vol. 208, pp. 313–14.

104 Thompson, R. K. R. and Herman, L. M. 1977. 'Memory for lists of sounds by the bottle-nosed dolphin: convergence of memory processes with humans?', *Science*, vol. 195, pp. 501–3.

105 Tormosov, D. D. 1975. '(Ecologo-physiological basis of different structures of sperm whale concentrations)' in *Morskie Mlekopitayushchie*, Kiev, pp. 127–9.

106 Tower, D. B. 1954. 'Structural and functional organization of mammalian cerebral

cortex: the correlation of neurone density with brain size. Cortical neurone density in the fin whale (*Balaenoptera physalus* L.) with a note on the cortical neurone density in the Indian elephant', *J. Comp. Neurol.*, vol. 101, pp. 19–51.

107   Wallace, R. A. 1979. *Animal Behavior – Its Development, Ecology, and Evolution*, Santa Monica, Ca, Goodyear Publishing Company.

108   Watkins, W. A. 1977. 'Acoustic behaviour of sperm whales', *Oceanus*, vol. 20, pp. 50–8.

109   Watkins, W. A. and Schevill, W. E. 1977. '*Sperm whale codas*', *J. Acoust. Soc. Am.*, vol. 62, pp. 1485–90.

110   Watson, A. P. 1976. 'The diurnal behaviour of the harbour porpoise (*Phocoena phocoena* L.) in the coastal waters of the Bay of Fundy', M.Sc. thesis, University of Guelph, Ontario.

111   Williams, G. C. 1966. *Adaptation and Natural Selection – A Critique of Some Current Evolutionary Thought*, Princeton, NJ, Princeton University Press.

112   Wilson, E. O. 1975. *Sociobiology*, Cambridge, Mass., Belknap Press, Harvard University Press.

113   Winn, H. E., Edel, R. K. and Taruski, A. G. 1975. 'Population estimate of the humpback whale (*Megaptera novaeangliae*) in the West Indies by visual and acoustic techniques', *J. Fish. Res. Bd. Canada*, vol. 32, pp. 499–506.

114   Würsig, B. 1978. 'Occurrence and group organization of Atlantic bottlenose porpoises (*Tursiops truncatus*) in an Argentine Bay', *Biol. Bull.*, vol. 154, pp. 348–9.

115   Würsig, B. 1979. 'Dolphins', *Scientific American*, vol. 240, pp. 136–48.

116   Würsig, B. and Würsig, M. 1979. 'Behavior and ecology of the bottlenose dolphin, *Tursiops truncatus*, in the South Atlantic', *Fishery Bulletin*, vol. 77, pp. 399–412.

117   Würsig, B. and Würsig, M. 1980. 'Behavior and ecology of the dusky dolphin, *Lagenorhynchus obscurus*, in the South Atlantic', *Fishery Bulletin*, vol. 77, pp. 871–90.

118   Würsig, M., Würsig, B. and Mermoz, J. F. 1977. 'Desplazamientos, comportamiento general y un varamiento de la marsopa espinosa, *Phocoena spinipinnis*, en el Golfo san Jose (Chubut, Argentina)', *Physis*, vol. 36, pp. 71–9.

119   Wynne-Edwards, V. C. 1962. *Animal Dispersion in Relation to Social Behaviour*, Edinburgh and London, Oliver & Boyd.

CHAPTER 5

Evolution of Cetacea

Palaeocene origins and Eocene differentiation

The high degree of morphological and anatomical adaptation to environment found in both living suborders of Cetacea – the Odontoceti (toothed whales) and Mysticeti (baleen whales) – has been the source of discussion and lively controversy among zoologists for decades. Two important questions have been posed: from which group or groups of Mammalia did the Cetacea originate? Did the two living suborders share a common ancestor? A number of workers have made careful anatomical, morphological and osteological comparisons between early unspecialized cetaceans and both living and extinct members of those orders of Mammalia which might conceivably have been directly ancestral to the whales and dolphins (58, 67, 80, 111, 118, 120). More recently, pertinent cytogenetic evidence has been published (5–9, 70) which can be considered in conjunction with somewhat older serological studies (18). My purpose in this section is to review classical and modern data pertaining to the origin of Cetacea, and re-examine the conclusions of the authors concerned.

Mammals demonstrably recognizable as cetaceans first appear in strata of the early Middle Eocene. These animals were primitive in comparison to modern whales and dolphins and less well adapted to a totally aquatic existence. They are classified within a separate and totally extinct suborder Archaeoceti; the name 'zeuglodont', after the generic name *Zeuglodon* applied by Richard Owen (88), is commonly used for some forms. Even by the late Middle and early Upper Eocene archaeocetes such as *Basilosaurus* were so specialized that they could not possibly have been ancestral to modern cetaceans. It is obviously necessary to look further back than the Middle Eocene for the ancestors of these groups.

The oldest verified cetacean remains are of *Pappocetus lugardi* from the Eocene of southern Nigeria and *Protocetus atavus* from the Middle Eocene of Egypt (3, 42, 61, 91). Both species belong to the family Protocetidae, and are quite possibly congeneric (111). *Anglocetus*, based on a fragment of scapula from the Middle Eocene strata of the Isle of Sheppey in southern England, was previously regarded as the earliest cetacean (106), but this remain is now recognized as being part of a bone from a turtle (41).

Another early archaeocete of considerable taxonomic and evolutionary significance was recently described from north-western India as *Indocetus ramani* sp. and *gen. nov.* (96).

The skulls of *Pappocetus, Protocetus* and *Indocetus* are typically zeuglodont: the opening of the nares lies halfway to the orbit in line with the first premolars of the upper jaw; turbinal bones are present; the pterygoid and palatine bones extend the palate posteriorly; a rather wide, terminally arched, supraorbital frontal process extends beyond the jugal; and a distinctive and characteristic saggital crest is present at the median boundary of the parietals, except in *Indocetus* where the frontal and parietal meet at an obtuse angle. In general, the bones of the cranial (and specifically the rostral) region in these three genera are little different in arrangement from those found in other mammals of the late Cretaceous and early Eocene, except for a narrowing of the nasal bones and the posterior rostral area. This narrowing and elongation of the posterior rostral region bears no direct resemblance to the 'telescoping' processes which have occurred in the skulls of odontocetes and mysticetes (80). In both genera of early zeuglodonts we find normal eutherian dentition, with three incisors, a single canine, four premolars and three molars in each jaw (58, 61). The incisors are widely spaced, and the cheek teeth particularly prominent and noteworthy. Most molar and premolar teeth bear a distinct cingulum with a trace of typical mammalian crown. There is a large paracone, and a posterior differentiated cusp that could be a metacone; no protocone is present in *Protocetus* and *Pappocetus* (110), but one is retained in *Indocetus*. In fact, the whole general appearance is that of a fairly typical late Cretaceous–early Eocene 'creodont' or condylarthran mammal, but with widely spaced incisors and large cheek teeth set in a narrow mouth. Specialization towards snapping and grasping of fast-moving prey such as fish, is strongly implied.

Some important groups of terrestrial mammals became differentiated in the late Cretaceous and Palaeocene (119), from ancestors which in turn are thought to have stemmed from an ancient insectivorous stock in the early to Middle Cretaceous. These taxa are all now extinct, but mammalogists are in general agreement that they were quite closely related to the Ungulata. The suborder Arctocyonia is probably ancestral to ungulates and their relatives (112), and the parallel and related suborder Mesonychia seems likely to have been ancestral to the Cetacea (112). These suggested relationships are supported by serological studies which suggest a slight but significant affinity between Artiodactyla and Cetacea (18).

Van Valen (110–12) proposed a specific family, the Mesonychidae, as the group from which the zeuglodonts (and all other cetaceans) diverged at the very end of the Cretaceous, taking to the sea in the Palaeocene. The Mesonychidae not only closely resemble the zeuglodonts in cranial and dental characters, but also fulfil another important requirement for being a possible group of origin for cetaceans; they were clearly differentiated and widespread by the late Cretaceous and Palaeocene. *Indocetus ramani* has several clear mesonychid characteristics (96), and in several respects it retains more primitive features than *Protocetus* or *Pappocetus*. Similarities between archaeocetes and mesonychids are particularly marked in the structure of the teeth. The third premolar of *Pappocetus lugardi* is almost identical to that of the Middle Palaeocene mesonychid *Dissacus navajovius* (111). A common lingual lobe arrangement and paracone structure is shared between the fourth premolar and the first and second molars of the zeuglodont jaw, and those of *Dissacus* and other mesonychids. Van Valen himself pointed out that *D. navajovius* was obviously too specialized with respect to phalange structure to have been a direct ancestor of Cetacea, but concluded that undoubtedly other species will be found which are less specialized. He also noted that there were two particularly important differences between zeuglodont and mesonychid cranial patterns, namely the absence of the preglenoid process in the zeuglodonts, and the zeuglodont divergence in basicranial proportions and arrangement from the mesonychids; however, both these could obviously be strongly adaptive.

Van Valen's arguments for the Hyaenodontidae (as proposed by D. D. Kulu (70), who appeared to be unaware of Van Valen's work), Miacidae, Oxyaenidae, or late Cretaceous insectivorous stock (30), *not* being likely zeuglodont ancestors seem decisive. Although some mesonychids appear to have been secondarily carnivorous (105, 111), a careful study of their anatomy indicates that they are clearly part of the same evolutionary stem as the ungulates (110). Despite the problems that remain, the Mesonychidae appear to be the most promising group for further study of cetacean ancestry, and certainly at present no one seems prepared seriously to argue a case for cetaceans originating other than from some kind of condylarthran stock.

Colonization of the sea

What factors directed the evolutionary progress of the Cetacea back into the sea and which adaptations permitted them to thrive there before the transition was complete? The distribution of the earliest zeuglodont remains suggests that they arose in the relatively restricted western arm of the Tethys in the Palaeocene (more or less approximating to the present position of the Mediterranean–Persian Gulf) and dispersed through the warm shallow coastal waters of the greatly re-enlarged Tethys during the Eocene. At the close of the Cretaceous the great Sea of Tethys still existed, as it had throughout the Mesozoic, as a huge stable warm-water basin extending from present southern and western Europe to the vicinity of northern Australia and South-East Asia. During this long period it functioned as a singularly important centre for evolution and radiation, and a dispersal route for marine and coastal fauna and flora (20, 32). During the Palaeocene, however, the western arm of the Tethys became much constricted, and formed a semi-enclosed shallow sea (29) approximately in the position of the modern Mediterranean.

We can envisage populations of terrestrial condylarthrans (or 'creodonts') colonizing the fringes of the slower-moving rivers emptying into the Southern and Western Tethys, perhaps gathering at trampled watering places as do savanna mammals of the tropics today. The earliest cetacean ancestors were undoubtedly little more aquatic than modern hippopotami and considerably less bulky and specialized. W. H. Flower (39) was one of the first to suggest that the ancestors of Cetacea probably inhabited late Mesozoic marshes. Freshwater and estuarine molluscs and sluggish fish could be grubbed from the mud, but as population pressure on resources became more intense, further selection would take place in favour of those forms with dentition and reflexes suited to exploitation of the faster-swimming nektonic and benthic fish species. If such selection was maintained and intensified over many generations, elimination of forms not totally adapted to a fish-eating diet would occur in a relatively short period of geological time. Selection for mechanisms or behaviour to escape from predators was likely to be of importance (58), but availability of food and habitat resources was probably the decisive factor. With the tremendous wave of mammalian speciation taking place in the Palaeocene and Eocene the pressures on territory and feeding areas were probably locally intense, with one population after another reaching a state of over-abundance and collapsing as a result of changes in ecological balance wrought by the populations themselves. Interactions within riverside communities were undoubtedly very dynamic and always in a state of flux. Exertion of such pressures on the ancestral populations could well stimulate a movement into the sea to exploit niches vacated at the end of the Cretaceous by the vanishing ichthyosaurs, plesiosaurs and mososaurs. Could it be that the whale ancestors were unable to colonize the coastal waters of the Tethys until the large marine reptiles had ceased to be of competitive significance? Alternatively, might not their appearance have contributed to the final decline of such reptiles, in concert with changes in tropical marine climate and food-web composition, correlated with alterations in continental configuration during the later part of the Mesozoic? These are intriguing ideas, but not supported by any direct evidence at present.

Evolutionary change is likely to be initiated during periods of relatively unfavourable conditions when population sizes and ranges are somewhat reduced. Although dealing successfully with their local environment, transitional taxa might be less 'successful' in global and numerical terms than the ancestors from which they had evolved or the forms into which they were evolving. As a consequence they may have restricted distributions requiring very fortuitous fossil discovery. Adaptive radiation, refinement of isolating mechanisms and increases in population sizes, with improved chances for fossilization, would occur subsequent to these critical periods. Nevertheless, some significant objections can be made to such an interpretation of 'transitionals' (48), and the problem remains unresolved.

I believe it is precisely because the evolution of the ancestral condylarthran or 'creodont' forms into cetaceans was rather rapid and geographically localized that the fossil record is so sparse. Many evolutionists now believe that in some animal orders rapid phyletic change may be the rule, rather than the exception (33, 48, 102). Possibly the ancestral forms first had their distributions restricted to island chains in the Western Palaeocene Tethys (Figure 5.1) (46). Sahni and Mishra (96) suggested the western Indian margin of the now Arabian Sea as the probable region within which the primitive archaeocetes first radiated. Although *Indocetus ramani* retains some of the most primitive characteristics of any archaeocete, the balance of evidence, however, indicates that *Indocetus* was probably a relict species even by the Middle Eocene. The Egyptian and Nigerian deposits seem to be older, and the Kutch sediments contain some primitive agorophiid proto-odontocetes, contemporaneous with *Indocetus*. The sediments of the western Kutch within which *Indocetus* remains were found give us some interesting clues concerning the possible habitats of these early true cetaceans. The basal Palaeocene deposits contain terrestrial plant remains and are non-marine in nature. The next, Lower Eocene in age, may not be fully marine. The archaeocetes were deposited in Middle Eocene strata from which *Protosiren* (a primitive sea cow) and one terrestrial mammal remain (probably a moerithiid) were also obtained. This strongly suggests a coastal, perhaps estuarine situation, but obviously somewhere with heavy sediment deposition facilitating fossilization.

W. Schäfer (99) discussed the process of fossilization of cetacean remains at some length; conditions necessary for preservation of a whole skeleton of a marine mammal are the exception rather than the rule, since the majority of animals die in the open sea and bodies in the open sea float for some weeks, fragmenting gradually. Strandings account only for a fraction of the number dying each year. The comparatively restricted land surface areas of small islands and their lack of large rivers and subsequent regions of heavy sediment deposition would not make them likely places

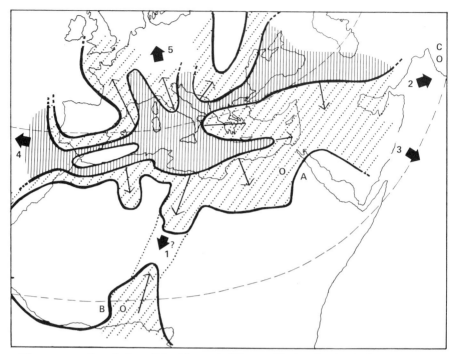

Figure 5.1   Restriction of the Mesozoic Western Tethys Sea in the Palaeocene
(vertical shading), forming the region in which the Cetacea appear to have
evolved. Thin arrows and dotted area indicate the approximate extent of the
temporarily re-enlarged Western Tethys in the Eocene. Circles A, B and C show
the earliest known remains of Eocene archaeocetes. Broad arrows 1, 2, 3, 4 and 5
show possible dispersal routes for early zeuglodonts and perhaps early
odontocetes into the Atlantic Basins, seas around northern Europe, and the
Eastern Tethys, then in transition to becoming the Indian Ocean as we know it
today. Redrawn and modified from the original in Gaskin (46).

for good fossilization of the earliest forms, if they were in fact archipelagic
in origin.

So 'suddenly' there were zeuglodonts. It is most unlikely that they were
as physiologically well adapted to the marine environment as are modern
cetaceans. Even the later archaeocetes were still essentially distributed in
warm water. They were probably capable of only relatively short and
shallow dives. There were apparently basic limitations to the archaeocete
body plan that were unsuited to changing environmental conditions, or
competition from more advanced derived forms – true (albeit primitive)
Odontoceti – or both. The Archaeoceti completely dominated the Eocene,
but began to dwindle in diversity during the Oligocene, though this was an
epoch noted as being one of low diversity of all cetaceans (71, 114) except
in the western South Pacific (40). The early Oligocene archaeocetes were

apparently quite large animals, for example, *Platyosphys* (from the southern European USSR) could have been 15 metres in length or more. The genus *Kekenodon*, from Middle Oligocene strata of New Zealand (65) was by best estimate about 7 metres in length (78). The last archaeocete remains may be those from early or early Middle Miocene of France (61), although the age of the strata in which they were found needs to be reconfirmed. In the course of the Miocene they were totally replaced by odontocetes and mysticetes, the early 'experimental' variants of which were making their appearance by the Middle Oligocene. Both were to become greatly diversified during the Miocene.

The slow deterioration of the warm marine climate of middle-latitude Tethys from conditions optimal for the archaeocete mode of existence, together with intense competitive pressure from other mammals for limited resources, would provide ideal conditions for vigorous selection at the species level (25). Cumulative favourable mutations (increasing the 'raw material' of variation on which natural selection can work) tend to spread most rapidly through isolated and relatively small populations (25). The opening up of what, in effect, represented whole new adaptive zones for this particular group also appears to have favoured very rapid macroevolutionary advances across a broad spectrum of forms (Figure 5.2).

Evolutionary development and characteristics of the suborders with living representatives

With their exceptional resistance to lactic acid accumulation, tolerance of oxygen debt in muscle tissue, high titre of muscle myoglobin for rapid transfer of oxygen to the cellular level, hypodermal blubber layer for food storage and sophisticated thermoregulatory control, the modern whales and dolphins reveal a history of intensive selection and progressive specialization. Those features not directly essential, or useful, in the aquatic environment were eliminated by fairly rapid selection, with much consequent modification of the basic tetrapod mammalian plan. Virtually all pelage, the fully mobile neck, functional hind limbs and ultimately most of the pelvic girdle were lost in this way. The aquatic mode of life favoured posterior and dorsal shift of the external nares with the perfection of methods for sealing them against water (58). The flukes developed as a new and distinct propulsion unit, with horizontal orientation for a dorso-ventral stroke action. The body became progressively more streamlined and in many groups a dorsal fin developed from the dorsal crest of the integument, becoming involved in both hydrodynamic control and thermoregulation, especially in the smaller species.

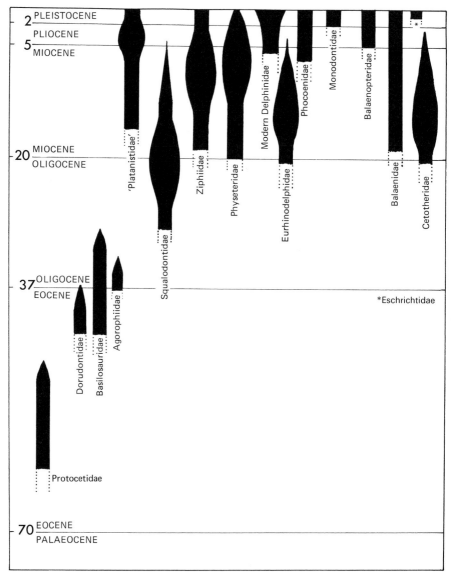

Figure 5.2   Evolutionary history of the major families of Cetacea and their approximate relative diversity (in terms of numbers of valid genera) over time. Data drawn in part from Kellogg (58), and Lipps and Mitchell (71).

1   *Odontoceti (toothed whales)*

Before we can consider the relationships between the two living suborders and the Archaeoceti we first need to pause and examine the characteristics which delineate them. The major characters of the zeuglodont cranial plan were described earlier (p. 160), and for detailed descriptions of species the reader should refer to the monograph on the Archaeoceti by R. Kellogg in 1936(61). The basic odontocete skull differs from that of the zeuglodont in a number of important features (Figure 5.3). The lachrymal bones, though still set at the anterior edges of the supraorbital processes of the frontal bones, abut on to the ventral area of the maxillaries, not on to their lateral surfaces. The maxillaries themselves have undergone migration posteriad to lie over the supraorbital region of the frontal bones. This could not have happened without involving a significant degree of reduction of the intraorbital region of the maxillaries (80).

The changes which have taken place in odontocete morphology and anatomy are perhaps nowhere as remarkable (and, when one attempts to trace the evolutionary development, bewildering!) as in the skull (Figure 5.4). Understanding these changes is easier if it is realized that many peculiarities of the odontocete skull are strongly adaptive to these animals' adoption and perfection of systems which scan acoustically, and which

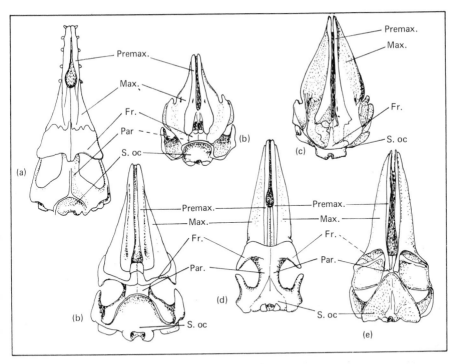

Figure 5.3 Cetacean skull morphology. (*a*) *Prozeuglodon stromeri*; (*b*) *Agorophius pygmaeus*; (*c*) *Aulophyseter morricei*; (*d*) *Physeter catodon*; (*e*) *Balaenoptera musculus*. Abbreviations for major bones: Fr. (frontal); Max. (maxillary); Par. (parietal); Premax. (premaxillary); S. oc. (Supraoccipital). Redrawn after Kellogg (58).

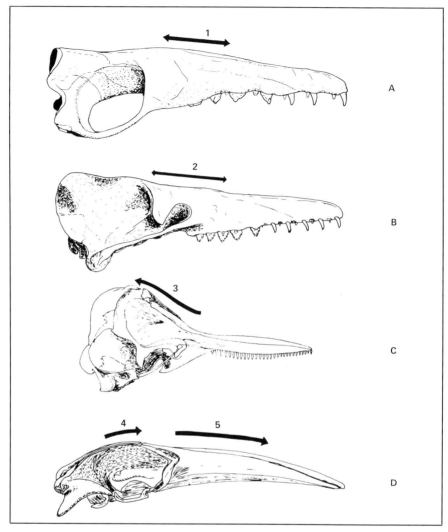

Figure 5.4   Typical cetacean skulls. A *Protocetus*; B *Prosqualodon*; C *Tursiops*;
D *Balaenoptera*; partly redrawn after Kellogg (58). In the first two, arrows 1 and
2 indicate 'telescoping' by elongation of the rostral region and narrowing the
lachrymals. In *Tursiops*, arrow 3 shows the type of telescoping found in the
modern odontocete skull, in which a posterior movement of the maxillary
spreads out over the supraoccipital region. In *Balaenoptera*, the telescoping is
directed anteriorly, with movement of the supraoccipital over the frontal (4), and
elongation of the rostral region (5); rostral and cranial bones have become very
closely associated in modern baleen whales. From top to bottom the dentition
shows the drastic modification which has occurred within the order; first, the
typical 'creodont' pattern; second, transitional dentition with considerable
modification from the typical eutherian plan; then, the fully homodont condition
of the modern delphinoid odontocete; and finally, the loss of teeth, with
replacement by baleen, in the mysticete whales. Redrawn from Gaskin (46).

collect the resulting information from the environment (35–7, 44, 45). A complex of specialized organs has been developed – the 'melon', spermaceti organ and nasal diverticula – which all appear to be associated in some way with production or reception of sounds, and also with diving. Much controversy still surrounds the ways in which sound is produced and received by odontocetes; these problems are considered more fully on pages 38–41. Needless to say, such an organ complex did not arise *de novo*, complete (Figure 5.5). There is evidence, which will be brought out in subsequent sections, to indicate that early odontocetes either lacked the capacities of modern species or had transitional systems of lower efficiency.

EVOLUTIONARY PATTERNS WITHIN THE ODONTOCETI

Agorophius and Xenorophus

R. Kellogg (58) recognized two genera of Agorophiidae as the earliest known true odontocetes: *Agorophius pygmaeus* and *Xenorophus sloanii*, from the Upper Eocene of the southern United States. He suggested that the first-named species represented a relatively early stage of mainstream odontocete evolution; F. W. True (108) believed that the genus was ancestral to the Squalodontidae, and Rothausen (94, 95) thought that the family probably contained possible precursors of all the Odontoceti. As often happens in science, further studies and discoveries demolished these attractive and tidy hypotheses. The Cooper Marl of the Ashley River in South Carolina, where the type specimens of *Agorophius* and *Xenorophus* were obtained, has now been redated as late Oligocene (74), that is about 22–25 million years of age. Since differentiated squalodonts are known from early Oligocene deposits in New Zealand (65), *Agorophius* itself can no longer be considered ancestral to this family. Furthermore, squalodonts are also known from Middle Oligocene deposits in Germany (94), New Zealand (65), Australia (47), and from late Oligocene strata of the USSR (76). Recognition by palaeobiologists of the redating of the Cooper Marl, therefore, was a crucial factor in the reinterpretation of these postulated relationships.

Nevertheless, the recent discovery of the remains of the mandibles of a primitive odontocete *Andrewsiphius* in the Middle Eocene sediments of the Kutch of north-western India (96) has served to tip the pendulum back the other way. Here we have an animal, assignable with some reservations to the Agorophiidae, with basic cranial characters unknown, but with mandibular morphology which would match that of the rostra of known Agorophiidae (only skulls are known). Yet the alveoli show that the number of teeth was as in the archaeocetes, and the specimens originated

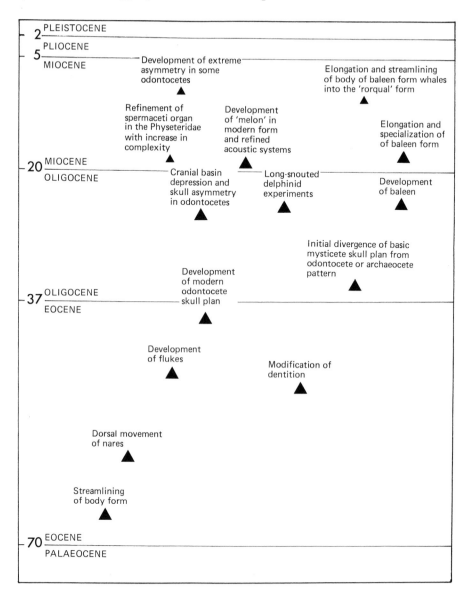

Figure 5.5   Guide to approximate timing of events during the modifications of the cetacean body form.

in sediments old enough to significantly pre-date any known true squalodont.

During the last few years A. E. Sanders of the Charleston Museum has obtained half a dozen more skulls of *X. sloanii*, and from a detailed study of these it has been concluded that the relationship between *Xenorophus* and

Agorophius is not close, and that they should not, in fact, be regarded as members of the same family (114). These authors suggested that retention of the Agorophiidae as a monotypic family had no systematic value, and believed that the name should be dropped from use for the time being. They also discussed skulls from two other unnamed odontocetes taken from the late Oligocene Alsea Formation of Oregon. One of these resembles *Agorophius*, but has a narrower rostrum, a wide frontal, a sagittal crest and a triangular supraoccipital reminiscent of that of mysticetes. The other specimen has a small parietal, rounded supraoccipital and the maxillae apparently overlaid the frontal bone. Both are clearly unrelated either to *Xenorophus* or the Squalodontidae.

The skull of *Xenorophus* reveals that while telescoping of rostral elements has taken place to a significant extent, no modification of the post-orbital region had occurred. There is extraordinary posterior extension of the maxilla and premaxilla beyond the orbital region. The premaxilla spreads outwards beneath the maxilla at its proximal extremity, another unusual feature. The large lachrymal overlies the supraorbital process. The nasal passages slope backwards; the nares themselves probably opened forward. All features but the last are singularly distinctive (114). In *Agorophius*, on the other hand, some anterior movement of the posterior occipital elements had clearly begun (although not as advanced as in the Squalodontidae), but it can still be regarded as having a number of primitive features. Differences between the two genera, as outlined by the above authors, are major. *Xenorophus* has a distinct sagittal crest; *Agorophius* has none. *Xenorophus* has a vertical occiput; that of *Agorophius* is thrust forward to the vicinity of the anterior portion of the orbit. Most immediately noticeable is the shape of the brain case; relatively broad and curved in *Xenorophus*, narrow and tabular in *Agorophius* with the parietals forming part of a prominent intertemporal constriction.

The place of these two species in the evolutionary sequence of odontocete must, unfortunately, await discovery of more fossil material. Several features of *Xenorophus* suggest that this animal was not in the mainstream of odontocete evolution but represented one of the first of a large number of 'experiments' within the group which led only to relatively rapid extinction (58). For example, although the lachrymals are in the typical odontocete position, the premaxillaries extend over the frontal supraorbital processes but *beneath* the maxillaries. In the later squalodonts telescoping of the skull has progressed to the point where the posterior margin of the maxillaries touches the supraoccipital crest. Although *Agorophius* cannot any longer be considered ancestral to the Squalodontidae, the type of telescoping pattern observed probably represents a stage in the evolutionary reorganization of the cranial elements of certain odontocetes, including the squalodonts. *Agorophius* was (judged by its skull dimensions) little larger than modern adult *Tursiops truncatus*. F. C. Whitmore and his colleague A. E. Sanders suggested (114) that such a small animal would seem 'ill-suited for the demands of a pelagic existence', and was likely coastal-dwelling in habit. This seems plausible; although modern odontocetes of similar size efficiently occupy pelagic niches, it is doubtful if *Agorophius* and its kin would have approached modern genera such as *Delphinus* and *Stenella* in anatomical and physiological efficiency.

Squalodontidae

Odontocetes did not become particularly abundant until the very end of the Middle Miocene. Among Oligocene odontocetes, the Squalodontidae appear to have been relatively abundant or, at least, are represented by the largest number of specimens (114).

The squalodonts branched into two quite divergent lines. A relatively short-beaked group, perhaps somewhat resembling the modern globicephalids (false killer, killer and pilot whales), dispersed through the southern hemisphere during the Miocene. This group is exemplified by *Prosqualodon davidi* from Tasmania and *P. australis* from southern Argentina, but remains of species such as *Squalodon gambierensis* of South Australia (47), and *Austrosqualodon trirhizodonta* of New Zealand (28, 65) show that Squalodontidae were already well diversified in the southern hemisphere during the Oligocene. The other relatively long-beaked group was more widespread but possibly had a more northern biased distribution, and is typified by *Squalodon zitteli* of the German Middle Miocene and *Neosqualodon assenzae* of the Sicilian Middle Miocene. Closely related species of *Squalodon* are known both from the Calvert deposits of Maryland and Virginia, and Anversian Sands of the Antwerp Basin in Belgium (64). Both groups were extinct by the Middle Pliocene. Even by the Middle Miocene they were being superseded by representatives of families with living relatives, for example, the Physeteridae (sperm whales), Ziphiidae (beaked whales), Delphinidae (true dolphins) and, in fresh and brackish waters, Platanistidae and Iniidae (river dolphins). We are fairly confident that the ziphiids can in fact be traced back to a squalodont ancestor, but the lineage of other families is much less certain (Figure 5.2).

Whitmore and Sanders have recently obtained enough new squalodont material from Oligocene strata of South Carolina to display the sequence of telescoping of cranial elements in this family (Figure 5.6) (114). Basically the two processes taking place were a forward thrust of the supraoccipital to cover the parietal, and posterior extension of the maxillae to make contact with the anterior margin of the supraoccipital. In one of

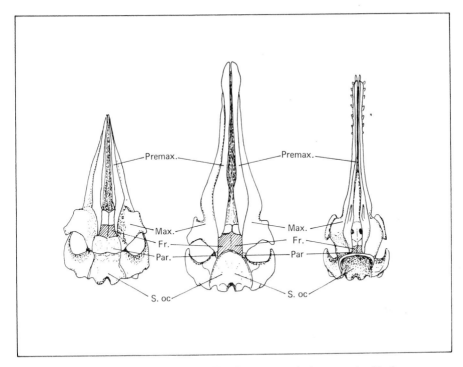

Figure 5.6   Telescoping process in *Patriocetus*, squalodont species Y of Whitmore and Sanders (114) and *Squalodon calvertensis*. Abbreviations for major bones: Fr. (frontal); Max. (maxillary); Par. (parietal); Premax. (premaxillary); S. oc. (supraoccipital). Redrawn partly from Kellogg (58).

the three unnamed genera, the telescoping is obviously age-related as well as a function of the evolutionary stage of the species, since the frontals are involved in the partial covering of the parietal in an old adult, but not in a juvenile specimen. Telescoping is generally, however, at a more advanced evolutionary stage in this genus than in the other two.

Kentriodontidae

Another extinct family of considerable interest is the Kentriodontidae, first described by E. J. Slijper in 1936 (103). They have recently been reconsidered by L. G. Barnes (14), who discussed their relationship to the Delphinoidea. In comparison to the latter they are decidedly structurally primitive, as was pointed out by earlier workers (57, 108). Kentriodontids lack the type of skull asymmetry characteristic of delphinids, and excavations for air sinuses around the middle-ear region are also absent from the bones of the ventral portion of the cranium. The relationships of the bones in the narial and vertex regions differ from those found in delphinids. The Kentriodontids may have been related to the family

Iniidae (freshwater dolphins) (62, 90), although all the characters shared with the Iniidae (long mandibular symphyses, rugose enamel on the teeth, large cranial crests and unfused cervical vertebrae) are essentially primitive (14). Unlike the iniids (and pontoporids), the kentriodontids have a more or less symmetrical cranial vertex, and show little or no sign of having had large basicranial air sinuses. The symmetrical cranial vertex, and the contact between the proximal extremities of both premaxillae and both nasal bones, distinguishes them from the Monodontidae, Phocoenidae and Delphinidae. The relatively short rostrum in the known species separates them from the Platanistidae, Eurhinodelphidae and Acrodelphidae. The symmetrical cranial vertex and the large aperture formed by the lacerate foramina serve in turn to distinguish them from the Ziphiidae.

The kentriodontids are distinguished from the Squalodontidae by having virtually homodont dentition and teeth with single roots. Kentriodont origins appear to date to the early Miocene (*c.* 22 million years ago), and it is almost certain that they were directly derived from a squalodont ancestor (14). There is close agreement among authorities concerning the importance of this extinct taxon (14, 54, 58), particularly the subfamily Kentriodontinae (containing the genera *Kentriodon*, *Delphinodon*, *Leptodelphis*, *Sarmatodelphis*, *Pithanodelphis* and *Microphocoena*) (14, 109). There are, for example, strong similarities between modern *Sotalia* and *Cephalorhynchus* (58) and *Kentriodon*. L. G. Barnes has gone further (14), suggesting that not only was the Kentriodontinae a very delphinid-like subfamily, but that the group could also have been ancestral to the whole family Delphinidae in its modern restricted form, as redefined by T. Kasuya in 1973 (54), that is excluding the monodontids (white whale and narwhal) and phocoenids (true porpoises).

The Middle Miocene subfamily Kampholophinae contains two interesting known genera; *Kampholophos* and *Liolithax*, of which the latter clearly seems to have possessed more derived characters. *Kampholophos*, on the other hand, appears to provide an almost perfect intermediate between the late Oligocene squalodont *Eosqualodon langewieschi* described by K. Rothausen in 1968 (94), and *Liolithax* (14). There is described fossil material (such as *Pontistes* and *Saurodelphis*) in collections which urgently needs to be re-examined in the light of the new discoveries and interpretations. Some of these forms may reveal relationships between the Kampholophinae, Iniidae and Pontoporiidae. The intriguing possibility exists that the two modern families may have risen from such kentriodontids.

The remaining kentriodontid subfamily, Lophocetinae, seems to show the most derived characters or advanced features in the whole family, but its affinities, though more likely to be with the Kentriodontinae than the

Kampholophinae, are still uncertain. There are distinct similarities between the cranial vertices of *Lophocetus* and the modern beaked whale *Berardius* (14), which, according to J. C. Moore (83), has the most primitively structured cranial vertex among all the modern Ziphiidae. This is more likely, however, to be a simple case of two genera retaining a rather primitive general odontocete character rather than indicating common ancestry.

Ziphiidae

Among the numerous cetacean types found in Miocene strata are the ancestors of the modern beaked whales, the Ziphiidae, which have reduced (and often highly modified) dentition and an elongate rostral region; the narial region of the cranium is noticeably elevated. Some species have characters which link them closely to the squalodonts of the Oligocene (79). True Ziphiidae appear initially in the early Miocene and are exemplified by *Notocetus* of Argentina, described by F. P. Moreno in 1892 (84). It may prove to be significant that these earliest known remains are southern hemisphere in origin. Although *Squalodelphis* (described from Italian skulls) has been attributed to early Miocene also, the dating of the strata is unconfirmed, and they may be Middle or even Upper Miocene. About nine or ten genera (some undescribed) are known from the Middle and Upper Miocene of Europe, North America and South America.

The osteology of modern Ziphiidae was full redescribed by Joseph Curtis Moore in 1968 (83), and in a recent paper James Mead of the Smithsonian Institution has attempted to make sense of the relationships of the various described fossil genera (79). The most primitive ziphiids, such as *Notocetus, Squalodelphis* and *Incacetus*, all probably from Lower or Lower Middle Miocene strata, are characterized by unmodified dentition, homodont teeth being present in both upper and lower jaws. Certain cranial elements of these genera closely resemble those found in generalized squalodonts of the Oligocene. The only living beaked whale with unreduced dentition is the (probably) circumpolar southern temperate *Tasmacetus shepherdi*, which has been regarded as the most primitive existing species (83). Once again, we must be aware of the danger of attaching relative importance to a character which is essentially one ancestrally common to all Ziphiidae. The modern genus *Mesoplodon* is generally regarded as more advanced than other genera, yet radiography will sometimes show a nearly complete complement of unerupted teeth in the gums of both jaws of *Mesoplodon grayi*.

On the basis of the morphology of skull elements Mead delineated two other groups, both showing more derived characters than the fossil genera discussed above. The first, characterized by having relatively flat premaxillae, contains the diverse modern genus *Mesoplodon* with up to twelve living species (depending on the authority consulted) and the extinct genera *Proroziphius* and *Belemnoziphius*. The second group, which exhibits mesorostral ossification of the vomer and has a median 'basin' formed of the lateral margins of the premaxillae (associated with the presence of an extensive 'melon' perinasal structure), is characterized by living *Ziphius*. Extinct genera possibly related to *Ziphius* are *Eboroziphius*, *Choneziphius*, *Pelycorhamphus* and *Ziphirostrum*. The latter genus may well represent a line ancestral to all the others in the group (79).

Recently it has been shown (11) that the ziphioid chromosome karyotype is $2n=42$, a number held in common only with the sperm whales. Nevertheless, the morphology of the ziphioid and the physeterid chromosomes is radically different; the ziphioid type does not seem to fit as an intermediate between the general cetacean karyotype and that of the sperm whales. Rather these seem to be two lines which diverged early, independently of the delphinid 'mainstream'.

Delphinidae, Phocoenidae and Monodontidae
Karyotypes of these modern Delphinidae, Phocoenidae and Monodontidae studied to date – *Phocoenoides dalli* (73), *Phocoena phocoena* (8), *Monodon monoceros* (4), *Globicephala macrorhynchus* (113), *Lagenorhynchus obliquidens* (31), *Stenella plagiodon* and *Delphinus delphis* (9) – reveal striking uniformity. C-heterochromatin content varies only between 10 and 15 per cent, the karyotype value is $2n=44$ and karyotype morphology is closely concordant (7, 8). Even the karyotype of the platanistid *Inia geoffrensis* conforms to the general $2n=44$ pattern (69). The one exception is *Orcinus orca* the killer whale (24, 53, 69); while the karyotype is $2n=44$, only one pair of t chromosomes is present in this species, and the short arms of these frequently have satellite structures. The m chromosomes are relatively small, and there are a number of other minor but noticeable differences from other delphinids. These characteristics of the killer whale would appear to be secondarily derived, rather than an indication of different evolutionary origin. The overwhelming mass of anatomical evidence points to the delphinid nature of *Orcinus*.

Delphinidae in the strict sense date from the late Miocene (*c.* ten million years ago) (13, 59) and remains are known from the latest Miocene deposits of California which closely resemble modern *Stenella* and *Tursiops*. Late Pliocene strata in the same region have produced similar fossils, and also a specimen which seems to be a globicephalid (13). The Pliocene was a period during which morphologically 'modern' delphinids became abundant, and these forms dominate the fossil record from Middle Pliocene to Recent strata. R. Kellogg discussed a sequence of specific fossils, apparently all of stages in the evolution of *Tursiops*, from the early Pliocene in Italy, in which a definite increase in the number of teeth is observed (59). Even the most recent of these skulls, however, has far fewer teeth (up to 66 in total) than modern *Tursiops truncatus* (100+). The Italian Middle Pliocene deposits have also produced fossils of an extinct species of *Orcinus*, and two species of *Steno* (19, 23, 89).

The ancestry of the Monodontidae and Phocoenidae is obscure. I indicated earlier that the relationship of *Delphinapterus* and *Monodon* is controversial. Kellogg (59) did not regard the phocoenids as distinct, and discussed possible Miocene precursors in the same paragraph with globicephalids. Barnes wrote in 1976 (13) that he had evidence (unpublished at that time) that the Middle Miocene genus *Loxolithax* 'may be involved in the ancestry of the Phocoenidae'. From late Miocene strata of California and the Baja, he had identified remains which were undoubtedly true phocoenids. *Loxolithax stocktoni* (116) seems to be 'the oldest proven phocoenid'. Late Miocene deposits of the west coast of North America have also produced true monodontid remains (two genera); the species have not yet been described. Forms attributable to these families, therefore, were extant at least five million years ago, and probably twice that. The monodontids, like the undescribed species recorded from Capistrano and San Diego late Pliocene formations, were basically delphinapterid types. Monodontids, therefore, are unlikely to have been Arctic in origin, even though the two modern species – beluga (white whale) and narwhal – are today virtually confined to Arctic and subarctic waters.

Discussion of the Delphinidae in isolation is difficult, principally because of lack of agreement among specialists as to the definitive characteristics and composition of the family. L. G. Barnes (14) justifiably claimed that the family tended to be treated as a taxonomic 'scrap-basket', although this was hardly the intent of the authors concerned. At various times the Stenidae (92) and Globicephalidae (86) have been removed from the delphinids and given the status of full families; alternatively, the Monodontinae and Phocoeninae have been retained within the Delphinidae as subfamilies.

Significant papers or chapters which examine the systematics of the Delphinidae include those of True (108), Winge (117), Slijper (103), Simpson (101), Fraser and Purves (45), Nishiwaki (86, 87), Fraser (43), Rice (92), Ness (85), Mitchell (82), Kasuya (54), Mead (79) and Barnes (14). There appear to be good anatomical grounds for excluding the Phocoenidae and Monodontidae from the Delphinidae according to Mead and Barnes. Mead pointed out that the form of the nasal vestibular sac in the phocoenids was quite different from that present in the delphinids, and that in the former group the structures around the inferior vestibule were relatively more complicated. Kasuya found distinctive features in the tympano-periotic bones of the Phocoenidae, specialized posterior processes, for example, which sharply distinguished them from the Delphinidae. The monodontids are divergent from the delphinids in several aspects of cephalic anatomy; *Monodon* itself also differs from *Delphinapterus* in a number of important characters. The tympano-periotic bones of these two genera diverge in several basic characteristics, causing Kasuya to remove *Delphinapterus* from the Monodontidae and give it monotypic family status close to the Phocoenidae (54). Both these genera were considered to share common ancestry with late Miocene *Delphinodon* (109), and to show a relationship to *Kentriodon* of the same period. This phylogeny is in close general agreement with that recently presented by Barnes (14), except that the latter author was not happy with such a major taxonomic segregation of *Monodon* and *Delphinapterus* on the basis of a single character, and retained both as subfamilies of the Monodontidae. Another interesting decision by Kasuya, based upon comparative anatomical reasoning which appears sound and with which Barnes has concurred, was the transfer of the genus *Orcaella* (the Irrawaddy dolphin) from the Delphinidae (subfamily Orcininae) to the Delphinapterinae.

Whether these or other groups of genera within the delphinids merit segregation into families or subfamilies is a controversial issue. Barnes (14) argued that establishment of the Globicephalidae and the Stenidae as separate families tended to mask or distort the evolutionary history of the delphinids. Mead (79) also concluded that on anatomical grounds the Delphinidae stood as a 'coherent assemblage'. He found the facial anatomy to be relatively conservative. On the evidence provided by facial anatomy one of the clear cases for subfamily status within the Delphinidae appeared to be for recognition of the Cephalorhynchinae, containing southern hemisphere *Cephalorhynchus*. This genus resembles *Phocoena* in several ways, and may represent convergence to the *Phocoena* pattern (14, 79, 82). There seem to be no consistent criteria for distinguishing the globi-cephalids, orcinids or stenids as separate taxa, beyond simple generic groupings. Mead regarded *Lissodelphis* as close to *Lagenorhynchus* on cranial characters, and as being a genus distinguished mainly by the narrow elongate form of the body, which was presumed to be a secondary locomotory specialization. The Orcininae seem to be a natural monophy-letic group if the morphology of the pterygoid air sinuses is emphasized (45), but in all other respects *Orcinus* really appears to be little more than just a large delphinid of generalized morphology, which has become specialized for feeding on large prey. Kasuya, of course, did not consider the smaller *Orcaella* to belong to the Delphinidae at all. Several authors have attempted to arrange *Orcinus, Pseudorca, Orcaella, Feresa* and *Globicephala* into an evolutionary sequence. The variable results reflect the adaptations which have occurred in the various structures used as a basis for each classification. Within the more 'typical' delphinids, *Delphinus*, *Stenella* and *Tursiops* form a relatively homogeneous group.

There is common agreement that *Tursiops* is anatomically the most generalized of modern delphinids. *Grampus* was thought to be closely related to *Tursiops* by Fraser and Purves (45) and E. Mitchell, but Mead was more doubtful. On the basis of the anatomy of the facial region of *Grampus*, which he found to be exceedingly divergent from other delphinids, he was tempted 'to put it in a subfamily by itself', but demurred on the basis of the other evidence pointing to a close relationship to *Tursiops*. Hybrids between these two genera are known.

Eurhinodelphidae, Acrodelphidae

Kellogg (58) was doubtful if these extinct delphinids, the 'long snouted dolphins', could justifiably be regarded even as a subfamily in their own right. Established as a subfamily by Miller (80) they are characterized by a greatly elongate premaxillary projecting some distance anterior to the termination of the maxillary. Some fossil forms from the United States, which on balance of features must probably be assigned to this group, do not possess this specific character (58). Modern authors tend to give them family status, for the time being at least, although there is no doubt that the group needs to be fully revised and the relationships of each described form completely re-evaluated (13, 14). Nevertheless, the eurhinodelphids are particularly characteristic of the early Miocene deposits of the west coast of North America (13, 81). *Eurhinodelphis* has also been found in the Miocene Calvert strata of Maryland and Virginia, and the Anversian sands of the Antwerp Basin of Belgium (64).

Eurhinodelphid types are apparently absent from the Oligocene strata of eastern and western American coasts and from European deposits, suggesting that their evolution and radiation in the early Miocene was quite rapid. As a group, they do not appear to have outlasted the Miocene epoch. The earlier forms are typified by the genus *Argyrocetus*, described originally from Argentina (21, 72), and now known to have occurred in other regions, including the west coast of North America (13). *Argyrocetus* and its allies exhibit extreme elongation of the rostrum; not only has anterior elongation of the snout occurred, but the proximal region of the maxillaries has ridden up the anterior face of the cranium to make intimate contact with the crest of the supraoccipital. Usually one-fifth of the snout region is made up only of the premaxillaries. Each side of the jaw contains about fifty teeth – relatively few considering the length of the maxillary and mandibular surfaces.

Reduction in the number of teeth occurred in this family as their development progressed (58); in the late Early Miocene the genus *Ziphiodelphis* had anterior teeth much reduced in size in comparison to those more posteriorly situated. No one has yet given a satisfactory explanation for this excessive development of the rostrum which, in the European species *Eurhinodelphis longirostris*, accounted for more than four-fifths of the total length of the skull (1). Some eurhinodelphids were quite small, for example *Acrodelphis (=Argyrocetus) bakersfieldensis* from California was only about a metre in length (13, 115). *Macrodelphinus kelloggi*, on the other hand, seems to have been the size of a modern killer whale (4–6 metres) (13), and some other widely distributed members of *Eurhinodelphis* attained lengths of about 5 metres. Suggestions that the long snouts of these animals were used for digging out prey from estuarine oozes can probably be discounted. I believe they were probably predators of pelagic schools of relatively small fish, feeding in the same way that the modern delphinids of the *Stenella longirostris* group feed. It may be possible to consider this problem of rostral elongation in the same way that bill shape and size has been analysed by ornithologists. It seems that a long slender bill is advantageous in securing small, relatively fast-moving prey (17,100). This still does not explain why the rostral elongation became so extreme in these animals. Yet during the course of the Middle and Upper Miocene, the eurhinodelphids became quite numerous, and their remains are common in most Miocene cetacean deposits. They disappear from the fossil record at the Miocene–Pliocene interface, and in the latter epoch were completely replaced by delphinids of the groups living today.

Three different lines of descent can be recognized within the eurhinodelphids (58): the direct line, containing *Argyrocetus–Ziphiodelphis–Eurhinodelphis*; a second including *Cyrtodelphis* and *Eoplatanista* with telescoping of cranial elements highly developed and modified dentition; and a third group, composed of *Acrodelphis* and *Champsodelphis*, originally described from southern and central European strata of the Lower and Lower Middle Miocene, and later found in North America. The systematic position of the large *Macrodelphinus* with respect to these three groups is not clear. *Cyrtodelphis* has the elongate rostrum common to most eurhinodelphids, and the type of telescoping characteristic of the family, but is also characterized by a flat cranial vertex with large exposure of the frontal bones. The dentition is striking; the anterior teeth are slender, with laterally compressed enamelled crowns, and are placed obliquely in the jaws. The posterior teeth are much more conical. This secondary modification of the odontocete homodont condition is less extreme than that found in the third, or acrodelphid group of eurhinodelphids. In *Acrodelphis* the anterior teeth have a slender crown, while posterior teeth have small accessory tubercles and scalloped cutting edge. Telescoping of cranial elements in this group is basically similar to, but less extreme than in *Cyrtodelphis* or *Eurhinodelphis*, and the nasal bones are relatively larger.

Platanistinae, Pontoporinae and Iniinae
The four living genera of the so-called 'freshwater dolphin' group – a misnomer, since not all of them are – have been subjected to almost every conceivable taxonomic permutation. F. C. Fraser and P. E. Purves (45) concluded that *Lipotes* (white fin dolphin – called white flag dolphin in the literature for many years, because of a minor error in translation – or 'Baiji' of the Upper Yangtze and Tun-T'ing Lake system in China) and the Amazon river dolphin *Inia* were related. M. A. C. Hinton (52) grouped *Pontoporia* (the Franciscana of eastern South America) with *Lipotes*. The Ganges dolphin, *Platanista*, seems to stand somewhat further apart from the other three. Recently Zhou and his colleagues (121) have re-examined fresh material of *Lipotes*, and concluded that it differs sufficiently from the other three genera to merit family status; the differences are of insufficient magnitude to really justify this. The balance of evidence (45, 52, 58) quite strongly supports the concept of the Platanistidae as monophyletic. Furthermore, I concur with Barnes (14) that monotypic families are of no systematic value and should be avoided where possible; they draw attention to differences rather than relationships.

Pontoporia (*Stenodelphis* in most pre-1970 literature) *blainvillei* was placed by G. S. Miller (80) and R. Kellogg (58) in the Stenodelphinae, a subfamily of the Delphinidae. Kellogg also assigned to this subfamily the extinct species '*Stenodelphis*' *sternbergi* (generic status not stabilized, but considered close to *Pontoporia* according to Barnes) (13), and the Lower Pliocene genus *Pontistes* from Argentina, which by all accounts was much larger than the modern representative. This group is characterized (58) (and distinguished from the other delphinids) by possession of pterygoids which overlie part of the adjacent alisphenoid, and separate cervical vertebrae (in my opinion the latter is only retention of a primitive character and cannot be used to prove a relationship with any other group).

In *Platanista* the outer maxillary margins have turned upwards above the orbits; these bones were free to continue adding to this margin, resulting in the peculiar fan-like maxillary crest characteristic of the facial region of the cranium in this genus. Kellogg referred the interesting genus *Zarhachis* to the Platanistidae also; the described species *Z. flagellator* from the Middle Miocene of the eastern United States had a rostrum five times as long as the actual brain case. In its skull the periotic bone resembles that of *Platanista*, and the maxillaries have contact with the supraoccipital, though being marginally curved upwards in conjunction with the supraorbital processes.

Inia and *Lipotes* also have elongate rostra, but differ from other odontocetes in possessing a portion of the maxillary projecting to the level of the sphenoid fissure. The facial depression is narrow and, as in *Platanista*, the external borders of the maxillaries bend upwards. The pterygoids are simple and do not overlie the alisphenoid as in *Pontoporia*.

The whole group requires reinterpretation, together with examination of all the described fossil forms and the unclassified material which might have affinities, but the case for splitting the Platanistidae is frankly rather weak.

The early Miocene species *Allodelphis pratti* from the west coast of the United States might well be a primitive platanistid or pre-platanistid (13), and could be related to *Zarhachis flagellator*. Kellogg (58) suggested a relationship between *Zarhachis* and *Platanista*, and also put forward the tentative proposal that a relationship might be established between *Inia*, *Platanista* and the Lower Pliocene genus *Ischyrorhynchus*; he remarked that, if anything, the resemblance was strongest between the two latter genera. As mentioned earlier, both iniids and pontoporiids may have had their origins in the extinct family Kentridontidae (14). Fossils of reputed iniids such as *Goniodelphis*, *Pontistes*, the presently unplaced *Liolithax*, certain other eastern North Pacific platanistid-type fossils such as '*Squalodon*' *errabundus* of the Middle and late Miocene deposits of California, '*Stenodelphis*' *sternbergi*, and an undescribed genus of late Pliocene strata in the same region need to be re-examined. Barnes believes that the latter at least was related to modern *Pontoporia*, based on his ideas of the steps which had taken place in the evolutionary modification of the tympano-periotic bones of the platanistid skull.

Kasuya, on the other hand (54), hypothesized that *Platanista*, *Lipotes*, *Inia* and *Pontoporia* arose from a squalodont rather than a kentriodont ancestor (14), with *Zarhachis* in the ancestry of *Platanista*, as suggested many years ago by Kellogg (58). He considered that *Platanista* had the most basic periotic structure, and that *Lipotes*, *Inia* and *Pontoporia* were more closely related to one another than to *Platanista*. *Lipotes* was thought to be the most primitive of this derived group, and *Pontoporia* the most specialized. Like most earlier workers (38, 45, 86, 117), he concluded that *Pontoporia* was allied to the other platanistiids, and should not remain part of the Delphinidae as defined by Miller (80) and Kellogg (58). Kasuya also pointed to some interesting structural features shared by *Platanista* and the Miocene genus *Schizodelphis*, but noted that in other important cranial features the latter showed more affinity to modern Delphinoidea. In particular the nature of the telescoping and spreading of the maxillary is very different in *Platanista* and *Schizodelphis*; it is unrealistic to suggest that platanistids were derived directly from a eurhinodelphid ancestor.

A. R. Ness (85) had some interesting points to make as a result of his study of the nature and development of asymmetry in odontocete skulls. In general, the measurements of cranial skew taken from platanistid skulls fell within two standard deviations of the mean regression line for delphinids. *Lipotes* and *Inia* lay below the delphinoid line and close together, while *Platanista* showed relatively more cranial skew than most other odontocetes. Specimens of *Pontoporia* showed virtually no measurable asymmetry; in this they are alone among the living odontocete whales. This is in accord with differences in structure of the nasal sacs in the platanistids: the nasal diverticulae are greatly developed on the right side in *Lipotes* (52); those of *Pontoporia*, on the other hand, are far less developed and lack such symmetry. Miocene and Pliocene species, which might have been on or close to the platanistid line, show little or no cranial asymmetry. This is in strong contrast to the asymmetry present in the delphinoid, ziphioid and physeterid lines. Ness suggested that asymmetry in the platanistids had arisen independently of that found in delphinids to accommodate extension and changes in the acoustical/upper respiratory structures. Since *Lipotes*, *Inia* and *Platanista* are fluvial and estuarine and *Pontoporia* is basically a marine animal, modifications might have been greater in the former as they penetrated turbid habitats where reliance on acoustical mechanisms became more important. In view of the marked asymmetry in other non-platanistid marine odontocetes, this explanation is obviously less than totally satisfactory. His suggestion that a comparative study of *Pontoporia* and other marine cetaceans might be fruitful is, however, a sound suggestion. *Pontoporia* may be found to have a poorly developed range of acoustical talents.

Physeteridae and Kogiinae

As with other groups of cetaceans, the appearance of physeterids in the fossil record is rather abrupt; and the earliest known examples, from the early Miocene, were already demonstrably sperm whales, with marked cranial asymmetry of the type peculiar to this family. The development of the characteristic spermaceti organ in association with the distal part of the respiratory track was obviously an early specialization in the physeterids. In the living sperm whale the organ consists of a large lower adipose structure or 'cushion', overlying which is a sinus system or reservoir filled with spermaceti oil which appears to have a role in buoyancy control (26, 27) and may also act as a sound resonator, according to K. S. Norris. In the early Miocene genus *Diaphorocetus* in South America, the right side of the nasal passage was partially surrounded by a well-developed adipose structure, the presence of which had become associated with asymmetric modifications in the underlying facial elements of the cranium (84). In the skull of this form the right premaxillary extends posteriorly to the crest of the supraoccipital bone and forms the floor of a kind of facial 'basin'. The maxillaries are also involved in this 'basin' and turn upward to form the lateral margins. Another related but considerably larger South American form of the same period was *Idiorophus* (72). Both these species had large grasping and tearing teeth in both jaws. In the modern *Physeter catodon* truly functional maxillary teeth are often unerupted. When protruding, they apparently serve only to provide oblique surfaces for sharpening the tips of the mandibular teeth. The individual teeth of the fossil forms were much larger than in their modern counterpart. Kellogg (58) suggested that the diet and feeding habits of these early Miocene sperm whales was more akin to that of modern killer whales than the living cachalot.

Reduction in size of mandibular teeth and perhaps the beginnings of loss of functional maxillary teeth can be seen in Middle Miocene *Aulophyseter*. The frontal basin seen in *Diaphorocetus* has attained a more advanced stage in this form. The general characteristics of the skull are such that it is quite possible that this species shared common ancestry with modern *Physeter*, as tentatively suggested by E. Mitchell (81). By the Middle Miocene sperm whales had spread through the northern hemisphere; their remains are known from both sides of the Pacific and also from western Europe. One Pacific Basin species of this period, *Ontocetus*, was probably up to 10 metres in length, judging by the skull measurements (56). Other genera from this period include *Idiophyseter* from the west coast of the United States and *Orycterocetus* from the east coast (63); both seem closely related to *Aulophyseter*.

The late Miocene saw further radiation and spread of physeterid forms. Several distinct genera have been described from the Antwerp region of Belgium, some of them rather small species of perhaps 3–5 metres in total body length. One of these genera, *Scaldicetus*, was widespread; it has been identified from Californian deposits of the same period, and persisted in that region well into the Pliocene. Remains of this form in Californian Pleistocene deposits probably result from redistributions from eroded Miocene/Pliocene strata (13). Only *Physeter*, however, seems to have survived and prospered during the Pleistocene and Recent epochs.

The kogiids have been variously grouped by different authors within the Physeteridae, sometimes with subfamily status and sometimes without it, or placed in a distinct family Kogiidae. The group is characterized by a facial basin basically similar to that of the physeterids, but the rostrum is shorter than the cranium (compare with the *Physeter*, where the rostrum is longer than the cranium) and the palatine bones are small, in contrast to the very large ones found in *Physeter*. On the other hand, while the pterygoid and lachrymal bones are small in *Physeter*, they are large and well developed in *Kogia*. Only two fossil pygmy sperm whales are known; one from the late Pliocene of Japan, which seems to be congeneric with the two modern species of *Kogia* (50), and the interesting primitive kogiid *Praekogia cedrosensis*, described from Miocene–Pliocene interface deposits of Baja California (12).

The origins and relationships of both physeterids and kogiids are poorly known. The karyotype differs from that of other cetaceans. Common ancestry with the squalodonts and ziphiids seems likely, based on the morphology of the tympano-periotic bones (54). Subsequent modifications of form, however, have been great. The basic form of the cranial asymmetry in *Physeter* and *Kogia* seems to be different from that of other odontocetes (85). The two genera are rather different from one another in facial region anatomy (79), but both are much more divergent from other toothed whales.

The karyotype composition and structure is particularly intriguing (10). The differences between the killer whale's C-heterochromatin distribution (which apparently shows either pericentric inversions or accumulation in the short arms of chromosomes) (9), and that of the rest of the $2n=44$ cetaceans may be the result of a relatively recent specialization, since the karyotype is basically the same. The $2n=42$ karyotype of the Ziphiidae seems to be the result of relatively simple secondary fusion of two pairs (11). The $2n=42$ sperm and pygmy sperm whales, on the other hand, have chromosome morphology significantly different from other Cetacea, which suggests that they diverged from all other odontocetes very early in the history of the line.

2 Mysticeti (baleen whales)

The odontocetes and mysticetes have long followed divergent modes of exploitation of food at quite different trophic levels, with very great consequent adaptations. Although the odontocete skull has become modified to contain acoustic apparatus, certain features of mysticete skulls, such as the great forward extension of the upper margin of the occipital shield, represent a response through structural modification to the various forces imposed upon the anterior end of these animals. The most constant of these strains is that imposed by forward motion against water resistance; an irregular but much more severe strain is placed on the cranial and mandibular system each time the animal opens its mouth wide while moving forward to sieve food from masses of sea water. Both groups of cetaceans are so highly adapted that it is very dangerous to consider any skull character, even a basicranial one, as purely ancestral. Consequently the mere enumeration of differences does not necessarily add strength to a case for separate ancestry of odontocetes and mysticetes.

The Mysticeti are clearly descended from some type of toothed ancestor, regardless of whether or not that ancestor was a true archaeocete. There is clear embryological evidence of dentition, before the development of the baleen plates (those remarkable feeding structures of secondary dermal origin) obscures the rudiments completely. No author appears to doubt that the baleen whales form a monophyletic group. To propose that such structures as unique as the baleen plates could have arisen independently in several closely related families would impose a severe strain on anyone's credulity.

The late Oligocene deposits of Europe and North America have been the source of five particularly interesting and intriguing cetacean fossils: *Patriocetus*, *Archaeodelphis*, *Mirocetus*, *Ferecetotherium* and *Aetiocetus*. These have all at one time or another been considered as possible ancestors of the Mysticeti (2, 58, 77, 114). *Patriocetus* can be quickly dealt with, as all its major cranial features are of odontocete character (94, 114); it appears to be related to *Agriocetus*, but perhaps not too closely.

Kellogg (58) was convinced that *Archaeodelphis* and the cetotheres were derived from a common stock, concluding that the construction of the orbit, the frontal, and the relationship of the lachrymal bone and the maxillary (with the latter partially covering the former), all seemed to be early stages in the process of conversion of archaeocete skull to mysticete skull. He drew particular attention to the ascending process of the maxillary which projected over the frontal, pointing out that this was 'the interlocking sort of maxillary found in all known whalebone skulls'. All that seemed to be required to turn this cranium into one of mysticete type was constriction of the ascending process of the maxillary, and further telescoping, since the skull of *Archaeodelphis* is otherwise little modified in most respects. The pterygoid fossae are similar to those found in mysticetes. These must be present in any precursor of the mysticetes so that an infraorbital extension of the maxillary could occur. They are also involved in the formation of the accessory air sinuses of the inner ear.

Ferecetotherium, *Mirocetus* and, most convincingly, *Aetiocetus* appear to be transitional forms between the Archaeoceti and Mysticeti. *Aetiocetus*, although excluded from the Mysticeti by its discoverer (34) because it was toothed, has a skull which is demonstrably mysticete in many other respects (111, 114). This skull has a posteriorly concave, almost vertical supraoccipital, and lacks a sagittal crest. The parietals visibly form part of the rounded brain case. In these three characters it shows clear archaeocete affinities. Teeth are present, but they are small and laminate. The rostrum is triangular, however, and the arrangement of the proximal ends of the maxillary and premaxillary is very mysticete in character. *Aetiocetus* has been quite reasonably designated as a true intermediate between Archaeoceti and Mysticeti (34, 107, 114). The deposits from which it was obtained have been interpreted as late Oligocene. *Aetiocetus* itself, therefore, is clearly too late to be the direct ancestor of other mysticetes, since it is contemporary with an early true cetothere from Europe, *Cetotheriopsis*. The lack of Oligocene cetothere remains in the relatively rich eastern North Pacific suggests that *Aetiocetus* was a relict species even by late Miocene (13).

R. E. Fordyce (40) argued that the key genus in the origin of true mysticetes was in fact *Mauicetus*, from New Zealand deposits of the Middle Oligocene (65). This fossil pre-dates both *Aetiocetus* and *Cetotheriopsis* by about five million years, more or less. Four species have been described. The long intertemporal region of *Mauicetus* resembles that of late Eocene Archaeocetes, as do certain other cranial features (15, 75, 76), but other characters, such as the forward-directed triangular supraoccipital and the long nasal bones partially enveloped by the premaxillaries and maxillaries, are typically mysticete (15, 16). There are few difficulties in classifying *Mauicetus* as a primitive but true cetothere, and the pattern of cranial telescoping is simple and clearly of the mysticete type. There is a discussion of this genus and the interesting ideas put forward by Fordyce concerning the possible factors which directed its evolution in Chapter 6.

EVOLUTIONARY PATTERNS WITHIN THE MYSTICETI

Cetotheridae and Eschrichtidae

The processes of 'telescoping' of the mysticete skull are not identical in the different families (80), although within the suborder they are not as different from one another as are all from the 'telescoping' process which has occurred in the odontocete skull. In the right whales, anteriad migration of the cranial supraoccipital bones has taken place, but the rostral and cranial regions as a whole have remained distinctly segregated. In the rorquals there has been the same general kind of migration, but the rostral and cranial bones have become very closely associated and sutured one to another. The Cetotheridae (and to some extent the Eschrichtidae) differ from both right whales and rorquals in that the parietal region remains, in general, very distinct. In the Cetotheridae the supraorbital processes of the frontal bones angle smoothly downwards to the orbital rims instead of dipping very sharply ventrad of the intraorbital regions to form conspicuous dorsal troughs on each side of the skull as in other mysticetes (58); nor are the nasal bones of the Cetotheridae and Eschrichtidae reduced as in the right whales and rorquals.

After first appearing in Middle Oligocene strata the family Cetotheridae speciated strongly during the early and Middle Miocene. The family dwindled in numbers of species during the late Miocene, and finally became extinct at the end of the early Pliocene. A study of their characteristics led Kellogg (58) to propose that the gray whales could be quite simply derived from the Cetotheridae through some relatively minor adaptations and modifications. There is, however, no conclusive evidence as yet to indicate that the early Cetotheridae were directly ancestral to the other families of modern mysticetes.

Several lines of cetothere evolution can be discerned among the rather abundant early and Middle Miocene remains that have been described. Two patterns can be recognized, based upon different trends in the progressive modification of the supraoccipital shield and whether the cranium remained primitively broad at the base or was secondarily narrowed. The early telescoping process observed in Oligocene cetotheres reached the stage of actual cranial and rostral bone articulation in the early Miocene species *Cetotherium furlongi*. The type of this interesting form is unfortunately lost, although a detailed description remains (13). The best fossils of cetotheres from North America date back about 13–15 million years (98) and have been retrieved from the Sharktooth Hill Bonebed in the Round Mountain area of California, and the Calvert formations of Maryland and Virginia. At least four genera of cetotheres have been recorded from California (13, 59, 60), and several species of the same or different genera from the east coast of the United States. *Parietobalaena palmeri* was an Atlantic cetothere which attained a length of about 4–5 metres (64). *Aglaocetus patulus* may have been somewhat larger; *Aglaocetus moreni* was described from Patagonian remains (72). Another species which may belong to the same genus has also been found in the Sharktooth Hill Bonebed (58). Cetothere remains are much rarer in late Miocene and Pliocene deposits; in the Californian deposits a genus close to *Herpetocetus* is the sole remaining representative of this family.

Balaeninae, Neobalaeninae and Balaenopteridae

The other four generally recognized families or subfamilies of Mysticeti have living relatives: Balaeninae (right whales), Neobalaeninae (pygmy right whale), Balaenopteridae (rorquals) and Eschrichtidae (gray whales). Rather modern balaenids start to appear in Californian deposits even by the Middle Miocene, and we find the remains of balaenopterids in Middle-Upper Miocene strata of the north-western Atlantic coast and in the Californian late Miocene. When they appear in the fossil record they are apparently already well differentiated: however, some early Miocene mysticete remains may have been misinterpreted and further study of these might show that intermediates do exist among known fossils.

It seems probable that both main evolutionary lines of modern cetaceans – the right whales with their arched jaws and the slender, more streamlined rorquals – were differentiating even at the end of the Oligocene. The primitive mysticete *Mesotaras* has been suggested as a possible link between the two main groups (97). Balaenids are known from the early Miocene, for example, *Morenocetus* from Patagonia (21). Even in this primitive balaenid the nasal bones, premaxillae and maxillae were all clearly anterior to the supraorbital processes (58). Balaenid fossils are reasonably common in Miocene and Pliocene deposits. One undetermined species has been recorded from the Middle Miocene deposits of

California, and at least two, one assigned to the genus *Balaenula*, from the Miocene–Pliocene strata of California (13).

There has been some argument as to whether *Neobalaena* is primitive or specialized – one problem seemed to be that of conflicting terminology, used with different meaning by various authors. The short rostrum is a primitive feature; in many ways it resembles that of the cetotheres. In other respects *Neobalaena* has a skeletal structure with many specialized characters; the cervicals are all fused, and the lumbar and caudal vertebrae are reduced in number. The ribs are stout and flattened, and eight or more are not articulated. It appears to be archaic but very specialized, and cannot easily be derived from any specific Pliocene or Miocene fossil form.

The oldest known balaenopterid remains from the Pacific are from the late Miocene, and include a species of humpback whale (55), named *Megaptera miocaena*. A 'rorqual' (*Balaenoptera ryani*), described by G. D. Hanna and M. E. McLellan (51) has been re-examined by Barnes (13), who pointed out that the skull lacked the breadth and interdigitation of the frontals and parietals characteristic of modern rorquals. He tentatively concluded that *ryani* was probably closer to the cetotherids. Indisputable Californian balaenopterids, however, occur in strata assigned to the very latest Miocene or earliest Pliocene. One of these seems close to the genus *Plesiocetus*, described originally from European remains. The same form is present in late Pliocene deposits in the San Diego region (13). The oldest balaenopterid remains appear to occur on the Atlantic margins (68). '*Eschrichtius*' *cephalus* Cope was re-examined by Kellogg (64), who concluded that it was in fact a true balaenopterid quite close to the modern fin whale. That differentiated humpback and rorqual forms can be identified from Middle and late Miocene strata points to differentiation occurring at least in the early Miocene. Balaenopterid remains are well known from the European Pliocene, including *Balaenoptera cortesii* from Italy, which shows a number of cranial specializations, such as exaggerated anterior extension of the supraoccipital shield. Other Pliocene species, for example *Balaenoptera cuvieri*, also from Italy, differ from modern rorquals only in relatively minor respects.

Are the Cetacea monophyletic or polyphyletic?

The very success and relative complexity of the adaptations found in the Odontoceti and Mysticeti obscures the answer to a fascinating and contentious question – are the Cetacea monophyletic, biphyletic or polyphyletic? The majority of published opinion currently appears to favour separate origins of odontocetes and mysticetes and probably archaeocetes too (66, 67, 104, 118, 120), although well-reasoned arguments in favour of monophyly are not lacking (49, 111). But how solidly are these opinions based and, especially considering some new evidence from cytogenetic studies, how valid are these interpretations of the available evidence? It is well worth spending some time pondering both the problem and the data.

Anatomical considerations

About fifty years ago G. S. Miller critically analysed the processes which had taken place in the cetacean skull during the re-modellings of the original 'creodont' pattern (80). He concluded that 'All the known members of each series, including the oldest fossils sufficiently well preserved to merit serious discussion, have developed in strict accordance with the definite, and, it would seem, mutually exclusive tendencies of their respective groups.' With respect to the taxal distance between the three suborders he stated '. . . this assumption does not imply that the separate lines represent convergence from widely different ancestral stocks . . . it now appears to me unnecessary to assume that the three points of reference were farther apart than adjacent families in some carnivore-like, perhaps early creodont stock'. Such a viewpoint now seems unnecessarily conservative; probably only a single family was involved (111).

The ascending process of the maxillary has a homologous relationship to other bones in both living suborders, but the jugal meets the maxillary in quite different positions in odontocetes and mysticetes. Miller's main objection to the zeuglodonts being considered ancestral to the mysticetes centred on the large horizontal plate formed from the orbital region of the maxillary in the latter, which occurred 'in a position which meets no recognizable mechanical need'. He pronounced that he was at a loss to see how a mysticete skull with this feature could have been derived from the zeuglodont condition, but admitted that he had not had the chance to examine creodont skulls as fully as he would have liked.

Because Miller could not think of a function does not necessarily mean that one is lacking. A. J. Cain adequately exposed the deficiencies of this type of reasoning in biological arguments (22). Miller also noted that the orbital-plate region of the maxillary appeared to be in an advanced state of degeneration, pointing out the presence of variable vacuities, the general thinness of the bone and the irregular form of the free margin. This conclusion is questionable. He was, however, probably quite correct in deciding that this plate added nothing to the structural strength of the skull, but that very fact makes it seem likely that some function other than that of a strengthening member was being served. Many of the cranial modifications in the baleen whale skull are highly adaptive to the peculiar feeding mode. Anyone who has seen a fin whale feeding is struck by the magnitude of the gape, the upper and lower jaw almost forming a right angle when the mouth is opened to its maximum extent (see Figures 2.9 and 2.10). One may postulate at least one way in which such a pair of plates above the back roof of the mouth, well-cushioned with connective tissue, could provide a flexible and elastic surface against which the back of the tongue could work during feeding. The thinness would be highly functional, and vacuities and irregularities might be present simply because, within broad limits, there was no selective disadvantages to a certain amount of variation in the basic plan.

In recent years the major proponents of polyphyly in the Cetacea have included such notable authorities as E. J. Slijper (104) and A. V. Yablokov (118). Both concluded that the archaeocetes were not directly ancestral to modern whales, but represented a third great suborder which had become extinct after considerable 'experimentation' with form and function. Yablokov argued that the similarities between the modern suborders, such as the loss of true vocal cords, lung shape and the oblique position of the diaphragm, the streamlined body shape with loss of pelage, and the dorsal migration of the external nares, are all clearly parallel adaptations to function in a common aquatic environment. He stressed the major differences between them. For example, the biochemical properties of odontocete and mysticete blubber are far from identical, the lower jaw is symphysial in the odontocetes but not in the mysticetes, the skull is symmetrical in the latter but asymmetrical in the former, ethmoturbinals are present in mysticetes but lacking in odontocetes, dimorphism is reversed in the two suborders, with the females larger in mysticetes and the males larger in odontocetes (although this is not the case in *Phocoena phocoena*), and so on. The list extends to twenty characters which need not be completely repeated here. Yablokov was not, however, able to pursue his argument to the point of being very specific about what the actual ancestors were supposed to have been, nor to indicate the degree of taxal difference between the ancestral forms in the Palaeocene when they took to the water. Despite this, he proposed that archaeocetes, odontocetes and mysticetes each be elevated to full ordinal status. Van Valen (111) and the present author find this step unnecessary and unacceptable. So did Miller as long ago as 1923, despite his belief in polyphyly (80).

Van Valen (111) rightly pointed out that giving a list of these differences is irrelevant to a consideration of phylogeny, since the differences are as adaptive as the similarities. Odontocetes and mysticetes have adopted radically different modes of life since the Palaeocene. Dimorphism has certain functional advantages and social structure and behaviour can have considerable selective impact on this character. The non-symphysial lower jaw of the mysticetes is surely functional in their mode of feeding and blubber composition could be influenced over a long period by a factor as simple as diet (see the book by D. W. Rice and A. A. Wolman in 1971 (93), discussing pigmentation changes in gray whale blubber). In addition, considerations of size and metabolism suggest that in the relatively large mysticetes, blubber functions more as a seasonal food reserve than it does in the relatively small odontocetes (with due allowance for the atypical sperm whale), in which thermoregulation is probably more important. Consequently, there is no particular reason, when both these factors are considered, to expect oil composition to be similar in the two suborders. Van Valen pointed to similarities in the structure of the tympanic bulla, not considered by Yablokov, which is almost identical in the three suborders except for relatively minor variations. He also pointed out that the structure of the mandibular condyle of the archaeocetes is intermediate in position with respect to the living whales, and stressed that the early zeuglodonts, *Protocetus* and *Pappocetus*, had cranial features rather nicely intermediate between mesonychid condylarthran 'creodonts' and both living cetacean suborders.

Karyotype studies

Recently, very strong evidence in favour of the monophyly of Cetacea has been provided by U. Arnason and his co-workers (5, 7, 8, 9) and D. D.

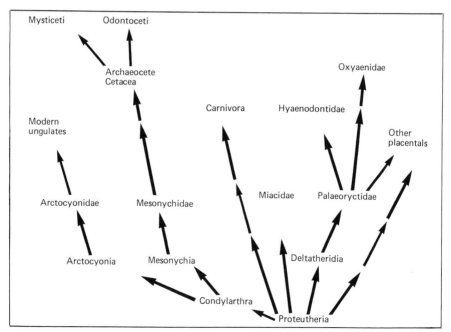

Figure 5.7 Apparent phylogeny of the Cetacea and related groups of mammals. Constructed from data in Van Valen (110–12).

Kulu (70), from studies of the cytogenetics of mysticetes and odontocetes. Their findings may be briefly summarized as follows. There is not only close karyotypic agreement between odontocetes and mysticetes in terms of detailed chromosome morphology, but the two groups share the same characteristic distribution of C-heterochromatin in the chromosomes. These authors found it inconceivable that this could have happened by chance in two separate groups. However, they found several divergent and

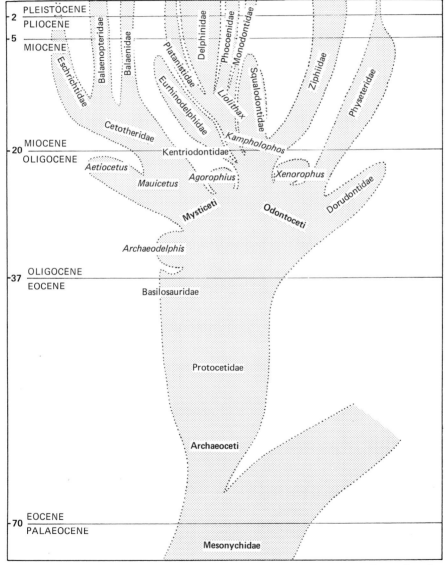

Figure 5.8 Apparent phylogenetic relationships within the Cetacea. Some data drawn from Kellogg (58), Whitmore and Sanders (114), Barnes (14) and other modern sources.

probably secondary karyotypes among the odontocetes. We must therefore consider the possibility that while the modern Cetacea as a whole are probably monophyletic, with archaeocete and, prior to that, probably mesonychid ancestry (Figures 5.7 and 5.8), the sperm whales might have diverged at a very early time. Nevertheless, physeterid fossils are at present known only as far back as the Lower Miocene (58), and the structural and functional similarities between the nasal diverticulae of all odontocetes, and the spermaceti organ of the sperm whale, on the one hand, and the 'melon' of the smaller odontocetes, such as the pilot whale, on the other, are too marked for one to readily discard the probability of common ancestry of all odontocetes. Further study and thought is needed here.

References

1   Abel, O. 1905. 'Les odontocètes du Bolderein (Miocene supérieur) d'Anvers', *Memoires du Musee Royal d'histoire naturelle de Belgique* (Bruxelles), vol. 3, pp. 1–155.
2   Abel, O. 1913. 'Die Vorfahren der Bartenwale', *Derkschr. der Math.-Naturwiss. kl. kais. Akad. Wissensch*, vol. 90, pp. 155–224.
3   Andrews, R. C. 1920. 'A description of new species of zeuglodont and of leathery turtle from the Eocene of Southern Nigeria', *Proc. zool. Soc. London* (1919), pp. 305–19.
4   Andrews, R. C., Dill, F. J., Masui, S. and Fisher, H. D. 1973. 'The chromosome complement of the narwhal (*Monodon monoceros*)', *Can. J. Zool.*, vol. 51, pp. 349–53.
5   Arnason, U. 1969. 'The karyotypes of the fin whale', *Hereditas*, vol. 62, pp. 273–84.
6   Arnason, U. 1970. 'Karyotypes of a male sperm whale (*Physeter catodon* L.) and a female sei whale (*Balaenoptera borealis* Less.)', *Hereditas*, vol. 64, pp. 237–42.
7   Arnason, U. 1972. 'The role of chromosomal rearrangement in mammalian speciation with special reference to Cetacea and Pinnipedia', *Hereditas*, vol. 70, pp. 113–18.
8   Arnason, U. 1974. 'Phylogeny and speciation in Pinnipedia and Cetacea – a cytogenetic study', Lund.
9   Arnason, U. 1974. 'Comparative chromosome studies in Cetacea', *Hereditas*, vol. 77, pp. 1–36.
10 Arnason, U. and Benirschke, K. 1973. 'Karyotypes and idiograms of sperm and pygmy sperm whales', *Hereditas*, vol. 75, pp. 67–74.
11 Arnason, U., Benirschke, K., Mead, J. G. and Nichols, W. W. 1977. 'Banded karyotypes of three whales: *Mesoplodon europaeus*, *M. carlhubbsi* and *Balaenoptera acutorostrata*', *Hereditas*, vol. 87, pp. 189–200.
12 Barnes, L. G. 1973. '*Praekogia cedrosensis*, a new genus and species of fossil pygmy sperm whale from Isla Cedros, Baja California, Mexico', *Los Angeles County Mus. Contrib. Sci.*, vol. 247, pp. 1–20.
13 Barnes, L. G. 1976. 'Outline of eastern North Pacific fossil cetacean assemblages', *Syst. Zool.*, vol. 25, pp. 321–43.
14 Barnes, L. G. 1978. 'A review of *Lophocetus* and *Liolithax* and their relationships to the Delphinoid family Kentriodontidae (Cetacea: Odontoceti)', *Nat. Hist. Mus. of Los Angeles County Museum, Sci. Bull.*, vol. 28, pp. 1–35.
15 Benham, W. B. 1939. '*Mauicetus*: a fossil whale', *Nature* (London), vol. 143, p. 765.

16 Benham, W. B. 1942. 'Fossil Cetacea of New Zealand. *V. Mauicetus*, a generic name substituted for *Lophocephalus* Benham', *Trans. Roy. Soc. New Zealand*, vol. 71, pp. 260–70.

17 Bock, W. J. 1966. 'An approach to the functional analysis of bill shape', *Auk*, vol. 83, pp. 10–51.

18 Boyden, A. and Gemeroy, D. 1950. 'The relative position of the Cetacea among the orders of Mammalia as indicated by precipitin tests', *Zoologica*, vol. 35, pp. 145–51.

19 Brandt, J. F. 1894. 'Ergäzungen zu dem Fossilen Cetaceen Europa's', *Mem. Acad. Imp. Sci. de St Petersburg* (7), vol. 21, no. 6, pp. iv, 54, plates 1–5.

20 Briggs, J. C. 1970. *Marine Zoogeography*, New York, McGraw-Hill.

21 Cabrera, A. 1926. 'Cetaceos fosiles del Museo de la Plata', *Revista del Museo de la Plata, Buenos Aires*, vol. 29, pp. 363–411.

22 Cain, A. J. 1964. 'The perfection of animals', *Viewpoints in Biology*, vol. 3, pp. 36–63.

23 Capellini, G. 1883. 'Di un'orca fossile, scoperta a Cetona in Toscana', *Mem. Acad. Sci. Ist. de Bologna*, vol. 4, pp. 665–87, plates 1–4.

24 Carr, D. H., Singh, R. P., Miller, I. R. and McGeer, P. L. 1966. 'The chromosome complement of the Pacific killer whale (*Orcinus rectipinna*)', *Mamm. Chromosomes Newsletter*, vol. 22, p. 208.

25 Clarke, G. L. 1954. *Elements of Ecology*, New York, John Wiley; London, Chapman & Hall.

26 Clarke, M. R. 1978. 'Physical properties of spermaceti oil in the sperm whale', *J. mar. biol. Ass. U.K.*, vol. 58, pp. 19–26.

27 Clarke, M. R. 1978. 'Buoyancy control as a function of the spermaceti organ in the sperm whale', *J. mar. biol. Ass. U.K.*, vol. 58, pp. 27–71.

28 Climo, F. M. and Baker, A. N. 1972. 'A new shark-toothed dolphin (Cetacea: Squalodontidae) from the upper Oligocene of New Zealand', *J. Roy. Soc. New Zealand*, vol. 2, pp. 61–8.

29 Cooke, H. B. S. 1972. 'The fossil mammal fauna of Africa' in A. Keast, F. C. Erk and B. Glass (eds.), *Evolution, Mammals and Southern Continents*, Albany, NY, State University of New York Press, pp. 89–139.

30 Deschaseaux, C. 1961. 'Cetacea' in J. Piveteau (ed.), *Traite de Paleontologie*, vol VI, Paris, Masson et Cie, pp. 831–56.

31 Duffield, D. H., Ridgway, S. H. and Sparkes, R. S. 1967. 'Cytogenetic studies of two species of porpoise', *Nature* (London), vol. 213, pp. 189–90.

32 Ekman, S. 1953. *Zoogeography of the Sea*, London, Sidgwick & Jackson.

33 Eldridge, N. 1980. 'An extravagance of species', *Natural History*, vol. 89, pp. 46–51.

34 Emlong, D. 1960. 'A new archaic cetacean from the Oligocene of northwest Oregon', *Bull. Mus. nat. Hist. Oregon*, vol. 3, pp. 1–51.

35 Fleischer, G. 1973. 'On structure and function of the middle ear in the bottlenosed dolphin (*Tursiops truncatus*)', *Proc. 9th Ann. Conf. on Biol. Sonar and Diving Mammals*, Menlo Park, Cal., pp. 137–79.

36 Fleischer, G. 1976. 'Hearing in extinct cetaceans as determined by cochlear structure', *J. Palaeontol.*, vol. 50, pp. 133–52.

37 Fleischer, G. 1976. 'Über Beziehungen zwischen Horvermögen und Schädelbau bei Walen', *Sonderdruck a. Saugetierk. Mitt.*, vol. 24, pp. 48–59.

38 Flower, W. H. 1867. 'On the osteology of the cachalot or sperm whale (*Physeter macrocephalus*)', *Trans. zool. Soc. London*, vol. 6, pp. 309–69.

39 Flower, W. H. 1883. 'On whales, present and past and their probable origin', *Proc. zool. Soc. London* (1883), pp. 466–513.

40 Fordyce, R. E. 1977. 'The development of the circum-Antarctic current and the evolution of the Mysticeti (Mammalia: Cetacea)', *Paleogeography, paleoclimatology, paleontology*, vol. 21, pp. 265–71.

41 Fordyce, R. E. 1977. Personal communication.

42 Fraas, E. 1904. 'Neue Zeuglodonten au dem unteren Mitteleocän vom Mokattam bei Cairo', *Geol. Paläont. Abh.* (n.s.), vol. 6, pp. 199–220.

43 Fraser, F. C. 1966. 'Comments on the Delphinoidea' in K. S. Norris (ed.), *Whales, Dolphins, and Porpoises*, Berkeley and Los Angeles, University of California Press, pp. 7–30.

44 Fraser, F. C. and Purves, P. E. 1954. 'Hearing in Cetaceans', *Bull. Brit. Mus. (Nat. Hist.) Zool.*, vol. 2, pp. 103–16.

45 Fraser, F. C. and Purves, P. E. 1960. 'Hearing in Cetaceans', *Bull. British Mus. (Nat. Hist.) Zool.*, vol. 7, pp. 1–140.

46 Gaskin, D. E. 1976. 'The evolution, zoogeography and ecology of Cetacea', *Oceanogr. Mar. Biol. Ann. Rev.*, vol. 14, pp. 247–346.

47 Glaessner, M. F. 1955. 'Pelagic fossils (Aturia, penguins, whales) from the Tertiary of South Australia', *Rec. South Australian Mus.*, vol. 11, pp. 353–71.

48 Gould, S. J. 1980. 'Is a new and general theory of evolution emerging?' *Paleobiology*, vol. 6, pp. 119–30.

49 Gregory, W. K. 1951. *Evolution Emerging, vol. I*, New York, Macmillan Company.

50 Handley, C. O., Jr. 1966. 'A synopsis of the genus *Kogia* (pygmy sperm whales)', in K. S. Norris (ed.), *Whales, Dolphins, and Porpoises*, Berkeley and Los Angeles, University of California Press, pp. 62–9.

51 Hanna, G. D. and McLellan, M. E. 1924. 'A new species of whale from the type locality of the Monterey Group', *Proc. Calif. Acad. Sci.* (ser. 4), vol. 13, pp. 237–41.

52 Hinton, M. A. C. 1936. 'Some interesting points in the anatomy of the freshwater dolphin *Lipotes* and its allies', *Proc. Linn. Soc.*, 148th session, 1935–6, vol. 3, pp. 183–5.

53 Horrall, J. F., Taylor, B. K. and Taylor, K. M. 1968. 'Karyotypes of the Pacific killer whale *Orcinus orca* (Linn. 1758), and the Brazilian Tapir, *Tapirus terrestris* (Gray 1843)', *Mammal. Chromosomes Newsletter*, vol. 9, pp. 244–5.

54 Kasuya, T. 1973. 'Systematic consideration of recent toothed whales based on the morphology of tympano-periotic bone', *Sci. Rep. Whales Res. Inst.*, vol. 25, pp. 1–103.

55 Kellogg, R. 1922. 'Description of the skull of *Megaptera miocaena*, a fossil humpback whale from the Miocene diatomaceous earth of Lompoc, California', *Proc. US Nat. Mus.*, vol. 61, pp. 1–18.

56 Kellogg, R. 1925. 'A fossil physeteroid cetacean from Santa Barbara County, California', *Proc. US Nat. Mus.*, vol. 66, pp. 1–8.

57 Kellogg, R. 1927. '*Kentriodon pernix*, a Miocene porpoise from Maryland', *Proc. US Nat. Mus.*, vol. 69, pp. 1–55.

58 Kellogg, R. 1928. 'The history of whales – their adaptations to life in the water', *Q. Rev. Biol.*, vol. 3, pp. 29–76, 174–208.

59 Kellogg, R. 1931. 'Pelagic mammals from the Trembler formation of the Kern River formation, California', *Proc. Calif. Acad. Sci.* (ser. 4), vol. 19, pp. 217–397.

60 Kellogg, R. 1934. 'A new cetothere from the Modelo Formation at Los Angeles, California', *Carnegie Inst. Publ.*, vol. 447, pp. 83–104.

61 Kellogg, R. 1936. 'A review of the Archaeoceti', *Carnegie Inst. Publ.*, vol. 482, pp. 1–366.

62 Kellogg, R. 1955. 'Three Miocene porpoises from the Calvert Cliffs, Maryland', *Proc. US Nat. Mus.*, vol. 105, pp. 101–54.

63 Kellogg, R. 1965. 'The Miocene Calvert sperm whale, *Orycterocetus*', *Bull. US Nat. Mus.*, vol. 247, pp. 47–63.

64 Kellogg, R. 1968. 'Fossil marine mammals from the Miocene Calvert formation of Maryland and Virginia', *Bull. Smithsonian Inst.*, vol. 247, pp. 103–201.

65 Keyes, I. W. 1973. 'Early Oligocene squalodont cetacean from Oamaru, New

Zealand', *N.Z.J. mar. Freshwat. Res.*, vol. 7, pp. 381–90.

66 Kleinenberg, S. E. 1958. 'The origin of the Cetacea', *Doklady Akad. Nauk. SSSR*, vol. 122, pp. 950–2.

67 Kleinenberg, S. E. 1959. 'On the origin of the Cetacea', *Proc. Int. Congr. Zool.*, vol. 15, pp. 445–7.

68 Klumov, S. K. 1963. '(Feeding and helminth fauna of whalebone whales (Mysticeti) in the main whaling grounds of the world ocean)', *Trudy Inst. Okeanol.*, vol. 71, pp. 94–194.

69 Kulu, D. D., Veomett, I. and Sparkes, R. S. 1971. 'Cytogenetic comparison of four species of cetaceans', *J. Mammal.*, vol. 52, pp. 828–32.

70 Kulu, D. D. 1972. 'Evolution and cytogenetics' in S. H. Ridgway (ed.), *Mammals of the Sea: Biology and Medicine*, Springfield, Ill., Thomas Company, pp. 503–27.

71 Lipps, J. H. and Mitchell, E. 1976. 'Trophic model for the adaptive radiations and extinctions of pelagic marine mammals', *Paleobiology*, vol. 2, pp. 147–55.

72 Lydekker, R. 1894. 'Cetacean skulls from Patagonia', *Anales del Museo de la Plata, Buenos Aires, Paleontologica Argentina*, vol. 2 (pt II), pp. 1–13.

73 Makino, S. 1948. 'The chromosomes of Dall's porpoise, *Phocoena dalli* (True) with remarks on the phylogenetic relation of the Cetacea', *Chromosoma*, vol. 3, pp. 220–31.

74 Malde, H. E. 1959. 'Geology of the Charleston phosphate area, South Carolina', *US Geol. Survey Bull.*, vol. 1079, pp. 1–105.

75 Marples, B. J. 1956. 'Cetotheres (Cetacea) from the Oligocene of New Zealand', *Proc. zool. Soc. London*, vol. 126, pp. 565–80.

76 Mchedlidze, G. A. 1970. 'Nekotorye obschchie cherty istorii kitoobraznykh' in *Metsniereba*, ch. 1, U.S. Geological Survey Translation TR71–14, Tblisi. (Not seen: cited in ref. 114 below.)

77 Mchedlidze, G. A. 1975. Written communication (not seen: cited in ref. 114 below).

78 McKay, A. 1882. 'On the lower deposits of Wharekauri Basin and the lower Waitaki Valley', *Repts Geol. Explor. 1881*, Colonial Museum and Geological Survey Dept, Wellington, New Zealand, 1881, pp. 98–106.

79 Mead, J. G. 1975. 'Anatomy of the external nasal passages and facial complex in the Delphinidae', *Smithsonian Contrib. Zool.*, vol. 207, pp. 1–72.

80 Miller, G. S. 1923. 'The telescoping of the cetacean skull', *Smithsonian Misc. Collections*, vol. 75, pp. 1–68.

81 Mitchell, E. 1966. 'Faunal succession of extinct North Pacific marine mammals', *Norsk Hvalfangsttid.*, vol. 55, pp. 47–60.

82 Mitchell, E. 1970. 'Pigmentation pattern evolution in delphinid cetaceans: an essay on adaptive colouration', *Can. J. Zool.*, vol. 48, pp. 717–40.

83 Moore, J. C. 1968. 'Relationships among the living genera of beaked whales, with classifications, diagnoses, and keys', *Fieldiana Zool.*, vol. 54, pp. 209–98.

84 Moreno, F. P. 1892. 'Lijeros apuntes sobre does generos de Cetaceros fosiles de la Republica Argentina', *Revista del Museo de la Plata, Buenos Aires*, vol. 3, pp. 393–400.

85 Ness, A. R. 1967. 'A measure of asymmetry of the skulls of odontocete whales', *J. Zool. London*, vol. 153, pp. 209–21.

86 Nishiwaki, M. 1963. 'Taxonomic consideration on genera of Delphinidae', *Sci. Rep. Whales Res. Inst.*, vol. 17, pp. 93–103.

87 Nishiwaki, M. 1964. 'Revision of the article *Taxonomic consideration on genera of Delphinidae*', *Sci. Rep. Whales Res. Inst.*, vol. 18, pp. 171–2.

88 Owen, R. 1839. 'Observations on the *Basilosaurus* of Dr Harlan (*Zeuglodon cetoides* Owen)', *Trans. Geol. Soc. London*, vol. 6, pp. 69–79.

89 Portis, A. 1885. 'Catalogo descrittivo dei Talasoterii rinvenuti nei Terreni Terziarii del Piemonte e dello Liguria', *Mem. R. Accad. Sci. Torino*, vol. 37, pp. 247–365.

90 Rensberger, J. M. 1969. 'A new iniid cetacean from the Miocene of California', *Univ.*

Calif. Publ. Geol. Sci., vol. 82, pp. 1–43.

91 Reyment, R. A. 1965. *Aspects of the geology of Nigeria*, Ibadan, Ibadan University Press.

92 Rice, D. W. 1967. 'Cetacea' in S. Anderson and J. Knox Jones (eds.), *Recent Mammals of the World : A Synopsis of Families*, New York, Ronald Press, pp. 291–324.

93 Rice, D. W. and Wolman, A. A. 1971. 'The life history and ecology of the gray whale (*Eschrichtius robustus*)', *Amer. Soc. Mammalogists*, Spec. Publ. no. 3.

94 Rothausen, K. 1968. 'Die systematische Stellung der europäischen Squalodontidae (Odontoceti: Mammalia)', *Palaont. Zeit.*, vol. 42, pp. 83–104.

95 Rothausen, K. 1970. 'Marine Reptilia and Mammalia and the problem of the Oligocene–Miocene boundary', *Giornale di Geologia* (2), vol. 35, pp. 181–9.

96 Sahni, A. and Mishra, V. P. 1975. 'Lower Tertiary vertebrates from western India', *Monogr. Palaeontol. Soc. India*, no. 3, pp. 1–49.

97 Sanderson, I. T. 1956. *Follow the Whale*. London, Cassell.

98 Savage, D. E. and Barnes, L. G. 1972. 'Miocene vertebrate geochronology of the west coast of North America' in E. H. Stinemeyer (ed.), *Proceedings of the Pacific Coast Miocene Biostratigraphic Symposium*, Bakersfield Calif., Soc. Econ. Paleontol. Mineralogists, pp. 124–45.

99 Schäfer, W. 1972. *Ecology and Palaeoecology of Marine Environments*, translated by I. Oetel, Edinburgh, Oliver & Boyd.

100 Schoener, T. W. 1965. 'The evolution of bill size differences among sympatric congeneric species of birds', *Evolution*, vol. 19, pp. 189–213.

101 Simpson, G. G. 1945. 'The principles of classification and a classification of mammals', *Bull. Amer. Mus. Nat. Hist.*, vol. 85, pp. 1–350.

102 Simpson, G. G. 1953. *The Major Features of Evolution*, New York, Columbia University Press.

103 Slijper, E. J. 1936. *Die Cetaceen Vergleichend-anatomisch und systematisch*, Den Hague, Capita. zool.

104 Slijper, E. J. 1962. *Whales*, London, Hutchinson.

105 Szalay, F. E. and Gould, S. J. 1966. 'Asiatic Mesonychidae (Mammalia: Condylarthra)', *Bull. Amer. Mus. nat. Hist.*, vol. 132, pp. 127–74.

106 Tarlo, L. B. H. 1964. 'A primitive whale from the London clay of the Isle of Sheppey', *Proc. Geol. Assoc.*, vol. 74, pp. 319–23.

107 Thenius, E. 1969. *Phylogenie der Mammalia*. Berlin, Walter de Gruyter.

108 True, F. W. 1889. 'Contributions to the natural history of the cetaceans, a review of the family Delphinidae', *Bull. US Nat. Mus.*, vol. 36, pp. 1–191.

109 True, F. W. 1912. 'Description of a new fossil porpoise of the genus *Delphinodon* from the Miocene Formation of Maryland', *J. Acad. Nat. Sci. Philadelphia* (ser. 2), vol. 15, pp. 165–94.

110 Van Valen, L. 1966. 'Deltatheridia, a new order of mammals', *Bull. Amer. Mus. Nat. Hist.*, vol. 132, pp. 1–126.

111 Van Valen, L. 1968. 'Monophyly or diphyly in the origin of whales', *Evolution*, vol. 22, pp. 37–41.

112 Van Valen L. 1969. 'The multiple origins of the placental carnivores', *Evolution*, vol. 23, pp. 118–30.

113 Walen, K. H. and Madin, S. H. 1965. 'Comparative chromosome analyses of the bottle-nosed dolphin (*Tursiops truncatus*) and the pilot whale (*Globicephala scammoni*)', *Amer. Natur.*, vol. 99, pp. 349–54.

114 Whitmore, F. C. and Sanders, A. E. 1976. 'Review of the Oligocene Cetacea', *Syst. Zool.*, vol. 25, pp. 304–20.

115 Wilson, L. E. 1935. 'Miocene marine mammals from the Bakersfield region, California', *Bull. Peabody Mus. Nat. Hist.*, Yale University, vol. 4, pp. 1–143.

116 Wilson, L. E. 1973. 'A delphinid (Mammalia: Cetacea) from the Miocene of Palos

Verdes Hills, California', *Univ. Calif. Publ. Geol. Sci.*, vol. 103, pp. 1–34.

117 Winge, H. 1912. *The interrelationships of the mammalian genera*, vol. III *Ungulata, Cetacea*, translated by E. Deichmann and G. M. Allen, Copenhagen, C. A. Reitzels.

118 Yablokov, A. V. 1964. 'Convergence or parallelism in the evolution of cetaceans', *Palaeontol. Zh.*, vol. 1, pp. 97–106.

119 Young, J. Z. 1958. *The Life of Vertebrates*, Oxford, Oxford University Press.

120 Zhemkova, Z. P. 1965. 'On the origin of Cetacea', *Zool. Zh.*, vol. 44, pp. 1546–52.

121 Zhou, K., Weijuan, Q. and Yuemin, L. 1978. '(Recent advances in the study of the Baiji) *Lipotes vexillifer*', *Chin. Inst. Biol. Sci.*, Nanjing, vol. 1, pp. 8–13.

Systematic list of living Cetacea, including probable synonyms which have been used as specific names in relatively recent literature

A systematic list of the Cetacea of the world is a necessary aid to guide the reader through the maze of nomenclature involved in a discussion of cetacean zoogeography, but unfortunately the problems discussed in Chapters 6 and 7 come into sharp focus when one attempts to compile such a list, especially one which will meet the approval of even the majority of cetacean taxonomists.

The following assemblage contains a number of genera and species of uncertain or unsatisfactory status. In most cases I have followed the names given by Rice and Scheffer (6) in their revised list of 1968, updated by Rice (5) in 1977, those compiled by Mitchell in 1975 (4), and those used by the Marine Mammal Commission (3). I cannot agree to the retention of the Phocoenidae as a generic group within the Delphinidae, as was done by Rice and Scheffer, and I concur with Kasuya (2) and Barnes (1) that *Orcaella* seems to fit best in the Monodontidae, but do not follow Kasuya in dividing that family into two. I retain the single family Platanistidae for all the 'freshwater' dolphins and *Pontoporia* – small cakes can only be divided into so many portions of sensible size – and I agree with Barnes that monotypic families are pointless systematic entities, emphasizing differences rather than relationships. That situation cannot, however, be avoided in the case of the gray whale, unless one suggests that the Eschrichtiinae could be made a living subfamily of the Cetotheridae.

ORDER CETACEA

Suborder Mysticeti (or Mystacoceti) (Baleen or whalebone whales)

Family Balaenidae (Right whales)

SUBFAMILY BALAENINAE
Balaena mysticetus Linnaeus, 1758

Greenland right whale or bowhead whale. Two to four isolated populations are generally recognized in the Arctic basin.

Eubalaena glacialis Müller, 1776
   Balaena seiboldii

Black right whale. Three nominal subspecies are recognized: *E. g. glacialis* in the North Atlantic; *E.g. japonica* Lacepede, 1818 in the North Pacific; *E. g. australis* Desmoulins, 1822 in the Southern Ocean.

SUBFAMILY NEOBALAENINAE
Caperea marginata Gray, 1846

Pygmy right whale. Southern Ocean.

Family Eschrichtidae (Gray whales)

Eschrichtius robustus Gray 1864
   Eschrichtius gibbosus
   Eschrichtius glaucus
   Rhachianectes glaucus

Pacific gray whale. In the North Pacific only. A North Atlantic population apparently became extinct only in historical times.

Family Balaenopteridae (Rorquals)

Balaenoptera musculus (Linnaeus, 1758)

Blue whale. All oceans. A pygmy form in the southern Indian Ocean has been given the name *B.m. brevicauda* Ichihara, 1966 (alternatively attributed to Zemsky and Boronin, 1964). *B. m. intermedia* Burmeister, 1871 has been applied to the Southern Ocean population, individuals of which are significantly larger at maturity than the *B. m. musculus* of the North Atlantic and North Pacific. This subspecific name is rarely used.

Balaenoptera physalus (Linnaeus, 1758)	Fin or finback whale. All oceans, but especially temperate and sub-polar waters. The larger form of the southern hemisphere sometimes has the name *B. p. quoyi* Fischer, 1830 applied to it.
Balaenoptera borealis (Lesson, 1828)	Sei whale. All oceans. *B. b. schlegeli* Flower, 1865 is the subspecific name sometimes applied to the Southern Ocean population.
Balaenoptera edeni Anderson, 1878 *Balaenoptera brydei*	Bryde's whale. Tropical waters.

Balaenoptera acutorostrata (Lacépède, 1804)
   Balaenoptera davidsoni
   Balaenoptera huttoni
	Minke or lesser piked whale. All oceans. The name *bonaerensis* Burmeister, 1867 is applied to the form lacking a white patch on the pectoral flippers.

Megaptera novaeangliae (Borowski, 1781) *Megaptera nodosa*	Humpback whale. All oceans.

Suborder Odontoceti (Toothed whales)

Family Physeteridae (*Sperm whales*)

SUBFAMILY PHYSETERINAE

Physeter catodon Linnaeus, 1758 *Physeter macrocephalus*	Sperm whale or cachalot. All oceans.

SUBFAMILY KOGIINAE

Kogia breviceps (de Blainville, 1838)	Pygmy sperm whale. All oceans, but not in polar or subpolar regions.
Kogia simus Owen, 1866	Dwarf sperm whale. All waters, but not in polar or subpolar regions.

Family Ziphiidae (*Beaked whales*)

Tasmacetus shepherdi Oliver, 1937	Shepherd's beaked whale. Probably circumpolar in Southern Ocean.
Berardius arnuxii Duvernoy, 1851	Southern bottlenosed whale. Temperate Southern Ocean.
Berardius bairdii Stejneger, 1883	Baird's beaked whale. Temperate North Pacific.
Hyperoodon planifrons Flower, 1882	Flat-headed bottlenosed whale. Temperate and polar Southern Ocean.

Hyperoodon ampullatus (Forster, 1770) *Hyperoodon rostratus*	North Atlantic bottlenosed whale. Temperate and polar North Atlantic.
Ziphius cavirostris G. Cuvier, 1823	Goose-beaked whale. All oceans outside polar regions.
Mesoplodon (Dioplodon) densirostris (de Blainville, 1817)	Blainville's beaked whale. All low-latitude waters.
Mesoplodon (Dolichodon) layardi (Gray, 1865)	Strap-toothed whale. Circumpolar in temperate latitudes of Southern Ocean.
Mesoplodon ginkodens Nishiwaki and Kamiya, 1958	Ginko-toothed beaked whale. Warm waters of the Indo-Pacific region.
Mesoplodon grayi von Haast, 1876	Gray's beaked whale. Circumpolar in the Southern Ocean.
Mesoplodon carlhubbsi Moore, 1963	Arch-beaked whale. Temperate North Pacific.
Mesoplodon europaeus (Gervais, 1855) *Mesoplodon gervaisi*	Gervais' beaked whale. Temperate and tropical waters of North Atlantic.
Mesoplodon mirus True, 1913	True's beaked whale. North and South Atlantic.
Mesoplodon stejnegeri True, 1885	Stejneger's beaked whale. Cooler waters of North Pacific.
Mesoplodon bowdoini Andrews, 1908	Andrew's beaked whale. Temperate waters of Indo-Pacific region, but not known from eastern South Pacific.
Mesoplodon bidens (Sowerby, 1804)	Sowerby's beaked whale. Temperate North Atlantic.
Mesoplodon hectori (Gray, 1871)	Hector's beaked whale. Circumpolar cool waters of Southern Ocean.
Mesoplodon (Indopacetus) pacificus (Longman, 1926)	Longman's beaked whale. Coral Sea.

Family Monodontidae (*White whales and narwhals*)

Monodon monoceros Linnaeus, 1758	Narwhal. Circumpolar in Arctic Basin.
Delphinapterus leucas (Pallas, 1776)	Beluga or white whale. Arctic Ocean, Bering Sea, Sea of Okhotsk, Hudson Bay and James Bay, St Lawrence estuary.
Orcaella brevirostris (Gray, 1866)	Irrawaddy dolphin. Coastal waters from Bay of Bengal to northern coast of Australia.

Family Phocoenidae (*True porpoises*)

Phocoena phocoena (Linnaeus, 1758)
   Phocoena vomerina

Common or harbour porpoise. The name *P. p. relicta* Abel, 1905 is applied to the isolated Sea of Azov–north Black Sea population.

Phocoena sinus Norris & McFarland, 1958

Gulf of California porpoise or Cochito. Upper Gulf of California. Population very small, may be extinct, or nearly so.

Phocoena spinipinnis Burmeister, 1865

Burmeister's porpoise. Coast of Peru to coast of southern Argentina.

Phocoena dioptrica Lahille, 1912

Spectacled porpoise. Coast of Argentina, Falkland Islands, South Georgia, Auckland Islands.

Phocoenoides dalli (True, 1885)

Dall's porpoise. Cool waters of the North Pacific, to south Bering Sea.

Neophocoena phocoenoides (G. Cuvier, 1829)
   Neomeris phocoenoides

Finless black porpoise. Warm coastal waters of the Indo-Pacific region, but not in central or eastern Pacific.

Family Delphinidae (*True dolphins*)

Orcinus orca (Linnaeus, 1758)
   Orcinus rectipinna
   Grampus rectipinna
   Grampus orca

Killer whale. All oceans.

Pseudorca crassidens (Owen, 1846)

False killer whale. All oceans except high latitudes.

Feresa attenuata Gray, 1875

Pygmy killer whale. Probably in all tropical and subtropical seas.

Peponocephala electra Gray, 1875

Melon-headed whale or many-toothed blackfish. All warm seas.

Globicephala melaena (Traill, 1809)

Pilot whale, pothead or common blackfish, North Atlantic. *G. m. edwardi* A. Smith, 1934, is circumpolar in the southern hemisphere, in cooler waters.

Globicephala macrorhynchus Gray, 1846
   Globicephala scammoni
   Globicephala seiboldi

Short-finned pilot whale. All tropical and subtropical waters. The form in the temperate North Pacific may deserve subspecific status; one of the synonymic names is available for it (*seiboldi*).

Lagenorhynchus obliquidens Gill, 1865

Pacific white-sided dolphin. Temperate waters of the North Pacific.

Lagenorhynchus cruciger (Quoy and Gaimard, 1824)
Lagenorhynchus wilsoni

Hour-glass dolphin. Probably circumpolar in the cooler waters of the Southern Ocean.

Lagenorhynchus australis (Peale, 1848)

Peale's or black-chinned dolphin. Cool waters of Falkland Islands and Argentina.

Lagenorhynchus obscurus (Gray, 1828)
Lagenorhynchus fitzroyi
Lagenorhynchus superciliosus

Dusky dolphin. Circumpolar in coastal waters of the southern hemisphere; confined to more temperate waters.

Lagenorhynchus acutus (Gray, 1828)

Atlantic white-sided dolphin. Temperate and subpolar waters of the North Atlantic.

Lagenorhynchus albirostris (Gray, 1846)

White-beaked dolphin. Temperate and subpolar waters of the North Atlantic.

Lagenodelphis hosei Fraser, 1956

Fraser's dolphin. Possibly through all warm waters of the world, or certainly in warm waters of the Indo-Pacific region.

Cephalorhynchus hectori (Van Beneden, 1881)
Cephalorhynchus albifrons

Hector's dolphin. Coastal waters of New Zealand.

Cephalorhynchus eutropia (Gray, 1846)
Cephalorhynchus albiventris

Black dolphin, white-bellied dolphin. Coast of Chile.

Cephalorhynchus commersoni (Lacépède, 1804)

Commerson's dolphin. Cool waters of southern South America and Falkland Islands.

Cephalorhynchus heavisidei (Gray, 1828)

Heaviside's dolphin. Coastal waters of southern South Africa.

Lissodelphis borealis (Peale, 1848)

Northern right whale dolphin. Temperate waters of North Pacific.

Lissodelphis peronii (Lacépède, 1804)

Southern right whale dolphin. Possibly circumpolar in Southern Ocean. Best-known from the Pacific sector.

Grampus griseus (G. Cuvier, 1812)
Grampidelphis griseus

Risso's dolphin. All tropical and temperate seas.

Tursiops truncatus (Montagu, 1821)
Tursiops absulam
Tursiops catalania
Tursiops gadamu
Tursiops nesarnack
Tursiops nuuanu

Bottlenosed dolphin. In coastal waters of most tropical, subtropical and warm temperate regions. *T. t. aduncus* (Ehrenberg, 1833) inhabits the Indo-Pacific core region; *T. t.*

Sotalia gadamu

Steno bredanensis (Lesson, 1828)
  Steno rostratus

Delphinus delphis Linnaeus, 1758
  Delphinus bairdii
  Delphinus capensis

Stenella coeruleoalba (Meyen, 1833)
  Stenella euphrosyne
  Stenella styx

Stenella longirostris (Gray, 1828)
  Stenella alope
  Stenella roseiventris
  Stenella microps

Stenella attenuata (Gray, 1846)
  Stenella dubia?
  Stenella frontalis?
  Stenella fraenata?
  Stenella malayana?
Stenella a. graffmani (Lönnberg, 1934)
  Prodelphinus graffmani
Stenella plagiodon (Cope 1866)

Sotalia fluviatalis (Gervais and Deville, 1853)
  Sotalia tucuxi
  Sotalia pallida
Sotalia guianensis (van Beneden, 1864)
  Sotalia brasiliensis

Sousa teuszii (Keukenthal, 1892)
  Sotalia teuszii

gilli Dall, 1873, the temperate North Pacific.
Rough-toothed dolphin. All tropical, subtropical and warm temperate seas.
Common or saddleback dolphin. All tropical, subtropical and warm temperate seas, including the Mediterranean and Black Sea. The subspecific name *D. d. bairdii* has been applied to a North Pacific form.
Blue–white, or striped dolphin. All tropical, subtropical and warm temperate seas, including Mediterranean.
Spinner dolphin. Probably in all tropical oceans. The taxonomy of the tropical forms of *Stenella* is in chaos; the genus presents some formidable taxonomic problems. This list is at best provisional. Some recognize *roseiventris* as a distinct species, others state that it can be graded into *longirostris* through known intermediate forms.
Spotted dolphin. Pelagic waters of the tropical Pacific, and probably other waters too.

Coastal waters of the tropical eastern Pacific.
Tropical Atlantic and possibly other waters. May be part of the *attenuata* complex.
Tucuxi. Amazon river system.

Coastal waters and river systems of South America. Relationship to *fluviatalis* requires more study.
Atlantic humpbacked dolphin. Coastal waters of West Africa. This genus is in chaos and needs thorough revision.

Sousa chinensis (Osbeck, 1765)
  Sotalia chinensis
  Sotalia sinensis
  Sousa (=Sotalia) plumbea?
  Sousa (=Sotalia) lentigenosa?
  Sousa borneensis?

Indo-Pacific humpbacked dolphin. Coastal waters from warm waters of eastern South Africa to Indonesia and southern China.

Family Platanistidae (River dolphins)

Pontoporia blainvillei (Gervais and d'Orbigny, 1844)
  Stenodelphis blainvillei

Franciscana, La Plata dolphin. Coastal waters and estuaries (apparently *not* rivers) of eastern South America from central Brazil to central Argentina.

Lipotes vexillifer Miller, 1918

White fin (=flag) dolphin, Baiji. Upper Yangtze River system and Tung-T'ing Lake, central China.

Inia geoffrensis (de Blainville, 1817)

Bouto, Bufeo, Amazon river dolphin. Amazon and Orinoco river basins of South America.

Platanista gangetica (Roxburgh, 1801)

Ganges dolphin or Ganges susu. Ganges and Brahmaputra river systems above tidal incursion limits.

Platanista indi Blyth, 1859
  Platanista minor (Owen, 1859)

Indus river dolphin, or Indus susu. Indus river system above tidal incursion limit.

References

1 Barnes, L. G. 1978. 'A review of *Lophocetus* and *Liolithax* and their relationships to the delphinoid family Kentriodontidae (Cetacea: Odontoceti)', *Nat. Hist. Mus. Los Angeles County Sci. Bull.*, vol. 28, pp. 1–35.

2 Kasuya, T. 1973. 'Systematic consideration of recent toothed whales based on the morphology of tympano-periotic bone', *Sci. Rep. Whales Res. Inst.*, vol. 25, pp. 1–103.

3 Marine Mammal Commission. 1976. *Marine mammal names used by the Marine Mammal Commission*, Washington.

4 Mitchell, E. 1975. *Porpoise, Dolphin and Small Whale Fisheries of the World-Status and Problems*, IUCN Monograph 3, pp. 1–129.

5 Rice, D. W. 1977. 'A list of the marine mammals of the world', NOAA Technical Report, NMFS SSRF–711.

6 Rice, D. W. and Scheffer, V. B. 1968. 'A list of the marine mammals of the world', *US Fish Wildl. Serv. Spec. Sci. Rep.*, vol. 579, pp. 1–16.

CHAPTER 6

The zoogeography of Cetacea

Introduction

Several difficulties are encountered when we attempt to interpret such patterns of cetacean distribution as our limited knowledge permits us to recognize. Some of these are the simple result of that familiar constraint – insufficient information. In addition to problems concerning the identification of species, that is, common agreement on the identity of the units under discussion (see Chapter 7), a number of forms are known only from fortuitous discoveries, often chance strandings. Apparent distributions of 'rare' species may be artifacts, therefore, merely the result of gross undercollecting. Even if reasonably sure of the identities and distributions of a species or genus, the zoogeographer is often further handicapped by deficiencies in knowledge concerning changes in past environmental conditions which, on the one hand, could have generated isolative barriers or, on the other, led to their breakdown.

But all these are really practical difficulties, which can be resolved to some degree, albeit not always to the investigator's complete satisfaction. More contentious are the differences of opinion among biogeographers concerning assumptions which can or cannot be made during systematic analyses of taxa, and the serious differences of opinion as to how biota dispersed and became established in the patterns we observe today. Before considering the zoogeography of the Cetacea in particular, it is worth examining the opposing viewpoints in some detail, since the respective interpretations of causative events and factors differ significantly.

Controversies in zoogeographic interpretation

For the purposes of the present discussion I am accepting the philosophical and actual reality of cetacean species, as indicated by Linnaean nomenclature, and leaving consideration of some of the problems inherent in the 'species concept' until the next chapter. (In permitting myself the luxury of putting the cart before the horse and discussing speciation processes before definitions of species, I would argue that zoogeography is almost always discussed in terms of units at or above the species level, and if the evolution of the Cetacea is the starting-point for this section, then the origins of the major distribution patterns we see today should logically follow next.)

Most recent authors have considered only one or two categories of speciation to be plausible: *allopatric* (or geographic) speciation and various forms of *sympatric* (that is, non-geographic) speciation. So-called 'instantaneous speciation' still has some proponents, but the difficulties of accepting any type of 'instantaneous' change in a population through mutation, massive chromosome alteration and so on, seem almost insurmountable at present (64) (see reference 48 in Chapter 5 also). It is not a concept, however, that should be confused in any way with what might be called 'rapid' speciation. Although we may not be able to calculate rates of evolution with any accuracy, we can accept that they vary considerably within the animal kingdom (see p. 163), on the evolution of the early Cetacea).

The two concepts can be summarized as follows: sympatric speciation by definition must imply the development of isolating mechanisms within the dispersal area of a single unit population. Allopatric speciation, on the other hand, requires that some kind of isolative barrier divide a unit population, which then ceases to have physical and genetic continuity. Reproductive isolating mechanisms can then develop as the two populations evolve separately under somewhat different conditions. These may or may not become strong enough to prevent interbreeding, should the barrier break down at some time in the future. The validity of the two 'accepted' categories of speciation has been debated at length in the literature, but this is not the place to review this controversy in any detail. The majority of biological opinion has been against hypotheses of sympatric speciation during the last twenty years or so, concluding that the essential component of speciation – that of the genetic repatterning of populations – can take place only if those populations are temporarily protected by extrinsic factors, that is, by spatial isolation (63). Spatial isolation appears to be normally effected by geographical barriers, but the possibility cannot be ruled out that certain kinds of animals or plants can become segregated by differing ecological requirements within an area, and that genetic divergence can occur without recognizable spatial isolation being present. There are some strong arguments to support this possibility, backed by quite convincing examples in the recent evolutionary literature, which should not be overlooked by the interested reader, though it does not seem to be applicable to any cases of cetacean speciation (some of these articles are included in the references on speciation processes in Chapter 7). The controversy will undoubtedly continue for years, even though at present the majority of biologists believe, as E. Mayr stated, that 'It is . . . clear that geographic speciation is of overwhelming importance in explaining the problem of multiplication of species' (64).

When considering opposing viewpoints among biogeographers, it is

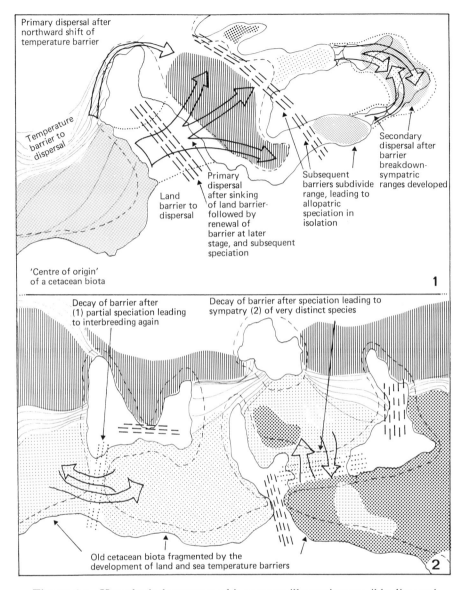

Figure 6.1 Hypothetical zoogeographic patterns illustrating possible dispersal, isolation and speciation patterns of cetaceans with reference to **1**. a 'centre of origin' concept, and **2**. fragmentation of an old widespread cetacean biota, with subsequent speciation occurring more along the lines of the 'vicariance' concept. In both models sympatric distributions frequently result. Both land barriers and ocean-front boundaries are indicated as possible agents through which populations of some cetacean species can become isolated.

important to keep in mind the fact that almost all of them adhere to the same belief in the essential role of allopatric processes in speciation. Polemic discourses in systematic and biogeographic journals over the last ten or fifteen years have done much to polarize published opinion into two camps (to the deteriment of rational discussion and appreciation of just how much common ground they share).

The division is superficially simple (Figure 6.1): 'orthodox' biogeography is defined as having its roots in the Darwinian concept of 'centres of origin' of taxa, from which the latter disperse by land, air, water or through the medium of a host species. Principal authors classically associated with this view include Darwin (23), Matthew (62), Simpson (97), Darlington (21, 22) and Mayr (63–5). 'New' or 'vicariance' biogeographers (19, 20, 74, 75, 92) dispute the existence of centres of origin, and doubt the associated explanations for assembly of the components of regional biota by dispersal from these centres in terms of over-water or over-land 'sweepstakes' (that is, by chance), and the influence of 'filter barriers' which permit passage of some taxa but not others.

The root of the 'schism' is this – does the term 'centre of origin' have real meaning, or can one conclude that '. . . within a particular geographic framework . . . plant and animal distributions may be interpreted without commitment to special assumptions other than allopatric speciation (vicariance)' (92). The *general features* of modern biotic distribution on a global basis are believed by this school of thought to have been determined by subdivision of ancestral biotas in response to changing geography alone. As early as the 1930s D. Rosa (91) suggested that biogeographic development should be viewed as consisting of '*a primitive cosmopolitanism succeeded by a process of localization taking place at the same time as the multiplication and differentiation of species*'.

'Vicariants' (allopatric species) arise when an extrinsic barrier develops and prevents gene exchange in a population which formerly represented a genetic continuum. Sympatric distributions of related species are recognized; these are considered to be the result of rearrangement of distribution patterns after the disappearance of former barriers. Sympatry can be maintained, providing the allopatric vicariants developed reproductive isolation during their period of separation. Vicariance biogeography is basically the systematic study of the history of *fragmentation* of ancestral biotas (that is, large *sets* of allopatric vicariants), and has much to recommend it.

Yet one can point to weaknesses in the theoretical underpinning of vicariance biogeography as currently proposed, which make it less than fully satisfying intellectually. In his formalization of the theory, the founder, Leon Croizat, defined 'dispersal' in a very particular way (19), combining the principles of adaptation, development of isolating mechanisms (that is, speciation) and spatial dispersal, into a two-phase unified concept. The first 'immobile' phase, which he described as '*form-building without translation in space*', is said to be followed by a more or less distinct 'mobile' phase, in which the vicariant 'disperses' in the more usual sense, which Croizat defines as '*translation in space with elimination of form-making*'.

To a considerable degree the first concept is not in accord with modern field data on population fluctuations. In the great majority of papers by vicariance biogeographers that I have read there is little real dynamic ecological content; the diagrams and maps of ranges of vicariants are static items, frozen in time and space. The very use of 'immobilist phase' by Croizat does not give one confidence that the dynamic ebb and flow, which can occur within short periods of time in the numbers and distributions of animals, has been recognized – Platnick's (87) insistence on the essential differences between 'dispersal' and dispersion notwithstanding. I find a casual dismissal of the importance of stochastic influences, and the conceptually static view of allopatric speciation is particularly difficult to accept when one considers pelagic marine species. For example, dynamic population shifts, largely under the influence of changes in environmental conditions, are responsible for 'invasions' of sei whales penetrating the high latitudes of the North Atlantic in some seasons (see p. 268). In fish populations, feeding in a short food-chain situation, the size of a 'good' year class may be fifty or sixty times greater than a 'poor' year class, and the area of distribution of the migrating population can differ by an order of magnitude (76).

Furthermore, the second phase of Croizat's hypothesis, '*spatial movement with elimination of form-making*', seems to me to be at variance with what we know of the real modes of action of natural selection and the pressures a population must encounter at all times. The 'form' will not cease to be affected by selection pressures when the vicariant disperses; as soon as it 'moves' it will almost certainly encounter different environmental conditions and come into contact with other species. It may have to compete for the basic resources that make up the carrying capacity of its environment, should these be seriously limited. This cannot help but direct further selective modification of the 'form'.

My own view of this controversy is that, as with most things, the real answers lie somewhere between the poles of the two opposing points of view. The importance of 'allopatric' speciation processes are probably not to be disputed. Vicariance theory is claimed to work best when used to study *biotas* rather than individual *taxa*, for, as its proponents admit (20), 'attempts to explain the distribution of individual plant and animal groups, based on their ecology and means of dispersal, may ignore and obscure existing generalized tracks [distribution patterns] and the ancestral biotas they represent'. Personally, I am in full agreement that the fragmentation of ancestral biotas has played a far more important role in the establishment of modern biogeographic distributions than would have been admitted thirty years ago. But I also believe that the real reason that examples can be found which do not conform in their analyses is that often the evolution of species and their dispersal simply does not take place in a manner in accord with the vicariance hypothesis or in a way that can realistically be analysed by the vicariance model or the cladistic systematics (43) which so frequently underlie its use (for argued objections to these, see Darlington (22), Mayr (65) and Sokal (101)). Although '*primitive cosmopolitanism*' is sometimes apparent (105), it is also frequently illusory and the result of lack of 'resolution' in data, particularly when taxa of great antiquity are considered. Rosa (91) also wrote of this cosmopolitanism being '*succeeded by a process of localization taking place at the same time as the multiplication and differentiation of species*'. I find less fault with this concept, but if such a 'localization' is confined to one continental area or one ocean basin, and the species differentiated in such an area then disperse more widely after breakdown of isolative barriers, I can see no reason why 'centre of origin' is not a perfectly applicable term in such a situation. When such a 'localization' also involves the development of a significant *evolutionary novelty*, and the fossil record suggests that this took place in a restricted area, with initial allopatric speciation occurring *within* that limited area, and dispersal and further speciation take place subsequently, then the term 'centre of origin' seems the only one which really describes what has happened. In other situations, however, the simple vicariance model probably accounts quite satisfactorily for distribution patterns that we observe.

Patterns of cetacean radiation and dispersal

What apparent evolutionary patterns are revealed when we turn to a specific study of the Cetacea? We have two significant 'evolutionary novelties' in the order: the nasal sacs and associated acoustic structures in the odontocetes, and the baleen plate-buccal filter beds of the mysticetes. Within both the suborders we have abundant examples of allopatric speciation processes at various stages, and the extrinsic barriers which were probably responsible can be identified in a number of cases. We have sympatric distributions of closely related species, almost certainly representing previous isolations which have since broken down subsequent to the development of isolating mechanisms. But we also have some nearly unique biogeographic situations – a small number of species, some the only living survivors of their genera – have distributions which are virtually worldwide.

The earliest archaeocetes do not, on the basis of what we presently know, show 'primitive cosmopolitanism'; that comes later. In the early and Middle Eocene they seemed to occur only in the western Tethyan periphery from West Africa, Egypt and India, and even the latter record may represent a secondary dispersal following a secondary expansion of the western Tethys Sea (see Chapter 5, p. 164). The Eocene record is quite good, relatively speaking, and these are large and distinctive fossils.

The primitive Squalodontidae, on the other hand, were quite widely distributed, as were the Cetotheridae. Yet there is no evidence to suggest this was the result of slow and steady allopatric speciation, in fact the number of species present at any given time seems to have been rather small, indicative of simple, rather rapid expansion of spatial range. This conflicts with neither 'orthodox' nor vicariance biogeographical hypotheses.

Of more interest is the distribution of the fossils of the earliest Mysticeti and of the earliest balaenopterid rorquals. As in the case of the earliest archaeocetes, present information indicates that the evolution of each of these new forms was a relatively localized event – the first mysticetes developing in what is now the western South Pacific, and balaenopterids in the temperate–subtropical North Atlantic. Once again, existing data appear to support a geographical 'centre of origin' for these taxa. In the case of the early mysticetes the western South Pacific seems to have been the one region which, during the otherwise unfavourable early Oligocene, appears to have favoured the evolution of this mode of feeding at a relatively low trophic level in the food-chain (pp. 219–221).

That these kinds of patterns should predominate in advanced mammals such as the Cetacea would seem logical. There are coastal and estuarine species, of course, which have arisen through the appearance of barriers to dispersal and the division of previous ranges. Many of these species appear to have become adapted to rather particular breeding and feeding requirements. Interspecific competition as well as environmental conditions may have played an important role in determining the composition of the cetacean fauna we now observe. Some neritic and pelagic species, on the other hand, are demonstrably successful opportunists. Cetacea are intelligent, and frequently have huge foraging ranges. Young adults often appear to explore aggressively new territory for suitable feeding. Although it may be difficult for a human to comprehend, an ocean basin may seem a relatively small place to animals which can swim as fast as a rorqual or dolphin at sustained speeds. The fact that, on average, most individuals might spend a considerable part of their life in one area, say part of the Sea of Japan, does not alter the fact that some impressive individual movements have been demonstrated by mark and recapture techniques. Some pelagic Cetacea, such as the sperm whale, have literally dispersed to encompass almost the whole world ocean and it seems impossible to deny that spatial dispersal has just about reached feasible limits in this case.

In the case of the sperm whale, sea temperature, salinity, currents and land-mass projections seem to be rather ineffectual barriers at present. Far from being in an 'immobile' phase from which we might expect (according to Croizat) subsequent speciation, the sperm whale appears to be maintaining sufficient genetic interchange among all its populations to retain specific integrity worldwide. Significant differences between populations can be demonstrated only with great difficulty (see pp. 256-8).

Some of the small odontocete genera display interesting distribution patterns which are obviously the result of sequences of allopatric speciation events. Where pelagic species are concerned, however, only in a few cases does isolation seem to have occurred within geographical areas much smaller than a hemispheric ocean basin. In some genera we can recognize allopatric species pairs that appear to date back to a transgression from one ocean to another, followed by re-establishment of an isolative barrier. In other cases, dispersal from tropical zones into respective northern and southern hemisphere cool zones, with subsequent adaptation and evolution away from the common ancestor, seems a more plausible explanation. Do we view such 'pairs' as 'vicariants', segregated from each other by the isolative barrier of the tropics? Or do we regard the tropical belt as a 'centre of origin' for the temperate species? Does, in fact, a 'centre of origin' heresy lurk even at the heart of the vicariance model, despite assertions to the contrary by its protagonists? The differences between the possible interpretations discussed above seem to me to have more semantic than practical importance in the case of the Cetacea. A little less determination in the quest to explain absolutely all distributions by the same hypothesis, and even an acceptance that exceptions can prove rules, might do much to cool present biogeographical controversies. In the meantime, I can only interpret cetacean zoogeography to the best of my ability, in ways which seem in accord with the few known facts.

The earliest phase of cetacean radiation appears to have been closely tied to events involving the constriction and later reopening of the Western Tethys Sea in the Lower Tertiary, as discussed in the previous chapter. Further radiations seem to have been associated with the completion of the circum-Antarctic current, changes in temperature regimes in the Middle Tertiary, and the intermittent availability of the Central American Seaway as a route for faunal dispersal (Figure 6.2).

Mesozoic–Caenozoic drift and the decay of Tethys

The majority of modern geologists believe that dramatic changes in the redistribution of continental masses were in progress during the latter part

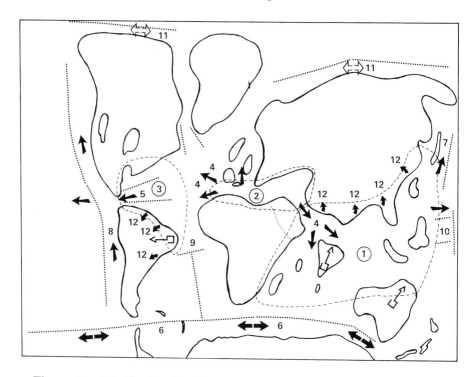

Figure 6.2   Distribution of land masses in the early Caenozoic, together with stylized representations of factors which appear to have been of significance in cetacean zoogeography. Circled numbers indicate major regions. 1. Eastern Tethys, now the 'Indo-Pacific core' of Ekman (26) and Davies (24); 2. Western Tethys, now represented only by the (secondary) Mediterranean region; 3. the 'Atlantic Tethyan Fringe' colonized by *Inia* and *Pontoporia*. Other numbers indicate: 4. dispersal routes of zeuglodonts and early odontocetes; 5. trans-isthmus routes into the Pacific, open more than once during the Caenozoic; 6. development of the circumpolar Southern Ocean, with the West Wind Drift available for dispersal after separation of Australia from Antarctica early in the Eocene; 7. warm water Kuroshio route by which Indo-Pacific core species were able to penetrate into the western North Pacific; 8. periodic cool-water corridor temporarily bridging the tropical eastern Pacific during late Caenozoic, permitting cool–temperate zone species to move from one hemisphere to another; 9. lack of a similar transgression of warm surface waters in tropical Atlantic precluding most such exchanges; 10. open central Pacific forming a barrier to dispersal of some species; 11. periodic Arctic circumpolar dispersal routes open during warm phases in Caenozoic history; 12. some secondary invasions of freshwater by Platanistidae and Iniidae, and *Orcaella*: Australian penetrations not shown – data lacking.

of the Cretaceous and the early Caenozoic, being brought about by sea-floor spreading at some of the margins of tectonic plates in the earth's crust. No totally satisfactory explanation of plate-movement mechanisms has yet been proposed, and there is still a small but significant geological minority which does not accept the tectonic-plate theory (6, 67–9). This is not the place to air the protagonistic and antagonistic arguments, which have been fairly presented and summarized elsewhere (53, 54). Yet, despite the continuing controversy, the majority of geological opinion currently accepts plate movement as a fact and, with the plate movements, changes in the distribution of continents.

The timetable of rifting of the continental juxtapositions of the late Palaeozoic and early Mesozoic is believed to be as follows. The North Atlantic gap between North America and western Europe opened about 120 million years ago (35). The sea-floor spreading occurring in the eastern part of the Endeavour Fracture resulted in increased distance between the New Zealand Plateau and Antarctica perhaps 80 million years ago (41). Separation of South America and Africa has been dated at about 75 million years ago (1, 46, 104), although there are still some discrepancies in data from different sources. Final separation of South America from Antarctica is dated at approximately 55 million years ago, and that of Australia from Antarctica at 43 million years ago (51, 102), with a widening stretch of the Southern Ocean opening around Antarctica. At the same time a gradual restriction of the Mesozoic Tethys Sea began, and this process has continued throughout the Caenozoic until today only the Mediterranean and Persian Gulf remain as possible (highly modified) relict areas. The former appears to be still in the process of contracting in area. This restriction of Tethys was recognized long before tectonic-plate theory was developed (26). There is little doubt that the decay of the Tethys Sea, the breaching of the Caribbean geosyncline through Central America, and the opening of the circumpolar Southern Ocean and the Caribbean have all played important roles in the history and dispersal of the Cetacea. Certainly changes in sea temperature, relative availability of migration routes, and competitive factors were involved.

The opening of the Caribbean was far enough advanced by the Middle Eocene for somewhat less primitive archaeocetes to penetrate as far as present day Texas and Louisiana. By the end of the Eocene their remains are found in northern Europe and western Canada (55). They probably reached the latter by traversing the shallow waters of the Caribbean geosyncline across Central America and spreading northwards along the Pacific coast. The inland Niobara Sea, present in North America and linked to the Gulf of Mexico throughout much of the Cretaceous, had vanished by the Middle Eocene. Virtually all these widely dispersed Eocene archaeocetes were, however, dorudontids and zygorhizids of the family Dorudontidae. These forms possessed more specialized anatomical and morphological features, almost certainly complemented by physiological adaptations, and were better able to colonize relatively cool waters than the earlier zeuglodonts.

By the late Oligocene all the early zeuglodonts were apparently extinct, some of the more specialized forms were in turn dwindling in abundance, but the early true odontocetes were able to colonize only relatively limited areas (55, 107). In fact, cetacean fossils as a whole are not common anywhere in Oligocene strata; this suggests that these relatively early warm-water forms of both suborders were not dealing successfully with the cooler conditions which followed the Eocene. The Oligocene might be regarded as a period of 'retrenchment' for the Cetacea, probably with a decline in population sizes and ranges of extant species. A great abundance of new forms appeared after the Oligocene–Miocene interface warming. Ten genera of Squalodontidae are known from the Lower Miocene, compared with two or three in the Upper Oligocene, and the first ziphiids, physeterids, delphinids and balaenids appear in the fossil record (55).

Ocean temperature fluctuations in the Caenozoic

The patterns of distribution we now observe among living Cetacea are as likely to be the result of responses to several major global climatic changes which occurred during the course of the Caenozoic, as to tectonic events which altered the juxtaposition of continental masses. Consequently, before examining these distribution patterns in more detail it is informative to review the history of ocean temperature fluctuations during the Caenozoic. In the Eocene, subtropical conditions extended far into what are now essentially temperate or even boreal regions (26). There is good evidence of a decline in temperatures at the Eocene–Oligocene interface, a relatively cool period lasting through the Oligocene, a brief warming phase at the Oligocene–Miocene interface, followed by rather drastic and steady cooling through the Miocene without any real recovery in the Pliocene (49, 56, 94). During this cooling the Antarctic mainland was rendered uninhabitable; most of its remaining fauna and flora became extinct (18). In the Pleistocene there were further declines and recoveries with the glacial advances and retreats. Temperate seas were perhaps 4–6°C cooler on average 15000 years ago during the last glacial period than today; this was followed by a short post-Pleistocene warm period about 6000 years ago (27). It is necessary to interpret data from different continents with caution. Australia, for example, is believed to have moved extensively during the Caenozoic, with significant changes in its latitudinal positions (51), but Europe and North America do not appear to have experienced significant latitudinal shifts in the Caenozoic, and data from coastal seas of the North Atlantic region imply a net decline in temperatures at all latitudes since the Eocene, despite occasional warm surges for varying periods of time (94). The sequence outlined above fits quite well with apparent bursts of cetacean evolution or massive changes in distribution and extensions of range represented in the fossil record by the relatively sudden appearance of new forms or an increase in the abundance of existing forms (Figure 6.3). Tables of relative abundance in the early and Middle Caenozoic have been provided by several authors (4, 39, 61, 83).

Did the Mysticeti evolve in the western South Pacific?

Ewan Fordyce (29) has suggested that the completion of the circumpolar Antarctic Current south of Australia by the mid-Oligocene (15, 50) led to cool waters upwelling against the Campbell Plateau, with a consequent dramatic increase in primary productivity (Figure 6.4). There is complementary evidence (95) that water temperatures over the Campbell Plateau declined from 11°C in the late Eocene to 7°C in the Oligocene, and that this was accompanied by increases in diatom deposits during the same period. Fordyce presumed that a significant increase in secondary productivity would result, and certainly the presence of abundant zooplanktonic remains in the Upper Oligocene strata of eastern New Zealand (28, 36) supports this idea.

Jere Lipps and Edward Mitchell (61) hypothesized that disappearance of cetacean taxa in the Oligocene was a direct result of decreased availability of upwelling zones generating sufficient secondary trophic production to support their populations. They concluded that near-shore upwellings had been the critical factor in the late Eocene radiation of the earlier archaeocete forms, and related the distribution of these during the Tertiary to the presence or absence of thick diatomaceous deposits indicating strong primary production. Lipps and Mitchell found it significant that such were absent during the early Palaeocene and Oligocene in the same areas where deposits occur abundantly in late Palaeocene, early Eocene and Miocene strata (47, 82). They attempted to relate upwelling activity to increase or decrease in the strength of the earth's thermal gradient. In view of what is known about the dissolution of some carbonate-rich zooplankton remains on the ocean floor under the influence of pressure and actions of ocean chemistry, however (99), such data have to be interpreted with caution.

In the light of the rich zooplankton deposits in New Zealand Oligocene strata, Fordyce (29) related the occurrence of *Mauicetus* remains to this apparent Lower Middle Oligocene upwelling region, postulating that evolution of baleen and a filter-feeding mode of life was favoured by

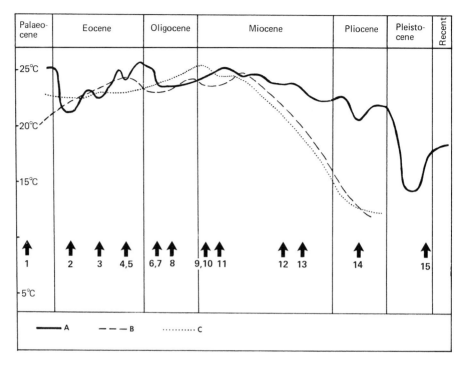

Figure 6.3   Mean annual temperature fluctuations in the Caenozoic based on figures by Jenkins (49), Keyes (56) and Schwartzbach (94). A From planktonic Foraminiferida; B Mollusca; C Scleractinian coral faunae. The extent of some fluctuations must be regarded with caution, since the best data are from the southern hemisphere, and some latitudinal movement of Australia and New Zealand apparently took place. Even so, there are remarkably good correlations between sudden changes and apparent 'bursts' of evolution in the Cetacea; perhaps neither are totally spurious! Events: 1. evolution of Cetacea, apparently in the Western Tethys Sea; 2. dispersal of early zeuglodonts; 3. more advanced archaeocetes reach Caribbean region and Gulf of Mexico; 4 and 5. archaeocetes reach northern Europe and Canada, while earliest true odontocetes appear in southern USA; 6 and 7. extinction of zeuglodonts, differentiation of true squalodonts in New Zealand region; 8. first cetotheres appear; 9 and 10. burst of squalodont evolution, and appearance of forms which may be the first Balaenidae; 11. appearance of several groups of modern odontocetes; 12. appearance of forms resembling early rorquals; 13. more modern odontocetes appear; 14. the last cetotheres and squalodonts present in fossil record; 15. establishment of modern antitropical distribution patterns in rorquals and others. Redrawn from Gaskin (39).

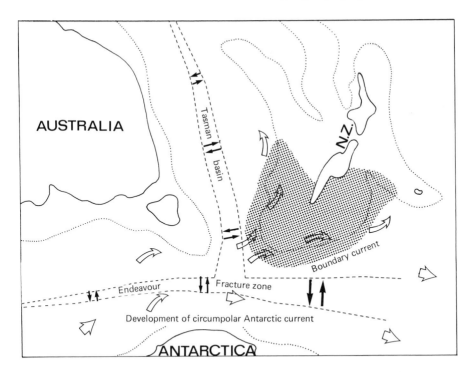

Figure 6.4 Events in the western South Pacific which appear to have been important in the origins of the Mysticeti during the late Eocene and early Oligocene. Black arrows indicate sea-floor spreading along the Endeavour Fracture zone, with sphenochasmic opening of the Tasman Basin. White arrows indicate the development of the circumpolar Antarctic Current (West Wind Drift) as Australia and Antarctica separate. The stippling indicates a zone of high primary and secondary productivity around the margin of the New Zealand Plateau as a result of topographic upwelling effects. The earliest Mysticeti are recorded from the New Zealand archipelago. In other parts of the world, the Oligocene appears to have been a time of decreased marine productivity. Partly redrawn and modified from Fordyce (29) and Griffiths and Varne (41).

generation of high primary, and hence secondary production of zooplankton over the relatively shallow Campbell Plateau. The occurrence of other cetacean forms in this region at the same time, including Squalodontidae (57), when remains are scarce in other parts of the world, is cited as further evidence of its trophic productivity. Fordyce suggested that since the short food-chain of the zooplankton-baleen whale trophic relationship provides more efficient exploitation of basic productivity, the mysticetes were able to prosper at a time when other cetacean groups appeared to be in retrenchment or decline. The occurrence of a toothed proto-baleen whale (*Aetiocetus*) in the North Pacific late Oligocene seems at first to be an anomaly in Fordyce's hypothesis, yet because it is clearly pre-dated by true baleen whales, there are obvious grounds for considering it a relict form.

Subsequent cooling throughout the Middle and Upper Miocene did not result in a new wave of net extinctions of major taxal units; even though some genera disappeared they were replaced by new ones, especially among the Ziphiidae, Physeteridae, Delphinidae and Mysticeti. It is evident that the later Miocene forms were well adapted to colonize relatively cool waters. If present continental drift timetables are correct (5), by the time these events occurred the gap between South America and Africa had long since become truly oceanic, the circumpolar Southern Ocean had developed, India was approaching its present position, and the Western Tethys was much reduced in comparison with its size in Eocene times.

Factors modifying cetacean distribution patterns

Although we can make some limited and general speculation about major cetacean taxa, it is very difficult to relate changes in the distribution of species or genera to particular pre-Pleistocene ocean regime shifts. The fossil record is fragmentary and shows almost as much correlation with the distribution of research centres as with real distributions. For example, North American and European deposits are far better known than those of Asia or Africa, with a few local exceptions such as Fayum in Egypt, where unusually abundant remains have attracted attention (55).

The modification of the distribution of a cetacean species will depend on a number of factors, namely the ability of the animal to adapt when faced with progressively higher or lower temperatures; its initial range before a change in ocean-temperature regime begins; and the disposition of that range with respect to major land masses or, where coastal-dwelling species are concerned, great stretches of open ocean.

Continental Africa has functioned as a barrier to some warm-water species, depending on their varying abilities to penetrate through the relatively cool waters off the Cape of Good Hope (24, 39, 85). Groups with a relatively long history, such as the Iniidae and Pontoporidae, may have developed in the tropical Atlantic, or reached that region while the subtropical Tethyan route south of Europe was still open. The Americas do not appear to have been a serious obstacle to cetacean dispersal. Species such as the gray whales, which spend part of their annual cycle in relatively warm waters, were undoubtedly able to cross the Central American isthmus at one time since this was broken by sea-ways on several occasions in the Caenozoic, especially during the Miocene. The same dispersal route was probably also used by the precursor of the sei whale (60).

Cold adapted forms have been able to penetrate around the southern extremity of the Americas – indeed in the Southern Ocean several species still do so today. On the other hand, the vast gap of the deep islandless eastern tropical and subtropical Pacific has acted as an effective barrier to eastward dispersal of coastal marine organisms (26), including those essentially inshore or freshwater cetaceans with relict Tethyan distribution (24). Such species as do succeed in crossing the gap then face the serious problem of colonization. The cool, north-flowing Peru Current has influence to about latitude 8°S, and the topography of the west coast of the Americas in low latitudes is quite different from the equivalent regions of the east coast; the continental shelf is very restricted, and there are no giant river systems comparable with the Orinoco and Amazon. The only coastal region of any size which might be considered remotely suitable as a west-coast warm-water cetacean 'haven' is the Gulf of California and the bays and lagoons of the Baja.

Relict Tethyan and simple pan-tropical distributions

The Pleistocene glacial periods probably had little influence upon species with purely tropical distributions, and in these cases we appear to see a 'Relict Tethyan' marine mammal fauna, albeit modified by local events during the Caenozoic. The area inhabited by these species today is generally referred to as the Indo-Pacific region (10, 24, 26). We find a number of freshwater, estuarine and coastal forms; *Platanista indi* and *P. gangetica* (blind river dolphins: Indus and Ganges systems) (52, 86), *Lipotes vexillifer* (white-fin dolphin: Tung-T'ing Lake and Yangtze system) (11), *Orcaella brevirostris* (Irrawaddy dolphin: Ganges to the Mekong, Indonesia and probably northern Australia) (90), and *Neophocoena phocoenoides* (finless porpoise: eastern Indian Ocean to western North Pacific) (89). Platanistid fossils from the Miocene and Pliocene are found in marine deposits, indicating that the freshwater habit is secondary (55). One ziphiid, *Indopacetus pacificus* (although not coastal in distribution as far as is known) from north-eastern Australia, and possibly *Mesoplodon ginkodens*, from the Indian Ocean and the south-western North Pacific Ocean, may also be Indo-Pacific core species (73).

An equivalent relict 'Tethyan Atlantic Fringe' fauna occurs in the coastal waters of the tropical and subtropical western Atlantic and the great river systems of eastern South America: *Inia geoffrensis* (Bouto or Amazon dolphin: Orinoco and Amazon basins) (90) and *Pontoporia blainvillei* (La Plata dolphin: Bahia de Santos to Golfo San Matias) (90). As *Neophocoena phocoenoides* has extended its range northwards into the North Pacific along the Kuroshio boundary, so *Pontoporia blainvillei* has spread southwards to about latitude 40°S on the coast of Argentina.

Some genera have clearly not found the cool waters off the Cape of Good

Figure 6.5   Family Delphinidae: killer whale, *Orcinus orca*, Peninsula Valdes, Argentina. Photograph courtesy of Drs B. and M. Würsig, Santa Cruz, University of California.

hope a barrier; there are several with an Atlantic and Indo-Pacific region distribution. These are the coastal *Sousa* (humpbacked dolphins: five described species some of which are of dubious status) (90), pelagic *Feresa attenuata* (pygmy killer whale) (8, 13, 14, 32, 77, 88), *Steno bredanensis* (rough-toothed dolphin) (90), *Peponocephala electra* (Electra dolphin) (79, 106), *Lagenodelphis hosei* (Fraser's dolphin) (31), and *Stenella* (long-beaked, spinner and spotted dolphins: number of valid species not known, taxonomy still in relative chaos) (34, 45, 84, 85). W. F. Perrin and his colleagues recently speculated (85) that the Cape of Good Hope may have acted as a one-way filter, admitting Indo-Pacific elements into the tropical Atlantic via the equivalents of the Agulhas and Benguela Currents, but not necessarily facilitating return dispersal of Atlantic elements.

Figure 6.6 Family Physeteridae: sperm whale, *Physeter catodon*. Photograph by the author, 1962.

S. coeruleoalba penetrates both northern and southern temperate latitudes, and should perhaps be considered as transitional between those species with a simple pan-tropical distribution and those discussed in the next section.

Colonization of the temperate, boreal and polar regions

A number of forms have penetrated into all the major oceans other than the Arctic Ocean. These are almost all monotypic genera: *Delphinus delphis* (common or saddleback dolphin: all tropical and temperate seas [see, however, p. 258] to a limit set by a surface temperature of approximately 14°C) (38); *Pseudorca crassidens* (false killer whale: range as for *Delphinus delphis* and perhaps extending further into temperate regions) (90); *Orcinus orca* (killer whale: range as for *Delphinus delphis* but more local, probably most common in cool temperate regions and subpolar seas, present right to the ice edge in suitable areas of both hemispheres) (90) (Figure 6.5); *Physeter catodon* (sperm whale: all oceans except high Arctic, but only males penetrating into cool waters of high latitudes) (Figure 6.6) (17); *Ziphius cavirostris* (goose-beaked whale) and *Grampus griseus* (Risso's dolphin), both with ranges similar to that of *Pseudorca crassidens*;

Figure 6.7   Family Physeteridae: pygmy sperm whale, *Kogia breviceps*.
Photograph courtesy of Seaworld, Orlando, Florida, USA (Dr E. Asper).

and *Kogia breviceps* and *K. simus* (pygmy sperm whales: range as for
Pseudorca crassidens, but *K. breviceps* not yet recorded from eastern
Atlantic) (Figure 6.7) (42). These species appear to have regional
populations, the extent of which is difficult to define at this time, but
between which enough mixing takes place to prevent genetic isolation.
Subspecific status for such populations is probably not justified (see
Chapter 7). Although the species clearly show adaptation to existence
within quite broad temperature regimes, this does not, of course, imply
that all individuals or even all local subpopulations have such tolerances,
unless extensive migrations occur.

Various degrees of population segregation and often speciation or
subspeciation have taken place, following the establishment of some
species in the northern and southern temperate zones. This type of
segregation, which was the result of Tertiary or Pleistocene events, has
been called antitropical distribution (24, 44).

The southern form of the pilot whale *Globicephala melaena edwardi* has
been distinguished from the northern subspecies *G. m. melaena* (96).
Tropical and subtropical waters between the northern and southern
temperate-zone populations are inhabited by the short-finned pilot whale
G. macrorhynchus, which is morphologically quite distinct from
G. melaena and presumed to be closer to the parent stock. D. E. Sergeant

(96) noted that the pectoral flippers of *G. melaena* show positive allometric growth throughout all but the earliest postnatal period; those of *G. macrorhynchus* do not. *G. seiboldii* (often called *scammoni*) of the North Pacific may be intermediate between *G. melaena* and *G. macrorhynchus*; the divergence within this group is so well marked that it probably predates the Pleistocene.

In the genus *Tursiops* (bottle-nosed dolphin) we find virtually identical northern and southern hemisphere populations, separated by smaller tropical and subtropical forms, slightly different in colour and morphology, referable to *T. aduncus* (93). The population from the Gulf of California region is usually given specific status as *T. gilli* (90). The status of other named warm-water forms is doubtful; G. J. B. Ross has recently concluded that *T. absulam* (Rüppell), *T. catalania* (Gray) and *Delphinus gadamu* (Owen) are all synonymous with *T. aduncus* (93). The distribution of these slightly differentiated populations might be ascribed to Pleistocene events. Among the right whale dolphins (genus *Lissodelphis*) two forms have been distinguished which have relatively minor pattern differences. *L. borealis* occurs in the North Pacific and *L. peronii* in the southern hemisphere (30). The ziphiid genus *Berardius* has a similar distribution pattern (*B. bairdii*, temperate North Pacific; *B. arnuxii*, temperate and polar waters of the Southern Ocean) (73). If the cool north-flowing Peru Current almost bridged the tropical Pacific on one or more occasions during the Pliocene and Pleistocene it could have provided a route by which a cold water-adapted species could move from one ocean to the other (24). It is difficult to say whether the colonizing movement was northward or southward. Perhaps northward movement is most likely, since some southern circumpolar ziphiid species are known which have no co-species in the northern hemisphere.

The temperate southern hemisphere may have been a major evolutionary centre for many odontocete groups. Many early odontocetes were differentiated in the southern hemisphere long before they appear in the northern fossil record (57). The absence of a cold-water corridor penetrating completely through the tropical Atlantic in the late Caenozoic is a simpler explanation for the absence of such genera from the North Atlantic, and gives more support to the hypothesis of a southern or southern-tropical origin for these and many other odontocete genera.

The low invertebrate faunal diversity of the temperate North Atlantic is in sharp contrast to the high diversity found in the North Pacific (10), and can be attributed to their different climatic histories during the Pleistocene (70). In the Wisconsin Glacial Stadial, average annual sea-surface temperatures may have been reduced by as much as 6°C in the North Atlantic, but only by about 3°C at most in the North Pacific as a whole. It has been implied therefore that the depauperate North Atlantic fauna can

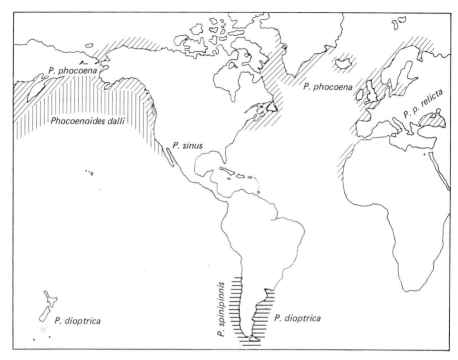

Figure 6.8   Distribution patterns of some odontocete cetacean genera, I:
Phocoena and *Phocoenoides*. The latter is confined to the northern temperate
region of the North Pacific (vertical striping). The distribution of the species of
Phocoena is complex. *P. sinus* is confined to the upper part of the Gulf of
California; *P. spinipinnis* to the western coast of South America and the part of
the south-eastern coast (horizontal striping) where its range overlaps with that
of *P. dioptrica* (stipple), which has also been recorded around the Auckland
Islands south of New Zealand; *P. phocoena* has a disjunct distribution in the cool
boreal North Pacific and North Atlantic, with subspecies *P. p. relicta* isolated in
the Black Sea (diagonal striping).

in many cases be attributed to extensive Pleistocene extinctions (10).
Considering that genera such as *Lissodelphis* and *Berardius* are successfully
cool-adapted in the North Pacific, it seems more likely that they never
succeeded in penetrating the North Atlantic. There seemed to be
relatively little evidence for the 'East Pacific Cool Corridor' in the fossil
record (10), and marine temperature fluctuations were certainly not that
striking in the tropical Pacific. In reality, however, simple relative
proximity of northern and southern cool-water surface streams would
probably have been sufficient to permit some cetaceans to cross the
equator, since most species are normally wide-ranging.

Much information on the ziphiids has been provided by the meticulous
work of J. C. Moore (73). The taxal distance between the two antitropical
temperate-polar species of *Berardius* is considerably less than between

Hyperoodon ampullatus of the North Atlantic and *Hyperoodon* (subgenus *Frasercetus*) *planifrons* of the Southern Ocean. The dispersal of these two pairs of species into the temperate zones could date to the Pleistocene and Pliocene, respectively. Moore also argued that the widespread *Ziphius cavirostris* is demonstrably closer to *Berardius* than any other ziphiid. Common ancestry could have been shared between the above species, the temperate-tropical genus *Mesoplodon* and tropical *Indopacetus* according to Moore. *Indopacetus* appears to be the least specialized of the group in a number of significant respects, but the southern hemisphere monotypic genus *Tasmacetus* is the most primitive of all living ziphiids. The single species *T. shepherdi* is known largely from New Zealand strandings (37), but it has been reported recently from the coasts of Argentina (66) and Chile (12), so the species is probably circumpolar in distribution.

The original stock of the family Phocoenidae seems to have radiated and dispersed from the tropics into temperate waters of both hemispheres (39). This probably occurred in the Miocene–Pliocene, and present-day *Neophocoena*, distributed in the Indo-Pacific core region, probably differs little from the warm-water ancestor in morphology and range. The derivative genus *Phocoenoides* has colonized temperate and subarctic waters of the North Pacific (Figure 6.8) but, peculiarly, not the South Pacific. Its range extends into the southern Bering Sea (89), and related fossil forms are known from the Upper Miocene and the Pliocene deposits of California (3). Two colour phases have been described as distinct species, *P. dalli* (Dall's porpoise) and *P. truei* (True's porpoise) (see Chapter 7, pp. 263–4).

The southern representatives of the genus *Phocoena* (Figure 6.8) are *P. dioptrica* (spectacled porpoise: Atlantic coast of South America in temperate latitudes and New Zealand subantarctic islands) (2), and *P. spinipinnis* (Burmeister's porpoise: southern Argentina from Rio de la Plata on the Atlantic coast, and from about latitude 40°S in Chile to about latitude 5°S in Peru. *P. sinus* (Gulf of California porpoise) has a relict distribution confined to the upper part of the Gulf of California (81), and may even be extinct (100). Equatorial transgressions of cooler tropical waters during the Pliocene, or in Pleistocene glacial intervals, followed by isolation in opposite hemispheres as tropical waters warmed again, have probably been a major factor in speciation in the genus (24, 108).

P. sinus bears a much stronger relationship to *P. spinipinnis* (80, 81) the northernmost range of which lies 4000 kilometres to the south on the west coast of South America, than to *P. phocoena*, which ranges to less than 1200 kilometres to the north of it (although if the double coastline length of the Baja is included, this distance is considerably increased). Norris and McFarland (81) concluded that *Phocoena sinus* probably evolved from an ancestor of *P. spinipinnis* which crossed the equator during late Pleistocene

Figure 6.9 Family Phocoenidae: common or harbour porpoise, *Phocoena phocoena*, Head Harbour Passage, New Brunswick, Canada. Photograph by D. E. Gaskin.

times and was embayed in the Gulf of California as tropical surface waters warmed again. It does not seem likely that *P. phocoena* (common or harbour porpoise) shared immediate ancestry with *P. sinus*.

P. phocoena (Figure 6.9) is the most specialized member of the genus and has diverged in a number of important characteristics from the others, suggesting that its specific segregation was associated with earlier events. Its present populations are discontinuously distributed in the North Pacific and North Atlantic (40), with a relict population of subspecific status in the Black Sea and Sea of Azov, but not in the Mediterranean (103). The species was reported from Pliocene strata in the USSR (58), so that its presence in the northern hemisphere certainly dates back at least to the Upper Pliocene. Records of Phocoenidae (*Protophocoena*, *Palaeophocoena*) from the European Miocene are at best dubious identifications, and despite some acceptance of these records at face value, they are probably best discounted (71). *Microphocoena*, included with these genera by myself (39) and earlier authors, is now regarded as a member of the extinct family Kentriodontidae (see p. 174). In the Pleistocene, *Phocoena* was certainly present in Asian waters (89).

The isolation of the northern Black Sea–Sea of Azov population of *P. phocoena* (Figure 6.8) is probably related to Pleistocene events. During one or more cooling periods *P. phocoena* presumably penetrated the Mediterranean at a time when it was cooler than today, and became isolated in the eastern marine extremity when subsequent warming occurred. Although there are a number of records of *P. phocoena* in the western Mediterranean, it is difficult to confirm all these (40, 108) and the species is certainly not common there. The delphinid fauna of the Mediterranean Sea seems to be largely composed of *Delphinus delphis*, *Stenella coeruleoalba* and *Tursiops truncatus*.

I have earlier suggested (39) that the genus is of southern origin and that *P. phocoena* diverged furthest from the stem stock as the result of an earlier bridging of the equator during the Pliocene. While this remains possible, D. B. Yurick has suggested (108) a plausible alternative, that is, that the genus had a northern origin with the initial equatorial transgression(s) being southwards. The abundance of fossil forms in the north certainly seems to favour this hypothesis. Two other considerations support this view. The southern fossil record includes only *Phocoenopsis*, from the New Zealand Pleistocene, but *P. phocoena* definitely was in the northern hemisphere in the Upper Pliocene at the very latest, and preceded by probably related forms.

P. dioptrica and *P. spinipinnis* are quite generalized, in comparison to *P. phocoena*, with little taxonomical distance separating them (81). Because their ranges overlap it is difficult to explain their dual evolution, if the genus is considered to be of southern origin. If a northern origin is proposed, however, temporally or spatially separated movements of ancestral forms south across the equator can be invoked (that is, along opposite coasts of South America at different times) (108). Movement of the northern ancestor from one ocean to another is likely to have been via the Caribbean geosyncline ('Central American Seaway') which did not close until the Upper Pliocene (107). Northward movement of the *P. sinus* ancestor during the Pleistocene is presumed to have occurred later and independently of this earlier dispersal.

The delphinid genus *Lagenorhynchus* demonstrates a rather complex and interesting antitropical distribution (Figure 6.10). The genus is still poorly known, and our knowledge of its relationships would benefit from a planned global collecting programme. Perhaps the best treatment of the genus is that by E. Mitchell (72). He recognized six distinct species, all distributed in temperate and subpolar regions. Three are restricted to the southern hemisphere, *L. cruciger* (hour-glass dolphin: circumpolar chiefly in waters adjacent to the Antarctic convergence); *L. australis* (black-

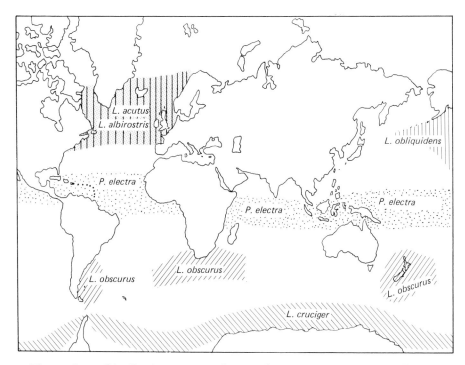

Figure 6.10   Distribution patterns of some odontocete cetacean genera, II: *Peponocephala and Lagenorhynchus.* The former genus is represented only by one species, *electra*, the distribution of which appears to be pan-tropical. The latter genus contains five recognized species. *L. cruciger* appears to have a circumpolar distribution along and south of the Antarctic convergence; *L. obscurus* is semi-circumpolar, but apparently absent from Australian waters and those of the central South Pacific; *L. obliquidens* is the representative in the temperate North Pacific, while *L. acutus* and *L. albirostris* have similar, if not sympatric, distributions in the North Atlantic. Other forms have been described and named in this genus, but their specific status is dubious.

chinned dolphin: temperate waters off South America and the Falkland Islands); and *L. obscurus* (dusky dolphin: partially circumpolar, but concentrated in coastal waters and apparently not through the central South Pacific) (Figure 6.11) (38). A single species, *L. obliquidens*, occurs in the North Pacific (North Pacific white-sided dolphin) while *L. acutus* (North Atlantic white-sided dolphin) and *L. albirostris* (white-beaked dolphin) have more or less similar ranges in temperate waters. Mitchell asserts that *L. acutus* has the most specialized colour patterns in the genus, and cannot easily be related to any of the others. The two species do not seem to occupy quite the same ecological niche despite their apparently sympatric geographical range, and probably did not enter or arise in the North Atlantic at the same time. *L. cruciger* and *L. obliquidens* appear to be a species pair with antitropical distribution. Some authors have considered them as

Figure 6.11 Family Delphinidae: dusky dolphin, *Lagenorhynchus obscurus*, Golfo San Jose, Argentina. Photograph courtesy of M. and B. Würsig, Santa Cruz, University of California.

conspecific (9), but having seen both on a number of occasions at close quarters, I am in full agreement with Mitchell that these are valid species. *L. obscurus* has the least specialized body pattern in the genus, and is probably closest in range to the hypothetical subtropical–temperate ancestor. Penetration of the North Atlantic may have occurred via the Central American Seaway during the Pliocene, at the same time as *P. phocoena*.

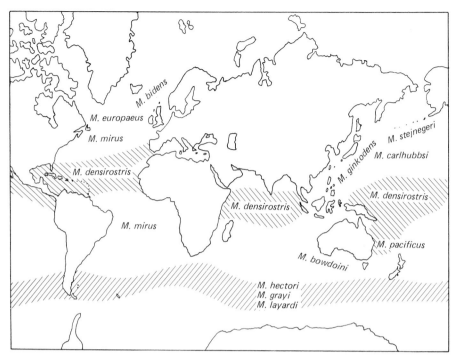

Figure 6.12 Distribution patterns of some odontocete cetacean genera, III:
Mesoplodon. *M. densirostris* appears to have a pan-tropical distribution; *M.
layardi*, *grayi* and *hectori* southern temperate and subtropical circumpolar
distributions; *M. mirus* is apparently more or less confined to the Atlantic and
adjacent seas; *M. europaeus* and *bidens* to the North Atlantic; *M. pacificus* to the
south-western tropical Pacific; and *M. bowdoini* to the temperate and subtropical
western South Pacific; and *M. ginkodens*, *stejnegeri* and *carlhubbsi* to sectors of the
temperate North Pacific.

The antitropical distributions of the ziphiid genus *Mesoplodon* exhibit
similar complexities (Figure 6.12). Among the Ziphiidae this genus
appears to have diverged farthest from its probable squalodont ancestors.
Like some delphinid genera, *Mesoplodon* seems to be in the process of
prolific speciation, possibly as a result of population isolation events which
began in the Pliocene and were completed in the Pleistocene. The number
of species is large for a cetacean genus, and many determinations have had
to be made on admittedly inadequate material. It is likely, therefore, that
some species will prove to have more extensive distributions than is at
present accepted.

Three subgenera have been recognized within *Mesoplodon* (73).
Mesoplodon itself contains nine species, and *Dolichodon* and *Dioplodon* one
each, namely *Dolichodon layardi* (strap-toothed whale) and *Dioplodon
densirostris* (dense-beaked whale). The latter occurs in the tropics of the

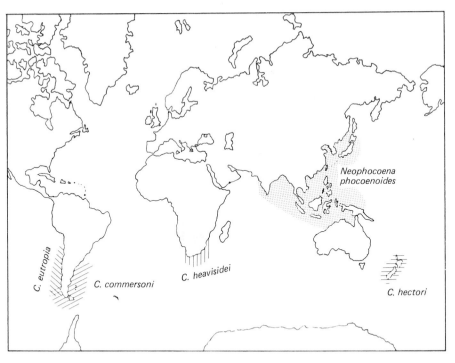

Figure 6.13 Distribution patterns of some odontocete cetacean genera, IV: *Neophocoena* and *Cephalorhynchus*. The former genus is largely confined to the classic Indo-Pacific core region, with extensions of range to southern coastal China and Japan. *Cephalorhynchus* is absent from Australia, but four other species occur in coastal waters of the southern hemisphere: *C. hectori* in New Zealand waters; *C. heavisidei* around South Africa; *C. eutropia* off south-western South America, and *C. commersoni* off southern and south-eastern South America.

Atlantic, Indian and Pacific Oceans, with a similar distribution pattern to that of *Feresa*. *Mesoplodon (Dolichodon) layardi* is circumpolar in the southern hemisphere.

Within the subgenus *Mesoplodon* proper *M. ginkodens* may be the remaining Indo-Pacific core species, and from the *M. ginkodens* ancestral stock *M. grayi* has colonized the Southern Ocean, *M. carlhubbsi* the North Pacific, and *M. europaeus* the North Atlantic, with a bias to the tropical and subtropical region in the latter case. One species, *M. mirus*, occurs only in the North and South Atlantic, a very unusual distribution pattern among Cetacea. In the Pacific Ocean the equivalent niche seems to be occupied by the antitropical species pair *M. stejnegeri* (North Pacific) and *M. bowdoini* (South Pacific and Indian Ocean). The affinities of southern circumpolar *M. hectori* are not clear, nor are those of *M. bidens* of the north-eastern North Atlantic and the North Sea.

One odontocete genus and one mysticete genus have relict southern

Figure 6.14 Family Balaenidae: the rarely seen pygmy right whale, *Caperea marginata*, photographed underwater in South Africa, Plettenberg Bay, December 1967, by the late Mr T. Dicks. Thanks are due to Mrs F. Hayes for permission to reproduce this photograph, and to Dr G. J. B. Ross of the Port Elizabeth Museum, who contacted Mrs Hayes on behalf of the author.

hemisphere distributions. *Cephalorhynchus* has four generally accepted species (Figure 6.13), namely, *C. hectori* (Hector's dolphin: New Zealand), *C. commersoni* (Commerson's dolphin: southern Chile and Argentina), *C. eutropia* (black dolphin: Chile between latitudes 33°S and 40°S) and *C. heavisidei* (the tonine: Cape Province, South Africa) (90). The relationships within this genus are still under study; it is interesting that the genus is not known from Australian waters. Two workers have discussed the possibility of *Cephalorhychus* and *Phocoenoides* once coming into competition on the south-western coast of South America (24, 72), but no phocoenid is known to have reached Tasmania, southern Australia or southern African waters. *P. dioptrica* occurs around the Auckland Islands (2), but *Cephalorhynchus hectori* has not been reported from the New Zealand subantarctic to the best of my knowledge.

The pygmy right whale, *Caperea marginata* (Figure 6.14), has a circumpolar distribution in the southern hemisphere. Traditionally the New Zealand–Tasmania–southern Australian region was regarded as its stronghold, but in recent years animals have been recorded from several areas of the open South Atlantic (48). This is one of the most primitive whalebone whales (25), yet possesses a number of specialized anatomical modifications, for example, in the thoracic skeleton, the functions of which are not at present understood.

Figure 6.15 Family Monodontidae: white whale or beluga, *Delphinapterus leucas* in the Saguenay River, Quebec. White adult female with young (bleuvet stage). Young white whales become progressively paler with time. Photograph courtesy of Mr Andrew Macfarlane, Ottawa, Canada.

Figure 6.16 Family Balaenidae: bowhead whale, *Balaena mysticetus*. A specimen taken in the Alaskan Eskimo hunt hauled out on the ice (upside down). The slender baleen can be seen, as can the absence of the calluses of the snout and jaw margin characteristic of the right whale *Eubalaena glacialis*. Photograph courtesy of Barbara Lipton, Newark Museum, Newark, New Jersey, USA.

Three odontocetes and one baleen whale have northern relict distributions. The narwhal, *Monodon monoceros*, is confined to the Arctic basin (103). The white whale or beluga, *Delphinapterus leucas* (Figure 6.15), is distributed in coastal waters of the polar-boreal region (59), and the North Atlantic bottlenosed whale, *Hyperoodon ampullatus*, is distributed pelagically in the same region (7, 16). The bowhead (Figure 6.16) and Greenland right whales are geographically segregated eastern and western populations of *Balaena mysticetus*, which are largely confined

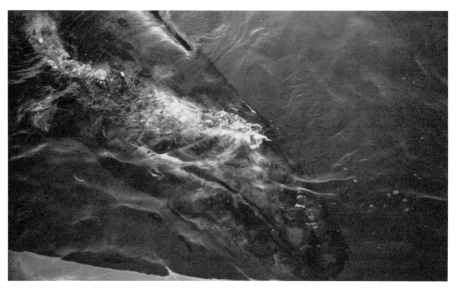

Figure 6.17   Family Eschrichtidae: Californian gray whale, *Eschrichtius robustus*. Photograph by D. E. Gaskin, 1971.

to the Arctic basin but in times of former abundance made migrations southward into the Bering Sea and the Denmark Strait region (103). The trapping of *Balaena*, *Monodon* and *Delphinapterus* in the Arctic basin during one of the cold periods of the Tertiary must have resulted in very rapid selection in favour of the whole life cycle being carried out in cold water (24). Antarctic species, of course, were able to retreat freely towards the equator in all zones of the Southern Ocean, virtually unimpeded by land masses.

The Californian gray whale, *Eschrichtius robustus* (Figure 6.17), is confined to coastal waters of the North Pacific. The eastern population on the west coast of North America is functionally stable at about 11 000 individuals – further recovery is believed to be limited by the magnitude of aboriginal catches in eastern Siberia – but the western population off Japan is virtually extinct (see Chapter 7, pp. 269–70) (78). Although the gray whale feeds in the Bering Sea region in summer, its winter movements were probably always such that it was able to avoid the southward movement of ice areas, and probably retreated entirely into the North Pacific during the Pleistocene. An Atlantic population is known from subfossil remains and may have survived until relatively recent times, but is now extinct (see also p. 270) (33). It is remarkable that the Tertiary deposits of California contain no gray whale remains earlier than the Pleistocene (4). We have to consider the possibility therefore that, like the modern walrus, the gray whale reached the North Pacific via the Arctic Ocean in the last warm period, unlikely as that might seem at first sight.

Figure 6.18   Family Balaenopteridae: blue whale, *Balaenoptera musculus*, off the Mingan Islands, Quebec, in the Gulf of St Lawrence. Photograph courtesy of Mr Richard Sears, Director, Mingan Island Cetacean Survey, East Falmouth, Mass., USA.

Figure 6.19   Family Balaenopteridae: fin whale, *Balaenoptera physalus*, near the Mingan Islands, Quebec, in the Gulf of the St Lawrence. Photograph courtesy of Mr Richard Sears, Director, Mingan Island Cetacean Survey, East Falmouth, Mass., USA.

The black right whales and almost all species of rorqual (Balaenopteridae) have distinct, antitropically distributed populations. All species of *Balaenoptera* (*B. musculus*, blue whale (Figure 6.18); *B. physalus*, finback whale (Figures 6.19 and 6.20); *B. borealis*, sei whale; *B. edeni*, Bryde's whale; and *B. acutorostrata*, minke or lesser piked whale (Figure 6.21)),

Figure 6.20   Family Balaenopteridae: fin whale, *Balaenoptera physalus*; a rare dorsal view of a specimen on the deck of the FF *Southern Venturer* in 1962. Photograph by D. E. Gaskin.

Figure 6.21   Family Balaenopteridae: minke whale, *Balaenoptera acutorostrata*, near mouth of the Saguenay River, St Lawrence estuary, Quebec. Photograph courtesy of Mr A. Macfarlane, Ottawa, Canada.

Eubalaena glacialis, the black right whale (three nominal subspecies – *E. glacialis*: North Atlantic, *E. australis*: Southern Ocean and *E. japonica*: North Pacific), and *Megaptera novaeangliae*, the humpback whale, occur in the Southern Ocean, North Atlantic and North Pacific. The relationships of these populations are considered in some detail in the next chapter.

Of these species, *Balaenoptera edeni* has the least well-defined populations. Its distribution is not completely known but appears to be composed of relatively localized subpopulations in tropical and subtropical regions, which carry out only limited migrations. Blue, finback, sei, humpback and right whales undertake extensive annual migrations. Humpbacks move from summer feeding grounds in the Antarctic to breeding grounds off such coasts as those of tropical Africa, Australia, Fiji and Tonga. As Figure 1.1 shows, northern and southern populations of baleen whales almost certainly do not interbreed at the present time. Whales of the northern hemisphere are nearest the equator during the northern winter, and at that time during the corresponding southern summer their austral counterparts are furthest from the equator. 'Crossing over' of rorquals has been invoked by some authors (98), but to the best of my knowledge has never been conclusively proved by whale-mark recoveries. If it occurs at all it is almost certainly very rare.

In general, however, the migratory patterns of baleen whales are much more marked than those of odontocetes. Their precursors were probably distributed in subtropical and tropical regions, as *B. edeni* is today, but responded favourably to cooling conditions during the Pleistocene. Following the retreating cold waters during and after glacial periods, they have taken advantage of the vast zooplanktonic production which occurs in high latitudes during summer months, even though most species must still return to warmer waters to calve.

The balaenopterids apparently arose and radiated in the temperate and subtropical waters of the North Atlantic (Figure 6.22) (60); the earliest fossils are known from the early Middle Miocene beds of North America and Europe (55). From here the balaenopterids seem to have crossed the equator and colonized the Southern Ocean, the Indian Ocean and the North Pacific. The sei whale does not penetrate as far into cool waters as the blue and finback, and S. Klumov suggested that it reached the Pacific Ocean via the seaway of the old Caribbean geosyncline which was still periodically open in the later half of the Tertiary (see Figure 6.2). This seems less likely when one considers that this species does not penetrate far into tropical waters now. Penetration through the Central American Seaway could conceivably have occurred prior to segregation of *B. borealis* and *B. edeni*, however.

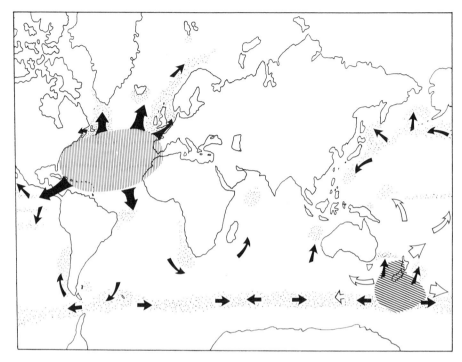

Figure 6.22 Hypothetical origins and dispersal of major baleen whale groups. Diagonal striping represents apparent area of origin of earliest baleen whale forms (early cetothere ancestors) and the white arrows indicate their dispersal into the Pacific and Indo-Pacific regions. Vertical striping indicates apparent original distribution of earliest Balaenopteridae in the warm temperate North Atlantic; the black arrows, major and lesser routes of dispersal of balaenopterids (with subsequent isolations due to changes in biotic barriers and adaptations in timing of reproduction to relatively local conditions). Stippled areas indicate probable zones of relatively high productivity during latter part of Caenozoic.

References

1 Allard, G. A. and Hurst, V. J. 1969. 'Brazil–Gabon geologic link supports continental drift', *Science*, vol. 163, pp. 528–32.
2 Baker, A. N. 1977. 'Spectacled porpoise, *Phocoena dioptrica*, new to the subantarctic Pacific Ocean (Note)', *N.Z.J. mar. Freshwat. Res.*, vol. 11, pp. 401–6.
3 Barnes, L. G. 1971. 'Comments on the Phocoenidae', *Abstracts, 1971 Meeting Geol. Soc. Am.*, Riverside, Ca., vol. 3, p. 79.
4 Barnes, L. G. 1976. 'Outline of eastern North Pacific fossil cetacean assemblages', *Syst. Zool.*, vol. 23, pp. 321–43.
5 Barron, E. J., Harrison, C. G. A. and Hay, W. W. 1978. 'A revised reconstruction of the southern continents', *Trans. Am. Geophys.*, vol. 59, pp. 436–49.
6 Beloussov, B. B. 1967. 'Against continental drift', *Science J.*, January 1967, pp. 2–7.
7 Benjaminsen, T. 1972. 'On the biology of the bottlenose whale, *Hyperoodon ampullatus* (Forster)', *Norw. J. Zool.*, vol. 20, pp. 233–41.
8 Best, P. B. 1970. 'Records of the pygmy killer whale, *Feresa attenuata*, from Southern Africa, with notes on behaviour in captivity', *Ann. S. Afr. Mus.*, vol. 57, pp. 1–14.
9 Bierman, W. H. and Slijper, E. J. 1948. 'Remarks upon the species of the genus *Lagenorhynchus* II', *Proc. K. ned. Akad. Wet.*, vol. 51, pp. 127–33.
10 Briggs, J. C. 1970. *Marine Zoogeography*, New York, McGraw-Hill.
11 Brownell, R. L., Jr and Herald, E. S. 1972. '*Lipotes vexillifer*', *Mammalian Species*, vol. 10, pp. 1–4.
12 Brownell, R. L., Jr, Aguayo, L. A. and Torres, N. D. 1976. 'A Shepherd's beaked whale, *Tasmacetus shepherdi*, from the eastern South Pacific', *Sci. Rep. Whales Res. Inst.*, vol. 28, pp. 127–8.
13 Cadenat, J. 1958. 'Notes sur les delphinidés ouest-africains. II. Un spécimen du genre *Feresa* capturé sur les côtes du Sénégal', *Bull. Inst.fr. Afr. noire* (A), vol. 20, pp. 1486–93.
14 Caldwell, D. K. and Caldwell, M. C. 1971. 'The pygmy killer whale, *Feresa attenuata*, in the western Atlantic, with a summary of world records', *J. Mammal.*, vol. 52, pp. 206–9.
15 Carter, R. M. and Landis, C. A. 1972. 'Correlative Oligocene unconformities in southern Australia', *Nature*, London, vol. 237, pp. 12–13.
16 Christensen, I. 1973. 'Age determination, age distribution and growth of bottlenose whales, *Hyperoodon ampullatus* (Forster), in the Labrador Sea', *Norw. J. Zool.*, vol. 21, pp. 331–40.
17 Clarke, R. 1956. 'Sperm whales of the Azores', *'Discovery' Rep.*, vol. 28, pp. 237–98.
18 Cranwell, L. M. 1963. '*Nothofagus*: living and fossil' in J. L. Gressitt (ed.), *Pacific Basin Biogeography: A Symposium*, Honolulu, Tenth Pacific Science Congress, pp. 287–400.
19 Croizat, L. 1964. *Space, Time Form: The Biological Synthesis*, Caracas, Venezuela, L. Croizat.
20 Croizat, L., Nelson, G. and Rosen, D. E. 1974. 'Centres of origin and related concepts', *Syst. Zool.*, vol. 23, pp. 265–87.
21 Darlington, P. J., Jr. 1957. *Zoogeography: The Geographical Distribution of Animals*, New York, John Wiley.
22 Darlington, P. J., Jr. 1970. 'A practical criticism of Hennig-Brundin *Phylogenetic systematics* and Antarctic biogeography', *Syst. Zool.*, vol. 19, pp. 1–18.
23 Darwin, C. 1859. *On the origin of species by means of natural selection, or the preservation of favoured races in the struggle for life*, London, John Murray.
24 Davies, J. L. 1963. 'The antitropical factor in cetacean speciation', *Evolution*, vol. 17, pp. 107–16.

25 Davies, J. L. and Guiler, E. R. 1957. 'A note on the pygmy right whale, *Caperea marginata* Gray', *Proc. zool. Soc. London*, vol. 129, pp. 579–89.

26 Ekman, S. 1953. *Zoogeography of the Sea*, London, Sidgwick & Jackson.

27 Fleming, C. A. 1962. 'New Zealand biogeography: a palaeontologist's approach', *Tuatara*, vol. 10, pp. 53–108.

28 Fleming, C. A. 1975. 'The geological history of New Zealand and its biota' in G. Kuschel (ed.), *Biogeography and Ecology in New Zealand*, The Hague, Dr W. Junk bv Publishers, pp. 1–86.

29 Fordyce, R. E. 1977. 'The development of the circum-Antarctic current and the evolution of the Mysticeti (Mammalia: Cetacea)', *Paleogeography, Paleoclimatology, Paleoecology*, vol. 21, pp. 265–71.

30 Fraser, F. C. 1955. 'The southern right whale dolphin *Lissodelphis peroni* (Lacepede), external characters and distribution', *Bull. Brit. Mus. (Nat. Hist.) Zool.*, vol. 2, pp. 339–46.

31 Fraser, F. C. 1956. 'A new Sarawak dolphin', *Sarawak Mus. J.* (n.s.), vol. 8, pp. 478–502.

32 Fraser, F. C. 1960. 'A specimen of the genus *Feresa* from Senegal', *Bull. Inst. fr. Afr. noire* (A), vol. 22, pp. 699–707.

33 Fraser, F. C. 1970. 'An early 17th century record of the Californian grey whale in Icelandic waters' in G. Pilleri (ed.), *Investigations on Cetacea*, Berne, Waldau, pp. 13–20.

34 Fraser, F. C. and Noble, B. A. 1970. 'Variation of pigmentation pattern in Meyen's dolphin, *Stenella coeruleoalba* (Meyen)' in G. Pilleri (ed.), *Investigations on Cetacea*, Berne, Waldau, pp. 147–63.

35 Funnel, B. M. and Smith, A. G. 1968. 'Opening of the Atlantic Ocean', *Nature*, London, vol. 219, pp. 1328–33.

36 Gage, M. 1957. 'The geology of Waitaki subdivision', *N.Z. Geol. Surv. Bull.* (n.s.), vol. 55, pp. 1–135.

37 Gaskin, D. E. 1968. 'The New Zealand Cetacea', *Fish. Res. Bull. N.Z. Mar. Dept.* (n.s.), vol. 1, pp. 1–92.

38 Gaskin, D. E. 1968. 'Distribution of Delphinidae (Cetacea) in relation to sea surface temperatures off eastern and southern New Zealand', *N.Z. J. mar. Freshwat. Res.*, vol. 2, pp. 527–34.

39 Gaskin, D. E. 1976. 'The evolution, zoogeography and ecology of Cetacea', *Oceanogr. Mar. Biol. Ann. Rev.*, vol. 14, pp. 247–346.

40 Gaskin, D. E., Arnold, P. W. and Blair, B. A. 1974. '*Phocoena phocoena*', *Mammalian Species*, vol. 42, pp. 1–8.

41 Griffiths, J. R. and Varne, R. 1971. 'Evolution of the Tasman Sea, Macquarie Ridge and Alpine Fault', *Nature*, London, vol. 235, pp. 83–6.

42 Handley, C. O., Jr. 1966. 'A synopsis of the genus *Kogia* (pygmy sperm whales)' in K. S. Norris (ed.), *Whales, Dolphins, and Porpoises*, Berkeley and Los Angeles, University of California Press, pp. 62–9.

43 Hennig, W. 1965. *Phylogenetic Systematics*, Urbana, Ill., University of Illinois Press.

44 Hubbs, C. L. 1952. 'Antitropical distribution of fishes and other marine organisms', *Seventh Pacific Sci. Congr.*, vol. 3, pp. 324–9.

45 Hubbs, C. L., Perrin, W. F. and Balcomb, K. C. 1973. '*Stenella coeruleoalba* in the eastern and central tropical Pacific', *J. Mammal.*, vol. 54, pp. 549–52.

46 Hurley, P. M. and Rand, J. R. 1968. 'Review of age data in west Africa and South America relative to a test of continental drift' in T. A. Phinney (ed.), *The History of the Earth's Crust*, Princeton, NJ, Princeton University Press, pp. 153–60.

47 Ingle, J. C., Jr. 1973. 'Summary comments on Neogene biostratigraphy, physical stratigraphy, and paleo-oceanography in the marginal northeastern Pacific Ocean' in L. D. Kulm et al. (eds.), *Initial Reports of the Deep Sea Drilling Project*, vol. 18, Washington, DC, US Government Printing Office, pp. 949–60.

48 Ivashin, M. V. 1972. '(Pygmy right whale *Caperea marginata* [Cetacea])', *Zool. Zh.*, vol. 51, pp. 1715–23.

49 Jenkins, D. G. 1968. 'Planktonic Foraminiferida as indicators of New Zealand Tertiary paleotemperatures', *Tuatara*, vol. 16, pp. 32–7.

50 Jenkins, D. G. 1974. 'Initiation of the proto circum-Antarctic current', *Nature*, London, vol. 252, pp. 371–3.

51 Jones, J. G. 1971. 'Australia's Caenozoic drift', *Nature*, London, vol. 230, pp. 237–9.

52 Kasuya, T. and Haque, A. K. M. 1972. 'Some information on the distribution and seasonal movement of the Ganges dolphin', *Sci. Rep. Whales Res. Inst.*, vol. 24, pp. 109–15.

53 Keast, A. 1968. 'Australian mammals: zoogeography and evolution', *Quart. Rev. Biol.*, vol. 43, pp. 373–408.

54 Keast, A., Erk, F. C. and Glass, B. (eds.). 1972. *Evolution, Mammals, and Southern Continents*, Albany, NY, State University of New York Press.

55 Kellogg, R. 1928. 'History of whales – their adaptation to life in the water', *Quart. Rev. Biol.*, vol. 3, pp. 29–76, 174–208.

56 Keyes, I. W. 1968. 'Cenozoic marine temperatures indicated by the Scleractinian coral fauna of New Zealand', *Tuatara*, vol. 16, pp. 21–5.

57 Keyes, I. W. 1973. 'Early Oligocene squalodont cetacean from Oamaru, New Zealand', *N.Z.J. mar. Freshwat. Res.*, vol. 7, pp. 381–90.

58 Kirpichnikov, A. A. 1951. 'O del'finakh iz otlozhenii aspheronskoga yarusa', *Dokl. Akad. Nauk SSSR*, vol. 79, pp. 1021–4.

59 Kleinenburg, S. E., Yablokov, A. V., Bel'kovitch, B. M. and Tarasevich, M. N. 1969. 'Beluga (*Delphinapterus leucas*) – Investigation of the species', *Akad. Nauk SSSR*, Jerusalem, Israel Program for Scientific Translation.

60 Klumov, S. K. 1963. '(Feeding and helminth fauna of whalebone whales (*Mystacoceti*) in the main whaling grounds of the world ocean)', *Trudy Inst. Okeanol.*, vol. 71, pp. 94–194.

61 Lipps, J. H. and Mitchell, E. 1976. 'Trophic model for the adaptive radiations and extinctions of pelagic marine mammals', *Paleobiology*, vol. 2, pp. 147–55.

62 Matthew, W. D. 1915. 'Climate and evolution', *Ann. N.Y. Acad. Sci.*, vol. 24, pp. 171–318.

63 Mayr, E. 1963. *Animal Species and Evolution*, Cambridge, Mass., Belknap Press, Harvard University Press.

64 Mayr, E. 1970. *Populations, Species, and Evolution*, Cambridge, Mass., Belknap Press, Harvard University Press.

65 Mayr, E. 1974. 'Cladistic analysis or cladistic classification?' *Zool. Syst. Forsch.*, vol. 42, pp. 94–128.

66 Mead, J. G. and Payne, R. S. 1975. 'A specimen of the Tasman beaked whale, *Tasmacetus shepherdi*, from Argentina', *J. Mammal.*, vol. 56, pp. 213–18.

67 Meyerhoff, A. A. 1970. 'Continental drift; implications of paleomagnetic studies, meteorology, physical oceanography, and climatology', *J. Geol.*, vol. 78, pp. 1–51.

68 Meyerhoff, A. A. 1970. 'Continental drift, II. High-latitude evaporite deposits and geological history of Arctic and North Atlantic Oceans', *J. Geol.*, vol. 78, pp. 406–44.

69 Meyerhoff, A. A. and Teichert, C. 1971. 'Continental drift, III. Late Paleozoic glacial centers, and Devonian–Eocene coal distribution', *J. Geol.*, vol. 79, pp. 285–321.

70 McIntyre, A. 1967. 'Coccoliths as paleoclimatic indicators of Pleistocene glaciation', *Science*, vol. 158, pp. 1314–17.

71 Miller, G. S. 1923. 'The telescoping of the cetacean skull', *Smithsonian Misc. Contrib.*, vol. 76, pp. 1–71.

72 Mitchell, E. 1970. 'Pigmentation pattern evolution in delphinid cetaceans: an essay

in adaptive coloration', *Can. J. Zool.*, vol. 48, pp. 717–40.

73 Moore, J. C. 1968. 'Relationships between the living genera of beaked whales with classifications, diagnoses, and keys', *Fieldiana zool.*, vol. 53, pp. 209–98.

74 Nelson, G. 1973. 'Comments on Leon Croizat's biogeography', *Syst. Zool.*, vol. 22, pp. 312–20.

75 Nelson, G. 1974. 'Darwin–Hennig classification. A reply to Ernst Mayr', *Syst. Zool.*, vol. 53, pp. 452–8.

76 Nikolskii, G. V. 1969. *Theory of fish population dynamics as the biological background for rational exploitation and management of fishery resources*, translated by J. E. S. Bradley, edited by R. Jones, Edinburgh, Oliver & Boyd.

77 Nishiwaki, M., Kasuya, T., Kamiya, T., Tobayama, T. and Nakajima, M. 1965. '*Feresa attenuata* captured at the Pacific coast of Japan in 1963', *Sci. Rep. Whales Res. Inst.*, vol. 19, pp. 65–90.

78 Nishiwaki, M. and Kasuya, T. 1970. 'Recent record of gray whale in the adjacent waters of Japan and a consideration on its migration', *Sci. Rep. Whales Res. Inst.*, vol. 22, pp. 29–37.

79 Nishiwaki, M. and Norris, K. S. 1966. 'A new genus, *Peponocephala*, for the odontocete cetacean species *Electra electra*', *Sci. Rep. Whales Res. Inst.*, vol. 20, pp. 95–100.

80 Noble, B. A. and Fraser, F. C. 1970. 'Description of a skeleton and supplementary notes on the skull of a rare porpoise *Phocoena sinus* Norris and McFarland', *J. Nat. Hist.*, vol. 5, pp. 447–64.

81 Norris, K. S. and McFarland, W. N. 1958. 'A new harbor porpoise of the genus *Phocoena* from the Gulf of California', *J. Mammal.*, vol. 39, pp. 22–39.

82 Orr, W. N. 1972. 'Pacific northwest siliceous phytoplankton', *Paleogeography, Paleoclimatology, Paleoecology*, vol. 12, pp. 95–114.

83 Orr, W. N. and Faulhaber, J. 1975. 'A middle Tertiary cetacean from Oregon', *Northwest Sci.*, vol. 49, pp. 174–81.

84 Perrin, W. F., Warner, R. R., Fiscus, C. H. and Holts, D. B. 1973. 'Stomach contents of porpoise (*Stenella* spp.) and yellowfin tuna (*Thunnus albacares*) in mixed species aggregations', *Fishery Bull. Fish. Wildl. Serv. US*, vol. 71, pp. 1077–92.

85 Perrin, W. F., Mitchell, E. D. and Van Bree, P. J. H. 1978. 'Historical zoogeography of tropical pelagic dolphins', *Abstract, II. Congressus Theriologicus Internationalis.*, 20–27 June 1978, p. 79.

86 Pilleri, G. 1970. 'Observations on the behaviour of *Platanista gangetica* in the Indus and Brahmaputra rivers' in G. Pilleri (ed.), *Investigations on Cetacea*, vol. II, Berne, Waldau, pp. 27–60.

87 Platnick, N. I. 1976. 'Concepts of dispersal in historical biogeography', *Syst. Zool.*, vol. 25, pp. 294–5.

88 Pryor, T., Pryor, K. and Norris, K. S. 1965. 'Observations on a pygmy killer whale (*Feresa attenuata* Gray) from Hawaii', *J. Mammal.*, vol. 46, pp. 450–61.

89 Rice, D. W. 1967. 'Family Phocoenidae Bravard, 1885 Porpoises' in S. Anderson and J. K. Jones (eds.), *Recent Mammals of the World: A Synopsis of Families*, New York, Ronald Press, pp. 319–21.

90 Rice, D. W. and Scheffer, V. B. 1968. 'A list of the marine mammals of the world', *US Fish. Wildl. Service*, Spec. Rep. no. 579, pp. 1–16.

91 Rosa, D. 1931. *L'ologénèse. Nouvelle théorie de l'evolution et de la distribution géographique*, Paris, Felix Alcon.

92 Rosen, D. E. 1975. 'A vicariance model of Caribbean biogeography', *Syst. Zool.*, vol. 24, pp. 431–64.

93 Ross, G. J. B. 1977. 'The taxonomy of bottlenosed dolphins *Tursiops* species in South African waters, with notes on their biology', *Ann. Cape Prov. Mus. (Nat. Hist.)*, vol. 11, pp. 135–94.

94 Schwartzbach, M. 1968. 'Tertiary temperature curves in New Zealand and Europe', *Tuatara*, vol. 16, pp. 38–40.

95 Shackleton, N. J. and Kennett, J. P. 1975. 'Paleotemperature history of the Cenozoic and the initiation of Antarctic glaciation: oxygen and carbon isotope analyses in DSDP sites 277, 279 and 281' in L. D. Kulm *et al.* (eds.), *Initial Reports of the Deep Sea Drilling Project*, vol. 29, Washington, DC, US Government Printing Office, pp. 743–55.

96 Sergeant, D. E. 1962. 'On the external characters of the blackfish or pilot whales (Genus *Globicephala*)', *J. Mammal.*, vol. 43, pp. 395–413.

97 Simpson, G. G. 1940. 'Mammals and land bridges', *Wash. Acad. Sci.*, vol. 30, pp. 137–63.

98 Slijper, E. J., Van Utrecht, W. L. and Naaktgeboren, C. 1964. 'Observations on the distribution and migrations of whales as observed from Netherlands ships', *Bijdr. tot de Dierk.*, vol. 34, pp. 3–93.

99 Sliter, W. V., Be, A. W. H. and Berger, W. H. (eds.). 1975. *Dissolution of Deep-Sea Carbonates*, Special Publication of the Cushman Foundation, no. 13.

100 Small Whale Subcommittee of the IWC Scientific Committee. 1978. 'Report to the Scientific Committee of the International Whaling Commission' in *Twenty-Eighth Report of the International Whaling Commission*, London, pp. 79–82.

101 Sokal, R. R. 1975. 'Mayr on cladism; and his critics', *Syst. Zool.*, vol. 24, pp. 257–63.

102 Sproll, W. P. and Dietz, R. S. 1969. 'Morphological continental drift fit of Australia and Antarctica', *Nature*, London, vol. 222, pp. 345–8.

103 Tomilin, A. G. 1967. *Cetacea : vol. 9, Mammals of the USSR and Adjacent Countries*, translation by Israel Program for Scientific Translation, and edited by V. G. Heptner, Jerusalem.

104 Valencio, D. A. and Vilais, J. F. 1969. 'Age of the separation of South America and Africa', *Nature*, London, vol. 223, pp. 1353–4.

105 Valentine, J. W. 1973. *Evolutionary Paleoecology of the Marine Biosphere*, Englewood Cliffs, NJ, Prentice-Hall.

106 Van Bree, P. J. H. and Cadenat, J. 1968. 'On a skull of *Peponocephala electra* (Gray, 1846) (Cetacea, Globicephalinae) from Senegal', *Beaufortia*, vol. 14, pp. 193–202.

107 Whitmore, F. C. and Sanders, A. E. 1976. 'Review of the Oligocene Cetacea', *Syst. Zool.*, vol. 25, pp. 304–20.

108 Yurick, D. B. 1977. 'Populations, subpopulations, and zoogeography of the harbour porpoise, *Phocoena phocoena* (L.)', MSc thesis, University of Guelph, Ontario, Canada.

Conceptual views of species and speciation in Cetacea, and recognition of degrees of polytypy*

Species and speciation – problems of definition

It is probably true to say that we still do not have *excellent* data in large quantities for even *one* of the large commercially exploited species. We have useful quantities of good, indifferent and poor data – which is not quite the same thing. If we lack clear understanding of the population distribution and structure of the large commercially exploited species, we know much less about those of no commercial interest. Some are represented in collections by such a small number of specimens (often only skeletal in nature) that we have but the sketchiest ideas of the normal range of variation in size and pigmentation patterns and changes in morphology with age, and we know virtually nothing of their life histories. The truth is, we are still quite ignorant of cetacean population genetics, inter-regional interactions, social structure, and a whole host of other aspects. Small wonder, then, that the definitions of species, subspecies and unit populations are often ambiguous and unsatisfactory, and the opinions of equal authorities at odds.

From time to time one comes across statements in the cetacean literature, as in other fields of biology, indicating that authors can hold markedly different concepts of 'species', and that some misapprehensions about what does or does not constitute a species are still quite widespread. I think it useful, therefore, to take some space to discuss in general terms what has been called 'the species problem', although of course students will have to draw their own conclusions when faced with divergent opinions about cetacean systematics, and view each interpretation on its merits.

---

*Population differentiation below the species level.

Originally, the concept of a 'species' related purely and simply to the need to classify animals, it was part of a desire to reduce the chaos (or rather, the bewildering diversity) of the animal and plant kingdoms to manageable proportions and, furthermore, to define in scientific terms those categories of animals and plants which were already recognized as 'units unto themselves' in the common tongues of the world. To extend the simple older definitions of species (and the larger groupings such as genus, tribe, family, order and phylum) to embrace ideas of common ancestry, phylogeny and evolution was to step on to entirely new ground – territory in which the original concepts of 'species' were soon found to be inadequate.

In the classical literature of modern biology we encounter three main definitions of the species: 'typological species', 'biological species' and 'nominalistic species' (30, 31, 94–6). More recently, among population geneticists, we find those who would like to see the concept of 'species' dropped altogether (except for use strictly confined to the discipline of taxonomy) and the 'deme', or unit breeding population, substituted. The deme, they argue with much force, is the raw material moulded by selective forces, and is the essential core of the evolutionary process. The species is considered by many in this field to represent nothing but a collection of demes, some of which may well have no genetic contact at all. The taxonomists of the past have recognized this genetic reality, albeit often in a crude way, by the use of subspecies, 'races' and sometimes 'forms'.

Although the 'biological species' has dominated most of the evolutionary literature during the last twenty years, one can still find authors in modern biological literature adhering consciously or subconsciously to one or other of the earlier concepts. The essence of the nominalistic concept, which proves immensely attractive to undergraduate students wearying of instruction in the mysteries of taxonomy, is that there exist continua of plant and animal *individuals*, any one of which is slightly different from any other. Though the ideological nominalist would admit to discontinuities in this spectrum, these are said to be the result of chance extinctions. The continuum of individuals is said to have been broken down by taxonomists into units of classification, referred to as 'species', which the nominalist considers to be purely arbitrary abstractions. This view is contrary to the observed realities of genetics; if all individuals were simply part of such a continuum there would be no way in which favourable recombinations could be preserved and no way for gradual 'improvement' (that is, adaptation) of the gene pool (94).

The 'typological species', on the other hand, implies not only an acceptance of the reality of 'species', but conceives of a plant or an animal as having a 'type' to which the individuals in the population conform within certain limits of variation. The concept of 'species' in this case, therefore, is based essentially on observed morphology, and species A is distinguished from species B by reasonably consistent differences in phenotypic characteristics. The continued existence of this concept is reinforced in many ways by the system of nomenclature instituted by Linnaeus, which forms the universally accepted basis of all latinized scientific names for all plants and animals. Furthermore, each description of a new species must be supported by a *type* specimen; perferably with a series of *paratypic* specimens, deposited in an accredited systematic institute or museum. In many cases, a definition of a species in strictly morphological terms is, in practice, quite acceptable for purposes of recognition and classification. Indeed, when one first studies a poorly known group such as the genus *Mesoplodon*, with relatively few specimens of each species available and their life histories unknown, virtually exclusive use of morphological characters is almost the only course open, however undesirable this may be in theory. The taxonomist must still rely heavily on diagnostic experience to make decisions concerning what constitutes a species in such cases, but classifying plants or animals in this fashion, in full realization of the degree of one's ignorance and limitations, is a very different thing in principle from a slavish belief that recognizable morphological differences *necessarily* imply specific differences. The fallacy of the latter approach can be easily demonstrated by reference to examples in which the same genetic pool is capable of producing distinct phenotypic forms under different conditions; pelt colour changes in fur-bearing mammals from subarctic regions, for example.

The 'biological species' is considered by its proponents as having conceptual reality. It is at the same time a reproductive community, an ecological unit and a genetic unit. Biological species are groups of interbreeding natural populations that are reproductively isolated from other such populations. A biological species can also be defined as 'a gene pool protected by isolating mechanisms', the reproductive isolation preventing the dilution of an integrated and co-adapted genetic system which has been produced as the result of natural selection within a specific environmental range (96). Such isolating mechanisms are also believed to function to increase the efficiency of mating.

The relative importance of the various types of isolating mechanisms which can develop is sometimes misunderstood. Some elementary biology texts still stress production of a sterile hybrid as the only true test of the specific status of two related forms. In practice, crossing two related species will produce fertile hybrids at least as often as sterile issue. Even the existence of indisputable spatial isolation is *no* guarantee that one will find the populations in question to be separated by reproductive isolating mechanisms, should individuals be brought into contact experimentally.

In reality, species often co-exist without interbreeding even when such crossing is, in the strictly technical sense, quite possible. *Lagenorhynchus albirostris* and *L. acutus* may be a case in point. On the other hand, some biologists worry about the practical difficulties of testing the biological species concept when populations are widely separated, or breeding cycles are out of phase, as with northern and southern hemisphere baleen whales, but, as Mayr pointed out, it becomes irrelevant whether reproductive isolating mechanisms in the technical sense exist or not when spatial or temporal isolation is complete.

Various combinations of different types of isolating mechanisms may operate, and at varying levels of efficiency in different populations of a single species, because the genetic assemblage that that term represents is a dynamic, not a static system, and does not need to be viewed as having consistent reactions on all its interfaces. Sometimes the isolating mechanisms may break down, and there is no reason not to expect this from time to time. Few cetologists, I think, would argue about the specific identities of Risso's dolphin *Grampus griseus* and the bottlenosed dolphin *Tursiops truncatus*. Yet there exist three specimens from Blacksod Bay in Ireland which appeared, in every respect, to be intermediates, hybrids, of the two species (48). Recently a calf was born in a Japanese seaquarium as the result of a successful *Tursiops–Grampus* mating, and the more extreme case of a *Tursiops–Steno* hybrid has also been recorded (42). There is little in the cetacean literature to suggest, however, that this is a common event among those species which we normally, and probably quite reasonably, consider to be well defined. There are of course other groups, such as the genus *Stenella*, where there is currently so much trouble defining species that a swarm of hybrid forms could be under our noses all the time.

Behavioural (that is, ethological) isolation is considered to be one of the most significant of all isolating mechanisms, especially in higher animals (96), and has probably played an important role in cetacean speciation. Some cetacean species have sharply delineated and consistent pigmentation patterns. They may not just represent camouflage of some form (100) but be clear species-identification display patterns that will not elicit a mating stimulus in a member of the opposite sex of a different species. Humpback whales 'sing' – in fact have a whole complex repertoire of underwater sounds (127) – other rorquals do not. Did this difference play an important role in the original divergence of *Megaptera* and *Balaenoptera*? Auditory stimuli and cues are certainly extremely important in Odontoceti. In a recent paper Watkins and Schevill of the Woods Hole Marine Laboratory showed that sperm whales within a small social unit all demonstrated highly specific individual acoustic signatures or 'codas', repeated during underwater communication by animals separated by hundreds of metres vertically and horizontally (157).

Trophic-niche differentiation can be recognized in Cetacea (see Chapter 2). Though sea-surface temperature is unlikely to be a primary factor *per se* in delimiting cetacean distributions, it can certainly reflect spatial and ecological isolation in the case of some delphinoid species (57, 139). The migratory populations of the large rorquals of the temperate-subpolar zones of the northern and southern hemisphere are spatially isolated, and chances of contact are further reduced to an absolute minimum by the migrations being six months out of phase. Even when several species of rorqual exploit the same feeding ground and clear trophic-niche differentiation cannot be demonstrated, they often move into the area in sequence, so that competition is minimized by a degree of temporal segregation (10). In all cases, whatever the manner in which populations first start to become reproductively isolated, the development of isolating mechanisms is probably never 'all or nothing', but rather stepwise (94).

The existence of variation, which greatly bothered the early Darwinians, is an intrinsic part of the biological species concept. Without the existence of such variation, there would be no 'raw material' on which natural selection could operate. Mutation merely increases the range of such variation. Evolution can, in fact, be defined as 'a change in the genetic composition of populations' (41).

Nevertheless, identifying the nature of and measuring the extent of variation in a species is a vexing problem for the systematic biologist, and must be dealt with before comparisons with similar species can be made satisfactorily. Variation occurs at two levels; there is individual variation, which is a familiar enough concept, and 'group' or population variation, which gives the taxonomist and systematist a lot more trouble. No species occupies a spatial range that is totally uniform, and the adaptations which have occurred in the overall population through different selective influences in different parts of the range become reflected in recognizable variation between local populations. At the genetic level, cohesion in these subpopulations is maintained and consolidated since, on average, an animal is more likely to mate with one of its neighbours in the local population than a far distant member of the opposite sex.

In fact most species are *polytypic*, that is, have recognizable local populations, and differences between these can range from virtual indistinguishability to levels of distinctness that merit subspecific or even specific status. When the range of a species is continuous, such adaptive variation still occurs, but the quantitative and qualitative changes in aspects of the phenotype are *clinal* (that is gradual, or stepwise). Species with wide distributions may have peripheral populations which are functioning genetically more or less as distinct species, yet are connected one to another by populations with intermediate characteristics (96). To further confuse the taxonomist, it is the rule rather than the exception for different characters to vary independently, and the perfection of isolating mechanisms may proceed at different rates of development in different local populations. If there is geographical (spatial) isolation, they may not develop at all.

Several situations produce serious obstacles to our attempts to define species (96): (1) the presence of clinal variation in phenotypic characters; (2) the acquisition of morphological differences within a population without corresponding reproductive isolating mechanisms, as is often the case in polymorphism (when used in the strict sense only, that is, discontinuous genetic variation), or polyphasy (having different colour phases within an interbreeding population); (3) acquisition of reproductive isolation without significant morphological change; this results in so-called *sibling species*, which seem, fortunately, to be rare in mammals, since the cetacean taxonomist has enough problems as it is! (4) the existence of recognizable local populations without clinal variation being demonstrated; (5) what appear on other counts to be well-defined species being separated by incomplete isolating mechanisms; and (6) reproductive isolation being dependent largely on habitat isolation – a change in environmental conditions bringing two such populations together will result in ready interbreeding.

In shadowy areas such as these only biological knowledge and wisdom and relevant taxonomic experience can act as guides. The rules of the International Commission on Zoological Nomenclature impose certain constraints; for example, subspecific names must only be applied when the populations differ by taxonomically acceptable criteria; otherwise local populations or 'races' must not be formally named (95). In general, the investigator has only the available data, previous literature (if any) and personal experience as a basis for making decisions which may have important practical ramifications. In the case of commercially exploited animals such as cetaceans, an underestimate of the degree of isolation of a local population, incorporated into a management decision, could lead to severe overexploitation or even functional extinction of the population.

So taxonomy, systematic analysis and population identification have vital roles to play in the study of Cetacea, and at all levels the research worker is hampered by inadequate data which are the result of past (and present) neglect of research by those countries which have gained most from the exploitation of these animals. Even if biologists have a clear idea of what they should be looking for in terms of species or population identifications, the data are rarely equal to the requirements. Our knowledge of every cetacean species and genus would benefit from further systematic study; this applies as much to relatively well-known genera, such as *Balaenoptera*, as to little-known genera, such as *Mesoplodon*. The systematic list of living Cetacea given on pp. 200–207 is at best only provisional and subject to almost immediate amendment and modification. Our nearly total ignorance of cetacean population genetics renders any further discussion of the role of the deme (gamodeme) in evolutionary processes beyond the scope of this volume, and I shall not even attempt to use the terminology of population genetics, but retain the traditional terminology of species, subspecies and populations in the sections which follow. For those students who would like to read some of the more cogent and thought-provoking essays in the modern general evolutionary literature, a selection of titles have been included in the bibliography of this chapter (26, 30, 39, 45, 46, 62, 67, 142, 144, 145, 158).

Differentiation of populations below the species level

Population segregation has been identified in a number of cetacean species and spans a wide range of differentiation, from the barely detectable to undoubted polytypy or subspeciation. In some cases, rather small differences in meristic or morphometric values occur from one geographical region to another. In other instances, biochemical characteristics or colour patterns have been reported from one area that differs significantly from those present in more distant populations. Sometimes a sequence of changes occur from one region to another in a series of characters, the phenomenon known as clinal variation. We also have rather clear-cut examples of morphological differences within a described species, with or without distinct geographical distributions. This is *polyphenism*, or the existence of one or more distinct phenotypes which may or may not represent valid species. In other species we observe two or more basic colour patterns, again with or without a corresponding difference in distribution patterns; this is *polyphasy*.

Degrees of polytypy

1 Low level population segregation

Three wide-ranging, well-known species are the humpback *Megaptera novaeangliae*, the minke whale *Balaenoptera acutorostrata* and the sperm whale *Physeter catodon*. In none of these species does apparent segregation of populations seem to have progressed far enough to permit subspecies status to be reasonably applied. Marking experiments have shown that significant transpopulation intermingling still occurs.

Some attempts have been made to detect humpback population

segregation through morphometric studies. R. G. Chittleborough (33) was unable to find any significant differences between eastern and Western Australian humpback morphometry: 'analysis showed greater differences between the measurements of two observers measuring whales from the same population than between measurements from whales of the two populations'. Another more recent attempt to analyse morphometric data was made by D. Machin and B. Kitchenham of the University of Stirling, who used principal component analysis methods to examine sets of measurements made in two southern hemisphere regions (88). Their conclusions were greatly limited by the differences in population composition of catches at South Georgia and South Africa (93); the sample means of the components at the latter locality were affected by a much larger percentage of immature animals being present. They were able to detect significant differences between size ranges of males and females, but there are easier and more direct ways of doing that! Nevertheless, the method is undoubtedly a powerful tool which is of great assistance for comparisons when aged samples are available. Studies of colour morphs in humpbacks have also been made (see section 3 of this chapter); these also suggest, but do not yet confirm, the existence of subpopulations in the North Pacific.

The minke whale *Balaenoptera acutorostrata* is the rorqual best known to coastal fishermen of temperate latitudes; it is generally abundant and attracts attention by its habit of sometimes closely approaching stationary or slow-moving boats (11). Despite detailed comparisons of the number of baleen plates, hyoid bones, ventral grooves and other characteristics there is little or no decisive evidence for recognizing significant differences between northern and southern populations on morphological grounds (5, 78, 115, 136).

Distinction of minke whale populations, even between hemispheres, remains, therefore, a frustrating problem which requires much more attention. The question is a particularly urgent one since the southern hemisphere minke whale catch jumped from virtually zero a few years ago to 3020 in 1971/2 and to 8676 by 1976/7. Furthermore, 80–90 per cent of these were taken in Antarctic area IV and the rest in area III in the first phase of this intensive hunting. If this trend of concentration of zonal effort continues for even a very few more seasons the area IV population will have been subjected to intense selective overexploitation.

The most recent study to describe possible recognizable subpopulations of minke whales at the time of writing is that of Wada and Numachi (156). They examined simultaneously both external and biochemical parameters in the same samples from a large range of Antarctic whaling areas. The former included the gradations of black, grey and white on the pectoral flippers (see also section 3 in this chapter), the proportion of dark banding on the baleen, and the degree to which the ventral grooves extended to the umbilical region of the body. On average, the commonest phenotypic combination was for an animal to have ventral grooves reaching the umbilicus, the flipper to be uniformly dark, and the baleen to have about half of each baleen plate banded with blackish. They were, however, quite unable to assign any morphological type to a particular longitudinally defined area, and were also worried that different observers might have reported intermediate patterns in various ways, introducing significant bias into the results.

The biochemical approach proved somewhat more useful. Large samples of liver tissue were examined for enzyme polymorphic phenotypes, nine of which were recognized. All alleles appeared to have equilibrated in each population examined. No genetic characters seemed to segregate the southern Atlantic minke from the western Indian Ocean stock. Both were distinguished, however, by at least one characteristic from populations in the eastern Indian Ocean, western Pacific and eastern Pacific respectively. The authors pointed out that none of the allele frequencies found most useful were very large, and differences were generally detectable at the 5 per cent significance level only. The practical use of these results, therefore, is rather limited.

Among odontocetes, the sperm whale has perhaps been subjected to the most intensive investigations in the major ocean regions. Some significant progress in the analysis and recognition of sperm whale breeding stocks has been made (8, 14–17, 35, 37, 40, 55, 91, 116).

Eight southern hemisphere populations have been proposed, defined by longitudinal zones, which might tentatively be considered as functional breeding stocks on the basis of whaling records and mark returns (17). These are: (1) eastern South America (60°W–20°W); (2) western Africa (20°W–20°E); (3) eastern Africa (20°E–60°E); (4) India (60°E–90°E); (5) Western Australia (90°E–140°E); (6) New Zealand and eastern Australia (140°E–160°W); (7) central South Pacific (160°W–100°W); and (8) western South America (100°W–60°W). In most respects this appears to represent a workable representation of distributions on which to base unit management. At least one division (that of 3 from 4) has been supported by serological typing results. In the 23rd report of the International Whaling Commission in 1973 (72), the Scientific Committee recommended increasing to nine the number of stocks for recognition; they included a separate New Zealand stock between 160°E and 170°W; however, I think 170°E–160°W would provide a more realistic regional definition of this population. The present author has analysed the western South Pacific catch and sighting data, and correlated these with summer and winter surface temperatures in the New Zealand region (59). The results indicate that the Tasman Sea and eastern New Zealand populations should be treated as separate units for management purposes. Summer surface temperatures directly south of the New Zealand archipelago are low enough to inhibit almost completely interchange of breeding schools containing females with calves. Indeed, the catches in that area have historically always been of males, even though females with calves may concentrate only one or two hundred kilometres to the north-east, on the shelf of the Canterbury Bight. Although the two populations are adjacent on the wintering grounds (Old French Rock and Kermadec grounds north and north-east of New Zealand), they have segregated to the west and east of the archipelago during the spring southward migration long before the peak of pairing in November. There is no interchange through Cook Strait; whales often enter the eastern side but invariably turn back when they encounter the shallower water west of Wellington and the Marlborough Sounds. Sperm whales not infrequently strand in this area.

There is a little information from Russian whale-mark returns to suggest that there is interchange between North and South Atlantic sperm whale populations, but studies by Robert Clarke on the population distributed around the Azores (35), suggested that the normal seasonal movement of this population is into the higher latitudes of the North Atlantic, with some males summering as far north as Iceland each year or penetrating north-westwards towards the New England and Canadian coastal shelf.

Three basic breeding units of sperm whales appear to occur in the North Pacific (91); one distributed to the west of longitude 170°E, and a second between 170°E and 150°W, migrating in summer as far north as the Aleutian Islands and wintering perhaps in the Hawaiian region, and the third between 150°W and the west coast of North America. Even so, a large degree of genetic homogeneity must be maintained by interchange of males above 40°N, as demonstrated by some whale-mark returns (109).

C. H. Townsend (150) plotted the catches of sperm whales recorded by a very large number of logbooks of old whale ships, and his work showed intensive concentrations throughout the Old World tropics in equatorial regions. In the light of this, discriminative morphometric studies by Robert Clarke and Obla Paliza (37), and by David Machin (87) are of great interest. Their results indicate a degree of genetic continuity between the whales of the North and South Pacific and those of the Indian Ocean, but there are significant differences in a number of principal morphological components between these 'greater Indo–Oceanic region' animals and those from the South Georgia–western South African region, which are presumably of South Atlantic origin. A third, somewhat less defined, group occurs between 95°E–150°E; this equates with Best's 'Western Australian' unit. These results are not incompatible with the published results of blood-typing studies (40), and the southern stock units proposed by P. B. Best (17) or the International Whaling Commission's Scientific

Committee. One important result of these studies is that the case for recognizing separate subspecies of northern and southern hemisphere sperm whales can be emphatically rejected.

These findings could, however, have an unfortunate consequence for rational management of global sperm whale populations. The Scientific Committee of the International Whaling Commission noted in 1974 (73) that K. Yonezawa of Japan disagreed with the proposal of nine functional southern stocks and considered that recognition of three might be more appropriate. The morphometric studies could be construed as providing support for such a view, since they indicate a considerable degree of genetic continuity. The present author is emphatically opposed to the adoption of this simplistic approach, unless it is totally politically unavoidable, for the following reasons. Data presented by the Scientific Committee even as early as 1973 and 1974 show conclusively that males have been depleted in virtually every area in which sperm whales have been hunted (72, 73). Although genetic exchange in post-Pleistocene times has been sufficient to suppress all but relatively minor genetic differentiation in sperm whale populations, the interchange is a relatively slow process. We may, therefore, conclude that the hunting pressures which the modern whaling industry can bring to bear will deplete local subunits far faster than they can be resupplied by slow immigration from other subunits even in the same oceanic region. Whaling fleets operate by a concentration of effort in relatively limited geographical areas, and it is precisely this mechanism, coupled with inaccurate population estimates (certainly still true in the case of the sperm whale), which has led to severe reduction of southern baleen whale stocks despite management attempts. I am convinced that in the long run recognition of only three huge stock units would prove a most unfortunate method of attempting to manage exploitation of sperm whales; on the other hand, the economic advantages of such a system to the industry (in the short term) are very obvious and do not require being spelled out.

In recent years similar studies have begun on some small cetacean species; results have been more decisive in some cases than in others. The problem of North Pacific population identities in the genus *Delphinus* was studied by R. C. Banks and R. L. Brownell (7). Their conclusion was that *D. bairdii* could be distinguished from *D. delphis* on the basis of a number of cranial characteristics. Their samples were, however, not age specific and on two counts the conclusions can be (and have been) challenged (152). The problem is an interesting one and their findings may be confirmed when larger regional samples become available. One cannot exclude the possibility of there being distinct inshore and offshore populations or tropical–subtropical distinctions; W. E. Evans has recently given evidence for the latter (47).

Population variation in the widespread blue–white dolphin *Stenella coeruleoalba* has been studied, based on samples obtained from the Mediterranean, North and South Atlantic, Indian Ocean and Pacific (51). Hampered by the small size and quality of some of the samples, the researchers confessed themselves unable to relate the common pigmentation patterns to any particular geographical area, although by considering the sum of the component variants it was possible in general terms to distinguish any individual of this species from any other *Stenella*. More recently, however, W. F. Perrin has used distributional data to indicate that two distinct populations of *S. coeruleoalba* might exist in the North Pacific (130).

Within the Delphinidae we find, in fact, some of the most frustrating taxonomic problems in the suborder Odontoceti. These must be solved before any real progress can be made in the detection of discrete population units within any single species. A number of attempts to make some sense of the welter of names within the genus *Stenella* have been published in recent years (51, 128, 129). E. Mitchell (100), admittedly working with samples of limited size, made a creditable attempt to provide a logical working explanation of the evolution of the subunits of colour pattern in *Stenella* from an adaptive point of view. W. F. Perrin carried out a similar analysis of pattern components and colour–field distribution in *S. attenuata* (East Pacific spotted dolphin) and *S. cf. longirostris* (128, 129). He was able to explain most geographical variation as the result of differences in the intensity of pigmentation of a discrete 'dark field system' which overlaid a basic ground–colour pattern. In later work Perrin analysed population segregation of these two species (130, 131). Based on colour pattern, length at a given age, number of vertebrae, condylbasal skull length and tooth diameter, he identified three distinct populations of *Stenella attenuata*. The first of these occurs in the vicinity of the Hawaiian archipelago (and may range into the western and south Pacific), and is most clearly characterized by the near-obsolescence of the typical spotted pattern. The pelagic ('offshore') form, *S. attenuata attenuata*, is found from the tropical and subtropical coasts of North and Central America westward to approximately longitude 145°W. In coastal waters from the Gulf of California to Ecuador are found animals with low dorso-ventral pigmentation contrast; this population also contains the largest adults with relatively large skull size; at first these were provisionally assigned by Perrin to subspecies *S. a. graffmani* (128), but this name has now been dropped (131).

He also identified four 'races' of spinner dolphin, *Stenella longirostris* in the eastern tropical Pacific. One occurs in Hawaiian waters and the western Pacific, and is characteristically elongate, with a white ventral surface. A second, called provisionally the 'Costa Rican form', is also relatively elongate, but grey. The third or 'Eastern spinner' is not noticeably elongate, but is also grey in colour. Its distribution extends westwards to about longitude 115°W. Its range, which varies seasonally along with that of the other forms, is overlapped to the west (about 150°W) and south (including the Galapagos Islands) by the relatively shorter, ventrally pale 'white-belly spinner' dolphin. Some intermediates have been taken; genetic isolation of these populations is obviously far from complete. In a more recent analysis (131), he and his co-workers presented evidence also indicating significant differences between this 'white-belly' population and that which occurs south of the equator and west of the Galapagos Islands. Specimens of *Stenella attenuata* sighted and taken in this area also showed consistent colour-pattern differences.

Apparent subspeciation in the harbour porpoise *Phocoena phocoena* has been the subject of considerable work and discussion. The species occurs even today as for north as Point Barrow, Alaska (65), the Beaufort Sea (153), Disco Island, Greenland (97), and has been sporadically reported at other localities as far north as southern Baffin Island (61, 98).

I suggested in 1976 (60) that the similarity of North Pacific and North Atlantic *Phocoena phocoena* was so great that fairly frequent mixing via the Canadian Arctic island channels had probably taken place during relatively warm periods since the last glaciation, and perhaps during Pleistocene interstadia. More recent work in my own laboratory indicates that this opinion needs re-evaluation and perhaps some revision. In a preliminary study, A. G. Tomilin of the USSR compared a series of North Pacific, North Atlantic and Sea of Azov–Black Sea skulls (149). He found significant difference in rostral lengths, with the greatest difference between rostral to total skull length ratio between the North Pacific and North Atlantic populations. This work, along with other aspects, was inconclusive because it had not been carried out using age-determined material. D. B. Yurick of the University of Guelph recently examined large osteological samples of age-determined *P. phocoena* from the Pacific and both sides of the Atlantic, and found significant differences between the jaws and dentition of North Atlantic and North Pacific *P. phocoena* (162). He concluded that this indicated that the two populations probably have *not* been in contact via Arctic seaways during the post-Pleistocene as frequently as previously suggested (60, 137). Occasional mixing, especially during the post-Pleistocene warm period about 5000–6000 years ago, as I had suggested (60), is not precluded. This may, in fact, have prevented further genetic and morphological divergence between the two populations. Although there have been several openings of the seaway during Pleistocene and recent periods, contact between the boreal faunas of the Atlantic and Pacific Oceans has apparently been minimal (21). The Arctic Ocean has been warmer over the last 700 000 to 1 million years than at any other time since the Pliocene (34).

The morphological differences that separate North Atlantic and North Pacific *P. phocoena* may have developed quite early or relatively recently, there is no way at present to tell for certain. Yurick provided another synthesis of information to explain the zoogeographic distribution of this species. Original divergence from a North Pacific ancestor in the late Miocene was proposed, followed by penetration of the North Atlantic by the Caribbean seaway in the Pliocene. Following closure of the seaway (which may also have been the route followed by the precursor of the walrus *Odobenus rosmarus* into the Atlantic at the same time), the North Atlantic and Pacific populations were segregated.

There is a strong possibility that with development of suitable techniques, we may be able to distinguish several populations of harbour porpoise in each of these oceans. M. C. Mercer suggested that possible genetic differences in North Atlantic population units were manifested in external pigmentation variations (97). More recently D. B. Yurick summarized the admittedly scanty evidence for as many as 14 functional subpopulations (162). He has since been able to demonstrate significant differences between the eastern and western North Atlantic animals (163).

Records of *P. phocoena* from West Africa are from the Strait of Gibraltar (27) and Agadir, Morocco (4) south to Cape Verde (28, 29, 49). Six of the records are from the latter area in May and June and, therefore, are unlikely to represent wintering animals from farther north (161). Winter sightings are known from the Cape Verde region as well (29), suggesting a year-round resident subpopulation. No significant differences between the proportions of Cape Verde and British *P. phocoena* skulls have been found (49), but there are differences in tooth count between the two populations (29).

Porpoises from the Baltic Sea appear to be consistently larger than their Sea of Azov–Black Sea counterparts (149), although measurements made on the samples used by these researchers were not corrected for age. It has been reported that as the animals grow, the anterior part of the body grows more slowly than the posterior region, so different rates can be recognized in different populations (151).

Much less effort has been expended in the study of subpopulations of other odontocetes, and correspondingly less information is available. The sighting and catch distributions of the North Atlantic bottlenosed whale reveal a tantalizing suggestion of two or more rather discrete stocks, one moving in summer into the Davis Strait and Labrador Sea and the other to Spitsbergen and coastal Norway respectively (12). Two colour forms of Dall's porpoise are known (see section 3) (77). The population of *P. dioptrica* in the New Zealand subantarctic (6) is probably distinct from that of coastal South America.

2   *Possible clinal variations*

The problem of high–low latitude coastwise population distribution has proved to be a vexing problem in the study of western North Atlantic fin whales. Three land stations operated until 1972 on the east coasts of Newfoundland (two) and Nova Scotia (one), and it was a matter of some contention and much importance to determine if these stations were exploiting the same population (3, 101). The catch data appeared to show that the fin whale stocks of the two areas were reacting quite differently to exploitation (3). Analysis of body-length frequencies from the three stations also showed statistically significant differences; however, the biological significance of this was much less clear. No unambiguous solution was obtained by whale marking, and with the cessation of whaling the probability of further marks being recovered is very small. Stranded individuals are of infrequent occurrence, and there is little chance of discovering marks in one of these. E. Mitchell suggested that the stations may be sampling a single population with clinal size variation (101). The population may consist of the interbreeding but generally discrete subunits which tend to segregate out into coastal feeding grounds at different latitudes in summer. As long ago as 1929 R. Kellogg suggested a simplified form of this population model. Kellogg's idea was that two overlapping populations existed, the southern one occupying the winter grounds of the northern population during summer, with southward movement of both in winter (82).

3   *Colour phases (polyphasy)*

D. G. Lillie (86) and L. H. Matthews (93) independently graded humpback whales taken in the vicinity of South Georgia into four major categories based on the amount of white on the ventral and vento-lateral surfaces. Matthews extended this analysis to include animals from South African and New Zealand waters, and showed that animals from areas II and III were predominantly dark, while New Zealand humpbacks were, on the whole, less heavily pigmented. H. Omura used large samples from Japanese Antarctic catches to show that there was in fact a decrease in proportional pigmentation from the South Atlantic sub-population eastwards to those feeding in summer in the vicinity of the Balleny Islands (118). R. G. Chittleborough examined the eastern and Western Australian humpback populations, and concurred with other authors in recognizing this trend (33). Humpbacks taken off eastern Australia included significantly less pigmented animals than the western Australian group. M. Nishiwaki carried out a similar study on the winter breeding-ground catches of Ryukyu Islands of the western North Pacific. No less than 92 per cent of the Ryukyu humpbacks were of the most heavily pigmented category (108).

Most of the humpback whales which winter in the vicinity of the eastern Hawaiian islands have been reported as having pectoral flippers which are dorsally white (68, 161). There seem to be some 200–250 individuals in this population, and they do not appear to be the same as the population found in winter off south-eastern Alaska. They may be representatives of the humpback population recently reported by T. Nemoto to spend the summer months on the continental shelf of the eastern Bering Sea (112). The Alaskan animals are reported to have black dorsal surfaces to their pectoral flippers.

Classically the minke is described as being distinguishable from small specimens of larger rorquals by the possession of a white patch or band on the exterior surface of the pectoral flipper. This is, indeed, a characteristic of North Atlantic minke, and the 'flash' of white is generally visible even when the whale is swimming some distance below the surface in reasonably clear water; however, this patch is not necessarily diagnostic for minke in all regions. G. Williamson (160) reported in 1961 that minke with and without flipper patches occurred in the Southern Ocean, and the problem has been discussed further by several other workers, none of whom have yet been able to fully resolve the problem of subspecific systematics of the minke whale (see pp. 255–6). The name *Balaenoptera acutorostrata* has been applied to the North Atlantic minke with the flipper patch, and *B. bonaerensis* to the southern form lacking the patch. S. Ohsumi and his colleagues (115), after studying quite extensive samples from the Antarctic, clearly doubted that both colour phases occurred in the southern hemisphere, since they were able to find only the *B. bonaerensis* type. More recent Russian and Japanese research has shown that both phases, and intermediates, are indeed present in the southern hemisphere (43, 156). Both colour phases occur in Australian and New Zealand coastal waters; I have long possessed monochrome and colour illustrations of animals stranded in Victoria and the South Island of New Zealand in which a white flipper patch is either clearly visible or clearly absent.

P. Brodie (22) related possession of this patch to a fish-eating diet (see also p. 44). There may also have been selection for presence or absence of this patch in the southern hemisphere. Coastal-dwelling populations are most likely to be feeding on schooling fish; pelagic populations of minke in the Southern Ocean are essentially euphausiid eaters (see p. 44, Figure 5.2).

Polyphasy has been little studied in the smaller cetaceans. Two colour forms of *Phocoenoides* occur in the North Pacific (69, 77, 106, 110); *dalli* and *truei* have been applied as specific names to these forms. Whether or not they represent valid species is unknown at this time (see pp. 2 and 299, for further discussion associated with the movements of *Phocoenoides*). The facts were recently marshalled by G. V. Morejohn (106) of California; and though there appear to be morphometric and weight differences which parallel the colour patterns, the balance of evidence supports the earlier view of J. Houck that these are morphs, not species. M. Nishiwaki (110) regarded these as subspecies, but there is a good record of a *truei* foetus in a pregnant *dalli* female (159). Polyphasic forms may well occur also in *Stenella attenuata* and *Stenella longirostris*, within otherwise identifiable population units.

4 Polyphenism

Bryde's whales *Balaenoptera edeni* appear to be discontinuously distributed through the tropical and subtropical zones to the very edge of the temperate regions. These are areas where relatively little whaling is carried out, and hence our information is somewhat limited. In some areas Bryde's whales have probably been observed but confused with sei whales, for example, 'sei' reported near the Canary Islands (83). The species has been identified in most major low-latitude regions of the world: Bay of Bengal (140), Malaysian region (76), western equatorial Africa (135), Brazil (121), South Africa (13, 16, 18), southern Western Australia (9), north-eastern New Zealand (58), Chile (1, 36), southern California (133), coastal southern Japan (120, 122), the Bonin Islands (109, 123), and the Caribbean and Gulf of Mexico (132, 146). Many other populations probably await identification. We have no knowledge as yet of intermixing of these stocks. It may be relatively limited, since local morphological differences certainly do occur.

We do know, however, that the taxonomy is more complex than was first believed. Not only do we have to consider the existence of a large number of probably semi-isolated populations, but P. B. Best (16) has confirmed the existence of two distinct forms of Bryde's whale from South African waters, and these appear to have allopatric ranges over quite a wide region of the world. These two forms have now been recorded from at least four different areas, namely, western South Africa, coast of Mexico, coast of Brazil and western Japan. Best has referred to one of these as the 'inshore form'. Populations of these occur within about 20 miles of offshore, are residential throughout the year, have no fixed breeding season and make only very limited local feeding migrations. These animals fit the classical description of Bryde's whales – upper surface of snout with dorso-lateral supplementary ridges, throat grooves extending to the umbilicus, slim but course and robust baleen plates, and attainment of sexual maturity at body lengths of about 11–13 metres. The second type, called the 'offshore form' by Best, may be found up to 200 miles from shore, and while resembling the first form in many ways, may easily be distinguished from it by having much wider baleen plates in proportion to body size, and by being significantly larger than the inshore form at any given age. Both forms will obviously require discrete management in every area in which they are identified. Their polyphenism seems partly related to dietary differences, which were examined by Best in a later paper (18) (see also pp. 63–4).

5   Near-polytypy and demonstrable polytypy

An inhabitant of the floating ice region of the Arctic Basin, the Greenland right whale or bowhead whale *Balaena mysticetus* appears to have three fairly distinct regional populations (63, 147, 155). The first, or so-called Spitsbergen stock, ranged from east Greenland to Novaya Zemlya. Ruthlessly hunted from the seventeenth century onwards, it has now been reduced to a tiny remnant. There is a good possibility that it is extinct. The occasional individuals reported in the region (perhaps one every few years) may be strays from one of the other two populations. The second, or west Greenland stock, is distributed in the Davis Strait–Baffin Bay–Hudson Bay region, and although known still to exist (101, 139) was certainly reduced to a level only a little above total extinction by whalers from Holland and northern Scottish ports (particularly Dundee), operating during the late nineteenth century in the west Greenland whaling which followed the Spitsbergen phase. The third stock, known to the Yankee whalers as the bowhead, moves from the Chukchi Sea and Beaufort Sea into the Bering Sea and back each year, sometimes entering the Sea of Okhotsk in winter (149). This population appears to have recovered to perhaps a few thousand (90). Some intermixing appears to occur among these three stocks, especially between the first and the third, and the evidence for this, based largely on embedded harpoons of known origin, was summarized by A. G. Tomilin (149). There are also rather scanty records for the Kara Sea, East Siberian Sea and Barents Sea.

The three isolated populations of black right whales *Eubalaena glacialis*, in the North Atlantic, North Pacific and Southern Ocean, have been given nominal subspecific status. Even in the southern hemisphere the migration streams of the once numerous *Eubalaena g. australis* are quite widely separated from one another, with most of the main zones of winter concentration adjacent to land masses (150). The seasonal movements follow patterns analagous (although far from identical) to those of the humbacks in the same regions. The right whales of the North Atlantic (*E. g. glacialis*) appear to have divided into rather distinct eastern and western coastal populations, of which the eastern is a remnant and the western is also small but thought by some to be possibly showing signs of slowly recovering in numbers (101). Studies indicate that the North Pacific population (*E. g. japonica*) exists in the low hundreds and is subdivided into three miniscule population remnants in the eastern Pacific, western Pacific and the Sea of Okhotsk (84, 119).

Although greatly reduced in numbers, the blue whale *Balaenoptera musculus* is present in all major oceans. Apparent segregation of North Atlantic blues into eastern and western populations has been suggested (74). The western element ranges from west Greenland in summer to the Carolinas in winter (2, 105). The eastern population winters in the vicinity of the Cape Verde Islands (83) and in summer may range as far north as the Barents Sea and Spitsbergen (74). In east Greenland waters and around Spitsbergen some intermingling may occur, since the high Arctic feeding grounds of this species are not very extensive. The North Pacific population similarly has eastern and western components (109); the former winters in the vicinity of Baja California southwards and ranges north to the Aleutians in summer. The eastern feeds in summer off Kamchatka and the Kuriles; its wintering grounds are not well known, but probably include the Bonin Islands.

The Southern Ocean blue whale population was originally considerably larger than those of both the North Atlantic and North Pacific combined. The relative size of the standing crops of euphausiids in the respective areas is probably the major factor involved (64). Some degree of population segregation among blue whales of the southern hemisphere has been recognized (89), which very roughly corresponds to the six Antarctic whaling areas, but the problem of distinguishing them is complex. Analysis of whale-mark returns strongly indicates that a much greater degree of dispersal and intermingling occurs during foraging than in the case of the humpback whale (23–5). Coherent segregation may not appear until the blues begin to leave on the northward migration at the end of summer.

The problem of identifying blue whale breeding units is further complicated by the presence of two recognizable components in the southern populations, with ranges which are semi-allopatric. It has been known for many years that the southern blue attains a greater size at physical and sexual maturity than its northern counterparts (140, 149) and to this form the subspecific name *Balaenoptera musculus intermedia* has been given with some justification. There is little likelihood of mixing across the equator (89, 141), but a second recognizable form *B. m. brevicauda* also exists, distributed largely across the Kerguelen–Gaussberg Ridge and probably wintering in the Indian Ocean. This matures at a much smaller size than *B. m. intermedia* populations. Even this 'pygmy' blue whale population may have rather distinct eastern and western components, judging from the distributions of catches (70). There are differences between pygmy blue and great blue in pattern, morpho-metrics, baleen plate size and other characteristics (126), and the distinctions are clear enough for stray individuals to be easily identified when taken outside the normal range (1, 56). Non-specialists, who have contended that the subspecies was 'invented' by Japanese biologists to justify continued catching of blue whales, are ignoring published data (143). Although one may argue (138) that the population might not deserve subspecific status, there is no doubt of its distinct status at some level. The pygmy blue population of the southern Indian Ocean has been very heavily overexploited, but after recovery it would in any case require separate management from the great blue populations, should whaling for these animals commence again in the Southern Ocean.

Recognizable populations of fin whales *Balaenoptera physalus* parallel those of the blue quite closely in all major oceans, although there are some important differences, and we have more information about this species. The fin ranges into warmer waters in winter, penetrating southwards in the North Atlantic to Florida (105), the Canary Islands and even into the western Mediterranean around Corsica, Sardinia and Tunisia (148). The North Pacific population has been studied intensively through catch analysis and marking (109), and serological typing (52). The results indicate the existence of quite well-marked eastern and western components, with a third semi-isolated in the East China Sea region. Interchange has been amply demonstrated between fin whales feeding in the Kamchatka–Kurile region and the eastern Aleutian region. Through study of the Ju antigen system of these populations, Fujino found, however, that the geographical distribution of the frequency of occurrence of the Ju_1 and Ju_2 antigen types was decidedly non-random, confirming that although there was interchange, there was also a high degree of population segregation. The East China Sea subpopulation in particular showed a high degree of isolation from the eastern Aleutian component of the North Pacific population. Fujino also discussed the possibility that the coastal American fin whales might represent a different subunit from those off Alaska and the eastern Aleutians, since no mark returns indicated interchange between the two; however, data were insufficient for firm conclusions to be drawn.

As in the case of the blue whale, the southern hemisphere animals are significantly larger at maturity than these of the North Atlantic and North Pacific (140). The subspecific name *B. physalus quoyi* is sometimes used for the southern hemisphere population.

The combined approaches of catch analysis, marking and serological typing have given us some information on the segregation of fin whale subpopulations in the Southern Ocean. R. M. Laws (85) found evidence of segregation by longitudinal zones, and the Antarctic area II population in particular could be distinguished from that of area III on mark returns and blood types, despite a degree of intermingling (23, 53, 54). Fujino's conclusion was that the Ju blood-type incidences of distribution suggested the presence of four breeding units between longitude 60°W and 130°E: Atlantic, western Indian Ocean, eastern Indian Ocean and low-latitude populations, the latter distributed analogously to the pygmy blue whale but without showing such overtly recognizable morphological features. Convincing evidence was obtained of overlap between Atlantic and western Indian Ocean animals on the middle-latitude Antarctic feeding grounds. The rate of intermixing was determined as being something less than 14 per cent per annum, perhaps 10 per cent might be a reasonably accurate annual figure. This would be enough to prevent significant genetic isolation of the breeding units, especially considering the rather long life-span of the fin whale (24–25 years according to Ohsumi (113, 114)). Conversely, however, the segregation is great enough to allow detectable differences to arise and be maintained.

J. A. Michalev (99) studied the morphology and position of Jacobson's organ (small hollows at the tip of the rostrum in baleen whales which may have some sensory function) in Antarctic fin whales as a possible guide to population differences. Although not all his results are conclusive, there do appear to be some differences between populations around the islands of the south-western Indian Ocean, the south-east Atlantic and the south-east Pacific. These findings parallel those of Fujino quite closely.

Sei whales, *Balaenoptera borealis*, range through the eastern North Atlantic to Spitsbergen waters and into the Barents Sea in association with the relatively warm waters of the North Atlantic Drift (38, 71). Norwegian workers (75) have used the term 'invasion years' to describe the sporadic penetrations of large numbers of the migrating population of the eastern North Atlantic sei whale into the more northerly latitudes at irregular intervals; it is not entirely certain if such appearances are completely dependent on food supply alone. In the cooler western North Atlantic sei can occur as far north as the Labrador Sea (101), but sighting and catch records suggest sporadic or cyclic occurrence only in waters north of southern Newfoundland. The species figured more regularly in catches from the Nova Scotia whaling station. Reports of sei as far south as Cape Verde must be treated with caution as mentioned earlier, since these may have been, or included, Bryde's whales. Similar records of sei to latitude 18°N in the North Atlantic (149) must also be regarded with care. Two populations have been tentatively identified in the western North Atlantic, one with its centre of summer abundance on the Nova Scotia shelf and the other in the Labrador Sea (103).

The North Pacific population has been subjected to heavy and very

intensive exploitation during the last decade, and as a result proportionately more information has accrued than for the North Atlantic
(79, 109, 117, 124, 125). A low-latitude and possibly semi-isolated
summer population is distributed in the vicinity of the Emperor Seamount
below latitude 40°N (79). It would appear that exploitation of the western
component of the North Pacific sei has been excessive. The decline in
catch per unit effort has been so great (from a catch per unit effort of 3.09 in
1968 to only 1.20 in 1972) that concern for the state of the stock is being
expressed. The maximum sustainable yield is probably being exceeded,
since there is no sign of the catch per unit effort stabilizing. Y. Masaki (92),
using four independent methods of analysis, concluded that three
population units of sei whales existed in the North Pacific, which can for
practical purposes be considered to be separated by longitudes 155°W and
175°W. The data are far from unambiguous.

The sei whale of the southern hemisphere, like the fin whale and blue
whales, is larger than its northern counterparts, and the name *Balaenoptera borealis schlegeli* has been applied to this form. There is a low-latitude
population in the Tasman sea analagous to that of the Emperor Seamount
(58, 107). The Southern Ocean populations have been subjected to
intensive study, but no firm conclusions have yet been reached on the
certain identification of discrete breeding-population units. For stock-
assessment and yield-calculation purposes, however, the Antarctic area
components are now being estimated separately (32). By comparing the
morphology and position of Jacobson's organ Michalev (99) argued for
distinctions being present between sei in the south-eastern Atlantic and
those in the south-western Indian Ocean. The method was less able to
distinguish between sei whales from the south-eastern Pacific and the
Indian Ocean. Sei are the last rorquals to reach the southern feeding
grounds, often not arriving until February or March, and even then many
may remain in the subantarctic latitudes to feed (19, 80). The possibility of
the sei population increasing as blue and fin whales declined during
intensive Atlantic hunting has been hinted at cautiously by a number of
authors (10) (see also p. 319), but since the diets are far from identical
such caution is probably justified. At present we have very little data on the
possibility of competitive exclusion during feeding by rorquals (and right
whales) (66, 81, 102). It is important that we try to obtain information on
this subject, since if such exclusion can occur (see pp. 319–20), it might have
considerable influence on the estimated recovery patterns of whale
populations after whaling ceases. Nor should feeding competition just from
other whale species be considered; sea-birds, fish, cephalopods and some
seals all take their share of the pelagic crustacean standing crop.

Only two populations of the gray whale, *Eschrichtius robostus*, are
known, and these migrate or migrated to the Bering Sea and back each

year, respectively from California, and Japan and Korea. The western Pacific population has been virtually or completely exterminated by whaling (20). The last remnant was probably killed during the period 1911–32; there is a reasonable case for the distinctness of the two populations (104). Two occurrences in Japan have been reported since 1959 (111), of which one specimen was eventually stranded after being wounded by a local fisherman. Japanese scientists concluded it was more likely that these were strays from the eastern population rather than a remnant of the western population showing signs of recovery. There are no data given by workers in the United States which might suggest that significantly different breeding subunits might occur within the Californian stock (134).

Subfossil remains of Atlantic gray whales have been recorded from several coastal localities of north-western Europe (154), and this population quite possibly entered the Baltic to feed during summer until about AD 500 (134). In a recent paper F. C. Fraser (50) presented tenuous but interesting evidence to suggest that the 'Scrag whale' described by Dudley in 1725 (44), and the 'Sandloegja' of Icelandic historical natural history refer to the now-extinct Atlantic gray whale, and that in the western North Atlantic this species survived until early colonial days.

Conclusions

It should be evident to the reader from the foregoing that we know little about cetacean population structure below the species level, not nearly enough, at any rate, to assist us as much as we would like in refined management of commercially exploited species (see further discussion, pp. 383–7). Some, such as the blue and right whales, had been reduced to remnant level long before any coherent attempt at defining regional breeding units could be made. The problem has resisted analysis by simple approaches; the differences between breeding units in many species are much too subtle and the segregation too recent. We require further sophisticated morphometric analysis based on large comparative age-specific samples, more telemetric studies on a much larger scale, more support for studies of naturally occurring markings on cetaceans to facilitate subpopulation identification through the distributions of recognisable individuals, a solution to the problem of a long-term visible tag, and a real 'breakthrough' in biochemical tissue typing. Accurately measuring the degrees of interchange from one oceanic area to another is as important as determination of stock identities. Concentration of effort on one local unit can deplete it to a low level in a very few seasons. It is distressing to learn too late that it will take scores of years for the unit to be repopulated by either reproductive recovery or immigration, yet we have evidence that this has happened over and over again in the last few decades to several rorqual species.

References

1 Aguayo, L., A. 1974. 'Baleen whales off continental Chile' in W. E. Schevill (ed.), *The Whale Problem: A Status Report*, Cambridge, Mass., Harvard University Press, pp. 209–17.

2 Allen, G. M. 1916. 'The whalebone whales of New England', *Mem. Soc. nat. Hist. Boston*, vol. 8, pp. 107–322.

3 Allen, K. R. 1971. 'A preliminary assessment of fin whale stocks off the Canadian Atlantic coast', *Rep. Int. Whal. Commn.*, vol. 21, pp. 64–6.

4 Aloncle, H. 1964. 'Premières observations sur les petits cétacés des côtes marocaines', *Bull. Inst. Pêch. marit. Maroc*, vol. 12, pp. 21–42.

5 Arseniev, R. K. 1960. 'Distribution of *Balaenoptera acutorostrata* Lacep. in the Antarctic', *Norsk Hvalfangsttid.*, vol. 49, pp. 380–2.

6 Baker, A. N. 1977. 'Spectacled porpoise, *Phocoena dioptrica*, new to the subantarctic Pacific Ocean (Note)', *N.Z.J. mar. Freshwat. Res.*, vol. 11, pp. 401–6.

7. Banks, R. C. and Brownell, R. L., Jr. 1969. 'Taxonomy of the common dolphins of the eastern Pacific Ocean', *J. Mammal.*, vol. 50, pp. 262–71.

8 Bannister, J. L. 1969. 'The biology and status of the sperm whale off Western Australia – an extended summary of results of recent work', *Rep. Int. Whal. Commn.*, vol. 19, pp. 70–6.

9 Bannister, J. L. 1974. 'Whale populations and current research off western Australia' in W. E. Schevill (ed.), *The Whale Problem: A Status Report*, Cambridge, Mass., Harvard University Press, pp. 239–54.

10 Bannister, J. L. and Gambell, R. 1965. 'The succession and abundance of fin, sei and other whales off Durban', *Norsk Hvalfangsttid.*, vol. 54, pp. 45–60.

11 Beamish, P. and Mitchell, E. 1973. 'Short pulse length audio frequency sounds recorded in the presence of a minke whale (*Balaenoptera acutorostrata*)', *Deep-Sea Res.*, vol. 20, pp. 375–86.

12 Benjaminsen, T. 1972. 'On the biology of the Bottlenose whale, *Hyperoodon ampullatus* (Forster)', *Norw. J. Zool.*, vol. 20, pp. 233–41.

13 Best, P. B. 1960. 'Further information on Bryde's whale (*Balaenoptera edeni* Anderson) from Saldanha Bay, South Africa', *Norsk Hvalfangsttid*, vol. 49, pp. 201–15.

14 Best, P. B. 1969. 'The sperm whale (*Physeter catodon*) off the west coast of South Africa. Pt 3. Reproduction in the male'. *Investl. Rep. Div. Sea Fish. S. Afr.*, vol. 72, pp. 1–20.

15 Best, P. B. 1970. 'The sperm whale (*Physeter catodon*) off the west coast of South Africa. Pt 5. Age, growth and mortality', *Investl. Rep. Div. Sea Fish. S. Afr.*, vol. 79, pp. 1–27.

16 Best, P. B. 1974. 'Status of whale populations off the west coast of South Africa, and current research' in W. E. Schevill (ed.), *The Whale Problem: A Status Report*, Cambridge, Mass., Harvard University Press, pp. 53–81.

17 Best, P. B. 1974. 'The biology of the sperm whale as it relates to stock management' in W. E. Schevill (ed.), *The Whale Problem: A Status Report*, Cambridge, Mass., Harvard University Press, pp. 257–93.

18 Best, P. B. 1977. 'Two allopatric forms of Bryde's whale off South Africa', *Rep. Int. Whal. Commn.* (Special Issue 1), pp. 10–38.

19 Best, P. B. and Gambell, R. 1968. 'The abundance of sei whales off South Africa', *Norsk Hvalfangsttid.*, vol. 57, pp. 168–74.

20 Bowen, S. L. 1974. 'Probable extinction of the Korean stock of the gray whale (*Eschrichtius robustus*)', *J. Mammal.*, vol. 55, pp. 208–9.

21 Briggs, J. C. 1970. *Marine Zoogeography*, New York, McGraw-Hill.

22 Brodie, P. F. 1977. 'Form, function and energetics of Cetacea: a discussion' in R. J. Harrison (ed.), *Functional Anatomy of Marine Mammals*, vol. 3, London, Academic Press, pp. 45–66.

23 Brown, S. G. 1954. 'Dispersal in blue and fin whales', *Discovery*, Rep. 26, pp. 355–84.

24 Brown, S. G. 1962. 'International co-operation in Antarctic whale marking 1957 to 1960, and a review of the distribution of marked whales in the Antarctic', *Norsk Hvalfangsttid.*, vol. 51, pp. 93–104.

25 Brown, S. G. 1962. 'The movements of fin and blue whales within the Antarctic zone', *Discovery*, Rep. 33, pp. 1–54.

26 Brussard, P. F. 1978. *Ecological Genetics: The Interface*, New York, Springer-Verlag.

27 Cabrera, A. 1914. *Fauna Iberica, Mamiferos*, publisher not indicated.

28 Cadenat, J. 1949. 'Notes sur les Cétacés observés sur les côtes du Senegal de 1941–1948', *Bull. Inst. fr. Afr. noire*, vol. 11, pp. 2–15.

29 Cadenat, J. 1959. 'Rapport sur les petits Cétacés ouest-africaines. Résultats des recherches enterprises sur ces animaux jusqu'au mois de mai 1959', *Bull. Inst. fr. Afr. noire*, vol. 21, pp. 1367–1440.

30 Cain, A. J. 1954. *Animal Species and their Evolution*, New York, Hutchinson's University Library.

31 Cain, A. J. 1958. 'Logic and memory in Linnaeus' system of taxonomy', *Proc. Linn. Soc. London*, vol. 169, pp. 144–63.

32 Chapman, D. G. 1974. 'Estimation of population parameters of Antarctic baleen whales' in W. E. Schevill (ed.), *The Whale Problem: A Status Report*, Cambridge, Mass., Harvard University Press, pp. 336–51.

33 Chittleborough, R. G. 1965. 'Dynamics of two populations of the humpback whale *Megaptera novaeangliae* (Borowski)', *Aust. J. mar. Freshwat. Res.*, vol. 16, pp. 33–128.

34 Clark, D. L. 1971. 'Arctic Ocean ice cover and its late Cenozoic history', *Bull. geol. Soc. Am.*, vol. 82, pp. 3313–24.

35 Clarke, R. 1956. 'Sperm whales of the Azores', *Discovery*, Rep. 28, pp. 237–98.

36 Clarke, R. and Aguayo, L. A. 1965. 'Bryde's whale in the southeast Pacific', *Norsk Hvalfangsttid.*, vol. 54, pp. 141–8.

37 Clarke, R. and Paliza, O. 1972. 'Sperm whales of the southeast Pacific. Part III: Morphometry', *Hvalrådets Skr.*, vol. 53, pp. 1–79.

38 Collett, R. 1912. *Norges Pattedyr*, Kristiana, H. Aschehoug.

39 Crowson, R. A. 1970. *Classification and Biology*, New York, Atherton Press.

40 Cushing, J. E., Fujino, K. and Calaprice, N. 1963. 'The Ju blood typing system of the sperm whale and specific soluble substances', *Sci. Rep. Whales Res. Inst.*, vol. 17, pp. 67–77.

41 Dobzhansky, Th. 1970. *Genetics of the Evolutionary Process*, New York, Columbia University Press.

42 Dohl, T. P., Norris, K. S. and Kang, I. 1974. 'A porpoise hybrid: *Tursiops × Steno*', *J. Mammal.*, vol. 55, pp. 217–21.

43 Doroshenko, N. V. 1979. 'Populations of minke whales in the southern hemisphere', *Rep. Int. Whal. Commn*, vol. 29, pp. 361–4.

44 Dudley, P. 1725. 'An essay upon the natural history of whales with a particular account of the ambergris found in the Sperma Ceti whale', *Phil. Trans. R. Soc.*, vol. 33, pp. 256–69.

45 Ehrlich, P. R. and Raven, P. H., 1969. 'Differentiation of populations', *Science*, vol. 165, pp. 1228–32.

46 Endler, J. A. 1977. *Geographic Variation, Speciation and Clines*, Princeton, NJ, Princeton University Press.

47 Evans, W. E. 1976. 'Distribution of stocks of *Delphinus delphis* Linnaeus in the northeastern Pacific', FAO of the UN, Scientific Consultation on Marine Mammals, Bergen, Norway, 31 August–9 September 1976, document ACMRR/MM/SC/18, pp. 1–72.

48 Fraser, F. C. 1940. 'Three anomalous dolphins from Blacksod Bay, Ireland', *Proc. R. Irish Acad.*, vol. 45(B), pp. 413–55.

49 Fraser, F. C. 1958. 'Common or harbour porpoises from French West Africa', *Bull. Inst. fr. Afr. noire*, ser. A., vol. 20, pp. 276–85.

50 Fraser, F. C. 1970. 'An early 17th century record of the Californian grey whale in Icelandic waters' in G. Pilleri (ed.), *Investigations on Cetacea*, Berne, Waldau, pp. 13–20.

51 Fraser, F. C. and Noble, B. A. 1970. 'Variation of pigmentation pattern in Meyen's dolphin, *Stenella coeruleoalba* (Meyen)' in G. Pilleri (ed.), *Investigations on Cetacea*, vol. II, Berne, Waldau, pp. 147–63.

52 Fujino, K. 1960. 'Immunogenetic and marking approaches to identifying subpopulations of the North Pacific whales', *Sci. Rep. Whales Res. Inst.*, vol. 15, pp. 85–142.

53 Fujino, K. 1963. 'Intra-uterine selection due to maternal-fetal incompatibility of blood types in the whales', *Sci. Rep. Whales Res. Inst.*, vol. 17, pp. 53–65.

54 Fujino, K. 1964. 'Fin whale subpopulations in the Antarctic whaling areas II, III, and IV', *Sci. Rep. Whales Res. Inst.*, vol. 18, pp. 1–28.

55 Fujino, K. and Cushing, J. E. 1959. 'Blood typing of dried whale erythrocytes with ^{131}I labelled antibody', *Sci. Rep. Whales Res. Inst.*, vol. 14, pp. 101–6.

56 Gambell, R. 1964. 'A pygmy blue whale at Durban', *Norsk Hvalfangsttid.*, vol. 53, pp. 66–8.

57 Gaskin, D. E. 1968. 'Distribution of Delphinidae (Cetacea) in relation to sea surface temperatures off eastern and southern New Zealand', *N.Z.J. mar. Freshwat. Res.*, vol. 2, pp. 527–34.

58 Gaskin, D. E. 1972. *Whales, Dolphins and Seals : With Special Reference to the New Zealand Region*, London and Auckland, Heinemann Educational Books.

59 Gaskin, D. E. 1973. 'Sperm whales in the western South Pacific', *N.Z.J. mar. Freshwat. Res.*, vol. 7, pp. 1–20.

60 Gaskin, D. E. 1976. 'The evolution, zoogeography and ecology of Cetacea', *Oceanogr. Mar. Biol. Ann. Rev.*, vol. 14, pp. 247–346.

61 Gaskin, D. E., Arnold, P. W. and Blair, B. A. 1974. '*Phocoena phocoena*', *Mammalian Species*, vol. 42, pp. 1–8.

62 Ghiselin, M. T. 1974. 'A radical solution to the species problem', *Syst. Zool.*, vol. 23, pp. 536–44.

63 Guldberg, G. 1904. 'Ueber die Wanderungen verschiedener Bartenwale', *Biol. Centrbl.*, vol. 23, pp. 803–16.

64 Gulland, J. A. 1974. 'Distribution and abundance of whales in relation to basic productivity' in W. E. Schevill (ed.), *The Whale Problem: A Status Report*, Cambridge, Mass., Harvard University Press, pp. 27–54.

65 Hall, E. R. and Bee, J. W. 1954. 'Occurrence of the harbor porpoise at Point Barrow, Alaska', *J. Mammal*, vol. 35, pp. 122–3.

66 Harwood, J. 1979. 'The effects of interspecific competition on the choice of management policies for fin and sei whales', *Rep. Int. Whal. Commn*, vol. 29, pp. 167–9.

67 Heywood, V. H. 1963. 'The "species aggregate" in theory and practice', *Regnum Veg.*, vol. 27, pp. 26–37.

68 Herman, L. M. and Antinoja, R. C. 1977. 'Humpback whales in the Hawaiian breeding waters: population and pod characteristics', *Sci. Rep. Whales Res. Inst.*, vol. 29, pp. 59–85.

69   Houck, W. J. 1976. 'The taxonomic status of the species of the porpoise genus *Phocoenoides*', FAO of the UN, Scientific Consultation on Marine Mammals, Bergen, Norway, 31 August–9 September 1976, document ACMRR/MM/SC/114, pp. 1–13.

70   Ichihara, T. 1966. 'The pygmy blue whale, *Balaenoptera musculus brevicauda*, a new subspecies from the Antarctic' in K. S. Norris (ed.), *Whales, Dolphins, and Porpoises*, Berkeley and Los Angeles, University of California Press, pp. 79–113.

71   Ingebrigtsen, A. 1929. 'Whales caught in the North Atlantic and other seas' *Rapp. Cons. Explor. Mer.*, vol. 56, pp. 1–26.

72   International Whaling Commission. 1973. 'Report of the Scientific Committee' in *Twenty-third report of the Commission*, London, pp. 28–43.

73   International Whaling Commission. 1974. 'Report of the Scientific Committee' in *Twenty-fourth report of the Commission*, London, pp. 39–54.

74   Jonsgård, Å. 1966. 'The distribution of Balaenopteridae in the North Atlantic Ocean', in K. S. Norris (ed.), *Whales, Dolphins, and Porpoises*, Berkeley and Los Angeles, University of California Press, pp. 114–24.

75   Jonsgård, Å and Darling, K. 1977. 'On the biology of the eastern North Atlantic sei whale', *Rep. Int. Whal. Commn* (Special Issue 1), pp. 124–9.

76   Junge, G. C. A. 1950. 'On a specimen of the rare fin whale, *Balaenoptera edeni* Anderson, stranded on Puli Sugi, near Singapore', *Zool. Verh., Leiden*, no. 9.

77   Kasuya, T. 1976. 'Preliminary report of the biology, catch, and populations of *Phocoenoides* in the western North Pacific', FAO of the UN, Scientific Consultation on Marine Mammals, Bergen, Norway, 31 August–7 September 1976, document ACMRR/MM/SC/21, pp. 1–20.

78   Kasuya, T. and T. Ichihara, 1965. 'Some information on minke whales from the Antarctic', *Sci. Rep. Whales Res. Inst.*, vol. 19, pp. 37–43.

79   Kawamura, A. 1973. 'Food and feeding of sei whale caught in the waters south of 40°N in the North Pacific', *Sci. Rep. Whales Res. Inst.*, vol. 25, pp. 219–36.

80   Kawamura, A. 1974. 'Food and feeding ecology in the southern sei whale', *Sci. Rep. Whales Res. Inst.*, vol. 26, pp. 25–144.

81   Kawamura, A. 1978. 'An interim consideration on a possible interspecific relation in southern baleen whales from the viewpoint of their food habits', *Rep. Int. Whal. Commn*, vol. 28, pp. 411–19.

82   Kellogg, R. 1929. 'What is known of the migrations of some of the whale-bone whales', *Ann. Rept Smithsonian Inst. 1928*, pp. 467–94.

83   Kirpichnikov, A. A. 1950. '(Observations on the distribution of large whale species in the Atlantic Ocean)', *Priroda*, vol. 10, pp. 63–4.

84   Klumov, S. K. 1962. '(Right whale (Japanese) of the Pacific Ocean)', *Trudy Inst. Okeanol.*, vol. 58, pp. 202–97.

85   Laws, R. M. 1961. 'Reproduction, growth and age of southern fin whales', *Discovery*, Rep. 31, pp. 327–486.

86   Lillie, D. G. 1915. 'Cetacea, British Antarctic 'Terra Nova' Expedition, 1910', *Brit. Mus. Nat. Hist. Rept. Zool.*, vol. 1, pp. 85–124.

87   Machin, D. 1974. 'A multivariate study of the external measurements of the sperm whale (*Physeter catodon*)', *J. Zool. London*, vol. 172, pp. 267–88.

88   Machin, D. and Kitchenham, B. L. 1971. 'A multivariate study of the external measurements of the humpback whale (*Megaptera novaeangliae*)', *J. Zool. London*, vol. 165, pp. 415–21.

89   Mackintosh, N. A. 1966. 'The distribution of southern blue and fin whales' in K. S. Norris (ed.), *Whales, Dolphins, and Porpoises*, Berkeley and Los Angeles, University of California Press, pp. 125–44.

90   Mansfield, A. W. 1971. 'Occurrence of the bowhead or Greenland right whale (*Balaena mysticetus*) in Canadian Arctic waters', *J. Fish. Res. Bd. Canada*, vol. 28, pp. 1873–5.

91 Masaki, Y. 1970. Paper Sp/9, Rept Special Meeting, sperm whale biology and stock assessments, Honolulu, Hawaii, 1970, under auspices of International Whaling Commission.

92 Masaki, Y. 1977. 'The separation of the stock units of sei whales in the North Pacific', *Rep. Int. Whal. Commn* (Special Issue 1), pp. 77–9.

93 Matthews, L. H. 1937. 'The humpback whale, *Megaptera nodosa*', *Discovery*, Rep. 17, pp. 7–92.

94 Mayr, E. 1963. *Animal Species and Evolution*, Cambridge, Mass., Belknap Press, Harvard University Press.

95 Mayr, E. 1969. *Principles of Systematic Zoology*, New York, MacGraw-Hill.

96 Mayr, E. 1970. *Populations, Species, and Evolution*, Cambridge, Mass., Belknap Press, Harvard University Press.

97 Mercer, M. C. 1973. 'Observations on distribution and intraspecific variation in pigmentation patterns of odontocete Cetacea in the western North Atlantic', *J. Fish. Res. Bd. Canada*, vol. 30, pp. 1111–30.

98 Mercer, M. C. 1974. in letter.

99 Michalev, J. A. 1979. 'Revealing of differences in the Antarctic baleen whale stocks on the basis of the analysis of the "Jacobson's Organ" position', *Rep. Int. Whal. Commn*, vol. 29, pp. 343–6.

100 Mitchell, E. 1970. 'Pigmentation pattern evolution in delphinid cetaceans: an essay in adaptive coloration', *Can. J. Zool.*, vol. 48, pp. 717–40.

101 Mitchell, E. 1974. 'Present status of northwest Atlantic fin and other whale stocks' in W. E. Schevill (ed.), *The Whale Problem: A Status Report*, Cambridge, Mass., Harvard University Press, pp. 108–69.

102 Mitchell, E. 1975. 'Trophic relationships and competition for food in northwest Atlantic whales', *Proc. Can. Soc. Zool. 1974*, pp. 123–33.

103 Mitchell, E. and Chapman, D. G. 1977. 'Preliminary assessment of stocks of northwest Atlantic sei whales (*Balaenoptera borealis*)', *Rep. Int. Whal. Commn* (Special issue 1), pp. 117–20.

104 Mizue, K. 1951. 'Gray whales in the east Sea of Korea', *Sci. Rep. Whales Res. Inst.*, vol. 5, pp. 71–9.

105 Moore, J. C. 1953. 'Distribution of marine mammals to Florida waters', *Am. Midl. Nat.*, vol. 49, pp. 117–58.

106 Morejohn, G. V. 1979. 'The natural history of Dall's porpoise in the North Pacific Ocean' H. E. Winn and B. L. Olla (eds.), *Behaviour of Marine Animals Current Perspectives in Research, vol. 3: Cetaceans*, New York and London, Plenum Press, pp. 45–83.

107 Nasu, K. 1973. 'Results of whale sighting by Chiyoda Maru No. 5 in the Pacific sector of the Antarctic and Tasman Sea in the 1966/67 season', *Sci. Rep. Whales Res. Inst.*, vol. 25, pp. 205–17.

108 Nishiwaki, M. 1959. 'Humpback whales in Ryukyuan waters', *Sci. Rep. Whales Res. Inst.*, vol. 14, pp. 49–87.

109 Nishiwaki, M. 1966. 'Distribution and migration of the larger cetaceans in the North Pacific as shown by Japanese whaling results' in K. S. Norris (ed.), *Whales, Dolphins, and Porpoises*, Berkeley and Los Angeles, University of California Press, pp. 171–91.

110 Nishiwaki, M. 1972. 'General biology' in S. H. Ridgway (ed.), *Mammals of the Sea; Biology and Medicine*, Springfield, Ill. Charles C. Thomas Company, pp. 3–204.

111 Nishiwaki, M. and Kasuya, T. 1970. 'Recent record of gray whale in the adjacent waters of Japan and a consideration on its migration', *Sci. Rep. Whales Res. Inst.*, vol. 22, pp. 29–37.

112 Nemoto, T. 1978. 'Humpback whales observed within the continental shelf waters of the eastern Bering Sea', *Sci. Rep. Whales Res. Inst.*, vol. 30, pp. 245–7.

113 Ohsumi, S. 1964. 'Examination on age determination of the fin whale', *Sci. Rep.*

Whales Res. Inst., vol. 18, pp. 49–88.

114   Ohsumi, S. 1973. 'Revised estimation of recruitment rate in the Antarctic fin whales', *Rep. Int. Whal. Commn*, vol. 23, pp. 192–9.

115   Ohsumi, S., Masaki, Y. and Kawamura, A. 1970. 'Stock of the Antarctic minke whale', *Sci. Rep. Whales Res. Inst.*, vol. 22, pp. 75–125.

116   Ohsumi, S. and Nasu, K. 1970. Paper Sp/7, Rept. Special Meeting, sperm whale biology and stock assessments, Honolulu, Hawaii, 1970, under auspices of International Whaling Commission.

117   Ohsumi, S. and Wada, S. 1974. 'Status of whale stocks in the North Pacific, 1972', *Rep. Int. Whal. Commn*, vol. 24, pp. 114–26.

118   Omura, H. 1953. 'Biological study on humpback whales in the Antarctic whaling areas IV and V', *Sci. Rep. Whales Res. Inst.*, vol. 8, pp. 81–102.

119   Omura, H. 1958. 'North Pacific right whale', *Sci. Rep. Whales Res.*, vol. 13, pp. 1–52.

120   Omura, H. 1959. 'Bryde's whales from the coast of Japan', *Sci. Rep. Whales Res. Inst.*, vol. 14, pp. 1–33.

121   Omura, H. 1962. 'Bryde's whale occurs on the coast of Brazil', *Sci. Rep. Whales Res. Inst.*, vol. 16, pp. 1–5.

122   Omura, H. 1962. 'Further information on Bryde's whale from the coast of Japan', *Sci. Rep. Whales Res. Inst.*, vol. 16, pp. 7–18.

123   Omura, H. 1966. 'Bryde's whale in the Northwest Pacific' in K. S. Norris (ed.), *Whales, Dolphins, and Porpoises*, Berkeley and Los Angeles, University of California Press, pp. 70–8.

124   Omura, H. and Fujino, K. 1954. 'Sei whales in the adjacent waters of Japan. II. Further studies on the external characters', *Sci. Rep. Whales Res. Inst.*, vol. 9, pp. 89–103.

125   Omura, H. and Fujino, K. 1955. 'Sei whales in the adjacent waters of Japan. III. Relation between movement and water temperature of the sea', *Sci. Rep. Whales Res. Inst.*, vol. 10, pp. 89–132.

126   Omura, H., Ichihara, T. and Kasuya, T. 1970. 'Osteology of pygmy blue whale with additional information on external and other characteristics', *Sci. Rep. Whales Res. Inst.*, vol. 22, pp. 1–27.

127   Payne, R. and McVay, S. 1971. 'Songs of humpback whales', *Science*, vol. 173, pp. 587–97.

128   Perrin, W. F. 1969. 'Color pattern of the eastern Pacific spotted porpoise *Stenella graffmani* Lönnberg (Cetacea, Delphinidae)', *Zoologica*, vol. 54, pp. 135–42.

129   Perrin, W. F. 1972. 'Color patterns of spinner porpoises (*Stenella cf. longirostris*) of the eastern Pacific and Hawaii, with comments on delphinid pigmentation', *Fishery Bull. Fish. Wildl. Serv. US*, vol. 70, pp. 983–1003.

130   Perrin, W. F. 1975. 'Distribution and differentiation of populations of dolphins of the genus *Stenella* in the eastern tropical Pacific', *J. Fish. Res. Bd. Canada*, vol. 32, pp. 1059–67.

131   Perrin, W. F., Sloan, P. A. and Henderson, J. R. 1979. 'Taxonomic status of the South-Western stocks of spinner dolphin *Stenella longirostris* and spotted dolphin *S. attenuata*', *Rep. Int. Whal. Commn*, vol. 29, pp. 175–84.

132   Rice, D. W. 1965. 'Bryde's whale in the Gulf of Mexico', *Norsk Hvalfangsttid.*, vol. 54, pp. 114–15.

133   Rice, D. W. 1974. 'Whales and whale research in the eastern North Pacific' in W. E. Schevill (ed.), *The Whale Problem: A Status Report*, Cambridge, Mass., Harvard University Press, pp. 170–95.

134   Rice, D. W. and Wolman, A. A. 1971. 'The life history and ecology of the gray whale (*Eschrichtius robustus*)'. *Amer. Soc. Mammal. Spec. Publ.*, No. 3.

135   Ruud, J. T. 1952. 'Catches of Bryde-whale off French Equatorial Africa', *Norsk Hvalfangsttid.*, vol. 41, pp. 662–3.

136   Satake, Y. and Omura, H. 1974. 'A taxonomic study of the minke whale in the

Antarctic by means of hyoid bone', *Sci. Rep. Whales Res. Inst.*, vol. 26, pp. 15–24.

137 Scheffer, V. B. 1967. 'Marine mammals and the history of Bering Strait' in D. M. Hopkins (ed.), *The Bering Land Bridge*, Standford, Ca., Standford University Press, pp. 350–63.

138 Sergeant, D. E. 1973. '*The Blue Whale*, by G. L. Small' (book review), *Can. Fld Nat.*, vol. 87, pp. 84–5.

139. Sergeant, D. E. 1974. Personal communication.

140 Slijper, E. J. 1962. *Whales*, London, Hutchinson.

141 Slijper, E. J., Van Utrecht, W. L. and Naaktgeboren, C. 1964. 'Remarks on the distribution and migration of whales based on observations from Netherlands ships', *Bijdr. tot de Dierk.*, vol. 34, pp. 3–93.

142 Sloan, P. R. 1972. 'John Locke, John Ray and the problem of the natural system', *J. Hist. Biol.*, vol. 5, pp. 1–53.

143 Small, G. L. 1971. *The Blue Whale*, Irvington, NY, Columbia University Press.

144 Sokal, R. R. 1973. 'The species problem reconsidered', *Syst. Zool.*, vol. 22, pp. 360–74.

145 Sokal, R. R. and Crovello, T. J. 1970. 'The biological species concept, a critical evaluation', *Amer. Nat.*, vol. 104, pp. 127–53.

146 Soot-Ryen, T. 1961. 'On a Bryde's whale stranded on Curaçao', *Norsk Hvalfangst-tid.*, vol. 50, pp. 323–32.

147 Southwell, T. 1898. 'Notes on the seal and whale fishery, 1897', *Zoologist*, vol. 4, pp. 69–77.

148 Tamino, G. 1953. 'Ricupero di una Balenottera arenata sul lido di Salerno il 10 Febbraio 1953', *Boll. Zool.*, vol. 20, pp. 51–4.

149 Tomilin, A. G. 1967. *Cetacea, Vol. 9, Mammals of the USSR and Adjacent Countries*, translation by Israel Program for Scientific Translation, edited by V. G. Heptner, Jerusalem.

150 Townsend, C. H. 1935. 'The distribution of certain whales as shown by logbook records of American whaleships', *Zoologica*, vol. 19, pp. 1–50.

151 Tsalkin, V. I. 1938. '(Morphological characteristics, systematic position and zoogeography of the common porpoise in the Sea of Azov and the Black Sea)', *Zool. Zh.*, vol. 17, pp. 706–33.

152 Van Bree, P. J. H. and Purves, P. E. 1972. 'Remarks on the validity of *Delphinus bairdii* (Cetacea, Delphinidae)', *J. Mammal.*, vol. 53, pp. 372–4.

153 Van Bree, P. J. H., Sergeant, D. E. and Hoek, W. 1977. 'A harbour porpoise *Phocoena phocoena* (Linnaeus, 1758) from the Mackenzie River delta, Northwest Territories, Canada (Notes on Cetacea, Delphinoidea VIII)', *Beaufortia*, vol. 26, pp. 99–105.

154 Van Deinse, A. B. and Junge, G. C. A. 1937. 'Recent and older finds of the California Gray whale in the Atlantic', *Temminckia*, vol. 2, pp. 161–84.

155 Vinogradov, M. P. 1949. 'Morskie Mlekopitayushchie Arktiki', *Trudy Arkticheskogo Instituta Bull.*, no. 202.

156 Wada, S. and Numachi, K. 1979. 'External and biochemical characters as an approach to stock identification for the Antarctic minke whale', *Rep. Int. Whal. Commn.*, vol. 29, pp. 421–32.

157 Watkins, W. A. and Schevill, W. E. 1977. 'Sperm whale codas', *J. Acoust. Soc. Am.*, vol. 62, pp. 1485–90.

158 White, M. J. 1978. *Modes of Speciation*, San Francisco, W. H. Freeman.

159 Wilke, F., Taniwaki, T. and Kuroda, N. 1953. '*Phocoenoides* and *Lagenorhynchus* in Japan with notes on hunting', *J. Mammal.*, vol. 34, pp. 488–97.

160 Williamson, G. 1961. 'Two kinds of minke whale in the Antarctic', *Norsk Hvalfangsttid.*, vol. 50, pp. 133–41.

161 Wolman, A. A. and Jurasz, C. M. 1977. 'Humpback whales in Hawaii: vessel census, 1976', *Mar. Fish. Rev.*, vol. 39, July 1977, pp. 1–7.

162   Yurick, D. B. 1977. 'Populations, subpopulations, and zoogeography of the harbour
       porpoise, *Phocoena phocoena* (L.)', M.Sc. thesis, University of Guelph, Ontario.
163   Yurick, D. B. 1980. Unpublished data.

CHAPTER 8

Analysis of cetacean populations

Introductory comments on population dynamics

I recall having problems defining 'population' earlier in this book, but if we are going to examine the functioning of populations as variable systems, obviously we require some kind of working definition for the purposes of this chapter. At the purely statistical level, a population can be considered as any group of numbers or items. In biology, on the other hand, the term almost always contains a strong implication of relationship. Unless otherwise specified, a biological population always refers to a group of organisms from a single species. The species in question must be as clearly defined as possible in taxonomic terms, and preferably the particular population under study should be definable with reference to any discontinuities which segregate it from other discrete or semi-discrete populations of the same species (29, 169). We therefore imply that the population is genetically and ecologically integrated, and that as a unit it can be described in terms of its size, birth rate, survival (or mortality) rate and age structure (31). Because populations are rarely arranged so tidily in nature, we also need to be able to measure the rate of any dispersal into and out of the population, that is, the rate of any immigration and emigration with respect to our study region.

In practice, it is almost impossible for a biologist to study a whole population. We are forced by the constraints of time, money or manpower to restrict our study in some way, either to one geographical locality, hoping that it is representative, or to taking smaller samples than we would really like from several parts of the population range. As a result of these nearly inevitable limitations hardly any data set for an animal population is going to meet the appropriate statistical ideal. The questions which the practising population dynamicist must therefore continually ask are:

1 I am assuming the population under study to be a genetically and ecologically distinct unit. Is this assumption really true?
2 If it is, are my sampling programmes providing a valid representation of the population distribution and structure?

For many years whale populations have been studied (and managed) using methods and assumptions largely developed within what are usually loosely called the 'fisheries sciences' (1, 16, 149), although it should be pointed out that one or two techniques of analysis now in common use in population dynamics were in fact originally applied to whales, their use then spreading to other population studies (109). To a certain extent these methods have worked reasonably well considering the difficult political situation and the miniscule research budgets with which the whale population scientists of the 1950s and 1960s were forced to function. Nevertheless, most of the methods contain specific underlying assumptions about homogeneity of distribution and interaction which are known not to be very realistic. Having the inevitable benefit of hindsight, with several decades of the use of these models behind us, we can point to numerous deficiencies. In several respects, for example, they are inappropriate for dealing with discontinuously distributed populations of large mammals that have many age classes, and in some cases, various levels of social organization.

In this chapter I want to outline the basic methods available for the analysis of whale populations, and discuss some of the theoretical and practical problems which are encountered in their application. The results of such use, including those resulting from misapplications, are largely discussed under management in Chapter 9. I hope that the reader appreciates that it is difficult to draw an absolute line between the two areas of discussion, and that I will be forgiven for sometimes wandering back and forth across the boundary when it seems appropriate.

Characteristics of populations

Like an individual organism, a population can be said to manifest growth, maintenance, decline and death, but it is unwise to pursue this analogy too far. A population is not really an 'entity', and is no greater than the sum of its components. We very rarely see the 'birth' of a population, even though we might discuss it in theoretical terms; a biologist inherits a population at some later stage of its career, and a large part of his job may involve deciding just which that stage is. Frequently the population is under some degree of commercial or incidental exploitation, and whatever 'natural' structure it may have had at one time has been distorted to a greater or lesser extent by that exploitation, which almost invariably involves some form of selective harvesting. Growth, in numbers or biomass or both, will differ under different environmental conditions, and according to the constraints imposed by the evolved reproductive 'strategies' of the population. We sometimes find it convenient to talk about the theoretical 'plateau' size of 'stable' populations, but in most cases the concept of such stability is illusory at worst and oversimplified at best; the size and composition of a natural population is generally changing continuously under a variety of extrinsic and intrinsic factors. For example, if viewed at a particular moment in time a population may appear to be declining towards extinction, yet an extended study may reveal that this is only a stage in a long-term cyclic change in population size, perhaps related to environmental conditions, predation or disease (114). Some animal populations are well known for fluctuating wildly over time as a matter of course, peaking and collapsing at regular or irregular intervals. The mechanisms underlying such catastrophic changes have greatly interested population dynamicists, and there are a number of fairly recent theoretical studies of the subject to which the reader might care to refer (61, 77). Such populations can still have structure and age-class composition, but the concept of 'average' population size becomes meaningless.

I do not wish to take up any more space than is absolutely necessary, discussing general population theory, and for those wishing to read further I have included some useful references to the modern general and theoretical population literature in the bibliography of this chapter (28, 32, 66, 113, 140, 143, 180). The readers new to this discipline must appreciate that there have been some basic differences of opinion about the mechanisms by which animal numbers are regulated and some degree of equilibrium maintained in nature. Some have argued that such regulation occurs largely through the operation of extrinsic factors, others maintain that intrinsic factors are involved. The conclusions one draws are often greatly influenced by the nature of the populations which have been studied, and some conclude that it is rarely possible in practice to distinguish fully between the two types of effects. The same population may respond differently at different levels of population size. There are obviously important implications in such controversies for interpreting the dynamics of cetacean populations, both under continued exploitation and during protected recovery periods.

Many cetacean populations are exploited, some heavily and a few have been reduced to remnants by excessive hunting. The questions which we have to ask are simple and straightforward, even though the process of obtaining answers may be complex.

1　What is the population size of each species?
2　Are the populations distributed homogeneously or heterogeneously?
3　Under what circumstances, for purposes of analysis, can we treat small isolated heterogeneous populations as if they were a single larger population?
4　Is catching effort evenly distributed over the whole range within which the species occurs?

5 What specific effects is the exploitation process having on each population?

6 If the exploitation process has introduced distortion into the population structure, what was the original age distribution?

7 Is the exploitation 'rational', that is, are operations directed to a sustained yield rather than a high-yield relatively short-term exploitation pattern?

Question 7 and others stemming from it will be discussed in Chapter 9. In order to answer the other questions we require a comprehensive array of information derived from catch statistics and various population parameters. There are several possible approaches, but it is perhaps easiest to start with methods for estimating distribution and abundance, which yield results that can help to answer questions 1–4.

Measurements of abundance

Direct visual estimates

Sometimes circumstances dictate that it is either not possible or not advisable to sample physically a population of a cetacean species to determine the age structure and other population parameters. No one these days, for example, would advocate biological sampling to determine the age and maturity status of the western North Atlantic right whale, when the total number of animals probably does not exceed one hundred individuals, and the population may not be increasing. (Nevertheless, such considerations did not stop the USSR doing precisely that to the minute right whale population in the Sea of Okhotsk (95) a couple of decades ago.) Problems can also arise at the other end of the scale of population size. If we were studying an unexploited species of very common tropical dolphin, the population of which could number in the millions of individuals, it would be most difficult to determine whether or not the largest sample that we could take in practice through scientific collecting was representative or not. Even in the case of populations which can be biologically sampled, it does no harm to have other methods for estimating abundance, and visual methods of assessment play an essential role in determining distribution when catching is not distributed over the whole geographical area occupied by the species.

Visual counting methods give us data which can be described as 'coarse-grained', in terms of the reliability of the estimates so obtained. They can be based on area, strip or line. Application of sampling theory to these methods can become quite complex, and in practice the results rarely satisfy the professional statistician, although they can provide the biologist with much useful information. In a few special situations where populations are strongly localized for part of the year, small in absolute size, and particularly in cases where a significant number of animals bear scars or other prominent marks that permit recognition of individuals, we can make quite accurate estimates of absolute abundance. Sometimes man-made tags or branding can be used instead of natural markings to study movements and dispersal, but we run the risk that handling the animals will either result in some actual mortality or alter the behaviour patterns of the tagged specimens so that they become unrepresentative. Tagging can also be used to estimate population size, although there are serious constraints to the methods (pp. 295–7).

CENSUS METHODS

Information obtained in this way is of limited application for several reasons. It gives us a temporally static picture of the population, and little if any data on the composition, unless there are striking differences in the appearance of the sexes or of particular age classes, as occurs in white whales, for example. As stated above, it is occasionally possible to carry out a near-total census; these have been made for the south-western population of the South Atlantic right whale (135), the migratory portion of the Californian gray whale population which passes through the inshore shallow coastal waters of southern California (148), and the white whale population in the St Lawrence estuary in Canada (142). Unfortunately, in most circumstances it is quite impractical to do this, and we must resort to one or other form of sampling survey. Studies can sometimes be conducted from suitable sites on shore, but census work is most often carried out from ships or aircraft. In many parts of the world, the distant waters of the Southern Ocean, for example, aerial surveys are beyond the economic limits of any ordinary research programme, although helicopters are sometimes deployed from factory ships for spotting in good weather. However the counts are made, we invariably run into problems at several different levels. If the results are to have any comparative quantitative value, they must be collected in such a way that they can be analysed statistically and confidence levels can be attached to the means. One can, of course, treat any data in this way, however collected, and still get what appears to be a reasonable answer, but the conclusions might only be valid if the observations have been collected according to the dictates of the statistical model being tested. In the strictest statistical sense confidence limits are only valid when the sampling has been carried out at random, and in fact most of the usual models assume that (a) the animals are distributed at random, and (b) that they have been counted along transects or within plots which have also been selected at random.

Unfortunately whales and dolphins are almost invariably distributed contagiously rather than randomly, and it is often very difficult in practice to ensure that sampling tracks are selected at random. Sometimes we can transform data mathematically into a suitable form, but more often we have to resort to stratagems for wringing the best we can out of the observations available. The quality of the counts can vary according to sea state, lighting conditions, wind speed, visibility, the experience of the observers and the behaviour of the animals. Under normal circumstances, for example, fin whales are highly visible animals, but sometimes individuals adopt a low-activity pattern (possibly representing sleep), drifting with the current, not showing their backs and only blowing at infrequent intervals. In such cases it is possible for experienced observers to steam through an area and miss most of the animals present. Sperm and bottlenosed whales that are widely dispersed and feeding deep will dive for long periods of tens of minutes at a time. It is almost impossible to estimate the numbers of animals present under these conditions.

Our problem is that we are trying to determine the *mean density* of populations that are heterogeneously distributed at best, and subject to intensive contagious clustering at worst (Figure 8.1). Under most circumstances we can sample only a relatively tiny fraction of the total range of a cetacean species at one time, with the fond hope that the estimate of density we arrive at is as representative of the unsampled areas as it is of the sampled one. The greater the number of replicate observations we can make, the better our estimate should be. A heavy sampling programme is particularly essential when the degree of distributional heterogeneity is high. In fact, Estes and Gilbert concluded that 40–56 per cent of survey strip areas needed to be surveyed to obtain a $\pm$ 10 per cent population count (for walrus, in their case) within 95 per cent confidence limits (43).

Most sighting data for baleen whales and sperm whales have been gathered from commercial hunting expeditions. These have to be used with great caution; such expeditions habitually concentrate their searches in regions where experience dictates that whales will be most frequently encountered. The result is that these observational data sets contain a built-in bias right from the start, and are likely to yield values of distribution densities which are significantly higher than the real mean. Such data can be useful, however, if it is possible to detach some vessels on controlled survey into adjacent regions. In this way the data can be combined to obtain synoptic, relatively independent measures of density over a much greater area.

When distribution patterns are strongly heterogeneous, or when any degree of clustering can be demonstrated in certain areas, we must resort to *stratified sampling*. This approach requires that we carry out estimates separately in areas known to contain different densities of the subject

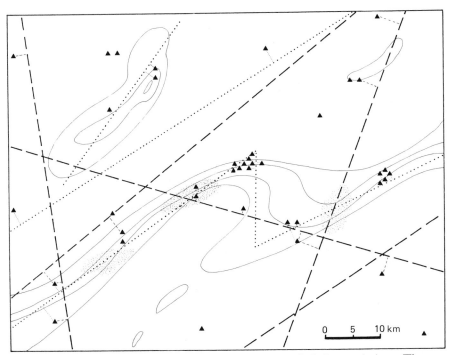

Figure 8.1   The problem of carrying out censuses of whale populations. The axioms of applicable statistical methods generally demand that the transects be carried out at random (broken lines). Unfortunately, they also usually require that the objects to be sighted are also distributed at random. Whales, on the other hand, are usually clustered in suitable areas. In this hypothetical illustration, the whales, indicated by triangles, are most abundant along the ocean front (thin lines, indicating isotherms) and the associated temperature anomalies. One solution to this kind of problem, as advocated by Caughley (21), is to abandon the purely random transect approach, and to carry out 'stratified' sampling. In this case, three stratified subset areas are established; the front itself, the major anomalies and all other areas. Within each of these one would attempt to census a set of randomly selected transect routes. Of course, in the case of a long narrow zone like the front, this is difficult or impossible. Method 1 would almost certainly undercount the animals. Method 2 would probably give a better estimate of real density, though perhaps with a bias on the high side because of over-survey of the front. Problems of density estimations are compounded by weather bringing about changes in visibility along the transects, fog for example (stipple). Cruise tracks of stratified survey indicated by dotted lines.

population, as determined by pilot surveys or general previous experience. There are a number of controlled studies in the literature which demonstrate that good stratified sampling frequently yields a higher degree of precision than the random approach which the professional statistician without field experience might initially consider more ideal. Within each zone of stratification the transects preferably should still be selected and laid out at random. Even this may not be feasible in areas with few landmarks or where Loran or Decca navigational aids are not available, and it may be necessary to resort to the less satisfactory but still useful method of evenly-spaced transects (21). If enough replicates are carried out, this method will still permit one to obtain quite a good estimate of the underlying animal distribution in the region, providing common-sense rules are not violated.

Most cetacean surveys are made from ships, using the 'strip census', or more correctly the 'line-transect' method. A good overview of both the theory and practice of 'line-transect models has been provided recently by K. P. Burnham and his co-workers (20). The reader is also referred to the useful summaries and review by G. Caughley of practical problems encountered during the application of these methods to vertebrates (21).

A range of formulae exist which can be applied in different circumstances. A relatively simple line-transect model developed by N. Höglund and others (64), and discussed by L. Eberhart (41) and G. Caughley (21), seems particularly applicable to many cetacean surveys, since it assumes that the chances of sighting an animal decrease exponentially with distance, and are largely dependent on visibility. One does not, therefore, have to define rigorously the outer boundaries of the strip being surveyed. It is important, however, that the behaviour of the animals is more or less consistent during the survey periods, or the results are not comparative. Personal experience leads me to suspect that the exponential decrease is not really valid for large baleen whales with a high blow and that, for these, some kind of sub-exponential fit is more realistic. One of the practical difficulties of analysing sighting data is that most observers use a mixture of naked eye and binocular scanning. The use of binoculars for long periods is very fatiguing and, paradoxically, can lead to animals close to the vessel being missed, even though it greatly increases the range at which whales can be sighted. During our studies of the harbour porpoise in eastern Canadian waters my research group developed a rather complex method for assessing correction factors based on sixteen different combinations of sea state, visibility and lighting conditions, and the number of observers. T. Doi has given much attention to the problem of quantifying observations of large whales from ships, and discussed several models for sighting theory in a series of papers during the last decade or so (39, 40).

In the formula of Högland *et al.*, mean density of animals (*D*) is estimated from

$$D = n \mid 2L\bar{x}$$

where *n* is the total number of animals seen, *L* is the length of the transect survey, and $\bar{x}$ is the mean of all the right-angle distances of all the animals seen each side of the transect. More sophisticated formulae take into account that the rate of decrease in probability of sighting with distance is more nearly sub-exponential than exponential (20).

COUPLED CENSUS

A difficult problem facing the Scientific Committee of the International Whaling Commission during the last fifteen years has been the estimation of recovery rates (if any) of those whale populations which were hunted to very low levels and finally given complete protection. Obviously the usual methods of population assessment and estimation employed by the Commission are inapplicable under these circumstances. Although whaling expeditions are required to collect detailed records of all species sighted, protected or not, these data are rarely sufficient in themselves to help us with these decisions. Nevertheless, if standard line-transect methods are used to estimate the densities of all species, the indices of population abundance obtained visually for the exploited species can be compared with those obtained from catch statistics and population parameters. If no correction factor appears necessary, then in the case of a randomized or randomized/stratified survey which produced sightings of 132 sei whales (exploited), 4 blues and 7 rights (protected) during the same period, the population densities of the latter species could be assumed to be 3.03 and 5.3 per cent respectively, of that of the exploited sei whales; that is, we 'couple' the two approaches.

Unfortunately, data obtained in this way can rarely be interpreted so simply, because the operative phrase is 'all relevant factors being equal'. They rarely are. Experienced observers doubt that one can realistically assume that all cetacean species have equal sightability, for a number of reasons. The minke whale is particularly difficult to see when surface conditions hide the back; the blow is frequently indistinguishable. The size and density of the 'blow' of the sei whale also varies greatly with behaviour, weather conditions and between individual animals. I recall occasions in the 1966–7 Antarctic season, working north of the Ross Sea with some Japanese colleagues, when sei whales of medium size were behaving and blowing in such a way in moderate seas that it was quite difficult to maintain contact with them even at distances of only four or five hundred metres. On another occasion a large sei, sighted through binoculars at a distance of more than three miles in good conditions, was at first mistaken for a blue whale by a Japanese officer in the crow's-nest who actually had over a dozen seasons of Antarctic whaling experience. His embarrassment at the subsequent actual identification at one mile was tempered by the fact that everyone on the bridge except the captain had agreed with his initial identification, and even the captain thought it more likely to be a fin whale!

The principal problem, however, is more serious. Only sei and minke whales are still exploited in the Southern Ocean, and the distributional range of both species differs significantly both in time and space from that of the other baleen whales. Sei whales do not penetrate nearly as far south as fin and blue whales in most regions and, as was mentioned in Chapter 2, arrive later on the feeding grounds than those species. Because it is unreasonable to expect factory-ship expeditions to spend time cruising in regions which are known to be unproductive for the remaining species which they are permitted to catch, there is virtually no way in which all the sighting data for the various protected and exploited species are going to be comparable. We could require the detachment of vessels from the main operational zone on scientific expedition to work these areas, but the data so obtained may not be strictly comparable, and must be used with great caution and only on the basis of considerable experience.

Mark-recapture or resighting methods

Whale marking has been carried out for many years using numbered stainless-steel darts, issued by the Discovery Committee in Britain or the scientific authorities for whale research in the Soviet Union and Japan. These darts are fired into the dorsal musculature, and a percentage are recovered during processing after the animal has been killed. Such internal marks yield only limited data; they provide little or no information about the movements of animals during the period between marking and capture. Sometimes, even though we suspect that the whale moved many hundreds or thousands of kilometres between the times of marking and recovery (19, 35), the animal is killed quite close to the original marking location. This is inevitable if whaling is being carried out in successive years in the same region during a relatively short season. The result is that only one part of a migration route is sampled each year, and always in the same months. There is often no way of proving conclusively that the animal had ever left the area, except perhaps by reference to fresh diatom film on the skin containing species characteristic of different latitudes (109).

For many years the Scientific Committee has been trying to develop a method for the long-term visible marking of large whales, with only the

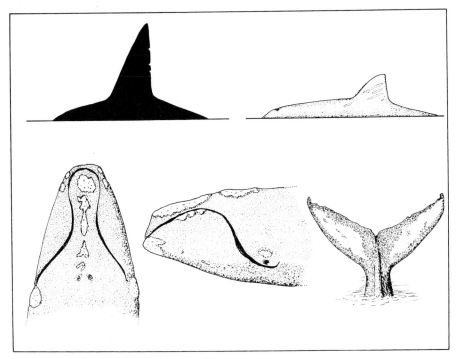

Figure 8.2 Valuable information on population composition and size has been obtained in cases where animals with distinctive individual markings can be observed. Successful studies have been made on killer whales with characteristic flaws in the dorsal fin outline by Dr M. Bigg, British Columbia (upper left); bottlenosed dolphins with nicked or scarred fins (upper right) by Dr B. Würsig in Argentina and H. P. Castello and M. C. Pinedo in southern Brazil; on callosity patterns of right whales off Argentina by Dr R. Payne and his associates, and in the Bay of Fundy and off the eastern coast of the USA by S. Kraus, S. Katona, W. A. Watkins, W. E. Schevill and others lower (lower left and centre); and on the markings on the underside of humpback flukes by S. Katona, H. E. Winn and others in many parts of the western North Atlantic (lower right).

most limited success. Branding is impractical for large species which cannot be handled, and dyes will not colour cetacean skin to any significant extent. Streamer marks have been employed, but the practical problems are severe. Sometimes the streamer does not deploy properly, or when it does, the water resistance is strong enough to pull the whole mark from the wound eventually. Stress on the streamer can also enlarge the entry point to such an extent that considerable tissue damage is caused. Dorsal fin tags have been used for small cetaceans; my own research group has had successful resightings of tagged harbour porpoises over periods varying from a few weeks to three years with no apparent tissue necropsy. Several other species of small cetacean have been successfully freeze-branded, although recently there has been some concern that delayed mortality can occur (144) as a result of severe muscle damage that is not superficially evident.

Certain species, particularly right whales with their variable parasitic head and jaw encrustations (135), humpback whales with their variable individual fluke markings (89) and killer whales and bottlenosed dolphins with their prominent, frequently nicked and scarred dorsal fins (17), have persistent natural markings which can be identified, catalogued and used as tools in population ecology studies through careful observational or photographic recording techniques (Figures 8.2–8.10).

In the last few years radio-tagging has been employed with some success for small cetaceans, using backpacks mounted on a harness, or bolted through the dorsal fin if the animal has one (44, 55, 75). In the past, results have been limited by technical problems related to the length of battery life, the general reliability of such equipment, the range of the

Figure 8.3   The markings on humpback flukes are distinct, and appear to persist over periods of many years. Photograph taken in the Head Harbour region of New Brunswick, Canada; courtesy of G. J. D. Smith, University of Guelph, Ontario.

Figure 8.4 Mr R. Sears of the Mingan Island cetacean survey, on the northern side of the Gulf of St Lawrence, Canada, has recently been attempting to identify individual blue whales using the method established for humpback whales. Blue whales do not show their flukes so frequently when diving. This individual has virtually no major fluke marks by which it could easily be re-identified. The mottled backs, on the other hand, have highly individual patterns. Photograph by R. Sears.

Figure 8.5 The flukes of gray whales have distinctive individual scars and encrustations. Photograph courtesy of Drs M. and B. Würsig, Santa Cruz, University of California, USA.

Figure 8.6   Encrustation and scar patterns on the back and flanks of gray whales have permitted workers to track animals and recognize individuals from season to season. There is reason to believe that these markings vary somewhat more than those in some other species, such as the right whales. They may become steadily more extensive with time. This animal, seen off Baja California, has mud streaming from the corner of its mouth, suggesting bottom feeding. Stomachs of whales examined on this southern part of the migration route however, have almost invariably been empty. Photograph courtesy of Drs M. and B. Würsig, Santa Cruz, University of California, USA.

Figure 8.7   Sometimes nature provides a free visible tag. This pilot whale, seen off the coast of Argentina, has a small cluster of highly visible stalked barnacles (*Xenobalanus*) hanging from the tip of its dorsal fin. Photograph courtesy of Drs M. and B. Würsig, Santa Cruz, University of California, USA.

Figure 8.8   On other occasions visible marks may have been provided by man. The white whale at the top of the picture has a deep healed wound in its back. Studies by L. Pippard, H. Malcolm, J. Hughes, J. Laurin, A. Macfarlane and the author in the Saguenay region of Quebec have made note of the large number of animals which bear such distinctive scars. Although they could be caused by gashes from propeller blades, L. Pippard is of the opinion that almost all result from healed bullet wounds. These animals are sometimes shot at by thoughtless hunters and, formerly, by a small number of professional cullers who took some animals for meat. Photograph courtesy of A. Macfarlane, August 1980.

Figure 8.9   Killer whale off coast of British Columbia, with distinctive back blaze and notches on trailing edge of dorsal fin. Photograph of whale A14 by M. Bigg, Pacific Biological Station, Nanaimo, BC, July 1975.

Figure 8.10   Killer whale B1, with large distinctive gash in dorsal fin. Photograph by M. Bigg, Pacific Biological Station, Nanaimo, BC, September 1977.

transmitters, and the technical difficulty of picking up and amplifying signals broadcast for fractions of a second as the animal fleetingly surfaces (111). Considerable improvements have been made in the last two or three years in all these aspects. The influence of the earlier, heavier transmitters on the behaviour of the animal was of some humane concern, and the fact that the behaviour might be somewhat altered from the norm, even if the life of the animal was not threatened directly, caused some scientific concern. Reduction in the size and weight of transmitters, and improvement in their streamlining and methods of attachment have lessened these fears.

Under some circumstances it has been possible to attach radio transmitters directly to large baleen whale species. A young gray whale held at Seaworld in California was liberated with a transmitter and tracked for a time (127). For many years researchers have been trying to develop a radio-tag which could be implanted in a large whale without the necessity of securing and handling the animal. The problems were formidable; the tag had to be small enough so that it could be fired from a gun without injuring the animal, the package had to be shaped in such a way that it presented the minimum resistance, and finally the electronic system had to be robust enough to withstand the accelerational forces encountered as the package was fired from the gun and upon impact. After several years the whale research group at Woods Hole and their co-workers have managed to develop such a radio dart (179). This tag has not only been used to track large baleen whales in coastal waters for extended periods, but has also permitted them to follow the long-distance movements of a fin whale in the North Atlantic for something close to 1500 kilometres (178). Visible and radio markers are particularly valuable because they provide data about movements of known individuals over extended periods of time in a way that no standard whale mark can.

For many years biologists have attempted to estimate abundance by dispersing a known number of marked specimens into a population. During a later sampling period, the percentage of recaptures is recorded and the proportion of marked animals recovered on this occasion should, if certain constraints are met, be equivalent to the proportion of marked animals in the total population; that is,

$$m/n = M/N$$

so that the population size can theoretically be estimated from

$$N = Mn/m$$

This method is usually known as the *Petersen estimate* or *Lincoln Index*, and the simple constraints are as follows.

(1) The marked animals must have dispersed back into the population at random.
(2) There must be no mortality, births, emigration or immigration between the sampling periods.
(3) The capture of one animal must not interfere with the capture of another.
(4) No individual must have a greater or lesser chance of recapture than any other because of heterogeneity in population distribution (even if the redispersal was originally at random).

In practice, some of these constraints are always violated, sometimes all of them, making the interpretation of mark recaptures a very unreliable basis for accurate estimation of population size. However, a number of methods have been developed that permit statistical confidence limits to be attached to the results, and further modifications involving multiple recaptures can, under some circumstances, improve the accuracy levels considerably, although none are fully satisfactory in field conditions.

N. J. T. Bailey (8) advocated the use of inverse sampling, where the number of required recaptures is decided upon in advance, and sampling is continued until that number is attained, at which point the population size is estimated from

$$N = \frac{n\,(M+1)}{m-1}$$

This result is relatively unbiased for large samples (but not for small ones), providing the two samples and the recaptures are large relative to the population size. When we are dealing with data obtained from commercial whale-marking returns this is really the only kind of approach that can be used, and other variants of this method have been published (3).

If births or deaths or significant emigration and immigration are known to occur during the course of the study, then we require data drawn from several mark and recapture sequences, if our estimate of N is to be remotely reliable. Bailey developed a triple-catch method (8) that is applicable in many circumstances, and G. M. Jolly (79) published a sophisticated model that takes stochastic fluctuations and population dilutions into account, and has been widely used. Although it is not really appropriate for standard whale marking where there can only be a single mark and a single capture event for each individual, it can be employed with much greater reliability when visible tags or markings are being used. Unfortunately this method can rarely be applied with complete success to cetacean population studies because Petersen/Lincoln estimates really demand that the initial markings be made more or less simultaneously. Furthermore, the recovery rate of standard whale marks in factory-ship deck and meat-processing operations may be less than 50 per cent of the real number taken, with the rest escaping detection (3). Ideally we need a foolproof model which takes into account marking being carried out over a period, or in successive batches, that does not rely too heavily on the expectation of random redistribution of marked animals into the population – something which probably hardly ever happens in the real situation (37, 161).

Some flexible models which are applicable with reasonable levels of reliability in the sort of commercial hunting operation represented by whaling have, in fact, been developed and given fresh field trials in recent years. These may employ the Poisson distribution, negative binomial or geometric distributions. The latter two methods allow for catchability being unequal at different times, whereas the Poisson works best when there is no change in catchability over time (21). Even these models can have some serious practical drawbacks, although the test developed by Orians (133) for equal catchability can estimate bias in recaptures in most cases. The reader who wishes to study these problems in more depth can refer to the work of Seber (163, 164), Johnson (78), Jones (80), Jolly (79), DeLury (37) and Caughley (21). These, in turn, provide many more references. This literature has direct relevance to the analysis of whale marking, inasmuch as there are relatively few papers in whaling research which have tackled the statistical problems of mark-recapture with anything approaching the rigour that has been applied in other areas of animal ecology.

Methods of calculating population abundance utilizing catch data of exploited species

It is a reasonable first-order assumption that in the unexploited state, the recruitment and mortality rates of populations of relatively (or absolutely) large and long-lived mammals such as cetaceans, with long reproductive cycles, will usually vary rather slowly. This can be contrasted with the situation in small mammals with short generation periods such as voles, mice and rabbits, in which population parameters can fluctuate quite widely in relatively short periods of time. If the structures of cetacean populations are relatively stable in the short term, as suggested above, then catches which are relatively large, or at least measurably large with respect to the total population size, should have an impact which can be recognized. This impact can be studied through changes in the catch per unit time by measured effort. It is first essential to be able to measure that catching effort, and in practice this proves to be far from simple.

Catch-per-unit-effort analysis

The impact of harvesting on cetacean populations is usually measured in terms of catch per unit effort (C/f), where f represents the unit effort. The theory is simple; one examines the industry and its hunting methods and determines a basic workable unit of effort, for example, one catcher-boat's day's work. We can then compare the number of whales taken per boat per day in different regions or in different seasons. We hope that (all things being equal) changes in these values reflect real changes in the availability of animals to the industry. We need to collect independent observational and oceanographic data to help us decide if this change in availability represents, in turn, a real change in the size of the population, rather than a change in distribution. If pushed to the wall, we can give some kind of limited policy advice based on catch-per-unit-effort value changes alone, providing we have good reason to believe them to be reliable. In practice, unfortunately, many problems arise. The effort exerted by British, Norwegian, Japanese and Russian whale chasers in the Antarctic in the 1950s and 1960s was found to differ significantly. The Russian vessels were modern, considerably larger, faster and more powerful than those of the west European nations, and operated more efficiently in conditions of lower whale density. On the other hand, the organizational deployment of Russian factory expeditions, sometimes with more than 30 chaser boats, appeared cumbersome, with perhaps significantly lower overall efficiency than in the Japanese or Norwegian expeditions.

Unfortunately, like the problem of age determination (see section on pp. 302–8), estimation of real effort is critical if any of several models of population analysis are to be used satisfactorily. That the issue is still being debated today, and refinements continue to be made, is a measure of the difficulty of standardizing effort over fleets, species, time and regions. S. J. Holt (69), for example, recently provided an analysis of the consequences of breaking down the 'catcher's day's work' into operational components and assuming that the whale density was actually proportional to catch per unit searching time. The searching time exerted by the boat is a dependent variable of population density; it will decrease when the daily catch rate is high, and introduces a consistent bias into density estimates.

Holt concluded that the rate of decline in whale density over time had been generally underestimated through catch-per-unit-effort values (69). G. P. Kirkwood examined this problem recently (93) and also concluded that catch per net catcher's day's operation overestimates whale density quite seriously when small fleet units are used. These are not new conclusions. When the present author analysed the catches of sperm whales made by the New Zealand industry in the 1960s (50) it was evident that catch per unit effort declined less steeply than sightings per unit effort (S/f) as real density decreased. I therefore preferred to rely more on sightings per unit effort for density estimations, despite the inherent problems with this approach that were examined earlier in the discussion of line transects and similar techniques.

Further problems, difficult to solve, arise when the industry has been taking two or more species during the same catching period. Virtually all that can be done in this case is to survey the total records very carefully, and retain for use those data for days or parts of days when only one species was in the area or being sought by the chasers. The problem is further complicated when boats of different horsepower and tonnage are involved. Gambell recently corrected all the southern hemisphere sperm whale catch-per-unit-effort data for these factors (48, 49). Japanese attempts to use catcher's hour's work instead of catcher's day's work could hardly be called successful, even by the admission of the authors (132). Recently J. R. Beddington presented a thoughtful review of the whole basis of the use of catch per unit effort in the estimation of whale population abundance (12).

Beddington contended that the usual method of estimating population density from catch-per-unit-effort data tended to overestimate abundance after the initial phase of exploitation, because any change over time in searching or handling efficiency resulted in a non-linear change in the relationship between catch and abundance. He concluded that simple comparisons of the catch per unit effort of different boats in different circumstances were not really valid. In the basic form, the simple relationship between catch (C), the number of working boats (k) per unit time (T) is usually expressed as

$$C = qkTN$$

where q is the 'coefficient of catchability'. This can be converted to an index of abundance by transforming it to

$$qN = C/kT$$

Beddington suggests that a more appropriate equation can be given by

$$C = kaNT / (1 + ahN)$$

where a is the efficiency of a boat and h is the time spent handling the catch. The modified expression for catch per unit effort can then be written as

$$C/kT = aN / (1 + ahN)$$

Beddington also developed a simple model for calculating modified catch per unit effort for sperm whale hunting, when boats normally co-operated in the hunt once one vessel had sighted a school. He concluded that a further modification could also be applied to situations where boats were fishing either for male and female sperm whales under separate quotas, or for more than one species of baleen whale. Time spent searching for, catching and handling the sex or species not under immediate consideration was incorporated into a 'time wasted' (T_w) component that could be deducted from the total operation time. In practice, unfortunately, the precise data for this kind of approach are not always available, as Ohsumi and Yamamura concluded in their paper in 1978 in which they attempted a detailed breakdown of operational components (132).

Nevertheless, leaving percentage over- or underestimates in abundance aside (with all due respect for their critical role in quota decisions from time to time), if we can estimate effort with some confidence, and the known catch is taken from a relatively small population upon which the catches have a measurable impact, it is sometimes possible to measure directly the changes in the 'catchability' of the population. By relating effort to the cumulative catch, using one or other of the methods developed by Leslie (102) and DeLury (Figure 8.11) (36), we can make a first-order estimate of the magnitude of the population size prior to exploitation. The methods depend on certain other basic assumptions, namely that for

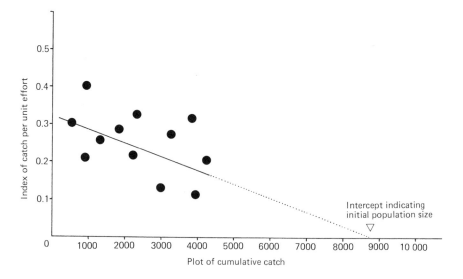

Figure 8.11   The Leslie method of determining population size relies on a plot of catch-per-unit-effort values over a period of time (solid circles) against cumulative catch. The method assumes balance of births and deaths by other causes, and any emigration and immigration. The intercept gives an approximate measure of the initial population size.

practical purposes there is no change in population composition during sampling (that is, if there is emigration and immigration, that they balance), and that birth and natural mortality rates also balance; that the probability of capture is equal for all units in the population, and that capture of one animal does not interfere with the capture of another.

The method of Leslie plots the simple linear-regression equation of catch per unit effort against cumulative catch

$$C/f = a - bC_c$$

where a is the coefficient of intercept, b is the coefficient of slope, and C_c is the cumulative catch. The DeLury modification uses logged C/f, since this can be shown to be linear on effort expended before a particular catching event. Readers not acquainted with the mechanics of these standard statistical manipulations can refer to the text by N. J. T. Bailey (9), or any other elementary statistics or biometrics book. The number obtained by extending the regression time until it cuts the x (that is, C_c) axis represents the approximate size of the initial population. There has been much argument about the validity of this method in different circumstances. Most workers are in agreement with W. E. Ricker (149) that careful weighting of data are probably not worth the effort, because periodic variations in catch per unit effort probably cancel out gains made through such correction factors. Nevertheless, the decline in catch per unit effort noted in a number of cases where these methods have been applied to whale populations has been highly statistically significant, indicating that they appeared to give some rough estimate of initial population size. Under most circumstances this is certainly better than nothing, and the results can be used to check estimates of abundance obtained by other methods. Just to give some examples, these methods have been used to determine initial population size in the Australian humpback whale populations by Chittleborough (26), in the sei whale population of Southern Ocean area III by Beddington (11) and Chapman (23), in the western North Atlantic pilot whale population by Mercer (116) and in the North Pacific Bryde's whale population by Tillman (171).

Analysis and determination of abundance through studies of intrinsic population parameters

None of the foregoing methods of determining abundance gives us much idea about changes taking place within exploited whale or dolphin populations. Their value is much enhanced if they can be used in combination with data on population composition or changes in that composition during exploitation.

Two types of model have been formulated to analyse animal populations; these provide the basis for hypothetical simulations of population reactions to exploitation under different conditions. The first, which has been used with varying degrees of success as a tool in fisheries management and was adapted to the management of whale populations by the statisticians and biologists of the International Whaling Commission Scientific Committee, is the surplus production model (56, 158, 159). Under ideal circumstances this predicts changes in the sustainable yield with changes in the size of the population, but few have been completely happy with the success obtained with this model in whale population studies. One of the problems has been that for many years the data available were so poor that it was not possible to measure accurately changes taking place in populations until these changes had reached a considerable magnitude.

The second type in common use, the so-called analytic models (16, 59), really form a family of methods. These too were first developed for use in fisheries (149); they provide far more detailed information than the simple yield models, but they also require the input of considerably more data. Various extensions and modifications of the analytic models have been used to study fish and, more lately, whale populations in recent years. Trends in population structure are examined through study of the changes in age composition and, where possible, by following the fate of each year class as it progresses through the 'age spectrum' of the population. This latter method is often called 'cohort analysis', and has been widely used in fish population studies. It has been much less extensively employed in whale population studies (see later section, pp. 308–9). To develop the model we require unbiased information on growth rates and maturity state, and an accurate method of age determination, which are then used in combination with catch and effort data. With this information we can calculate not only total mortality rates, but also, by indirect methods (1, 2, 16), separate values for hunting (usually called fishing) and natural mortality rates.

The analytic approach usually reveals that hunting mortality rates (and therefore presumably catchability) are far from equally distributed throughout the life-span of the exploited species. One of the major problems of applying this type of model in practice is that commercially obtained samples are almost always biased, perhaps by time of year (limited season), region (closed areas), sex (protection of lactating females), age–class composition (minimum-size restrictions), or any of these in various combinations. The interim conservation measures which may be imposed by management agencies prior to complete biological analyses being carried out are well intentioned, but sometimes the catch results in samples with such inherent bias that they may be virtually impossible to analyse. It may be necessary to request special hunting licences to obtain samples of animals of age classes not normally taken in the commercial operation or from restricted areas.

AGE AND AGE DETERMINATION IN CETACEA

An accurate measure of age (preferably absolute, but at least relative) is an essential prerequisite for application of any analytic approach to a biological population. As a consequence, a significant fraction of cetacean research during the last forty years has been directed to this end.

A wide variety of tissues have been utilized in the search for 'ideal' or at least completely reliable methods of age determination for both suborders of Cetacea. The research literature prior to about 1966 was summarized by Å. Jonsgård in a generally available symposium text (81). The number of articles published since that time has more or less doubled, but doubts about all the tried and tested methods remain. A symposium on age determination in odontocetes held late in 1978 (74) found much to criticize in existing methods, drew attention to the fact that the underlying endogenous mechanism governing the formation of seasonal layering in different types of tissues is still not really understood, and opened several new lines of possible investigation for the future.

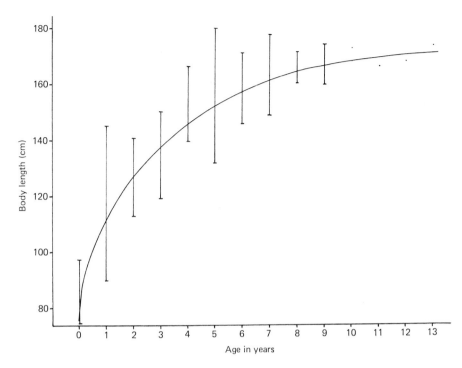

Figure 8.12   The relationship of body length and age in years for the female harbour porpoise *Phocoena phocoena* in the western North Atlantic. Bars give approximate range of variation determined for each value, indicating that estimation of age by body length alone, without reference to dentine layers in the teeth is highly suspect. Redrawn from Gaskin and Blair (54).

Body length was used as the original rough guide to relative age of large cetaceans (110), but although approximately linear during the foetal stage, the annual growth increment becomes progressively smaller and smaller after adolescence. Furthermore, individual variation in growth rates is considerable (Figure 8.12). Many workers have tried to correlate the rate of accumulation of corpora albicantia in the ovaries with increase in body size. Others have attempted to use this method to give information about the number of pregnancies but, despite suggestions to the contrary (45), it has yet to be convincingly demonstrated that a consistent difference exists between the corpora of ovulation and the corpora of pregnancy once they have regressed to the albicans stage. The active corpus luteum of pregnancy can be distinguished from a corpus luteum of ovulation by its central vesicle (96, 98, 139, 150, 166, 173).

The rate of accumulation of corpora albicantia is variable, and highly dependent upon the reproductive history of the individual. During the

1950s and 1960s the rate of accumulation of corpora was variously interpreted for blue, fin and humpback whales to lie between a low of 0.5 per year and a high of 1.64 per year (26, 98, 108, 124, 129, 151, 176), with the lower values being supported by some data from capture of marked animals. Accumulation rates in odontocetes fall within the lower part of the range given above; 0.5 in the bottlenosed whale (27), 0.69 in *Stenella coeruleoalba* (84) and 0.41 in *S. attenuata* (84, 92).

Scoresby (162) was the first to suggest that the age of the Greenland right whale might be recorded in the grooves and ridges of the baleen plates. For a long time no successful way of quantifying such features was found, until a method was devised to mechanically record changes in zone thickness and transfer them to recording paper (153–5). Unfortunately, this seems to give an apparently reliable means of measuring age in blue and fin whales only up to about the fifth year (156). Subsequent work has shown that the deposition of these zones is indeed about one per year (81, 109, 174). The nature of the structures in the baleen has also been studied histologically (176). Nevertheless, the method cannot be used reliably for adult specimens because of the wear on the baleen plates which occurs during life.

The needed break-through in the ageing of baleen whales was provided by P. E. Purves (145), who reported the presence of layers in the wax plug which occurs in the external auditory meatus of whalebone whales. The number of laminations in this structure was closely correlated with body length and presumably, therefore, with age. This gave a most useful relative measure of age in adult baleen whales for the first time, but serious problems were encountered when trying to determine the rate of deposition so that the values could be converted to the all-important measure of absolute age. There were other difficulties too. It was hard to extract the plug entire in young specimens, where it is rather fragile. The smaller plugs are poorly pigmented and, furthermore, the earliest-formed laminations tend to become compressed at the apex of the plug core as the animal ages so that they are hard to discern (25). A consistent error in age estimation can be introduced in both adults and young because of these factors.

The rate of deposition was originally suggested as being annual or semi-annual (145). Many subsequent studies were made (99, 125) and it was in many ways unfortunate that the first real correlative data from marked whales came from quite young animals (25, 34). For a time the results reinforced the view of those who believed that two growth layers were deposited each year, and ageing of commercial baleen whale samples (especially fin whales) was for some time conducted quite confidently on this basis.

As whale-mark returns accumulated, members of the Scientific

Committee of the International Whaling Commission came to doubt more and more that the value of two growth layers per year could be maintained as a realistic figure (109). Information from significant numbers of mark returns from both the Southern Ocean and the North Pacific led S. Ohsumi (128, 129) to conclude that the number laid down was never less than one, but nowhere near two per annum, except perhaps during the first few years of life. The average increments seemed to be about 1.5 per year until after sexual maturity had been attained. The absolute chronological age of North Atlantic fin whales by ear-plug determinations was likewise considered to be 'open to interpretation' (117). Doubling the postulated age of fin and blue whales naturally had considerable ramifications. In effect, it meant more or less halving the value for the annual rate of population production per unit time which had been previously accepted. There was a sudden realization that quotas had been set far too high for several years, and the abrupt change in the advice from the Scientific Committee led to a crisis of confidence within the Commission (115). A firm report on the sequence of laminations in the baleen whale ear plug was provided by Roe in 1967, who described their formation in detail (152). Overestimation of the number of growth layers per annum in young animals was caused by the deposition of 'false' laminations. In the normal course of events an alternating sequence of light and dark laminations are laid down, the pair making up a single annual growth layer. We still do not understand the physiological basis of this formation, but it may be dictated endogenously, as are the changes in layering in the dentine of odontocetes, rather than resulting simply from changes in food availability. Nevertheless, it is important to remind ourselves that it *could* conceivably be related directly to deposition under the control of food intake in the large baleen whales, since they fast or take only small amounts of food during the period of migration in low latitudes. The ear plugs of all the smaller species, such as sei, Bryde's whale and minke, present difficult problems, especially since the growth layers are very thin and hard to count in these species (131). Recently Lockyer (104) found that bleaching the plugs with hydrogen peroxide greatly increased the readability of the layers in such cases; readability increases with age, but the laminations of young specimens often still yield ambiguous results.

In the case of odontocete whales, the majority of age-determination studies have been made on the basis of growth layers in teeth, sometimes using those in cementum (if present), but more often those in the dentine (165). Laws (97) and Nishiwaki (126) have described layering in certain zones of the mandible of the sperm whale, but these become difficult to read after the first decade of life.

Complex layers (18) apparently deposited in annual sets of one narrow translucent and one broader opaque lamination, have been found in the dentine of virtually every odontocete whale examined. The readability of these layers varies from species to species, and they are almost impossible to interpret in the specialized teeth of certain beaked whales (119). This is not a problem in the North Atlantic bottlenosed whale, however (27). In some odontocetes readable layers can be clearly discerned in the cementum, but this is not the case in all species. There has been much argument about the mechanism governing the formation of layering in both tissues; some authors have speculated that the effect is the result of significant changes in the feeding rate during the course of the year or of calcium levels in the food. Work carried out in our laboratory on dentinal layering in the harbour porpoise revealed that the timing of the onset of deposition of an opaque or a translucent lamination in this species appeared to follow an annual sequence originally dictated by the time of birth (54). Since the calving season extends over a period of several months in the population of the harbour porpoise in the western North Atlantic, we were not surprised to find different animals in that same population with either opaque or translucent laminations being formed simultaneously. In one case, two animals taken as a pair had different types of lamination being laid down. We concluded, therefore, that seasonal changes in diet, either in quantitative or qualitative terms, were most unlikely to provide adequate explanation for the alternating sequence, and that some form of direct endogenous control was responsible, although we did not exclude the possibility that this was being triggered, in turn, by changes in some external factor, such as photoperiod or the level of vitamin D in the food during the season.

Subsequent to this study, other authors have also affirmed their belief in the role of endogenous rhythms in this process (18, 71, 94). Nevertheless, the problems encountered in the interpretation of layering in odontocete teeth are essentially the same as those discussed above with respect to the baleen whale ear plug. Although one of each type of major lamination appears to be deposited as a growth layer each year as long as the pulp cavity remains open and the tissue within the cavity remains actively involved in the deposition of dentine, high magnification of tooth sections, either untreated or enhanced by staining or etching (141), can reveal several to many subsidiary laminations. Sometimes these are prominent enough to cause confusion during counting. It has been suggested that these subsidiary or accessory laminations may represent (lunar) monthly depositions (122). Counts of the numbers of growth layers in dentine or cementum can differ significantly between observers looking at the same material (92), and there can also be some variability within the dentine deposits in different teeth from the same specimen (72), although this does not seem to be too serious a problem with most species. Tetracycline is one of the compounds which can be used to deposit visible traces in growing dentine; either oral or injected doses can be applied. The zone of deposition can later be detected by ultraviolet light (14, 123). This method has been used to check the rate of dentine accumulation over time in captive odontocetes. In practice, its use seems to be limited to relatively young animals in most species, because of problems of possible pulp cavity occlusion or increasing dentinal compression with increasing age, which makes the zone hard to find (60). Several other innovative methods to detect annual changes in tissues have been developed in recent years, with varying degrees of success. Study of the racemization of D/L-aspartic acid in the crowns of odontocete teeth shows promise (7, 63). Micro-radiography and scanning electronmicroscopy have also been attempted, but results are somewhat inconclusive (65). Acetate peels have been used as a method of preserving surface microfeatures of etched tooth-section surfaces (112).

On the basis of present results, the absolute life-span among odontocete cetaceans seems to vary from a low of about 13–16 years in two of the smallest species *Pontoporia blainvillei* (87) and *Phocoena phocoena* (54, 175), to a maximum of about 50 years in the sperm whale *Physeter catodon* (15) and 70 years in Baird's beaked whale *Berardius bairdii* (85). Odontocetes of intermediate sizes have life-spans which fall between these maxima and minima; about 15–18 years in *Phocoenoides* (86), 20+ years in *Platanista gangetica* (83), 17–22 years in *Stenella longirostris* (137), 25 years in *Tursiops truncatus* (168), 27–30 years in *S. coeruleoalba* (120) (or possibly as much as 45 years in *Stenella* species) (84), 30–40 years in *S. attenuata* (88), 25–27 years in the white whale *Delphinapterus leucas* (167), and up to 37 years in the North Atlantic bottlenosed whale *Hyperoodon ampullatus* (27). Maximum age for baleen whales appears to fall within the same general range, but perhaps towards the upper end of the scale. Values for minke and sei are still uncertain because of the problems encountered in reading their ear plugs successfully. Southern humpback whales are believed to live to at least 30 years of age (24), and marking returns from southern fin whales indicate a maximum in the region of 25 to perhaps 40 years (73, 129).

If we are to grasp the essential dynamics of an animal population, we must determine not only the size of that population and the age structure, but also its balance of production, that is, the rates at which animals are being born, recruited into the reproductively active segment, and lost by natural causes or mortality as a result of hunting. Once we have a reasonably reliable method of determining age, we can investigate age-specific birth rates, the frequency distributions of age classes, survival by age, the overall death rate, and ultimately the rate of increase or decrease of the population. All this presupposes that we have accurate catch and effort data to use with the information on population parameters. Sometimes we do not know the absolute size of the population under exploitation, have only a series of relative estimates of abundance, and can estimate only relative ages. Nevertheless, changes in the composition over a period of time will, if sampling is unbiased, still tell us quite a lot about the effect the exploitation process is having on the population.

PREGNANCY, BIRTH AND RECRUITMENT RATES, AND COHORT ANALYSIS

Fecundity is quite low in the Cetacea in comparison to many other mammals. At best potential production in this order is probably about half that of humans, and sometimes considerably less than that. Although multiple births have been recorded, and the incidence of twinning is between 0.25 and 0.5 per cent, it is most unlikely that both offspring survive; frequently both may die. For all intents and purposes, therefore, the average 'litter' size is one. The season of births is relatively restricted in most species, and so is the peak of pairing. Not all females are necessarily impregnated even in those years that conception is theoretically possible. The phenomenon of a 'resting year' between periods of pregnancy and lactation has been recorded frequently in Cetacea. The fact that the calving period is protracted can lead to computation difficulties in some cases; Caughley (21) provided summaries of several alternative methods for handling the birth statistics in mammalian populations, and estimating the modal point of births. These are applicable to whale populations with some modifications, and one of the adaptations he suggests can be used in cases where animals are neither killed nor captured (21, 22).

In commercial operations the pregnancy rate can be determined directly, since there is no practical way of protecting this segment of the population from capture, by simple regulation, as there is in the case of females with offspring. One has to have reason to assume, of course, that the sampling for pregnant females is indicative of their true proportion in the population. Minor complications are sometimes introduced by whaling practices, such as the slitting of the body cavity at sea to cool the tissue masses and slow the rate of decomposition. This used to be done in whaling operations on the east coast of Canada, and many foetuses were lost at sea (117). It was necessary to check the uterine condition to make sure that a foetus had or had not been present. Observational information on the percentage of females with calves can be used in conjunction with estimates of pregnancy rates, each set of data being used to provide a rough check on the accuracy of the other. If we had reason to believe that the values obtained were accurate and representative, then we could obtain some idea of the percentage of still births or immediate post-natal mortality, although as far as I know this has rarely been done for cetaceans.

The length of the complete female reproductive cycle varies from species to species; in most some variation is also the rule. Cycle patterns may overlap; it is not that unusual in some species (for example, harbour porpoise) to find females which are simultaneously pregnant and lactating, indicating that calves can indeed be produced in subsequent years. Whether the mother can rear the second one successfully is debatable, however (181). In most species production of a calf every second, or even every third year, is probably more typical (106). The sperm whale female generally appears to calve only once in each four-year period; production in this species is perhaps the lowest in the Cetacea (13, 15).

The study of 'recruitment' developed within the context of fisheries population dynamics, because estimation of the 'strength' of year classes (that is, numbers or biomass relative to the average) is of great importance from the point of view of predicting the magnitude of contribution to the fishery which the incoming recruits will make. Study of the fate of sequential cohorts over the years as they progress through the population structure and the fishery often yields valuable information. If a good measure of natural and fishing mortality is available, one can utilize equations which have been developed by several workers to estimate the probable fate of a particular cohort over time (57, 59, 121, 149, 160). For a number of reasons – one being that the number of age classes is large relative to the size of the sampled catch, and usually accompanied by considerable sampling variation – cohort analysis has only been rarely applied to cetacean populations, and not always with great success (10, 15). Recently, however, K. R. Allen and G. Kirkwood have developed a computer program for cohort analysis and prediction in the sperm whale providing sufficient data are available (4).

MORTALITY SOURCES AND RATES

Although the bullet or harpoon may be the major sources of cetacean mortality at the hands of man, it is worth keeping in mind that incidental kills can occur as a result of entanglement in fishing gear and, depending on the size and distribution of the cetacean population, such kills can contribute significantly to losses from the population (82,136) (see discussion of tuna–porpoise problem and humpback whale entrapments in next chapter, pp. 349–52 and 354–5). Sometimes such entrapment particularly affects females which have moved into coastal waters to calve and feed their young. The populations which have been most subject to incidental catching, however, are those of the tropical spinner and spotted dolphins of the Pacific, taken in tuna purse-seining operations (138), where the catch has run to many tens of thousands per annum (see Chapter 9).

Total mortality is usually expressed as the instantaneous coefficient of mortality (Z) for ease of calculation. This is not quite the same as the crude annual rate, since the instantaneous mortality value is a differential coefficient. Mortalities are additive, so we can separate hunting or fishing mortality (F) from natural mortality (M) in the simple form:

$$F + M = Z$$

If M can be calculated, then it follows that the effect of fishing or hunting is easily defined as

$$F = C/N$$

where C is the catch and N is the exploitable fraction of the population available to the operation. It therefore follows in turn that

$$N = C/F$$

All this sounds very easy in theory, but in practice values of population abundance obtained by these few simple calculations are usually wildly inaccurate. Many sophisticated modifications have been developed during the last twenty years; for summaries the reader is referred to selected major works in the bibliography of this chapter – the list is far from exhaustive (1, 16, 21, 59, 149).

Hunting operations are invariably selective, and reduce the survival rates of certain year classes more than others (juveniles are protected in virtually all whale fisheries). The normal age structure of the population (that is, in the unexploited state) often just has to be guessed at. One might think that we should be able to estimate the relative intensity of hunting and its effects from recognizable changes in the age composition over a period of years, but in practice it is rather difficult to do this in such a way that one has much confidence in the conclusions. Caughley discussed this problem in some detail (21), and provided useful references to this subject in the mammalian population literature. It can be considered almost axiomatic that an exploited population must show some kind of recognizable symptom of decline, either in abundance or in return per effort, before regulatory action is taken (58). The literature on whale populations contains many estimates of initial stock size; most are little better than educated guesses, yet despite this, some values have become almost part of the 'folklore' of the sequential citation process. It is fascinating to trace some of these values back through the literature and see on what slender evidence they were derived in the first place! Nevertheless, realistic comparisons can be made between age classes within the stock at different times as long as reliable estimates of hunting effort are available, and there is no significant hunting bias (59).

The direct estimation of natural mortality (M) in cetaceans presents in practice some formidable problems. Attempts to study M through the survival of successive age classes have yielded indifferent results (13). Cetaceans often carry a heavy load of gut parasites (and in the case of porpoises, lung and pancreatic parasites as well), but under normal circumstances these may not be a significant factor in annual mortality as long as the nutritional demands of the host population are being adequately met. When these inputs fall below a critical minimum level from time to time however, parasites may be responsible for a considerable increase in the death rate, as has been observed in crabeater and North Pacific fur seals. Carcinomas are apparently rather rare in these animals (30). Predation by killers and sharks on the young, even of the largest baleen whales, may be significant. On the other hand, predation of killer whales on adult animals is likely to be slight, albeit spectacular (see pp. 32–3). Adult natural mortality rates seem to be rather low. I suspect that genetic maladaptations, post-weaning starvation deaths, and accidents at or immediately following birth, may account for most natural juvenile mortality.

Some reasonable estimate of M can be obtained by using the total mortality rate Z in cases where the population is still in a virtually unexploited state (13), and it can be assumed that hunting will have contributed only a negligible fraction to the total mortality in the first few years of operation. A common assumption is that natural mortality rates will decrease with increased exploitation. There are several good theoretical reasons for assuming this (130), but frankly, they are not necessarily all that sound in practice. The basic idea is that as the population declines, food availability will be enhanced and, because there will be less intraspecific competition for it, starvation is less likely. But this is only likely to apply if one is dealing with a very simple single-species density-dependence situation. In animals such as whales, where a significant fraction of the natural mortality presumably occurs in infancy, in practice there may be no particular reason to expect this to decrease as the population is exploited. Whaling operations select for the largest animals, which is likely to mean in most cases the oldest and most experienced parents. Juvenile mortality rates in these animals have not been examined from the point of view of success perhaps being correlated with the age of the mother and whether the offspring is a first-born or subsequent birth. There is reason to speculate that young mothers, with less experience in finding alternative feeding grounds if the regular locations fail, might have higher natural mortality rates among their young. This would not necessarily occur because of poor feeding in the year the calf is with the mother; if feeding had been inadequate the year before, the depot fat reserves might be insufficient to carry both the calf and the mother through the period of lactation. This would be particularly dangerous if two poor-feeding years were experienced in a row. Lockyer (105) has stressed (Chapter 3) that we have to remember that the energy budget of a reproductively active migratory female whale must be examined from the point of view of the 'carry-over' of food store from one year to the next.

An elegant and simple method of calculating M indirectly was developed by Beverton and Holt (16). The total mortality coefficient Z is graphed with respect to time t against effort f_t, and the regression line estimated. The critical point is where the line cuts the axis of Z_t, for when effort is zero, obviously the hunting/fishing mortality F_t is zero, and hence the fraction of Z falling below the intercept must represent the natural mortality M_t.

INDIVIDUAL GROWTH RATES

A complex of factors has influenced the evolution of each population and species of the Cetacea, and in the process, selection has occurred for rather specific ranges of body sizes and individual growth rates. Needless to say, there are periods when the actual growth *rate* of a large species and a small species could be exactly the same. Whereas the time periods required for selection of optimal ranges of these various parameters could be quite long, there is clear evidence that changes of food supply in the relatively short term, that is, over a few seasons, can produce measurable changes in growth rates within a population, and also influence the average age at which the onset of sexual maturity occurs (107). If we relate the growth rate of the individual animals in a population to its potential exploitability, it could be a key factor in making decisions about the value of that particular population as a commercial resource. If the growth rate was slow, and the body size relatively small, then even if maturity was attained at a relatively early age, the population might be a less attractive exploitation prospect from the economic point of view than another population in which body size was larger, and growth rates faster, even if sexual maturity occurred relatively late.

Foetal and post-natal growth is rapid in all cetaceans (26, 109), and remains so during the juvenile years, falling off asymptotically as physical maturity is approached. Most cetologists have been satisfied to describe the growth of cetaceans after birth by the equation of Von Bertalanffy introduced in Chapter 3,

$$L_t = L \infty \left[1 - e^{-k(t-t_0)} \right]$$

Some scientists have drawn attention to a characteristic 'growth spurt' as puberty approaches, and suggested that in cases where the age–length relationship has a large standard deviation at each value, growth can for all

practical purposes be effectively described by two straight-line regressions
for the periods before and subsequent to this growth spurt (46). Of course,
the problem encountered here is that one has to make an arbitrary decision
about where the cut-off point between the two data sets should lie, and this
is likely to be influenced by the particular set of data points available at any
time. When examining the age/length curves for male and female harbour
porpoises, Blair and I (54) found that the fit provided by the Von
Bertalanffy equation was relatively poor; the relationship could be more
accurately described by the curvilinear equations:

$$d - [b/-1.30b + 209.35)] - 1 \qquad \text{for males}$$

$$d = [b/-0.84b + 156.15)] - 1 \qquad \text{for females}$$

where b is body length and d is number of completed dentinal layers. The
problem with these equations, of course, is that they are purely
descriptive, whereas the Von Bertalanffy equation to some extent
attempts to represent the interaction of factors actually occurring in the
growth process.

In recent years several workers have been interested in comparative
growth rates in a single species where one or more regional populations are
being exploited at different rates. If competition from similar whale
species (and other upper-trophic-level animals) could be reasonably
discounted, and if surplus food was available in some areas as a result of
reduction of whale numbers, then juvenile growth rates might be expected
to be most rapid in those areas. In practice, clear-cut results in the short
term have been hard to find (see also pp. 380–1 in Chapter 9). Food
supply at any location fluctuates both in biomass and distribution from
season to season, and even from day to day. If euphausiid concentrations in
one area were to sink just an extra hundred feet or so through the
epipelagic layer and become half as densely distributed during the course
of a week, for example, that zone would rapidly become far less attractive
(and useful) to baleen whales. Other groups of organisms, especially large
pelagic or demersal fish and sea-birds, can gather to feed on food patches in
very short periods of time. Competition is probably rarely eliminated
completely, and may often be locally significant for certain whale species
(52, 118), although it would be difficult to collect data to test whether this
were true or not because of the practical problems. Surpluses of food,
therefore, may often be too short-lived to exert an influence in the way
suggested above. Nevertheless, if the right information is available, it can
be readily demonstrated that within the same species, growth rates and the
age at which maturity is attained vary from one geographic region to
another, for example, in the sperm whale (15, 51) and the harbour porpoise
(54, 175, 182). Such differences may have evolved over quite long periods

in response to subtle regional environmental differences, rather than being the result of exploitation. Over periods of decades, on the other hand, significant reductions in the age of maturity of some baleen whale species has been demonstrated (47, 107).

Whatever one's viewpoint about these kinds of responses, and the manipulations that have been suggested (67), an appreciation that individuals of different ages have very different proportions of their energy intake going into growth or maintenance has been a very basic factor in the development of the management methodologies which have been applied to whale populations under commercial exploitation during the last thirty years or so.

POPULATION PRODUCTION AND RATES OF CHANGE

I earlier implied that the net annual production of cetacean populations varies considerably from species to species; this has the result of making some subjects more desirable for commercial exploitation than others. It is also worth mentioning that for human consumption the meat of baleen whales and dolphins is preferred to that of large and medium-sized toothed whales; this also has bearing on the nature and general desirability of exploitation. Differences in the rates of population production obviously have important bearing on potential recovery rates (these can be measured in terms of biomass as well as numbers) (59) after over-exploitation. In some whale species the sustainable and/or economic yields may be negligible at certain population levels (68).

The elementary dynamics of population increase have been ably summarized by a number of authors in available texts (Gulland (59), and Caughley (21), for example) and only the basic essentials are considered here. Under conditions when no checks to growth are in operation, the population will grow exponentially according to the form:

$$N_t = N_0 e^{-rt}$$

where N_0 is the initial population, N_t is the population at a later time t, and e^r is the exponential rate of increase. At any point on the line obtained by graphing numbers against time, the slope has the value rN. If one converts to natural logarithms the plotted line is straight, and much simpler to work with.

Only in rare circumstances, of course, do populations increase in this fashion for more than a short period of time. Food supply dwindles, intra-specific competition increases, and the population tends in the normal course of events, especially where large mammals are concerned, to oscillate for extended periods around a numerical plateau, known as the K value. This can perhaps be expressed as the size at which the population is in equilibrium with the mean level of available resources, and can therefore be considered a measure of the 'carrying capacity' of the environment for that population. Of course, things are rarely that simple in reality, but nevertheless, when we are talking about long-lived mammals such as whales with extended reproductive cycles, minimum litter size and relatively low mortality rates, the concept of K, at least in the short term of a few decades, probably has some reality. Lower down the food-chain, on the other hand, animal populations tend to respond much more rapidly to changes in availability of food supply, or to other favourable or unfavourable changes in environmental conditions. If those conditions improve, there is a tendency to maximize for numbers. These two extremes of population response have led some authors to categorize species as either K or r strategists. The classification is not exclusively dichotomous, and the response may depend on circumstances. Nevertheless, the magnitude of response that can occur per unit time in those species with long reproductive periods and small litter sizes is quite strictly limited (42). For a fuller treatment of this subject the reader is referred to Pianka's *Evolutionary Ecology*, which provides leads into the major literature, and many useful insights (140), and the interesting paper by Estes which deals specifically with marine mammals (42).

This model of density–dependent growth is usually referred to as 'logistic', and is described by

$$\frac{dN}{dt} = rN \left[\frac{K-N}{K} \right]$$

or, if written in terms of the rate of increase per generation,

$$\frac{dN}{dt} = N \log_e R \left[\frac{K-N}{K} \right]$$

In the first case, the size of population N at any given time t is described by:

$$N = \frac{K}{1 + e^{a-rt}}$$

where a is the constant of integration defining the position of the curve relative to the origin. Thus, when $t=0$, a has the value

$$a = \log_e \left[\frac{K-N}{N} \right]$$

In animal population literature the symbol r_m is generally used to designate the theoretical 'intrinsic rate of increase' of a population under no constraints. Year to year comparisons are made by examining ratios, either of total numbers, or with respect to selected year classes, in terms of

N at time t and N at time $t+1$. With a series of such comparisons, one can build a simple table of survivorship. The value of r_m, of course, is determined by the balance of birth rate and death rate in a particular population. Caughley (21) has argued that r is a fair measure of the 'ecological fitness' of a population, or 'demographic vigour' as it has also been called. One also has to appreciate that both survivorship and fecundity are age- and resource-dependent, and this is as true of Cetacea as any other animal. The specific rate of increase r_s (that is, the increase occurring under the prevailing balance of fecundity, birth rate and mortality) can be used to denote the maximum rate of increase. It can be seen that r_m is only a special case of r_s (21). Nevertheless, there are several good reasons for wanting to know the approximate value of r_m, for the limits of any management strategy, if nothing else. Sometimes, if we can detect changes in first-year survival or fecundity rates in young adults, we might suspect that increase or decrease in the rate of population production is occurring, but in general, as Caughley pointed out, changes in age composition alone are rarely a sound indication of increase or decrease unless accompanied by some independent evidence.

In recent years, many workers, for example, Poole (143) and Williamson (180) in the general ecological literature and M. B. Usher (172) in whale population studies, have advocated methods of analysis using the fecundity/survival matrices developed by Leslie (100). These are a powerful tool for population modelling, and save enormous amounts of time when applied through a computing language which can handle matrix calculations with great facility (APL, for example, does this far more easily than most). Unfortunately, as Caughley indicated, the method has a number of important limitations when it comes to handling real field data. He discussed alternative methods for calculating trial values for the various forms of r through simple algebraic manipulations.

It is now generally accepted by most biologists that animal populations are usually regulated by density-dependent factors, although this was a matter of considerable dispute a couple of decades ago, and one can still find some examples of populations which do not always seem to conform. Quite what the key factors are in many circumstances is still hotly debated. This is not to deny, however, that there are many fish and insect populations which can fluctuate in size by one or more orders of magnitude in successive years. The role of predation in competition was examined by Cramer and May (32) but others, Dempster for example, have argued strongly that predation (and in many cases, probably diseases as well) often appears to exercise only an incidental effect in comparison with food supply (38). Changes in other environmental conditions, such as temperature, may often leave adults unscathed but kill a large fraction of the young. It is well known, for example, that the limits of tolerance of fish fry are far less than those of adults.

In three papers on the impact of infectious diseases on populations, Anderson and May (5, 6, 114) modelled relationships for both direct and indirect host–parasite relationships to determine possible influences for regulation of the host populations. One of their interesting conclusions was that during epidemics at high population densities, host mortalities were not so much the result of enhanced transmission but brought about by the close relationship between pathogenicity and nutritional or other stress associated with the high population levels. I have noted elsewhere that 100 per cent of harbour porpoise adults carry a lungworm infestation; during good feeding years this is probably not harmful (see also Figure 6.3). These authors also presented data (6) that indicated the possible role of parasitic infections in generating long-term cycles in population size in some invertebrate species. We have no evidence, however, to suggest that such population cycling occurs to any extent in cetaceans.

There obviously *are* factors limiting the size of cetacean populations. I have argued in several publications and again in this volume that one of the most important will prove to be the *distribution* of food that can be obtained at a bioenergetic profit. Others have estimated that the total biomass of zooplankton food sources in the Antarctic is far in excess of that required for whale, seal, bird and fish populations – but that figure is irrelevant, much of that food supply is too thinly dispersed to be of any use. There is no reason at this stage to look for exotic behavioural or endogenous endocrinological controls that might serve to limit the size of whale populations until we have fully considered data which would prove or disprove whether a simple mechanism was operating. But as long as we lack a rigorous understanding of the factors underlying natural regulation of numbers, simulations of cetacean populations must, to some extent, remain only tentative analogues, and rather suspect ones at that. As Dempster (38) suggested with respect to animal ecology as a whole, we have passed, or are passing, through a phase which (largely as a result of intense love-affairs with high-speed computing systems) has seen a surfeit of models and a minimum of field data. This is as true of whale population studies as any other discipline. They have become a favourite field for theoretical modellers and indeed lend themselves rather nicely to simulations, but the paucity of fresh field information is glaringly obvious. Time and again one sees the same old whaling statistics being recycled in new forms. Some of us who saw how many of these data were collected, often under appalling field conditions, still have great reservations about their reliability, and no amount of recycling will improve that. To give two examples; as a whaling inspector twenty years ago I encountered whalers who admitted to 'stretching' whale lengths in the records (because they were sympathetic to catcher crews, who were paid by a length bonus).

These same men admitted that in the past, if no inspector or biologist was on duty, they were not above filling in some of the data on foetus presence and size 'at the end of the shift' (that is, they sat down and invented them!). Why? Because this was easier than picking their way across a deck or shore station plan (a dangerous journey) to check each whale. These men were, of course, experienced enough to know roughly what size of foetus might be expected to occur in each species at any given time of the season. Sometimes I ask myself if 'increases in pregnancy rates' from, say, 1930 to 80 don't just result to some extent from much more accurate reporting in recent years.

In conclusion, there is probably no one in whale population studies at present who would deny that the really definitive field experimental ecology has not, and is not, being carried out except on a very small scale in very restricted locations. It is not just a matter of lack of research funds; the will to fund such research has simply not been there among those governments with the resources to do it.

Analysis of multispecific interactions

There are still serious limitations to the methodologies available for determining the sizes, production, mortalities and composition of whale populations. Partly this results from deficiencies in the data themselves; published values for estimates of fin whale recruitment as late as the early 1970s, for example, ranged from 0.01 to 0.057 – almost a sixfold difference. Partly it occurs because the models used are not, on the whole, designed in such a way that they can take into account external influences such as competition for food resources by two or more species. Some authorities still seriously doubt that we can calculate the maximum-sustainable-yield level of *any* whale population accurately enough to permit us to talk, for example, about 'fishing that population at 10 per cent below the maximum-sustainable-yield level' (12, 67). The obvious limitations of single-species surplus production models have stimulated some workers to suggest that they are useless, and should be discarded in favour of more comprehensive models which analyse and take into account the ecological relationships of the species. Almost all these proposals are still experimental or speculative. Unfortunately, there is no real workable scheme of methodologies simply sitting in the wings waiting to take the place of the deterministic approach in day-to-day fisheries management, and it will be at least a decade before we can even anticipate a total change in the structure of the management process. Furthermore, as development of 'ecological models' proceeds, all kinds of pitfalls are continually being discovered. At present the best approach where whales are concerned is to stick with the existing system, and add sophistications as and when it can be done effectively. The analysis of population and system energetics has made significant strides during the last decade, and the availability of high-speed computers greatly accelerates the process of examining, trial-testing and either accepting models for further refinement or rejecting their applicability. More and more research workers are conscious of the importance of identifying and quantifying inter-specific relationships, and much study is being devoted to this end. The crying deficiency, however, is in terms of real data, not modelling abilities or potential.

The fact that has to be recognized is that we *have* operated multi-species whale fisheries in many regions for decades. Some critics will ask how, if we cannot fully understand single-species population fluctuations, can we even contemplate trying to examine more complex situations? For two reasons. First, as indicated above, multi-species whale fisheries are a reality. Second, it may well be that we will never fully understand the dynamics of one species *until* we begin to study its interactions with other components in the trophic complex. Is population recovery a simple problem which will be self-resolving with time if no further hunting is permitted, or is it a complex problem? E. Mitchell (118) speculated, for example, that the western North Atlantic right whale population might be prevented from fully exploiting its summer feeding resources off the eastern seaboard of America by competition from sei whales. There is also speculation, supported by some catch-per-unit-effort data and apparent changes in reproductive parameters, that the sei whale population of the Southern Ocean has undergone a significant increase in size during the post-1930 period, coincident with the decline in the size of the populations of fin, blue and humpback whales (47).

A useful and concise discussion of this type of problem as it affects fish communities and aquatic ecosystems was provided recently by H. A. Regier (147), and the reader may also be interested in earlier articles by Kesteven (91), Paulik (134) and Ryther (157). Regier argues that, within certain limits of accuracy, the deterministic approach works relatively well for what he refers to as 'class A populations', that is, those which have large, relatively stable stocks, with a more or less linear relationship with the food-web components on which they feed. The limits of these methods are reached rapidly, however, when the exploitation attains a level where the biomass of the major components begins to change rapidly or when more interactions start to operate, stimulated, for example, by other species being caught in large quantities.

The elementary mathematical structures for examining the interactions of different trophic levels are already defined, and these have been summarized by Caughley (21, pp. 126 ff.). Put briefly, the primary producers are basically limited by light values and sometimes by nutrient availability. At first the limitations to population increase may appear to be density independent, but this soon changes and density-dependent growth becomes evident, so that the logistic equation generally applies. In the case of the second trophic level the growth rate of populations is controlled by the availability of food resources; as the populations of secondary consumers grow, they reduce the populations of primary producers, an action which has drastic consequences for their own continued growth prospects. If a third trophic level (for example, baleen whales) is added, it has been found through simulation that the herbivore population will be shifted to a new (and lower) equilibrium level than existed when there were only two levels of interaction.

A number of workers, such as Caughley (21) and earlier May (113), have examined this kind of relationship, based on developments of the simple differential equations of the Lotka–Volterra pattern for interactions of a prey species with a predator species. These well-known equations take the following forms:

$$\frac{dN_1}{dt} = (r_1 - b_1 N_2)N_1$$

$$\frac{dN_2}{dt} = (-d + b_2 N_1)N_2$$

where N_1 is the density of the prey population, N_2 that of the predator, r_1 and r_2 are the intrinsic rates of increase, b_1 and b_2 are constants expressing the relationship of the density of one population as it affects the other, and d is the intrinsic death rate of the population N_2. The steps by which these simple concepts (which frankly do not apply in reality because they contain too many assumptions) have been developed into more realistic models by workers such as Leslie (101), Leslie and Gower (103), May (113) and Wangersky and Cunningham (177), for two-level interactions, have been summarized by Poole (143) and Williamson (180), among others.

When these analyses are applied to three levels of interaction, as with the trophic web components suggested above, Caughley pointed out that we obtain some interesting insights into the working of these systems which are not at all immediately obvious. He listed these as follows, and they provide some useful raw material for thinking about the exploitation of whales and the limitations of possible new 'ecological' policies which might be developed.

(1)   The intrinsic rate of increase of the edible vegetation has no influence on the biomass equilibrium achieved while grazing is taking place, that is, any increase is countered, after a short time-lag, by an increase in the biomass of herbivores.

(2)   This is also true of the equilibrium biomass achieved when there is no grazing pressure; it has no relationship to the equilibrium attained under grazing.

(3)   If the feeding rate of the herbivores increases, the equilibrium biomass of the vegetation does not alter (as one might think), but the biomass of the herbivores is reduced at equilibrium.

(4)   Should the intrinsic rate of production of the herbivore population increase, this results in increased biomass of herbivores at equilibrium, but a lower equilibrium biomass of vegetation.

(5)   As a general rule, changes in population parameters of the vegetation exert no influence on its biomass, but any alteration in any parameter of the herbivore population can alter the equilibrium biomass of both.

As might be expected, the situation becomes even more complex if we move on to add the effect of the secondary consumers to the pyramid. In the simplest sense, the response of the secondary consumers parallels that of the herbivores. Some systems are vertically stable, or relatively so, while others can oscillate seasonally. Increase in the number of secondary consumers can result in a fall in herbivore equilibrium biomass and, as a further result, an increase in equilibrium biomass of vegetation occurs. Some problems arise, however, when we try to apply this type of model to the diatom–zooplankton–whale situation. First, much of the published work results from studies of terrestrial ecosystems, and there is considerable debate regarding the basic similarities or differences between terrestrial and marine ecosystems. One of the prime factors in relative stability (66) in ecosystems would appear to be the 'protection' of a segment of any prey from any predator or, in practice, the protection of a segment of any trophic level from those in the next level which prey upon it (53, 103). This applies as much to vegetation as to animals. One major difference between the two systems is that 'protection' of the vegetation of the temperate or polar sea takes a totally different form from that which occurs in the terrestrial system (53), since not only is a 'permanent' vegetation lacking in the sea, but it is apparent that in many circumstances the vegetation, that is, diatoms and other planktonic algae, is grazed down as fast as it is produced, eventually to quite low levels of density by the late autumn in temperate zones.

We have an obvious interest in the stability of marine ecosystems, as witness the number of 'doom-watch' popular articles that have appeared during the last ten years or so. Looking at point (1) above, we could speculate that if some universal pollutant caused a halving of the rate of production of edible vegetation, then the whole of the second trophic level would undergo a drastic change downwards in equilibrium biomass. This would be followed, after a short time-lag, by a similar downward readjustment of the population biomass of the third-trophic-level species.

That is a view from one end of the telescope – a subject for speculative coffee-break discussion only, we hope! Of more immediate concern are possible major changes at the other end of the system. What actually happens when we remove a large fraction of the third trophic level? The simplistic type of trophodynamic thinking which dominated such discussions in the 1960s (and still today in some government-agency circles) was that by 'creaming off' most of this level, we could substantially increase the yield of usable second-trophic-level animals. The inference implicit in some documents has been that it hardly matters if whales or seals remain at low population levels, since they compete with fisheries (or potential krill harvesting) and in their absence we can take a greater lower-trophic-level harvest. In reality there are simply too many horizontal or multiple links in marine food webs for such a straightforward reaction to occur. Mixed feeders which normally function at both as first and second-level consumers may switch to consumption at the primary or the secondary levels only when such a major adjustment is made in the system. There are, for example, copepods which are both phytophagous and carnivorous (170), and fish which are both phytophagous and carnivorous (for example, anchoveta) (33). If food availability changes, it is presumably no great problem for a shift in feeding habits to take place. Probably there are few baleen whales which similarly could not make a shift from fish eating to euphausiid feeding or vice versa as circumstances dictated. Removing all the whales, for example, might not necessarily result in a higher available biomass of euphausiids for the shrimp meal industry, but instead the same biomass of euphausiids and a higher equilibrium biomass of some other small (and commercially useless) predator of euphausiids, which had hitherto fed only in part on euphausiids.

Regier (147) suggested that aquatic ecosystems perhaps have conservative features which dictate the number of trophic levels and horizontal pathways for energy transfer, so that even the most major 'tinkering' which man might contemplate at any level would have much less result than might be expected. Issacs (76), among others, has argued that highly productive marine ecosystems (in terms of fisheries yields) are often rather unstructured. Examples of these are the 'upwelling ecosystems' discussed in some detail in Chapter 1. The kinds of manipulations aimed at increasing yield which have been suggested would certainly fail in this sort of situation, with massive component removals at one level probably simply permitting the types of feeding shifts described above.

'Time-lag' effects are important in moderating or 'damping down' the amplitude of changes both in terrestrial and marine ecosystems. Variations in phytoplankton population densities are considerable; and increases can take place relatively rapidly because of the short generation times. Zooplankton generation cycles are slower, but some species can still have several each year under favourable conditions. Responses by planktonophagous fish populations takes correspondingly longer, and those by larger predatory fish and whales usually take longer still. Over relatively short periods of time, therefore, the impact of whales and other upper-trophic-level animals on the lowest part of the trophic hierarchy could well be assumed to be constant from the point of view of some modelling approaches (59). In such simulations it is perhaps wise to take relatively little notice of changes in numerical values obtained – and certainly not to try to use them in any quantitative predictive sense – but to focus upon the *types* of system changes and responses that are obtained when specific changes in inputs are made (21). At this stage of our understanding this would likely be far more valuable.

In the last few years some workers have begun to employ these kinds of processes and approaches to studies of the possible interactions between different whale species. Horwood (70) calculated the possible equilibrium yield for the southern sei whale populations for a range of fishing effort and in circumstances that took into account the best estimates for the biomass of the other species of baleen whales. The proportion of the stock that could be taken as sustainable yield at various times only varied from less than 1 per cent in about 1940 to perhaps 2 per cent at present. The numbers of whales produced from such a yield differed by far more than the percentage figures would indicate; 300 in 1940, but 13 800 at present. A small catch in the early years would have had a much more significant effect on a population that was presumably close to or at its K value than a much larger catch today. The yield was found to be very sensitive to a difference of only 1–2 per cent change in the theoretical natural mortality rate, varying by a factor of 2 in response. Data suggest that the southern sei whale is now maturing earlier, but at the same body length, indicating an increase in the growth rate (107) and in the rate of physiological maturation. The simplest explanation of increased food supply enhancing the well-being of the population has been accepted for the time being by most cetologists, in lieu of any other explanation, but that may not be all there is to the story by any means.

The model proposed by Horwood effectively assumed that a total overlap in feeding competition existed between the baleen whale species concerned. As we have seen in Chapter 2, this is not realistic, except in certain conditions of low availability of some items, and high availability and concentration of others. In these circumstances optimal foraging theory would presumably dictate that the feeding strategies of all species should converge (146). The degree and nature of dietary differences under normal conditions have been summarized by A. Kawamura and myself in recent reviews (52, 90), and also discussed in detail in Chapter 2 of this book. There is good reason to expect partial competition between southern blue and fin, and between right and sei in the North Atlantic, but it must be remembered that in the case of the former species in the Southern Ocean the degree of their spatial and temporal overlap is far from complete. Kawamura drew attention to the possible errors which can be introduced into this kind of study if only cetaceans are considered in relation to the food supply, particularly in view of the very large biomass of pinnipeds and sea-birds present in the Southern Ocean.

J. Harwood (62) designed a specific model to investigate equilibria in sei and fin whale populations where the two species were feeding together in the Icelandic whaling industry area. He specified a catch of adult animals with a two-year calving interval, and applied a pair of time-lagged Lotka–Volterra equations. He observed that for any particular value of the yield there were an infinite number of equilibrium values, as might be expected, except at the point where the rate of change of both yields was zero. He then explored the relative sensitivity of different quota policies by examining the behaviour of the equilibrium populations following the experimental input of a relatively small perturbation. I will consider some of his conclusions and the apparent implications for management in the next chapter.

Summary and conclusions

Advances in the simulation of both simple and relatively complex population systems have been striking and rapid during the last decade (28, 77), but as indicated earlier in this chapter, the collection of more sophisticated data about real whales has lagged considerably astern of the fleets of models now available to us. As one of my colleagues remarked, 'if we could only manage the real populations and the industry half as well as we can handle paper whales with the aid of the silicon chip we would be in good shape' (Figure 8.13).

The major areas of deficiency are quite evident. I am certainly *not* advocating that we throw out the (relatively) venerable methods of single-species population analysis. As Regier wrote, 'whatever the reasons, the "simplified trophic dynamics" tradition has heretofore provided little useful advice, and has contributed to a great deal of confusion, e.g. concerning the potential yields, from a practical viewpoint, of protein from the ocean'. The confident belief prevalent a few years ago that ecosystem modelling would soon solve all our problems has failed to deliver workable methodologies as yet. The approach has much promise,

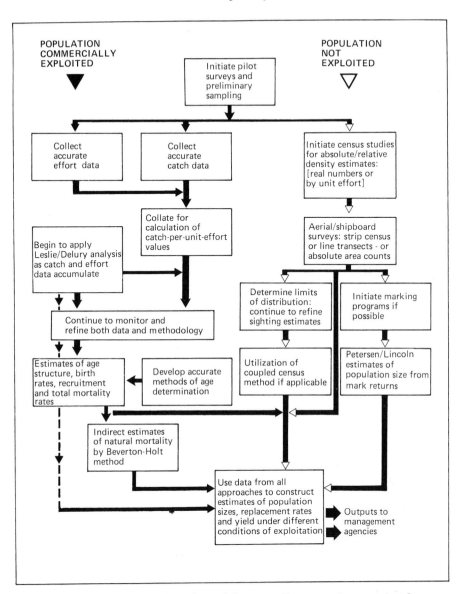

Figure 8.13 A schematic flow chart of the generally accepted approaches for determination of the population dynamics of cetacean species. Certain types of data are almost impossible to obtain without killing animals. Census methods and marking programmes (using visible tags) give some significant information on population size and dispersal, but not usually on age structure.

and there are certainly good things to come from it. On the other hand, if many whale species tend to feed selectively in relatively unstructured ecosystems with short food-chains, as I have suggested in appropriate sections of this book, then there may be very definite limits to what we may expect this type of modelling to do for us in terms of providing data for tight management policies. We will have to continue to assume that whales have a high degree of independence within the systems in which they live, and do our best to improve the basic understanding and accuracy of data for important population parameters. We need more precise methods of age determination quite urgently; but despite the considerable research being carried out on this aspect it may be that we should not anticipate very much greater accuracy, and much less variance, than we have at present. It would be useful to know more about causes and partitioning of natural mortality in whale and porpoise populations, but except at the level of occasional observation and anecdotal reporting, this problem is likely to continue to be intractable, and we will probably have to be satisfied with continued indirect estimation. In view of the depleted condition of most populations of large whales in the North Atlantic, North Pacific and Southern Ocean, probably the most valuable information we could obtain in the relatively near future would be good field data on the degree of competition between species, and between whales and other groups of upper-trophic-level animals. Our knowledge of these basic ecosystem interactions is at present no more than fragmentary, and the recovery of some whale populations may depend quite crucially on such factors.

References

1 Allen, K. R. 1966. 'Some methods for estimating exploited populations', *J. Fish. Res. Bd. Canada*, vol. 23, pp. 553–74.

2 Allen, K. R. 1969. 'An application of computers to the estimation of exploited populations', *J. Fish. Res. Bd. Canada*, vol. 26, pp. 179–89.

3 Allen, K. R. and Chapman, D. G. 1977. 'Whales' in J. A. Gulland (ed.), *Fish Population Dynamics*, London, John Wiley, pp. 335–58.

4 Allen, K. R. and Kirkwood, G. P. 1977. 'A sperm whale population model based on cohorts (SPCOH)', *Rep. Int. Whal. Commn*, vol. 27, pp. 268–71.

5 Anderson, R. M. and May, R. M. 1979. 'Population biology of infectious diseases: Part I', *Nature*, vol. 280, pp. 361–7.

6 Anderson, R. M. and May, R. M. 1980. 'Infectious diseases and population cycles of forest insects', *Science*, vol. 210, pp. 658–61.

7 Bada, J. L., Brown, S. and Masters, P. M. 1978. 'Age determination of marine mammals based on aspartic acid racemization in the teeth and lens nucleus', *Proceedings of International Conference on Determining Age of Odontocete Cetaceans*, Scripps Institution of Oceanography, La Jolla, Ca., 5–7 September 1978, p. 8.

8 Bailey, N. J. T. 1951. 'On estimating the size of mobile populations from recapture data', *Biometrika*, vol. 38, pp. 293–306.

9 Bailey, N. J. T. 1959. *Statistical Methods in Biology*, London, English Universities Press.

10 Bannister, J. L. 1969 'The biology and status of the sperm whale off Western Australia – an extended summary of results of recent work', *Rep. Int. Whal. Commn*, vol. 19, pp. 70–6.

11 Beddington, J. R. 1978. 'On the dynamics of the sei whales under exploitation', *Rep. Int. Whal. Commn*, vol. 28, pp. 169–72.

12 Beddington, J. R. 1979. 'On some problems of estimating population abundance from catch data', *Rep. Int. Whal. Commn*, vol. 29, pp. 149–54.

13 Best, P. B. 1974. 'The biology of the sperm whale as it relates to stock management' in W. E. Schevill (ed.), *The Whale Problem: A Status Report*, Cambridge, Mass., Harvard University Press, pp. 257–93.

14 Best, P. B. 1976. 'Tetracycline marking and the rate of growth layer formation in the teeth of a dolphin (*Lagenorhynchus obscurus*)', *S. Afr. J. Sci.*, vol. 72, pp. 216–18.

15 Best, P. B. 1979. 'Social organization in sperm whales' in H. E. Winn and B. L. Olla (eds.), *Behavior of Marine Animals – Current Perspectives in Research. Vol. 3: Cetaceans*, New York, Plenum Press, pp. 227–89.

16 Beverton, R. J. H. and Holt, S. J. 1957. 'On the dynamics of exploited fish populations', *Min. Agr. Fish and Food, Fisheries Investigations*, (ser. 2), vol. 19, pp. 1–533.

17 Bigg, M. A. 1976. 'Photographic identification of individual killer whales', a working paper submitted to the meeting of the Subcommittee on Small Cetaceans, Scientific Committee, International Whaling Commission, London, 7–9 June 1976.

18 Boyde, A. 1978. 'Histological study of odontocete dental tissues', *Proceedings of International Conference on Determining Age of Odontocete Cetaceans*, Scripps Institution of Oceanography, La Jolla, Ca., 5–7 September 1978, p. 17.

19 Brown, S. G. 1966. 'Whale marks recovered in the Antarctic whaling season 1965/66', *Norsk Hvalfangsttid.*, vol. 55, pp. 31–5.

20 Burnham, K. P., Anderson, D. R. and Laake, J. L. 1980. 'Estimation of density from line transect sampling of biological populations', *Wildl. Monogr.*, vol. 44, pp. 1–202.

21 Caughley, G. 1977. *Analysis of Vertebrate Populations*, New York, John Wiley.

22   Caughley, G. and Caughley, J. 1974. 'Estimating median date of birth', *J. Wildl. Mgmt.*, vol. 38, pp. 552–6.

23   Chapman, D. G. 1974. 'Status of Antarctic rorqual stocks' in W. E. Schevill (ed.), *The Whale Problem: A Status Report*, Cambridge, Mass., Harvard University Press, pp. 218–38.

24   Chittleborough, R. G. 1959. 'Determination of age in the humpback whale, *Megaptera nodosa* (Bonnaterre)', *Aust. J. mar. Freshwat. Res.*, vol. 10, pp. 125–43.

25   Chittleborough, R. G. 1960. 'Marked humpback whale of known age', *Nature*, vol. 187, p. 164.

26   Chittleborough, R. G. 1965. 'Dynamics of two populations of the humpback whale, *Megaptera novaeangliae* (Borowski)', *Aust. J. mar. Freshwat. Res.*, vol. 16, pp. 33–128.

27   Christensen, I. 1973. 'Age determination, age distribution and growth of bottlenose whales, *Hyperoodon ampullatus* (Forster), in the Labrador Sea', *Norw. J. Zool.*, vol. 21, pp. 331–40.

28   Clark, C. W. 1976. *Mathematical Bioeconomics: The Optimal Management of Renewable Resources*, New York, John Wiley.

29   Clarke, L. R., Geier, P. W., Hughes, R. D. and Morris, R. F. 1967. *The Ecology of Insect Populations in Theory and Practice*, London, Methuen.

30   Cockrill, R. 1960. 'Pathology of the Cetacea: a veterinary study on whales', *Brit. vet. J.*, vol. 116, pp. 133–44 (Part I), pp. 175–90 (Part II).

31   Cole, L. C. 1957. 'Sketches of general and comparative demography', *Cold Springs Harb, Symp., Quant. Biol.*, vol. 22, pp. 1–15.

32   Cramer, N. F. and May, R. M. 1972. 'Inter-specific competition, predation and species diversity: a comment', *J. Theor. Biol.*, vol. 34, pp. 289–93.

33   Cushing, D. H. 1978. 'Upper trophic levels in upwelling areas' in R. Boje and M. Tomczack (eds.), *Upwelling Ecosystems*, Berlin, Heidelberg and New York, Springer-Verlag, pp. 101–10.

34   Dawbin, W. H. 1959. 'Evidence of growth-rates obtained from two marked humpback whales', *Nature*, vol. 183, pp. 1749–50.

35   Dawbin, W. H. 1964. 'Movements of humpback whales marked in the southwest Pacific Ocean 1952 to 1962', *Norsk Hvalfangsttid.*, vol. 53, pp. 68–78.

36   DeLury, D. B. 1947. 'On the estimation of biological populations', *Biometrics*, vol. 3, pp. 145–67.

37   DeLury, D. B. 1958. 'The estimation of population size by a marking and recapture procedure', *J. Fish. Res. Bd. Canada*, vol. 15, pp. 19–25.

38   Dempster, J. P. 1975. *Animal Population Ecology*, London and New York, Academic Press.

39   Doi, T. 1970. 'Re-evaluation of population studies by sighting observation of whale', *Bull. Tokai Regional Fish. Res. Lab.*, vol. 63, pp. 1–10.

40   Doi, T. 1974. 'Further development of whale sighting theory' in W. E. Schevill (ed.), *The Whale Problem: A Status Report*, Cambridge, Mass., Harvard University Press, pp. 358–68.

41   Eberhardt, L. L. 1968. 'A preliminary appraisal of line transects', *J. Wildl. Mgmt.*, vol. 32, pp. 82–8.

42   Estes, J. A. 1979. 'Exploitation of marine mammals: *r*-selection of *K*-strategists?', *J. Fish. Res. Bd Canada*, vol. 36, pp. 1009–17.

43   Estes, J. A. and Gilbert, J. R. 1978. 'Evaluation of an aerial survey of Pacific Walruses (*Odobenus rosmarus divergens*)', *J. Fish. Res. Bd Canada*, vol. 35, pp. 1130–40.

44   Evans, W. E., Hall, J. D., Irvine, A. B. and Leatherwood, J. S. 1972. 'Methods for tagging small cetaceans', *Fishery Bull.*, vol. 70, pp. 61–5.

45   Fisher, H. D. and Harrison, R. J. 1970. 'Reproduction in the common porpoise (*Phocoena phocoena*) of the North Atlantic', *J. Zool.*, vol. 161, pp. 471–86.

46 Gambell, R. 1972. 'Sperm whales off Durban', *Discovery*, Rep. 35, pp. 199–358.

47 Gambell, R. 1975. 'Variations in reproductive parameters associated with whale stock sizes', *Rep. Int. Whal. Commn*, vol. 25, pp. 182–9.

48 Gambell, R. 1977. 'Southern hemisphere sperm whale catch and effort data', *Rep. Int. Whal. Commn*, vol. 27, pp. 280–6.

49 Gambell, R. 1977. 'Further analyses of tonnage corrected catch per unit effort data for male sperm whales in the southern hemisphere', *Rep. Int. Whal. Commn*, vol. 27, pp. 287–94.

50 Gaskin, D. E. 1968. 'Analysis of sightings and catches of sperm whales (*Physeter catodon* L.) in the Cook Strait area of New Zealand in 1963–4', *N.Z.J. mar. Freshwat. Res.*, vol. 2, pp. 260–72.

51 Gaskin, D. E. 1971. 'Sperm whales (*Physeter catodon* L.) in the Cook Strait region of New Zealand: some data on age, growth and mortality', *Norw. J. Zool.*, vol. 21, pp. 45–50.

52 Gaskin, D. E. 1976. 'The evolution, zoogeography and ecology of Cetacea', *Oceanogr. Mar. Biol. Ann. Rev.*, vol. 14, pp. 247–346.

53 Gaskin, D. E. 1979. 'Change of particle size in diatom populations as a possible factor in pelagic marine ecosystem resilience', *Tuatara*, vol. 24, pp. 23–39.

54 Gaskin, D. E. and Blair, B. A. 1977. 'Age determination of harbour porpoise, *Phocoena phocoena* (L.), in the western North Atlantic', *Can. J. Zool.*, vol. 55, pp. 18–30.

55 Gaskin, D. E., Smith, G. J. D. and Watson, A. P. 1975. 'Preliminary study of movements of harbour porpoises (*Phocoena phocoena*) in the Bay of Fundy using radiotelemetry', *Can. J. Zool.*, vol. 53, pp. 1466–71.

56 Graham, M. 1939. 'The sigmoid curve and the overfishing problem', *Rapp. Proc. Verb. Cons. Int. Mer.*, vol. 110, pp. 15–20.

57 Gulland, J. A. 1965. 'Estimation of mortality rates, annex to Arctic Fisheries Working Group Report', Int. Counc. Expl. Sea, annual meeting 1965 (cyclo.).

58 Gulland, J. A. 1971. 'Science and fishery management', *J. Cons. int. Explor. Mer.*, vol. 33, pp. 471–7.

59 Gulland, J. A. (ed.) 1977. *Fish Population Dynamics*, London and New York, John Wiley.

60 Gurevich, V. and Stewart, B. 1978. 'The use of tetracycline marking in age determinations of *Delphinus delphis*', *Proceedings of International Conference on Determining Age of Odontocete Cetaceans*, Scripps Institution of Oceanography, La Jolla, Ca., 5–7 September 1978, p. 9.

61 Harmsen, R., Rose, M. R. and Woodhouse, B. 1978. 'A general mathematical model for insect outbreak', *Proc. Ent. Soc. Ont.*, vol. 107, pp. 11–18.

62 Harwood, J. 1979. 'The effects of inter-specific competition on the choice of management policies for fin and sei whales', *Rep. Int. Whal. Commn*, vol. 29, pp. 167–70.

63 Helfman, P. M. and Bada, J. L. 1976. 'Aspartic acid racemization in dentine as a measure of ageing', *Nature*, vol. 262, pp. 279–81.

64 Höglund, N., Nilsson, G. and Ståfelt, F. 1967. 'Analysis of a technique for estimating willow grouse (*Lagopus lagopus*) density', *Trans. 8th Int. Cong. Game Biologists*, pp. 156–9.

65 Hohn, A. 1978. 'Comparisons of *Tursiops* tooth laminae using microradiography, SEM, and light microscopy', *Proceedings of International Conference on Determining Age of Odontocete Cetaceans*, Scripps Institution of Oceanography, La Jolla, Ca., 5–7 September 1978, p. 10.

66 Holling, C. S. 1973. 'Resilience and stability of ecological systems', *Ann. Rev. Ecol. Syst.*, vol. 4, pp. 1–23.

67 Holt, S. J. 1976. 'Objectives of management, with particular reference to whales', FAO of the UN, Scientific Consultation on Marine Mammals, Bergen, Norway,

31 August–9 September 1976, document ACMRR/MM/SC/99.

68 Holt, S. J. 1977. 'Does the bottlenose whale necessarily have a sustainable yield, and if so is it worth taking?', *Rep. Int. Whal. Commn*, vol. 27, pp. 206–8.

69 Holt, S. J. 1979. 'A simple model of pelagic whaling', *Rep. Int. Whal. Commn.*, vol. 29, pp. 155–7.

70 Horwood, J. W. 1978. 'The effect of interspecific and intraspecific competition on the population dynamics of the sei whale (*Balaenoptera borealis*)', *Rep. Int. Whal. Commn*, vol. 28, pp. 401–10.

71 Hui, C. A. 1978. 'Reliability of using dentine layers for age determination in *Tursiops truncatus*', *Proceedings of International Conference on Determining Age of Odontocete Cetaceans*, Scripps Institution of Oceanography, La Jolla, Ca., 5–7 September, 1978, p. 19.

72 Hui, C. A. 1980. 'Variability of dentin deposits in *Tursiops truncatus*', *Can. J. Fish. Aquat. Sci.*, vol. 37, pp. 712–16.

73 Ichihara, T. 1966. 'Criterion for determining age of fin whale with reference to ear plug and baleen plate', *Sci. Rep. Whales Res. Inst.*, vol. 20, pp. 17–82.

74 International Conference on Determining Age of Odontocete Cetaceans. 1978. *Proceedings (Abstracts)*, Sumner Auditorium, Scripps Institution of Oceanography, La Jolla, Ca., 5–7 September 1978.

75 Irvine, A. B., Scott, M. D., Wells, R. S., Kaufmann, J. H. and Evans, W. E. 1976. *A study of the movements and activities of the Atlantic bottlenosed dolphin*, Tursiops truncatus, *including an evaluation of tagging techniques*, final report for US Marine Mammal Commission, contracts MM4AC004 and MM5AC0018.

76 Isaacs, J. D. 1972. 'Unstructured marine food webs and pollutant analogues', *Fish. Bull.*, vol. 70, pp. 1053–9.

77 Jeffers, J. N. R. 1978. *An Introduction to Systems Analysis: with ecological applications*, Baltimore, University Park Press.

78 Johnson, D. H. 1974. 'Estimating survival rates from banding adult and juvenile birds', *J. Wildl. Mgmt.*, vol. 38, pp. 290–7.

79 Jolly, G. M. 1965. 'Explicit estimates from capture–recapture data with both death and immigration – stochastic model', *Biometrika*, vol. 52, pp. 225–47.

80 Jones, R. 1977. 'Tagging: theoretical methods and practical difficulties' in J. A. Gulland (ed.), *Fish Population Dynamics*, London, John Wiley, pp. 46–66.

81 Jonsgård, Å. 1969. 'Age determination of marine mammals' in H. T. Andersen (ed.), *The Biology of Marine Mammals*, New York, Academic Press, pp. 1–30.

82 Kapel, F. O. 1977. 'Catch of belugas, narwhals and harbour porpoises in Greenland, 1954–75, by year, month and region', *Rep. Int. Whal. Commn*, vol. 27, pp. 507–20.

83 Kasuya, T. 1972. 'Some information on the growth of the Ganges dolphin with a comment on the Indus dolphin', *Sci. Rep. Whales Res. Inst.*, vol. 24, pp. 87–108.

84 Kasuya, T. 1976. 'Reconsideration of life history parameters of the spotted and striped dolphins based on cemental layers', *Sci. Rep. Whales Res. Inst.*, vol. 28, pp. 73–106.

85 Kasuya, T. 1977. 'Age determination and growth of the Baird's beaked whale with a comment on the fetal growth rate', *Sci. Rep. Whales Res. Inst.*, vol. 29, pp. 1–20.

86 Kasuya, T. 1978. 'The life history of Dall's porpoise with special reference to the stock off the Pacific coast of Japan', *Sci. Rep. Whales Res. Inst.*, vol. 30, pp. 1–63.

87 Kasuya, T. and Brownell, R. L. Jr. 1979. 'Age determination, reproduction, and growth of Franciscana dolphin *Pontoporia blainvillei*', *Sci. Rep. Whales Res. Inst.*, vol. 31, pp. 45–67.

88 Kasuya, T., Miyazaki, N. and Dawbin, W. H. 1974. 'Growth and reproduction of *Stenella attenuata* in the Pacific coast of Japan', *Sci. Rep. Whales Res. Inst.*, vol. 26, pp. 157–226.

89 Katona, S., Baxter, B., Brazier, O., Kraus, S., Perkins, J. S. and Whitehead, H. 1979. 'Identification of humpback whales by fluke photographs' in H. E. Winn and B. L.

Olla (eds.), *Behavior of Marine Animals – Current Perspectives in Research. Vol. 3 : Cetaceans*, New York, Plenum Press, pp. 33–44.

90 Kawamura, A. 1978. 'An interim consideration on a possible interspecific relation in southern baleen whales from the viewpoint of their food habits', *Rep. Int. Whal. Commn*, vol. 28, pp. 411–19.

91 Kesteven, G. L. 1972. 'Management of the exploitation of fishery resources' in B. J. Rothschild (ed.), *World Fisheries Policy, Multidisciplinary Views*, Seattle, University of Washington Press, pp. 229–61.

92 Kimura, M. 1978. 'Variability in dentinal layer counts (age estimations) by different observers on the tooth of a known age bottlenose dolphin *Tursiops truncatus*', *Proceedings of International Conference on Determining Age of Odontocete Cetaceans*, Scripps Institution of Oceanography, La Jolla, Ca., 5–7 September 1978.

93 Kirkwood, G. P. 1979. 'The net catcher day as a measure of effort', *Rep. Int. Whal. Commn*, vol. 29, pp. 163–6.

94 Kleve'zal, G. A. 1978. 'Layers in the hard tissues of mammals as a record of growth rhythms of individuals', *Proceedings of International Conference on Determining Age of Odontocete Cetaceans*, Scripps Institution of Oceanography, La Jolla, Ca., 5–7 September 1978, p. 20.

95 Klumov, S. K. 1962. '(Right whale (Japanese) of the Pacific Ocean)', *Trudy Inst. Okeanol.*, vol. 58, pp. 202–97.

96 Laws, R. M. 1958. 'Recent investigations on fin whale ovaries', *Norsk Hvalfangsttid.*, vol. 47, pp. 225–54.

97 Laws, R. M. 1960. 'Laminated structure of bones from some marine mammals', *Nature*, vol. 187, pp. 338–9.

98 Laws, R. M. 1961. 'Reproduction, growth and age of southern fin whales', *Discovery*, Rep. 31, pp. 327–486.

99 Laws, R. M. and Purves, P. E. 1956. 'The ear plug of the Mysticeti as an indication of age with special reference to the North Atlantic fin whale (*Balaenoptera physalus* Linn.)' *Norsk Hvalfangsttid.*, vol. 45, pp. 413–25.

100 Leslie, P. H. 1948. 'Some further notes on the use of matrices in population analysis', *Biometrika*, vol. 35, pp. 213–45.

101 Leslie, P. H. 1958. 'A stochastic model for studying the properties of certain biological systems by numerical methods', *Biometrika*, vol. 45, pp. 16–31.

102 Leslie, P. H. and Davis, D. H. S. 1939. 'An attempt to determine the absolute number of rats on a given area', *J. Anim. Ecol.*, vol. 8, pp. 94–113.

103 Leslie, P. H. and Gower, J. C. 1960. 'The properties of a stochastic model for the predator–prey type of interaction between two species', *Biometrika*, vol. 47, pp. 219–34.

104 Lockyer, C. 1974. 'Investigation of the ear plug of the southern sei whale, *Balaenoptera borealis*, as a valid means of determining age', *J. Cons. int. Explor. Mer.*, vol. 36, pp. 71–81.

105 Lockyer, C. 1976. 'Growth and energy budgets of large baleen whales from the southern hemisphere', FAO of the UN, Scientific Consultation on Marine Mammals, Bergen, Norway, 31 August–9 September 1976, document ACMMR/MM/SC/41.

106 Lockyer, C. 1978. 'A theoretical approach to the balance between growth and food consumption in fin and sei whales, with special reference to the female reproductive cycle', *Rep. Int. Whal. Commn*, vol. 28, pp. 243–50.

107 Lockyer, C. 1979. 'Changes in a growth parameter associated with exploitation of southern fin and sei whales', *Rep. Int. Whal. Commn*, vol. 29, pp. 191–6.

108 Mackintosh, N. A. 1942. 'The southern stocks of whalebone whales', *Discovery*, Rep. 22, pp. 197–300.

109 Mackintosh, N. A. 1965. *The Stocks of Whales*, London, Fishing News Books.

110 Mackintosh, N. A. and Wheeler, J. F. G. 1929. 'Southern blue and fin whales', *Discovery*, Rep. 1, pp. 257–540.
111 Martin, H., Evans, W. E. and Bowers, C. A. 1971. 'Methods for radio tracking marine mammals in the open sea', *Transactions of the IEEE Conference on Engineering in the Ocean Environment*, September 1971, San Diego, Ca., pp. 44–9.
112 Mate, B. and Harvey, J. 1978. 'Acid etching and acetate peels for microresolution of dental laminations', *Proceedings of International Conference on Determining Age of Odontocete Cetaceans*, Scripps Institution of Oceanography, La Jolla, Ca., 5–7 September 1978, p. 11.
113 May, R. M. 1973. *Stability and Complexity in Model Ecosystems*, Princeton, NJ, Princeton University Press.
114 May, R. M. and Anderson, R. M. 1979. 'Population biology of infectious diseases: Part II', *Nature*, vol. 280, pp. 455–61.
115 McHugh, J. L. 1974. 'The role and history of the International Whaling Commission' in W. E. Schevill (ed.), *The Whale Problem: A Status Report*, Cambridge, Mass., Harvard University Press, pp. 305–35.
116 Mercer, M. C. 1975. 'Modified Leslie–DeLury population models of the long-finned pilot whale (*Globicephala melaena*) and annual production of the short-finned squid (*Illex illecebrosus*) based upon their interaction at Newfoundland', *J. Fish. Res. Bd Canada*, vol. 32, pp. 1145–54.
117 Mitchell, E. 1974. 'Present status of northwest Atlantic fin and other whale stocks' in W. E. Schevill (ed.), *The Whale Problem: A Status Report*, Cambridge, Mass., Harvard University Press, pp. 108–69.
118 Mitchell, E. 1975. 'Trophic relationships and competition for food in northwest Atlantic whales', *Proc. Can. Soc. Zoologists, 1974*, pp. 123–33.
119 Mitchell, E. 1978. 'Readability of growth layers in teeth of beaked whales', *Proceedings of International Conference on Determining Age of Odontocete Cetaceans*, Scripps Institution of Oceanography, La Jolla, Ca., 5–7 September 1978, p. 6.
120 Miyazaki, N. 1977. 'Growth and reproduction of *Stenella coeruleoalba* off the Pacific coast of Japan', *Sci. Rep. Whales Res. Inst.*, vol. 29, pp. 21–48.
121 Murphy, G. I. 1965. 'A solution of the catch equation', *J. Fish. Res. Bd. Canada*, vol. 22, pp. 191–202.
122 Myrick, A. C., Jr. 1978. 'The use of the petrographic microscope in examination of ultra-structure in hard tissues of odontocetes', *Proceedings of International Conference on Determining Age of Odontocete Cetaceans*, Scripps Institution of Oceanography, La Jolla, Ca., 5–7 September 1978, p. 12.
123 Nielsen, H. G. 1972. 'Age determination of the harbour porpoise *Phocoena phocoena* (L.) (Cetacea)', *Vidensk. Medd. Dan. Naturhist. Foren. Khobenhaven*, vol. 135, pp. 61–84.
124 Nishiwaki, M. 1952. 'On the age determination of the Mystacoceti, chiefly blue and fin whales', *Sci. Rep. Whales Res. Inst.*, vol. 7, pp. 87–111.
125 Nishiwaki, M. 1957. 'Age characteristics of ear plugs of whales', *Sci. Rep. Whales Res. Inst.*, vol. 12, pp. 23–32.
126 Nishiwaki, M., Ohsumi, S. and Kasuya, T. 1961. 'Age characteristics in the sperm whale mandible', *Norsk Hvalfangsttid.*, vol. 50, pp. 499–507.
127 Norris, K. S. and Gentry, R. L. 'Capture and harnessing of young California gray whales *Eschrichtius robustus*', *Mar. Fish Rev.*, vol. 36, pp. 58–64.
128 Ohsumi, S. 1962. 'Biological material obtained by Japanese expeditions from marked fin whales', *Norsk Hvalfangsttid.*, vol. 51, pp. 192–8.
129 Ohsumi, S. 1964. 'Examination on age determination of the fin whale', *Sci. Rep. Whales Res. Inst.*, vol. 18, pp. 49–88.
130 Ohsumi, S. 1970. 'A trial to get mathematical models of population for sperm whale', document, Scientific Committee of the International Whaling Commission, 22nd

meeting (not seen, cited by Best, 1974).

131   Ohsumi, S. and Masaki, Y. 1978. 'Age-length keys and growth curves of the southern hemisphere sei whale', *Rep. Int. Whal. Commn*, vol. 28, pp. 431–6.

132   Ohsumi, S. and Yamamura, K. 1978. 'Catcher's hour's work and its correction as a measure of fishing effort for sei whales in the Antarctic', *Rep. Int. Whal. Commn*, vol. 28, pp. 459–68.

133   Orians, G. H. and Leslie, P. H. 1958. 'A capture–recapture analysis of a shearwater population', *J. Animal. Ecol.*, vol. 27, pp. 71–86.

134   Paulik, G. J. 1972. 'Fisheries and the quantitative revolution', in B. J. Rothschild (ed.), *World Fisheries Policy, Multidisciplinary Views*, Seattle, University of Washington Press, pp. 219–28.

135   Payne, R. S. 1972. 'Report from Patagonia: the right whales', *New York Zoological Society*.

136   Perkins, J. S. and Beamish, P. C. 1979. 'Net entanglements of baleen whales in the inshore fishery of Newfoundland', *J. Fish. Res. Bd. Canada*, vol. 36, pp. 521–8.

137   Perrin, W. F., Holts, D. B. and Miller, R. B. 1977. 'Growth and reproduction of the eastern spinner dolphin, a geographical form of *Stenella longirostris* in the eastern tropical Pacific', *Fishery Bull.*, vol. 75, pp. 725–50.

138   Perrin, W. F., Smith, T. D. and Sakagawa, G. T. 1975. 'Status of populations of spotted dolphin, *Stenella attenuata*, and spinner dolphin, *Stenella longirostris*, in the eastern tropical Pacific', FAO of the UN, Scientific Consultation on Marine Mammals, Bergen, Norway, 31 August–9 September 1976, document ACMRR/MM/SC/27.

139   Peters, N. 1939. Über Grösse, Wachstum, und Alter des Blauwales (*Balaenoptera musculus* L.) und Finnwales (*Balaenoptera physalus* L.)', *Zool. Anz.*, vol. 127, pp. 193–204.

140   Pianka, E. R. 1974. *Evolutionary Ecology*, New York, Harper & Row.

141   Pierce, K. V. and Kajimura, H. 1978. 'Acid etching and highlighting for defining growth layers in cetacean teeth', *Proceedings of International Conference on Determining Age of Odontocete Cetaceans*, Scripps Institution of Oceanography, La Jolla, Ca., 5–7 September 1978, p. 5.

142   Pippard, L. and Malcolm, H. 1978. 'White whales (*Delphinapterus leucas*): observations on their distribution, population and critical habitats in the St Lawrence and Saguenay Rivers', Department of Indian and Northern Affairs, and Parks Canada, project C1632, contract 76/190.

143   Poole, R. W. 1974. *Quantitative Ecology*, New York, McGraw-Hill.

144   Price, W. S. 1980. Personal communication.

145   Purves, P. E. 1955. 'The wax plug in the external auditory meatus of the Mysticeti', *Discovery*, Rep. 27, pp. 293–302.

146   Rapport, D. J. and Turner, J. E. 1975. 'Feeding rates and population growth', *Ecology*, vol. 56, pp. 942–9.

147   Regier, H. A. 1977. 'Fish communities and aquatic ecosystems' in J. A. Gulland (ed.), *Fish Population Dynamics*, London, John Wiley, pp. 134–55.

148   Rice, D. W. and Wolman, A. A. 1971. 'The life history and ecology of the gray whale (*Eschrichtius robustus*)', *Am. Soc. Mammalogists, Special Publ.*, no. 3.

149   Ricker, W. E. 1958. 'Handbook of computations for biological statistics of fish populations', *Bull. Fish. Res. Bd Canada*, vol. 119, pp. 1–300.

150   Robins, J. P. 1954. 'Ovulation and pregnancy corpora lutea in the ovaries of the humpback whale', *Nature*, vol. 173, pp. 201–3.

151   Robins, J. P. 1960. 'Age studies on the female humpback whale, *Megaptera nodosa* (Bonnaterre), in east Australian waters', *Aus. J. mar. Freshwat. Res.*, vol. 11, pp. 1–13.

152   Roe, H. S. J. 1967. 'Seasonal formation of laminae in the ear plug of the fin whale', *Discovery*, Rep 35, pp. 1–30.

153 Ruud, J. T. 1940. 'The surface structure of the baleen plates as a possible clue to age in whales', *Hvalråd Skr.*, vol. 23, pp. 1–23.

154 Ruud, J. T. 1945. 'Further studies on the structure of the baleen plates and their application to age determination', *Hvalråd. Skr.*, vol. 29, pp. 1–69.

155 Ruud, J. T. 1950. 'Investigations of the age of blue whales in the Antarctic pelagic catches 1945/46–1948/49', *Norsk Hvalfangsttid.*, vol. 39, pp. 245–61.

156 Ruud, J. T., Jonsgård, Å. and Ottestad, P. 1950. 'Age studies on blue whales', *Hvalråd. Skr.*, vol. 33, pp. 1–71.

157 Ryther, J. H. 1969. 'Photosynthesis and fish production in the sea', *Science*, vol. 166, pp. 72–6.

158 Schaefer, M. B. 1954. 'Some aspects of the dynamics of populations important to the management of commercial marine fisheries', *Inter-Amer. Trop. Tuna Comm. Bull.*, vol. 1, pp. 26–56.

159 Schaefer, M. B. 1957. 'A study of the dynamics of the fishery for yellowfin tuna in the eastern tropical Pacific Ocean', *Inter-Amer. Trop. Tuna Comm. Bull.*, vol. 2, pp. 247–85.

160 Schumacher, A. 1970. 'Bestimmung der fischereilichen Sterblichkeit beim Kabeljaubestand von Westgrönland', *Ber. Dt. Wiss. Komm. Meeresforsch.*, vol. 21, pp. 248–59.

161 Schumacher, F. X. and Eschmeyer, R. W. 1943. 'The estimation of fish populations in lakes and ponds', *J. Tenn. Acad. Sci.*, vol. 18, pp. 228–49.

162 Scoresby, W. 1820. *An Account of the Arctic Regions, with a History and Description of the Northern Whale Fishery*, Edinburgh.

163 Seber, G. A. 1970. 'Estimating time-specific survival and reporting rates for adult birds from band returns', *Biometrika*, vol. 57, pp. 313–18.

164 Seber, G. A. 1972. 'Estimating survival rates from bird-band returns', *J. Wildl. Mgmt.*, vol. 36, pp. 405–13.

165 Sergeant, D. E. 1959. 'Age determination in odontocete whales from dentinal growth layers', *Norsk Hvalfangsttid.*, vol. 48, pp. 273–88.

166 Sergeant, D. E. 1962. 'The biology of the pilot or pothead whale *Globicephala melaena* (Traill) in Newfoundland waters', *Bull. Fish. Res. Bd Canada*, vol. 132, pp. 1–84.

167 Sergeant, D. E. 1973. 'Biology of white whales (*Delphinapterus leucas*) in Western Hudson Bay', *J. Fish. Res. Bd Canada*, vol. 30, pp. 1065–90.

168 Sergeant, D. E., Caldwell, D. K. and Caldwell, M. C. 1973. 'Age, growth and maturity of bottlenosed dolphin (*Tursiops truncatus*) from northeast Florida', *J. Fish. Res. Bd Canada*, vol. 30, pp. 1009–11.

169 Solomon, M. E. 1969. *Population Dynamics*, London, The Institute of Biology/ Edward Arnold.

170 Steele, J. H. 1974. *The Structure of Marine Ecosystems*, Oxford, Blackwell Scientific Publications.

171 Tillman, M. F. 1978. 'Modified DeLury estimates of the North Pacific Bryde's Whale stock', *Rep. Int. Whal. Commn*, vol. 28, pp. 313–14.

172 Usher, M. B. 1976. 'Leslie matrix models and whale populations', FAO of the UN, Scientific Consultation on Marine Mammals, Bergen, Norway, 31 August–9 September 1976, document ACMRR/MM/SC/126.

173 Van Lennep, E. W. 1950. 'Histology of the corpora lutea in blue and fin whale ovaries', *Proc. Kon. Ned. Acad. Wet.*, vol. 53, pp. 593–9.

174 Van Utrecht, W. L. 1966. 'On the growth rate of the baleen plate of the fin whale and the blue whale', *Bijdr. Dierk.*, vol. 35, pp. 1–38.

175 Van Utrecht, W. L. 1978. 'Age and growth in *Phocoena phocoena* Linnaeus, 1758 (Cetacea, Odontoceti) from the North Sea', *Bijdr. Dierk.*, vol. 48, pp. 16–28.

176 Van Utrecht-Cock, C. N. 1966. 'Age determination and reproduction in female fin whales, *Balaenoptera physalus* (Linnaeus, 1758) with special regard to baleen

plates and ovaries', *Bijdr. Dierk.*, vol. 35, pp. 39–100.

177 Wangersky, P. J. and Cunningham, W. J. 1957. 'Time lag in population models', *Cold Springs Harbor Symp. Quant. Biol.*, vol. 22, pp. 329–38.

178 Watkins, W. A. 1981. 'Radio tagging of finback whales – Iceland, June–July 1980', technical report, Woods Hole Oceanographic Institution, WHOI–81–2, pp. 1–46.

179 Watkins, W. A., Wartzok, D., Martin, H. B. and Maiefski, R. R. 1980. 'A radio whale tag' in F. P. Diemer, F. J. Vernberg and D. Z. Merkes (eds.), *Advanced Concepts in Ocean Measurements for Marine Biology*, Columbia, SC, The Belle W. Baruch Library in Marine Science Publication, no. 10, University of South Carolina Press, pp. 227–41.

180 Williamson, M. 1972. *The Analysis of Biological Populations*, London, Edward Arnold.

181 Yasui, W. Y. 1980. 'Morphometrics, hydrodynamics, and energetics of locomotion for a small cetacean, *Phocoena phocoena* L.', M.Sc. thesis, University of Guelph, Ontario.

182 Yurick, D. B. 1977. 'Populations, subpopulations, and zoogeography of harbour porpoise, *Phocoena phocoena* (L.)', M.Sc. thesis, University of Guelph, Ontario.

Table 8.1 Summary of best estimates of present population sizes of commercially exploited Cetacea, subdivided by regions where possible

Species	Region	Best estimate of population size	References and comments
Bowhead or Greenland right whale (*Balaena mysticetus*)	West American Arctic	2200 (1783–2865)	Apparently showing signs of real recovery from near-extinct state: aboriginal hunting needs tight control in this critical phase. *Rep. Int. Whal. Commn.* (1979), vol. 29, pp. 84; Braham *et al.* 1979.
	East American Arctic	50 + ?	Remnant; no sign of real recovery; Mansfield, 1971.
	European Arctic	Low tens to extinct?	Tiny remnant if exists at all: sightings may be strays from East Arctic.
	Asiatic Arctic	No estimate available	
Some aboriginal hunting only		*Total* about 2500?	
Black right whale (*Eubalaena glacialis*)	Western North Atlantic	High tens to low hundreds	Mitchell, 1974. Apparently recolonizing southern part of original range: possibly increasing in numbers.

Species	Region	Best estimate of population size	References and comments
	Eastern North Atlantic	No estimate available	Tiny remnant: no evidence of recovery.
	Western North Pacific	134	Ohsumi and Wada, 1974; Wada, 1976; no evidence of increase.
	Eastern North Pacific	120	Ohsumi and Wada, 1974; Wada, 1976; no evidence of increase.
	Okhotsk Sea	High tens?	Klumov, 1962
	Southern Ocean	1500–3000	Doi *et al.*, 1971; Best, 1974; Masaki, 1979. Slow recovery possibly occurring in South African sector, but little or no indication of clear overall population growth in other sectors.
[Protected]		*Total* Perhaps 3500	
Gray whale (*Eschrichtius robustus*)	Eastern North Pacific	11 000 (7000–15 000)	Apparently stable. Wolman and Rice, 1979; Rugh and Braham, 1979.
[Protected]		*Total* 11 000 (7000–15 000)	
Great blue whale (*Balaenoptera musculus*)	Western North Atlantic	Low hundreds to 1500	Mitchell, 1974.
	Eastern North Atlantic	No recent estimate; high tens or low hundreds.	Remnant: hunted to near extinction by coastal and pelagic whalers from Norway in early 1900s.
	Western North Pacific	480	Ohsumi and Wada, 1974; Wada, 1976; no clear increase seen.
	Eastern North Pacific	1290	Ohsumi and Wada, 1974; Wada, 1976; no clear increase seen.

Species	Region	Best estimate of population size	References and comments
	Southern Ocean	8400 (6400–10600)	Changes in factory ship distributions in the last fifteen years make interpretation of sighting data very difficult; no definite trends can be established, despite assertions that some recovery is occurring.
[Protected]		*Total* 7000–13000	
Pygmy blue whale (*B. m. brevicauda*)	Southern Ocean	Low hundreds	Slow recovery probable, but data are not unequivocal.
[Protected]		*Total* Low hundreds	
Humpback whale (*Megaptera novaeangliae*)	Western North Pacific	1000	Ohsumi and Masaki, 1972; Wada, 1976.
	Eastern North Pacific	1000	Ohsumi and Masaki, 1972; Wada, 1976.
	Western North Atlantic	1380–2300	Mitchell, 1974; *Rep. Int. Whal. Comm.* (1979), vol. 29, p. 85.
	Eastern North Atlantic	No estimate	Remnant.
	Southern Ocean (areas)	I High tens to low hundreds	
		II 170+	Best, 1974.
		III 340+	Best, 1974.
		IV 800+	Ohsumi and Masaki, 1972.
		V and VI 200+	Ohsumi and Masaki, 1972; Masaki, 1979.
[Protected, except for limited aboriginal hunting]		*Total* 3000–5000	
Fin whale (*Balaenoptera physalus*)	Western North Pacific	6000	Omura and Ohsumi, 1974; Wada, 1976.

Species	Region	Best estimate of population size	References and comments
	Eastern North Pacific	9000	Omura and Ohsumi, 1974; Wada, 1976.
	East China Sea	High hundreds to low thousands	
	Western North Atlantic	3000	Average of several methods; Mitchell, 1974.
	Central and eastern North Atlantic	6000–11000	Jonsgård, 1974; Rørvik *et al.*, 1976; Sergeant, 1977.
	Southern Ocean	70000–85000	Chapman, 1974; Masaki, 1979; Chapman and Breiwick, 1979. There are significant differences in the state of stocks in the various Antarctic areas. That of area VI is probably in best condition (*Rep. Int. Whal. Commn.* (1979), vol. 29, p. 85).
[Partially protected]		*Total* probably substantially less than 88000	
Sei whale (*Balaenoptera borealis*)	Western North Pacific	17660	Ohsumi and Wada, 1974; Wada, 1976. Estimates are probably too high.
	Eastern North Pacific	18040	,,
	Western North Atlantic	1800–2500	Mitchell, 1974.
	Eastern North Atlantic	High hundreds to low thousands?	Jonsgård, 1974.
	Southern Ocean	70000–100000?	Chapman, 1974; Masaki, 1979.
[Partially protected]		*Total* probably less than 130000	

Species	Region	Best estimate of population size	References and comments
Bryde's whale (*Balaenoptera edeni*)	Western North Pacific	18 200 (Bonin Islands), + 36 800 (pelagic)	Ohsumi, 1978.
	Eastern North Pacific	*c.* 10 000	Rice, 1974, 1979; unexploited.
	North Pacific total	15 000	Privalikhin and Berzin, 1978.
	North Pacific total	17 800	Tillman, 1978.
	South Pacific	No estimate – 20 000?	—
	South African waters	15 500	Best, 1974: stable.
		Total Well in excess of 80 000; unexploited in most warm water regions.	
Minke whale (*Balaenoptera acutorostrata*)	Eastern North Atlantic	50 500	Jonsgård, 1974; Christensen & Rørvik, 1979.
	Western North Atlantic	No good estimate: some thousands?	Mitchell, 1974.
	North Pacific	9000	Wada, 1976.
	Southern Ocean	224 600	Ohsumi, 1978.
		108 900–389 200	Report of the Scientific committee, 1979 (p. 79).
		Total 113 000– 646 780	Masaki, 1979.
Sperm whale (*Physeter catodon*)	North Atlantic South Atlantic (above 30°S)	22 000? 27 000?	E. Mitchell's rough estimate – probably at least of the right order of magnitude.
	North Pacific total	118 000 (male); 210 000 (female)	Chapman, 1977.
	North Pacific total	138 000–233 000	Wada, 1976 (for 1973, 1974, based on sightings).
	North pacific total	215 500	Ohsumi and Fukuda, 1974.

Species	Region	Best estimate of population size	References and comments
	East tropical Pacific	81 000 ± 30 000	Rice, 1977.
	Southern Ocean (areas)	I 34 000	Rough estimate based on sightings (International Whaling Commission, 1973).
		II and III 33 500 IV 47 000+ females 31 400+ males V 32 000+ VI 15 700+	International Whaling Commission, 1973. Bannister, 1974; based on estimate of female stock of 47 000: Bannister, 1969, for male estimates.
	All Southern Ocean areas	c. 202 000 (193 600)	Summed from area estimates.
	Eastern South Pacific (coasts of Peru–Chile)	45 000	International Whaling Commission, 1973.
	Central Pacific	38 000+	International Whaling Commission, 1973.
	Central Indian Ocean	29 000+ ?	International Whaling Commission, 1973.
	Total 567 800+		Despite local over-exploitation of males, the global sperm whale population appears at present in a satisfactory condition.
Pacific spotted dolphin (*Stenella attenuata*)	Eastern tropical Pacific	3 674 000	Rep. Sci. Committee, 1978.
Pacific spinner dolphin (*Stenella longirostris*)	Eastern tropical Pacific	1 292 000	Rep. Sci. Committee, 1978.
Common dolphin (*Delphinus delphis*)	Eastern tropical Pacific	1 430 000	Rep. Sci. Committee, 1978.
Bottlenosed dolphin (*Tursiops sp.*)	Eastern tropical Pacific	588 000	Rep. Sci. Committee, 1978.

References

1   Bannister, J. L. 1969. 'The biology and status of the sperm whale off Western Australia – an extended summary of results of recent work', *Rep. Int. Whal. Commn*, vol. 19, pp. 70–6.

2   Bannister, J. L. 1974. 'Whale populations and current research off Western Australia' in W. E. Schevill (ed.), *The Whale Problem: A Status Report*, Cambridge, Mass., Harvard University Press, pp. 239–54.

3   Best, P. B. 1974. 'Status of the whale populations off the west coast of South Africa, and current research' in W. E. Schevill (ed.), *The Whale Problem: A Status Report*, Cambridge, Mass., Harvard University Press, pp. 53–81.

4   Braham, H. W., Krogman, B., Leatherwood, J. S., Marquette, W., Rugh, D., Tillman, M., Johnson, J. and Carroll, G. 1979. 'Preliminary report of the 1978 spring bowhead whale research program results', *Rep. Int. Whal. Commn*, vol. 29, pp. 291–306.

5   Chapman, D. G. 1974. 'Status of Antarctic rorqual stocks' in W. E. Schevill (ed.), *The Whale Problem: A Status Report*, Cambridge, Mass., Harvard University Press, pp. 218–38.

6   Chapman, D. G. and Breiwick, J. 1979. 'Updated estimates of fin whale stocks in southern oceans', appendix I to the Report of the Scientific Committee, Annex G, *Rep. Int. Whal. Commn*, vol. 29, p. 86.

7   Christensen, I. and Rørvik, C. J. 1979. 'Stock estimate of minke whales in the Svalbard–Norway–British Isles area from markings and recoveries 1974–77', *Rep. Int. Whal. Commn*, vol. 29, pp. 461–2.

8   Doi, T., Ohsumi, S. and Shimadzu, Y. 1971. 'Status of baleen whales in the Antarctic, 1970/71', *Rep. Int. Whal. Commn*, vol. 21, pp. 90–9.

9   International Whaling Commission. *Rep. Int. Whal. Commn*, 1973. vol. 23, pp. 28–43; 1978, vol. 28, pp. 38–89; 1979, vol. 29, pp. 38–105.

10 Jonsgård, Å. 1974. 'On whale exploitation in the eastern part of the North Atlantic Ocean' in W. E. Schevill (ed.), *The Whale Problem: A Status Report*, Cambridge, Mass., Harvard University Press, pp. 97–107.

11 Klumov, S. K. 1962. '(Right whale (Japanese) of the Pacific Ocean)', *Trudy Inst. Okeanol.*, vol. 8, pp. 206–19.

12 Mansfield, A. W. 1971. 'Occurrence of the bowhead or Greenland right whale (*Balaena mysticetus*) in Canadian arctic waters', *J. Fish. Res. Bd Canada*, vol. 28, pp. 1873–5.

13 Masaki, Y. 1979. 'Japanese pelagic whaling and whale sighting in the 1977/78 Antarctic season', *Rep. Int. Whal. Commn*, vol. 29, pp. 225–52.

14 Mitchell, E. 1974. 'Present status of northwest Atlantic fin and other whale stocks' in W. E. Schevill (ed.), *The Whale Problem: A Status Report*, Cambridge, Mass., Harvard University Press, pp. 108–69.

15 Ohsumi, S. 1978a. 'Assessment of population sizes of the southern hemisphere minke whales adding the catch data in 1976/77', *Rep. Int. Whal. Commn.*, vol. 28, pp. 273–6.

16 Ohsumi, S. 1978b. 'Bryde's whales in the North Pacific in 1976', *Rep. Int. Whal. Commn*, vol. 28, pp. 277–80.

17 Ohsumi, S. and Fukuda, Y. 1974. 'Revised sperm whale population model and its application to the North Pacific sperm whale', *Rep. Int. Whal. Commn*, vol. 24, pp. 91–101.

18 Ohsumi, S. and Masaki, Y. 1972. 'Status of stocks of baleen whales in the Antarctic, 1971/72', *Rep. Int. Whal. Commn*, vol. 22, pp. 60–8.

19 Ohsumi, S. and Wada, S. 1974. 'Status of whale stocks in the North Pacific, 1972', *Rep. Int. Whal. Commn*, vol. 24, pp. 114–26.

20 Omura, H. and Ohsumi, S. 1974. 'Research on whale biology of Japan with special

reference to the North Pacific stocks' in W. E. Schevill (ed.), *The Whale Problem : A Status Report*, Cambridge, Mass., Harvard University Press, pp. 196–208.

21 Privalikhin, V. I. and Berzin, A. A. 1978. 'Abundance and distribution of Bryde's whale (*Balaenoptera edeni*) in the Pacific Ocean', *Rep. Int. Whal. Commn*, vol. 28, pp. 301–2.

22 Rice, D. W. 1974. 'Whales and whale research in the eastern North Pacific' in W. E. Schevill (ed.), *The Whale Problem: A Status Report*, Cambridge, Mass., Harvard University Press, pp. 170–95.

23 Rice, D. W. 1977. 'Sperm whales in the equatorial eastern Pacific: population size and social organization', *Rep. Int. Whal. Commn*, vol. 27, pp. 333–6.

24 Rice, D. W. 1979. 'Bryde's whales in the equatorial eastern Pacific', *Rep. Int. Whal. Commn*, vol. 29, pp. 321–4.

25 Rørvik, C. J., and Jongsård, Å., 1976. 'Review of balaenopterids in the North Atlantic Ocean', FAO of the UN, Scientific Consultation on Marine Mammals, Bergen, Norway, 31 August–9 September 1976, document ACMRR/MM/SC/13.

26 Rugh, D. J. and Braham, H. W. 1979. 'California gray whale (*Eschrichtius robustus*) fall migration through Unimak Pass, Alaska, 1977: a preliminary report', *Rep. Int. Whal. Commn*, vol. 29, pp. 315–20.

27 Sergeant, D. E. 1977. 'Stocks of fin whales *Balaenoptera physalus* L. in the North Atlantic Ocean',*Rep. Int. Whal. Commn.*, vol. 27, pp. 460–73.

28 Tillman, M. F. 1978. 'Estimates of abundance determined from catch per unit effort and age distribution data for stocks of southern hemisphere sei whales', *Rep. Int. Whal. Commn*, vol. 28, pp. 473–5.

29 Wada, S. 1976. 'Indices of abundance of large-sized whales in the North Pacific in the 1974 whaling season', *Rep. Int. Whal. Commn*, vol. 26, pp. 382–91.

30 Wolman, A. A. and Rice, D. W. 1979. 'Current status of the gray whale', *Rep. Int. Whal. Commn*, vol. 29, pp. 275–80.

CHAPTER 9

Management of cetacean populations

Introduction

There is a tendency for many people, including biologists, to view 'whale population management' simply in terms of the policies of the International Whaling Commission. Although this is not surprising, it is far too narrow a view, and broader issues are involved. Successful long-term management, or even just simple preservation in some cases, may depend on actions taken far beyond the confines of a single commission controlling hunting.

This is not to deny that hunting has played a singular role in the collapse of the populations of the large baleen whales. 'What of the right, humpback and blue whales?' one might ask. 'Surely there is no doubt that these species were hunted to the point of extinction?' True enough, but in each case there were special reasons why this happened. For one thing, the value of the products from a single right whale was so high a century and a half ago that even difficult hunting under conditions of low population densities was worth the economic risk. Yet if the blue whale had been the *only* species of large rorqual worth taking on the high seas by modern whaling vessels, simple economic considerations would have dictated that pelagic hunting cease long before the Southern Ocean population reached the residual level existing at the time it was given final protection in the mid-1960s. The North Atlantic population, on the other hand, would have fared badly in any case, because too many of its temperate and subarctic feeding grounds can be exploited by relatively inexpensive whaling operations using shore-based catchers. In southern pelagic seas the decline of the blue whale continued below what has been called 'the primary level of economic extinction' for two reasons; (a) there were still abundant fin whale and sei whale stocks to sustain factory ship operations in Antarctic waters, and (b) disagreements within the International Whaling Commission permitted the capture of blue whales when encountered during the search for other species. This continued long after the majority of scientists had demanded full protection. One can make a case for genuine disbelief in certain segments of the industry that the species which had sustained them for so long could be in such a parlous state. Some captains, conscious of the vagaries of feeding ground stability, argued for several years that the blue whales were either staying north of the 40°S parallel, where the expeditions were not allowed to hunt, or alternatively had gone right down into the leads of the fast ice on the Antarctic margin where the chasers dare not follow. Man has considerable capacity for self-delusion when the truth is unpalatable. On the other hand, there is evidence, and some sound economic theory (17), to suggest that senior officials of industry knew precisely what was going on, and had no intention of ceasing the hunt for blues until literally forced to. Furthermore, it has been argued that industries of this type have not, do not and never will have a basic commitment to the concept of sustainable yield fishing or hunting, because it makes less economic sense (in the narrow view of making money, and especially in times of inflation) than intensive rapid-return exploitation, regardless of the biological consequences. I will return to this discussion later (pp. 375–7). There is also evidence that in some countries this attitude by industry was actively or passively supported by those very government agencies naively believed by the general public to be deeply committed to the preservation or conservation of national and international renewable resources. Caughley (13) discussed the well-known case of the last years of the Australian humpback whale fishery, when quotas continued to be set by the government and accepted by the industry, which were known to be far greater than the catch levels that the surviving populations could tolerate. Justification for this was based in part on the hypothesis that the pelagic nations were not toeing the line on humpback protection – so the coastal whaling nations saw no reason to do so either. If we look back at those days, even the most pessimistic of us is forced to admit that we have seen some improvements in public and government attitudes since then.

I indicated above that the humpback and right whales should also be considered as special cases. Humpbacks too were taken after the point of 'economic extinction', as they were encountered during the search for fin and sei, but an additional factor was involved. Coastal whaling industries and pelagic expeditions operating in temperate coastal waters were able to inflict significant damage on humpback populations, as their predecessors had done to the right whale populations a hundred and fifty years before, because right whales aggregate in temperate shallow waters to breed, and humpbacks pass through these areas on the way to tropical breeding grounds. As a result of this concentration in easily accessible regions, the populations of both species are vulnerable to unsophisticated hunting operations using small vessels of limited range.

Safeguarding populations which are not protected or have never been deliberately hunted

Habitat protection

It is difficult for the average person to accept the idea that habitat modification or destruction could play anything other than a very minor role in the decline of cetacean populations, simply because we have come to accept, with a fair degree of evidence, that excessive hunting is the greatest danger that these animals face. Yet, as Caughley (13) has pointed out, in the case of terrestrial animal populations (and this applies to freshwater populations as well), habitat modification is almost always the major cause of declines or extinctions, *not* hunting or fishing operations, even though these contribute.

Humpbacks, right whales, the Californian gray whale and some small odontocetes have rather critical need for shallow water conditions during part of their reproductive cycles. This is clearly recognized, even though the reasons for this requirement are poorly understood (36) (see Chapter 1). Consequently, these species are not only vulnerable to shore-based hunting operations, but also to habitat modifications and destruction. Although we are generally accustomed to think of this in terms of the actions of man, it can take many other forms, especially over long periods of time. Volcanic subsidence of an atoll region, for example, could, over the course of a few hundred to a few thousand years, or even shorter periods, eliminate major breeding grounds for humpback whales. Extensive silting of bays as a result of run-off, caused by increases in rainfall in a region, could destroy calving areas for some of the three large species of baleen whale mentioned above. Humpback whales, for example, have been noted to detour around turbid areas when passing through shallow New Zealand coastal waters on migration (19).

Under normal circumstances, changes of this nature might take place over hundreds, thousands or tens of thousands of years, allowing long periods of time during which it is highly likely that some populations could adopt to new conditions. Variations in sea level during the Pleistocene certainly caused extensive coastline modification. The changes wrought by man, on the other hand, can begin to take effect after periods of months or just a very few years. In tropical Australia, the Caribbean, among the Pacific islands such as Hawaii, in the Gulf of California and the estuary of the St Lawrence coastal areas important to these species of large whale are being threatened by the development of hotel resort areas, military facilities, wharves and breakwaters which change the local current patterns and facilitate silting, and the acoustic disturbance that comes with vast increases in boat traffic of all kinds. There are data, for example, which support the view that the population of white whales in the outer estuary of the St Lawrence, Canada, was seriously affected by the hydroelectric developments on the Manicouagan River, which closed important feeding (and probably mating areas) to these animals (82). The Mexican government took action in recent years to close off access to the crucial breeding lagoons occupied by the Californian gray whale population during the southern phase of the coastal migration. Efforts are under way in Hawaii to have particular coastal areas used by humpbacks in the winter declared sanctuaries, and for boat traffic to be required to detour around those areas during certain times. Most attention is naturally drawn to the plight of the large species, but threats to the habitats of small odontocetes should not be overlooked. In the last few years the International Whaling Commission (93) and other conservation agencies have expressed concern over the conservation of fluvial and estuarine species such as *Phocoena sinus* (the Cochito) in the upper regions of the Gulf of California, and the various river dolphins such as *Inia* and *Platanista*. These populations have obviously survived long periods of hunting by man, and this is not the most serious danger faced by some species. Modifications to the flow of the Indus, Ganges and Brahmaputra rivers in the Indian subcontinent, especially by the introduction of barrages for hydroelectric development, have caused some serious habitat changes. The barrages have the effect of cutting the populations into small, possibly non-viable segments which are unable to interchange and interbreed (50, 51). Studies were initiated on these populations a few years ago, and there seem to be grounds for a reasonably encouraging outlook in some cases (79). Progress has been made in reducing hunting by river-dwelling communities and trying to cut down on incidental net catches, and with this mortality check removed, *Platanista* appears to be increasing again in one or two areas where it was considered threatened (81).

Potentially, one of the most widespread threats to the well-being of cetacean populations is the cumulative effect of toxic chemicals reaching the sea from urban, industrial and agricultural effluent, and becoming incorporated into the food-chain. This problem is discussed in detail in Chapter 10, but I can say now that at present we have no firm idea how real this threat is, or could prove to be in the future. The only sensible course of action is to devote considerable effort to ensure that these inputs are minimized, since obviously they cannot be curtailed completely.

Harassment

There is little doubt that strong pressure through the newspapers, magazines, television, radio, petitions and other forms of lobbying have had marked effects on the official policies of some nations towards commercial whaling. Public awareness, however, can be a two-edged sword. Intentional harassment of cetaceans is sporadic and essentially random, like any other form of cruelty to animals. Often those bearing down on large baleen whales in fast speedboats have little idea that they may be causing discomfort or outright distress to the animals; they merely want the excitement of being very close to one of the largest animals on the earth, or to take photographs.

It is ironic that persistent interference on coastal feeding or breeding grounds should come from those who would not dream of harming whales or dolphins. There may be some correlation between the huge increase in tourist traffic into Alaskan waters and the decline of feeding humpbacks in areas such as Glacier Bay in the last few years. Concern has been expressed about the unintentional interference of tourist boats with the normal behaviour of gray whales in southern California and humpback whales in Hawaiian waters. The same phenomenon is taking place in the estuary of the St Lawrence river in Canada, where the number of tour boats leaving towns in Quebec has more than doubled since 1977.

In the United States legislation has been enacted to minimize this kind of interference. Legal minimum distances for approaching large whales have been established, and guidelines set out for the operation of vessels in the vicinity of these animals. Although the regulations may be excessive in some cases and somewhat inadequate in others, as a general rule they provide a good yardstick which other nations can follow. Small power-boats with high revving outboard engines cause most of the problems; in my experience large baleen whale species in coastal waters are quite accustomed to the presence of medium-sized fishing boats with low-frequency engine noise, and take little or no notice of these vessels. Nevertheless, there is some evidence that whales will eventually move away from areas with steady increases in boat and ship traffic. If the regions in question are prime feeding areas, or essential for mating or calving, then this is cause for concern, and some ameliorative action may be needed.

The problem of 'incidental catch'

Two kinds of incidental catch may occur. First, cetaceans may be taken deliberately, but 'in passing' during the course of another fishery. Second, cetaceans may be killed accidentally during the activities of another fishery. The problems involved with protecting whales and dolphins in the first situation can be solved relatively simply; if the incidental harvesting appears to present a real threat to the cetacean population, it can be prevented by legislation and enforced by fines or the threat of confiscation of fishing gear. Although some infractions will still continue, the number of catches invariably decreases, especially if the value of the cetacean catch is small in comparison to the financial risks of flouting the law. An example of this kind of incidental catch is provided by the small whaling operations of St Lucia (12, 37) in the West Indies. There are a few full-time whalers working out of this island, perhaps no more than three or four boats in most years (84). Many other fishermen, however, who normally go to sea to catch reef or flying fish, will harpoon dolphins or short-finned pilot whales if the opportunity presents itself, and sell the meat on the local market. The level of hunting pressure on the populations seems not to be critical at the time of writing, but there are no reliable catch-per-unit-effort figures (83).

The other kind of incidental catch can be much more difficult to control or curtail, and has provided some of the more intractable problems with which national and international agencies have had to wrestle in recent years. Although many species of cetacean may be caught in fishing gear all over the world from time to time, some particularly difficult situations can be pinpointed. Species for which some concern has been expressed are the spinner, spotted and common dolphins of the tropical eastern Pacific, Dall's porpoise in the western North Pacific, the Franciscana or La Plata dolphin off the south-east coast of South America, the harbour porpoise in north-eastern Canadian and west Greenland waters, and the humpback whale off the east coast of Newfoundland. This list is by no means exhaustive.

If we measure importance in terms of the number of animals killed, the incidental take of dolphins by the pelagic tuna fleets of the tropical Pacific has presented the greatest problem. The dolphin catch is a result of the methods used by these boats to capture tuna. The vessels are rigged for purse-seining and the tuna are sought in the same way that whales are, by using experience and oceanographic data to determine the most likely regions in which the preferred species (yellowfin) might occur, and then searching for individual schools with the naked eye. Spotter aircraft can be used near the coast, but usually the traditional method of rotating masthead lookouts is employed. Until the late 1950s, almost all the tuna fishing effort of the United States vessels was by pole fishing or trolling, but the advent of light-weight nylon netting and other technical advances completely revolutionized the industry, so much so that by about 1960 almost the whole fleet had been converted to purse-seining operations (72, 73).

There is very close association between feeding yellowfin tuna and some species of pelagic dolphins (78) and their diets have many food items in common. The association is such that if even a few dolphins get out of the encircling seine and escape, most of the tuna school may follow. To prevent this, the tuna captains use one or two 'pongas' (fast skiffs or power-boats) which circle the dolphin school and try to drive the animals into a tight group within easy distance of the parent ship. The tuna vessel then begins to pay out the purse seine, which can be a kilometre in length, around the dolphins. Because the tuna school is almost always immediately beneath or mingled with the dolphin school, a successful corralling of the cetaceans usually results in a heavy catch of tuna.

The annual kill during the late 1960s and early 1970s was estimated to be about 113 000 dolphins of all species (77); most of these were spinner or spotted dolphins, with perhaps 21 000 common dolphins also being taken (28). The industry was reluctant to face the adverse publicity which grew around this incidental kill during the 1970s, but co-operated with the National Marine Fisheries Service to devise methods for reducing or even eliminating this kill. The industry was not indifferent to the situation, if only from the pragmatic point of view that purse-seining operations would be jeopardized should the dolphin populations be drastically reduced. If the easily visible cetaceans were not there to run with the tuna, the latter would be that much harder to find. Furthermore, the presence of the dolphins in the purse seine (sometimes there might be a thousand or more) was not conducive to efficient tuna retrieval operations; hours had to be expended attempting to free as many as possible or removing dead dolphins from the net. One relatively early method used to liberate them was known as 'backing down'. It had been noticed that the dolphins tended to congregate at the far end of the seine, that is, as far from the vessel as they could get. By 'backing down' on the net, and reducing the tension, the captain could usually drop the distal-section float line of the seine under the surface, so that some dolphins could escape (72). This was a delicate manoeuvre; one mistake and the tuna could be lost as well. Unfortunately the net margin would rarely stay down long enough or deep enough for more than a fraction of the dolphins to escape. Experiments carried out by Perrin and his co-workers revealed that dolphins rarely crossed a float line at the surface (75). They would cross thin gill netting or polythene sheeting, on the other hand, suggesting that they were avoiding the obstacle by sight, not echolocation. They would also pass through an opening not less than 1 metre deep and/or 1.5 metre across, but not a smaller one. Great reductions in the incidental mortality rates were eventually brought about by such studies. The best results to date have been obtained by building a special panel into the net which can be manipulated to provide an avenue of escape for most of the dolphins. The relative success of this programme can be gauged from the fact that by 1980 the kill of all species in this fishery had dropped from 113 000 to about 17 000.

Needless to say, plenty of questions were asked about the effect of such large catches on the dolphin populations. Data now available make it seem unlikely that the species were ever in danger of extirpation as a result of this kill, but nevertheless, the useless slaughter of hundreds of thousands of large mammals year after year was a tragedy of considerable magnitude.

Population size of the offshore Pacific spotted dolphin and the eastern spinner dolphin have been estimated on the basis of detailed studies of survey data and catch patterns, as between 3.1–3.5 million and 1.1–1.2 million animals respectively (74, 77). There are still uncertainties, partly because a change in the catch structure has occurred. The average number of dolphins encircled at each set has been increasing as a result of improved techniques, and the number of animals killed per set has been drastically reduced (76). The proportion of calves and lactating females in the catch has increased, however, presumably because the calves are less able to escape than adult animals, and the mothers are reluctant to leave their offspring (76). Other complications are introduced by the existence of at least four distinct geographical populations of spinner dolphins (see Chapter 7). The latest published data available at the time of writing (74) suggest that the incidental kill has had most impact on the eastern spinner; cumulative fishing pressure is believed to have reduced this population to about 55 per cent of its original size. The effect on white-belly spinners has been much less, with a reduction to between 71–94 per cent of the original size. It is necessary to point out that the range of potential error about the mean estimate of reduction of the eastern spinner population is large (approximately 20 per cent), so that it is not surprising to learn that the evidence for any reaction to the exploitation is ambiguous. If the population of the eastern spinner prior to exploitation was at or near the carrying capacity of the environmental complex it inhabits and has since been reduced to about 55 per cent of its original size, then density-dependent limitation theory (96) would lead us to believe that the rate of production of that population will have increased by now, in fact in marine mammal populations the maximum-sustainable-yield point may be well above the logistic-curve 50 per cent point (24). In fact the data provide no positive indication that such an increase has occurred (74). There are several possible explanations of these results.

(1)   The data may simply be too coarse-grained to reveal the effect.
(2)   Population estimates may be too low, so that the population size has not yet reached a level where the effect would be significant. The potential error in the estimate of mean reduction admits to this possibility.
(3)   Competition between tuna and several species of pelagic dolphin (not all of which are equally susceptible to tuna purse-seining) may be such that we cannot necessarily expect a density-dependent response in a single heavily exploited species of the complex. If the

distribution of food supply in patches *is* limiting, then the reductions in one or two exploited populations might result in marginally better survival rates in, say, four or five other unexploited species with overlapping prey, thus damping down the response of the exploited populations below their full potential.

In any event, there is no definite evidence that these populations have yet been permanently damaged by the incidental catches; estimates of the fecundity levels and annual production rates do not support concern that the populations have been experiencing a level of exploitation that could have brought about a collapse in the near future (74, 77). The magnitude of the incidental catch of pelagic dolphins by United States tuna boats is now far less than it was a few years ago, however, and studies continue, although it may not be possible to eliminate accidental kills completely. The long period of time during which dolphins in the Black Sea have been exploited by Russian and Turkish hunters, taking catches of many thousands each year, suggest that some populations have considerable resilience. M. M. Sleptsov (92) reported that the catch of *Delphinus delphis* near the shores of the Crimea and Caucasus in 1938 alone totalled 135 000 animals. This figure did not take into account possible catches west of the Crimea or on the southern shores of the Black Sea. There is relatively little information on the Black Sea dolphin fishery, although some years ago the Russian press published an announcement that hunting of dolphins in their waters was to be curtailed. Estimated Turkish catches in 1971–3 were about 176 000 per year (48).

The next largest incidental kill is probably that of Dall's porpoise, *Phocoenoides dalli* by Japanese salmon gill-netting operations in the north-west Pacific. Estimates vary, but the number killed each year seems to be between 10 000 (70) and 20 000 (67), with a best estimate of 11 800 (68). As with the spinner dolphins, the Japanese salmon-fishing captains would like to solve this problem, if only because many valuable hours are wasted extracting dead porpoises from the nets, and repairing damage caused by their death struggles. The situation was recently reviewed by S. Ohsumi (70). Because these nets are strained astern of the vessels against anchored buoys, and fishing may take place at night, there does not seem to be a simple solution to the incidental kills in this case. Various possibilities have been examined by Japanese researchers, including decoy models of killer whales and play-backs of recorded killer whale sounds, which worked well to keep white whales away from fishing gear in Alaska (31). There is no reliable measure of the total population of Dall's porpoise, nor whether the catch is large enough to have any serious effect on that population.

A similar problem is experienced in the north-western North Atlantic, where harbour porpoises are caught in drift nets set for salmon by Greenland vessels or fishing boats from other countries, such as Canada. The catch of this species is much smaller than that of the spinner and spotted dolphins, but may have far more impact because *P. phocoena* appears to be relatively short-lived, and does not usually calve every year. This species therefore is likely to have a low rate of annual production and resilience under exploitation. There is some mortality of *P. phocoena* in herring weirs in southern New Brunswick and Nova Scotia, but investigations carried out by workers in my laboratory indicate that it is probably no more than a few dozen individuals each year in the whole region. More are caught, but a percentage are liberated alive. The worst kills occur off south-west and west Greenland, and perhaps off Newfoundland. Annual catch statistics have been collected and reviewed by Canadian, Danish and Norwegian scientists (54, 58). There is a basic hunted catch of 400–900 per annum taken by shooting and harpooning from dories and skiffs off the coast of Greenland, but the incidental catch in salmon drift nets is far more significant. It is interesting to note that set gill nets close to shore take hardly any porpoises; it is the drift nets which do the damage. Neither *Phocoenoides* or *Phocoena phocoena* appear to be able to avoid these nets under normal circumstances, suggesting that they use their sonar only when actively chasing food or exploring their environment, and not when on passage in areas which might reasonably be expected to be obstacle-free. The catch by non-Greenland vessels may total as many as 1500 per annum, and that by Greenland nets about 1200; that is, about 2500–2700 animals in all. Attempts to compare the catch per unit time have not been really successful, because of difficulties of calculating effort in such a catch (58). There have been quite drastic changes in the kill during the last twenty years, which Kapel attributed more to changes in fishing effort and fishing methods rather than population changes (54). The use of drift-net fishing for salmon by Greenlanders was at a relatively low level until about 1967; but between 1967 and 1971 there was a significant increase in the use of this gear. During the initial phase of this change the kills of harbour porpoise may have been much higher than the numbers given above. Much more work needs to be done on this problem, because the influence of these catches on this population may be very significant. Unfortunately the distances are vast in Davis Strait, the working conditions severe and the expense of research considerable.

A similar kind of incidental catch in nets has been studied recently in the western South Atlantic. Between 1500 (80) and 2000 (11) specimens of the Franciscana or La Plata dolphin *Pontoporia blainvillei* are taken in nets set for sharks by commerical fishermen off the coast of Uruguay and the adjacent nations. The impact of the catch on the population is not known, and once again the animals do not seem to be able to avoid the nets. G.

Pilleri (80) noted that neither the mesh size nor the thickness of the net cord made any difference to the numbers taken. Brownell (10) noted that the catch was a coastal phenomenon; boats setting nets 3–40 kilometres offshore took no dolphins.

The incidental catch problem which has drawn most attention in Canada and significant coverage in the press of the eastern United States in recent years is that involving the trapping of humpback whales in fishing gear off eastern Newfoundland. The situation is regarded as potentially rather serious because, although the western North Atlantic population of humpback whales appears to have recovered in numbers in the last few decades, the absolute size of the population is still relatively low, probably somewhere in the region of 1200–1500 (66, 97). Although larger numbers have been suggested by other workers, it is safer to take the most conservative estimates. The humpback whales have long been noted for mingling with vessels fishing on the banks of Newfoundland (91), but during the 1970s humpbacks began to appear much closer inshore in large numbers, coincident with the near collapse of the offshore capelin catches (59). Although there is no proof that the inshore movement was correlated with this collapse, some circumstantial evidence has been indicated as supporting this view, although changes in the nature of Newfoundland fishing effort may be a much more significant factor.

The coastal fisheries of Newfoundland rely quite heavily on set-nets at the surface (for salmon), on the bottom (for ground fish), and cod traps. Perkins and Beamish summarized reported entrapments of minke, humpback and fin whales in this region during recent years (71). Since 1969 at least seven humpbacks and ten minke whales are known to have died or been killed after entanglements; this must be considered a minimum number. Many more whales become entangled with gear but are either released, succeed in escaping or die without being reported, usually inflicting considerable damage in the process. Reduced manoeuvrability while hampered by lines and netting, coupled with persistent attempts to escape, probably lead to exhaustion and finally death, and at the very least, prevent the animals from feeding (4). A number of animals are freed alive each season, but the whole process has become an expensive one for fishermen and government alike. The increased incidence of entrapments was recently linked to a significant increase in the effort put into the inshore cod fishery (59).

It is simply not possible to prescribe a single, universally applicable management response to these varying kinds of incidental kill. If the industry can be encouraged to look for a solution, with or without government financial assistance, well and good. The situation is rarely improved by extremist conservation groups adopting a posture of immediate confrontation with fishermen or government, although a steady but moderate pressure from public opinion is healthy, and usually stimulates all concerned to greater activity. Progress has been significant in the case of the so-called 'tuna–porpoise problem' because it has been possible to re-design the nets, yielding a specific solution to a specific situation. There is no denying that a solution to the salmon gill net and cod-trap kills may be much more difficult. Experiments using sonic and ultrasonic warning devices have been tried, but their long-term success is doubtful. The whales are following food, and are likely to habituate to these 'pingers' once they are seen to provide no direct threat. This is really just another version of the seemingly endless conflict between pigeons and public works departments, and seagulls and airport management authorities. No one has yet been ingenious enough to design a net that will effectively catch cod or salmon, but not take porpoises or larger whales. Such solutions may not be impossible, but if some method is not found within the next ten years or so, the outlook for harbour porpoise and North Atlantic humpbacks may be grim.

Exploitation and management of whale populations in theory and practice

Harvesting methods and the structure of the whaling industry, past and present

At the mention of 'killing whales' the mind's eye immediately conjures up a vision of a steel-hulled whaling ship using an explosive harpoon, and a carcass buoyed with compressed air being towed to a mother ship. Certainly this is how many large whales are taken today, but the diversity of the whaling industry even today should not be overlooked. In the last twenty years the pelagic whaling industry has shrunk to a small fraction of its original size, the Antarctic effort being reduced from 21 expeditions in 1961/2 to only two or three in the last few years. At the time of writing there are rumours that the USSR and perhaps the Japanese are planning to withdraw completely from pelagic whaling in the North Pacific. There are still shore whaling stations operating at widely scattered locations around the world, for example, in Iceland and Japan, but many of the famous stations, such as those of South Georgia, South Africa, Australia, New Zealand and Canada, are now nothing but a minor part of national histories (34). The shift in public opinion has been so drastic that few can be found who would admit to viewing their demise with any nostalgia. Some of the surviving whaling stations operate with standard modern whaling boats and equipment, but there are still a few, such as those in the Azores and St Lucia, which operate with open boats, and the most primitive of fired or hand-thrown harpoons. The catch of bowhead whales by Alaskan

Eskimos using small boats has been a source of bitter contention in recent years (47); gray whales are taken by modern Russian chasers for aborigines in coastal waters of north-eastern Siberia, white whales and narwhal by Eskimos in the Canadian Arctic; and pilot whales are periodically driven ashore in large numbers by fishing communities in the Faeroes and eastern Newfoundland. These drives have exerted a significant impact on the population size of pilot whale populations in Newfoundland waters (65). The degree of control exerted by agencies over the plethora of small operations differs considerably. The bowhead hunt has been described as having more conservationists, government biologists and administrators directly or indirectly involved in the studies, regulation of the hunt, and the defence of the US position at international meetings than there are whales landed in an average year! At the other end of the scale, the Caribbean small whale fisheries are barely regulated at all, although the governments of St Vincent and St Lucia are making an active appraisal of the situation at the time of writing. The legal control of the International Whaling Commission over small cetaceans is a debatable issue.

The modern whaling industries of a relative handful of nations, however, have done most of the damage to the populations of large whales in the last sixty or seventy years. This is not the book in which to provide a detailed history of this industry; useful accounts have been given elsewhere (24, 34, 60, 62, 88) some dealing with the global pattern of whaling, some with national histories of exploitation. In brief, the pattern of development has been as follows.

The foundations of the last great phase of whaling were laid by the Norwegians, with a decade of successful operations using the first steam-powered chaser firing explosive harpoons, hunting for rorquals off the coast of Finmark. By 1886 the Finmark industry had grown to 19 stations operating 35 boats (56), catching fin, blue and sei whales. The local operations came to end with a government decision in 1904 to ban coastal whaling, after serious conflict between the whalers and fishermen who claimed that the offal and waste was destroying coastal fishing grounds. The Finmark catches were already declining by 1895, however, probably as a result of intensive local overexploitation of whale stocks. During the period 1885–1912 the Norwegian companies expanded across the North Atlantic in compensation for the decline at home, directly or indirectly setting up stations in Iceland, Newfoundland, the Faeroes, Shetland, the Hebrides, Spitsbergen and Greenland. Whale population decline and economic factors brought virtually all these enterprises to an end by 1915. The early years of Norwegian coastal whaling have been documented by Juel (53), the middle phase of expansion by Southwell (94) and the declining years by Fairford (29).

Captain C. Christensen was one of the first to give substance to a

Figure 9.1 The perfection of the factory ship for whaling freed the industry from its European and subarctic coastal bases. FF *Southern Harvester* in Cumberland Bay, South Georgia, 1961. Photograph by D. E. Gaskin.

growing belief that the future of rorqual hunting lay with pelagic whaling and mobile factories (Figures 9.1–9.3). His tentative operations in Spitsbergen waters in 1903–4 were the forerunners of the great Antarctic pelagic whale fishery, which began with the *Admiralen* working in the Falkland Islands and South Shetlands in 1905. The expansion of Antarctic whaling between 1905 and 1915 was quite remarkable; by 1912 over a dozen enterprises were taking whales from the South Shetlands to South Georgia, and the United Kingdom government became painfully aware how tenuous was its jurisdiction in these distant regions over which it claimed control. Yet signs of serious decline in the catches could be seen even by 1911. The early phase of southern factory-ship whaling has been documented by Salvesen (87) and Nippgen (69).

In 1924, the *Larsen* was designed with a stern slipway which would permit whales to be hauled directly on to the deck instead of being flensed in the water beside the ship. This innovation proved so successful that it

Figure 9.2   The addition of a stern slipway and tail grab in turn freed factory ships from operating in sheltered coves and bays of the Antarctic islands, and opened up mobile whaling operations throughout the Southern Ocean. Grab going down for a fin whale on FF *Southern Venturer*, 1962. Photograph by D. E. Gaskin.

Figure 9.3   Few shore whaling stations survived the economic changes which took place in the industry and the end of the ready availability of whales in the 1960s. Leith Harbour, South Georgia, 1961. Photograph by D. E. Gaskin.

Figure 9.4   First victim of the 'Southern Holocaust'; the blue whale was commercially extinct by the early 1960s. FF *Southern Venturer*, 1962. Photograph by D. E. Gaskin.

triggered off a tremendous surge in southern whaling activity (Figure 9.4). The number of truly pelagic factory ships rose from two in 1925/6 to eight in 1928/9, and to 41 in 1930/1, a number never equalled or surpassed since. Light aircraft were used for whale spotting for the first time in 1929/30. This phase has been documented by many authors, of which Harmer (42), Bennett (8) and Jenkins (49) provide good accounts in English. The great economic depression, then the Second World War, both led to almost total cessations of the hunting for short periods. Southern whaling regained impetus fairly slowly after the end of hostilities; the pre-war whaling factories had either been sunk or converted to tankers. Two Japanese expeditions sailed to the Antarctic in 1946–7, joined by vessels

Figure 9.5   Victim of massive 'pulse fishing' enterprises, the humpback whale populations have nevertheless succeeded in bouncing back again and again. FF *Southern Venturer*, 1962. Photograph by D. E. Gaskin.

from the Netherlands and the USSR, in addition to the traditional presence of the Norwegians and the British. None of the major whaling nations can be absolved from blame for the disaster which was about to befall most of the remaining southern whale populations. Southern coastal nations, such as New Zealand and Australia (13), were responsible for a significant fraction of the damage to humpback whale stocks (Figures 9.5 and 9.6). By 1958 the Australian shore stations had taken nearly twice as many of this species as all the pelagic whaling nations put together (38). In the pre-war years the southern industry had been supported largely by blue whales; subsequent changes in the industry are well known and need not be dwelt on at length. The catch following the war largely consisted of fin whales (Figure 9.7), with a decreasing percentage of blues and humpbacks; by 1962 sei began to figure prominently in the catches. This species supported the industry through the late 1960s and early 1970s (Figure 9.8). In the mid-1970s the pelagic industry was taking significant numbers of minke whales, and had clearly reached the end of the line. The European industries were in desperate straits even by 1962/3, when the British dropped out, their quota passing with the sale of vessels to Japan. The Dutch followed the British out a little later, but the Norwegian enterprises lingered on until 1967, at which time the Japanese and the

Figure 9.6 A sad picture of unrealized productivity. The inability of the Commission to provide any practical way of protecting pregnant females has vexed scientists and laymen alike, inside and outside the Commission and the industry. Foetal humpback and its membranes on the FF *Southern Venturer* in 1962. Photograph by D. E. Gaskin.

Figure 9.7 Penultimate phase of large whaling. The overexploitation of southern fin whales during the 1950s and 1960s was halted before the populations were depressed to quite the remnant levels of blue and humpback whales. Buoy boat delivers more fin whales to the FF *Southern Venturer* in 1962. Photograph by D. E. Gaskin.

Figure 9.8   The sei whale (later supplemented by catches of minke) has supported both the Southern Ocean and North Pacific whaling industries during the 1970s. FF *Southern Venturer*, 1962. Photograph by D. E. Gaskin.

USSR had the Southern Ocean to themselves. From a peak of 21 factory-ship expeditions in 1961/2 the industry dwindled rapidly to 15 in 1965, and only nine even as long ago as 1967. In 1966, at the eleventh hour for the southern fin whale, the International Whaling Commission finally managed to reach agreement on quotas estimated to be slightly below the sustainable yields of the surviving populations of fin and sei. Humpbacks and blue whales had been given complete protection in 1963 and 1964. It is hardly surprising, therefore, with this sorry record, that the whaling industry has become an object lesson for students of resource management as a case history in which national greed overpowered common sense, and economic considerations overpowered biological realities. In fact between 1946 and 1967 the International Whaling Commission was an example of how control of renewable resources beyond national jurisdiction should *not* be attempted. The rigidity of the Commission structure and its limited mandate were major reasons for the failure.

Existing management structure: the Whaling Commission – composition, mandate and history

The first international agreements on whale catches pre-date the formation of the International Whaling Commission by about nine years, although it is certain that the Commission would have been formed earlier if the war had not intervened. Whale quotas before 1937 had been largely a matter of joint consultation between Britain and Norway, although by 1938/9 Germany had five expeditions active and a financial interest in two more. The International Whaling Agreement was signed in 1937, requiring the signatories to observe a three-month season, and to limit the number of vessels taking part. There was some reference to conservation, but frankly, the participants were far more interested in the regulation of whale-oil prices to their best mutual interest. Nevertheless, the whaling nations did agree to the establishment of minimum-size lengths to permit some animals to reach maturity before being taken.

The International Convention for the Regulation of Whaling, drawn up in 1946, has formed the basis of whale-population management as we know it today. The Convention is made up of eleven Articles, and an accompanying Schedule containing all the regulatory provisions. Under the authorizations of Article 5, regulations in the Schedule can be amended as deemed necessary by a three-quarter majority of the voting commissioners in any given year. The history of the Commission and the problems which it has encountered have been documented by D. G. Chapman (14) J. A. Gulland (40), N. A. Mackintosh (60) and J. L. McHugh (64). The paper by the latter is a particularly comprehensive and well-rounded account, and I need only document briefly the highlights of the Commission's history.

At its inception, the International Whaling Commission was completely dominated by whaling nations, as might be expected. With any idea of a 'global village' some ten or fifteen years in the future, it would hardly have occurred to the governments of most non-whaling nations that they might be able to play a valuable role by joining and participating in the Commission. The budget provided to the Commission secretariat was miniscule even by the standards of the times; if it had not been for the supporting role of the Bureau of International Whaling Statistics in Oslo, it is doubtful if it could ever have functioned to any effect at all. Each one of the original participating nations of the Commission had an almost unblemished record of voting based on self-interest and realization of short-term economic gain, until such time as they divested themselves of all or most of their whaling interests. Since which time some of those with the worst records in the early years (and this has to include the British and the Australians, for example) have found it expedient (and inexpensive) to support politically popular conservation measures. Their records of supporting such measures at the times when they could have been effective to conserve blue, humpback and even fin whale populations were usually lamentable, even when those measures were recommended by a majority of the Scientific Committee of the International Whaling Commission.

The Articles and Schedule for regulation of whaling might have been successful, despite some of the shortcomings of the participants, had not several fatal errors been made right at the outset.

First, despite scientific advice to the contrary, the Commission did not adopt species quotas, but instead agreed to use the blue whale unit (BWU), in which the major species were rated by respective oil yields (1 blue = 2 fin whales = $2\frac{1}{2}$ humpbacks = 6 sei whales). This decision doomed the blue whale population as surely as if no kind of quota system was in use at all.

Second, the Commission determined that it was not going to use a formal system of national quotas, but have instead one Southern Ocean quota. The role played by the United States in getting this adopted is sometimes carefully overlooked by many American writers, who tend to reserve the role of major villains for the Russians, Japanese and Norwegians. The overall quota vote, purporting to be to the benefit of free enterprise and competition which would lead to higher efficiency, has rightly been accused of delaying effective conservation measures for fifteen years (26). Fortunately the major pelagic whaling nations soon adopted a rough and ready method of parcelling up the total quota between themselves, or the whole system might have soon collapsed into complete anarchy.

Third, the Commission was deprived of real 'teeth' for most of its existence by the provision which enabled any nation to enter an objection to proposed amendments to the Schedule within a 90-day period following the annual meeting. A nation doing this was then not bound by the amendment. This built-in veto made it almost impossible to implement any serious conservation measures during the 1950s. As Chapman (14) has pointed out, the combination of the blue whale unit quota, together with the lack of national quotas and the requirement for unanimous decisions rendered the Commission virtually impotent during ten crucial years. There is a strong comparison to be made here between the International Whaling Commission and the other international commissions attempting to regulate high seas activities. The management of tuna stocks has suffered from the problem of fragmented jurisdictions and lack of co-ordinated research (52).

The pelagic whaling industry – faced with lack of agreement on desperately needed conservation measures and, as a result, dwindling catches, more and more surplus effort available, rising costs and fewer and fewer options as each year passed – may merely be the first major casualty among all distant-water fishing industries. In 1973 Gulland (39) prophesized the decline of most such operations as the world economic situation became progressively more unfavourable. This is now beginning to come to pass; it is doubtful that Gulland would have imagined just how great the magnitude of rises in fuel prices would be in the eight years subsequent to the publication of his article.

Several periods of acute crisis can be recognized in the history of the International Whaling Commission; some of these were certainly worse or more dramatic than others. It is often not realized by what might be called the 'concerned public' that the Commission has never had the power to enforce its decisions. Even if the Commissioners are in total agreement on an issue, that agreement will in some cases not become binding on their own nations until equivalent domestic legislation is passed. This is certainly true of the United States, where the legislative and judicial branches of government must be party to all decisions of the executive branch (64).

Most of the major crises developed in connection with whaling in the Southern Ocean; it is only in the last few years that the major catch of baleen and sperm whales has been made in the North Pacific – a measure of the decline of the populations in the Antarctic and the impact of the rising cost of expeditions. Effort in the Southern Ocean increased significantly during the 1950s, not necessarily just because of increase in the numbers of catchers or expeditions, but because newer and more efficient vessels were coming into operation. Even during the early 1950s the pelagic fleets were having some difficulty reaching the excessive quota of first 16 000, and then 15 000 BWU. Attempts to reduce the quota by a significant amount were begun in 1958, but these efforts were not successful until the 1965/6 season. During a two-year period there were no agreed quotas at all, except for voluntary limits imposed by the five pelagic whaling nations. These came to a generous total of 17 780 BWU, and during this same period, the Netherlands government, with Norway following its lead, temporarily withdrew from the Convention, as was their right under Article 11. Their actions may have helped the situation, although it did not seem that way at the time. Both nations subsequently re-entered the Convention, the Netherlands on condition that at long last national quotas be set and agreed upon. The turning-point came between 1962 and 1963. In the 1962/3 season, the catches in the Antarctic fell short of the quota by nearly 4000 BWU and, for the first time, the respective governments began to take the scientific advice quite seriously. Much surplus effort was removed, and the number of expeditions sharply reduced. A reduction of 5000 BWU in the quota was agreed, but the Scientific Committee warned that the industry probably would not be able to take that quota in the available time, given the decreased whale densities. Again there was a shortfall, and the Commission and industry advisers were in turmoil. The 1964 meeting was disastrous (64) and could well have spelled the end of the Convention. No quota could be agreed on for the 1964/5 season, and again the catch dropped by about 1500 BWU. Yet, somehow the organization survived this, perhaps its worst crisis, and the industries and governments of the major whaling nations accepted an unprecedented drop in the quota from 10000 to only 4500 BWU. Subsequent to this meeting, the quota was reduced in three more steps, to an all-time low of 2700 BWU in 1970/1. There is no doubt that the whaling industries of Japan and the USSR went through severe periods of stressful readjustment during the post-1962 period; the Norwegian industry was almost completely destroyed.

McHugh (64) was careful to point out that the crisis in age determination of baleen whales (see Chapter 8, pp. 304–5) fortunately happened to coincide with the temporary withdrawal of the Norwegians from Antarctic whaling, since in 1968 the underestimations of age and concurrent overestimations of population production led the Scientific Committee to request the withdrawal of another 700 BWU from the quota, if the maximum sustainable yield of the fin whale population was to be attained.

Another important turning-point occurred at the 1971 meeting. Agreements included acceptance in principle of a scheme for the exchange of international inspectors; implementation of species quotas for 1972; a significant upgrading of the strength and finances of the Commissariat; and pledges to make determined efforts to bring into the Commission all those nations which were not signatories to the Convention, but hunted species which fell within its jurisdiction. It is fair to say that the International Whaling Commission was eventually successful in virtually all these proposals. The 1970s have seen several trends. First, growing support for a complete moratorium on all whaling, rejected by a slimmer and slimmer margin each year. This has received much publicity in the press in recent years, rarely qualified with the observation that it would only affect signatory nations and that a very significant fraction of all whales taken are now caught by non-signatory countries. A second trend has been the entry of a substantial number of non-whaling nations into the Commission, including some which have *never* had any sort of whaling industry. The 'hard-line' nations, such as the USSR, Japan, newly recruited South Korea (and many would add Canada), have felt progressively more beleaguered and defensive within a Commission which musters more votes in favour of complete abolition each year. The inherent danger in this has to be the potential dissolution of the Commission, if a time came when it appeared to no longer have a function. As it stands, the Commission is presently the *only* existing organization which can hope to bring non-signatory nations into line with conservative hunting policies.

In 1975 the Commission took another major step forward when the so-called New Management Policy was introduced (46). The policy involved the definition of three types of category for describing whale populations, and with different methods of managing each.

The first of these is the *protection stock*. Species falling into this category are those in which the sustainable yield has fallen more than 10 per cent below the maximum-sustainable-yield level. In these cases, hunting is completely prohibited (for example, blue and humpback whales).

The second category is the *sustained management stock*, in which the best estimate of population size falls between 10 per cent below and 20 per cent above that giving the maximum sustainable yield. For stocks deemed to be below the maximum sustainable yield the permitted catch can be no more than is indicated by a straight line from 0 at the lower limit to 90 per cent of the maximum sustainable yield at the upper limit. Above maximum sustainable yield, catches will be permitted to total 90 per cent of the maximum sustainable yield.

The third category is the *initial management stock*. This category includes those species with population levels estimated to be more than 20 per cent above the level needed to take the maximum sustainable yield. The permitted catch is once again 90 per cent of this maximum sustainable yield.

This classification scheme requires annual review, and if new evidence is brought forward to suggest that a stock has moved from one category to another, or the population abundance was previously miscalculated, then appropriate management action is taken to reclassify the stock. Although the new management policy was considered an improvement on the unworkable blue-whale-unit system, there are still serious drawbacks to this modified scheme for species quotas (see p. 383). It is worth pointing out here that 'trophic-level management', that is, joint management of fish species that feed at the same trophic level, seems to be coming into vogue again in some government agencies. All I can say is that they should take a hard look at the failures of the blue whale unit, which was just this sort of system, before they substitute trophic-level management for single species quotas.

Objectives of whale management

Objectives are subjective, that is, their validity depends strictly on your point of view. What alternative objectives might there be in whale management? At present there are strong pressures from environmentalist groups to accept only one objective, namely, to cease all hunting, end all incidental killing, and leave whales totally alone to prosper and recover from the unpleasant attentions they have received from man over the last few hundreds of years. It is necessary to indicate that this is by and large an urban, middle-class, college-educated viewpoint. I am not belittling such an opinion, merely describing it. In contrast, the perspective of the Caribbean fisherman whose mind is frequently drawn to the subject of tomorrow's meal, or that of the Newfoundland fisherman who has just lost two thousand dollars' worth of uninsured net to a passing humpback whale may differ significantly from that of a Harvard University student or a well-to-do Kensington solicitor. The latter individuals can afford to adopt what might be kindly described as the 'global view'; the fishermen are totally concerned with the intensely local and here-and-now situation of daily subsistence. The conflict of objectives begins here, in clashes between perspectives, cultures and perceived needs.

It is probably true that most biologists, for example, see all fisheries management problems in a strictly biological context, but as Gulland wrote, although it may be true that the fishery will end if the resource is exterminated, it does not follow, however, that continued existence of the stocks is an automatic guarantee of a healthy fishery and a prosperous industry. We can establish an overall schedule of 'conservation objectives', that may in practice form an umbrella to contain shades of opinion that range from the adamant preservationist to whom the killing of a single animal is unacceptable, even for food, to the 'rational' conservationist. Let me say immediately that the use of the word 'rational' is not selected to imply that the preservationist is, by contrast, irrational. In management 'rational usage' has become synonymous with exploitation that permits harvesting without destruction of the resource stock. Most biologists would probably view such exploitation as being required to take place with the aim of maintaining a sustainable yield. There are other methods of exploitation, however, which, though not providing a stable sustainable yield, are not necessarily 'irrational'.

If we establish a conservation ethic as our major goal, however, it will still be necessary to appreciate that others involved in the industry carrying out the exploitation will have their own objectives, which may range from labour stability, providing new employment, supplying a scarce product to the nation, allocating resources in some national or international scheme, to simply making as much money out of the operation as possible. These might be broadly grouped as socio-economic objectives (2). Obviously the possibilities for conflict with the conservation ethic are substantial.

Some years ago, Larkin and Wilimovsky (57) discussed the general pattern which emerges during uncontrolled exploitation or 'non-management' of a fishery. They noted that any fishery under these conditions develops successive periods of limited stability (compare right, blue, fin, sei whaling phases), and that while operations might start with a high degree of selectivity (for example, for right whales), they pass shortly into a phase where any available species are harvested to keep the operators solvent (for example, mixed fin and sei whale phase), and then eventually to a few species which can stand the pressure. The industry may stabilize at this stage, or it may not. In whaling it has not shown any particular sign of doing so, perhaps for two reasons. First, the rise in operating costs coincident with the last phase of Antarctic and North Pacific pelagic whaling has been rapid and of great magnitude. Second, the industry cannot stabilize in the sense of these authors because there is no such thing as a whale population which will stand intense fishing pressure. The biological realities of population productivity rates are quite different for fish and whales; the optimal fishing mortality for tuna is close to 0.80, and that for halibut about 0.30, but that for baleen whales only 0.04–0.06. The ratio of sustainable yield to standing stock is far smaller in whales than in fish (14).

There are subtle dangers in adhering to a simplistic conservation ethic. Gulland (40) suggested that there are cases when a management agency orientated primarily towards conservation of an exploited resource will not necessarily be geared to take action until it sees clear signs that stocks are in decline. During the initial exploitation phase, furthermore, many management structures have no clear philosophy directed to controlling the influx of new operational effort. Once that effort becomes entrenched in the industry, it usually proves very difficult to coax or legislate its removal or reduction at a later date. If we take a wider view of management objectives from the outset – that is, studying efficiency, full development of the resource to the maximum advantage of the communities concerned, but with minimum threat to the exploited population – then contraction of effort in case of misjudgements can be much easier.

Nevertheless, the basic conservation objective, the determination of what represents the biological 'bottom line' for rational exploitation, is of fundamental importance if we are to produce a workable management package (Figure 9.9) which will produce economic benefit, yet not permit the kind of overexploitation which characterized the whaling industry of the past. I want to examine in a little more detail what we mean when we talk about 'sustainable yield', and what the concept can provide us in terms of information and insight when viewed within the perspective of the different kinds of management objective which must be taken into account.

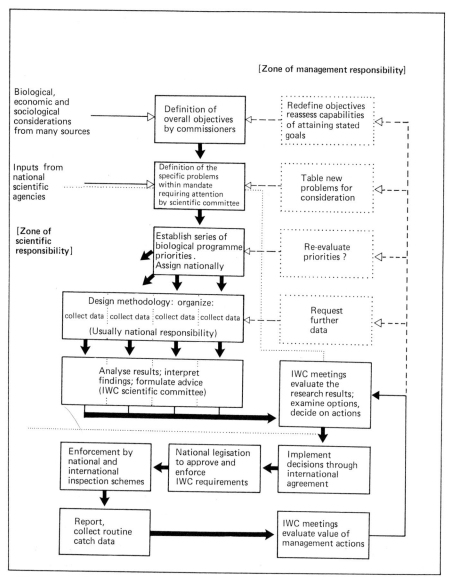

Figure 9.9   Schematic chart for the idealized flow of the management process for the global whaling industry, from the original formulation of objectives to the evaluation of the results of management actions after a period of operation. In practice, there have been tactical failures at several different levels, with particular respect to problems with the quality of available scientific information, which cannot really be blamed on anyone, and the slow movement of implementation of recommendations at the national level, which certainly can.

Sustained yield models in the theory and practice of whale management

The 1946 Convention contains statements about the 'optimal development' of whale population resources, but nothing about the concept of sustainable yield (44). From about 1964 to 1970 the scientific advisers to the International Whaling Commission appear to have interpreted the plea for optimalization as being more or less synonymous with exploitation to obtain the maximum sustainable yield. From the purely biological point of view this was not unreasonable, because maintaining populations at a size which produced the maximum sustainable yield would, indeed, represent 'optimal development'. Since 1970 the concept of establishing maximum sustainable yield as a desirable management objective has come under increasing attack both from biologists (44), and economists (17). Concurrently, several Commission advisers began to press for consideration of optimal sustainable yield as a more suitable management goal for controlled exploitation of whales. Unfortunately, precisely which aspects were to be optimalized was often unclear (17).

Any population that is neither standing at zero size nor at its plateau of absolute stability will have some kind of sustainable yield, because the yield at any given size is a function of the surplus of births over deaths, that is, it is proportional in the simplest terms to the production ratio, and can be described by

$$Y_s = N\,(r-M)$$

where Y_s is sustainable yield, N the population size at any given time, r the recruitment rate, and M the mortality rate. The yield curve is parabolic (89, 90), and parallels the changes observed in the logistic growth model between o and K (Figure 9.10). The sustainable yields which can be selected from this curve are abstract conceptions in a simple mathematical model; biological experience, however, reveals to us that species often have yield curves which do not necessarily conform to the theoretical parabola. Some curves are characteristically skewed, some acutely dome-shaped and yet others can be almost flat-topped, so that for a considerable range of population size there is little change in yield with increased or decreased effort (18). It may require many years of exploitation and careful interpretation of data before it is possible to identify the type of yield curve generated during population change in a particular species (24, 25).

One of the principle criticisms of maximum sustainable yield as a biological goal of management is (assuming a significant degree of error to be present in all our estimates of population parameters) that it simply cannot be calculated with enough accuracy (24, 61). The Scientific Committee of the International Whaling Commission has applied a 10 per

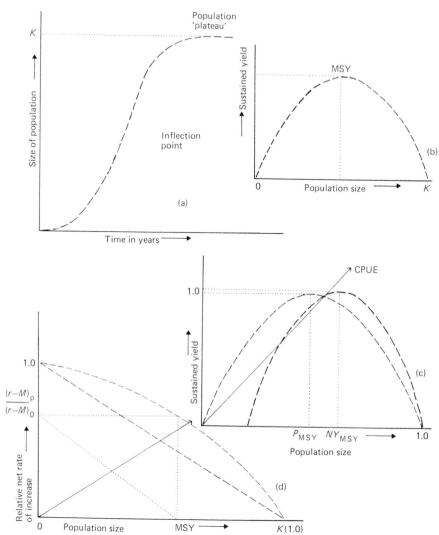

Figure 9.10   The logistic curve (a) defines population growth under density-dependent conditions; the maximum sustainable yield (MSY) is attained at the inflection point of this curve. The yield can be expressed by a curve (parabolic in form), showing the value of the yield at any given population size (b). Holt (44) explored the problems of determining and operating the maximum-sustainable-yield concept, and its relationship to catch per unit effort (CPUE). He showed (c) that there were significant differences between (i) sustainable yield relative to maximum sustainable yield against stock size relative to initial size (left-hand curve), and (ii) net yield, relative to net yield at P_{MSY}, against stock size relative to initial population size (right-hand curve). Holt also pointed out that the estimation of P_{MSY} was so sensitive to the degree of density-dependence of the net rate of increase (at points removed from 0 to 1.0 in (d)) that it was hard to see how the maximum sustainable yield could possibly be calculated with accuracy bettern than ±20 per cent.

cent safety margin to estimated maximum sustainable yields for exploited baleen and sperm whales, but Holt (45) and Beddington (5) have both suggested that it still seems unlikely, given disputes about mortality rates and recruitment rates (see p. 318), that the 10 per cent margin is enough to account for potential error. The counterarguments run to the effect that this is the best that can be done at present, and if warning signs such as declines in catch per unit effort become evident without significant correlated changes in efficiency or methods of operation within the industry, then we will have evidence that the maximum sustainable yield is being exceeded. Nevertheless, the maximum sustainable yield remains a goal largely in terms of the maximization of the biological production of the population only, and need not coincide with the optimum yield from the point of view of best deployment of the resources of the industry. For example, consider the shape of the yield curve; at certain population sizes a relatively small application of effort will result in very significant gains in yield. As the maximum sustainable yield is approached, however, the curve flattens significantly, revealing that further input of effort (that is, more catchers or expeditions) will not produce a significantly greater yield per unit than was already being obtained. If the population is decreased well below the maximum-sustainable-yield level, the magnitude of the *sustainable* catch declines rapidly, although this does not necessarily mean that *catches* could not be maintained by increased effort. Providing the industry is prepared to co-operate with the idea of a sustainable yield pattern of exploitation, then a suitable optimal-yield level cannot be established unless the needs of the industry (within the constraint above) are taken into account. When all these factors have been carefully examined and calculated in terms of cost per unit effort, *then* we might be in a position to set as our management goal a catch level which we could call the optimal sustainable yield, in which there was a clear understanding among all concerned as to the precise nature of the specific long-range objectives (61).

There have been some useful books and essays written on the problems of estimating and optimalizing yield, including some which take both biological and economic factors into account. These models are generally based on the maximization of the present value of net revenues. Those by Clarke (17), and Anderson (3) are among the best. Although the former may initially appear too mathematical for some readers, the ideas are also clearly developed and expressed in writing. Shorter treatments by Gulland and Robinson (41) and Regier (85) are worth reading first. Holt (44) drew our attention to the important point that the maximum sustainable yield in whale management has been related to maximization for numbers, ignoring that *weight* may be far more important from the point of view of best yield.

Economics of whale fisheries, and their influence on industry policy

One of the most significant phrases used in the brief outline above is 'providing . . . the industry is prepared to co-operate with the idea of a sustainable yield'. The immediate reaction from many biologists and lay readers might be one of bewilderment – surely it is to the benefit of all concerned if renewable resources are harvested in such a way that there is always a yield to be had? The short-term economic answer to this question is often 'no'.

Fishing, like any other kind of industry, is a function of cost–benefit balance. If the cost of fishing becomes too high with respect to the price which can be obtained for the product, then those involved will stop fishing and do something else. One of the problems of 'effort-in-place', that is, a developed industry which gets into difficult economic straits, is that the capital and labour are relatively immobile. It may be possible to redeploy some workers and some capital, but frequently not enough to make a significant difference. The modern pelagic whaling industry is a case in point. It has endured long enough so that perhaps two or three working generations have been supported in all the major whaling nations and this is also long enough for a tradition to develop, together with the narrow specializations which the industry demands. The sense of tradition reinforces the desire of personnel to continue trying to do what they know best. Without a change of direction enforced by the government, especially if subsidies are applied, the industry may slowly collapse into ruin without making any significant effort to adapt.

The demise of pelagic whaling to some degree parallels the collapse of the anchoveta fishery in Peru in the early 1970s. The population was probably being fished near its limit, but since it was largely a recruit fishery this might not have been too dangerous under normal circumstances. With the change in oceanographic conditions which periodically strikes this region (the El Niño phenomenon) came a collapse of the fishery. Had it been possible to reduce effort drastically until the stock recovered all might have been well, because the Peruvian government had certainly made a valiant attempt to run the fishery on the basis of the best scientific advice available. But, as C. W. Clark (17) put it, by about 1973 that government seemed to lose control of the political level of management. By that year the capacity of the industry had been permitted to grow until it had twice the potential effort necessary to take the estimated maximum sustainable yield (26). Heavy fishing was allowed to continue. The result was a predictable slide into deeper trouble. Yet not *all* operators were ruined by these events. The lucky ones were those who had been consistently successful for the duration of the major period of the fishery, had good fish meal inventories to sell in the following season, and whose equipment had just about reached the point where it was near the end of its useful life at the time the collapse came. With their investment more than recovered and capital in the bank, these companies were in a position to shift their assets into something else. The investors who were badly hurt financially were those who had entered the industry late, had overextended themselves in credit arrangements, and were in desperate need of cash return on their investment. Needless to say, those who suffered most were the workers. For them the development of the anchoveta industry had represented the first regular work other than subsistence fishing that had ever been available in many coastal towns and villages.

One of the major reasons for the bitter resistance of the whaling nations to demands for a complete moratorium in the last decade, and all lesser attempts to cut back effort in the past, relates to the high-risk and high-discount rate in the industry. Maintenance costs are very high; the deterioration of equipment is continuous once exposed to the potent mix of salt-water and blood. 'Moth-balling' factory ships is really not a practical proposition; the decay would continue even if they were not operating. Because prices would continue to increase during a period of moratorium, re-entry into pelagic whaling would be a costly process. The industry could also remember the disappointingly small recovery of Antarctic blue whale stocks which occurred during the five-year respite of the Second World War. A ten-year moratorium would mean in practice that they were out of the industry for good, unless they were prepared to completely rebuild their fleets at great cost at the end of the moratorium. Many of the vessels taking part in whaling in the mid-1960s had been built fifteen or twenty years before, and were close to the end of their useful life. The British, for example, were able to leave the industry with a minimum of economic hardship for the companies concerned. They pleaded hard luck and hard times, as such companies will do, but it could have been far worse. Some ships of the USSR were relatively new, however, so it was economically logical for them to attempt to stay in the business of whaling for as long as they could hold out and still balance the cost–benefit production equation.

For, as Chapman indicated, the rate at which depleted whale stocks rebuild is painfully slow, perhaps 4 per cent per annum, yet the interest rate on risk capital during the later phase of pelagic whaling has probably been of the order of 10 per cent or more (14). Clark (17) made the same point, contrasting in simple terms the value of whales caught now with whales saved for capture at a future date. Even allowing for the fact that the cost of catching 'whales now' will increase as density declines, the balance of the economic argument still favours taking whales now rather than in the future. I am sure the industry was far more aware of this economic reality than most of its conservationist and preservationist critics in the 1960s and early 1970s. The whaling industry was also far more specialized than most other fishing fleets – in fact it was equipped and trained for nothing except taking whales. The cost of conversion to fish-factory operations has been almost prohibitively expensive even for the younger vessels, and out of the question for the older ships.

One can therefore make a strong argument that the whaling industry, for some or all of the reasons suggested above, never was, is not and never would be really interested in sustainable-yield exploitation, simply because it makes no economic sense. The life of the average unit of whaling equipment is probably just about equal to the time span which an average baleen whale stock can be fished until the two sides of the cost–benefit equation equalize. At this point, under unmanaged conditions, and especially if only one species was being hunted, the classic open-access fishery would reach its equilibrium some time before the species became economically extinct. If the stock was then left alone to recover, perhaps even for some decades, the process could be repeated, yet never with the species being in danger of extinction. This approach has been called 'pulse fishing' (40). Gulland pointed out that southern humpback whale stocks have been exploited, particularly by coastal whaling nations such as Australia, in precisely this fashion. It is also characteristic of the actions of factory-ship fleets working ground fish stocks; when one area has been virtually cleaned out (in economic terms), the expeditions leave it alone for several seasons until some recovery occurs. Because many commercial fish species have very high fecundity rates, and there is not necessarily an obvious relationship between spawning success and the size of the spawning group (86), recovery may be remarkably rapid. Nevertheless, there are other cases where no recovery occurs at all, perhaps because of ecological displacement effects. Clark (17) emphasized two important considerations, as did Chapman (24). First, predictions based on the logistic model of population growth can be totally unreliable (a point also made strongly by Holt (44) (see Figure 9.10). There are other models which may give more explicit prediction, even if they have not been widely used by whale population dynamicists. Second, the recovery rate of whale populations is very slow, limited by the low fecundity and the long period before sexual maturity (24, 27).

The whaling industry has, in fact, carried out a huge and long drawn out version of pulse fishing with respect to the Southern Ocean and North Pacific baleen whale populations. It is impossible for any biologist to approve of this, whatever the economic logic behind the events. Because of poor management response and lack of control in multi-species fishing operations, with the quota system exercising only a limited degree of restraint, the prospect of *real* extinction for some species, such as the blue whale, became a possibility. This, I suppose, brings us to the point where we should see just what we can learn from the failures and limited successes obtained by the International Whaling Commission between 1946 and 1980.

Harvesting strategies and the route of optimal whale fisheries management

It may be that the cost–benefit equation will catch up with the pelagic whaling industry during the next three or four years, leaving only a few shore stations and some pirate whaling operations working on a rather small scale but still doing a lot of local damage, perhaps to totally protected species. What will happen to the International Whaling Commission after that is a matter for serious conjecture. If events take their usual course, it will be abandoned by the respective governments to slowly (or rapidly) wither. At the same time some of those governments will declare the 'whale problem' to be effectively solved, and a significant section of public opinion will believe that a great victory has finally been won. But if fuel prices stabilize in the future, or the need for extra protein and lipid becomes desperate enough in some nations, the whole sorry business will start all over again.

If it does, have we learned anything? I think we have. During the next decade or so we need a breathing space to make a careful review of management procedures, not only in whaling, but in all pelagic fishing operations of any scale. Basically, the management tools that we have at our disposal can be said to have two modes of operation, either to reduce the level of effort or to increase the cost of fishing. These are often, but not always, mutually interdependent. Many of the measures that can be taken to restrict effort may indeed directly or indirectly increase the cost of fishing. Simple management methods include limited entry licences, specific gear regulations, closed seasons and closed areas. The first may bring about stagnation and inefficiency, the second may reduce the effectiveness of fishing operations, the third result in seasonally idle men and equipment, and the fourth, unless the distribution of effort can be strictly controlled, may lead to cyclic overexploitation of areas and a very unstable fish catch. This in turn can generate market-price oscillations severe enough to cause operators serious problems.

In fact the determination of optimal fishing effort in real situations is far from simple; it has been given rather a comprehensive mathematical review by Clark (17). He points out that a family of solutions which relies on the maximization of sustained economic rent also includes the supposition that the industry will submit to arbitrary restrictions and sacrifices for the benefit of future generations. Frankly, when it comes down to the line, few of us are very good at doing that, especially those driven by the profit motive.

One comes to the inevitable conclusion, assuming whales will continue to be hunted by some nations despite the earnest pleas of preservationists, that we had better develop mechanisms in the near future whereby we can control that hunting. Despite all the criticism that has been levelled at it during the last decade, the International Whaling Commission still provides that focus, and the best thing that could happen during the next few years is for the nations which are now leaving whaling to maintain a strong and indefinite commitment to the Commission or to some re-negotiated international body, and for *all* non-signatory whaling nations to be brought into the orbit of the Commission. Significant strides have been made in the last few years in both these respects. The Netherlands and New Zealand, both of which had withdrawn from the Convention at one time or another, were encouraged to return, even though they are not now engaged in whaling operations. Several 'hold-outs', such as Spain and Chile, have finally joined the Convention, and others are at least supplying data to the Commission. I do not think that this trend is in any way aided by confrontations; steady pressure is more effective.

Review of actual management methods can lead even biologists, let alone economists, to some interesting conclusions (41). All the simple management methods, to which I will now add quota systems, not listed before, have some advantages as well as disadvantages. But it has to be understood that, from the point of view of the industry or the independent fisherman, management may confer very few obvious long-term benefits and may actually add to their costs. It is possible to maintain an ongoing fishery with all its operators in a state of chronic poverty or indebtedness. Whether or not they eventually get out and do something else may depend on the strength of their traditions, and their own view of their employability in other occupations.

Perhaps all the biggest benefits of sensible management are economic, rather than biological. We may talk about managing populations, but we are probably far more successful at managing industries, for in fact that is what we almost always do. It is invariably easier, furthermore, to take action to limit or improve economic returns than it is to tune fishing effort to the real maximum-sustained-yield level of the population (41).

Would-be managers of whale fisheries have tried most of these methods. The British attempted to limit entry, or at least take money from operators, in the old pre-First World War operations in the Falklands and Falkland dependencies. A sanctuary area was maintained in the Southern Ocean by the International Whaling Commission for many seasons, but it was not a zone of prime whale density or interest to pelagic operators. Closed seasons have been operated for many years. In the case of humpbacks the season was of only three or four days' duration by the late 1950s and early 1960s, and restricted to certain areas. The contagious distribution of humpback whales on the feeding grounds, however, made it easy to take them in numbers, providing one was in the right place at the right time.

The most basic method of limiting catches was obviously the quota. There was a general realization, and not just within the Scientific Committee of the International Whaling Commission, that the quotas set in the 1950s were far too high. The inability of the industry to agree on reductions does not mean that they did not realize this too – the reasons were given earlier in this chapter.

Although we have now abandoned the blue-whale-unit system, whaling will continue to be regulated by species quotas, and there has been much study and discussion on the suitability of fixed quotas, sliding quotas, joint quotas and effort quotas, and their respective long-term effects on populations, especially when two or more species are being hunted. There is no doubt that industry likes quotas, not only for whaling, but for all types of major fishing operations. Its representatives have argued for national quotas and for subdivisions well below that level to companies and even individual boats (26). Whether a fixed quota based on number of animals, or in the case of fish a given landed wet weight of each species, is actually the most desirable method of regulating catches from the point of view of best yield or stability is a moot point, however.

The effort that a fishery can exert if circumstances permit is probably the most crucial factor. In the anchoveta fishery in the early 1970s, for example, the industry could take a catch of ten million tonnes in only 80–100 days; not only did much of that effort lie idle for the rest of the year, but even during the season there was still capacity to spare (26). This is a dangerous situation which can stimulate just the kind of acute pressure to which the Peruvian government was subjected. If we are to operate a quota system with any hope of long-term success, the amount of effort potential present in the fishery should never be more than slightly greater than that necessary to take the quota in an average year. Anderson (3) discussed the impacts of quotas on the industry in some detail. Any form of overall quota (covering more than one nation, more than one fleet, more than one boat) will tend to encourage fishermen to increase their fishing power to maximize their share of the quota before closure. As they try to do this their costs will increase with each attempted improvement in fishing technique. Instead of promoting 'free enterprise' (the original US ideal for the whaling industry) the result will be loss of profitability in many cases. The operation of a 'peak-loading factor' brought about by quotas taken during a relatively short season can introduce stresses into the fishing, processing and marketing sections of the industry, and yet still not prevent overcapitalization. Anderson suggested that although ameliorative measures are possible, a carefully designed tax structure might in the long run be more beneficial than direct tampering with the fishery. As Elliot noted, despite the experience of the last couple of decades the business of management by quotas is still in its infancy (26).

The whaling operations carried out in most parts of the world generally involve more than one species, and despite the possible interactions between these species, it is still necessary to establish management procedures and regulate the industry. This is now done almost invariably by numerical quotas. In the last chapter I discussed the study carried out by Harwood on the mixed fin and sei whale fishery off Iceland (43). In this he considered the relative merits of three different types of quota that could possibly be applied (Figure 9.11):

(1) a fixed quota for each species;
(2) a quota based on partitioned effort;
(3) a joint quota for both species.

Fixed quotas had previously been shown to give undesirably fragile equilibria (17), and effort-based quotas were difficult to set because of objections by the industry and the practical problems of the partition of that effort. Although Harwood preferred the effort quota in theory, he opted for the joint quota in this case because fin and sei arrive at different times of the season, and some effort could in practice be partitioned for the two species. The conclusion drawn was that stability was quite sensitive to changes in the competition-coefficient component of the Lotka–Volterra equations. In his simulations stability deteriorated rapidly in the unexploited populations as competition increased. In the exploited populations, on the other hand, an *increase* in stability was favoured by increased competition for food. At high levels of competition all three policies demonstrated convergent results under exploitation, but both fixed and joint quotas had low stability at low rates of competition. If good data were available in such a case, the kinds of specific advice which could be given to a management agency are quite obvious.

Unfortunately, as can be imagined, direct calculation of competition coefficients for real whale population interactions is extremely difficult. Harwood therefore concluded that despite difficulties of application, a quota based on partitioned effort was to be preferred because it provided a far easier situation for population management. If this was impossible, then the next best approach was a joint quota, but only if it could be demonstrated that a lot of competition occurred between the two species. Beddington and Grenfell (5, 6) also examined the relative merits of harvesting models regulated by quota and effort, and came to the conclusion that under certain applications of effort regulation, fishing at

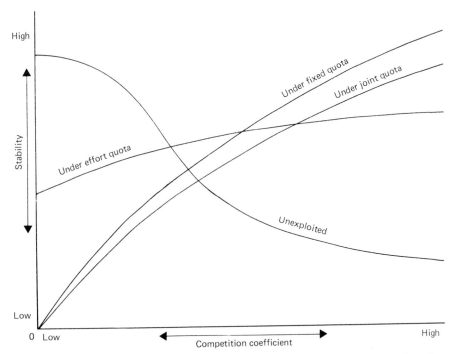

Figure 9.11 The problem of determining which type of quota is best employed under different circumstances in multispecific whale fisheries is a vexing one. J. Harwood and J. W. Horwood have explored the patterns of population stability which occur during competition between two simulated baleen whale species under fixed numerical, joint numerical, or effort quotas.

maximum-sustainable-yield levels could be shown to give a more stable population size than would occur in the unexploited stock. Horwood and his co-workers (45) studied the results of harvesting whale populations under different levels of stochastic variation. Their object was to see whether oscillations around the maximum-sustainable-yield level, or within 10 per cent of it, could lead to significant reductions in population size in a varying environment. This time-lagged simulation did not suggest that the influence of such variation was very great under the present management scheme. The main reason for the insignificant level of variability was considered to be the rather flat nature of the yield curve in whale populations, which means that at or near the maximum-sustainable-yield level the percentage of stock harvested was small in relation to the overall size of the population. Nevertheless, even if the variability is not regarded as significant, the difficulties of being able to accurately define the true maximum sustainable yield for a population are still formidable (33, 42). We have a hierarchy of population estimates of greater or lesser precision, and these have to be combined with what we hope are reasonably accurate relationships based on conjecture (33). The quantification of these problems in the last two or three years had led Allen (1) and others to suggest amendments to the new management procedure which had been adopted by the International Whaling Commission in 1974–5.

The weaknesses of the present scheme, however much of an improvement it is on the old blue-whale-unit management, Allen saw as follows. It contains no generally acceptable definition of optimum stock level for use in formulating management strategies. The form of whale yield curves are still not that well known, yet the Commission has been using maximum sustainable yield as a target even though its relationship to unexploited population sizes is unknown. This puts an unreasonable strain on the Scientific Committee when asked to project population estimates and yields. This is serious, because small changes in the scientific opinion concerning the values of population parameters can lead to advice requiring abrupt and sometimes large changes in catch levels, to the distress of planners in the industry. Each population currently has to be thoroughly reassessed each year, putting an enormous peak-loading strain on the Scientific Committee over a short period of time. The strategy of trying to bring all stocks to maximum-sustainable-yield level as soon as possible also prevents the Committee from learning about changes in biological parameters at different population sizes. Such information is critically important for developing future advice, and could be used for determining a sound basis for optimum population levels. There is no provision for adjustment of catch levels according to the degree of reliability of yield or abundance estimates.

Allen's new proposals would include the following changes: he would like to see the concept of optimum population level retained as the ultimate target, but the strategy for achieving this should be changed to permit *all* populations to increase until there was firm evidence that any further increase would not add to the available sustainable yield. Catches which would certainly lead to reduced population levels would only be permitted when there was strong evidence that such reductions would result in increased yield. The concept of protection stocks would be retained, and abundance estimates would be accepted at the most conservative level. In the process of determining the state and abundance level of a population for classification, the best estimate of the population prior to modern whaling would be used, rather than what appeared to be the present maximum-sustainable-yield level. In fixing quotas, the current replacement yield should be used as the main criterion, *not* the estimated maximum-sustainable-yield level. When determining this replacement yield, the Committee should take into account both the rate at which they would prefer the population to increase, and the degree of reliability of the estimate of the replacement yield. Quotas would be fixed for periods of several years for comparative study, and only changed abruptly if new information came to light which indicated that action was urgently necessary. Stock assessment would be carried out on a rotating basis, and if any previously unexploited stocks were added, then an initial quota would be set as a fixed proportion of the original stock size, with a reasonable margin of error included.

The main advantages of this revised strategy are seen as not establishing the maximum sustainable yield even as a temporary target of management, and permitting populations to increase until they are clearly above the optimum level. At this point 'downward revisions' can be made with relative safety. The revised method also substantially reduces quotas in cases where there is significant uncertainty about yields. The primary disadvantage of the revised methodology is seen by some as its extreme conservatism. If adopted, it could stop several operations presently permitted under the new management policy.

Until now we have considered the exploitation of the population as if it were one homogeneous unit. This is not the case, and the International Whaling Commission has always recognized this fact with certain catch restrictions, particularly with the regulations pertaining to minimum-size limits, and the protection of mothers with calves. Because whaling is a highly selective industry, and mean weight of animals as well as the mean length has decreased significantly, even in those populations which are still relatively numerous (the average weight of sperm whales, for example, has decreased dramatically in the last two decades, from about 45 tons to 28 tons (95)), it is well worth examining the effects that this may have had on the behaviour and general viability of populations. There is always the additional possibility to be considered that the yield by weight may *never* recover, even if the numbers do. The attention of the reader is drawn to work by Favro, Kuo and McDonald (30) who, studying the effects of selective fishing on trout, found that animals were not necessarily large because they were older – some proportion of the population were also large because their genetic make-up dictated that they would be larger at any given age than their fellows. Selective removal of these strains during the exploitation resulted in repopulation of the habitat with animals with less intrinsic capability to grow to the size of the former largest animals in the population. I do not believe that the implications of this work have been taken into account in the case of possible yields from recovered whale populations.

The basic unit of a large mammal population is the family group, often with some segregation of mothers with young. Above the family level – although such a term is hard to apply in the case of gregarious or polygynous species such as the sperm whale – we may have 'herd' structure, and several 'herds' may be found in the same region moving in the same direction with a common purpose, as during migration. It has been suggested that killing whole family groups of whales at a time, regardless of size or age, might make more sense in terms of mammalian biology than a fisheries biology-based selective culling for the largest animals (32). This would be in drastic contrast to the regulations which have to date governed whaling *within* quota limitations. If this suggested management approach was brought into effect we would have to take great care that the killing of family groups was tightly controlled so that the catching effort was evenly distributed through any subunits of the population. Although I tend to agree that this management proposal has some decided advantages in principle, the difficulties are considerable. Industry would almost certainly object strenuously, because if still held to a numerical quota, they would be forced to take many animals with a negligible yield of meat or oil within that number.

A further major difficulty can best be illustrated by a schematic study of the Antarctic areas IV–V humpback whale interactions (35), based on the studies of Chittleborough (15, 16) and Dawbin (19–23) (Figure 9.12). In some respects the model is speculative, because so little whaling is or was carried out among the Pacific islands for baleen whales (except at Tonga) that no mark recoveries in low latitudes could really be expected. But the pattern seems to be as follows. During the summer feeding period the western Australian, eastern Australian and the New Zealand–western South Pacific populations concentrate in the Antarctic between longitudes 70°E and about 160°W to about latitude 70°S. One feeding ground, centred between about 80°E and 90°E, seems (as determined by whale-mark recoveries) to be occupied solely by Western Australian animals, but another, centred between about 105°E and 130°E, is frequented by animals of both the eastern and western Australian populations and perhaps by relatively few from the New Zealand stock. Further east still, between longitudes 150°E and 180°, another feeding ground is occupied by eastern Australian and New Zealand animals. Some level of interchange between area IV and area V animals has been proved by marking, so that the subpopulations are not completely segregated or genetically isolated. Nevertheless, on average the majority of western Australian animals tend to return to western breeding grounds, the majority of eastern Australian animals to eastern breeding grounds, and so on. Consequently, although subpopulation segregation is not complete, it is a functional reality which must be taken into account for management purposes. Further complexity is revealed as the animals leave the feeding grounds and move northwards to their breeding grounds. Whereas the western and eastern Australian populations remain more or less

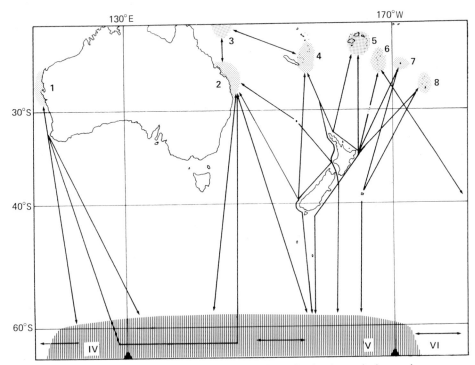

Figure 9.12 Separate stocks of humpback whales in the Australasian region are known to segregate on the breeding grounds of the tropics to a considerable extent, but also to intermingle on the feeding grounds of Antarctic areas (vertical striping) IV, V and VI. Breeding areas are: 1. subtropical coast of Western Australia; 2. subtropical–tropical coast of Queensland; 3. Louisiade archipelago; 4. New Caledonia–Loyalty Island region; 5. Fiji; 6. Tonga; 7. Niue; and 8. Cook Islands. Arrows indicate both apparent migration routes and positive movements indicated by whale-mark returns. Redrawn from Gaskin (35), formerly compiled largely from data in several papers by R. G. Chittleborough and W. H. Dawbin.

concentrated in continental coastal waters between 10°S and 35°S, the group V New Zealand population passes that archipelago and Norfolk Island, then divides into further subgroups which breed in the coastal waters of the Chesterfield Islands, New Caledonia, Loyalty Islands, New Hebrides, Fiji, Tonga, Niue and the Cook Islands. One animal marked in Tongan waters was eventually recovered near Peter I Island in the Bellingshausen Sea (21).

Whales from all these subgroups appear to mingle on the Antarctic feeding grounds – or at least we have no practical way of distinguishing them. Do the Fijian breeding herds tend to stay more or less together in the same localized part of the Southern Ocean during the summer, or at least move together? Might not a total family group kill in one region touch no Tongan breeders but perhaps totally exterminate the Cook Island herd?

We have no way of knowing at present, although data suggesting some recovery around Tonga but not near some other islands might indicate that this did indeed happen during the intensive humpback whaling, both from factory ships and land stations, during the 1950s and early 1960s. It is evident that no simple improved substitute exists for the imperfect forms of management at present used, although some method of enforcing a take of a given proportion of immature animals might give some protection to the proportion of the stock containing the older, more experienced, individuals.

Concluding thoughts: should we harvest whales at all?

Earlier I alluded to the possible end to pelagic whaling even before the publication of this volume, leaving serious residual problems for the member nations to wrestle with according to their will. If non-signatory nations can be brought into the regulatory system, some good measure of control can be operated. The same economic pressures and low whale population densities which have forced out several major whaling nations may soon force non-member countries from the industry as well. Boycotts against nations dealing with pirated products have proved to be quite effective if enforced with determination, and the marshalling of public opinion in this regard can be particularly useful. However, there are dangers even in this 'running-down' stage. As the expeditions dwindle in numbers, their effort is distributed over progressively smaller and smaller zones of the ocean. This can lead to excessive damage to local stock groups that may introduce bias into recovery estimates or yield estimates based on a population covering a much wider area.

Let us assume that the industry does run down almost completely, and several decades can pass so that populations recover to a large extent – with the proviso that the species ratios may never again be the same, and that if intensive krill fisheries also begin, the recovery population plateaux may be much lower than we anticipate. What then? Will the preservationist ideal of totally protected populations for the indefinite future be realized? Frankly, I doubt it. The pressures of human population increase; climatic changes and uncertainties in grain crops as a result of those changes will almost certainly dictate that some form of whaling would begin again in some parts of the world. If this does happen, let us at least be ready for it. This involves working hard to resolve the economic controversy of 'open access' versus 'common property' with respect to living resources of the high seas, and developing a sound basis for establishing control over entry into fisheries for those resources. We also need a strong commissariat *in situ* and equipped with strong and rational management policies and methods to take over if whaling begins again on a large scale. The preservation of the nucleus of the International Whaling Commission and its experience and expertise is essential, even if that organization metamorphoses into something else. It does not matter if the Commission does nothing but pure research on cetaceans for the next twenty or thirty years, in fact that would be splendid, bearing in mind how little we know about these animals. During this period the Commission's management functions could be kept in the idle mode, but ready to shift into gear the moment they were needed.

If this kind of future is to be realized then strong and far-sighted commitment is needed from maritime governments for an indefinite period. I do not regard this as unreasonable; these countries have done enough 'taking' in the past that it is only common justice that they put something back for a change. The rapid growth of the philosophy of 'coastal states' rights' and 200-mile limits is a serious threat to the International Whaling Commission and similar international organizations. Finally, I would urge the reader to study the review by G. L. Kesteven with respect to what he calls the 'necessary revolution' – really a revolution in attitudes as much as technical innovations (55). I quote, 'In its inability to predict, fisheries biology sits squarely and sadly beside ecology.' We may bluster, we may protest, but at heart we know that statement has an unpleasant ring of truth. We may need a completely new look at our techniques at this stage and even, as Kesteven puts it, our 'symbolic apparatus'.

Possibly deeper insights will be obtained through innovative application of dynamic systems analysis to marine ecological problems (7, 9, 63). Personally I think that even though our analytical techniques may have been too primitive to cope with complex ecological situations, the major failures have been ethical ones. We could have conserved many other resources than just the stocks of large baleen whales, if the dead-end philosophy of the economic industrial growth ethic could be circumvented, and if the aces in the deck of cards with which we play were not invariably short-term economic gain and political expediency.

References

1   Allen, K. R. 1979. 'Towards an improved whale management procedure', *Rep. Int. Whal. Commn*, vol. 29, pp. 143–5.

2   Alverson, D. L. and Paulik, G. J. 1973. 'Objectives and problems of managing aquatic living resources', *J. Fish. Res. Bd. Canada*, vol. 30, pp. 1936–47.

3   Anderson, L. G. 1977. *The Economics of Fisheries Management*, Baltimore and London, Johns Hopkins University Press.

4   Beamish, P. C. 1979. 'Behaviour and significance of entrapped baleen whales' in H. E. Winn and B. L. Olla (eds.), *Behavior of Marine Animals – Current Perspectives in Research Vol. 3 : Cetaceans*, New York, Plenum Press, pp. 291–309.

5   Beddington, J. R. 1978. 'On the dynamics of the sei whales under exploitation', *Rep. Int. Whal. Commn*, vol. 28, pp. 169–72.

6   Beddington, J. R. and Grenfell, B. 1979. 'Risk and stability in whale harvesting', *Rep. Int. Whal. Commn*, vol. 29, pp. 171–3.

7   Beddington, J. R. and May, R. M. 1977. 'Harvesting natural populations in a randomly fluctuating environment', *Science*, vol. 197, pp. 463–5.

8   Bennett, A. G. 1931. *Whaling in the Antarctic*, London, Blackwood.

9   Botkin, D. B. and Sobel, M. J. 1975. 'Stability in time varying ecosystems', *American Nat.*, vol. 109, pp. 625–46.

10 Brownell, R. L., Jr. 1975. 'Progress report on the biology of the Franciscana dolphin, *Pontoporia blainvillei*, in Uruguayan waters', *J. Fish. Res. Bd. Canada*, vol. 32, pp. 1073–8.

11 Brownell, R. L., Jr and Ness, R. 1970. 'Preliminary notes on the biology of the Franciscana, *Pontoporia blainvillei* (Cetacea: Platanistidae)' in *Proc. 6th Ann. Conf. on Biological Sonar and Diving Mammals*, Stanford Res. Inst., Palo Alto, California, 23–8.

12 Caldwell, D. K. and Caldwell, M. C. 1975. 'Dolphin and small whale fisheries of the Caribbean and West Indies: occurrence, history, and catch statistics – with special reference to the lesser Antillean island of St Vincent', *J. Fish. Res. Bd. Canada*, vol. 32, pp. 1105–10.

13 Caughley, G. 1977. *Analysis of Vertebrate Populations*, New York, John Wiley.

14 Chapman, D. G. 1973. 'Management of international whaling and North Pacific fur seals: implications for fisheries management', *J. Fish. Res. Bd. Canada*, vol. 30, pp. 2419–26.

15 Chittleborough, R. G. 1958. 'An analysis of recent catches of humpbacks from the stocks in groups IV and V', *Norsk Hvalfangsttid.*, vol. 47, pp. 109–37.

16 Chittleborough, R. G. 1959. 'Australian marking of humpback whales', *Norsk Hvalfangsttid.*, vol. 48, pp. 47–55.

17 Clark, C. W. 1975. *Mathematical Bioeconomics: The Optimal Management of Renewable Resources*, New York, John Wiley.

18 Cushing, D. H. 1973. 'Dependence on recruitment on parent stock', *J. Fish. Res. Bd. Canada*, vol. 30, pp. 1965–76.

19 Dawbin, W. H. 1956. 'The migrations of humpback whales which pass the New Zealand coast', *Trans. R. Soc. N.Z.*, vol. 84, pp. 147–96.

20 Dawbin, W. H. 1956. 'Whale marking in South Pacific waters', *Norsk Hvalfangsttid.*, vol. 45, pp. 485–508.

21 Dawbin, W. H. 1959. 'New Zealand and South Pacific whale marking and recoveries to the end of 1958', *Norsk Hvalfangsttid.*, vol. 48, pp. 213–38.

22 Dawbin, W. H. 1964. 'Movements of humpback whales marked in the southwest Pacific Ocean 1952 to 1962', *Norsk Hvalfangsttid.*, vol. 53, pp. 68–78.

23 Dawbin, W. H. 1966. 'The seasonal migratory cycle of humpback whales' in K. S. Norris (ed.), *Whales, Dolphins, and Porpoises*, Berkeley and Los Angeles, University of California Press, pp. 145–70.

24 Eberhardt, L. L. 1977. 'Optimal policies for conservation of large mammals, with special reference to marine ecosystems', *Env. Conserv.*, vol. 4, pp. 205–12.

25 Eberhardt, L. L. and Siniff, D. B. 1977. 'Population dynamics and marine mammal management policies', *J. Fish. Res. Bd. Canada*, vol. 34, pp. 183–90.

26 Elliot, G. H. 1973. 'Problems confronting fishing industries relative to management policies adopted by governments', *J. Fish. Res. Bd. Canada*, vol. 30, pp. 2486–9.

27 Estes, J. A. 1979. 'Exploitation of marine mammals: r-selection of K-strategists?', *J. Fish. Res. Bd. Canada*, vol. 36, pp. 1009–17.

28 Evans, W. E. 1976. 'Distribution and differentiation of stocks of *Delphinus delphis* Linnaeus in the northeastern Pacific', FAO of the UN, Scientific Consultation on Marine Mammals, Bergen, Norway, 31 August–9 September 1976, document ACMRR/MM/SC/18.

29 Fairford, F. 1916. 'Whale hunting in the North Atlantic', *Empire Rev.*, June 1916, pp. 222–4.

30 Favro, L. D., Kuo, P. K. and McDonald, J. F. 1979. 'Population-genetic study of the effects of selective fishing on the growth rate of trout, *J. Fish. Res. Bd. Canada*, vol. 36, pp. 552–61.

31 Fish, J. F. and Vania, J. S. 1971. 'Killer whale, *Orcinus orca*, sounds repel white whales, *Delphinapterus leucas*', *Fishery Bull.*, vol. 69, pp. 531–5.

32 Fox, W. W., Talbot, L. M., Aron, W. and Scheffer, V. B. 1974. 'Biological rationale and evidence for ceasing to take Antarctic fin whales', *Rep. Int. Whal. Commn.*, vol. 24, pp. 190–3.

33 Garrod, J. and Horwood, J. W. 1979. 'Whale management: strategy and risks – a comment', *Rep. Int. Whal. Commn*, vol. 29, pp. 215–18.

34 Gaskin, D. E. 1972. *Whales, Dolphins and Seals – With Special Reference to the New Zealand Region*, London and Auckland, Heinemann Educational Books.

35 Gaskin, D. E. 1976. 'The evolution, zoogeography and ecology of Cetacea', *Oceanogr. Mar. Biol. Ann. Rev.*, vol. 14, pp. 247–346.

36 Gaskin, D. E. 1978. 'Form and function in the digestive tract and associated organs in Cetacea, with a consideration of metabolic rates and specific energy budgets', *Oceanogr. Mar. Biol. Ann. Rev.*, vol. 16, pp. 313–45.

37 Gaskin, D. E. and Smith, G. J. D. 1977. 'The small whale fishery of St Lucia, W.I.', *Rep. Int. Whal. Commn*, vol. 27, p. 493.

38 Gates, D. J. 1963. 'Australian whaling since the war', *Norsk Hvalfangsttid.*, vol. 52, pp. 123–7.

39 Gulland, J. A. 1973. 'Distant-water fisheries and their relation to development and management', *J. Fish. Res. Bd. Canada*, vol. 30, pp. 2456–62.

40 Gulland, J. A. 1974. *The Management of Marine Fisheries*, Seattle, University of Washington Press.

41 Gulland, J. A. and Robinson, M. A. 1973. 'Economics of fisheries management', *J. Fish. Res. Bd. Canada*, vol. 30, pp. 2042–50.

42 Harmer, S. F. 1929. 'Southern whaling', *Proc. Linn. Soc. Lond.*, vol. 142, pp. 85–163.

43 Harwood, J. 1979. 'The effects of inter-specific competition on the choice of management policies for fin and sei whales', *Rep. Int. Whal. Commn*, vol. 29, pp. 167–9.

44 Holt, S. J. 1975. 'The concept of maximum sustainable yield (MSY) and its application to whaling', FAO of the UN, Scientific Consultation on Marine Mammals, Bergen, Norway, 31 August–9 September 1976, document ACMRR/MM/SC/4.

45 Horwood, J. W., Knight, P. J. and Overy, R. W. 1979. 'Harvesting of whale populations subject to stochastic variability', *Rep. Int. Whal. Commn*, vol. 29, pp. 219–24.

46 International Whaling Commission. 1977. 'Classification of whale stocks' (pp. 6–8) in

'Chairman's Report of Twenty-Seventh Meeting', *Rep. Int. Whaling Commn*, vol. 27, pp. 6–15.

47 International Whaling Commission. 1978. 'Protection stocks, review of status' (pp. 66–8) in 'Report of the Scientific Committee', *Rep. Int. Whal. Commn*, vol. 28, pp. 38–89.

48 International Whaling Commission. 1979. 'Report of the sub-committee on small cetaceans. Annex H' (pp. 87–9) in 'Report of the Scientific Committee', *Rep. Int. Whal. Commn*, vol. 29, pp. 38–105.

49 Jenkins, J. T. 1932. *Whales and Modern Whaling*, London, Witherby Press.

50 Jones, S. 1975. 'A suggestion for the introduction of the Indus Susu and Gangetic Susu into new sectors and river systems in the Indian subcontinent and for the establishment of sanctuaries for them', FAO of the UN, Scientific Consultation on Marine Mammals, Bergen, Norway, 31 August–9 September 1976, document ACMRR/MM/SC/16.

51 Jones, S. 1976. 'The present status of the Gangetic Susu, *Platanista gangetica* (Roxburgh)', FAO of the UN, Scientific Consultation on Marine Mammals, Bergen, Norway, 31 August–9 September 1976, document ACMRR/MM/SC/15.

52 Joseph, J. 1973. 'Scientific management of the world stocks of tunas, billfishes, and related species', *J. Fish. Res. Bd. Canada*, vol. 30, pp. 2471–82.

53 Juel, N. 1888. 'Hvalfangsten i Finmarken', *Norsk Fiskgritidende*, pp. 1–231.

54 Kapel, F. O. 1977. 'Catch of belugas, narwhals and harbour porpoises in Greenland, 1954–75, by year, month and region', *Rep. Int. Whal. Commn*, vol. 27, pp. 507–20.

55 Kesteven, G. L. 1972. 'Management of the exploitation of fishery resources' in B. J. Rothschild (ed.), *World Fisheries Policy – Multidisciplinary views*, Seattle, University of Washington Press, pp. 229–61.

56 Kükenthal, W. 1890. '(Finmark whaling)', *Deutche Geographische Blaetter*, vol. 18, p. 14.

57 Larkin, P. A. and Wilimovsky, N. J., 'Contemporary methods and future trends in fishery management and development', *J. Fish. Res. Bd. Canada*, vol. 30, pp. 1948–57.

58 Lear, W. H. and Christensen, O. 1975. 'By-catches of harbour porpoise (*Phocoena phocoena*) in salmon driftnets at West Greenland in 1972', *J. Fish. Res. Bd. Canada*, vol. 32, pp. 1223–8.

59 Lien, J. and Merdsoy, B. 1979. 'The humpback is not over the hump', *Nat. Hist.*, vol. 88, pp. 46–9.

60 Mackintosh, N. A. 1965. *The Stocks of Whales*, London, Fishing News (Books).

61 Marine Mammal Commission. 1977. *The concept of optimum sustainable populations*, Washington, Marine Mammal Commission.

62 Matthews, L. H. 1974. *The Whale*, New York, Crescent Books.

63 May, R. M. 1973. *Stability and complexity in model ecosystems*, Princeton, NJ, Princeton University Press.

64 McHugh, J. L. 1974. 'The role and history of the International Whaling Commission', in W. E. Schevill (ed.), *The Whale Problem: A Status Report*, Cambridge, Mass., Harvard University Press, pp. 305–35.

65 Mercer, M. C. 1975. 'Modified Leslie–DeLury population models of the long-finned pilot whale (*Globicephala melaena*) and annual production of the short-finned squid (*Ilex illecebrosus*) based upon their interaction at Newfoundland', *J. Fish. Res. Bd. Canada*, vol. 32, pp. 1145–54.

66 Mitchell, E. 1973. 'Draft report on humpback whales taken under special scientific permit by eastern Canadian land stations, 1969–1971', *Rep. Int. Whal. Commn*, vol. 23, pp. 138–54.

67 Mizue, K. and Yoshida, K. 1965. '(On the porpoises caught by the salmon fishing gill net in Bering Sea and the North Pacific Ocean)', *Bull. Fac. Fish. Nagasaki Univ.*, vol. 19, pp. 1–36.

68 Mizue, K., Yoshida, K. and Takemura, A. 1966. '(On the ecology of Dall's porpoise in Bering Sea and the North Pacific Ocean)', *Bull. Fac. Fish. Nagasaki Univ.*, vol. 21, pp. 1–21.

69 Nippgen, J. 1921. 'L'industrie de la balaeine aux Iles Falkland', *La Geographie*, vol. 36, p. 3.

70 Ohsumi, S. 1975. 'Incidental catch of cetaceans with salmon gillnet', *J. Fish. Res. Bd. Canada*, vol. 32, pp. 1229–35.

71 Perkins, J. S. and Beamish, P. C. 1979. 'Net entanglements of baleen whales in the inshore fishery of Newfoundland', *J. Fish. Res. Bd. Canada*, vol. 36, pp. 521–8.

72 Perrin, W. F. 1968. 'The porpoise and the tuna', *Sea Frontiers*, vol. 14, pp. 166–74.

73 Perrin, W. F. 1969. 'The problem of porpoise mortality in the US tropical tuna fishery', *Proc. 6th Ann. Conf. on Biol. Sonar and Diving Mammals*, Stanford Research Institute, Menlo Park, California, pp. 45–8.

74 Perrin, W. F. and Henderson, J. R. 1979. 'Growth and reproductive rates in two populations of spinner dolphins, *Stenella longirostris*, with different histories of exploitation', Southwest Fisheries Center, National Marine Fisheries Service, Administrative Report LJ–79–29.

75 Perrin, W. F. and Hunter, J. R. 1972. 'Escape behavior of the Hawaiian spinner porpoise (*Stenella* cf. *S. longirostris*)', *Fishery Bull.*, vol. 70, pp. 49–60.

76 Perrin, W. F., Miller, R. B. and Sloan, P. A. 1977. 'Reproductive parameters of the offshore spotted dolphin, a geographical form of *Stenella attenuata*, in the eastern tropical Pacific, 1973–75', *Fishery Bull.*, vol. 75, pp. 629–33.

77 Perrin, W. F., Smith, T. D. and Sakagawa, G. T. 1976. 'Status of populations of spotted dolphin, *Stenella attenuata*, and spinner dolphin, *Stenella longirostris*, in the eastern tropical Pacific', FAO of the UN, Scientific Consultation on Marine Mammals, Bergen, Norway, 31 August–9 September 1976, document ACMRR/MM/SC/27, addendum 1.

78 Perrin, W. F., Warner, R. R., Fiscus, C. H. and Holts, D. B. 1973. 'Stomach contents of porpoise, *Stenella* sp., and yellowfin tuna, *Thunnus albacares*, in mixed species aggregations', *Fishery Bull.*, vol. 70, pp. 1077–92.

79 Pilleri, G. 1970. 'Observations on the behaviour of *Platanista gangetica* in the Indus and Brahmaputra Rivers' in G. Pilleri (ed.), *Investigations on Cetacea*, vol. II, Berne, Waldau, pp. 27–60.

80 Pilleri, G. 1971. 'On the La Plata dolphin *Pontoporia blainvillei* off the Uruguayan coasts' in G. Pilleri (ed.), *Investigations on Cetacea*, vol. III, Berne, Waldau, pp. 59–67.

81 Pilleri, G. and Bhatti, N. U. 1978. 'Status of the Indus dolphin population (*Platanista indi* Blyth, 1859) between Gudda Barrage and Hyderabad in 1978' in G. Pilleri (ed.), *Investigations on Cetacea*, vol. IX, Berne, Waldau, pp. 25–38.

82 Pippard, L., Hughes, J. and Gaskin, D. E. *In preparation*. 'Distribution, movements and population size of the white whale (*Delphinapterus leucas*) in the estuary of the St Lawrence, Canada'.

83 Price, W. S. 1980. Personal communication.

84 Price, W. S. and Rozee, B. A. 1978. 'Small and large cetacean hunting in the Lesser Antilles, 1978', a report prepared for the International Fund for Animal Welfare.

85 Regier, H. A. 1973. 'Sequence of exploitation of stocks in multispecies fisheries in the Laurentian Great Lakes', *J. Fish. Res. Bd. Canada*, vol. 30, pp. 1992–9.

86 Ricker, W. E. 1958. 'Handbook of computations for biological statistics of fish populations', *Bull. Fish. Res. Bd. Canada*, vol. 119, pp. 1–300.

87 Salvesen, T. E. 1912. 'The whaling industry of today', *J.P. Soc. Arts, London*, vol. 60, pp. 515–23.

88 Sanderson, I. T. 1956. *Follow the Whale*, London, Cassell.

89 Schaefer, M. B. 1954. 'Some aspects of the dynamics of populations important to the management of commercial marine fisheries', *Inter-Amer. Trop. Tuna Comm. Bull.*, vol. 1, pp. 26–56.

90 Schaefer, M. B. 1957. 'A study of the dynamics of the fishery for yellowfin tuna in the eastern tropical Pacific Ocean', *Inter-Amer. Trop. Tuna Comm. Bull.*, vol. 2, pp. 247–85.

91 Sergeant, D. E. 1975. 'An additional food supply for humpback (*Megaptera novaeangliae*) and minke whales (*Balaenoptera acutorostrata*)', Int. Counc. Expl. Sea Marine Mammals Committee, document C.M. 1975/N:13.

92 Sleptsov, M. M. 1957. 'Determination of the age of *Delphinus delphis* L.', translation from *Bull. MOIP, otdel. biologii*, vol. 49, no. 2, pp. 43–51, Office of the Secretary of State, Washington, DC, 6 September 1957.

93 Small Whale Subcommittee of the International Whaling Commission Scientific Committee. 1978. 'Report to the Scientific Committee of the International Whaling Commission' in *Twenty-Eighth Report of the International Whaling Commission, London*, pp. 79–82.

94 Southwell, T. 1905. 'Some results of the North Atlantic fin whale fishery', *Ann. Mag. Nat. Hist.*, vol. 16, pp. 403–21.

95 Tillman, M. F. 1975. 'Assessment of North Pacific stocks of whales', *Marine Fisheries Review*, vol. 37, pp. 1–4.

96 Williamson, M. 1972. *The Analysis of Biological Populations*, London, Edward Arnold.

97 Winn, H. E., Edel, R. K. and Taruski, A. G. 1975. 'Population estimate of the humpback whale (*Megaptera novaeangliae*) in the West Indies by visual and acoustic techniques', *J. Fish. Res. Bd. Canada*, vol. 32, pp. 499–506.

CHAPTER 10

Environmental contaminants and trace elements: their occurrence and possible significance in Cetacea

Introduction

The literature on this subject is now considerable. Fifteen years ago this was not the case, testimony not only (as some have rather unjustly remarked) to the occurrence of fads in science as well as in fashion, but also to the fact that a problem has to be recognized before any resources can be marshalled to study it. Is there a problem? This is an issue which I want to examine in this chapter. If the situation is serious, then the juxtaposition to the chapter on management is no whim of arrangement; control over hunting of cetaceans and other direct human interferences will mean nothing if a steady, deadly deterioration in habitat is taking place. If there is one lesson which modern ecological science has for us, it is that if one protects the habitat, then animal populations can show remarkable resilience in the face of other external pressures, even those such as intensive predation by man.

There is no dispute that man-made contaminants occur in cetacean tissues, sometimes in what are considered by any standards to be significant quantities. These compounds have been found in most other kinds of marine organism also. The compounds usually referred to as 'contaminants' fall into three broad groups: the chlorinated hydro-carbons, exemplified by DDT (dichlorodiphenyltrichloroethane); compounds containing heavy metal atoms such as mercury; and finally the hydrocarbons derived from petroleum oils. There is dispute about the origins of the second group of compounds, since many metallic elements occur naturally in sea-water marine sediments, and find their way into all levels of marine food-chains. The amounts present per unit weight of tissue may, in some organisms, have been derived partly from natural sources, and partly from industrial, agricultural or urban effluent. In localized cases almost all heavy metal contamination may result from man-made inputs, but in practice it has proved extraordinarily difficult to identify sources of these elements in marine situations. For this reason, I think it more accurate to consider the metallic compounds as 'trace elements' at this time, rather than grouping them with the organochlorine hydrocarbons, which may more firmly be considered as being present as a result of our industrial activities. Most petroleum hydrocarbons also occur naturally. In many areas oil seepage into the sea is a natural and common event, for example, in the Santa Barbara Channel off California, and on parts of the Beaufort Sea shelf in the Canadian western Arctic.

Almost all discussion, apart from the points considered above, centres on two questions; first, do these compounds present a risk to the cetacean individuals, populations or species, or not? Second – in either case, because contaminants or trace elements may be present in high concentrations in some tissues or organs, such as the blubber and liver, to a much greater extent than in the animal's body as a whole – is there any danger presented to humans who might eat these tissues?

Compounds identified in cetacean tissues

The list of contaminants or potentially harmful trace elements found in the tissues of cetacean species is growing rapidly; this does not necessarily reflect a swiftly deteriorating situation, but the fact that far more routine analyses are now made than even five years ago. Furthermore, some analytical methods, although not particularly difficult to carry out with modern equipment, are highly specific as to compound or chemical group. In order to locate certain contaminants, it is necessary to look for them using specific tests; their presence is not always revealed by broad spectrum 'scattergun' analyses. Some may be masked by related compounds, perhaps of lower toxicity and not generally regarded as presenting a serious problem. A degree of foresight is required when searching for previously unrecorded contaminants. However, as one of my colleagues remarked, what is particularly depressing is that whatever we decide to search for, we all too often find.

Chlorinated hydrocarbons

The presence of chlorinated hydrocarbons in the tissues of marine mammals was first recorded in 1967, and the harbour seal and harbour porpoise were among the first species to be examined (40). The existence of significant levels of chlorinated pesticides in the depot fat of ocean-going sea-birds was established at about the same time (44, 59), in several widely scattered regions of the world (10, 77, 82).

The common chlorinated hydrocarbons belong to three basic chemical groups: DDT (dichlorodiphenyltrichloroethane) and allied compounds, the endrin-dieldrin group, and the polychlorinated biphenyl (PCB) compounds. Other organic contaminants undoubtedly occur in tissues of these animals. Organophosphorus compounds have not, to the best of my knowledge, been identified in tissues of these animals as yet; some seem to be very short-lived in mammalian tissues. Some are so toxic that they could cause rapid death.

DDT is an efficient stomach and/or contact poison which affects a wide range of insect groups. It was synthesized in 1874, but its insecticidal properties were not put to use until just before the Second World War (76). Treated surfaces remain poisonous to insects for weeks or months. It is synthesized from chlorine and petroleum chemicals, but the usual commercial product is a mixture, containing about 75–80 per cent p,p'-DDT, which is highly toxic, and 10–12 per cent each of p,p'-TDE and the other isometric form o,p'-DDT. The latter has little or no insecticidal effect. All three compounds are virtually insoluble in water, but highly soluble in lipids. In the soil, it takes a few years for micro-organisms to detoxify p,p'-DDT, but if it reaches freshwater or marine sediments the breakdown becomes far slower. Since DDT is insoluble in water, application in solid form to dry pasture and forest leads to rapid aerial transport (15); it is probably by this route that most finds its way into the sea. Suspended solids in river water can contain less than one-thirtieth or less of the amounts recorded in aerial dust samples (15). There seem to be no precise estimates of the relative percentages of DDT and its metabolites in the water column, as against presence in sediments or the living components of the marine food-chains. One of the most notorious breakdown products is p,p'-DDE (dichlorodiphenyldichloroethylene), implicated in thinning of eggshells in birds, including some sea-birds (13).

Some marine mammals appear to have detoxification mechanisms which can deal with mercury and cadmium, by converting toxic forms to less toxic compounds, or into a form in which they can be readily excreted (see pp. 424–5). Animal tissues in many cases do not seem to be able to break down chlorinated hydrocarbons to any great extent (although exceptions do occur, see p. 424). The tissues of marine organisms have evolved methods to deal with heavy metals at least to a degree, presumably because these elements were always there. This is not the case with the chlorinated hydrocarbons, which have only been present in the environ-ment for the last forty years or so (66).

Since DDT compounds are soluble in lipids, they become concentrated in those tissues with high lipid content; in the case of marine mammals by far the greatest amount is present in the blubber, as would be expected. Much of the earlier work on upper-trophic-level marine organisms was carried out on sea-birds, since these are considerably easier to collect than marine mammals under most circumstances. It became customary, as a result of these studies, to conclude that biological activity broke down DDT fairly rapidly into TDE (2,2-bis (p-chlorophenyl)-1, 1-dichloro-ethane) (DDD) and DDE, with the highly persistent DDE molecule predominating in the sea and the tissues of marine organisms, especially sea-birds (13, 71). This has not proved to be the case in marine mammals; in both seals and porpoises the proportion of p,p'-DDT recorded is often 40–50$^+$ per cent of the total in the depot fat (26–8). In the liver, however, DDE usually predominates (27). This suggests that much of the lipid intake is moved directly to the blubber without 'processing'.

The search for more highly specific or short-lived insecticides led to the development of a whole family of other compounds chemically related, to a greater or lesser extent, to DDT. Although the DDT compounds contain five chlorine atoms, and DDD and DDE four each, the cyclodiene compounds contain six or more chlorine atoms. This is a large family, with numerous isomeric forms. The breakdown products are often no less toxic than the primary cyclodiene compounds. All are neurotoxins, but have varying degrees of persistence and toxicity. Endrin proved to be so toxic to wildlife that it was rapidly banned in wide areas of the western nations. Somewhat less toxic, but exceedingly persistent, aldrin and dieldrin are two other well-known compounds of this group. Endrin is a stereoisomer of dieldrin, and was employed during the late 1950s and in the 1960s against foliage and orchard pests. Careless use resulted in some serious accidents for farm workers and orchardists. One advantage with aldrin was that it tended to volatilize rapidly under normal conditions. Dieldrin is the most persistent of the three compounds, and has seen much use since first marketed. It can still be used under certain stringent restrictions, and found wide employment in the tobacco industry against a range of serious pests. Dieldrin has been identified frequently in marine mammal tissues (27, 39). Endrin and aldrin are not normally detected in routine analyses, but both are toxic to a wide variety of vertebrates; they leave relatively little trace under most circumstances. Endrin traces have been reported in a dolphin from Japan and in another from the eastern tropical Pacific (64). Aldrin is rapidly converted to dieldrin in most animal tissues. Two other members of this group of compounds are heptachlor (found in small quantities in dolphin blubber off California, Japan and in the eastern tropical Pacific (64)), which has a relatively high vapour pressure and long residual action period, and chlordane, which has several isomers. The research group at Guelph has located only traces of *trans*-chlordane in porpoise tissues from the Bay of Fundy, but significant amounts in the tissues of great and sooty shearwaters (*Puffinus gravis* and *P. griseus*) from the same region (29). Oxychlordane has been found in small quantities in cetacean tissues from California and Japan (64), and *cis*-chlordane occasionally in specimens from Uruguay, southern California and the eastern tropical Pacific (64). Both *trans*- and *cis*-nonachlor were reported by the same authors, the former on a global basis, the latter from California. Hexachlorobenzene compounds (HCB), probably lindane or gammexane (=γ-benzene hexachloride) have also been detected in harbour porpoises from the same region (25). There are usually up to six isomeric compounds in commercial preparations of benzene hexachlorides; these molecules have the same chemical composition as the dieldrin group, but differ significantly in structure. Among the more 'exotic' pesticides, toxaphene has been recorded from Japan and the open Pacific (64).

Like the DDT and dieldrin group compounds, the polychlorinated biphenyls are based on a pair of linked rings with varying levels of chlorine atom inclusion or substitution for hydrogen atoms. Marketed since the 1930s, PCBs, as they are usually known, have found use in many branches of industry. They have been major constituents of transformer and hydraulic oils, various types of paint, electrical components and different types of plastics (86). Many isomeric forms are known, and well over fifty of these are common components of most commercial mixtures, and detailed analysis and individual identification of polychlorinated biphenyls is an exacting test for any organic chemist (45). The commonest commercial mixtures include Arochlor 1254, Arochlor 1260, Clophen A50 and Phenochlor DP6. These are used as reference mixtures in analyses, and the patterns observed in gas chromatographs of tissue residues can be compared against these standards (48, 52). The presence of polychlorinated biphenyl compounds in samples drawn from many parts of the world was given wide publicity in 1968 (70), but there is little evidence that they are distributed in atmospheric dust like DDT (35).

Polychlorinated biphenyls are almost insoluble in water, but soluble in lipids, and are always found in close association with DDT and its metabolites and dieldrin-type compounds. This is one of the reasons why it is so difficult to pinpoint these compounds as the specific cause of problems in the wild. Not only are polychlorinated biphenyls insoluble in water, but they are also singularly resistant to chemical reagent attack – hence their applicability to many industrial purposes. Almost all the commercially-used polychlorinated diphenyls have from five to eight chlorine atoms per molecule. Bio- and chemical degradability generally decrease as one goes up the chlorine atom scale; this may correlate quite closely with metabolism of the compounds and hence also with their relative toxicity. Accumulation, as with DDT and dieldrin compounds, varies from one locality to another, and with exposure time, and can therefore also be a function of age. Because marine mammals are relatively long-lived compared to most marine organisms, their exposure time is long, and because they also have lipid depot reserves which are very extensive in proportion to their body size and weight, they become ideal repositories for high concentrations of all persistent chlorinated hydrocarbons.

Heavy metals

Trace elements were for a long time the domain of the metallurgist searching for alloys, or, in a biological context, the nutritionist interested in the identification of dietary deficiencies. The widely publicized occurrence of acute mercury poisoning in Japan in the 1950s (54) – Minamata disease, as it came to be known – changed all that. The point on which most attention focused was the fact that the fishermen of Minamata Bay were poisoned *through the local marine food-chain*, by eating heavily contaminated fish and other marine organisms. This stimulated a reaction in government-sponsored research in other areas of the world in which such pollution was at least a remote possibility. There is no doubt that there was a great deal of over-reaction, but some interesting facts emerged. First, the general ignorance of oceanographers, marine chemists and marine biologists concerning the role of metallic elements in marine processes became glaringly evident. Second, the concentrations of heavy metals in the sea is so low that even minor contamination in an area could result in levels with which the marine life there had never previously had to cope (15). Third, although some metallic elements are minute but vital components of certain enzymic reactions, they can also act as reaction inhibitors if present in excess concentrations, with resulting toxic effects (15).

Initially studies were more or less confined to mercury, then cadmium and lead, but in recent years the term 'heavy metals' has been used to cover all metals except the light alkali metals such as lithium and sodium, and the alkaline earth elements. When present in the tissues of marine animals a number of metals, known to be essential for normal growth, are always found in the form of metalloproteins, of which the best known examples are the haemoglobins and the haemocyanins, respiratory pigment proteins containing iron and copper respectively. Zinc, iron, manganese and copper have been identified as essential components in enzymatic reactions. Zinc and copper can be acutely toxic, however, when present in excess; mercury, lead and cadmium are also toxic, but do not normally occur as essential elements in enzyme reactions.

These metallic elements may be transported as aerial dust, as in the case of DDT and related compounds, and reach the sea that way; they may be released from deep sea sediments or by volcanic action under water, or they can be eroded from watershed or river-bottom lodes and transported into the sea by normal coastal processes. It is generally thought that metallic elements most commonly arrive in the sea in particulate form.

In solution these elements are usually mixed together in several forms: as minute colloidal particles not in true solution, free metal ions, ion pairs and inorganic salt complexes. In oceanic waters most elements are probably in the form of inorganic complexes, or metallic 'salts', as they would have been called under the terminology of a generation ago. Chlorides are obviously likely to be the most common. In coastal waters a number of organic complexes are commonly found. The chemistry of these is poorly understood; some workers have suggested that they may be the result of treatment within living organisms (23). These bound organic fractions may be exceedingly stable, and not in any kind of equilibrium with the soluble inorganic fractions under normal conditions. A large fraction of the heavy metals in the sea may be subjected to biological action, and as much as 90 per cent may be vertically transported by organisms rather than physical processes (56). Death of organisms may result in some metals becoming temporarily or permanently locked up in deep sediments.

Most interest since Minamata has been directed to the fate of heavy metals once they enter biological systems. Some of their salts (for example, mercurous chloride) are not dangerous; others (for example, mercuric chloride) are acutely toxic. The methylated form of mercury (methyl-mercuric chloride) is the one which has caused most concern. Mercury entering fish tissues (and hence becoming available as food for man, marine birds and marine mammals) is largely in methylated form. There has been some argument whether or not this form is produced within the tissue or taken up in that form; A. Jernelöv has shown that the conversion of inorganic mercury into mono- or di-methyl mercury compounds can be carried out by micro-organisms found in surface layers of aquatic sediments (46). The organic mercury is returned to the water column from these sediments, and from there finds its way into the food-chains.

Petroleum hydrocarbons

The literature on the effects of oil pollution on marine life is huge; at the simplest level the organisms are killed by simple smothering. The tolerance of marine animals to oil varies; it is important to remember that oil compounds occur naturally in the sea in many areas, and many groups, or at least local populations, have evolved coincidently with oil seepage.

Tolerances therefore vary significantly from organism to organism. Periwinkles, for example, are quite notorious for their resistance to oil. Tiny pelagic larvae, on the other hand, often show extreme sensitivities. In addition, certain fractions of petroleum compounds are considerably more toxic than others.

These compounds are usually referred to as polynuclear aromatic hydrocarbons. They have a whole range of molecular sizes and structures, but the basic building blocks are always units of benzene hexagons ('aromatic rings'). In physical state they range from light and highly volatile compounds to heavy tars. Like the DDT group, they have very low true solubility in water. Unlike the DDT and PCB (polychlorinated biphenyl) species they are quite chemically reactive, which can make them more toxic in some circumstances, but can also result in much more rapid breakdown and biodegradation than occurs with the organochlorine pesticides and their chemical allies. I am not going to discuss these compounds in detail in this chapter. Although the carcinogenic substance 3,4-benzpyrene, for example, has been identified in a number of marine organisms, I am not aware that it or related compounds have yet been specifically isolated from cetacean tissues.

Contaminant levels in cetacean species

Chlorinated hydrocarbons

Some authors have reported DDT simply as total of *p,p'*-DDT, including its metabolites, others have given detailed breakdowns of each component (all are cited as parts per million of wet weight of tissue in this section unless otherwise specified).

At the time of writing, data are available for six species of baleen whale; blue, fin, sei, minke, humpback and gray whale (Table 10.1). On the whole, they are not as heavily contaminated as many odontocetes, but organochlorine levels in fatty tissues are certainly high enough that they should not be ignored. Samples from sperm whales have been analysed from several widely dispersed areas (Table 10.2); data from a series of dwarf and pygmy sperm whales from Florida are presented in the same table.

Data for ziphiid whales, monodontids and globicephalids are similarly rather limited; these are presented in Table 10.3. The smaller odontocetes of the families Platanistidae, Phocoenidae and Delphinidae have attracted considerable attention in recent years; in Tables 10.4 and 10.5 data on sixteen species are given. It is evident that Arctic and tropical cetaceans are relatively free of these contaminants, but species in temperate-zone

Table 10.1 Chlorinated hydrocarbon residues in baleen whales (p.p.m., wet weight)

Species	Locality	Tissue	Total DDT	Dieldrin	cis-Chlordane	Polychlorinated biphenyls	Others	References
Blue whale	Antarctic Ocean[1]	Blubber oils	0.18	ND[2]	NA[3]	ND	NA	5
Fin whale	Eastern Canada	Blubber	4.24–32.33	NA	NA	7.00	NA	5
	Eastern Canada	Blubber	0.67–2.56	NA	NA	0.01–0.18	NA	72
	South-east Greenland	Blubber	2.88	0.17	NA	3.6	NA	39
	France	Blubber	47.70	NR[4]	NR	NR	NR	6
	St Lawrence River, Canada	Blubber	3.00	NR	NA	10.00	NR	74
Sei whale	Antarctic Ocean	Blubber oils	0.31	ND	NA	ND	NA	5
Minke whale	St Lawrence estuary, Canada	Blubber	1·09	NA	NA	27.45	NA	74
Humpback whale	Nova Scotia	Blubber	23.10	ND	ND	5.40	NA	79
	Eastern USA	Blubber	7.60	1.20	0.20	6.00	NA	79
	Lesser Antilles	Blubber	1·40–2·10	0.10	0.10	1.30–1.50	NA	79
Gray whale	Californian coast, 1968–9	Blubber	0.50	0.07	NA	NA	NA	85
		Brain	trace	trace	NA	NA	NA	85
		Liver	trace	trace	NA	NA	NA	85

Notes:
1. Thirty-year-old stored samples. 2. Not detected. 3. Not analysed.
4. Not reported.

Table 10.2　Chlorinated hydrocarbon residues in sperm whales (p.p.m., wet weight)

Species	Locality	Tissue	Total DDT	Dieldrin	cis-Chlordane	Polychlorinated biphenyls	Others	References
Sperm whale	Antarctic	Blubber oils[1]	34.98	ND[2]	NA[3]	1.0	NA	5
	Nova Scotia	Blubber	7.60	trace	NA	1.0	NA	5
	North Pacific	Blubber	1.82–9.43	trace – 0.02	NA	NA	NA	85
		Liver	0.35	ND	NA	NA	NA	85
		Brain	0.07	ND	NA	NA	NA	85
	Eastern USA	Blubber	8.90	ND	0.30	2.10	NA	79
	Caribbean	Blubber	1.10–15.50	ND	ND	0.70–4.00	NA	79
Pygmy sperm whale	Florida coast, USA	Blubber	1.15–12.13 (6.74)	NA	NA	NA	NA	62
		Liver	0.10–1.74 (0.38)	NA	NA	NA	NA	62
		Muscle	0.03–0.79 (0.36)	NA	NA	NA	NA	62
		Kidney	0.03–0.43 (0.19)	NA	NA	NA	NA	62
		Brain	0.03–0.17 (0.12)	NA	NA	NA	NA	62
		Spermaceti organ	0.70–13.14 (4.32)	NA	NA	NA	NA	62
		Intramandibular fat body	0.47–13.80 (6.24)	NA	NA	NA	NA	62
		Melon	1.40–16.40 (6.26)	NA	NA	NA	NA	62
		Milk	1.67	0.037	NA	1.20	NA	43

Notes:
1. Thirty-year-old stored oils.　2. Not detected.　3. Not analysed.

Species	Locality	Tissues	Total DDT	Dieldrin	cis-Chlordane	Polychlorinated biphenyls	Others	References
Bottlenose whale	Western North Atlantic	Blubber	11.60	NR[1]	NA[2]	1.00	NA	5
Dense-beaked whale	Eastern USA	Blubber	38.20-65.10	0.20-0.30	0.10-0.30	14.00-29.00	NA	79
White whale	North-West Territories, Canada	Blubber	3.90±0.89	NR	NR	NA	NA	1
	Hudson Bay, Canada	Blubber	7.40	ND[3]	NA	1.00	NA	1
	St Lawrence estuary, Canada	Blubber (adult ♀)	21.50-34.00	NR	NR	171-183	NA	74
		Blubber (juvenile ♀)	827	NR	NR	800	NA	74
Pygmy killer whale	Florida coast, USA	Blubber	4.80	ND	NA	0.80	ND	22
		Liver	2.90	ND	NA	2.60	ND	22
		Kidney	0.50	trace	ND	1.20	traces of HBC[4] and lindane	22
		Melon and intramand. fat body	21.10-27.10	trace	ND	29.00-79.00	trace of heptachlor	22
Pilot whale	Newfoundland	Blubber	19.40-40.35	NA	NA	1.00	NA	5
	Eastern USA	Blubber	30.30-268	1.10-3.00	0.60-1.40	42.00-114	NA	79
	South-west England	Blubber	42.70	2.30	NA	93	NA	40
	France	Blubber	NR	NR	NR	6.9-840	NR	6
	Faeroe Islands	Blubber	68.80	NR	NR	NR	NR	55
Short-finned pilot whale	St Vincent, West Indies	Blubber	1.25-2.28	0.01-0.04	ND	0.69-1.60	ND	31
		Muscle	0.01-0.59	trace	ND	0.05-0.50	ND	31
		Liver	0.01-0.10	trace	ND	0.05-0.72	ND	31
		Kidney	0.04-0.39	trace	ND	0.06-0.64	ND	31
	California[4]	Blubber	255.30	0.40	ND	46.00	ND	79
	California	Blubber	35.08-130.10	ND	ND	8.80-14.00	ND	64
		Muscle	0.53-7.46	ND	ND	ND-0.88	ND	64
	Japan	Blubber	1.00-14.44	ND-1.20	ND	0.60-32.00	0.01-0.06 HCB, 0.08-0.14 toxaphene	64

Notes:
1. Not recorded. 2. Not analysed. 3. Not detected. 4. Hexachlorobenzene. 5. Captive specimen.

Table 10.4 Chlorinated hydrocarbon residues in platanistid and phocoenid cetaceans (p.p.m., wet weight)

Species	Locality	Tissue	Total DDT	Dieldrin	cis-Chlordane[1]	Polychlorinated biphenyls	Others	References
Franciscana dolphin	Uruguay	Blubber	9.28-30.90	0.22-1.00	ND[1]	3.60-18.00	ND-0.18 HCB[2] / ND-0.24 trans-nonachlor	64
		Brain	ND	NR[3]	NR	0.35-0.65	NR	64
		Muscle	ND	NR	NR	ND-0.25	NR	64
Dall's porpoise	California	Blubber	245.80	0.40	ND	94	0.28 HCB	64
	Japan	Muscle	3.97	NR	NR	0.53	NR	64
		Blubber	8.58	0.40	NR	3.40	0.28 HCB	64
		Brain	ND	NR	NR	ND	0.56 transnonachlor	64
		Muscle	ND	NR	NR	0.16	ND	64
Finless porpoise	Japan	Blubber	12.08-131.80	2.00-38.00	0.12-0.46 (oxychlordane)	18.00-96.00	0.22-0.64 HCB / ND-0.22 toxaphene / 0.28-0.82 heptachlor e.o. / 0.40-1.10 trans-nonachlor	64
		Brain	0.15-0.26	NR	NR	1.30-1.80	NR	64
		Muscle	ND-0.65	NR	NR	0.43-1.20	NR	64
Harbour porpoise	California	Blubber	334.80	1.00	ND	84.00	0.18 HCB / 0.18 heptachlor e.o. / 5.0 trans-nonachlor	64
	East Scotland	Brain	2.35	NR	NR	0.65	NR	64
		Muscle	2.20	NR	NR	0.50	NR	64
	North Sea	Blubber	27.00-56.00	4.90-18.00	NR	NR	NR	38-40
	Eastern USA	Blubber	250	0.54	NR	35.00-148.00	0.01-0.95 HCB	40
	Bay of Fundy,[4] Canada	Blubber	57.5	1.50	2.60	74.00	NR	79
		Blubber	22.83-227.00 (103.42 ♂) 21.48-55.69 (39.35 ♀)	1.52-9.54 (4.01 ♂) 0.98-6.56 (3.97 ♀)	ND-8.56 (2.32 ♂) 0.13-6.78 (1.78 ♀)	16.00-310.00 (72.28 ♂) 1.30-150.00 (42.83 ♀)	0.23 HCB (♂)	25, 27, 28
		Liver	0.21-2.03 (0.79 ♂) 0.10-0.30 (0.21 ♀)	ND-0.10 0.02-0.07 (0.05 ♀)	ND-0.70 (0.05 ♂) ND-0.03 (0.01 ♀)	0.30-23.00 (1.86 ♂) 0.11-7.30 (0.96 ♀)	0.20-0.25 (0.23 ♀) trace ♂	25, 27, 28
		Kidney	0.12-0.47 (0.22 ♂)	ND-0.03 (0.005 ♂)	ND	0.06-9.90 (0.62 ♂, 1.17 ♀)	0.01 ♀ ND	25, 27, 28

	Tissue	Total DDT	Dieldrin	cis-Chlordane	Polychlorinated biphenyls	Others	References
	Brain	0.08–1.53 (0.38 ♀) 0.11–0.58 (0.37 ♂)	ND–0.06 (0.02 ♀) 0.02–0.04 (0.03 ♂)	ND–0.06 (0.01 ♀) ND	0.11–3.70 (0.85 ♀) 0.10–4.50 (0.95 ♂, 0.63 ♀)	ND	25, 27, 28

Notes:
1. Not detected. 2. Hexachlorobenzene compounds. 3. Not recorded. 4. Data from most recent years' collecting: 1975–7 inclusive.

Table 10.5 Chlorinated hydrocarbon residues in delphinid cetaceans (p.p.m., wet weight)

Species	Locality	Tissue	Total DDT	Dieldrin	cis-Chlordane	Polychlorinated biphenyls	Others	References
Hector's dolphin	New Zealand	Blubber	45	NR[1]	NR	5	NR	9
Dusky/common dolphins[2]	New Zealand	Blubber	4.25–177.00	0.02–0.05	NR	0.05–4.80	NR	50
Pacific white-sided dolphin[3]	Eastern North Pacific	Blubber	1023	4.10	NR	147	NR	79
Atlantic white-sided dolphin	Eastern USA	Blubber	40.7	1.40	NR	37	NR	79
Common dolphin	Eastern USA	Blubber	71	1.5	1.2	74	NR	79
	Southern UK	Blubber	1.28	0.64	NR	NR	NR	40
	French Mediterranean	Blubber	NR	NR	NR	34.5–278	NR	6
	California	Blubber	450.4–1831	ND[4]–1.40	ND–1.2 (oxy)	80–300	ND–0.34 HCB[5] ND–2.0 heptachlor ND–10 trans-nonachlor	64
	Japan	Brain	10.4–47.9	NR	NR	ND–4.2	NR	64
		Muscle	4.78–40.68	NR	NR	ND–3.3	NR	64
		Blubber	1.28–8.72	0.14–0.62	ND	2.4–6.4	0.06–0.26 HCB ND–0.04 heptachlor e.o. 0.14–0.36 toxaphene ND–0.46 trans-nonachlor	64
		Muscle	ND–0.28	NR	NR	0.30–0.35	NR	64
Blue-white dolphin	Eastern USA	Blubber	70–231	1.40–2.40	NR	39–69	NR	79
	France	Blubber	56.8–706	NR	NR	47–833	NR	7

Species	Locality	Tissue	Total DDT	Dieldrin	cis-Chlordane	Polychlorinated biphenyls	Others	References
Striped dolphin	St Lucia, WI	Blubber	1.44–7.38	0.007–0.05	NA[6]	2.00–5.00	NA	31
		Liver	0.06–0.13	trace	NA	0.15–0.24	NA	31
		Kidney	0.06–0.14	trace	NA	0.17–0.26	NA	31
		Muscle	0.04–0.06	trace	NA	0.03–0.10	NA	31
	Eastern tropical Pacific	Blubber	0.62–182.50	0.14–0.84	ND	ND–12.00	4.0–5.6 toxaphene / 0.26–0.30 HCB / 0.18–0.64 trans-nonachlor	64
	Japan	Brain	ND–1.26	NA	NA	ND–0.40	NA	64
		Muscle	ND–1.78	NA	NA	ND	NA	64
		Blubber	1.26–18.92	ND–0.34	ND	1.20–5.00	0.08 HCB / 0.12–0.18 toxaphene / 0.24 trans-nonachlor	64
Fraser's dolphin	Eastern tropical Pacific	Brain	ND–0.96	NA	NA	ND	NA	64
		Muscle	ND–1.75	NA	NA	ND–1.60	NA	64
	Japan	Blubber	11.02	ND	ND	5.20	ND	64
		Muscle	0.17	ND	ND	ND	ND	64
Rough-toothed dolphin	Hawaii	Blubber	ND–28.80	0.32–0.66	ND	ND–38.00	0.5–1.0 trans-nonachlor	64
		Brain	ND–0.78	NA	NA	ND–1.30	NA	64
		Muscle	ND–0.25	NA	NA	ND–0.45	NA	64
Bottlenosed dolphin	France	Blubber	NR	NR	NR	34.5–98.2	NR	6
	Netherlands	Blubber	13.90–67.90	0.05–0.065	NA	29.0–41.0	0.013–0.032 HCB	50
	California	Blubber	1796.6–2695	ND–6.4	3.4–4.0 (oxy)	420–450	0.34–0.40 HCB / ND–0.62 heptachlor e.o. / 14–21 trans-nonachlor	64
Risso's dolphin	France	Muscle	18.70–55.04	NR	NR	5.50–15.0	NR	64
		Blubber	NR	NR	NR	19.0–33.6	NR	6
	South Africa	Blubber	0.26[7]	6	6	6	6	8
Surinam dolphin	Surinam	Blubber	2.77	0.19	NR	<0.4	NA	50

Notes:
1. Not recorded.   2. Species combined by analysts.   3. Captive specimen in New York.   4. Not detected.
5. Hexachlorobenzene compounds.   6. Not analysed.   7. Value includes all organochlorines, not separated from DDT species.

waters, especially those found in coastal habitats, frequently have heavy loading of chlorinated hydrocarbons in their depot fat and insulating layers.

Mention may be made of some of the most striking examples of organochlorine contamination in small cetaceans (further detail is provided in the appropriate tables indicated above). The worst recorded incidence of contamination concerns bottlenosed dolphins from the coast of California (64), DDT levels in their blubber ranged from 1796 to 2695 p.p.m., with 420–450 p.p.m. polychlorinated biphenyls. Common dolphins taken in the same area contained 450–1831 p.p.m. DDT and 80–300 p.p.m. polychlorinated biphenyls. A Pacific white-sided dolphin *Lagenorhynchus obliquidens* held in captivity in New York was found to contain 1023 p.p.m. DDT, 4.1 p.p.m. dieldrin and 147 p.p.m. polychlorinated biphenyls (79). The authors did not speculate on the cause of death. A heavily contaminated juvenile white whale *Delphinapterus leucas* from the St Lawrence estuary in Canada contained 827 p.p.m. DDT and 800 p.p.m. polychlorinated biphenyls (74). A blue–white dolphin *Stenella coeruleoalba* from the coast of France had 706 p.p.m. DDT and 833 p.p.m. polychlorinated biphenyls. The average level of DDT contamination in the blubber of harbour porpoise males from the Bay of Fundy region in eastern Canada was 306.74 p.p.m. in 1969 and 1970, with 9.24 p.p.m. dieldrin (27, 28). Levels in pregnant and lactating females were significantly lower, although resting and immature females had levels as high as those of adult males. The highest male level of DDT species was 520 p.p.m., that of a female 447.9 p.p.m. Polychlorinated biphenyl levels in this population are highest in males; although the maximum blubber level recorded was 310 p.p.m., the average was considerably less, about 50–80 p.p.m., depending on the year of sampling.

Heavy metals

More information has been published on residues of heavy metals in tissues of seals than in cetaceans (2, 4, 26, 33, 40, 49–51) principally because specimens are easier to obtain. Unlike the chlorinated hydrocarbons, some heavy metals, particularly mercury, cadmium, arsenic and copper, have little or no affinity for lipids, and are consequently not deposited in depot fat, but rather in major metabolic organs, specifically the liver and kidneys. In many ways this makes it more likely that excessive levels will cause problems for the animal. When potentially toxic compounds are deposited in depot fat a significant load will be released into the bloodstream only under conditions of starvation, when the animal is forced to call upon its reserves. Chromium, lead, zinc and manganese, on the other hand, may be found in similar amounts in lipid-rich and lipid-poor tissues (62).

A number of metals and semi-metallic elements have been detected in pygmy sperm whale carcasses recovered as stranded specimens from the coast of Florida (62). Levels of chromium, cadmium, zinc and silver were not spectacular, but the distributions of lead were most peculiar. In all but two specimens the element could not be detected in any of the range of organs assayed, except for 1.15 p.p.m. in the liver on one animal. In the other two specimens, however, the remarkable values of 42.8 p.p.m. in the spermaceti organ and 43.9 p.p.m. in the brain were found. It is difficult to avoid speculating that lead poisoning contributed to the death of the latter animal. Copper was generally present in small quantities (Table 10.6); usually less than 1 p.p.m. in any tissue. One animal had 2.1 p.p.m. in the liver, but in three specimens the livers contained from 17.3 to 144.4 p.p.m. Zinc, as might be expected from the range of enzymatic reactions in which it plays a role (15), was more generally abundant in all tissues examined. Concentrations were never less than 1 p.p.m., and attained a maximum value of about 15 p.p.m. in the liver of one animal. These values seem low relative to studies of zinc residues in marine mammals carried out by Dutch workers (50) and a Japanese team (33). Cadmium results for these animals were consistent with those found by the Dutch.

Other studies on metals in Cetacea include analyses of tissues from several species from the Mediterranean (81), harbour porpoises from the Bay of Fundy region (30, 32), white whales from the St Lawrence estuary in Canada (12, 73), striped dolphins from the Lesser Antilles (31), and Surinam and dusky dolphins from Surinam and New Zealand respectively (50). Titanium, iron and vanadium have been reported, in quantities considered by that author to represent a potential hazard, in several species of cetacean from the western Mediterranean (81).

Naturally, mercury has attracted most attention, although to date most studies have been made on tissues of odontocete cetaceans, with the exception of a single study of fin whale residues by Viale (81). Two of the first published accounts of levels of this metal in dolphins and porpoises were by Dutch (50) and Canadian (30) teams, reporting on residues in harbour porpoises from the North Sea and the Bay of Fundy. In the muscle of the Canadian specimens mercury was virtually all in methylated form, but in the liver, on the other hand, the methylated fraction ranged from 7.4 to 41 per cent, being lowest in those livers with the highest total mercury. In Caribbean dolphins the methylated fraction in muscle was not as high as in the Canadian specimens (31), suggesting that for some reason the methylation of mercury reaches a plateau in this tissue at about 2.6 p.p.m. The highest reported mercury levels in cetacean tissues have been in common dolphins and a Cuvier's beaked whale from the western

Mediterranean: greater than 604 p.p.m. and greater than 440 p.p.m. respectively (81) (Table 10.6).

Impact of oil on cetaceans

Considering the volume of literature on oil pollution and its impact on marine organisms, it is surprising to discover that there are to date *no* definitive studies on the effect of oil contamination on cetaceans. This is a glaring gap in our knowledge and ability to respond to potential crisis situations, which the United States National Marine Fisheries Service is attempting to rectify at the time of writing with a series of linked research projects being undertaken by J. R. Geraci of the University of Guelph in Canada.

There are scattered reports, most of them anecdotal, of the lack of response of whales to oil slicks; gray whales have been reported to swim through slicks off California without appearing to react to them, and there are some similar reports concerning the behaviour of rorquals off the eastern shores of the United States.

Oil could clog the baleen plates; this is likely to be a more serious problem for the right whales, with fine-fringed baleen plates, than any other group. Presumably, the colder the water and the heavier the grade of oil, the more serious the clogging problem would be. On the other hand, the heavier grades of oil might be less toxic than medium grades. Ingestion of oil can lead to the formation of alimentary system lesions, and a number of physiological problems. Inhalation of oil into the lungs in any quantities will almost certainly lead to intense tissue reaction, and pneumonic symptoms which are frequently fatal. All this one can deduce from reactions of small test mammals to oil immersion or ingestion, but at this time, as spokesmen for the oil industry are not slow to point out, no one appears to have a single record of a cetacean that was killed by an oil spill. Because our knowledge of delayed lethal effects on cetaceans or of more subtle sublethal effects on behaviour, feeding or reproduction is virtually nil, statements that oil presents little or no hazard to cetaceans cannot be challenged. Well-meaning radical preservationist organizations, totally opposed to any experimentation of this kind on cetaceans, have helped to perpetuate this situation to some extent. In the case of a massive and unexpected entrapment of whales by oil, it is to be doubted that veterinarians would even have the knowledge to treat the victims on a symptomatic basis, given the highly specialized and poorly known physiology of these animals.

Table 10.6　Metallic and semi-metallic elements in Cetacea (p.p.m., wet weight)

Species	Locality	Tissue	Hg	Cd	Pb	Se	Cr
Fin whale	Western Mediterranean	Various	0.05–0.42	0.001–0.016	0.02–0.17	NA[1]	0.20–3.0
Sperm whale	Western Mediterranean	Various	0.65–3.70	0.02–2.76	0.08–10.15	NA	0.40–1.0
Pygmy sperm whale	Florida	Blubber	NA	0.34–0.54	ND[2]	NA	3.62–6.
		Spermaceti organ	NA	0.19–0.65	ND–42.84	NA	3.09–6.
		Melon	NA	0.19–0.41	ND	NA	1.55–25
		Liver	NA	0.22–7.60	ND–1.15	NA	0.84–4.
		Kidney	NA	3.43	ND	NA	3.33
		Muscle	NA	0.25	ND	NA	4.83
		Brain	NA	0.22	43.89	NA	4.76
Cuvier's beaked whale	Western Mediterranean	Various	1.60–440+	0.02–28.73	0.03–8.53	NA	0.25–2.
White whale	St Lawrence, Canada	Liver	8.70–36.90	NA	NA	NA	NA
Short-finned pilot whale	St Lucia, West Indies	Liver	19.20–157	NA	NA	NA	NA
		Kidney	6.00–14.00	NA	NA	NA	NA
		Muscle	2.76–4.00	NA	NA	NA	NA
Harbour porpoise	North Sea	Liver	5.70–192	0.05–1.20	NA	3.20–79.00	NA
		Brain	0.09–2.00	0.01–0.15	NA	0.11–1.90	NA
	Bay of Fundy	Liver	0.55–91.3	0.007–0.20	0.06–0.08	0.20–2.40	NA
		Muscle	0.21–2.58	0.01–0.016	0.017–0.18	0.30–0.33	NA
		Brain	0.17–3.02	0.003–0.01	ND–0.033	0.03–0.04	NA
		Kidney	0.45–4.34	0.02–0.53	0.006–0.017	0.03–0.04	NA
Dusky/common dolphins[3]	New Zealand	Liver	35.00–72.00	0.21–1.55	NA	9.30–24.00	NA
Common dolphin	Western Mediterranean	Various	5.30–604+	0.01–1.20	0.16–0.21	NA	0.04–0.
Blue–white dolphin	Western Mediterranean	Various	1.57–2.83	NA	NA	NA	0.05
Striped dolphin	St Lucia West Indies	Liver	6.00–13.00	NA	NA	NA	NA
		Kidney	2.28–2.68	NA	NA	NA	NA
		Muscle	0.87–1.33	NA	NA	NA	NA
Bottlenosed dolphin	Western Mediterranean	Various	0.67–14.60	0.03–2.22	0.23–4.25	NA	0.07–1.0
Surinam dolphin	Netherlands[4]	Liver	2.20–62.00	0.05–0.30	NA	1.40–19.00	NA
	Surinam	Liver	0.37–11.00	0.02–0.06	NA	0.60–3.20	NA

Notes:
1.　Not analysed.　　2.　Not detected.　　3.　Combined samples by analysts.　　4.　Captive specimens.

	Ag	Cu	Zn	Fe	Ti	V	As	References
	NA	NA	NA	20.00–295+	0.26–10.50+	0.05–0.93	NA	81
	NA	NA	NA	18.00–204	0.30–3.16	0.30–2.04	NA	81
-1.02	NA	0.31–2.29	2.92–3.51	NA	NA	NA	NA	62
-0.40	NA	0.12–0.48	1.41–5.88	NA	NA	NA	NA	62
-0.52	NA	0.30–2.06	1.47–4.33	NA	NA	NA	NA	62
-4.06	0.10–0.65	2.10–144.44	10.09–15.04	NA	NA	NA	NA	62
	NA	2.15	NA	NA	NA	NA	NA	62
	NA	1.39	12.02	NA	NA	NA	NA	62
	0.07	3.16	5.32	NA	NA	NA	NA	62
	NA	NA	NA	28.30–174	0.10–2.65+	0.20–3.30	NA	81
	NA	NA	NA	NA	NA	NA	NA	12, 74
	NA	NA	NA	NA	NA	NA	NA	31
	NA	NA	NA	NA	NA	NA	NA	31
	NA	NA	NA	NA	NA	NA	NA	31
	NA	NA	35.00–64.00	NA	NA	NA	0.03–1.90	50
	NA	NA	7.30–15.00	NA	NA	NA	0.01–0.16	50
	NA	NA	NA	NA	NA	NA	NA	30, 32 and unpublished
	NA	NA	NA	NA	NA	NA	NA	30, 32 and unpublished
	NA	NA	NA	NA	NA	NA	NA	30, 32 and unpublished
	NA	NA	NA	NA	NA	NA	NA	30, 32 and unpublished
	NA	NA	30.00–40.00	NA	NA	NA	0.13–0.80	50
	NA	NA	NA	22.00–380+	0.12–1.60	0.02–0.10	NA	81
	NA	NA	NA	20.00–280+	0.50+	NA	NA	81
	NA	NA	NA	NA	NA	NA	NA	31
	NA	NA	NA	NA	NA	NA	NA	31
	NA	NA	NA	NA	NA	NA	NA	31
	NA	NA	NA	13.60–669+	0.05–7.30	0.01–2.12	NA	81
	NA	NA	42.00–66.00	NA	NA	NA	0.13–0.18	50
	NA	NA	59.00–66.00	NA	NA	NA	0.15–0.19	50

Global patterns of contaminants in cetaceans

Chlorinated hydrocarbons

There is no co-ordinated plan among marine mammalogists and regulatory agencies as yet to monitor the global patterns of contamination in these animals. The work that has been carried out to date has been, for obvious reasons, opportunistic and sporadic in nature. This reflects the difficulty of obtaining specimens in many areas, the concentration of specialists in a very few countries, lack of directed funding, or combinations of these factors.

At least with respect to the distribution of chlorinated hydrocarbon residues we can see some kind of pattern for those species, and within those areas that have been studied (Figure 10.1). In general, the higher up the food-chain a whale feeds, the greater the concentrations in its tissues. We can probably rank euphausiid, squid and fish eaters in a rough linear sequence. Relatively low residue levels might be expected to characterize baleen whales in most seas; one can point to quite high levels of DDT and polychlorinated biphenyls in blubber of North Atlantic rorquals, but this almost certainly reflects the major role of lipid-rich Atlantic herring and capelin in their diets. Most of the smaller toothed whales take squid or fish depending on which prey are available; all are opportunistic feeders.

Although wind systems have distributed DDT around the world, even into the Antarctic seas, the major zones of contamination are largely concentrated in the coastal waters or semi-enclosed seas of the northern hemisphere. The marine mammal fauna of the high Arctic is only lightly contaminated with chlorinated hydrocarbons (1, 4); this is also true of the Antarctic. Weddell seals *Leptonychotes weddelli* had 0.025–0.105 p.p.m. in depot fat (14), and a single example of a crab-eater seal *Lobodon carcinophagus* had 0.39 p.p.m. of DDT compounds in its blubber (77). A moderately contaminated sperm whale taken in Antarctic waters may have recently moved there after feeding in much lower latitudes. Although dolphins from coastal waters of the Rio de Plata region have 9–30 p.p.m. of blubber DDT (64), the single Risso's dolphin examined in South Africa can be cited as evidence that DDT compounds are not present in significant quantities in the eastern South Atlantic (8). Little DDT or polychlorinated biphenyl was present in dolphin or pilot whale tissue sampled from the southern or eastern Caribbean (31). At first sight the high levels of DDT in all specimens from New Zealand appear anomalous, but use of pesticides has been extensive on the grasslands of both main islands (9). Polychlorinated biphenyl levels do not match those of the DDT compounds.

Although the DDT levels in migrating gray whales off the west coast of the United States were low, this should not be taken as implying that there

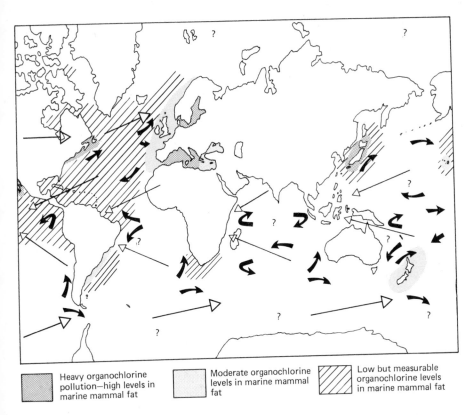

Heavy organochlorine pollution—high levels in marine mammal fat

Moderate organochlorine levels in marine mammal fat

Low but measurable organochlorine levels in marine mammal fat

Figure 10.1 Levels of organochlorine pollution of the world ocean, as judged by amounts recorded in the depot fat of Cetacea. Solid shaded area indicates heavy organochlorine pollution, with levels often in excess of 50 p.p.m.; light shaded area: moderate levels, generally less than about 20 p.p.m. in adult depot fat; striping: relatively low levels, zero to 5 p.p.m. in depot fat. DDT and related compounds and polychlorinated biphenyl compounds are considered together in this scheme. It is impossible to describe global pollution other than in the most general and approximate terms. Data are not available from many regions. Solid arrows indicate ocean currents; arrows with open heads: prevailing wind directions.

is no contamination problem in those waters for, as the reader should recall from Chapter 2, there is little evidence that gray whales feed extensively while in the southern part of their range. The results could be testimony to the low levels of contamination in the fringes of the Bering Sea, or to the loss of organochlorines as depot fat is metabolized, or a combination of both. Studies on resident and semi-resident seals and sea otters off the coast of California reveal quite a different picture (75). Sea otter fat residues of DDT ranged from 0.41 to 33 p.p.m.; the diet is very varied in this species, but the major proportion of the food eaten is usually molluscan or crustacean in nature. This diet is probably the reason why the fat titre of DDT is not excessive in this animal. Californian harbour seals, on the other hand, feeding about 93 per cent by volume on fish, a diet presumably yielding a far higher lipid content than shellfish and crabs, had blubber residue levels of DDT of 16–158 p.p.m. (75). Even higher levels of DDT, and significant concentrations of polychlorinated biphenyl, were found in the tissues of Californian dolphins and porpoises (64) (see Tables 10.4 and 10.5), and Californian sea-lions (19); blubber levels in female sea-lions giving birth to premature pups in these island populations ranged from 626–1039 p.p.m., in comparison to 51–203 p.p.m. in females bearing pups to full term. Respective polychlorinated biphenyl concentrations were 85–145 p.p.m. and 12–25 p.p.m.

Almost all the other information we have comes from eastern Canadian waters, eastern and western United States coastal waters, the eastern tropical Pacific, Hawaii, Japan, Uruguay, and the inshore waters of the United Kingdom, the North Sea, the Baltic Sea and the Gulf of Bothnia. Swedish studies suggest that the Baltic region and the Gulf of Bothnia may have the unenviable distinction of being the most severely polluted region of any of the world's seas, although a series of conference proceedings on the Mediterranean, particularly the eastern part between France and Italy, suggests that this dubious status may soon be claimed by Europe's southern enclosed sea. The massive contamination of small cetaceans off southern California was found to be related to highly specific local industrial pesticide manufacturing inputs (64). With respect to the pattern of chlorinated hydrocarbon contamination in cetaceans off eastern North America we can array the results roughly from north to south. Harbour porpoise tissues from Newfoundland examined by the University of Guelph group contain far lower levels of DDT and polychlorinated biphenyls than those from southern Nova Scotia and southern New Brunswick. Residue levels are still quite high in those sampled from Maine, but decrease as one examines animals taken from further south. There is evidently a significant contribution from the urbanized and industrialized St Lawrence, and a major source of contamination by DDT has undoubtedly been the intensive spraying in earlier years of the forests of Nova Scotia, New Brunswick and Quebec. Forestry and agricultural use of DDT, and urban sources of polychlorinated biphenyls in the heavily populated lower New England seaboard have probably contributed significant quantities of pollutants as particulate matter into the northward flowing margin of the Atlantic Drift. The prevailing eastward movement of weather and wind systems across the continent has also served to put much DDT into the western North Atlantic by the aerial route. Although there is some evidence that the levels of chlorinated hydrocarbons in the surface waters of the North Atlantic have decreased significantly since restrictions on the use of DDT and polychlorinated biphenyls (34), there is now so much in the sediments that we can expect the contamination to last for many years, even if no new inputs are made (see last section, p. 427). Some workers have pointed to an apparent gradient in the tissues of humpback whales from north to south, with the lowest levels occurring in those animals sampled in the northern fringe of the Caribbean (79). Once again, as with gray whales, this may represent reduced exposure to contaminants in the lower latitudes, or removal of chlorinated hydrocarbons from depot fat as the latter is mobilized for energetic use during the non-feeding migration.

Mercury

Mercury is the only heavy metal present in marine mammal tissues which one can even begin to discuss in terms of global distribution. Although some kind of pattern can be dimly perceived in the distribution of the organochlorines as broadly correlating with areas of industry and intensive agriculture, or with areas receiving water flow or prevailing winds from such regions, the situation is much less clear in the case of mercury. Mercury levels are relatively high in many of the same areas where high chlorinated hydrocarbon residues have been recorded; for example, coastal European waters, the Mediterranean, the Baltic and Gulf of Bothnia, the St Lawrence, Bay of Fundy and Atlantic coast of Nova Scotia, off California, and around New Zealand. In contrast, however, seals with low DDT species in the Arctic Basin often have high mercury levels in their livers, and dolphins and short-finned pilot whales in the Caribbean with negligible chlorinated hydrocarbon residues have been found to have very high levels of mercury both in muscle and liver.

Industrial and agricultural use of mercury compounds has been blamed for part of the contamination of the fauna of the Baltic and the Gulf of Bothnia. It is much less certain that this is the case in tropical regions such as the Caribbean. The amount used in the southern, eastern and western fringing nations of that sea is much too low to account for the 155 p.p.m. found in the liver of *Globicephala macrorhynchus* from St Lucia, for example. Analysis of the prevailing winds and currents of the Gulf of Mexico and the Caribbean (31) provided no support for the hypothesis that the source is industry and intensive agriculture in the southern states of the USA. In the absence of any other data, the initial hypothesis is that the probable source of this mercury is largely natural (Figure 10.2), and that its presence in marine mammal tissues is quite a normal occurrence in areas of high tectonic activity such as the Lesser Antilles and New Zealand.

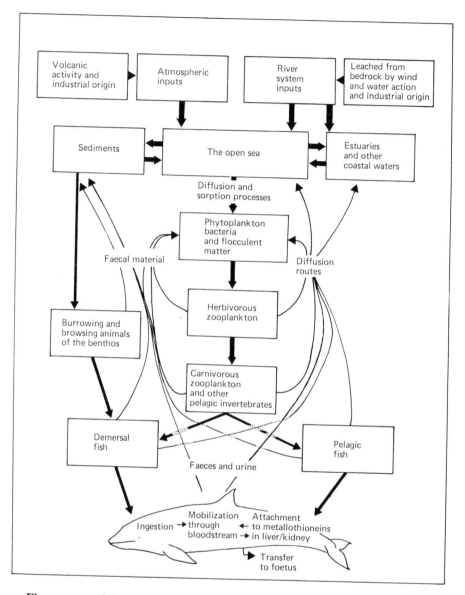

Figure 10.2   Schematic flow chart of the input of heavy metal contaminants into the marine food-chains with special reference to mercury, and simplified indication of the movement of the element through the food web and into the tissues of Cetacea. Narrow arrows indicate losses, returns and general outputs from components that provide feedback loops in the system. Highly approximate representation.

Variation of contaminant levels

In the previous sections I have been careful to give ranges of both chlorinated hydrocarbons and heavy metals when authors provided a series of values from several specimens. The reader will also have noted that the spread of many ranges is extremely wide, for example the 16 p.p.m. and 158 p.p.m. recorded in two specimens of harbour seal sampled in California. A number of factors may act singly or in combination to yield such variation. Both chlorinated hydrocarbons (especially DDT) and mercury can show a marked correlation of concentration with size and age (3, 26–8, 32). In the case of mercury this may be so for both males and females, but for DDT compounds the pattern is for increase with age in males and decrease in females. The conclusion of several workers, studying both cetaceans and pinnipeds, has been that lactation is a major route for loss of organochlorine compounds for the female (2, 4, 20, 27, 28), although there is also proven transfer of these compounds across the placenta to the foetus (20, 27).

Residue levels have been found to be significantly higher in captive than in wild specimens of harp seals (24); this suggests that monospecific diets of captive animals may exert some influence on retention, or that rates of assimilation are different. The tenuous data from the few North Atlantic and Caribbean humpback whale specimens (see p. 401) suggest that changes within a season may occur in depot fat residue levels of organochlorines, but perhaps the most serious problem is that of identifying relatively long-term differences in residue levels that may occur. Combining data from scattered years can lead to erroneous conclusions. If the data are also drawn from specimens of both sexes and different ages, the conclusions could be quite meaningless (32).

Bay of Fundy harbour porpoise population: a case history of variation in residue levels

My reason for singling out this population for particular discussion is not really to highlight the work of my own unit and colleagues at the University of Guelph, despite what the reader might think! Because we have collected specimens over a ten-year period in relatively large numbers, there are at present more data for this population than any other.

Variation in compound levels within the body

CHLORINATED HYDROCARBONS

As one would expect from the solubility patterns of these compounds, there is concentration of residues in the lipid-rich tissues (Figure 10.3).

Other than the blubber, tissues or organs with significant fat levels are the active mammary gland and the milk produced by it, and the brain. Lipid levels in the cerebrum of *Phocoena phocoena* can attain 15 per cent, and cerebellar fat content can reach nearly 20 per cent. The research group at Guelph is still in the process of examining organochlorine residues in up to a dozen kinds of tissue from over a hundred animals obtained during 1969–80. Results are not yet fully analysed, but there seems no apparent correlation between DDT residue levels and the lipid content of cerebrum, cerebellum, liver or kidney, but a rather broad relationship exists between DDT, polychlorinated biphenyl, dieldrin and lipid content in muscle tissue.

Organochlorine levels in blubber are always one or two orders of magnitude higher than in any other tissue except active mammary gland; in one specimen about 15 p.p.m. was found in pancreatic tissue with 8.3 per cent lipid content, but this was an exception. We also analysed residues in heart, lungs, spleen, stomach, intestine, uterus, testis, lymph nodes from the abdomen, thymus and thyroid. In no case was there significant deposition of chlorinated hydrocarbons in these tissues.

MERCURY

The distribution of mercury within the body is known in general terms from analyses (see Figure 10.3); the reasons for the great differences in residue levels which are found are less well understood. Mercury residues in the liver are not infrequently two orders of magnitude above that present in other organs. This possibly relates to different distributions of certain proteins, transport of mercury on a differential basis to particular organs, or perhaps the inability of mercury–protein combinations to pass certain cellular barriers, leading to accumulation in specific organs, or a combination of these factors.

Highest levels are almost invariably found in the liver, the next highest in the kidney, as in seals (32, 40). In some specimens those found in muscle may approach the levels in kidney, but only rarely exceed them in the same animal. Brain residues are generally about one-half to one-quarter those present in muscle, but exceptions to these generalizations can be found in any long series of analyses. Residues in the pancreas are very variable; in the harbour porpoise we have found them to be as low as 0.13 p.p.m. and as high as 15 p.p.m. Levels in the mammary gland are similar to those in brain or muscle; activity of the gland does not seem to make any significant difference, although we have been hampered in making a firm decision about this by the relatively small number of samples available from lactating females. Mercury levels in heart, lung, stomach and spleen are all

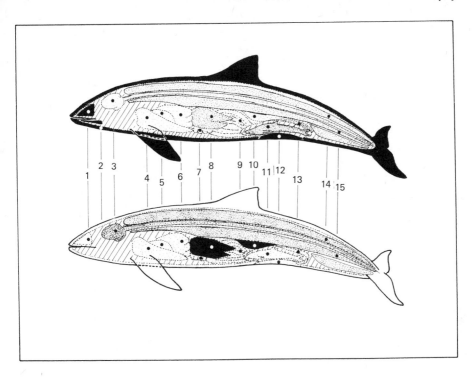

Figure 10.3 Diagrams to represent the approximate levels of relative contamination/accumulation of organochlorine compounds (above) and mercury and cadmium (below) in the tissues of the harbour porpoise. The former compounds accumulate in the depot fat and acoustic fat ('melon' and mandibular region), whereas the metals are most abundant in the liver and kidney, that is, the major metabolic and excretory organs. Codes: black, high levels; stipple, moderate levels; light stipple, low levels; white, virtually absent; diagonal striping, body cavity or bony areas (not examined). Numbers refer to organs or tissue systems: 1. melon fat; 2. blubber; 3. cerebrum and cerebellum; 4. lungs; 5. heart; 6. stomach; 7. pancreas; 8. liver; 9. intestines; 10. kidney; 11. foetus; 12. mammary gland; 13. placenta; 14. epaxial musculature; 15. hypaxial musculature.

similar, and of about the same magnitude as those in brain tissue. Stomach wall levels are rather low, and those of the upper intestine lower still. It seems unclear which part of the digestive tract might be most involved in absorption of mercury in cetaceans, but in any case it does not follow that mercury will necessarily be deposited in the walls of the organs of absorption.

Ratios of methylated to non-methylated mercury in the harbour porpoise are highest in muscle as mentioned earlier (about 89 per cent), next highest in kidney (41 per cent) and mammary gland (46.5 per cent), then in cerebellum (28.5 per cent), then liver (17 per cent), then finally cerebrum (10.5 per cent), among those tissues examined. Ratios for mammary gland, cerebrum and cerebellum must be regarded with some caution as they were based on small samples (32).

Variation in compounds in harbour porpoises by local region, body weight, sex and age

CHLORINATED HYDROCARBONS

Only single specimens were obtained from various localities in the coastal western North Atlantic during our study of this species, so comparisons with the material from the Bay of Fundy must be made with caution, even though we have some idea of what might be considered 'average' for an animal of known sex and age in that region. Levels in a five-year-old male from Prince Edward Island were much higher than the mean values for an equivalent Bay of Fundy specimen. A young animal from southern Maine had almost exactly comparable residue levels with the Bay of Fundy population. Animals were obtained from several localities on the Atlantic coast of Nova Scotia, these had residue levels that were similar, or slightly lower than those for Fundy; this was also true for specimens from Rhode Island (one examined by other workers) (79). A specimen from south-eastern Newfoundland had far smaller amounts of organochlorine residues than any Bay of Fundy specimen, and curiously, this was also true for an eight-year-old female from St Mary's Bay, Nova Scotia on the south-east fringe of the Bay of Fundy. In that animal the ovarian history indicated several pregnancies, and the diet was dissimilar to that of animals in the rest of the Bay of Fundy proper.

No relationship was evident between organochlorine residue levels and body weight (28) within age classes. When DDT and polychlorinated biphenyl levels in blubber of males and females are compared year class by year class in this species, the results differ significantly. In the males we found a 50–300 per cent increase from yearlings to eight-year-old animals, but in the females there is, on average, a net decrease in residues after maturity (at about four years of age), with loss of organochlorines by transfer to the foetus or through lactation to the calf, as indicated earlier in this chapter. A similar pattern of different net accumulation patterns in the two sexes has been observed in Atlantic gray seals (2), in ringed seals from the Canadian Arctic and the Baltic Sea (4, 36), and is suspected to occur in the harp seal as well (3).

MERCURY

As indicated in the previous section, we were only able to obtain a nominal number of specimens from regions distant from the Bay of Fundy and southern Nova Scotia during our studies (32). Our tentative conclusions were that a single Prince Edward Island specimen has mercury residue levels comparable to Fundy animals, but that specimens from Newfoundland, southern Maine and Rhode Island all had lower levels than one would expect in equivalent specimens of their sex and age in the Bay of Fundy region.

Statistical comparisons of subsets of specimens taken on different sides of the Bay of Fundy revealed only one significant difference, that females on the Nova Scotian side had somewhat higher muscle mercury than those on the New Brunswick side. At this time we do not attach much biological significance to this result.

Preliminary studies of a sample of moderate size (30) indicated a strong correlative relationship between body length (and in this species, therefore, weight) and mercury levels in both liver and muscle. In subsequent years we were able to age this species, and with a larger sample show a strong positive correlation of mercury residues with increasing age which was only slightly different for males and females (32). This parallels the results of other workers studying seal populations (40, 50). We also examined the possibility that the principle correlation was with weight rather than age, by examining a sample of individuals of known weights, lengths and ages, and comparing the relative fits. Mercury levels in the cerebrum were correlated with age only. For muscle tissue, there were significant correlations in all three cases, but the strongest was between residue level and age. For kidney the highest correlation was once again with age, but in the case of liver tissue, the highest correlation was with body weight, then body length, and then with age. All three relationships, however, were statistically highly significant. With a somewhat smaller sample we looked for correlations of residual level with weight and length *within* year classes; no significant relationship was found, except possibly in the liver, although the results were of marginal statistical significance only.

Changes in compound levels in Bay of Fundy harbour porpoises with time

CHLORINATED HYDROCARBONS

Although analyses are not complete at the time of writing, we have found no changes immediately evident in the residue levels of these compounds during the four-month period that most animals pass in the coastal waters of the western Bay of Fundy. We are unable to obtain specimens between autumn and early spring as the population moves offshore.

Polychlorinated biphenyl levels in this population were assessed between 1971 and 1977; no clear trends could be distinguished. With due respect for 'normal' variation, residues in both sexes seem to have remained more or less within the same range for the entire period, although significantly lower in female blubber than in that of males. DDT residues show a different pattern. In both males and females a fairly steep decline was noted from 1969 to 1973 (28). At the time that the cited publication was prepared (1975), it was assumed that this decline in residue levels was to have been expected, since use of DDT in the region had been discontinued some years before. It seemed reasonable to conclude that either some kind of plateau of low levels might be attained because of the large amount locked in the coastal western North Atlantic sediments, or that a steady continued decline would occur, but at a decreased rate. Neither of these predictions proved correct. Specimen collecting continued in 1975–7, and in both sexes the residues of DDT show a consistent increase in each year, from 55.9 p.p.m. to 133.5 p.p.m. in blubber of males, and from 31.3 p.p.m. to 43.8 p.p.m. in blubber of females (25). This may represent the effect of reintroductions of the use of DDT in the New England states when no substitute appears to work as well (for example, against Tussock moth (80)), justified on the basis of the low toxicity of DDT to birds and mammals in comparison to many of the alternatives. On the other hand, it may result from a combination of factors, perhaps involving changes in oceanographic conditions in the Bay of Fundy approaches between 1971 and 1974, which could have released more DDT stored in the sediments (see pp. 427–8). At present there is not enough evidence to decide one way or the other. What we can say is that the 'DDT problem' in marine mammals has not 'faded away' as we hoped a few years ago.

The proportion of *p,p'*-DDE to total DDT is only rarely as high in harbour porpoise as it is in sea-birds. I examined the possibility that the proportion might have changed between 1969 and 1977, indicating more metabolism of this compound within porpoise tissues or in the food-chain. The proportion of DDE varied from a low of about 36 per cent in 1969 to a high of 49 per cent in 1975, but no really striking trend is evident, except that it was lowest in the first two years studied, 1969 and 1970, and has been between 40 and 50 per cent ever since (25).

MERCURY

While studying tissue samples from this population we were aware that as well as varying with age, mercury might vary during the course of the year. Although we were unable to obtain animals from the winter months, no significant changes could be detected in the period which spans the onset, peak and decline of intensive summer feeding by these animals in the western Bay of Fundy.

Plotting all available data for mercury in porpoise muscle for the period 1969–77 gave the impression of a general, but not completely consistent, increase in average annual totals. This was misleading; when the data for males and females were segregated, the trend was found to be restricted to males and very young females. Mature females appeared to have suffered a net loss of mercury in muscle between 1971 and 1974 (32). This was matched by changes in levels within the liver of both sexes; and the trend was further supported by more limited data on residues from kidney and cerebrum. In the post-1974 period, however, levels increased rapidly again in three successive years, with liver levels for 1977 far exceeding those for the 1969–71 period.

There was some evidence of an environmental change in the waters of the inshore region of the western Bay of Fundy starting in 1971, with surface temperatures rising from barely 11°C in the late 1960s to a peak of over 12°C in 1971, then declining to 10.9°C in 1978, but with relatively high values still maintained during 1971 and 1972. The steepest decline took place between 1974–7. There was, therefore, an indication of a significant intrusion of Gulf of Maine water occurring in 1971–3. This water is warmer than that of the Bay of Fundy, which is normally partly fed by cool water from the Nova Scotia Current. Judging by a comparative study of mercury levels in harbour seals inside the Bay of Fundy and in the south-western part of the Gulf of Maine (26), the latter is mercury-poor in contrast to the Bay waters. The food web in the Bay of Fundy was then presumably exposed to lower than 'normal' concentration levels of mercury for two to three years. Oceanographic changes of this magnitude have been documented in earlier decades in this region. The Nova Scotia Current water appears to be affected by the discharge levels of the Gulf of St Lawrence at certain times of year (78). Mercury levels are relatively high within the Gulf fauna (12). Levels of mercury accumulating in migratory fauna entering the Bay of Fundy may therefore be greatly influenced by the relative dominance of the Nova Scotia Current water versus a Gulf Stream salient during a summer feeding season of about 120 days duration. On the basis of data presented for the half-life elimination of mercury in fish (42), this should be ample time for a significant change in mercury levels to occur in the food species of the harbour porpoise. A change would not necessarily be expected in porpoise tissues in a single season, since there are no gills across which a direct flux could occur, and no evidence that transport is likely to take place through the skin, in contrast to fish (42). Furthermore, the porpoise has a much smaller surface–volume ratio than its prey species.

Metabolism of chlorinated hydrocarbons

A definitive study of chlorinated hydrocarbon metabolism in a cetacean has yet to be carried out; at this stage of our knowledge it is necessary to refer, with some caution as to its applicability, to the work done on ringed seal and guillemot in the Baltic by a Swedish team (36, 37, 41, 63). DDT and polychlorinated biphenyl resemble one another chemically in that both molecules are based on phenyl rings. In the former compound these are attached to an aliphatic group (straight carbon chain). Three chlorine atoms are included in the molecule. By substitution of one of these chlorine atoms the DDT molecule can be degraded to DDE or TDE. It is well known that various micro-organisms can carry out this dechlorination in nature (17, 47). DDE can become bound to mammalian serum proteins (73), and cellular actions are known to be able to degrade DDT under other conditions to the second-stage metabolite DDA (2-bis (*p*-chloro-phenyl) acetic acid) (83). DDE is *not* an intermediate step between DDT and DDA. DDA can be found in the free molecular state, in glucuroinide form, or as conjugates of glycine and alanine (83). Several studies suggest that degradation pathways of DDT differ in birds and mammals, so results from these groups should be combined with caution. The degree to which organisms can degrade DDT differs considerably. In some cases, for example domestic chickens, up to fourteen different metabolites of DDT have been identified after single oral doses (21). In other instances only DDE or TDE is found, or no metabolism seems to occur (18). Conversion of DDT to TDE is common in living organisms, and may be mediated by the presence of reduced porphyrins (58, 87). Formation of the hydroxyl form of DDE also occurs (41).

The Swedish team found some evidence of metabolism and breakdown of biphenyl in the liver of the seals and guillemots; breakdown or conversion of DDT to DDA was apparent, and polychlorinated biphenyl appeared to undergo some conversion into tetrachlorobiphenyl metab-olites. These products were eliminated in faeces (41). In nature, further breakdown to DBP (dimethoxyhexachlorobiphenyl) is known to be mediated by some aquatic micro-organisms (47).

Metabolism of mercury

Mercury and selenium occur together in some marine mammal tissues, and appear to be bound to proteins by sulphur-based links (65). In the metabolizing organs such as liver, relatively little is in methylated form (30, 51). The presence of mercury in liver and kidney appears to stimulate biosynthesis of a specific type of protein called metallothioneins (68, 69). Atoms of mercury and cadmium, and possibly other heavy metals as well, become bound to these proteins (69). The formation of metallothioneins may render the mercury much less toxic to the organism than when it is in methylated form (84). The presence of selenium may be necessary for this to occur, and the readiness with which mercury is transferred from site to site within the body seems to be sensitive to changes in blood or tissue selenium levels. In the presence of selenium, however, mercury can be transferred from organ to organ, for example, from kidney to liver, and from metallothioneins to soluble and non-histone protein fractions (53). When mercury is mobilized in this way it may once again become active as a toxin. Protein-bound mercury is certainly mobile to some degree, and presumably has to travel through the bloodstream if moving from one organ to another. It is most likely to be eliminated from the body while in transition; the biological half-life of mercury in blood is barely one-third that of mercury in the body as a whole (61). Although mercury can be readily eliminated from the kidney when in ionic form (60), the usual route appears to be through the faeces. While bound to protein, mercury does not seem to be able to pass through the filter-bed system of the kidney into the urine (60).

There is reason to believe that mercury is in dynamic association in liver and kidney, so residue levels in these organs might change more readily in response to alterations of background level in the food than those in some other tissues such as muscle. Retention of mercury in non-living tissues such as hair is well-known (11). Mercury has been studied much less in muscle than in other major tissues and organs, but seems to replace calcium there, and is bound through carbon–mercury and sulphydryl linkages. Fluctuations in mercury in porpoise muscle over a nine-year period in the Bay of Fundy were much less than in liver on a proportional basis (32). The biological half-life of mercury in marine mammals seems to be much longer than in man (16), up to 700 days or more instead of 70–80 days, and the exchange rates for mercury in cetacean muscle are likely to be much slower than those in liver. Even the passage of mercury in and out of the brain seems to be retarded by the blood–brain barrier (11). In mature females bearing young, transfer of mercury is likely to occur, and during conditions with a reduced environmental background of mercury, this may become apparent as a net loss in tissues. A time-lag is to be expected, because of the length of the biological half life. In experimental studies with test mammals recognizable toxic symptoms begin to appear when mercury levels in the brain reach 6–8 ppm (11).

Do high organochlorine and heavy metal contaminants represent a threat to cetacean populations?

Sensationalism and careful environmental studies notwithstanding, it is not possible to point with certainty to a single proven case of detrimental impact of these compounds on cetaceans at this time. This is not to say that harm has not or is not occurring, but simply to state a fact – we do not know, because data are extremely difficult to obtain.

LD_{50} values for a range of small and medium-sized mammals have been determined experimentally; they can be summarized as follows from the literature (67):

Aldrin	54–150 mg/kg of body weight
Chlordanes	100–590 mg/kg of body weight
DDT	60–800 mg/kg of body weight
Dieldrin	50–200 mg/kg of body weight
Endrin	5–50 mg/kg of body weight
Heptachlor	90–? mg/kg of body weight
Lindane	100–200 mg/kg of body weight
Mirex	300–600 mg/kg of body weight
Toxaphene	15–240 mg/kg of body weight

Despite the numerous studies on these compounds (which would fill a fair-sized volume even in basic bibliographic form as references and abstracts only), we still do not know how they work. What is certain is that they are all neurotoxins that prevent the passage of normal impulses in neurons; this is also the mode of action of some mercury compounds. The neurons eventually start to send impulses spontaneously, causing tremors, then convulsions and death, usually by interruption of respiration. In some way the balance of sodium and potassium around and in the neuron is destroyed. Careful experimentation reveals that not all these compounds, DDT and dieldrin for example, work in quite the same way.

Polychlorinated biphenyls have been pinpointed as the cause of liver damage when heavy ingestion has occurred. At lower concentrations they have been implicated in more subtle hepatic enzyme disturbance and interference with oestradiol by stimulating liver microsome activity, and possibly play a role in the disruption of calcium metabolism leading to eggshell thinning in sea-birds (13, 71). It is difficult to attribute any specific problem to one particular contaminant, since in all the regions of significant contamination we find several or many of these compounds present together. Perhaps the most serious specific effect that has been attributed to chlorinated hydrocarbons is the influence of polychlorinated biphenyl and DDT in reduced reproduction in seals in the Baltic region (36, 63). About half the females which were not pregnant at a time of year when they should have been carrying foetuses were found instead to have enlarged uteri and corpora lutea but with scars instead of foetuses, pointing to abortion, resorption or maceration of embryos after implantation. These animals all had significantly higher levels of organochlorine hydrocarbon residues than the normally pregnant individuals (36). In a further study, pathological changes in uterine tissue were correlated with high DDT and polychlorinated biphenyl levels (37).

In this case we are looking at what amount to severe sublethal effects on individual seals. If these results are accepted, it seems likely that pinnipeds, and cetaceans, could be facing serious threats in other parts of the world where residue levels of chlorinated hydrocarbons are similar to those present in the Baltic. Although not actually killing individuals, a decrease in the successful pregnancy rate of the magnitude reported, will lead to extinction of populations. There could be other more subtle sublethal effects on reproduction taking place. It could be years before their impact becomes recognizable. Alternatively, there may be no threat to cetaceans at all. It is some consolation that most populations have evolved with metal trace element 'contamination' from natural sources, and have cellular mechanisms which appear able to mitigate the toxic effects of these elements to some extent. These animals are much more likely to be at risk from synthetic toxins for which there are no natural analogues, except in cases in which local industrial inputs of metallic elements are excessive. As I indicated earlier, even evidence of sublethal effects of contaminants on marine mammals is still largely circumstantial and correlative. If we know little about the direct effects of such compounds, we know far less about potential synergistic impacts where two or more contaminants are present together. We do, however, have cases where the level of some pollutants in cetacean tissues appear to have attained a steady state at, close to, or of the same order of magnitude as known LD_{50} values for experimental animals (see p. 426) in the case of organochlorines, or near the brain levels at which toxic symptoms have been recorded in mammals in the case of mercury. On this basis we can identify areas of the world in which contaminant levels are such that it seems not unreasonable to conclude that some coastal populations of Cetacea might be at risk (Table 10.7). Pressure on government agencies and industries must be intensified to ensure that at the very least no further deterioration takes place in these regions.

If cetaceans prove to be adversely affected by chlorinated hydrocarbons or other chemical pollutants, what would we be able to do? In the short term we could do nothing except wait and hope that segments of the populations proved resistant. From what we know of the flexibility of vertebrate genetic material, in the long term the likelihood of this is fortunately quite high. We could call for intensive experimental work to determine more precisely what the effects of these compounds are; this would give us more information, but what then could be done? Use of many potentially harmful compounds has been banned already. That the sediments now contain large quantities of organochlorine hydrocarbons is

Table 10.7   Major regions in which some cetacean populations are considered to be potentially at risk from contaminants

Area	Populations	Compounds	References
Western Mediterranean	Fin whale, common dolphin, bottlenosed dolphin, Cuvier's beaked whale	Fe, Ti, Hg	81
Coastal waters of France	Pilot whale	PCB	6
	Blue–white dolphin	PCB, DDT	7
Southern California	Bottlenosed dolphin, common dolphin, harbour porpoise	DDT, PCB	64
North Sea	Harbour porpoise	Hg	50
Bay of Fundy	Harbour porpoise	DDT, PCB	25, 27, 28

a fact, and nothing can be done about it. Biodegradation will occur, but in the case of DDT and the cyclodeines this may take twenty or thirty years, possibly longer for polychlorinated biphenyls. If some kind of marvellous antidote was developed for physiological problems as yet undetermined in cetaceans, it could not possibly be administered to wild populations. We searched for stable and persistent insecticides, and were only too successful. There may be no dramatic consequences for cetacean populations, but if there are then nothing can be done except wait and see. As K. Mellanby stated in 1977 (57), we have to learn to live with pesticides.

References

1 Addison, R. F. and Brodie, P. F. 1973. 'Occurrence of DDT residues in beluga whales (*Delphinapterus leucas*) from the Mackenzie Delta, NWT, *J. Fish. Res. Bd. Canada*, vol. 30, pp. 1733–6.

2 Addison, R. F. and Brodie, P. F. 1977. 'Organochlorine residues in maternal blubber, milk, and pup blubber from grey seals (*Halichoerus grypus*) Sable Island, Nova Scotia', *J. Fish. Res. Bd. Canada*, vol. 34, pp. 937–41.

3 Addison, R. F., Kerr, S. R., Dale, J. and Sergeant, D. E. 1973. 'Variation of organochlorine residue levels with age in Gulf of St Lawrence harp seals (*Pagophilus groenlandicus*)', *J. Fish. Res. Bd. Canada*, vol. 30, pp. 595–600.

4 Addison, R. F. and Smith, T. G. 1974. 'Organochlorine residue levels in Arctic marine seals: variation with age and sex', *Oikos*, vol. 25, pp. 335–7.

5 Addison, R. F., Zink, M. E. and Ackman, R. G. 1972. 'Residues of organochlorine pesticides and polychlorinated biphenyls in some commercially produced Canadian marine oils', *J. Fish. Res. Bd. Canada*, vol. 29, pp. 349–55.

6 Alzieu, C. and Duguy, R. 1978. 'Teneurs en composes organochlorines chez les cétaces et pinnipedes frequentant les côtes françaises', *Cons. Int. l'explor. Mer.*, Doc. C.M. 1978/N: 8.

7 Alzieu, C. and Duguy, R. 1978. 'Contamination du dauphin bleu et blanc de Mediterranée *Stenella coeruleoalba* par les composes organochlorines', XXVIᵉ Congrès, Assemblée plénière, Antalya, 24 novembre–2 decembre 1978.

8 Aucamp, P. J., Henry, J. L. and Stander, G. H. 1971. 'Pesticide residues in South African Marine Animals', *Mar. Pollut. Bull.*, vol. 3, pp. 190–1.

9 Baker, A. N. 1978. 'The status of Hector's dolphin *Cephalorynchus hectori* (Van Beneden), in New Zealand waters', *Rep. Int. Whal. Commn*, vol. 28, pp. 331–4.

10 Bennington, S. L. 1975. 'Patterns of chlorinated hydrocarbon contamination in New Zealand sub-antarctic and coastal marine birds', *Environ. Conserv.*, vol. 8, pp. 135–47.

11 Berglund, F., *et al.* (12 others). 1971. 'Methylmercury in fish. A toxicological–epidemiologic evaluation of risks. Report from an expert group', *Nord. Hyg. Tidskr.*, vol. 4, pp. 1–363.

12 Bligh, E. G. and Armstrong, F. A. J. 1971. 'Marine mercury pollution in Canada', ICES Council Meeting 1971 (E:34), pp. 1–3.

13 Bourne, W. R. P. 1976. 'Seabirds and pollution' in R. Johnston (ed.), *Marine Pollution*, London, Academic Press.

14 Brewerton, H. V. 1969. 'DDT in fats of Antarctic animals', *New Zealand J. Sci.*, vol. 12, pp. 194–9.

15 Bryan, G. W. 1976. 'Heavy metal contamination in the sea' in R. Johnston (ed.), *Marine Pollution*, London, Academic Press, pp. 185–302.

16 Clarkson, T. W. 1977. 'Mercury poisoning' in S. S. Brown (ed.), *Clinical Chemistry and Chemical Toxicology of Metals*, Amsterdam, Elsevier, pp. 189–200.

17 Collins, J. A. 1969. 'Chlorinated hydrocarbon pesticides: degradation and effect on the growth of bacteria', *Diss. Abstr.*, vol. 30B, no. 4, pp. 1426–7.

18 Cooke, A. S. 1970. 'The effect of *p,p'*-DDT on tadpoles of the common frog (*Rana temporaria*)', *Environ. Pollut.*, vol. 1, pp. 57–71.

19 DeLong, R. L., Gilmartin, W. G. and Simpson, J. G. 1973. 'Premature births in Californian sea lions: associated with high organochlorine pollutant residue levels', *Science*, vol. 181, pp. 1168–9.

20 Duinker, J. C. and Hillebrand, M. Th. J. 1979. 'Mobilization of organochlorines from female lipid tissue and transplacental transfer to fetus in a harbour porpoise (*Phocoena phocoena*) in a contaminated area', *Bull. Environm. Contam. Toxicol.*, vol. 23, pp. 728–32.

21   Feil, V. J., Lamoureux, C. H. and Zaylskie, R. G. 1975. 'Metabolism of *o,p'*-DDT in chickens', *J. Agric. Food Chem.*, vol. 23, pp. 382–8.

22   Forrester, D. J., Odell, D. K., Thompson, N. P. and White, J. R. 1980. 'Morphometrics, parasites, and chlorinated hydrocarbon residues of pygmy killer whales from Florida', *J. Mammal.*, vol. 61, pp. 356–60.

23   Foster, P. and Morris, A. W. 1971. 'The seasonal variation of dissolved ionic and organically associated copper in the Menai Straits', *Deep Sea Res.*, vol. 18, pp. 231–6.

24   Frank, R., Ronald, K. and Braun, H. E. 1973. 'Organochlorine residues in harp seals (*Pagophilus groenlandicus*) caught in eastern Canadian waters', *J. Fish. Res. Bd. Canada*, vol. 30, pp. 1053–63.

25   Gaskin, D. E., Frank R., and Holdrinet, M. 'PCB, chlordanes and hexachlorobenzene in harbour porpoises from eastern Canadian waters', in preparation.

26   Gaskin, D. E., Frank, R., Holdrinet, M., Ishida, K., Walton C.J. and Smith M. 1973. 'Mercury, DDT and PCB in harbour seals (*Phoca vitulina*) from the Bay of Fundy and Gulf of Maine', *J. Fish. Res. Bd. Canada*, vol. 30, pp. 471–5.

27   Gaskin, D. E., Holdrinet, M. and Frank, R. 1971. 'Organochlorine pesticide residues in harbour porpoises from the Bay of Fundy region', *Nature*, vol. 233, pp. 499–500.

28   Gaskin, D. E., Holdrinet, M. and Frank, R. 1976. 'DDT residues in blubber of harbour porpoises, *Phocoena phocoena* (L.) from eastern Canadian waters during the five year period 1969–1973', FAO of the UN, Scientific Consultation on Marine Mammals, Bergen, Norway, 31 August–9 September 1976, document ACMRR/MM/SC/96.

29   Gaskin, D. E., Holdrinet, M. and Frank, R. 1978. 'Organochlorine residues in shearwaters from the approaches to the Bay of Fundy, Canada', *Arch. Environm. Contam. Toxicol.*, vol. 7, pp. 505–13.

30   Gaskin, D. E., Ishida, K. and Frank, R. 1972. 'Mercury in harbour porpoise (*Phocoena phocoena*) from the Bay of Fundy region', *J. Fish. Res. Bd. Canada*, vol. 29, pp. 1644–6.

31   Gaskin, D. E., Smith, G. J. D., Arnold, P. W., Louisy, M. V., Frank, R., Holdrinet, M. and McWade, J. W. 1974. 'Mercury, DDT, dieldrin, and PCB in two species of Odontoceti (Cetacea) from St Lucia, Lesser Antilles', *J. Fish. Res. Bd. Canada*, vol. 31, pp. 1235–9.

32   Gaskin, D. E., Stonefield, K. I., Suda, P. and Frank, R. 1979. 'Changes in mercury levels in harbor porpoises from the Bay of Fundy, Canada, and adjacent waters during 1969–1977', *Arch. Environm. Contam. Toxicol.*, vol. 8, pp. 733–62.

33   Hamanaka, T., Kato, H. and Tsujita, T. 1977. 'Cadmium and zinc in Ribbon Seal, *Histriophoca fasciata*, in the Okhotsk Sea', *Res. Inst. N. Pac. Fish.*, Hokkaido Univ., spec. vol., pp. 547–61.

34   Harvey, G. R., Bowen, V. J., Backus, R. H. and Grice, G. D. 1973. 'Chlorinated hydrocarbons in open ocean Atlantic organisms' in D. Green and D. Jagney (eds.), *The Changing Chemistry of the Oceans*, New York, Wiley Interscience, pp. 177–86.

35   Harvey, G. R. and Miklas, H. P. 1972. 'Chlorinated hydrocarbons', IDOE workshop on baseline studies of pollution in the marine environment, Brookhaven, 24–26 May 1972.

36   Helle, E., Olsson, M. and Jensen, S. 1976. 'DDT and PCB levels and reproduction in ringed seal from the Bothnian Bay', *Ambio*, vol. 5, pp. 188–9.

37   Helle, E., Olsson, M. and Jensen, S. 1976. 'PCB levels correlated with pathological changes in seal uteri', *Ambio*, vol. 5, pp. 261–3.

38   Holden, A. V. 1972. 'Monitoring organochlorine contamination of the marine environment by the analysis of residues in seals' in M. Ruivo (ed.), *Marine Pollution and Sea Life*, West Byfleet, Surrey, Fishing News Books, pp. 266–72.

39   Holden, A. V. 1975. 'The accumulation of oceanic contaminants in marine mammals', *Rapp. P.-v. Reun. Cons. int. Explor. Mer.*, vol. 169, pp. 353–61.

40 Holden, A. V. and Marsden, K. 1967. 'Organochlorine pesticides in seals and porpoises', *Nature*, vol. 216, pp. 1274–6.

41 Jansson, B., Jensen, S., Olsson, M., Renberg, L., Sundström, G. and Vaz, R. 1975. 'Identification by GC–MS of phenolic metabolites of PCB and p,p'-DDE isolated from Baltic Guillemot and seal', *Ambio*, vol. 4, pp. 93–7.

42 Järvenpää, T., Tillander, M. and Miettinen, J. K. 1970. 'Methyl-mercury: half-time of elimination flounder, pike and eel', *Suom. Kemistilenti*, vol. B43, pp. 439–42.

43 Jenness, R. and Odell, D. K. 1978. 'Composition of milk of the pygmy sperm whale (*Kogia breviceps*)', *Comp. Biochem. Physiol.*, vol. 61A, pp. 383–6.

44 [Jensen, S.]* 1966. 'Report of a new chemical hazard', *reported in *New Scientist*, vol. 32, p. 612.

45 Jensen, S. and Sundström, G. 1974. 'Metabolic hydroxylation of a chlorobiphenyl containing only isolated unsubstituted positions – 2,2ʹ4,4ʹ,5,5ʹ-hexachlorobi-phenyl', *Nature*, vol. 251, pp. 219–20.

46 Jernelöv, A. 1972. 'Factors in the transformation of mercury to methyl mercury' in R. Hartung and B. D. Dinman (eds.), *Environmental Mercury Contamination*, Ann Arbor, Mich., Ann Arbor Science Publishers, pp. 167–72.

47 Johnson, B. T. 1969. 'The degradation of DDT by soil-borne bacteria', *Diss. Abstr.*, vol. 29B, no. 9, p. 3156.

48 Johnston, R. 1976. 'Mechanisms and problems of marine pollution in relation to commercial fisheries' in R. Johnston (ed.), *Marine Pollution*, London, Academic Press, pp. 3–156.

49 Jones, D., Ronald, K. and Lavigne, D. M. 1976. 'Organochlorine and mercury residues in the harp seal (*Pagophilus groenlandicus*)', *The Science of the Total Environment*, vol. 5, pp. 181–95.

50 Koeman, J. H., Peeters, W. H. M., Smit, C. J., Tijoe, P. S. and Goeij, J. J. M. de 1972. 'Persistent chemicals in marine mammals', *TNO-nieuws*, vol. 27, pp. 570–8.

51 Koeman, J. H., Peeters, W. H. M., Koudstaal-Hol, C. H. M., Tijoe, P. S. and Goeij, J. J. M. de 1973. 'Mercury–selenium correlations in marine mammals', *Nature*, vol. 245, pp. 385–6.

52 Koeman, J. H., Ten Noever der Brauw, M. C. and Vos, R. H. de 1969. 'Chlorinated biphenyls in fish, mussels and birds from the river Rhine and the Netherlands coastal area', *Nature*, vol. 221, pp. 1126–8.

53 Komsta-Szumska, E. and Chmielnicka, J. 1977. 'Binding of mercury and selenium in subcellular fractions of rat liver and kidneys following separate joint adminis-tration', *Arch. Toxicol.*, vol. 38, pp. 217–28.

54 Kurland, L. T., Faro, S. N. and Siedler, H. 1960. 'The outbreak of a neurological disorder in Minamata, Japan, and its relation to the ingestion of seafood contaminated by mercuric compounds', *World Neurol.*, vol. 1, pp. 370–95.

55 Lehman, J. W. and Peterle, T. J. 1971. 'DDT in Cetacea' in G. Pilleri (ed.), *Investigations in Cetacea*, Vol. III, Berne, Waldau, pp. 349–51.

56 Lowman, F. G., Rice, T. R. and Richards, F. A. 1971. *Radioactivity in the Marine Environment*, Washington, National Academy of Sciences, pp. 169–99 (not seen, cited in G. W. Bryan, 1976, ref. 15).

57 Mellanby, K. 1977. 'The future prospect for man' in F. H. Perring and K. Mellanby (eds.), *Ecological Effects of Pesticides*, London, Academic Press, published for the Linnean Society of London, pp. 181–4.

58 Metcalf, R. L., Sanborn, J. R., Lu, P.-Y. and Nye, D. 1975. 'Laboratory model ecosystem studies of the degradation and fate of radio-labelled tri-, tetra- and penta-chlorobiphenyl compared with DDE', *Arch. Environ. Contam. Toxicol.*, vol. 3, pp. 151–65.

59 Moore, N. W. and Tatton, J. O'G. 1965. 'Organochlorine insecticide residues in the eggs of sea birds', *Nature*, vol. 207, pp. 42–3.

60 Nomiyama, K. and Foulkes, E. C. 1977. 'Reabsorption of filtered cadmium–

metallothionein in the rabbit kidney', *Proc. Soc. Exp. Biol. Med.*, vol. 156, pp. 97–9.

61 Nordberg, G. F., Berlin, M. H. and Grant, C. A. 1970. 'Methyl mercury in the monkey: autoradiographical distribution and neurotoxicity', *Proc. 16th Int. Congr. Occup. Health, Tokyo.*

62 Odell, D. K. and Asper, E. D. 1976. 'Studies on the biology of *Kogia* (Cetacea: Physeteridae) in Florida'; preliminary report to the Small Whales Subcommittee on the International Whaling Commission, London.

63 Olsson, M., Johnels, A. G. and Vaz, R. 1975. 'DDT and PCB levels in seals from Swedish waters' in *Proceedings from the Symposium on the Seal in the Baltic*, 4–6 June, Lidingö, Sweden; Solna, Sweden, National Swedish Environmental Protection Board, publication 591, pp. 43–65.

64 O'Shea, T., Brownell, R. L. Jr, Clark, D. R. Jr, Walker, W. A., Gay, M. L. and Lamont, T. G. 1980. 'Organochlorine pollutants in small cetaceans from the Pacific and South Atlantic Oceans, November 1968–June 1976', *Pesticides Monitoring Journal*, vol. 14, pp. 35–46.

65 Parizek, J., Benes, I, Ostalova, A., Babicky, A., Benes, J. and Lener, J. 1969. 'Metabolic interrelations of trace elements: the effect of some inorganic compounds of selenium on the metabolism of cadmium and mercury in the rat', *Physiologia Bohemoslovaca*, vol. 18, pp. 95–103.

66 Peterle, T. J. and Lehman, J. W. 'DDT in Cetacea II' in G. Pilleri (ed.), *Investigations on Cetacea*, Vol. IV, Berne, Waldau, pp. 275–7.

67 Pimentel, D. 1971. 'Ecological effects of pesticides on non-target species', Washington, Executive Office of the President, Office of Science and Technology.

68 Piotrowski, J. K., Trojanowska, B. and Sapota, A. 1974. 'Binding of cadmium and mercury by metallothionein in the kidneys and liver of rats following repeated administration', *Arch. Toxicol.*, vol. 32, pp. 351–60.

69 Piotrowski, J. K., Bem, E. M. and Werner, A. 1977. 'Cadmium and mercury binding to metallothionein as influenced by selenium', *Biochem. Pharmacol.*, vol. 26, pp. 2191–2.

70 Risebrough, R. W., Reiche, P., Herman, S. G., Peakall, D. B. and Kirven, M. N. 1968. 'Polychlorinated biphenyls in the global ecosystem', *Nature*, vol. 220, pp. 1098–102.

71 Risebrough, R. W. 1971. 'Chlorinated hydrocarbons' in D. W. Hood (ed.), *Impingement of Man on the Oceans*, New York, Wiley Interscience, pp. 259–86.

72 Saschenbrecker, P. W. 1973. 'Levens of DDT and PCB compounds in North Atlantic fin-back whales', *Can. J. Comp. Med.*, vol. 37, pp. 203–6.

73 Schoor, W. P. 1973. '*In vivo* binding of p,p'-DDE to human serum proteins', *Bull. Environ. Contam. Toxicol.*, vol. 9, pp. 70–4.

74 Sergeant, D. E. 1980. 'Levels of mercury and organochlorine residues in tissues of sea mammals from the St Lawrence estuary', ICES, document CM 1980/E:55 (cyclo.).

75 Shaw, S. B. 1971. 'Chlorinated hydrocarbon pesticides in California sea otters and harbor seals', *Calif. Fish and Game*, vol. 57, pp. 290–4.

76 Short, J. R. T. 1963. *Introduction to Applied Entomology*, London, Longman.

77 Sladen, W. J. L., Menzie, C. M. and Reichel, W. L. 1966. 'DDT residues in Adelie penguins and a crabeater seal from Antarctica', *Nature*, vol. 210, pp. 670–3.

78 Sutcliffe, W. H., Jr, Loucks, R. H. and Drinkwater, K. F. 1976. 'Coastal circulation and physical oceanography of the Scotian Shelf and Gulf of Maine', *J. Fish. Res. Bd. Canada*, vol. 33, pp. 98–115.

79 Taruski, A. G., Olney, C. E. and Winn, H. E. 1975. 'Chlorinated hydrocarbons in cetaceans', *J. Fish. Res. Bd. Canada*, vol. 132, pp. 2205–9.

80 Train, R. E. 1974. 'Use of DDT to control the douglas fir tussock moth', *US Environmental Protection Agency, Fed. Reg.*, vol. 39, pp. 8377–81.

81 Viale, D. 1978. 'Evidence of metal pollution in Cetacea of the western Mediterranean', *Ann. Inst. océanogr.*, Paris, vol. 54, pp. 5–16.

82   Walker, W., Mattox, W. G. and Risebrough, R. W. 1973. 'Pollutant and shell thickness determinations of Peregrine eggs from West Greenland', *Arctic*, vol. 26, pp. 256–8.

83   Wallcave, L. and Gingell, R. 1974. 'Species differences in the acute toxicity and tissue distribution of DDT in mice and hamsters', *Toxicol. Appl. Pharmacol.*, vol. 28, pp. 384–94.

84   Wisniewska, J. M., Trojanowska, B., Piotrowski, J. K. and Jakubowski, M. 1970. 'Binding of mercury in the rat kidney by metallothionein', *Toxicol. Appl. Pharmacol.*, vol. 16, pp. 754–63.

85   Wolman, A. A. and Wilson, A. J. 1970. 'Occurrence of pesticides in whales', *Pestic. Monit. J.*, vol. 4, pp. 8–10.

86   Zitko, V. and Choi, P. M. K. 1971. 'PCB and other industrial halogenated hydrocarbons in the environment', *Fish. Res. Bd. Canada*, Tech. Rep., no. 272.

87   Zoro, J. A., Hunter, J. M., Eglinton, G. and Ware, G. C. 1974. 'Degradation of *p,p'*-DDT in reducing environments', *Nature*, vol. 247, pp. 235–7.

Author Index

Index of scientific and common names

Subject index